SUPERMAN

THE ADVENTURES OF
NIGHTWING AND FLAMEBIRD

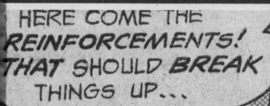

HERE COME THE
REINFORCEMENTS!
THAT SHOULD BREAK
THINGS UP...

IT SHOULDN'T HAVE
HAPPENED, FLAMEBIRD! THERE
SHOULD NEVER HAVE BEEN A
CONFRONTATION IN
THE F...

Dan DiDio **SVP – Executive Editor**
Murray Boltinoff Dennis O'Neil E. Nelson Bridwell **Editors – Original Series**
Georg Brewer **VP – Design & DC Direct Creative**
Bob Harras **Group Editor – Collected Editions**
Bob Joy **Editor**
Robbin Brosterman **Design Director – Books**

DC COMICS
Paul Levitz **President & Publisher**
Richard Bruning **SVP – Creative Director**
Patrick Caldon **EVP – Finance & Operations**
Amy Genkins **SVP – Business & Legal Affairs**
Jim Lee **Editorial Director – WildStorm**
Gregory Noveck **SVP – Creative Affairs**
Steve Rotterdam **SVP – Sales & Marketing**
Cheryl Rubin **SVP – Brand Management**

Cover art by Curt Swan and Rodney Ramos with Pete Pantazis

SUPERMAN: THE ADVENTURES OF NIGHTWING AND FLAMEBIRD

DC Comics, 1700 Broadway, New York, NY 10019
A Warner Bros. Entertainment Company
First Printing.
ISBN: 978-1-4012-2525-4
Printed by World Color Press, Inc, St-Romauld, Canada. 9/23/09

SUSTAINABLE FORESTRY INITIATIVE Certified Fiber Sourcing
Fiber used in this product line meets the sourcing requirements of the SFI program. www.sfiprogram.org PWC-SFICOC-260

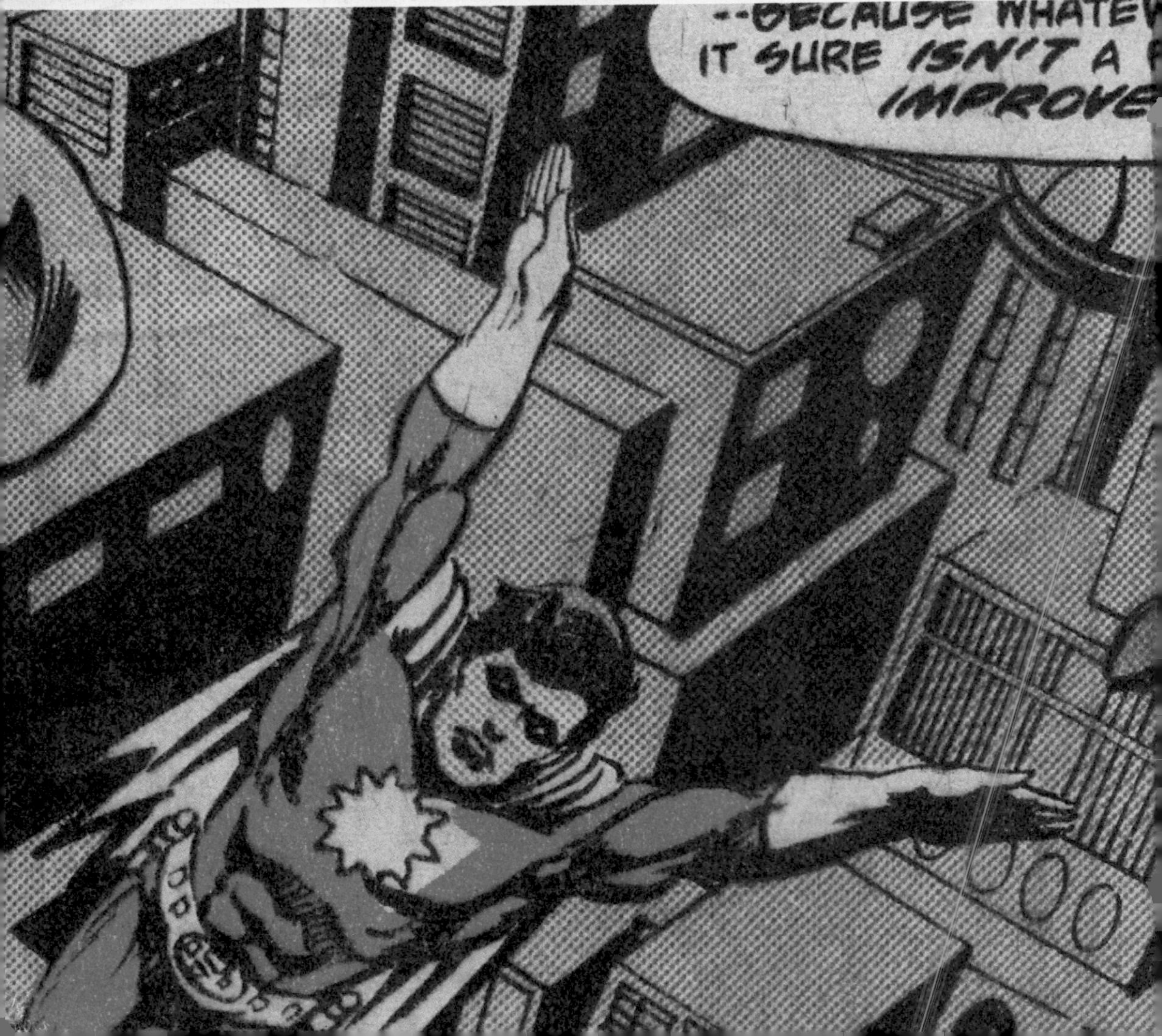
--BECAUSE
IT SURE ISN'T A

SUPERMAN

THE ADVENTURES OF NIGHTWING AND FLAMEBIRD

SUPERMAN CREATED BY JERRY SIEGEL AND JOE SHUSTER

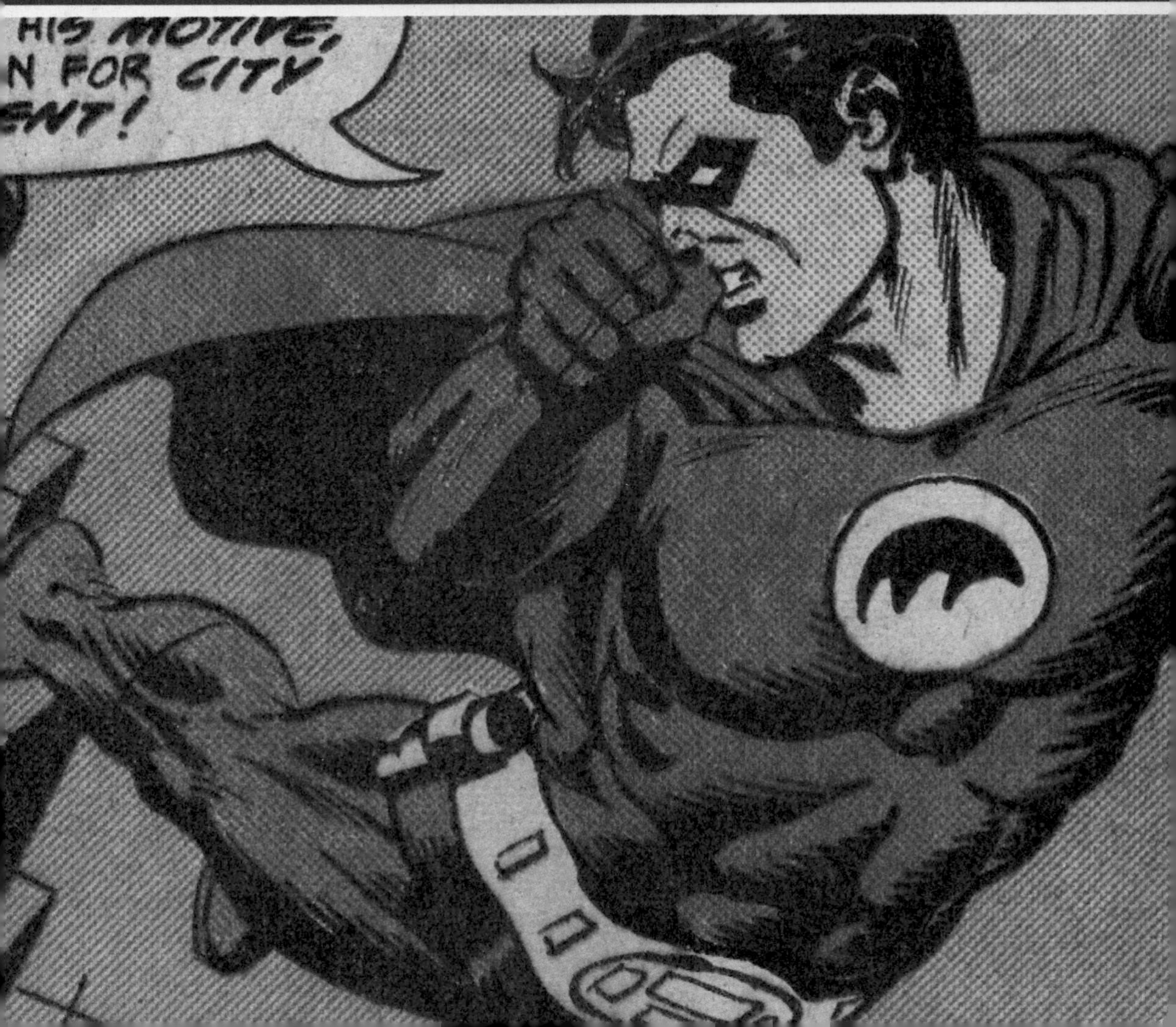
HIS MOTIVE,
N FOR CITY
ENT!

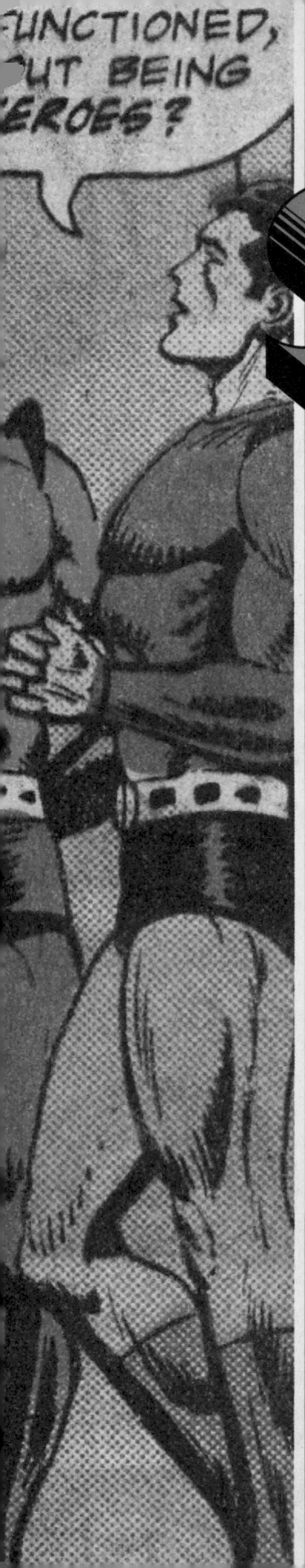

SUPERMAN
THE ADVENTURES OF NIGHTWING AND FLAMEBIRD

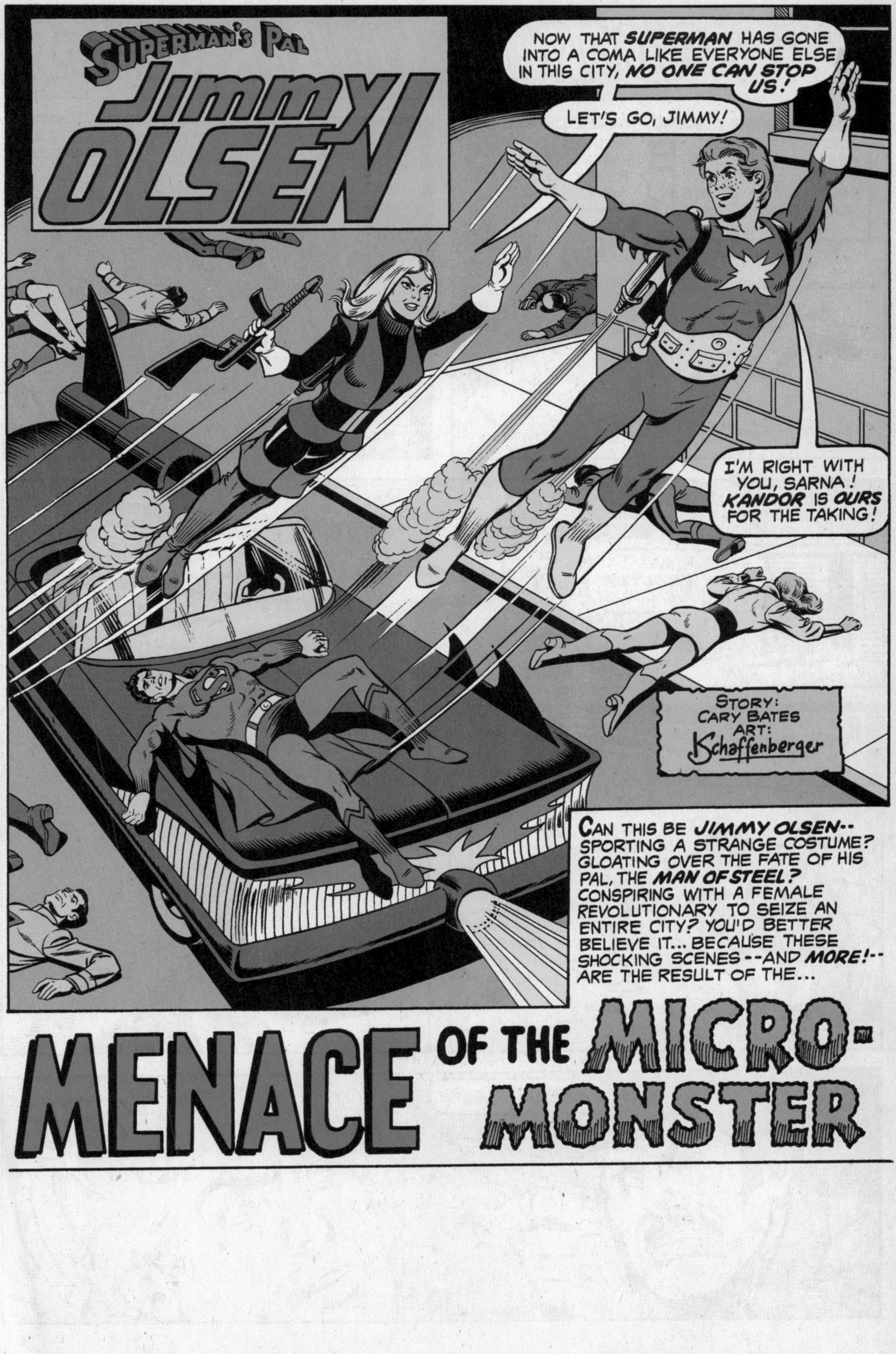
SUPERMAN'S PAL
JIMMY OLSEN
NOW THAT SUPERMAN HAS GONE INTO A COMA LIKE EVERYONE ELSE IN THIS CITY, NO ONE CAN STOP US!
LET'S GO, JIMMY!
I'M RIGHT WITH YOU, SARNA! KANDOR IS OURS FOR THE TAKING!
STORY: CARY BATES ART: KSchaffenberger
CAN THIS BE JIMMY OLSEN-- SPORTING A STRANGE COSTUME? GLOATING OVER THE FATE OF HIS PAL, THE MAN OF STEEL? CONSPIRING WITH A FEMALE REVOLUTIONARY TO SEIZE AN ENTIRE CITY? YOU'D BETTER BELIEVE IT... BECAUSE THESE SHOCKING SCENES--AND MORE!--ARE THE RESULT OF THE...
MENACE OF THE MICRO-MONSTER

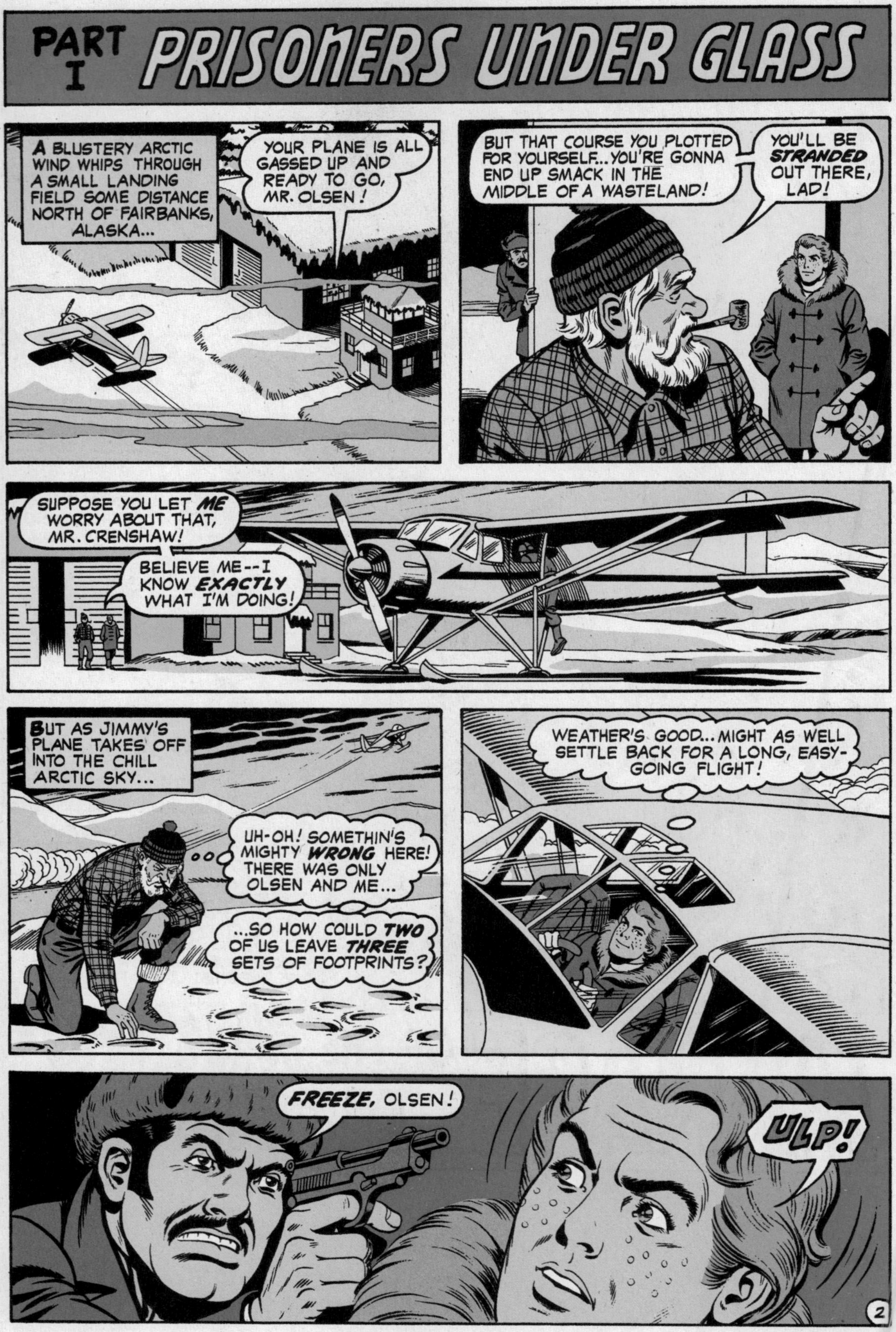
PART I
PRISONERS UNDER GLASS
A BLUSTERY ARCTIC WIND WHIPS THROUGH A SMALL LANDING FIELD SOME DISTANCE NORTH OF FAIRBANKS, ALASKA...
YOUR PLANE IS ALL GASSED UP AND READY TO GO, MR. OLSEN!
BUT THAT COURSE YOU PLOTTED FOR YOURSELF... YOU'RE GONNA END UP SMACK IN THE MIDDLE OF A WASTELAND!
YOU'LL BE STRANDED OUT THERE, LAD!
SUPPOSE YOU LET ME WORRY ABOUT THAT, MR. CRENSHAW!
BELIEVE ME--I KNOW EXACTLY WHAT I'M DOING!
BUT AS JIMMY'S PLANE TAKES OFF INTO THE CHILL ARCTIC SKY...
UH-OH! SOMETHIN'S MIGHTY WRONG HERE! THERE WAS ONLY OLSEN AND ME...
...SO HOW COULD TWO OF US LEAVE THREE SETS OF FOOTPRINTS?
WEATHER'S GOOD... MIGHT AS WELL SETTLE BACK FOR A LONG, EASY-GOING FLIGHT!
FREEZE, OLSEN!
ULP!
2

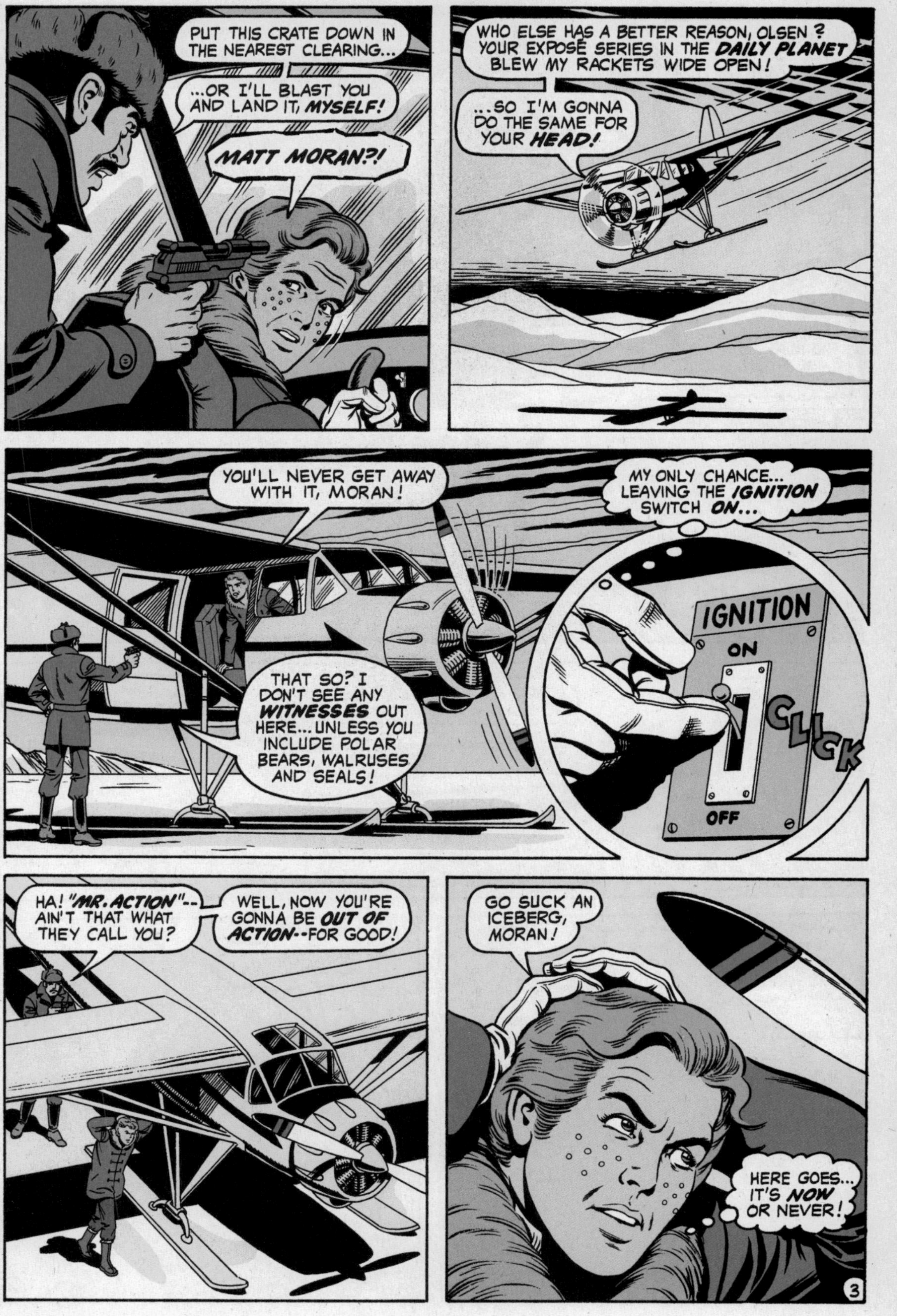
PUT THIS CRATE DOWN IN THE NEAREST CLEARING...
...OR I'LL BLAST YOU AND LAND IT, MYSELF!
MATT MORAN?!
WHO ELSE HAS A BETTER REASON, OLSEN? YOUR EXPOSÉ SERIES IN THE DAILY PLANET BLEW MY RACKETS WIDE OPEN!
...SO I'M GONNA DO THE SAME FOR YOUR HEAD!
YOU'LL NEVER GET AWAY WITH IT, MORAN!
THAT SO? I DON'T SEE ANY WITNESSES OUT HERE... UNLESS YOU INCLUDE POLAR BEARS, WALRUSES AND SEALS!
MY ONLY CHANCE... LEAVING THE IGNITION SWITCH ON...
IGNITION
ON
OFF
CLICK
HA! "MR. ACTION"-- AIN'T THAT WHAT THEY CALL YOU?
WELL, NOW YOU'RE GONNA BE OUT OF ACTION--FOR GOOD!
GO SUCK AN ICEBERG, MORAN!
HERE GOES... IT'S NOW OR NEVER!
3

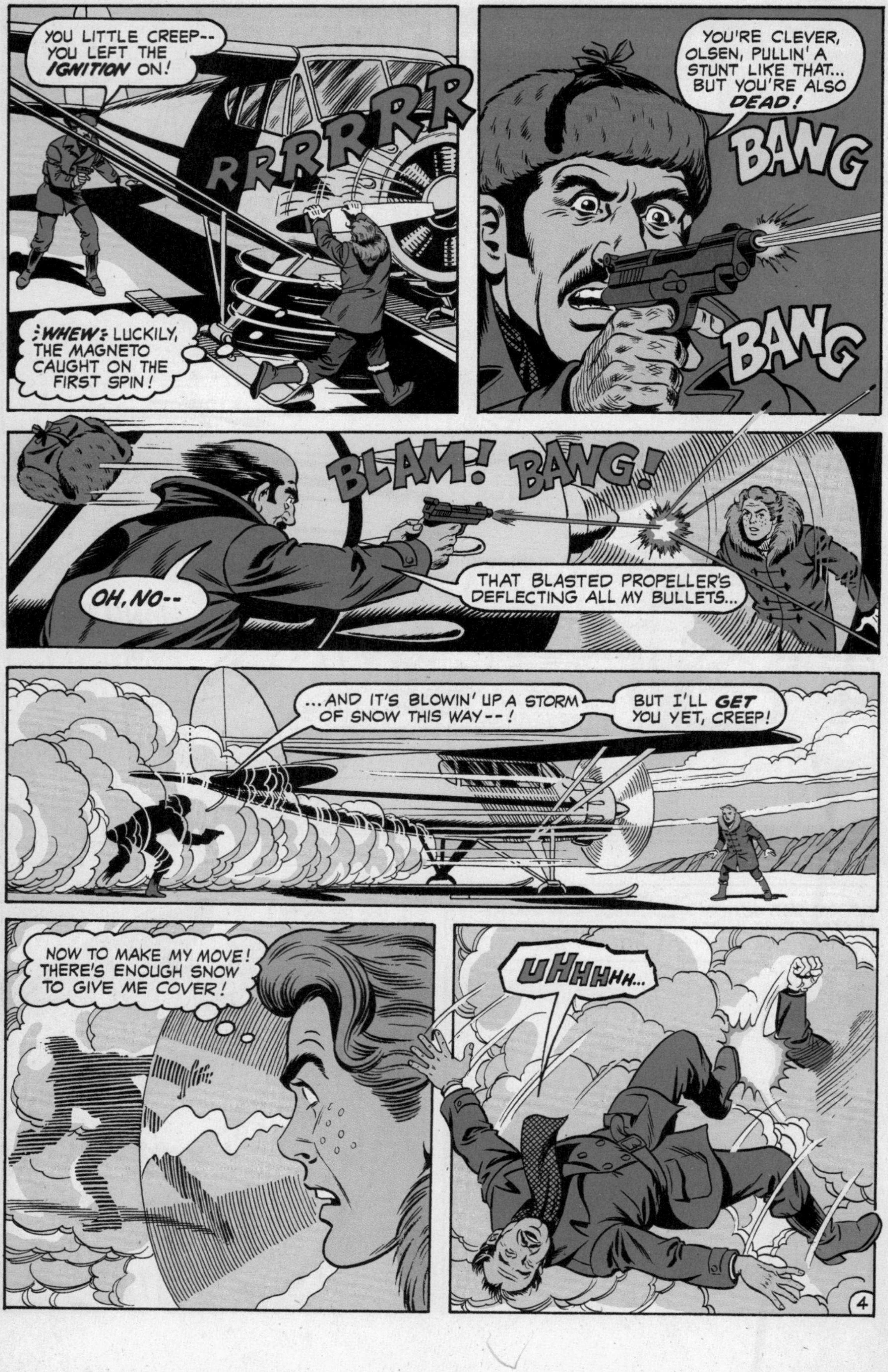
YOU LITTLE CREEP-- YOU LEFT THE IGNITION ON!
RRRRRRR
WHEW! LUCKILY, THE MAGNETO CAUGHT ON THE FIRST SPIN!
YOU'RE CLEVER, OLSEN, PULLIN' A STUNT LIKE THAT... BUT YOU'RE ALSO DEAD!
BANG
BANG
BLAM! BANG!
OH, NO--
THAT BLASTED PROPELLER'S DEFLECTING ALL MY BULLETS...
...AND IT'S BLOWIN' UP A STORM OF SNOW THIS WAY--!
BUT I'LL GET YOU YET, CREEP!
NOW TO MAKE MY MOVE! THERE'S ENOUGH SNOW TO GIVE ME COVER!
UHHHHH...
4

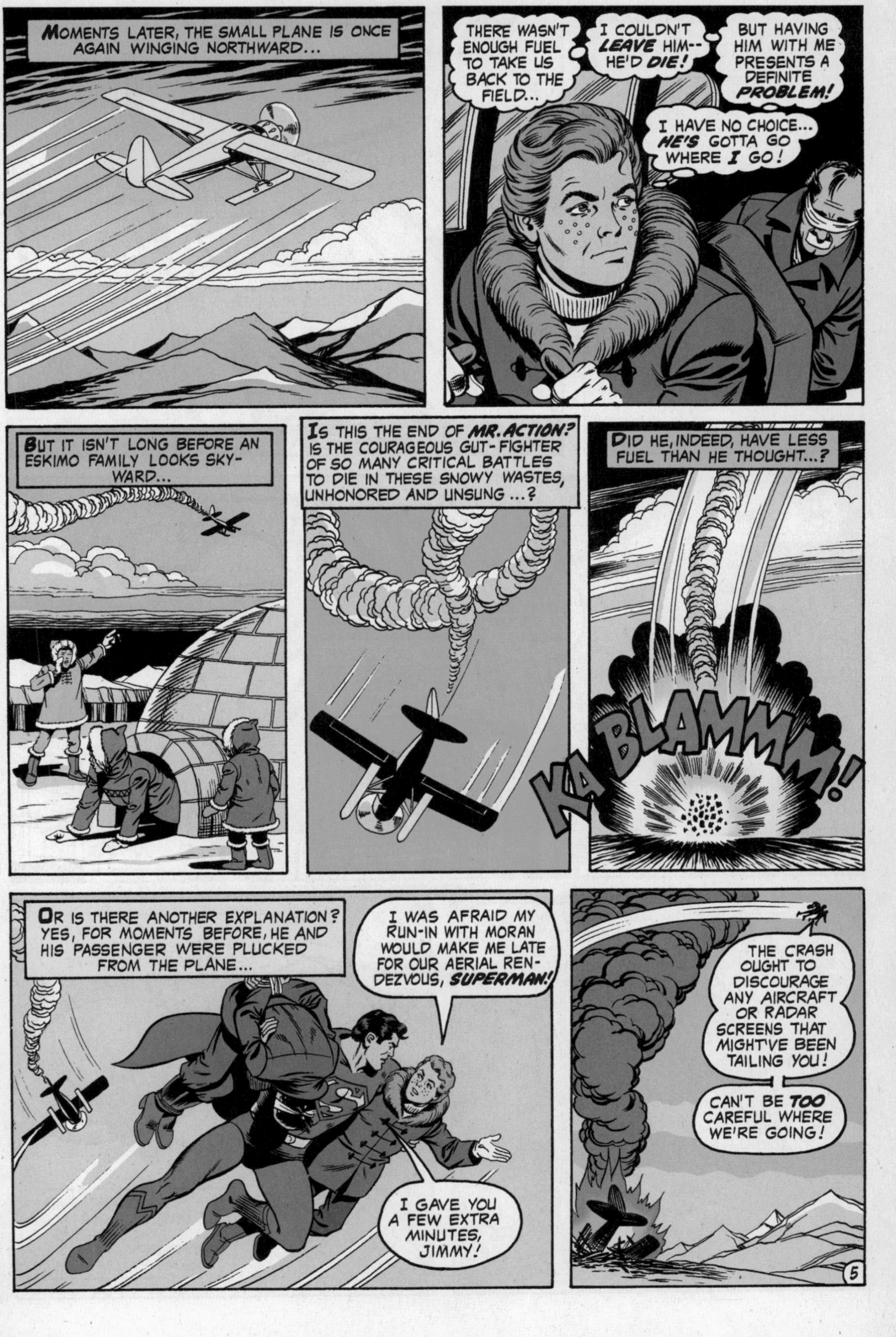
MOMENTS LATER, THE SMALL PLANE IS ONCE AGAIN WINGING NORTHWARD...
THERE WASN'T ENOUGH FUEL TO TAKE US BACK TO THE FIELD...
I COULDN'T LEAVE HIM-- HE'D DIE!
BUT HAVING HIM WITH ME PRESENTS A DEFINITE PROBLEM!
I HAVE NO CHOICE... HE'S GOTTA GO WHERE I GO!
BUT IT ISN'T LONG BEFORE AN ESKIMO FAMILY LOOKS SKYWARD...
IS THIS THE END OF MR. ACTION? IS THE COURAGEOUS GUT-FIGHTER OF SO MANY CRITICAL BATTLES TO DIE IN THESE SNOWY WASTES, UNHONORED AND UNSUNG ...?
DID HE, INDEED, HAVE LESS FUEL THAN HE THOUGHT...?
KA BLAMMM!
OR IS THERE ANOTHER EXPLANATION? YES, FOR MOMENTS BEFORE, HE AND HIS PASSENGER WERE PLUCKED FROM THE PLANE...
I WAS AFRAID MY RUN-IN WITH MORAN WOULD MAKE ME LATE FOR OUR AERIAL RENDEZVOUS, SUPERMAN!
I GAVE YOU A FEW EXTRA MINUTES, JIMMY!
THE CRASH OUGHT TO DISCOURAGE ANY AIRCRAFT OR RADAR SCREENS THAT MIGHT'VE BEEN TAILING YOU!
CAN'T BE TOO CAREFUL WHERE WE'RE GOING!
5

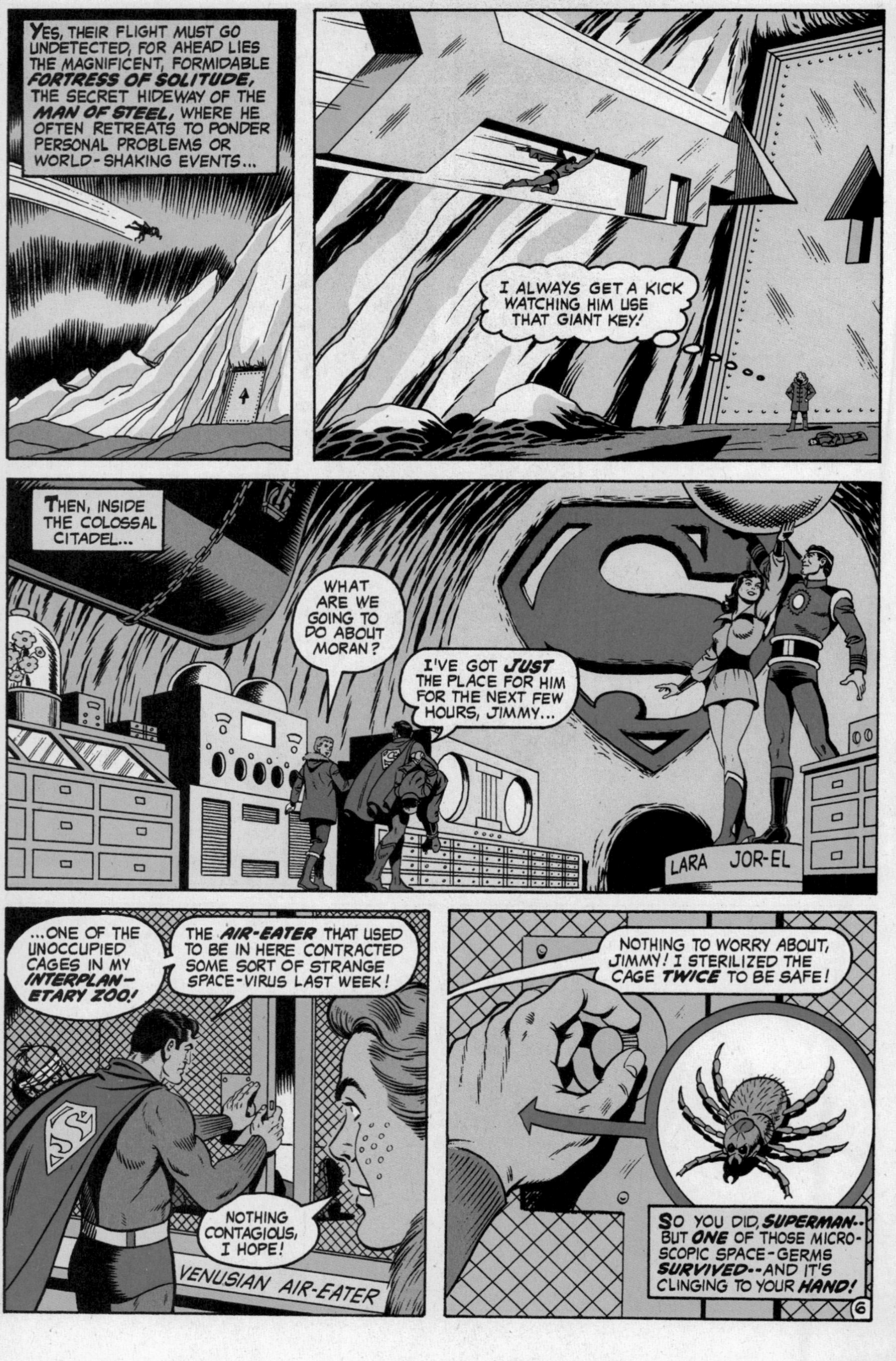
YES, THEIR FLIGHT MUST GO UNDETECTED, FOR AHEAD LIES THE MAGNIFICENT, FORMIDABLE **FORTRESS OF SOLITUDE,** THE SECRET HIDEWAY OF THE **MAN OF STEEL,** WHERE HE OFTEN RETREATS TO PONDER PERSONAL PROBLEMS OR WORLD-SHAKING EVENTS...
I ALWAYS GET A KICK WATCHING HIM USE THAT GIANT KEY!
THEN, INSIDE THE COLOSSAL CITADEL...
WHAT ARE WE GOING TO DO ABOUT MORAN?
I'VE GOT **JUST** THE PLACE FOR HIM FOR THE NEXT FEW HOURS, JIMMY...
LARA JOR-EL
...ONE OF THE UNOCCUPIED CAGES IN MY **INTERPLAN-ETARY ZOO!**
THE **AIR-EATER** THAT USED TO BE IN HERE CONTRACTED SOME SORT OF STRANGE SPACE-VIRUS LAST WEEK!
NOTHING CONTAGIOUS, I HOPE!
VENUSIAN AIR-EATER
NOTHING TO WORRY ABOUT, JIMMY! I STERILIZED THE CAGE **TWICE** TO BE SAFE!
SO YOU DID, **SUPERMAN**-- BUT **ONE** OF THOSE MICRO-SCOPIC SPACE-GERMS **SURVIVED**--AND IT'S CLINGING TO YOUR **HAND!**
6

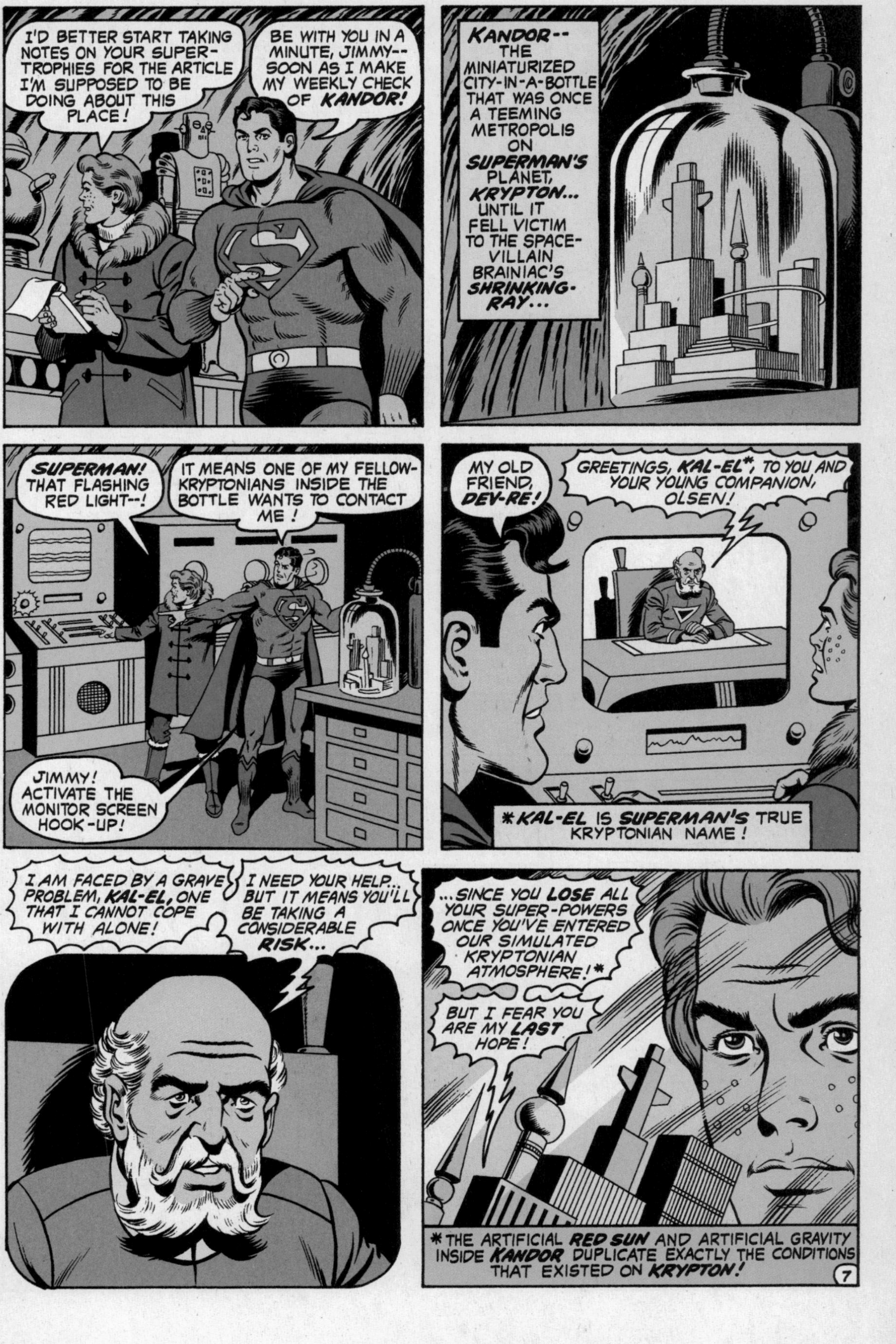
I'D BETTER START TAKING NOTES ON YOUR SUPER-TROPHIES FOR THE ARTICLE I'M SUPPOSED TO BE DOING ABOUT THIS PLACE!
BE WITH YOU IN A MINUTE, JIMMY-- SOON AS I MAKE MY WEEKLY CHECK OF KANDOR!
KANDOR-- THE MINIATURIZED CITY-IN-A-BOTTLE THAT WAS ONCE A TEEMING METROPOLIS ON SUPERMAN'S PLANET, KRYPTON... UNTIL IT FELL VICTIM TO THE SPACE-VILLAIN BRAINIAC'S SHRINKING-RAY...
SUPERMAN! THAT FLASHING RED LIGHT--!
IT MEANS ONE OF MY FELLOW-KRYPTONIANS INSIDE THE BOTTLE WANTS TO CONTACT ME!
JIMMY! ACTIVATE THE MONITOR SCREEN HOOK-UP!
MY OLD FRIEND, DEV-RE!
GREETINGS, KAL-EL*, TO YOU AND YOUR YOUNG COMPANION, OLSEN!
*KAL-EL IS SUPERMAN'S TRUE KRYPTONIAN NAME!
I AM FACED BY A GRAVE PROBLEM, KAL-EL, ONE THAT I CANNOT COPE WITH ALONE!
I NEED YOUR HELP... BUT IT MEANS YOU'LL BE TAKING A CONSIDERABLE RISK...
...SINCE YOU LOSE ALL YOUR SUPER-POWERS ONCE YOU'VE ENTERED OUR SIMULATED KRYPTONIAN ATMOSPHERE!*
BUT I FEAR YOU ARE MY LAST HOPE!
*THE ARTIFICIAL RED SUN AND ARTIFICIAL GRAVITY INSIDE KANDOR DUPLICATE EXACTLY THE CONDITIONS THAT EXISTED ON KRYPTON!
7

AS SOON AS JIMMY HAS TAKEN OFF HIS ARCTIC CLOTHING AND DONNED HIS SPECIAL ANTI-GRAVITY SHOES, HE AND SUPERMAN ARE PREPARED FOR AN INCREDIBLE JOURNEY...
ALL SYSTEMS GO!
I'VE ACTIVATED THE MICRO-WAVE BEAMER! ALL WE HAVE TO DO IS STAND IN ITS BEAM, AND WE'LL BE SHRUNK TO MICROSCOPIC SIZE!
BUT WHILE MAKING PREPARATIONS FOR THE TRIP, SUPERMAN IS UNAWARE THAT HIS HAND HAS DEPOSITED THE DEADLY, MICROSCOPIC SPACE-GERM ON THE OUTSIDE OF KANDOR'S BOTTLE-NECK...
YOU KNOW, IF THE KANDORIANS EVER LEFT THEIR BOTTLE-WORLD, THEY'D BE AS SUPER AS YOU!
TEN MILLION MICROSCOPIC SUPERMEN! WHEW!
AFTER YOU, JIMMY!
ONE QUESTION--
SINCE YOU WON'T BE ABLE TO FLY ONCE YOU'RE INSIDE, WHAT WILL KEEP US FROM FALLING ALL THE WAY DOWN TO KANDOR?
NO PROBLEM! AT THE BOTTOM OF THE TUBE, YOU'LL FIND TWO ANTI-GRAV PACKS LEFT BY THE KANDORIANS FOR VISITORS LIKE US!
RIGHT ON, SUPERMAN!
AND RIGHT WHERE YOU SAID THEY'D BE!
BUT BEFORE THEY CAN DON THEIR PACKS, AN EAR-SHATTERING EXPLOSION BLASTS JIMMY AND SUPERMAN FROM THEIR PERCHES...
BARR-ROOOM
SUPERMAN! HELP!
GRAB ONE END OF MY CAPE!
8

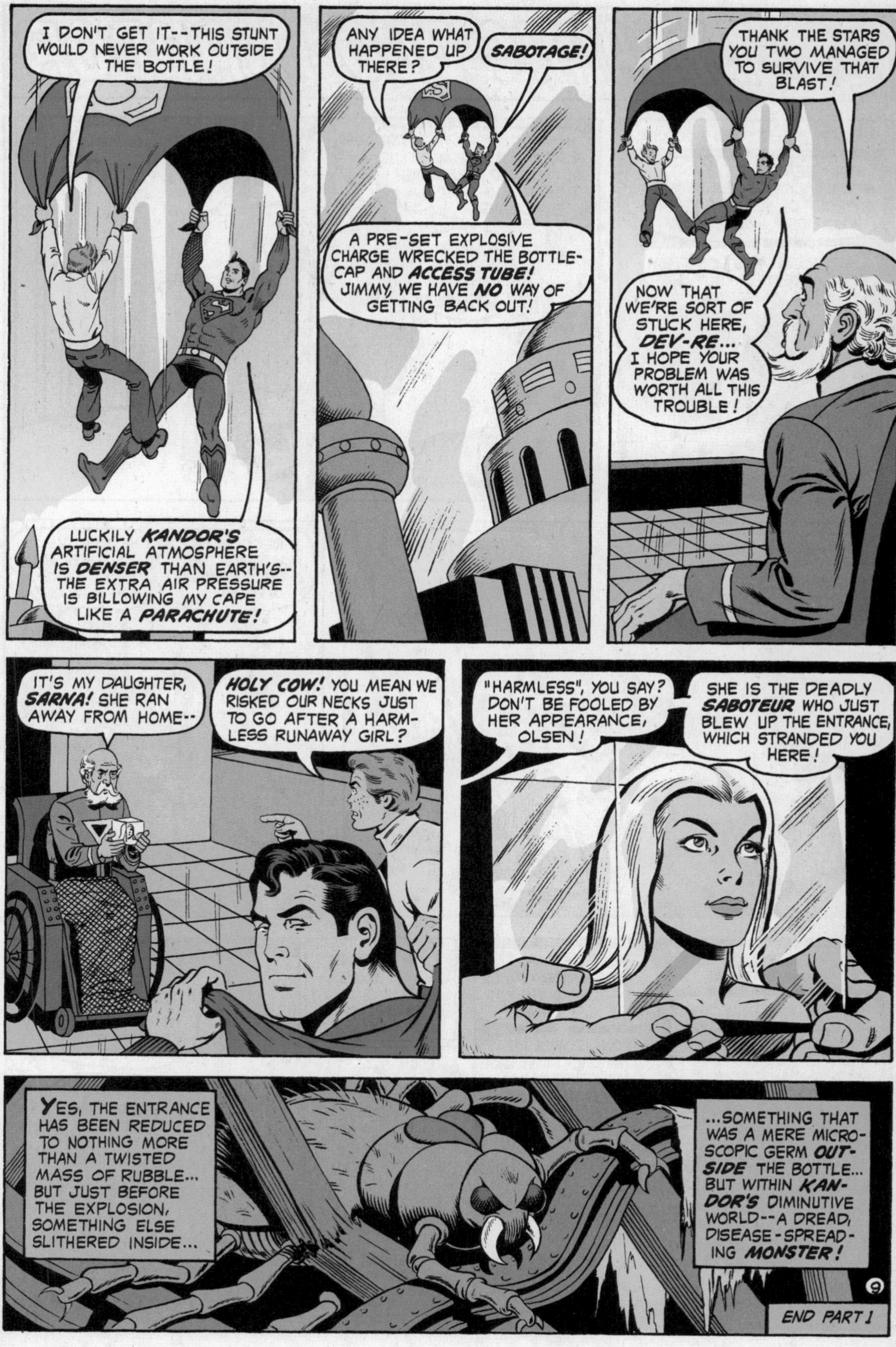
I DON'T GET IT--THIS STUNT WOULD NEVER WORK OUTSIDE THE BOTTLE!
LUCKILY KANDOR'S ARTIFICIAL ATMOSPHERE IS DENSER THAN EARTH'S--THE EXTRA AIR PRESSURE IS BILLOWING MY CAPE LIKE A PARACHUTE!
ANY IDEA WHAT HAPPENED UP THERE?
SABOTAGE!
A PRE-SET EXPLOSIVE CHARGE WRECKED THE BOTTLE-CAP AND ACCESS TUBE! JIMMY, WE HAVE NO WAY OF GETTING BACK OUT!
THANK THE STARS YOU TWO MANAGED TO SURVIVE THAT BLAST!
NOW THAT WE'RE SORT OF STUCK HERE, DEV-RE... I HOPE YOUR PROBLEM WAS WORTH ALL THIS TROUBLE!
IT'S MY DAUGHTER, SARNA! SHE RAN AWAY FROM HOME--
HOLY COW! YOU MEAN WE RISKED OUR NECKS JUST TO GO AFTER A HARMLESS RUNAWAY GIRL?
"HARMLESS", YOU SAY? DON'T BE FOOLED BY HER APPEARANCE, OLSEN!
SHE IS THE DEADLY SABOTEUR WHO JUST BLEW UP THE ENTRANCE, WHICH STRANDED YOU HERE!
YES, THE ENTRANCE HAS BEEN REDUCED TO NOTHING MORE THAN A TWISTED MASS OF RUBBLE... BUT JUST BEFORE THE EXPLOSION, SOMETHING ELSE SLITHERED INSIDE...
...SOMETHING THAT WAS A MERE MICROSCOPIC GERM OUTSIDE THE BOTTLE... BUT WITHIN KANDOR'S DIMINUTIVE WORLD--A DREAD, DISEASE-SPREADING MONSTER!
9
END PART I

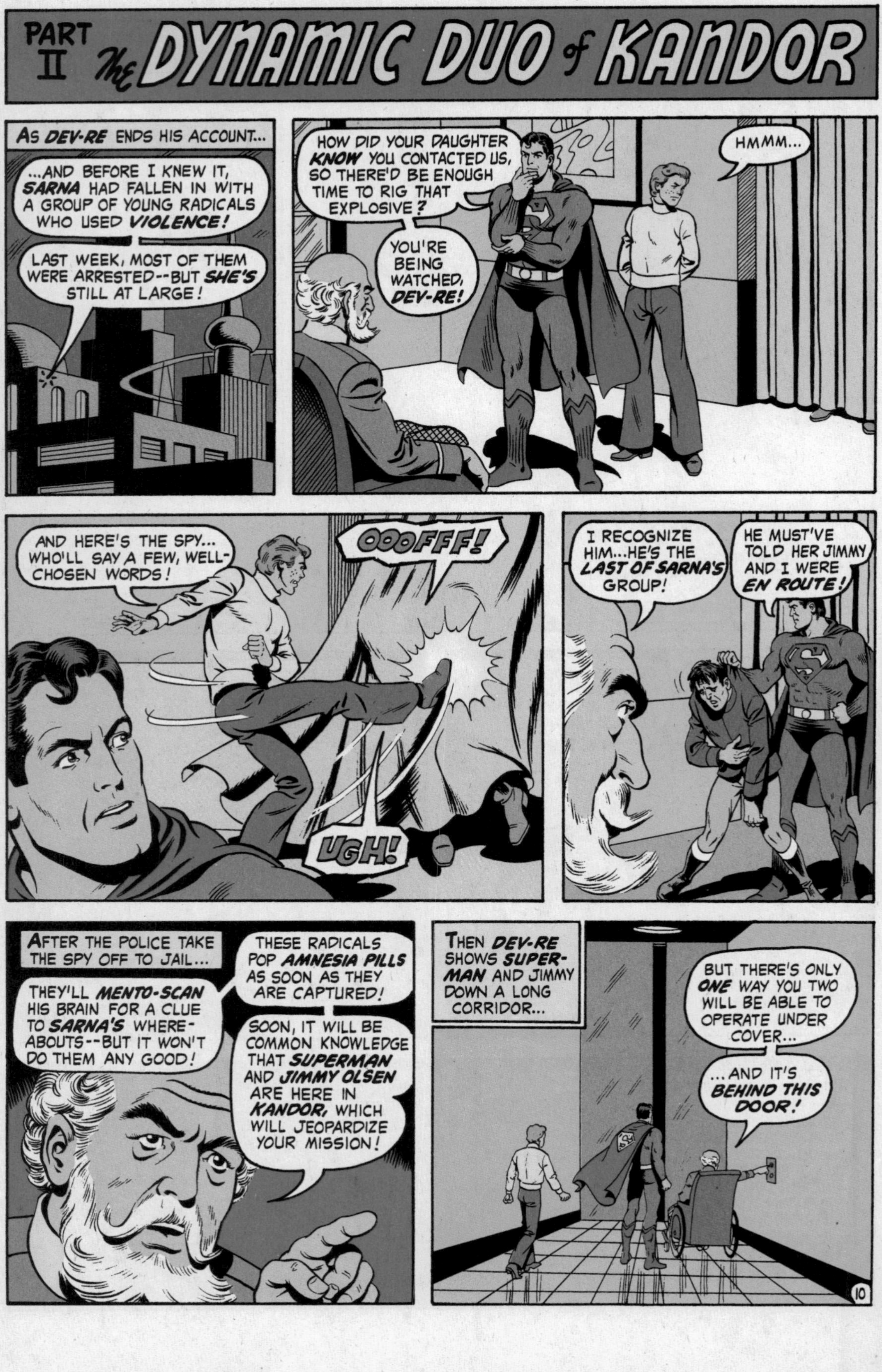
PART II THE DYNAMIC DUO of KANDOR
AS DEV-RE ENDS HIS ACCOUNT...
...AND BEFORE I KNEW IT, SARNA HAD FALLEN IN WITH A GROUP OF YOUNG RADICALS WHO USED VIOLENCE!
LAST WEEK, MOST OF THEM WERE ARRESTED--BUT SHE'S STILL AT LARGE!
HOW DID YOUR DAUGHTER KNOW YOU CONTACTED US, SO THERE'D BE ENOUGH TIME TO RIG THAT EXPLOSIVE?
YOU'RE BEING WATCHED, DEV-RE!
HMMM...
AND HERE'S THE SPY... WHO'LL SAY A FEW, WELL-CHOSEN WORDS!
OOOFFFF!
UGH!
I RECOGNIZE HIM...HE'S THE LAST OF SARNA'S GROUP!
HE MUST'VE TOLD HER JIMMY AND I WERE EN ROUTE!
AFTER THE POLICE TAKE THE SPY OFF TO JAIL...
THEY'LL MENTO-SCAN HIS BRAIN FOR A CLUE TO SARNA'S WHERE-ABOUTS--BUT IT WON'T DO THEM ANY GOOD!
THESE RADICALS POP AMNESIA PILLS AS SOON AS THEY ARE CAPTURED!
SOON, IT WILL BE COMMON KNOWLEDGE THAT SUPERMAN AND JIMMY OLSEN ARE HERE IN KANDOR, WHICH WILL JEOPARDIZE YOUR MISSION!
THEN DEV-RE SHOWS SUPER-MAN AND JIMMY DOWN A LONG CORRIDOR...
BUT THERE'S ONLY ONE WAY YOU TWO WILL BE ABLE TO OPERATE UNDER COVER...
...AND IT'S BEHIND THIS DOOR!
10

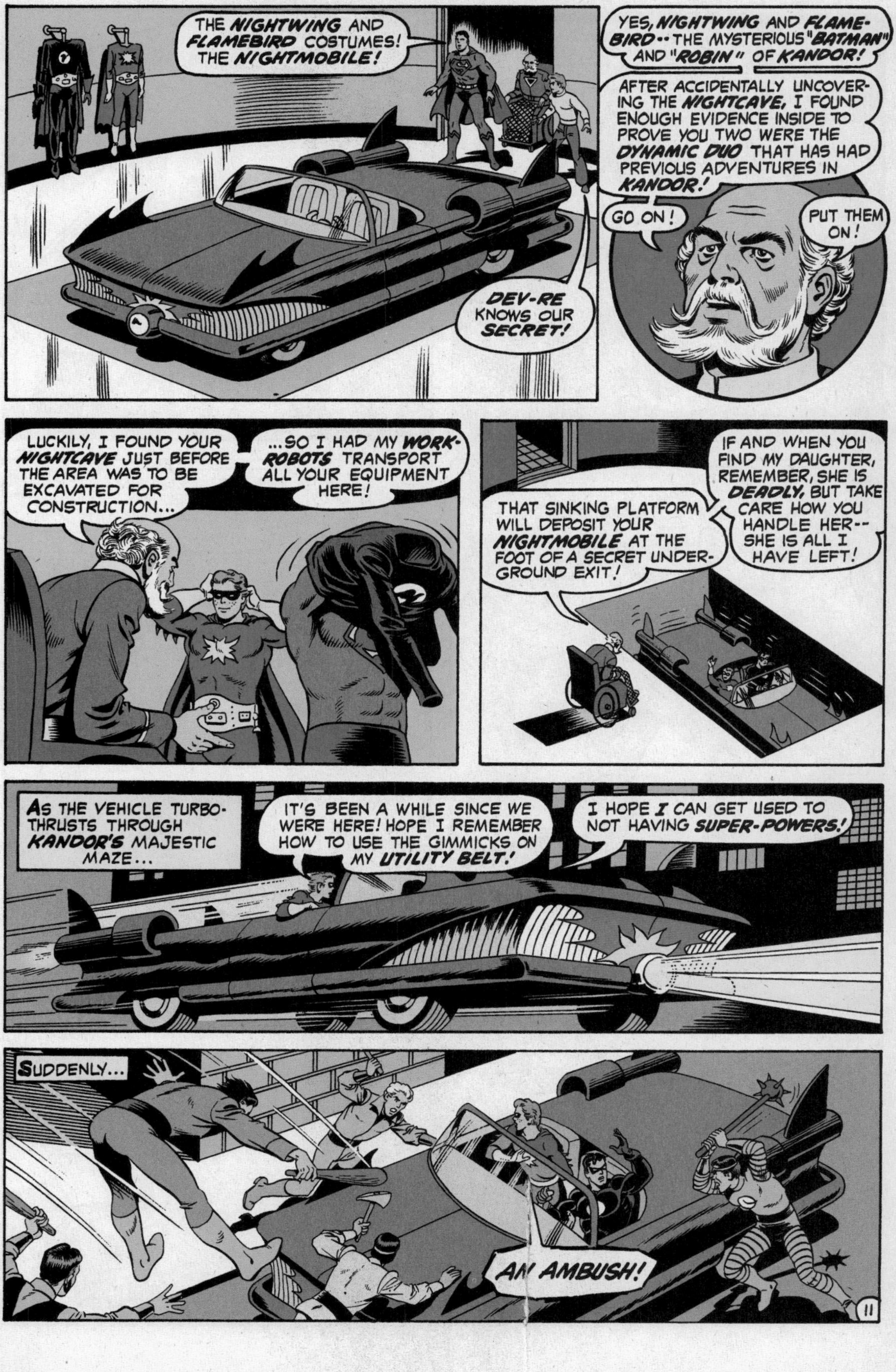
THE NIGHTWING AND FLAMEBIRD COSTUMES! THE NIGHTMOBILE!
DEV-RE KNOWS OUR SECRET!
YES, NIGHTWING AND FLAME-BIRD -- THE MYSTERIOUS "BATMAN" AND "ROBIN" OF KANDOR!
AFTER ACCIDENTALLY UNCOVER-ING THE NIGHTCAVE, I FOUND ENOUGH EVIDENCE INSIDE TO PROVE YOU TWO WERE THE DYNAMIC DUO THAT HAS HAD PREVIOUS ADVENTURES IN KANDOR!
GO ON!
PUT THEM ON!
LUCKILY, I FOUND YOUR NIGHTCAVE JUST BEFORE THE AREA WAS TO BE EXCAVATED FOR CONSTRUCTION...
...SO I HAD MY WORK-ROBOTS TRANSPORT ALL YOUR EQUIPMENT HERE!
THAT SINKING PLATFORM WILL DEPOSIT YOUR NIGHTMOBILE AT THE FOOT OF A SECRET UNDER-GROUND EXIT!
IF AND WHEN YOU FIND MY DAUGHTER, REMEMBER, SHE IS DEADLY, BUT TAKE CARE HOW YOU HANDLE HER-- SHE IS ALL I HAVE LEFT!
AS THE VEHICLE TURBO-THRUSTS THROUGH KANDOR'S MAJESTIC MAZE...
IT'S BEEN A WHILE SINCE WE WERE HERE! HOPE I REMEMBER HOW TO USE THE GIMMICKS ON MY UTILITY BELT!
I HOPE I CAN GET USED TO NOT HAVING SUPER-POWERS!
SUDDENLY...
AN AMBUSH!
11

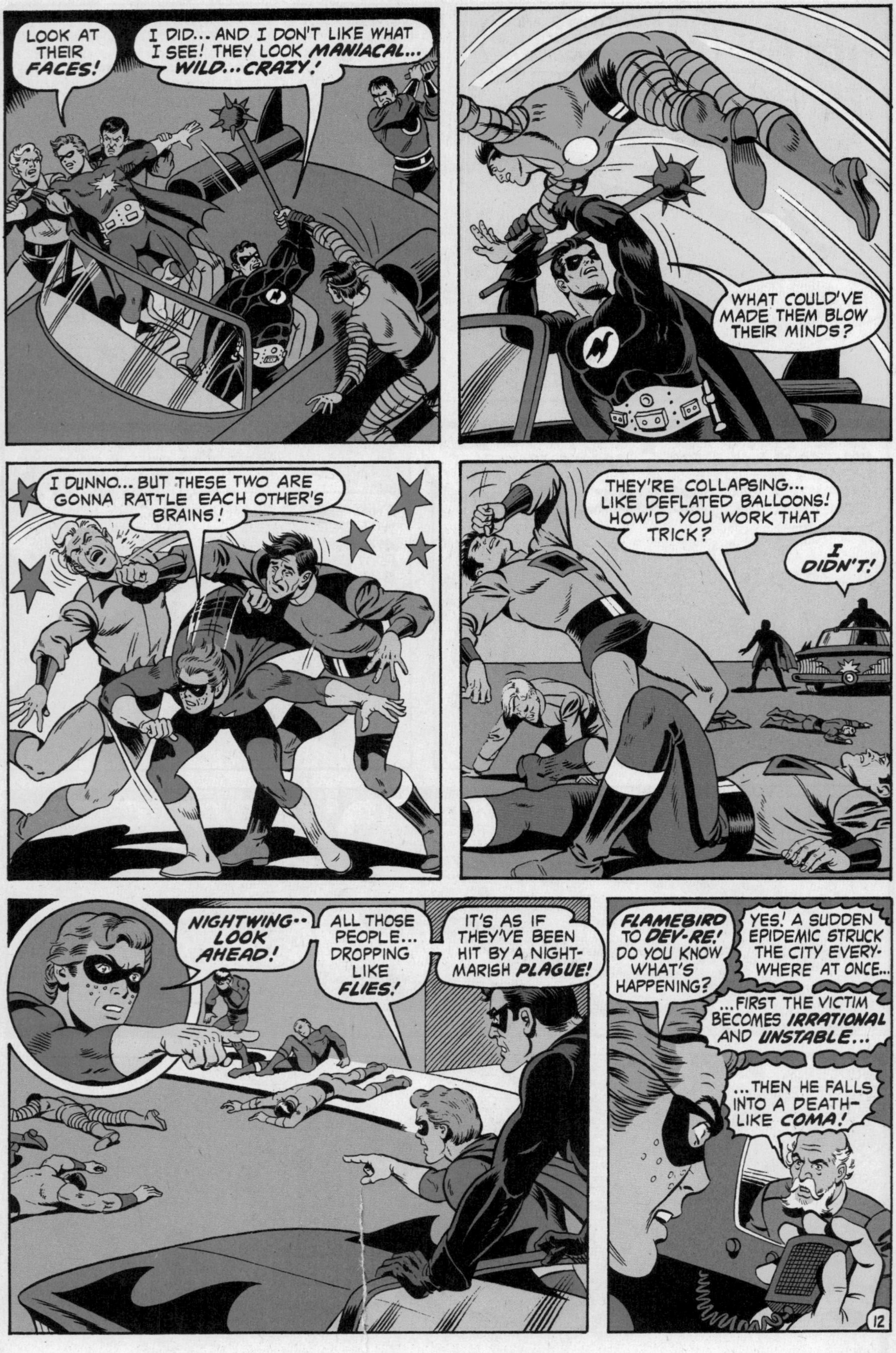
LOOK AT THEIR FACES!
I DID... AND I DON'T LIKE WHAT I SEE! THEY LOOK MANIACAL... WILD...CRAZY!
WHAT COULD'VE MADE THEM BLOW THEIR MINDS?
I DUNNO... BUT THESE TWO ARE GONNA RATTLE EACH OTHER'S BRAINS!
THEY'RE COLLAPSING... LIKE DEFLATED BALLOONS! HOW'D YOU WORK THAT TRICK?
I DIDN'T!
NIGHTWING.. LOOK AHEAD!
ALL THOSE PEOPLE... DROPPING LIKE FLIES!
IT'S AS IF THEY'VE BEEN HIT BY A NIGHT-MARISH PLAGUE!
FLAMEBIRD TO DEV-RE! DO YOU KNOW WHAT'S HAPPENING?
YES! A SUDDEN EPIDEMIC STRUCK THE CITY EVERY-WHERE AT ONCE...
...FIRST THE VICTIM BECOMES IRRATIONAL AND UNSTABLE...
...THEN HE FALLS INTO A DEATH-LIKE COMA!
12

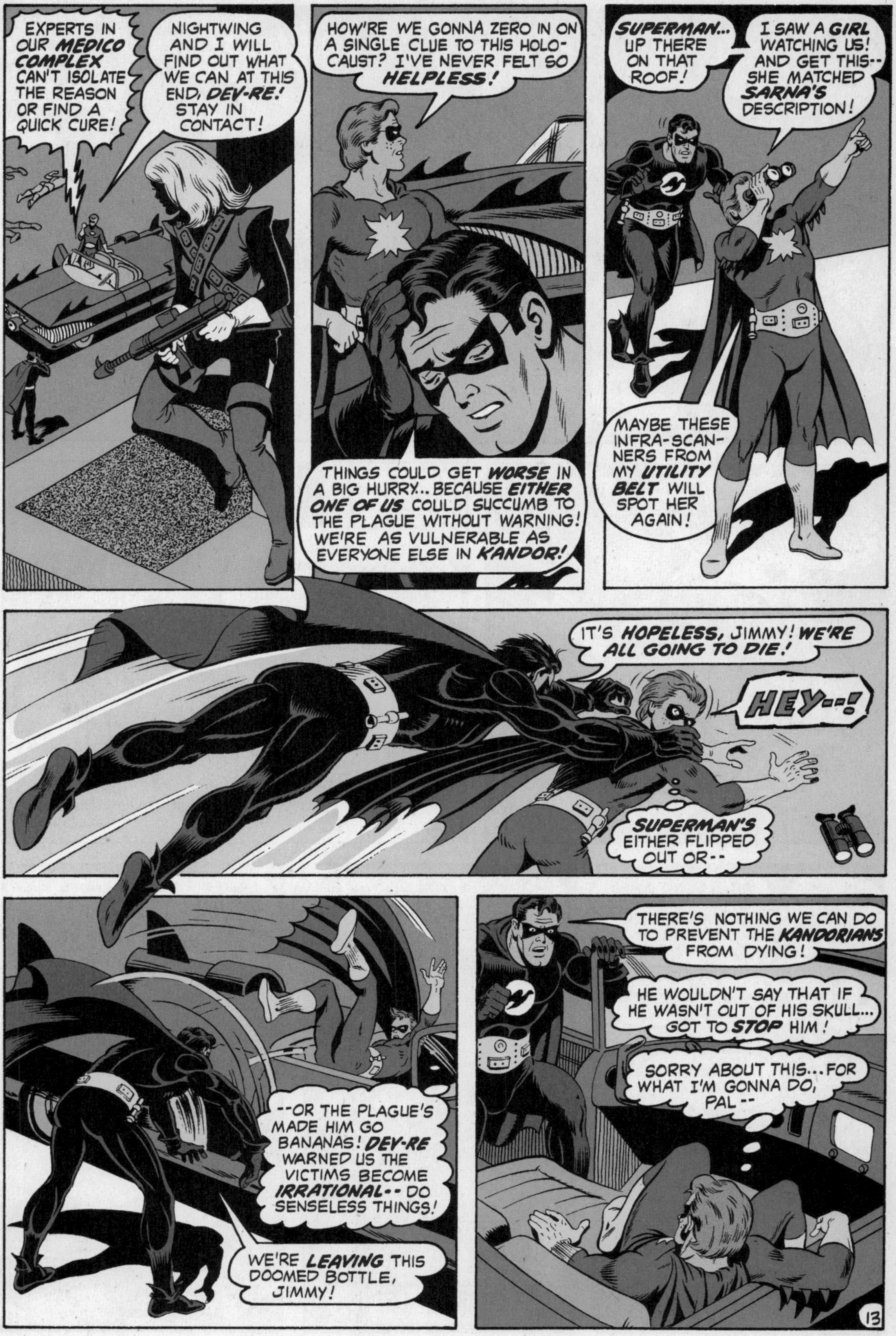

EXPERTS IN OUR MEDICO COMPLEX CAN'T ISOLATE THE REASON OR FIND A QUICK CURE!
NIGHTWING AND I WILL FIND OUT WHAT WE CAN AT THIS END, DEV-RE! STAY IN CONTACT!
HOW'RE WE GONNA ZERO IN ON A SINGLE CLUE TO THIS HOLOCAUST? I'VE NEVER FELT SO HELPLESS!
THINGS COULD GET WORSE IN A BIG HURRY... BECAUSE EITHER ONE OF US COULD SUCCUMB TO THE PLAGUE WITHOUT WARNING! WE'RE AS VULNERABLE AS EVERYONE ELSE IN KANDOR!
SUPERMAN... UP THERE ON THAT ROOF!
I SAW A GIRL WATCHING US! AND GET THIS-- SHE MATCHED SARNA'S DESCRIPTION!
MAYBE THESE INFRA-SCANNERS FROM MY UTILITY BELT WILL SPOT HER AGAIN!
IT'S HOPELESS, JIMMY! WE'RE ALL GOING TO DIE!
HEY--!
SUPERMAN'S EITHER FLIPPED OUT OR--
--OR THE PLAGUE'S MADE HIM GO BANANAS! DEV-RE WARNED US THE VICTIMS BECOME IRRATIONAL-- DO SENSELESS THINGS!
WE'RE LEAVING THIS DOOMED BOTTLE, JIMMY!
THERE'S NOTHING WE CAN DO TO PREVENT THE KANDORIANS FROM DYING!
HE WOULDN'T SAY THAT IF HE WASN'T OUT OF HIS SKULL... GOT TO STOP HIM!
SORRY ABOUT THIS... FOR WHAT I'M GONNA DO, PAL--
13

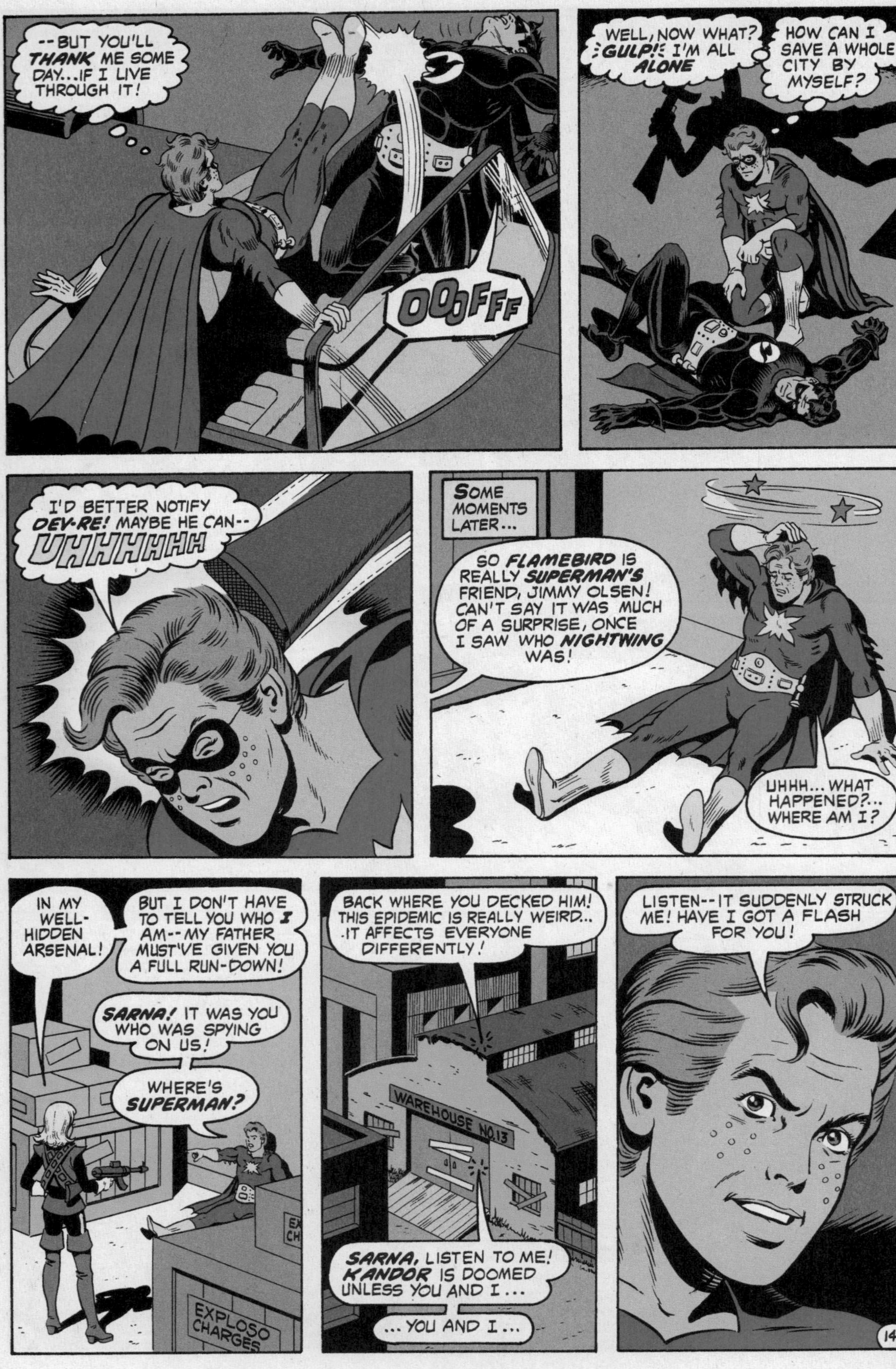
--BUT YOU'LL THANK ME SOME DAY...IF I LIVE THROUGH IT!
OOOFFFF
WELL, NOW WHAT? GULP! I'M ALL ALONE
HOW CAN I SAVE A WHOLE CITY BY MYSELF?
I'D BETTER NOTIFY DEV-RE! MAYBE HE CAN--
UHHHHHH
SOME MOMENTS LATER...
SO FLAMEBIRD IS REALLY SUPERMAN'S FRIEND, JIMMY OLSEN! CAN'T SAY IT WAS MUCH OF A SURPRISE, ONCE I SAW WHO NIGHTWING WAS!
UHHH... WHAT HAPPENED?... WHERE AM I?
IN MY WELL-HIDDEN ARSENAL!
BUT I DON'T HAVE TO TELL YOU WHO I AM--MY FATHER MUST'VE GIVEN YOU A FULL RUN-DOWN!
SARNA! IT WAS YOU WHO WAS SPYING ON US!
WHERE'S SUPERMAN?
EXPLOSO CHARGES
BACK WHERE YOU DECKED HIM! THIS EPIDEMIC IS REALLY WEIRD... IT AFFECTS EVERYONE DIFFERENTLY!
WAREHOUSE NO.13
SARNA, LISTEN TO ME! KANDOR IS DOOMED UNLESS YOU AND I...
...YOU AND I...
LISTEN--IT SUDDENLY STRUCK ME! HAVE I GOT A FLASH FOR YOU!
14

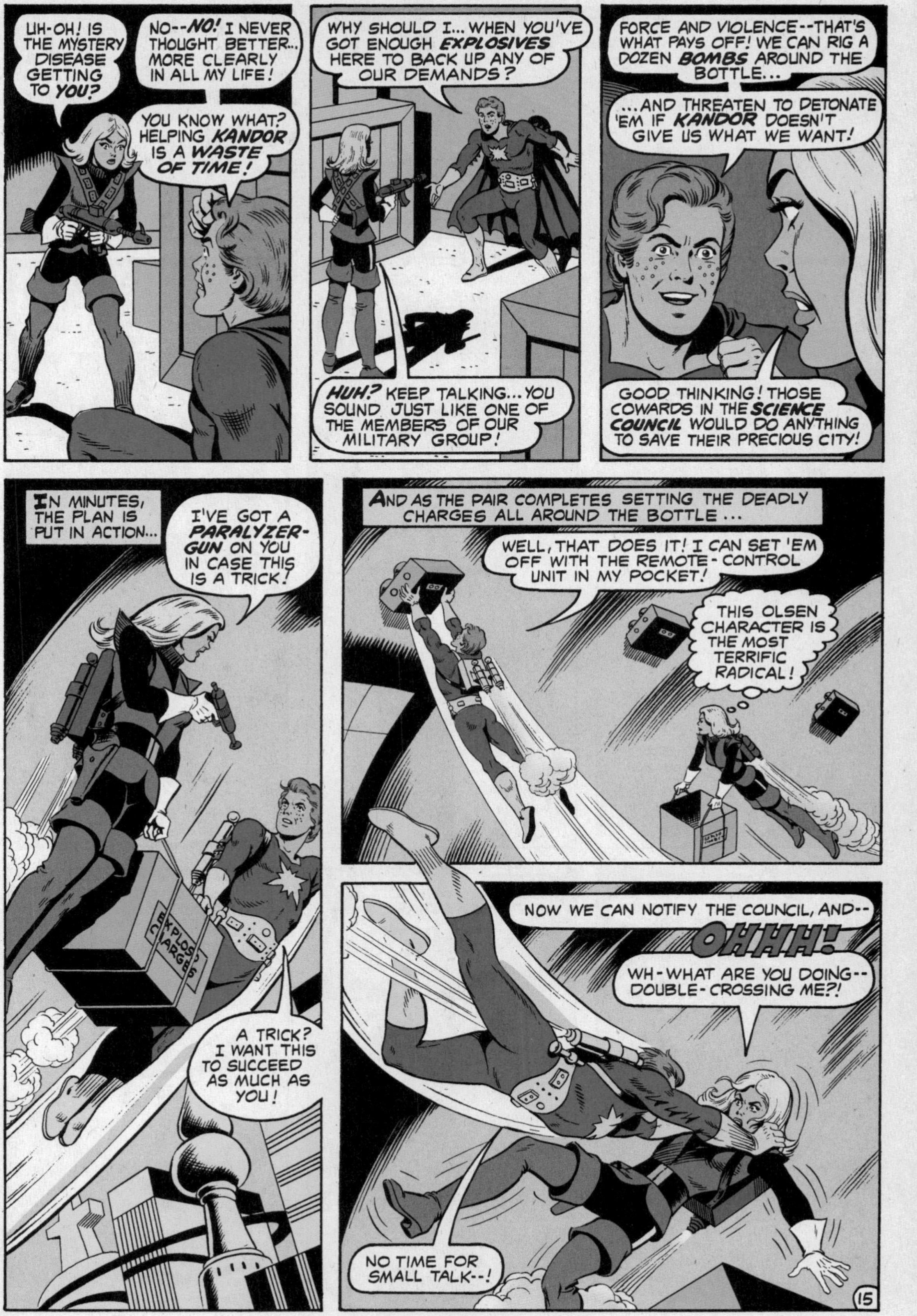
UH-OH! IS THE MYSTERY DISEASE GETTING TO YOU?
NO--NO! I NEVER THOUGHT BETTER... MORE CLEARLY IN ALL MY LIFE!
YOU KNOW WHAT? HELPING KANDOR IS A WASTE OF TIME!
WHY SHOULD I... WHEN YOU'VE GOT ENOUGH EXPLOSIVES HERE TO BACK UP ANY OF OUR DEMANDS?
HUH? KEEP TALKING... YOU SOUND JUST LIKE ONE OF THE MEMBERS OF OUR MILITARY GROUP!
FORCE AND VIOLENCE--THAT'S WHAT PAYS OFF! WE CAN RIG A DOZEN BOMBS AROUND THE BOTTLE...
...AND THREATEN TO DETONATE 'EM IF KANDOR DOESN'T GIVE US WHAT WE WANT!
GOOD THINKING! THOSE COWARDS IN THE SCIENCE COUNCIL WOULD DO ANYTHING TO SAVE THEIR PRECIOUS CITY!
IN MINUTES, THE PLAN IS PUT IN ACTION...
I'VE GOT A PARALYZER-GUN ON YOU IN CASE THIS IS A TRICK!
A TRICK? I WANT THIS TO SUCCEED AS MUCH AS YOU!
AND AS THE PAIR COMPLETES SETTING THE DEADLY CHARGES ALL AROUND THE BOTTLE...
WELL, THAT DOES IT! I CAN SET 'EM OFF WITH THE REMOTE-CONTROL UNIT IN MY POCKET!
THIS OLSEN CHARACTER IS THE MOST TERRIFIC RADICAL!
NOW WE CAN NOTIFY THE COUNCIL, AND--
OHHH!
WH-WHAT ARE YOU DOING--DOUBLE-CROSSING ME?!
NO TIME FOR SMALL TALK--!
15

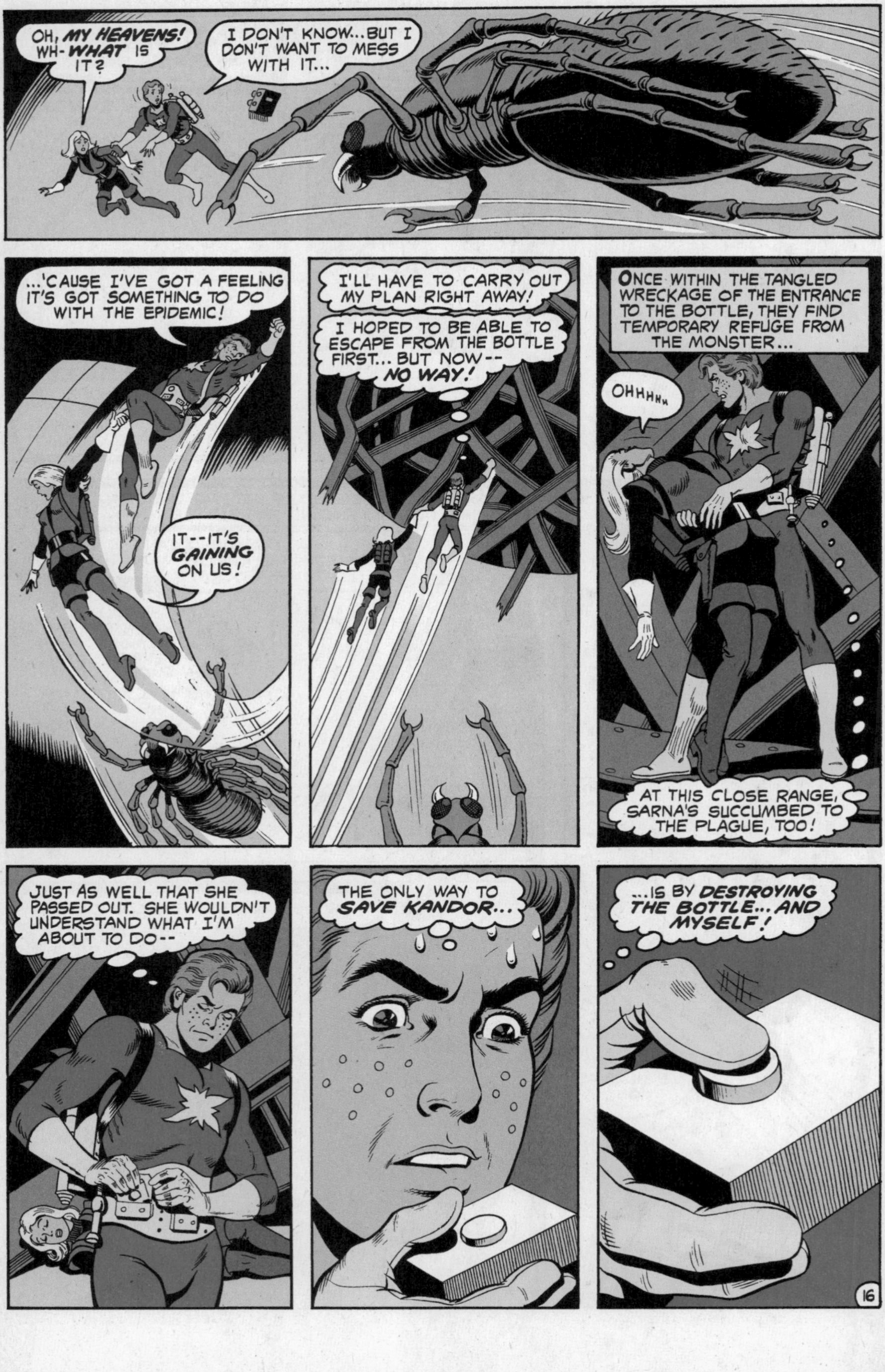
OH, MY HEAVENS! WH-WHAT IS IT?
I DON'T KNOW... BUT I DON'T WANT TO MESS WITH IT...
...'CAUSE I'VE GOT A FEELING IT'S GOT SOMETHING TO DO WITH THE EPIDEMIC!
IT--IT'S GAINING ON US!
I'LL HAVE TO CARRY OUT MY PLAN RIGHT AWAY!
I HOPED TO BE ABLE TO ESCAPE FROM THE BOTTLE FIRST... BUT NOW-- NO WAY!
ONCE WITHIN THE TANGLED WRECKAGE OF THE ENTRANCE TO THE BOTTLE, THEY FIND TEMPORARY REFUGE FROM THE MONSTER...
OHHHHH
AT THIS CLOSE RANGE, SARNA'S SUCCUMBED TO THE PLAGUE, TOO!
JUST AS WELL THAT SHE PASSED OUT. SHE WOULDN'T UNDERSTAND WHAT I'M ABOUT TO DO--
THE ONLY WAY TO SAVE KANDOR...
...IS BY DESTROYING THE BOTTLE... AND MYSELF!
16

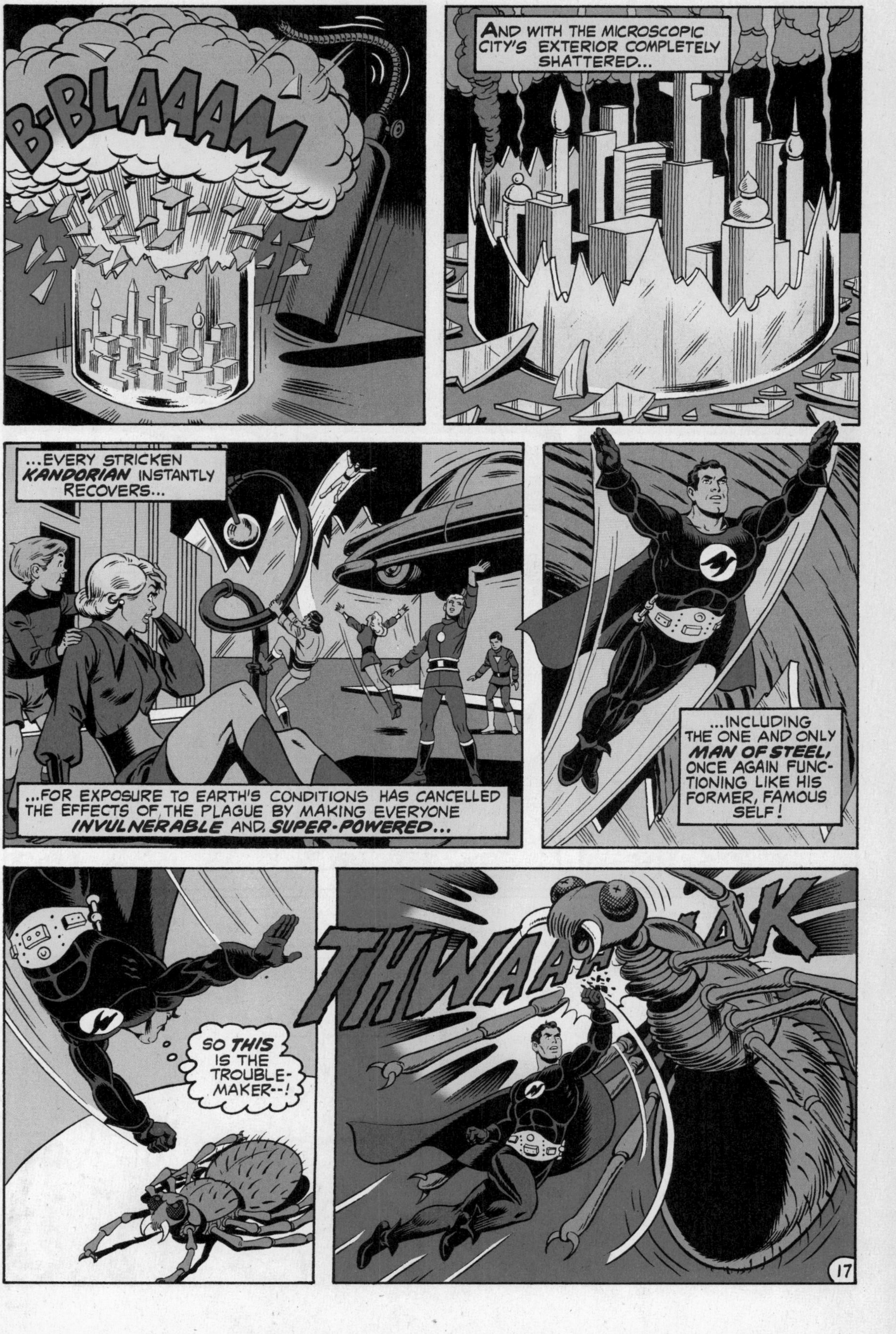
B-BLAAAM
AND WITH THE MICROSCOPIC CITY'S EXTERIOR COMPLETELY SHATTERED...
...EVERY STRICKEN KANDORIAN INSTANTLY RECOVERS...
...FOR EXPOSURE TO EARTH'S CONDITIONS HAS CANCELLED THE EFFECTS OF THE PLAGUE BY MAKING EVERYONE INVULNERABLE AND SUPER-POWERED...
...INCLUDING THE ONE AND ONLY MAN OF STEEL, ONCE AGAIN FUNCTIONING LIKE HIS FORMER, FAMOUS SELF!
SO THIS IS THE TROUBLE-MAKER--!
THWAA K
17

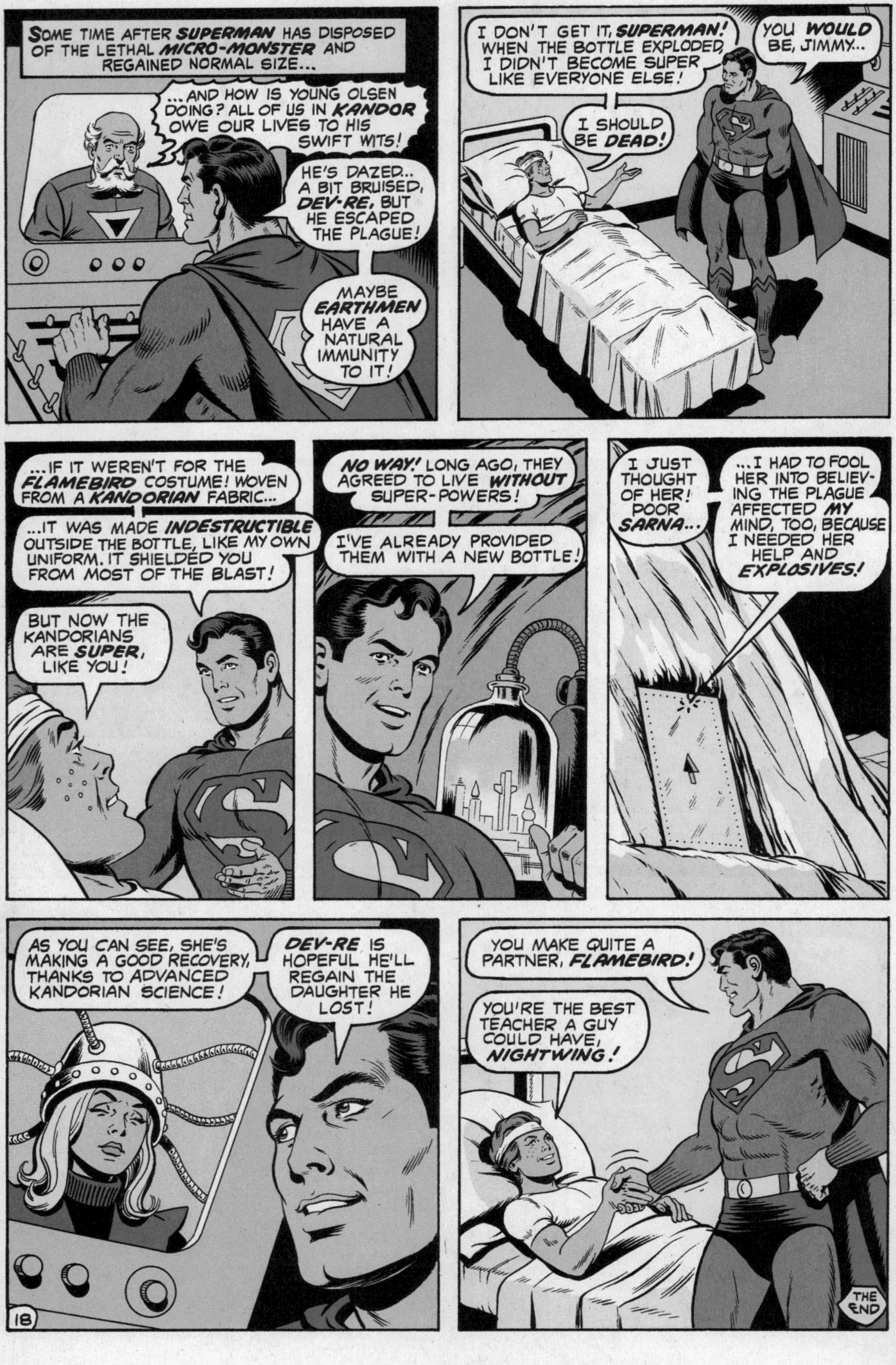
SOME TIME AFTER SUPERMAN HAS DISPOSED OF THE LETHAL MICRO-MONSTER AND REGAINED NORMAL SIZE...
...AND HOW IS YOUNG OLSEN DOING? ALL OF US IN KANDOR OWE OUR LIVES TO HIS SWIFT WITS!
HE'S DAZED.. A BIT BRUISED, DEV-RE, BUT HE ESCAPED THE PLAGUE!
MAYBE EARTHMEN HAVE A NATURAL IMMUNITY TO IT!
I DON'T GET IT, SUPERMAN! WHEN THE BOTTLE EXPLODED, I DIDN'T BECOME SUPER LIKE EVERYONE ELSE!
I SHOULD BE DEAD!
YOU WOULD BE, JIMMY...
...IF IT WEREN'T FOR THE FLAMEBIRD COSTUME! WOVEN FROM A KANDORIAN FABRIC...
...IT WAS MADE INDESTRUCTIBLE OUTSIDE THE BOTTLE, LIKE MY OWN UNIFORM. IT SHIELDED YOU FROM MOST OF THE BLAST!
BUT NOW THE KANDORIANS ARE SUPER, LIKE YOU!
NO WAY! LONG AGO, THEY AGREED TO LIVE WITHOUT SUPER-POWERS!
I'VE ALREADY PROVIDED THEM WITH A NEW BOTTLE!
I JUST THOUGHT OF HER! POOR SARNA...
...I HAD TO FOOL HER INTO BELIEVING THE PLAGUE AFFECTED MY MIND, TOO, BECAUSE I NEEDED HER HELP AND EXPLOSIVES!
AS YOU CAN SEE, SHE'S MAKING A GOOD RECOVERY, THANKS TO ADVANCED KANDORIAN SCIENCE!
DEV-RE IS HOPEFUL HE'LL REGAIN THE DAUGHTER HE LOST!
18
YOU MAKE QUITE A PARTNER, FLAMEBIRD!
YOU'RE THE BEST TEACHER A GUY COULD HAVE, NIGHTWING!
THE END

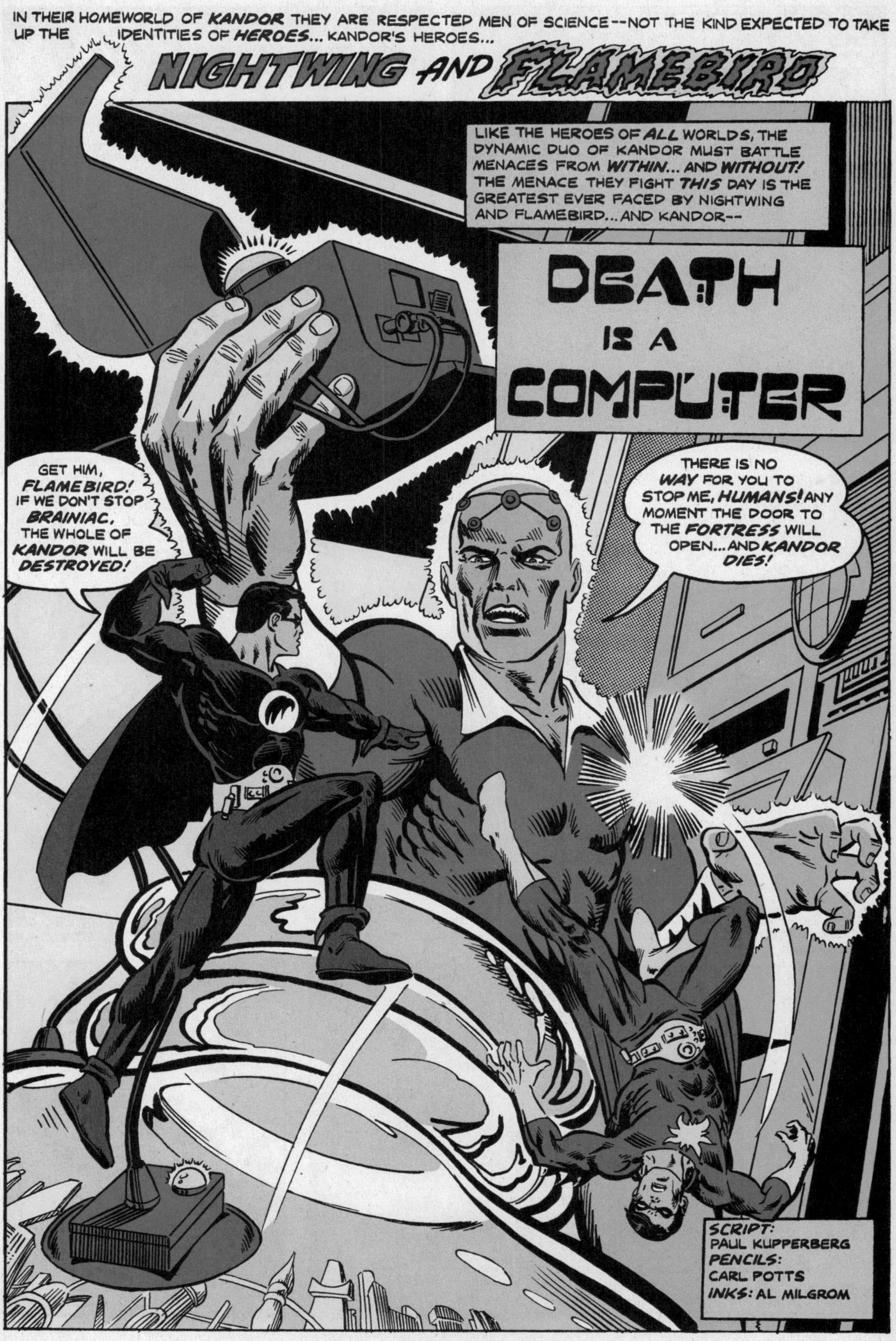
IN THEIR HOMEWORLD OF KANDOR THEY ARE RESPECTED MEN OF SCIENCE--NOT THE KIND EXPECTED TO TAKE UP THE IDENTITIES OF HEROES... KANDOR'S HEROES...
NIGHTWING AND FLAMEBIRD
LIKE THE HEROES OF ALL WORLDS, THE DYNAMIC DUO OF KANDOR MUST BATTLE MENACES FROM WITHIN... AND WITHOUT! THE MENACE THEY FIGHT THIS DAY IS THE GREATEST EVER FACED BY NIGHTWING AND FLAMEBIRD... AND KANDOR--
DEATH IS A COMPUTER
GET HIM, FLAMEBIRD! IF WE DON'T STOP BRAINIAC, THE WHOLE OF KANDOR WILL BE DESTROYED!
THERE IS NO WAY FOR YOU TO STOP ME, HUMANS! ANY MOMENT THE DOOR TO THE FORTRESS WILL OPEN... AND KANDOR DIES!
SCRIPT: PAUL KUPPERBERG
PENCILS: CARL POTTS
INKS: AL MILGROM

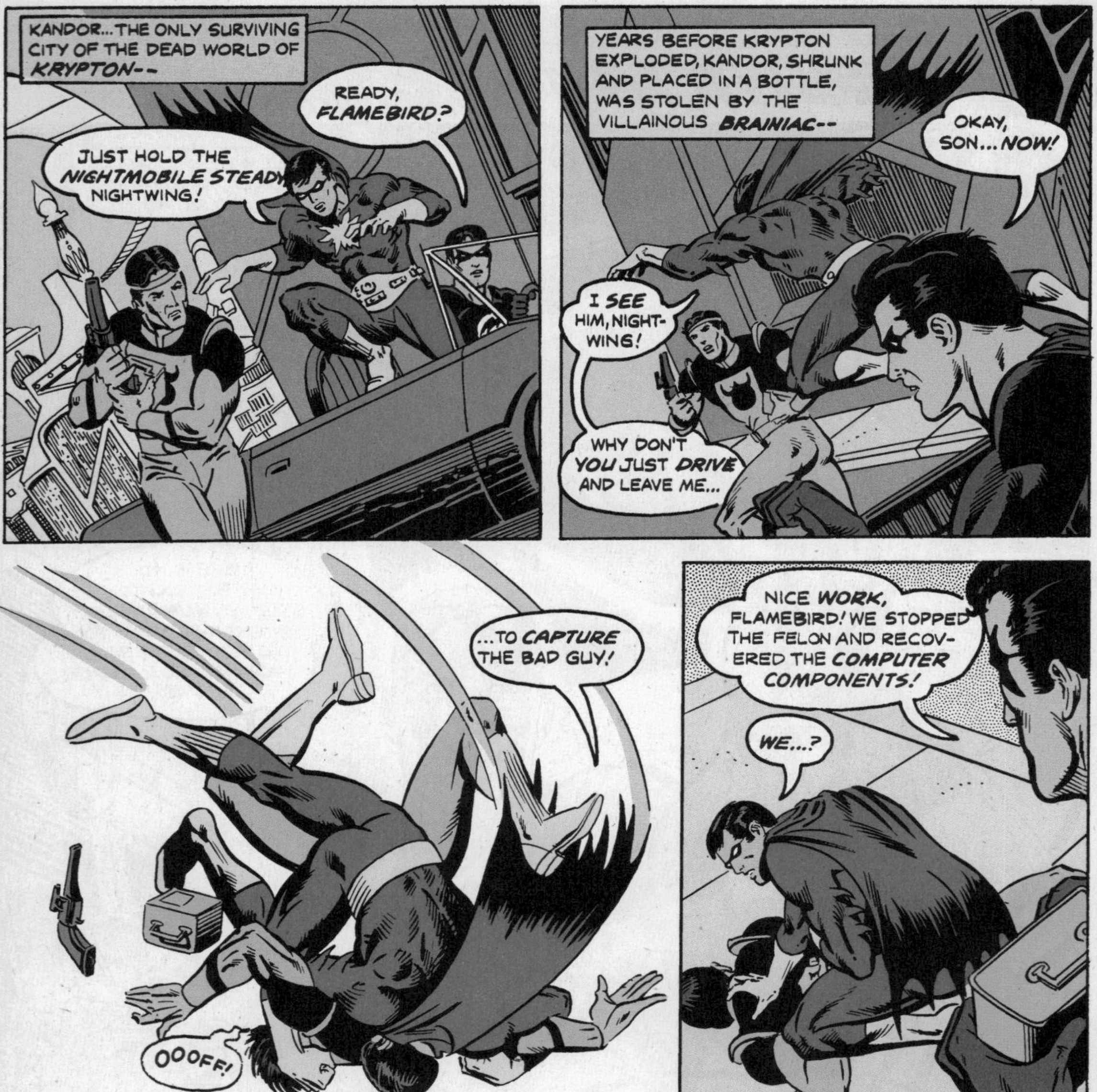
KANDOR... THE ONLY SURVIVING CITY OF THE DEAD WORLD OF KRYPTON--
READY, FLAMEBIRD?
JUST HOLD THE NIGHTMOBILE STEADY, NIGHTWING!
YEARS BEFORE KRYPTON EXPLODED, KANDOR, SHRUNK AND PLACED IN A BOTTLE, WAS STOLEN BY THE VILLAINOUS BRAINIAC--
OKAY, SON... NOW!
I SEE HIM, NIGHT-WING!
WHY DON'T YOU JUST DRIVE AND LEAVE ME...
...TO CAPTURE THE BAD GUY!
OOOFF!
NICE WORK, FLAMEBIRD! WE STOPPED THE FELON AND RECOVERED THE COMPUTER COMPONENTS!
WE...?

HIDDEN SECRETLY IN THE FORTRESS OF SOLITUDE OF THE FAMED *MAN OF STEEL*, SUPERMAN, THE BOTTLED CITY OF KANDOR SITS SECURE, GUARDED BY THICK WALLS OF ARCTIC ICE AND ROCK FROM THE OUTSIDE WORLD AND ITS DANGERS...

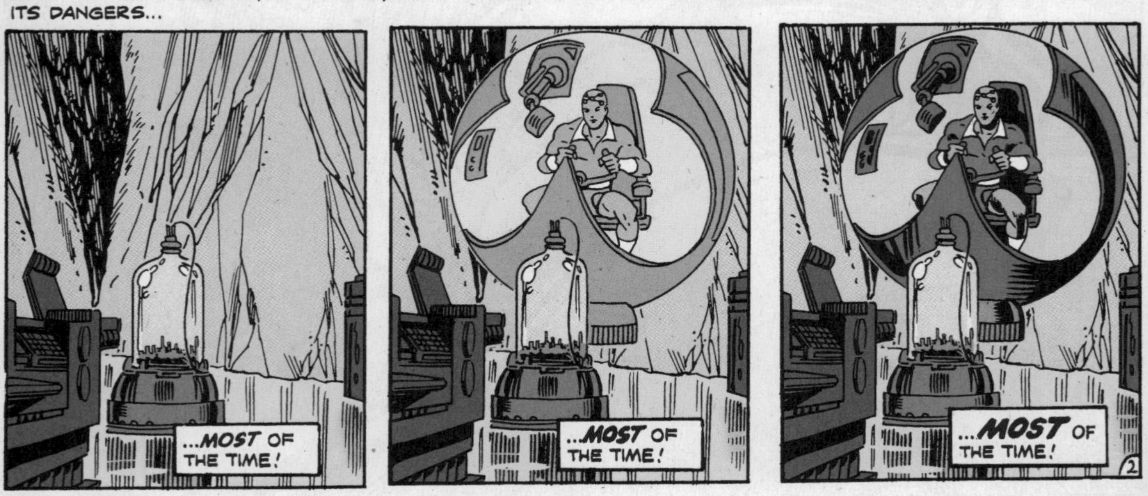
...MOST OF THE TIME!
...MOST OF THE TIME!
...MOST OF THE TIME!
2

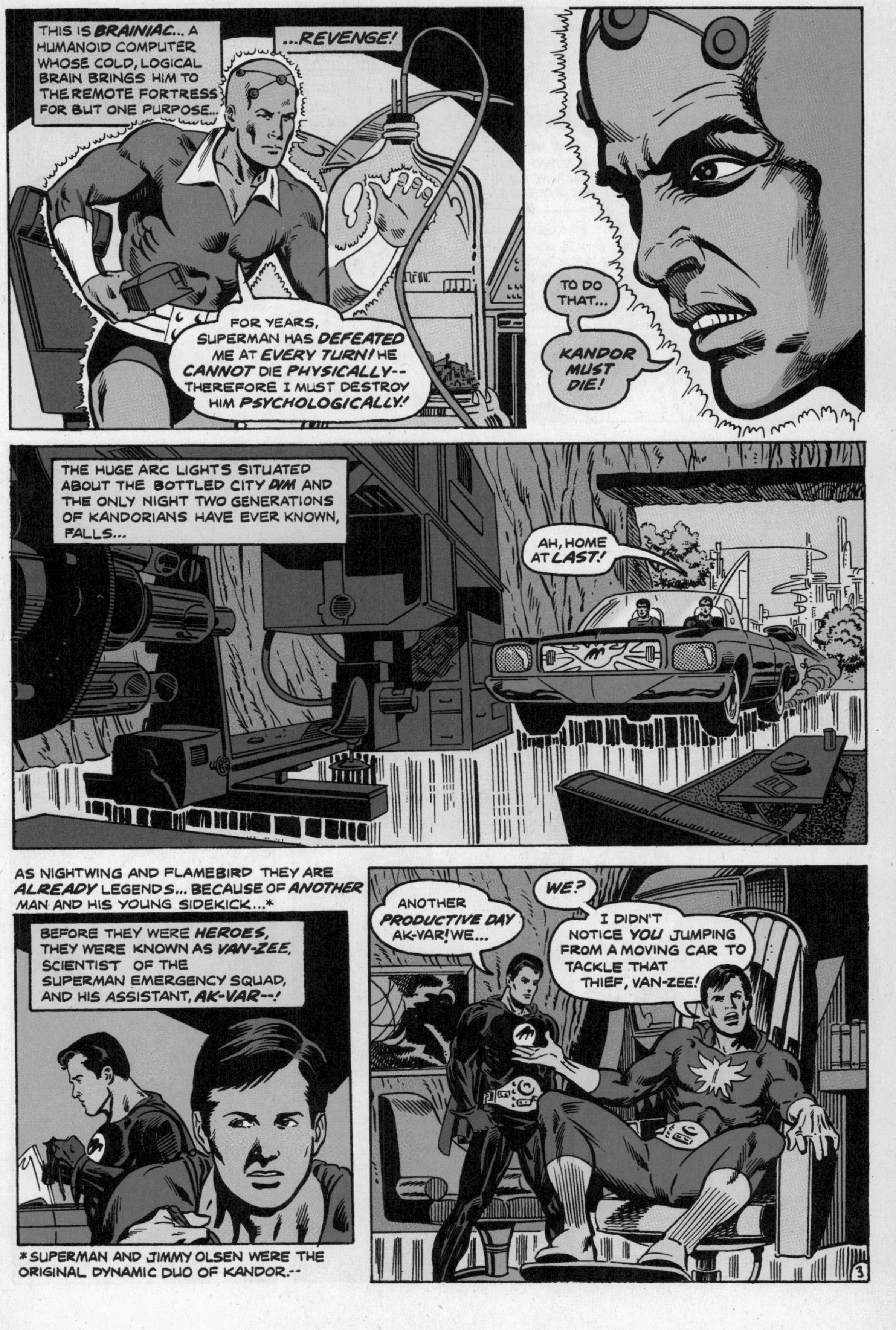

THIS IS BRAINIAC... A HUMANOID COMPUTER WHOSE COLD, LOGICAL BRAIN BRINGS HIM TO THE REMOTE FORTRESS FOR BUT ONE PURPOSE...
...REVENGE!
FOR YEARS, SUPERMAN HAS DEFEATED ME AT EVERY TURN! HE CANNOT DIE PHYSICALLY-- THEREFORE I MUST DESTROY HIM PSYCHOLOGICALLY!
TO DO THAT...
KANDOR MUST DIE!
THE HUGE ARC LIGHTS SITUATED ABOUT THE BOTTLED CITY DIM AND THE ONLY NIGHT TWO GENERATIONS OF KANDORIANS HAVE EVER KNOWN, FALLS...
AH, HOME AT LAST!
AS NIGHTWING AND FLAMEBIRD THEY ARE ALREADY LEGENDS... BECAUSE OF ANOTHER MAN AND HIS YOUNG SIDEKICK...*
BEFORE THEY WERE HEROES, THEY WERE KNOWN AS VAN-ZEE, SCIENTIST OF THE SUPERMAN EMERGENCY SQUAD, AND HIS ASSISTANT, AK-VAR--!
*SUPERMAN AND JIMMY OLSEN WERE THE ORIGINAL DYNAMIC DUO OF KANDOR.--
ANOTHER PRODUCTIVE DAY AK-VAR! WE...
WE?
I DIDN'T NOTICE YOU JUMPING FROM A MOVING CAR TO TACKLE THAT THIEF, VAN-ZEE!
3

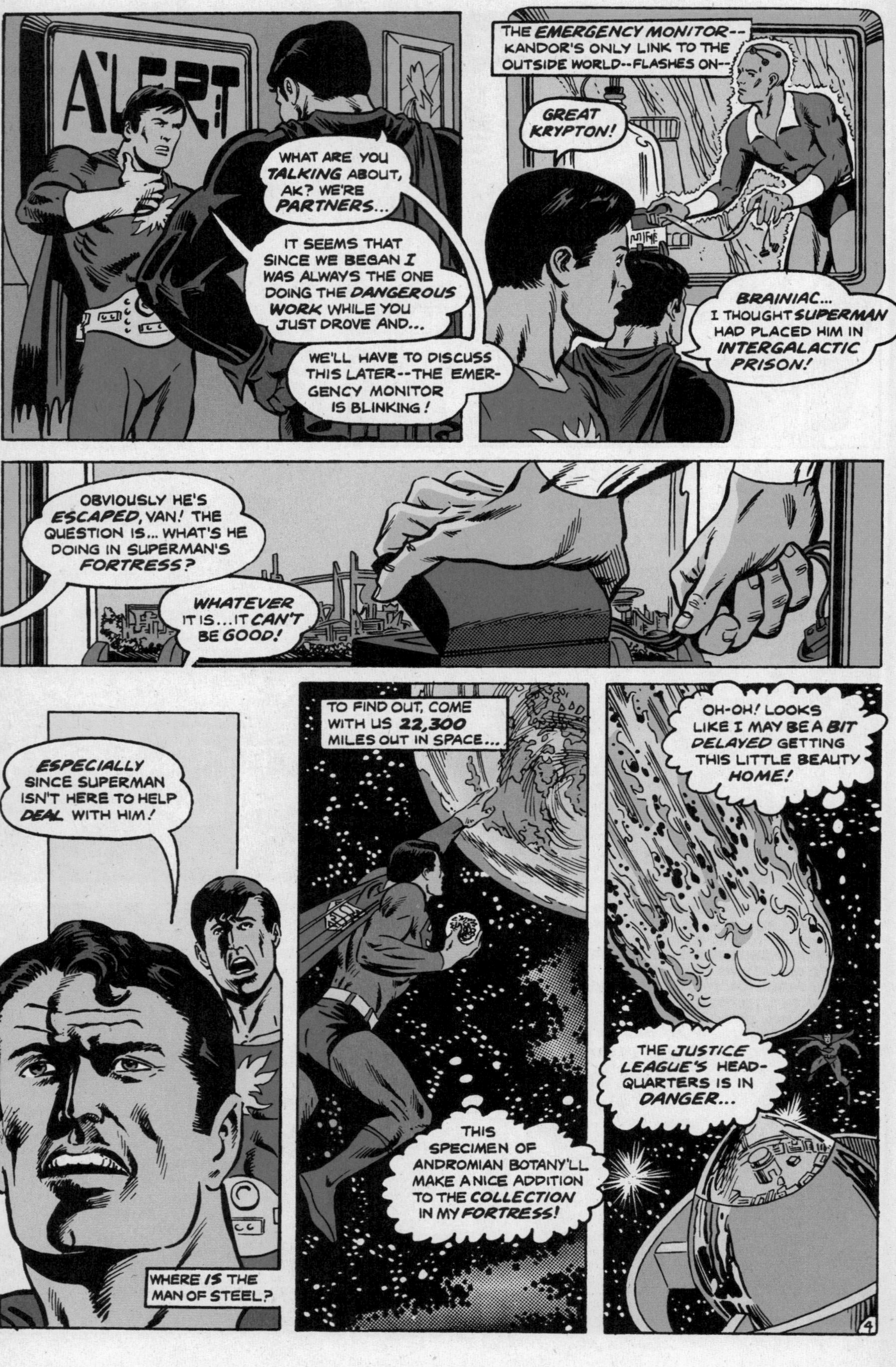

WHAT ARE YOU TALKING ABOUT, AK? WE'RE PARTNERS...
IT SEEMS THAT SINCE WE BEGAN I WAS ALWAYS THE ONE DOING THE DANGEROUS WORK WHILE YOU JUST DROVE AND...
WE'LL HAVE TO DISCUSS THIS LATER--THE EMERGENCY MONITOR IS BLINKING!
THE EMERGENCY MONITOR--KANDOR'S ONLY LINK TO THE OUTSIDE WORLD--FLASHES ON--
GREAT KRYPTON!
BRAINIAC... I THOUGHT SUPERMAN HAD PLACED HIM IN INTERGALACTIC PRISON!
OBVIOUSLY HE'S ESCAPED, VAN! THE QUESTION IS... WHAT'S HE DOING IN SUPERMAN'S FORTRESS?
WHATEVER IT IS... IT CAN'T BE GOOD!
ESPECIALLY SINCE SUPERMAN ISN'T HERE TO HELP DEAL WITH HIM!
WHERE IS THE MAN OF STEEL?
TO FIND OUT, COME WITH US 22,300 MILES OUT IN SPACE...
THIS SPECIMEN OF ANDROMIAN BOTANY'LL MAKE A NICE ADDITION TO THE COLLECTION IN MY FORTRESS!
OH-OH! LOOKS LIKE I MAY BE A BIT DELAYED GETTING THIS LITTLE BEAUTY HOME!
THE JUSTICE LEAGUE'S HEADQUARTERS IS IN DANGER...
4

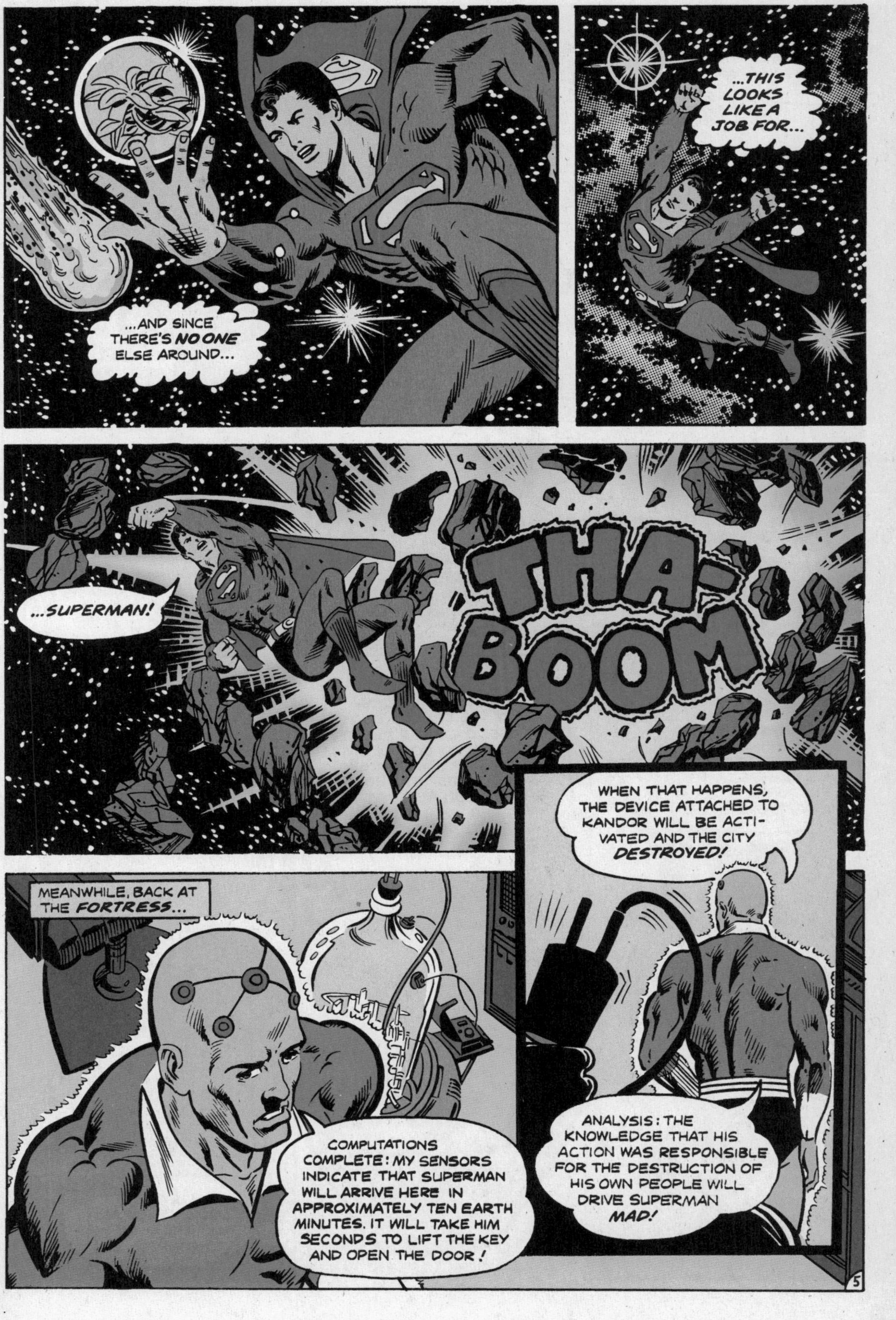
...AND SINCE THERE'S NO ONE ELSE AROUND...
...THIS LOOKS LIKE A JOB FOR...
...SUPERMAN!
THA-BOOM
MEANWHILE, BACK AT THE FORTRESS...
COMPUTATIONS COMPLETE: MY SENSORS INDICATE THAT SUPERMAN WILL ARRIVE HERE IN APPROXIMATELY TEN EARTH MINUTES. IT WILL TAKE HIM SECONDS TO LIFT THE KEY AND OPEN THE DOOR!
WHEN THAT HAPPENS, THE DEVICE ATTACHED TO KANDOR WILL BE ACTIVATED AND THE CITY DESTROYED!
ANALYSIS: THE KNOWLEDGE THAT HIS ACTION WAS RESPONSIBLE FOR THE DESTRUCTION OF HIS OWN PEOPLE WILL DRIVE SUPERMAN MAD!
5

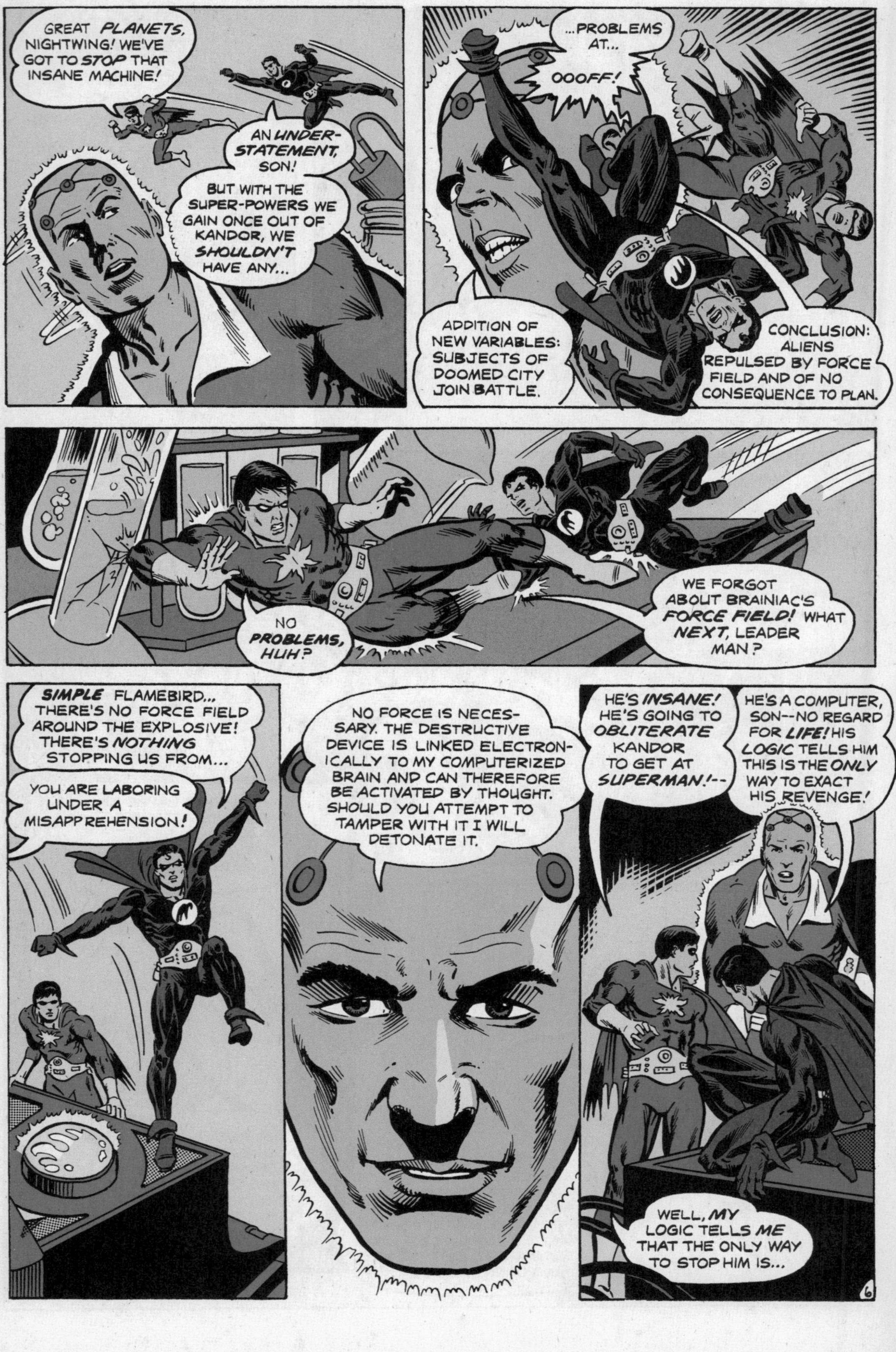
GREAT PLANETS, NIGHTWING! WE'VE GOT TO STOP THAT INSANE MACHINE!
AN UNDER-STATEMENT, SON!
BUT WITH THE SUPER-POWERS WE GAIN ONCE OUT OF KANDOR, WE SHOULDN'T HAVE ANY...
...PROBLEMS AT...
OOOFF!
ADDITION OF NEW VARIABLES: SUBJECTS OF DOOMED CITY JOIN BATTLE.
CONCLUSION: ALIENS REPULSED BY FORCE FIELD AND OF NO CONSEQUENCE TO PLAN.
NO PROBLEMS, HUH?
WE FORGOT ABOUT BRAINIAC'S FORCE FIELD! WHAT NEXT, LEADER MAN?
SIMPLE FLAMEBIRD... THERE'S NO FORCE FIELD AROUND THE EXPLOSIVE! THERE'S NOTHING STOPPING US FROM...
YOU ARE LABORING UNDER A MISAPPREHENSION!
NO FORCE IS NECES-SARY. THE DESTRUCTIVE DEVICE IS LINKED ELECTRON-ICALLY TO MY COMPUTERIZED BRAIN AND CAN THEREFORE BE ACTIVATED BY THOUGHT. SHOULD YOU ATTEMPT TO TAMPER WITH IT I WILL DETONATE IT.
HE'S INSANE! HE'S GOING TO OBLITERATE KANDOR TO GET AT SUPERMAN!--
HE'S A COMPUTER, SON--NO REGARD FOR LIFE! HIS LOGIC TELLS HIM THIS IS THE ONLY WAY TO EXACT HIS REVENGE!
WELL, MY LOGIC TELLS ME THAT THE ONLY WAY TO STOP HIM IS...
6

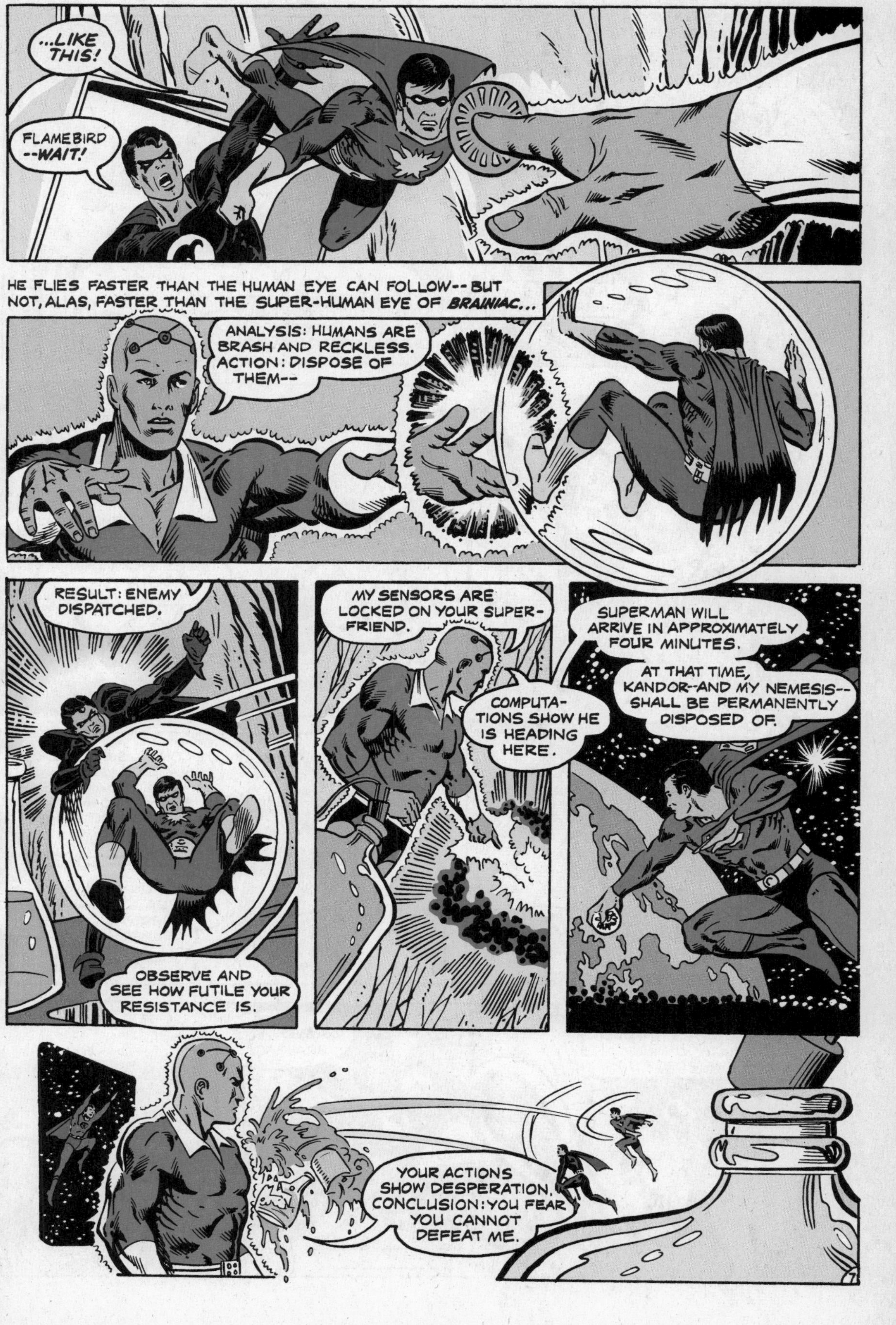
...LIKE THIS!
FLAMEBIRD --WAIT!
HE FLIES FASTER THAN THE HUMAN EYE CAN FOLLOW-- BUT NOT, ALAS, FASTER THAN THE SUPER-HUMAN EYE OF BRAINIAC...
ANALYSIS: HUMANS ARE BRASH AND RECKLESS. ACTION: DISPOSE OF THEM--
RESULT: ENEMY DISPATCHED.
OBSERVE AND SEE HOW FUTILE YOUR RESISTANCE IS.
MY SENSORS ARE LOCKED ON YOUR SUPER-FRIEND.
COMPUTATIONS SHOW HE IS HEADING HERE.
SUPERMAN WILL ARRIVE IN APPROXIMATELY FOUR MINUTES.
AT THAT TIME, KANDOR--AND MY NEMESIS--SHALL BE PERMANENTLY DISPOSED OF.
YOUR ACTIONS SHOW DESPERATION. CONCLUSION: YOU FEAR YOU CANNOT DEFEAT ME.

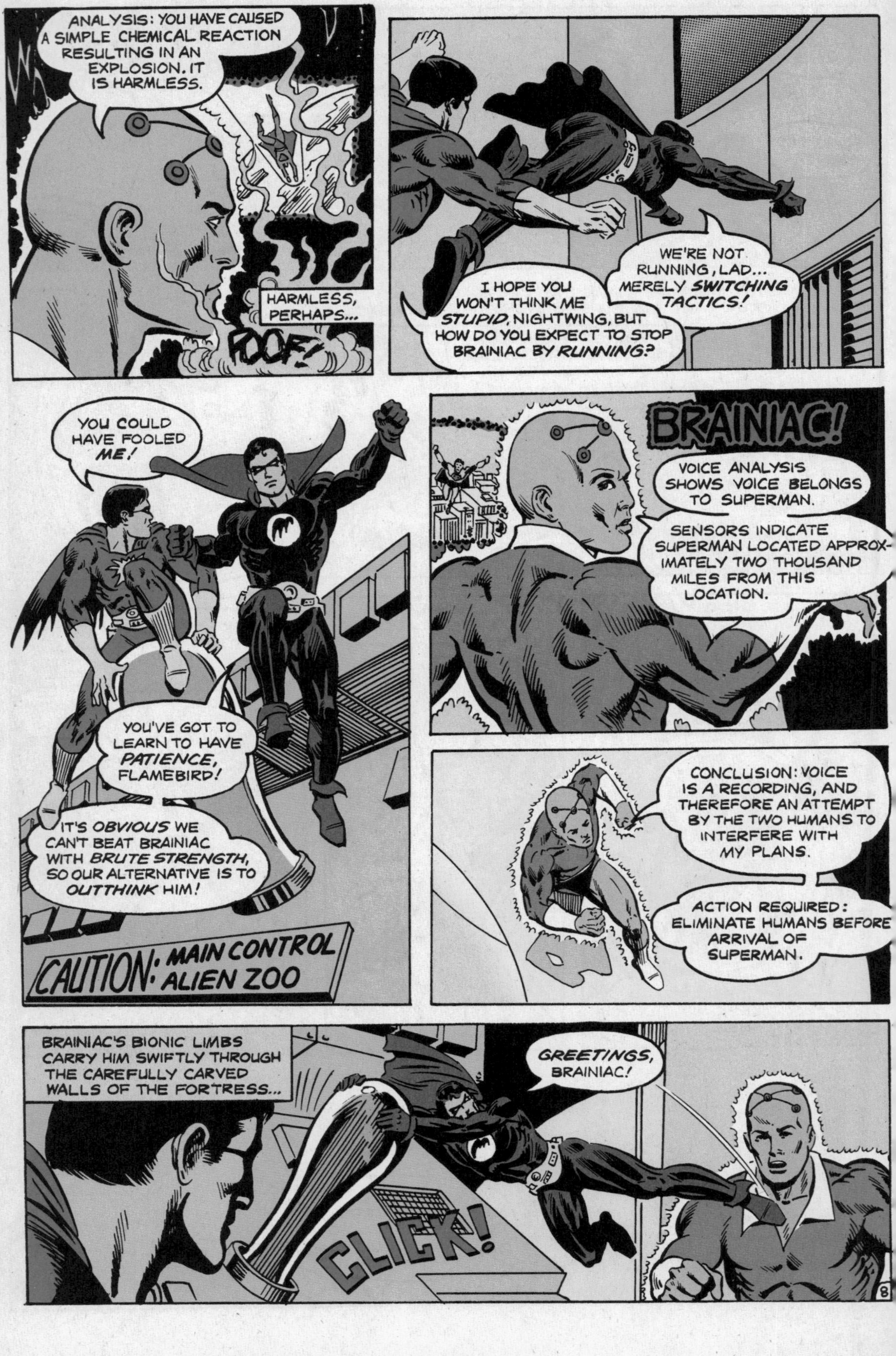

ANALYSIS: YOU HAVE CAUSED A SIMPLE CHEMICAL REACTION RESULTING IN AN EXPLOSION. IT IS HARMLESS.
HARMLESS, PERHAPS...
POOF!
I HOPE YOU WON'T THINK ME STUPID, NIGHTWING, BUT HOW DO YOU EXPECT TO STOP BRAINIAC BY RUNNING?
WE'RE NOT RUNNING, LAD... MERELY SWITCHING TACTICS!
YOU COULD HAVE FOOLED ME!
YOU'VE GOT TO LEARN TO HAVE PATIENCE, FLAMEBIRD!
IT'S OBVIOUS WE CAN'T BEAT BRAINIAC WITH BRUTE STRENGTH, SO OUR ALTERNATIVE IS TO OUTTHINK HIM!
CAUTION: MAIN CONTROL ALIEN ZOO
BRAINIAC!
VOICE ANALYSIS SHOWS VOICE BELONGS TO SUPERMAN.
SENSORS INDICATE SUPERMAN LOCATED APPROXIMATELY TWO THOUSAND MILES FROM THIS LOCATION.
CONCLUSION: VOICE IS A RECORDING, AND THEREFORE AN ATTEMPT BY THE TWO HUMANS TO INTERFERE WITH MY PLANS.
ACTION REQUIRED: ELIMINATE HUMANS BEFORE ARRIVAL OF SUPERMAN.
BRAINIAC'S BIONIC LIMBS CARRY HIM SWIFTLY THROUGH THE CAREFULLY CARVED WALLS OF THE FORTRESS...
GREETINGS, BRAINIAC!
CLICK!
8

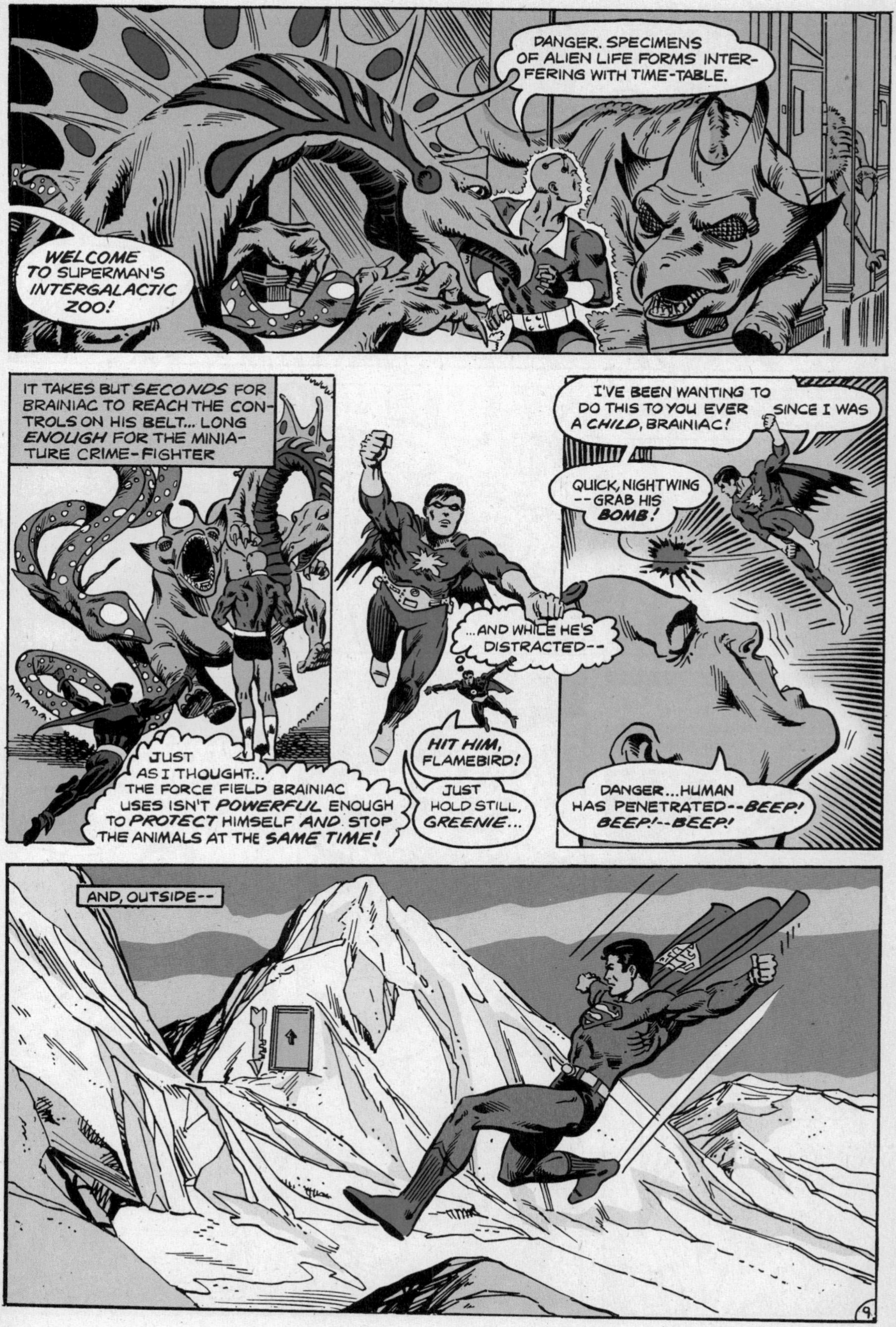
DANGER. SPECIMENS OF ALIEN LIFE FORMS INTERFERING WITH TIME-TABLE.
WELCOME TO SUPERMAN'S INTERGALACTIC ZOO!
IT TAKES BUT SECONDS FOR BRAINIAC TO REACH THE CONTROLS ON HIS BELT... LONG ENOUGH FOR THE MINIATURE CRIME-FIGHTER
JUST AS I THOUGHT... THE FORCE FIELD BRAINIAC USES ISN'T POWERFUL ENOUGH TO PROTECT HIMSELF AND STOP THE ANIMALS AT THE SAME TIME!
...AND WHILE HE'S DISTRACTED--
HIT HIM, FLAMEBIRD!
JUST HOLD STILL, GREENIE...
I'VE BEEN WANTING TO DO THIS TO YOU EVER SINCE I WAS A CHILD, BRAINIAC!
QUICK, NIGHTWING --GRAB HIS BOMB!
DANGER...HUMAN HAS PENETRATED--BEEP! BEEP!--BEEP!
AND, OUTSIDE--
9

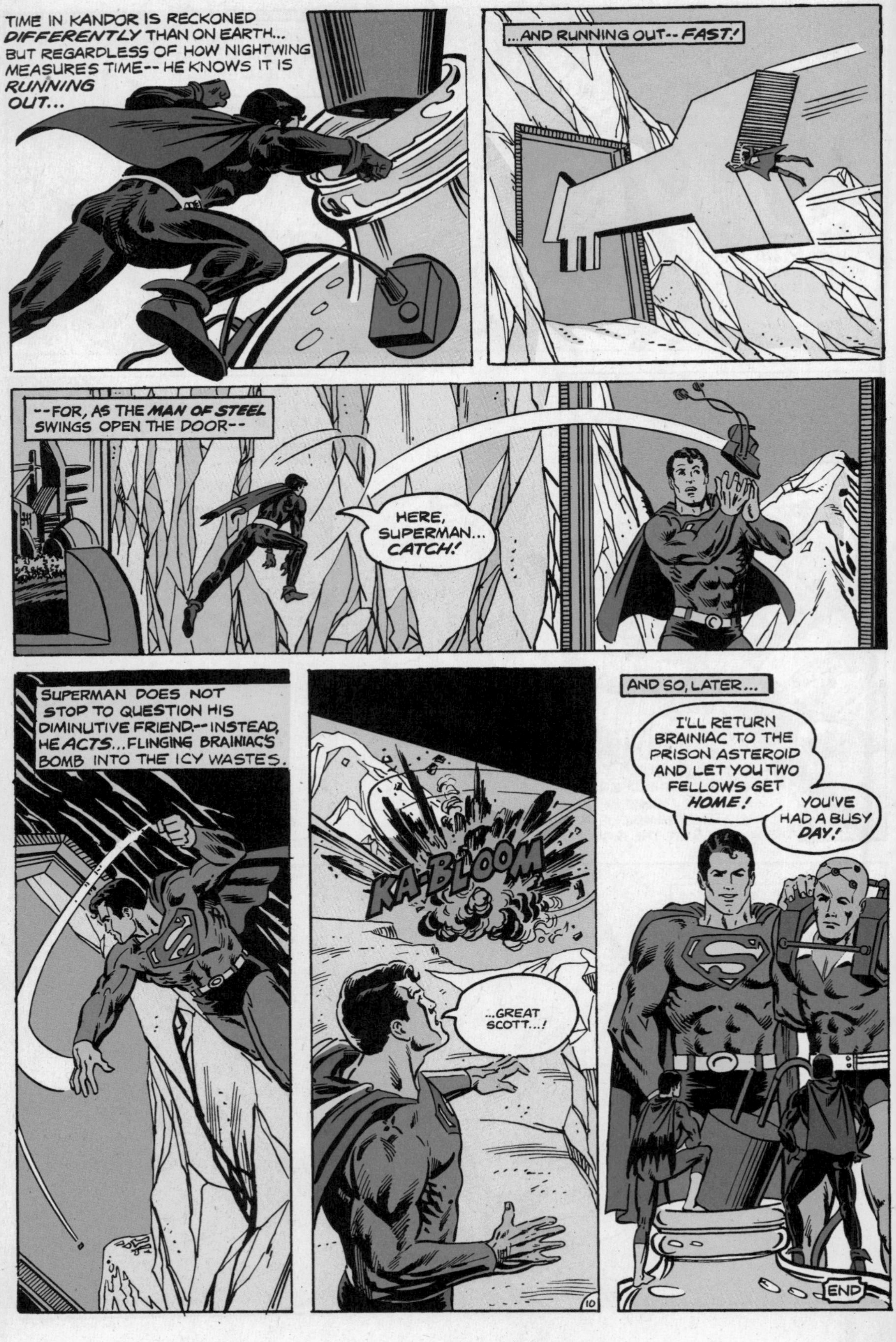
TIME IN KANDOR IS RECKONED DIFFERENTLY THAN ON EARTH... BUT REGARDLESS OF HOW NIGHTWING MEASURES TIME-- HE KNOWS IT IS RUNNING OUT...
...AND RUNNING OUT-- FAST!
--FOR, AS THE MAN OF STEEL SWINGS OPEN THE DOOR--
HERE, SUPERMAN... CATCH!
SUPERMAN DOES NOT STOP TO QUESTION HIS DIMINUTIVE FRIEND.-- INSTEAD, HE ACTS...FLINGING BRAINIAC'S BOMB INTO THE ICY WASTES.
KA-BLOOM
...GREAT SCOTT...!
10
AND SO, LATER...
I'LL RETURN BRAINIAC TO THE PRISON ASTEROID AND LET YOU TWO FELLOWS GET HOME!
YOU'VE HAD A BUSY DAY!
END

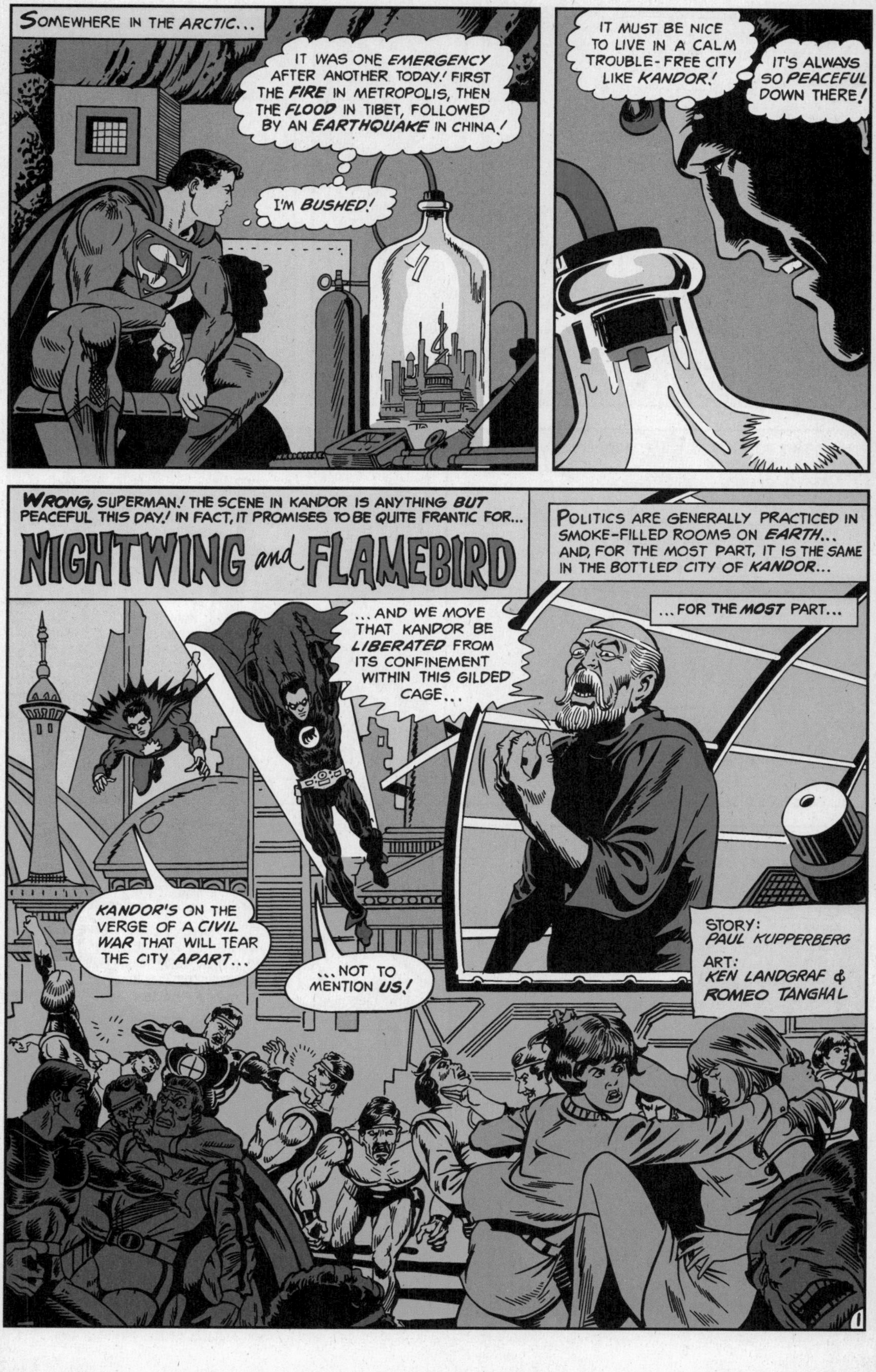
SOMEWHERE IN THE ARCTIC...
IT WAS ONE EMERGENCY AFTER ANOTHER TODAY! FIRST THE FIRE IN METROPOLIS, THEN THE FLOOD IN TIBET, FOLLOWED BY AN EARTHQUAKE IN CHINA!
I'M BUSHED!
IT MUST BE NICE TO LIVE IN A CALM TROUBLE-FREE CITY LIKE KANDOR!
IT'S ALWAYS SO PEACEFUL DOWN THERE!
WRONG, SUPERMAN! THE SCENE IN KANDOR IS ANYTHING BUT PEACEFUL THIS DAY! IN FACT, IT PROMISES TO BE QUITE FRANTIC FOR...
NIGHTWING and FLAMEBIRD
POLITICS ARE GENERALLY PRACTICED IN SMOKE-FILLED ROOMS ON EARTH... AND, FOR THE MOST PART, IT IS THE SAME IN THE BOTTLED CITY OF KANDOR...
...FOR THE MOST PART...
...AND WE MOVE THAT KANDOR BE LIBERATED FROM ITS CONFINEMENT WITHIN THIS GILDED CAGE...
KANDOR'S ON THE VERGE OF A CIVIL WAR THAT WILL TEAR THE CITY APART...
...NOT TO MENTION US!
STORY: PAUL KUPPERBERG
ART: KEN LANDGRAF & ROMEO TANGHAL
1

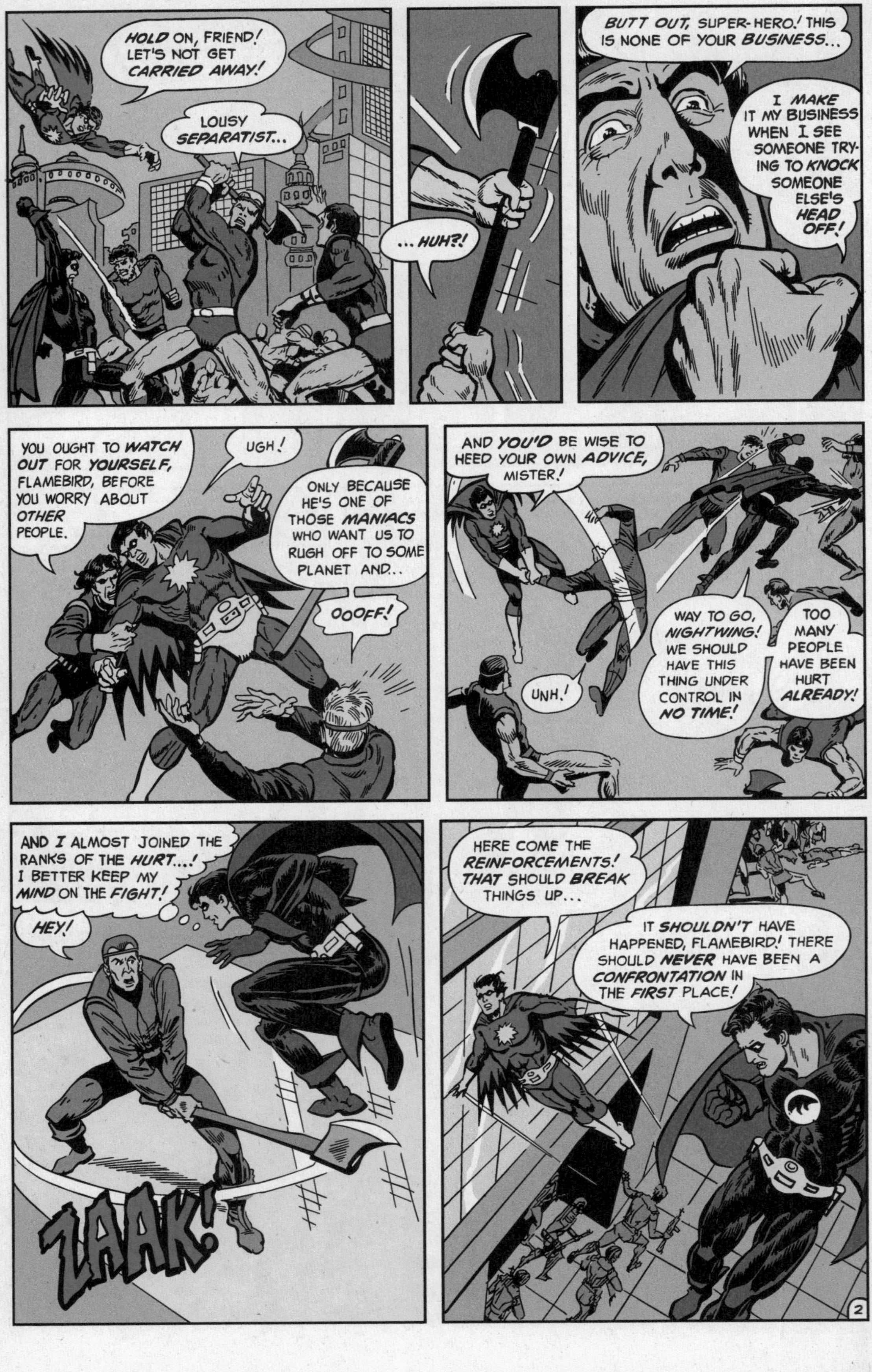
HOLD ON, FRIEND! LET'S NOT GET CARRIED AWAY!
LOUSY SEPARATIST...
...HUH?!
BUTT OUT, SUPER-HERO! THIS IS NONE OF YOUR BUSINESS...
I MAKE IT MY BUSINESS WHEN I SEE SOMEONE TRYING TO KNOCK SOMEONE ELSE'S HEAD OFF!
YOU OUGHT TO WATCH OUT FOR YOURSELF, FLAMEBIRD, BEFORE YOU WORRY ABOUT OTHER PEOPLE.
UGH!
ONLY BECAUSE HE'S ONE OF THOSE MANIACS WHO WANT US TO RUSH OFF TO SOME PLANET AND...
OOOFF!
AND YOU'D BE WISE TO HEED YOUR OWN ADVICE, MISTER!
UNH!
WAY TO GO, NIGHTWING! WE SHOULD HAVE THIS THING UNDER CONTROL IN NO TIME!
TOO MANY PEOPLE HAVE BEEN HURT ALREADY!
AND I ALMOST JOINED THE RANKS OF THE HURT...! I BETTER KEEP MY MIND ON THE FIGHT!
HEY!
ZAAK!
HERE COME THE REINFORCEMENTS! THAT SHOULD BREAK THINGS UP...
IT SHOULDN'T HAVE HAPPENED, FLAMEBIRD! THERE SHOULD NEVER HAVE BEEN A CONFRONTATION IN THE FIRST PLACE!
2

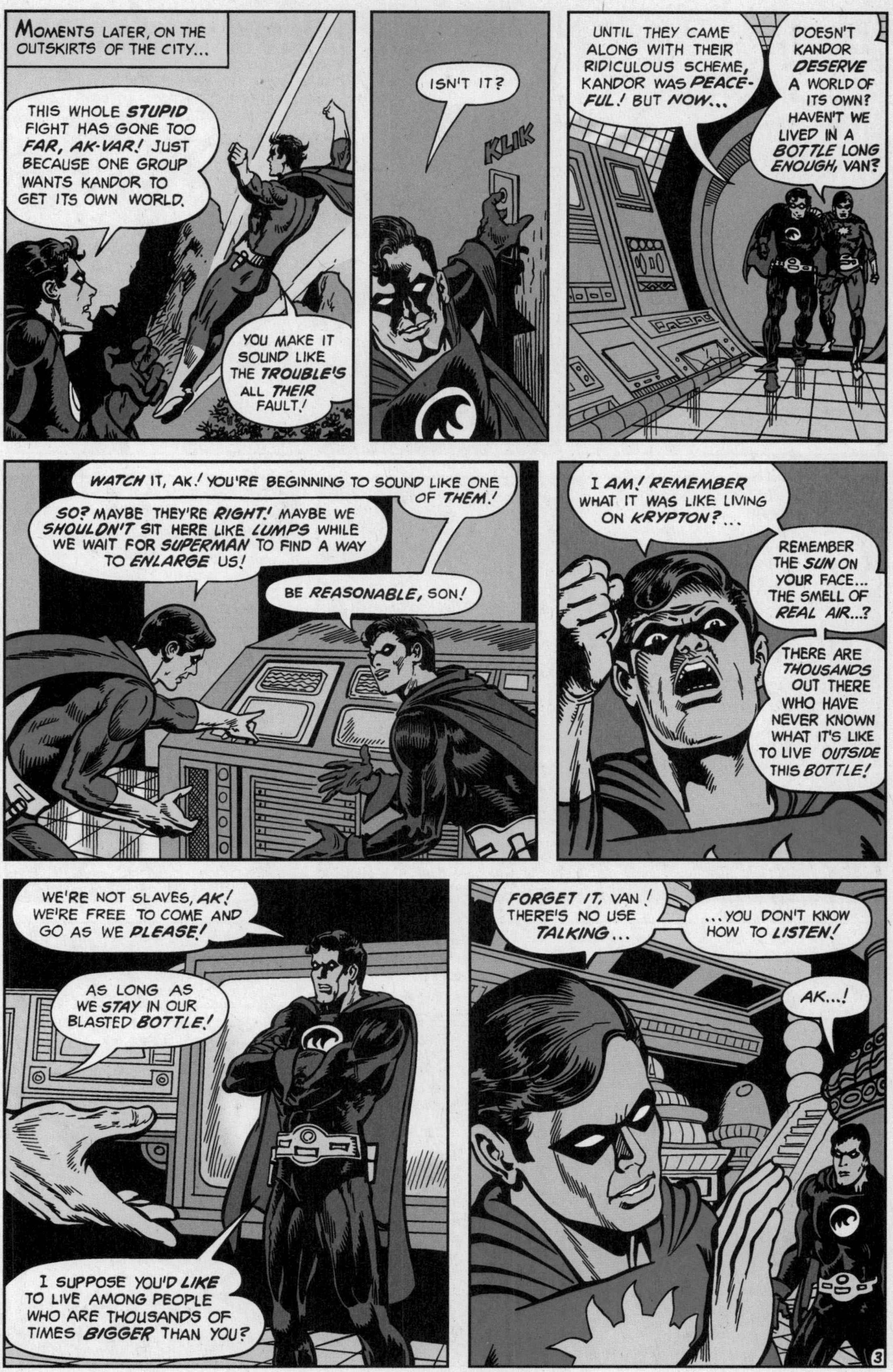
MOMENTS LATER, ON THE OUTSKIRTS OF THE CITY...
THIS WHOLE STUPID FIGHT HAS GONE TOO FAR, AK-VAR! JUST BECAUSE ONE GROUP WANTS KANDOR TO GET ITS OWN WORLD.
YOU MAKE IT SOUND LIKE THE TROUBLE'S ALL THEIR FAULT!
ISN'T IT?
KLIK
UNTIL THEY CAME ALONG WITH THEIR RIDICULOUS SCHEME, KANDOR WAS PEACE-FUL! BUT NOW...
DOESN'T KANDOR DESERVE A WORLD OF ITS OWN? HAVEN'T WE LIVED IN A BOTTLE LONG ENOUGH, VAN?
WATCH IT, AK! YOU'RE BEGINNING TO SOUND LIKE ONE OF THEM!
SO? MAYBE THEY'RE RIGHT! MAYBE WE SHOULDN'T SIT HERE LIKE LUMPS WHILE WE WAIT FOR SUPERMAN TO FIND A WAY TO ENLARGE US!
BE REASONABLE, SON!
I AM! REMEMBER WHAT IT WAS LIKE LIVING ON KRYPTON?...
REMEMBER THE SUN ON YOUR FACE... THE SMELL OF REAL AIR...?
THERE ARE THOUSANDS OUT THERE WHO HAVE NEVER KNOWN WHAT IT'S LIKE TO LIVE OUTSIDE THIS BOTTLE!
WE'RE NOT SLAVES, AK! WE'RE FREE TO COME AND GO AS WE PLEASE!
AS LONG AS WE STAY IN OUR BLASTED BOTTLE!
I SUPPOSE YOU'D LIKE TO LIVE AMONG PEOPLE WHO ARE THOUSANDS OF TIMES BIGGER THAN YOU?
FORGET IT, VAN! THERE'S NO USE TALKING...
...YOU DON'T KNOW HOW TO LISTEN!
AK...!
3

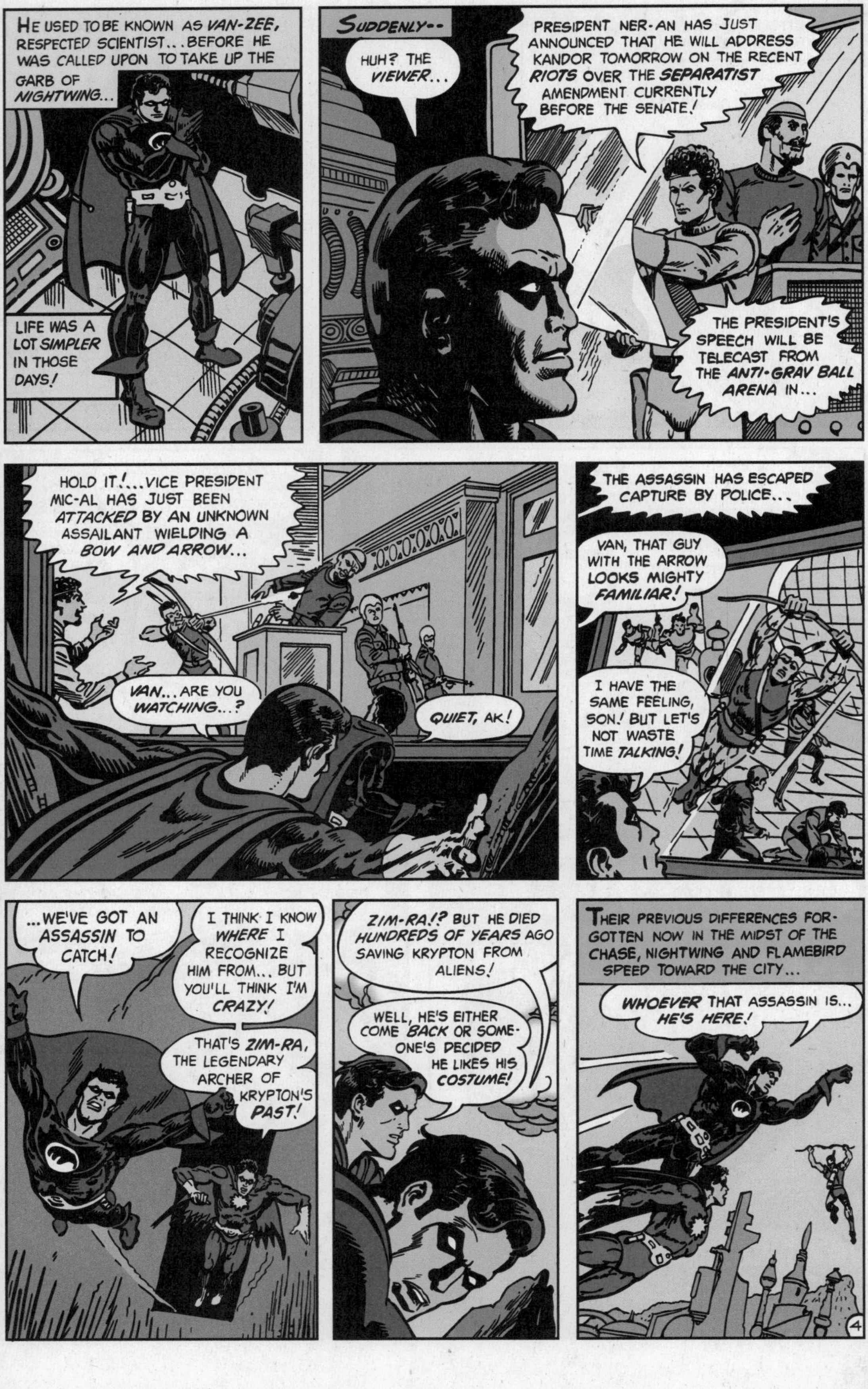
HE USED TO BE KNOWN AS VAN-ZEE, RESPECTED SCIENTIST... BEFORE HE WAS CALLED UPON TO TAKE UP THE GARB OF NIGHTWING...
LIFE WAS A LOT SIMPLER IN THOSE DAYS!
SUDDENLY--
HUH? THE VIEWER...
PRESIDENT NER-AN HAS JUST ANNOUNCED THAT HE WILL ADDRESS KANDOR TOMORROW ON THE RECENT RIOTS OVER THE SEPARATIST AMENDMENT CURRENTLY BEFORE THE SENATE!
THE PRESIDENT'S SPEECH WILL BE TELECAST FROM THE ANTI-GRAV BALL ARENA IN...
HOLD IT!...VICE PRESIDENT MIC-AL HAS JUST BEEN ATTACKED BY AN UNKNOWN ASSAILANT WIELDING A BOW AND ARROW...
VAN... ARE YOU WATCHING...?
QUIET, AK!
THE ASSASSIN HAS ESCAPED CAPTURE BY POLICE...
VAN, THAT GUY WITH THE ARROW LOOKS MIGHTY FAMILIAR!
I HAVE THE SAME FEELING, SON! BUT LET'S NOT WASTE TIME TALKING!
...WE'VE GOT AN ASSASSIN TO CATCH!
I THINK I KNOW WHERE I RECOGNIZE HIM FROM... BUT YOU'LL THINK I'M CRAZY!
THAT'S ZIM-RA, THE LEGENDARY ARCHER OF KRYPTON'S PAST!
ZIM-RA!? BUT HE DIED HUNDREDS OF YEARS AGO SAVING KRYPTON FROM ALIENS!
WELL, HE'S EITHER COME BACK OR SOME-ONE'S DECIDED HE LIKES HIS COSTUME!
THEIR PREVIOUS DIFFERENCES FOR-GOTTEN NOW IN THE MIDST OF THE CHASE, NIGHTWING AND FLAMEBIRD SPEED TOWARD THE CITY...
WHOEVER THAT ASSASSIN IS... HE'S HERE!
4

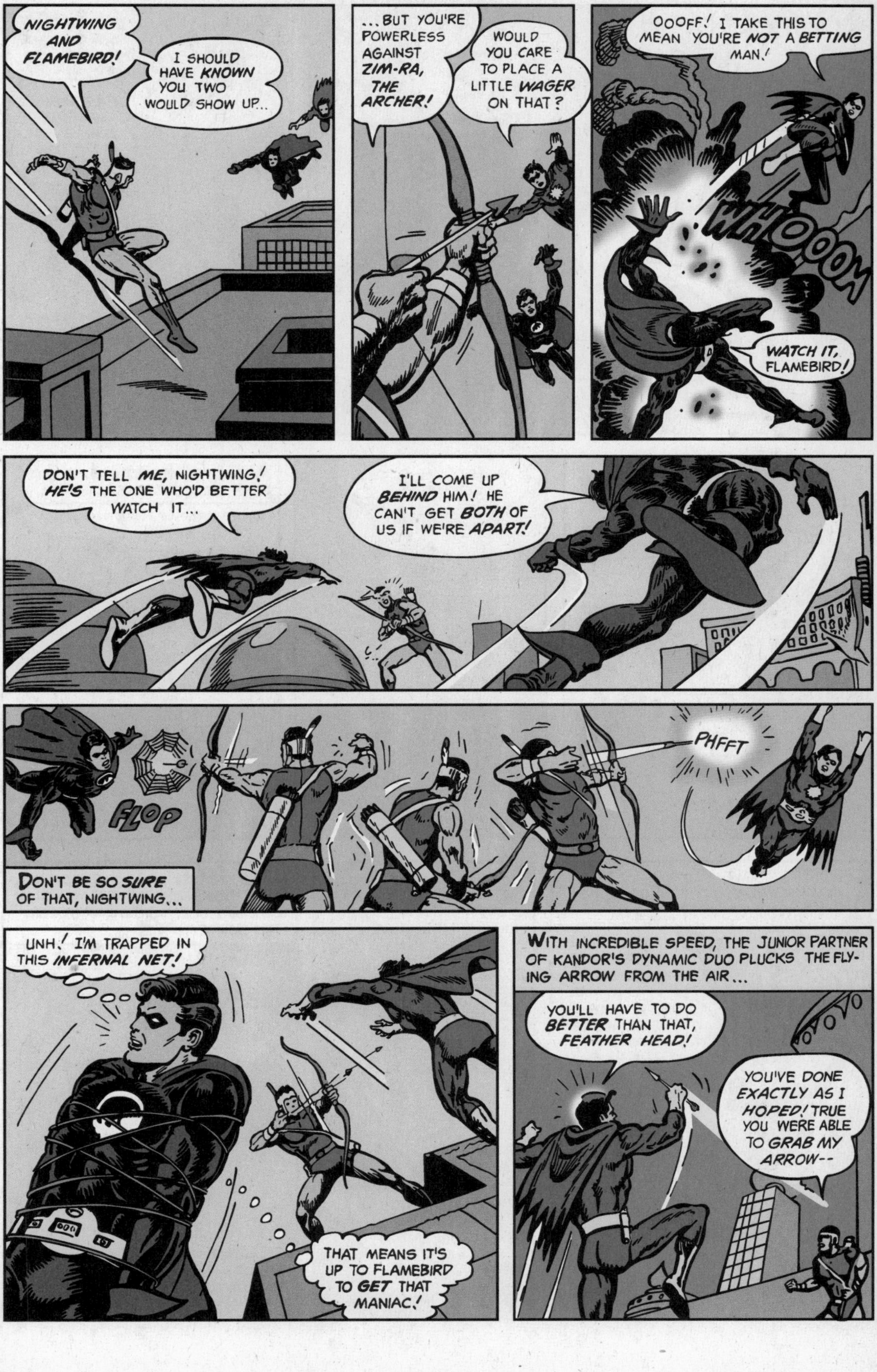
NIGHTWING AND FLAMEBIRD!
I SHOULD HAVE KNOWN YOU TWO WOULD SHOW UP...
...BUT YOU'RE POWERLESS AGAINST ZIM-RA, THE ARCHER!
WOULD YOU CARE TO PLACE A LITTLE WAGER ON THAT?
OOOFF! I TAKE THIS TO MEAN YOU'RE NOT A BETTING MAN!
WHOOOM
WATCH IT, FLAMEBIRD!
DON'T TELL ME, NIGHTWING! HE'S THE ONE WHO'D BETTER WATCH IT...
I'LL COME UP BEHIND HIM! HE CAN'T GET BOTH OF US IF WE'RE APART!
FLOP
PHFFT
DON'T BE SO SURE OF THAT, NIGHTWING...
UNH! I'M TRAPPED IN THIS INFERNAL NET!
THAT MEANS IT'S UP TO FLAMEBIRD TO GET THAT MANIAC!
WITH INCREDIBLE SPEED, THE JUNIOR PARTNER OF KANDOR'S DYNAMIC DUO PLUCKS THE FLYING ARROW FROM THE AIR...
YOU'LL HAVE TO DO BETTER THAN THAT, FEATHER HEAD!
YOU'VE DONE EXACTLY AS I HOPED! TRUE YOU WERE ABLE TO GRAB MY ARROW--

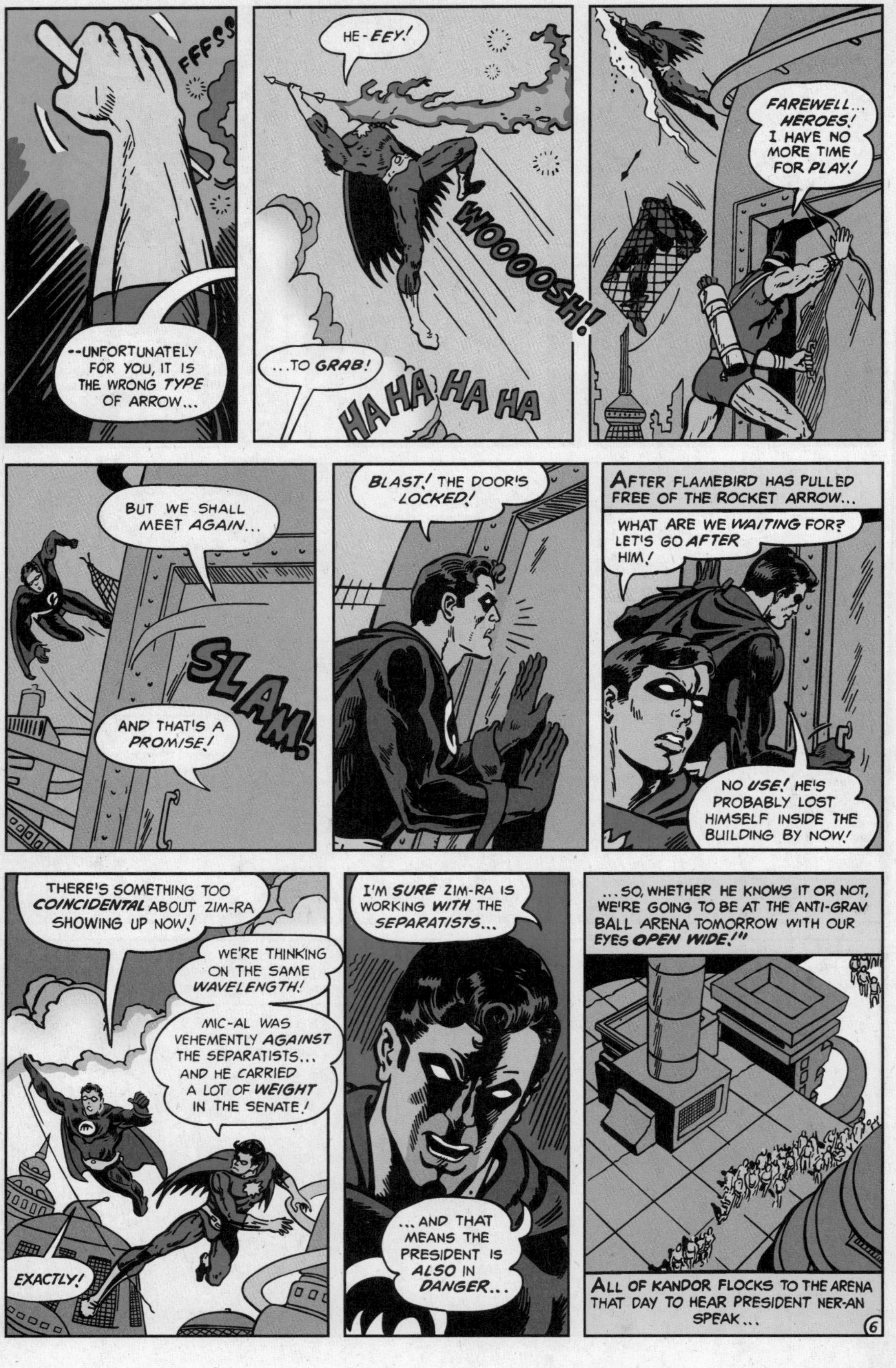
FFFSS
--UNFORTUNATELY FOR YOU, IT IS THE WRONG TYPE OF ARROW...
HE-EEY!
...TO GRAB!
WOOOOSH!
HA HA HA HA
FAREWELL... HEROES! I HAVE NO MORE TIME FOR PLAY!
BUT WE SHALL MEET AGAIN...
SLAM!
AND THAT'S A PROMISE!
BLAST! THE DOOR'S LOCKED!
AFTER FLAMEBIRD HAS PULLED FREE OF THE ROCKET ARROW...
WHAT ARE WE WAITING FOR? LET'S GO AFTER HIM!
NO USE! HE'S PROBABLY LOST HIMSELF INSIDE THE BUILDING BY NOW!
THERE'S SOMETHING TOO COINCIDENTAL ABOUT ZIM-RA SHOWING UP NOW!
WE'RE THINKING ON THE SAME WAVELENGTH!
MIC-AL WAS VEHEMENTLY AGAINST THE SEPARATISTS... AND HE CARRIED A LOT OF WEIGHT IN THE SENATE!
EXACTLY!
I'M SURE ZIM-RA IS WORKING WITH THE SEPARATISTS...
...AND THAT MEANS THE PRESIDENT IS ALSO IN DANGER...
...SO, WHETHER HE KNOWS IT OR NOT, WE'RE GOING TO BE AT THE ANTI-GRAV BALL ARENA TOMORROW WITH OUR EYES OPEN WIDE!"
ALL OF KANDOR FLOCKS TO THE ARENA THAT DAY TO HEAR PRESIDENT NER-AN SPEAK...
6

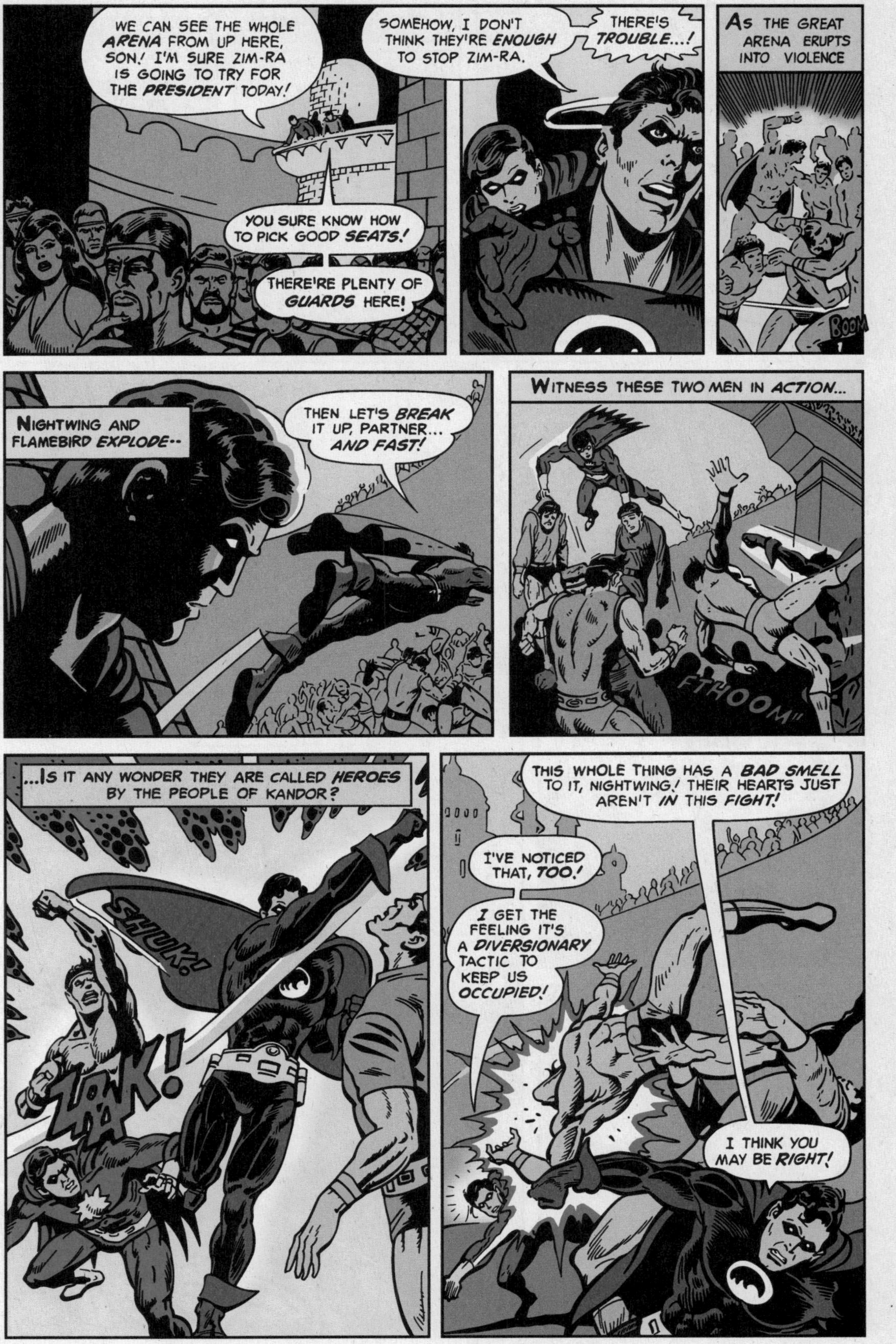
WE CAN SEE THE WHOLE ARENA FROM UP HERE, SON! I'M SURE ZIM-RA IS GOING TO TRY FOR THE PRESIDENT TODAY!
YOU SURE KNOW HOW TO PICK GOOD SEATS!
THERE'RE PLENTY OF GUARDS HERE!
SOMEHOW, I DON'T THINK THEY'RE ENOUGH TO STOP ZIM-RA.
THERE'S TROUBLE...!
AS THE GREAT ARENA ERUPTS INTO VIOLENCE
BOOM
NIGHTWING AND FLAMEBIRD EXPLODE--
THEN LET'S BREAK IT UP, PARTNER... AND FAST!
WITNESS THESE TWO MEN IN ACTION...
FTHOOM
...IS IT ANY WONDER THEY ARE CALLED HEROES BY THE PEOPLE OF KANDOR?
SHUK!
ZAAK!
THIS WHOLE THING HAS A BAD SMELL TO IT, NIGHTWING! THEIR HEARTS JUST AREN'T IN THIS FIGHT!
I'VE NOTICED THAT, TOO!
I GET THE FEELING IT'S A DIVERSIONARY TACTIC TO KEEP US OCCUPIED!
I THINK YOU MAY BE RIGHT!

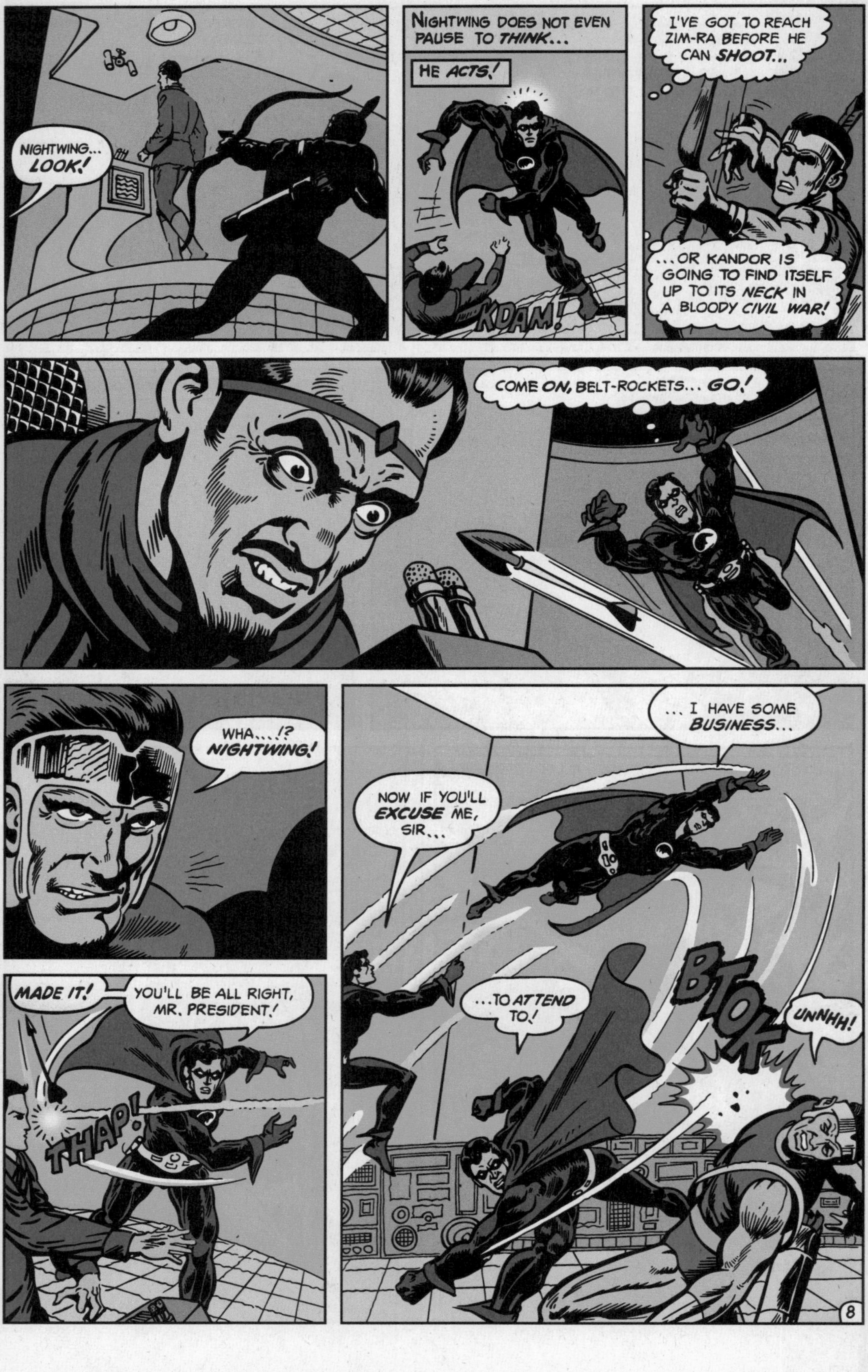

NIGHTWING... LOOK!
NIGHTWING DOES NOT EVEN PAUSE TO THINK...
HE ACTS!
KDAM!
I'VE GOT TO REACH ZIM-RA BEFORE HE CAN SHOOT...
...OR KANDOR IS GOING TO FIND ITSELF UP TO ITS NECK IN A BLOODY CIVIL WAR!
COME ON, BELT-ROCKETS... GO!
WHA...!? NIGHTWING!
MADE IT!
YOU'LL BE ALL RIGHT, MR. PRESIDENT!
THAP!
... I HAVE SOME BUSINESS...
NOW IF YOU'LL EXCUSE ME, SIR...
...TO ATTEND TO!
BTOK
UNNHH!
8

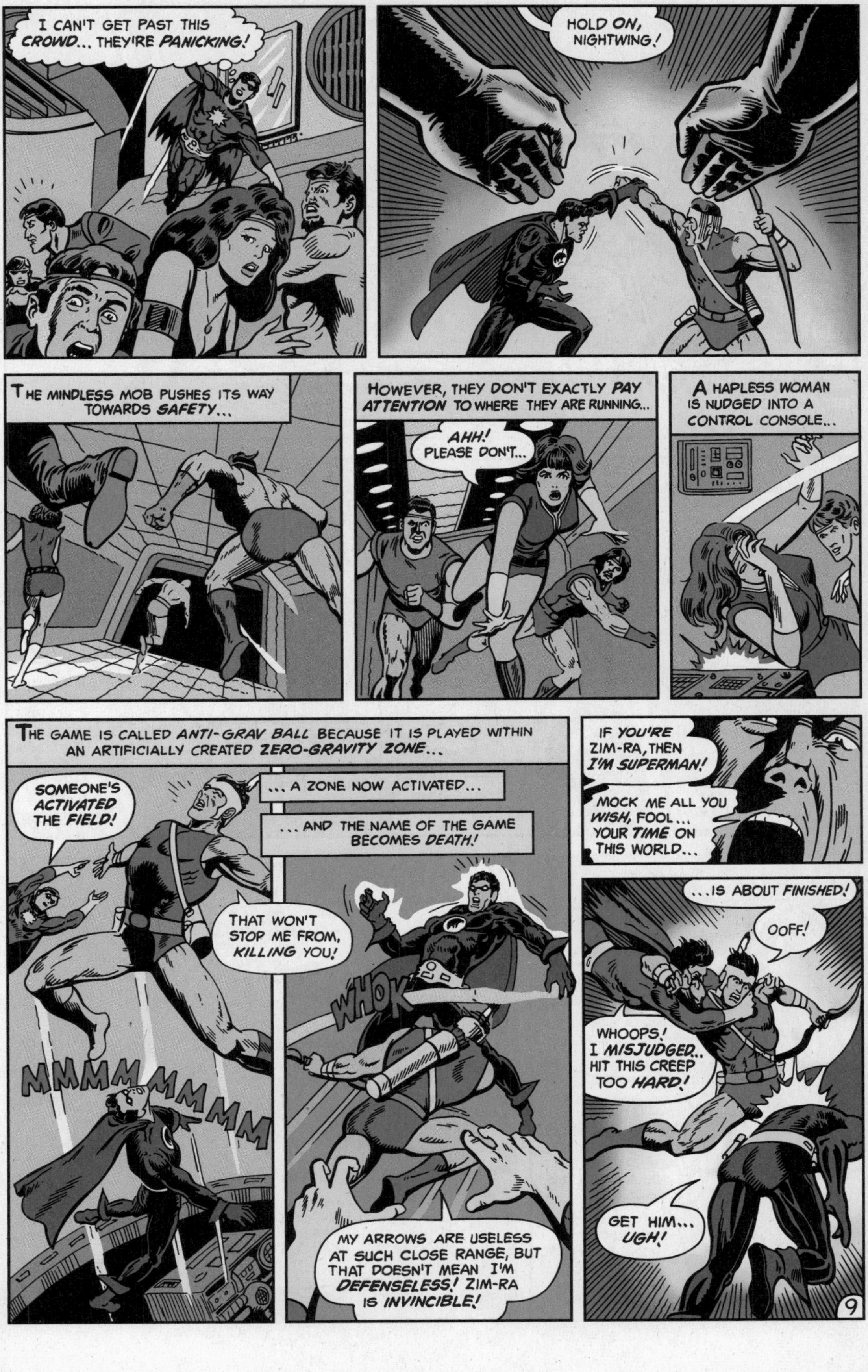

I CAN'T GET PAST THIS CROWD... THEY'RE PANICKING!
HOLD ON, NIGHTWING!
THE MINDLESS MOB PUSHES ITS WAY TOWARDS SAFETY...
HOWEVER, THEY DON'T EXACTLY PAY ATTENTION TO WHERE THEY ARE RUNNING...
AHH! PLEASE DON'T...
A HAPLESS WOMAN IS NUDGED INTO A CONTROL CONSOLE...
THE GAME IS CALLED ANTI-GRAV BALL BECAUSE IT IS PLAYED WITHIN AN ARTIFICIALLY CREATED ZERO-GRAVITY ZONE...
SOMEONE'S ACTIVATED THE FIELD!
... A ZONE NOW ACTIVATED...
... AND THE NAME OF THE GAME BECOMES DEATH!
THAT WON'T STOP ME FROM, KILLING YOU!
MMMMMMMMM
WHOK
MY ARROWS ARE USELESS AT SUCH CLOSE RANGE, BUT THAT DOESN'T MEAN I'M DEFENSELESS! ZIM-RA IS INVINCIBLE!
IF YOU'RE ZIM-RA, THEN I'M SUPERMAN!
MOCK ME ALL YOU WISH, FOOL... YOUR TIME ON THIS WORLD...
...IS ABOUT FINISHED!
OOFF!
WHOOPS! I MISJUDGED... HIT THIS CREEP TOO HARD!
GET HIM... UGH!
9

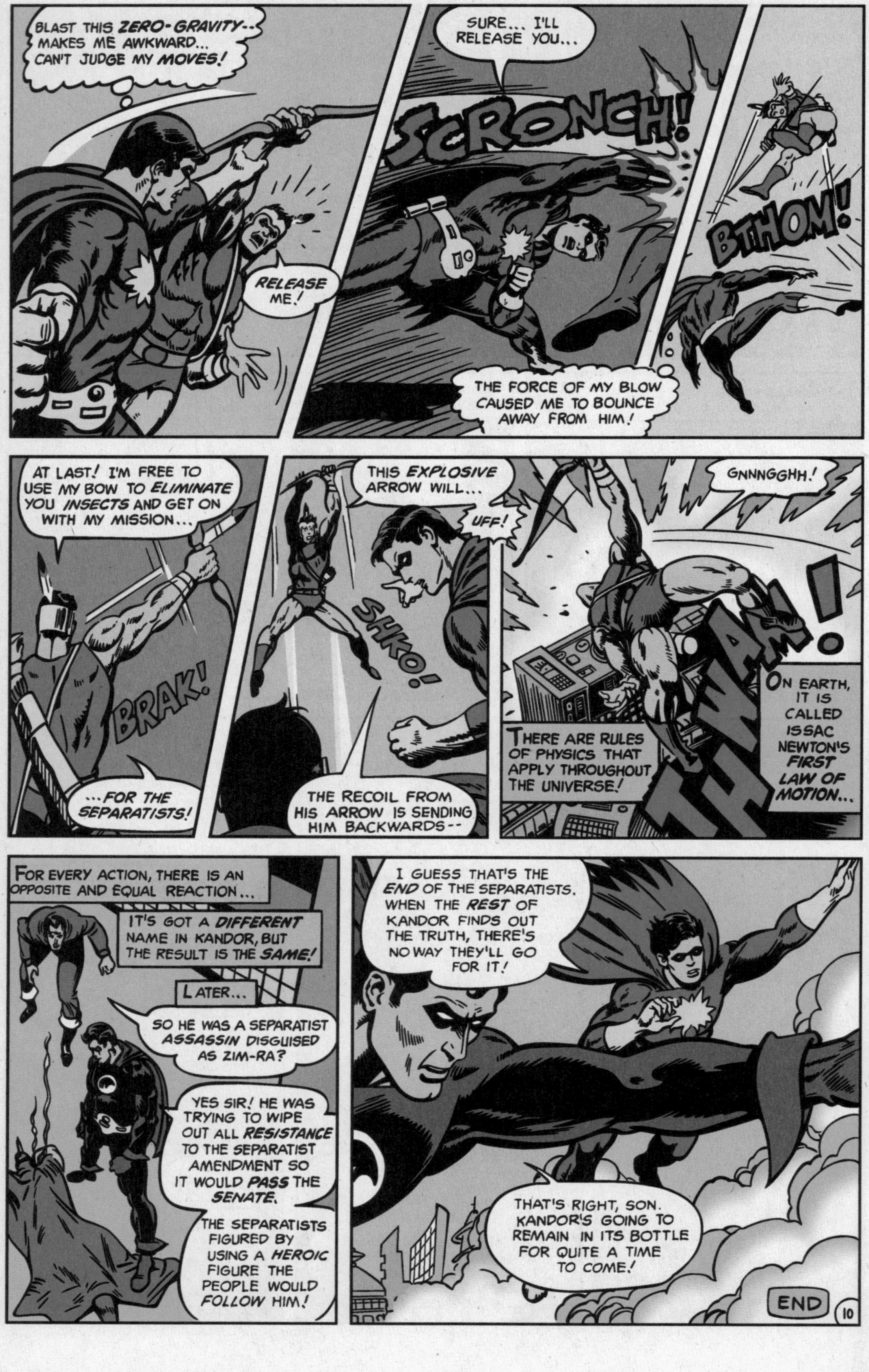

BLAST THIS ZERO-GRAVITY-- MAKES ME AWKWARD... CAN'T JUDGE MY MOVES!
RELEASE ME!
SURE... I'LL RELEASE YOU...
SCRONCH!
BTHOM!
THE FORCE OF MY BLOW CAUSED ME TO BOUNCE AWAY FROM HIM!
AT LAST! I'M FREE TO USE MY BOW TO ELIMINATE YOU INSECTS AND GET ON WITH MY MISSION...
BRAK!
...FOR THE SEPARATISTS!
THIS EXPLOSIVE ARROW WILL...
UFF!
SHKO!
THE RECOIL FROM HIS ARROW IS SENDING HIM BACKWARDS--
GNNNGGHH!
THWAM!
THERE ARE RULES OF PHYSICS THAT APPLY THROUGHOUT THE UNIVERSE!
ON EARTH, IT IS CALLED ISSAC NEWTON'S FIRST LAW OF MOTION...
FOR EVERY ACTION, THERE IS AN OPPOSITE AND EQUAL REACTION...
IT'S GOT A DIFFERENT NAME IN KANDOR, BUT THE RESULT IS THE SAME!
LATER...
SO HE WAS A SEPARATIST ASSASSIN DISGUISED AS ZIM-RA?
YES SIR! HE WAS TRYING TO WIPE OUT ALL RESISTANCE TO THE SEPARATIST AMENDMENT SO IT WOULD PASS THE SENATE.
THE SEPARATISTS FIGURED BY USING A HEROIC FIGURE THE PEOPLE WOULD FOLLOW HIM!
I GUESS THAT'S THE END OF THE SEPARATISTS. WHEN THE REST OF KANDOR FINDS OUT THE TRUTH, THERE'S NO WAY THEY'LL GO FOR IT!
THAT'S RIGHT, SON. KANDOR'S GOING TO REMAIN IN ITS BOTTLE FOR QUITE A TIME TO COME!
END
10

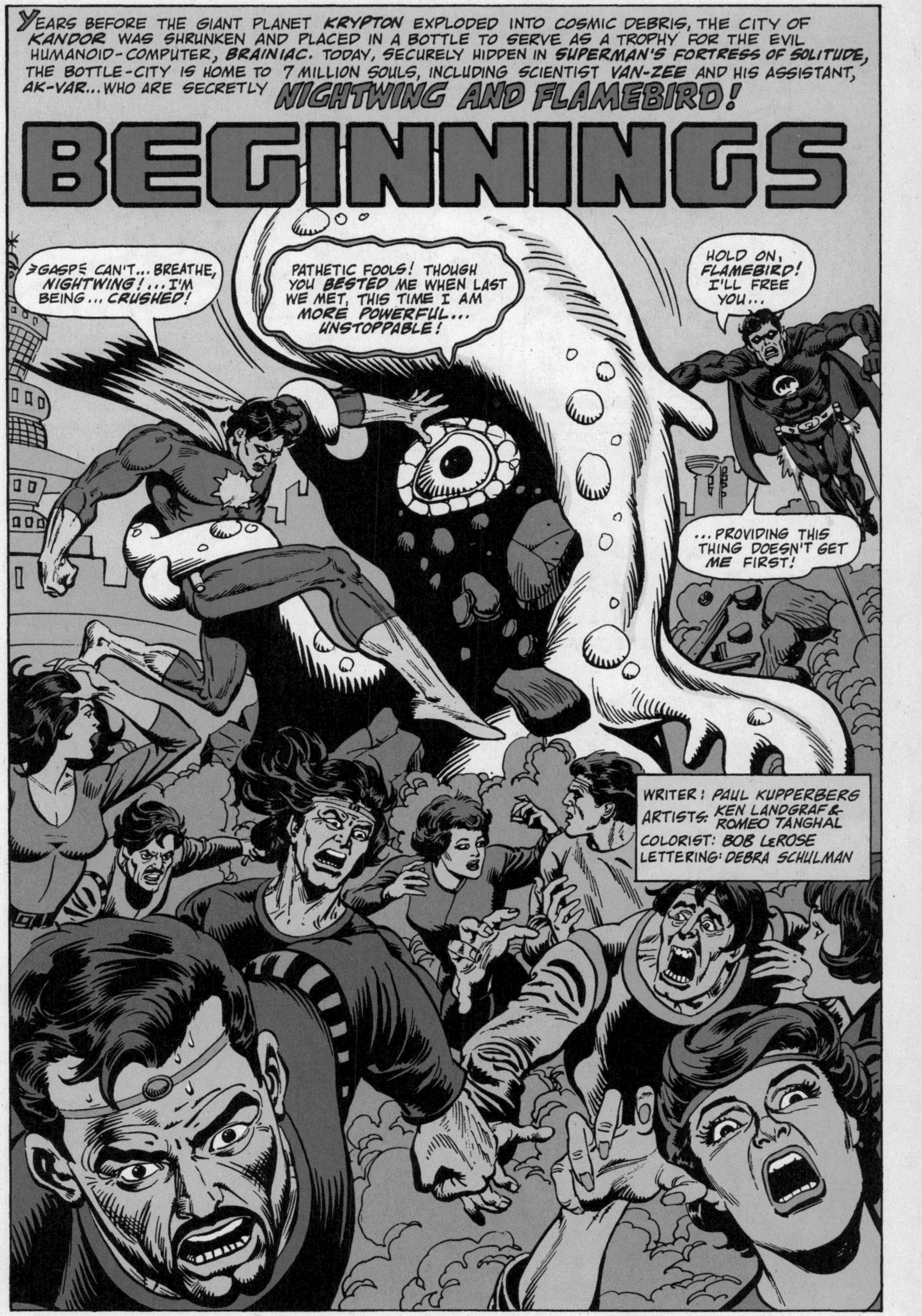
YEARS BEFORE THE GIANT PLANET KRYPTON EXPLODED INTO COSMIC DEBRIS, THE CITY OF KANDOR WAS SHRUNKEN AND PLACED IN A BOTTLE TO SERVE AS A TROPHY FOR THE EVIL HUMANOID-COMPUTER, BRAINIAC. TODAY, SECURELY HIDDEN IN SUPERMAN'S FORTRESS OF SOLITUDE, THE BOTTLE-CITY IS HOME TO 7 MILLION SOULS, INCLUDING SCIENTIST VAN-ZEE AND HIS ASSISTANT, AK-VAR... WHO ARE SECRETLY NIGHTWING AND FLAMEBIRD!
BEGINNINGS
GASP CAN'T... BREATHE, NIGHTWING!... I'M BEING... CRUSHED!
PATHETIC FOOLS! THOUGH YOU BESTED ME WHEN LAST WE MET, THIS TIME I AM MORE POWERFUL... UNSTOPPABLE!
HOLD ON, FLAMEBIRD! I'LL FREE YOU...
...PROVIDING THIS THING DOESN'T GET ME FIRST!
WRITER: PAUL KUPPERBERG
ARTISTS: KEN LANDGRAF & ROMEO TANGHAL
COLORIST: BOB LeROSE
LETTERING: DEBRA SCHULMAN

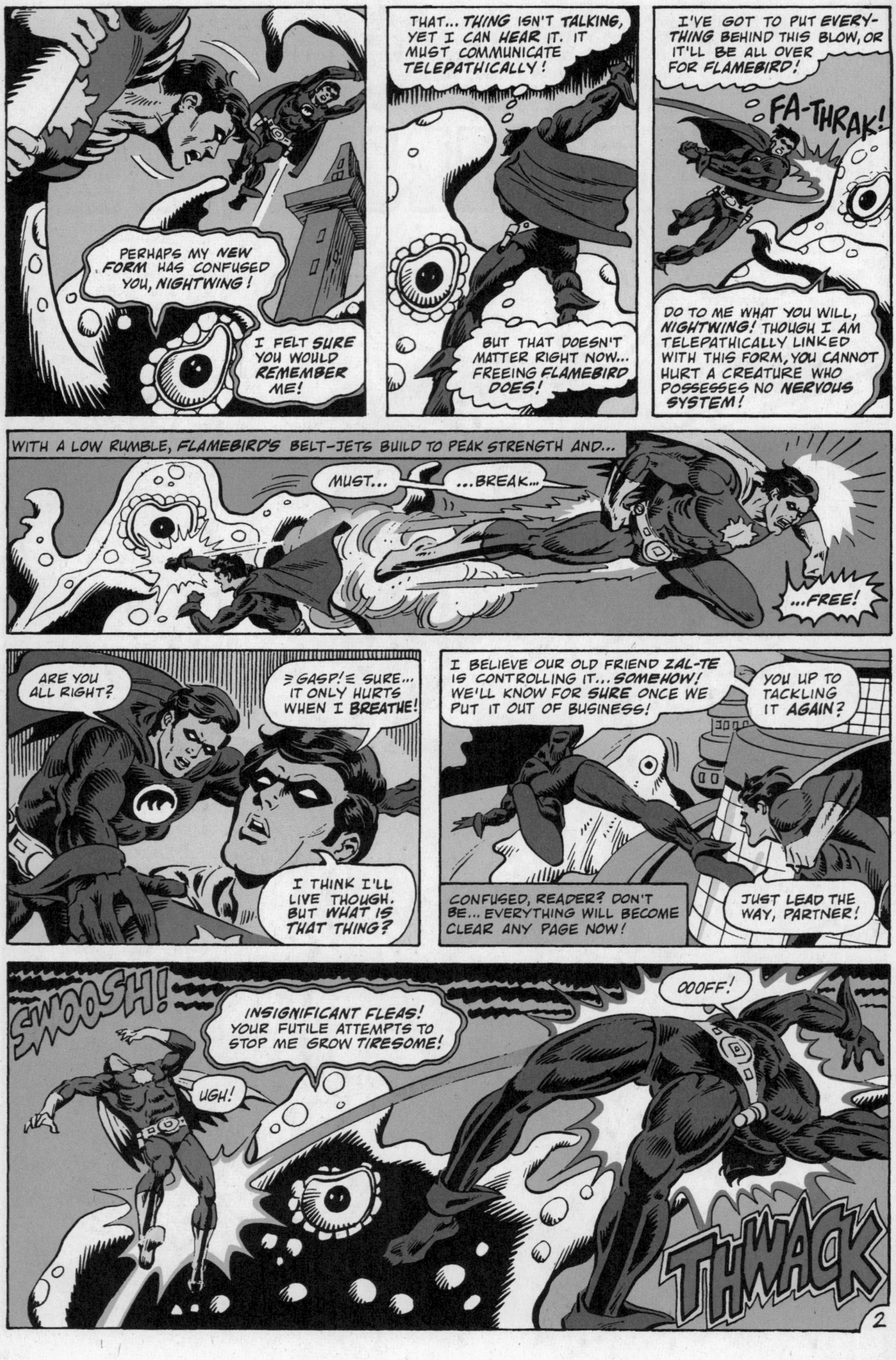
PERHAPS MY NEW FORM HAS CONFUSED YOU, NIGHTWING!
I FELT SURE YOU WOULD REMEMBER ME!
THAT... THING ISN'T TALKING, YET I CAN HEAR IT. IT MUST COMMUNICATE TELEPATHICALLY!
BUT THAT DOESN'T MATTER RIGHT NOW... FREEING FLAMEBIRD DOES!
I'VE GOT TO PUT EVERYTHING BEHIND THIS BLOW, OR IT'LL BE ALL OVER FOR FLAMEBIRD!
FA-THRAK!
DO TO ME WHAT YOU WILL, NIGHTWING! THOUGH I AM TELEPATHICALLY LINKED WITH THIS FORM, YOU CANNOT HURT A CREATURE WHO POSSESSES NO NERVOUS SYSTEM!
WITH A LOW RUMBLE, FLAMEBIRD'S BELT-JETS BUILD TO PEAK STRENGTH AND...
MUST...
...BREAK...
...FREE!
ARE YOU ALL RIGHT?
≥GASP!≤ SURE... IT ONLY HURTS WHEN I BREATHE!
I THINK I'LL LIVE THOUGH. BUT WHAT IS THAT THING?
I BELIEVE OUR OLD FRIEND ZAL-TE IS CONTROLLING IT... SOMEHOW! WE'LL KNOW FOR SURE ONCE WE PUT IT OUT OF BUSINESS!
YOU UP TO TACKLING IT AGAIN?
CONFUSED, READER? DON'T BE... EVERYTHING WILL BECOME CLEAR ANY PAGE NOW!
JUST LEAD THE WAY, PARTNER!
SWOOSH!
INSIGNIFICANT FLEAS! YOUR FUTILE ATTEMPTS TO STOP ME GROW TIRESOME!
OOOFF!
UGH!
THWACK
2

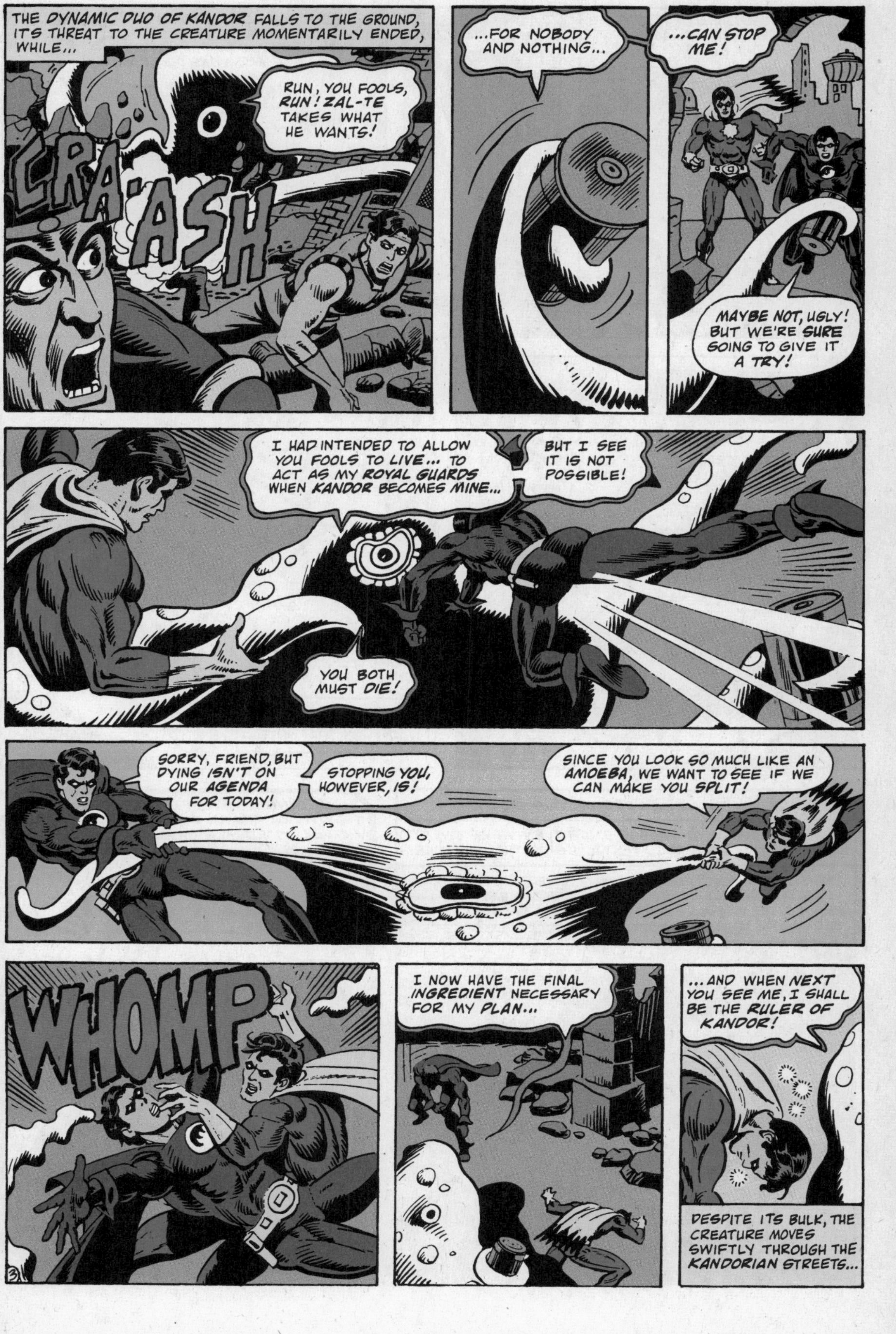
THE DYNAMIC DUO OF KANDOR FALLS TO THE GROUND, ITS THREAT TO THE CREATURE MOMENTARILY ENDED, WHILE...
RUN, YOU FOOLS, RUN! ZAL-TE TAKES WHAT HE WANTS!
CRA-ASH
...FOR NOBODY AND NOTHING...
...CAN STOP ME!
MAYBE NOT, UGLY! BUT WE'RE SURE GOING TO GIVE IT A TRY!
I HAD INTENDED TO ALLOW YOU FOOLS TO LIVE... TO ACT AS MY ROYAL GUARDS WHEN KANDOR BECOMES MINE...
BUT I SEE IT IS NOT POSSIBLE!
YOU BOTH MUST DIE!
SORRY, FRIEND, BUT DYING ISN'T ON OUR AGENDA FOR TODAY!
STOPPING YOU, HOWEVER, IS!
SINCE YOU LOOK SO MUCH LIKE AN AMOEBA, WE WANT TO SEE IF WE CAN MAKE YOU SPLIT!
WHOMP
I NOW HAVE THE FINAL INGREDIENT NECESSARY FOR MY PLAN...
...AND WHEN NEXT YOU SEE ME, I SHALL BE THE RULER OF KANDOR!
DESPITE ITS BULK, THE CREATURE MOVES SWIFTLY THROUGH THE KANDORIAN STREETS...

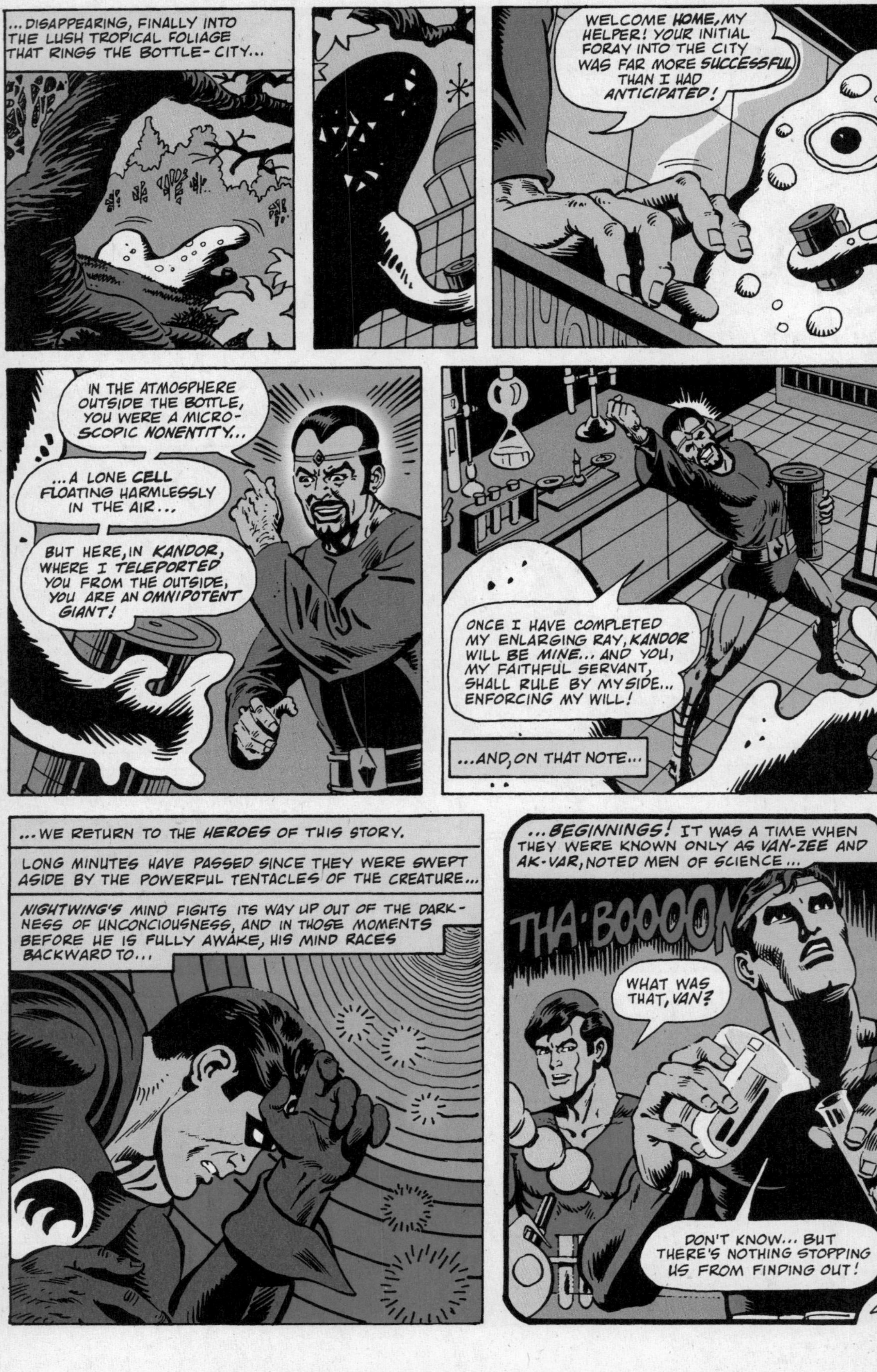

...DISAPPEARING, FINALLY INTO THE LUSH TROPICAL FOLIAGE THAT RINGS THE BOTTLE-CITY...
WELCOME HOME, MY HELPER! YOUR INITIAL FORAY INTO THE CITY WAS FAR MORE SUCCESSFUL THAN I HAD ANTICIPATED!
IN THE ATMOSPHERE OUTSIDE THE BOTTLE, YOU WERE A MICRO-SCOPIC NONENTITY...
...A LONE CELL FLOATING HARMLESSLY IN THE AIR...
BUT HERE, IN KANDOR, WHERE I TELEPORTED YOU FROM THE OUTSIDE, YOU ARE AN OMNIPOTENT GIANT!
ONCE I HAVE COMPLETED MY ENLARGING RAY, KANDOR WILL BE MINE... AND YOU, MY FAITHFUL SERVANT, SHALL RULE BY MY SIDE... ENFORCING MY WILL!
...AND, ON THAT NOTE...
...WE RETURN TO THE HEROES OF THIS STORY.
LONG MINUTES HAVE PASSED SINCE THEY WERE SWEPT ASIDE BY THE POWERFUL TENTACLES OF THE CREATURE...
NIGHTWING'S MIND FIGHTS ITS WAY UP OUT OF THE DARK-NESS OF UNCONCIOUSNESS, AND IN THOSE MOMENTS BEFORE HE IS FULLY AWAKE, HIS MIND RACES BACKWARD TO...
...BEGINNINGS! IT WAS A TIME WHEN THEY WERE KNOWN ONLY AS VAN-ZEE AND AK-VAR, NOTED MEN OF SCIENCE...
THA-BOOOOM
WHAT WAS THAT, VAN?
DON'T KNOW... BUT THERE'S NOTHING STOPPING US FROM FINDING OUT!
4.

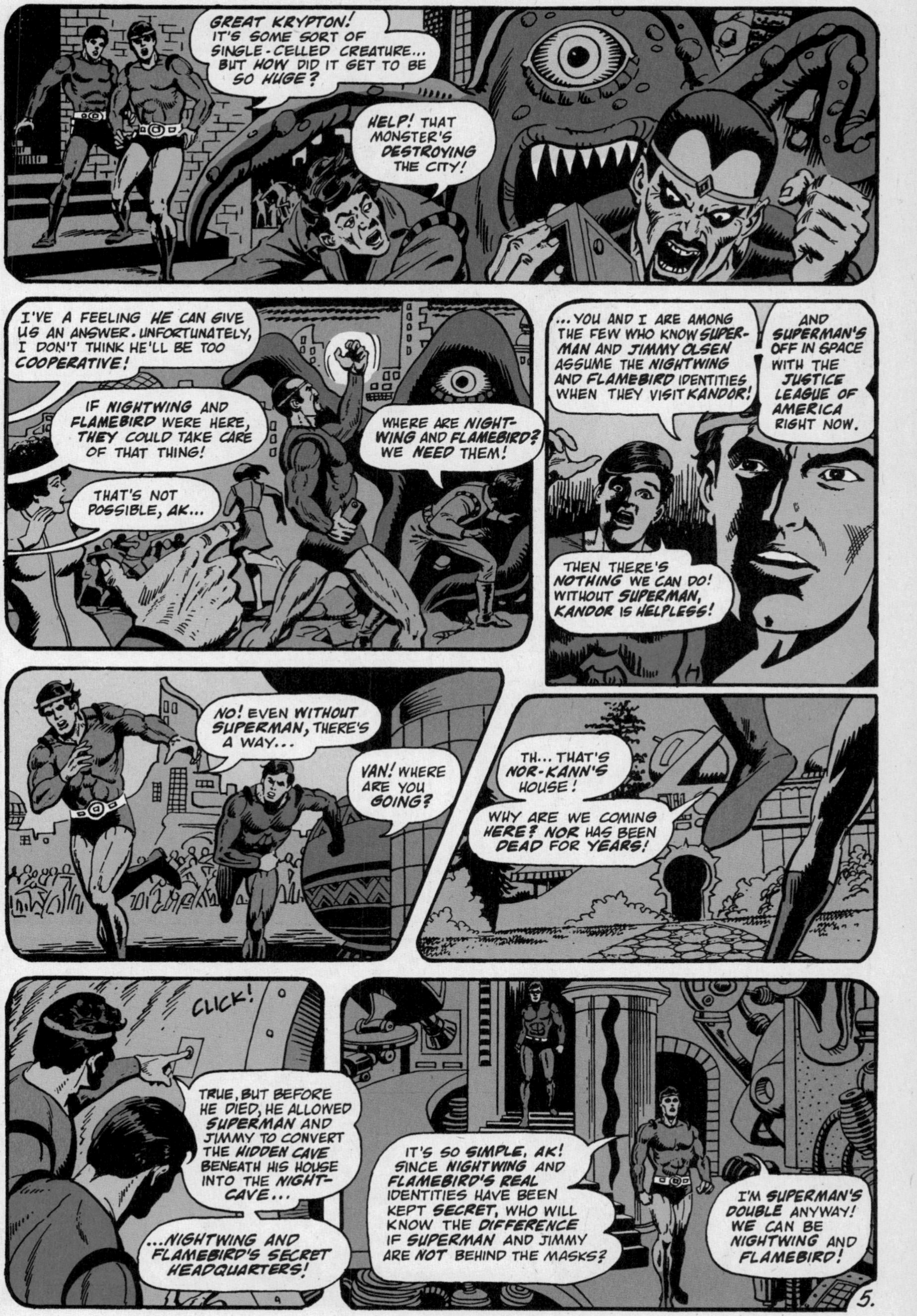
GREAT KRYPTON! IT'S SOME SORT OF SINGLE-CELLED CREATURE... BUT HOW DID IT GET TO BE SO HUGE?
HELP! THAT MONSTER'S DESTROYING THE CITY!
I'VE A FEELING HE CAN GIVE US AN ANSWER. UNFORTUNATELY, I DON'T THINK HE'LL BE TOO COOPERATIVE!
IF NIGHTWING AND FLAMEBIRD WERE HERE, THEY COULD TAKE CARE OF THAT THING!
WHERE ARE NIGHT-WING AND FLAMEBIRD? WE NEED THEM!
THAT'S NOT POSSIBLE, AK...
...YOU AND I ARE AMONG THE FEW WHO KNOW SUPER-MAN AND JIMMY OLSEN ASSUME THE NIGHTWING AND FLAMEBIRD IDENTITIES WHEN THEY VISIT KANDOR!
AND SUPERMAN'S OFF IN SPACE WITH THE JUSTICE LEAGUE OF AMERICA RIGHT NOW.
THEN THERE'S NOTHING WE CAN DO! WITHOUT SUPERMAN, KANDOR IS HELPLESS!
NO! EVEN WITHOUT SUPERMAN, THERE'S A WAY...
VAN! WHERE ARE YOU GOING?
TH... THAT'S NOR-KANN'S HOUSE!
WHY ARE WE COMING HERE? NOR HAS BEEN DEAD FOR YEARS!
CLICK!
TRUE, BUT BEFORE HE DIED, HE ALLOWED SUPERMAN AND JIMMY TO CONVERT THE HIDDEN CAVE BENEATH HIS HOUSE INTO THE NIGHT-CAVE...
...NIGHTWING AND FLAMEBIRD'S SECRET HEADQUARTERS!
IT'S SO SIMPLE, AK! SINCE NIGHTWING AND FLAMEBIRD'S REAL IDENTITIES HAVE BEEN KEPT SECRET, WHO WILL KNOW THE DIFFERENCE IF SUPERMAN AND JIMMY ARE NOT BEHIND THE MASKS?
I'M SUPERMAN'S DOUBLE ANYWAY! WE CAN BE NIGHTWING AND FLAMEBIRD!
5.

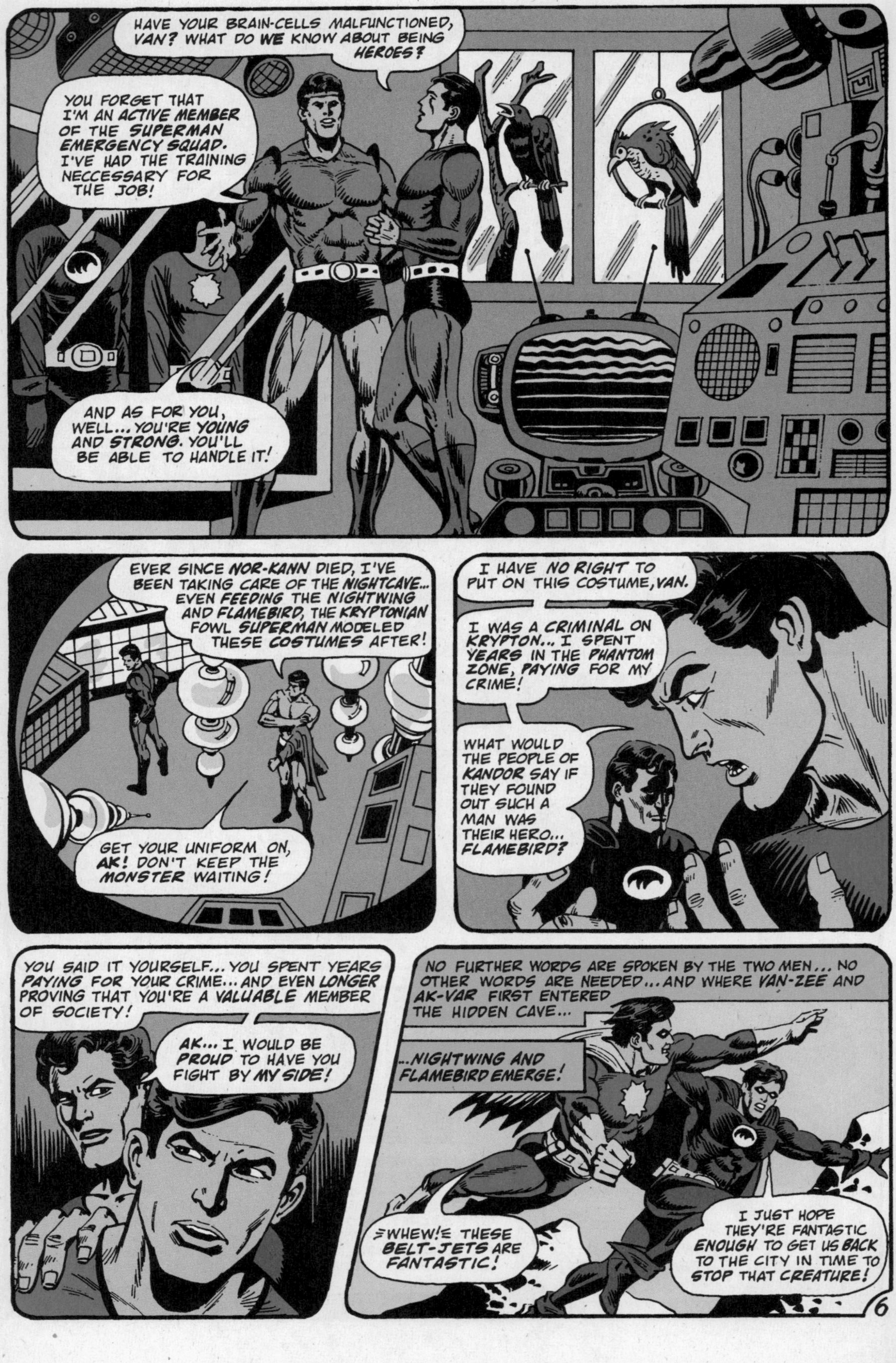
HAVE YOUR BRAIN-CELLS MALFUNCTIONED, VAN? WHAT DO WE KNOW ABOUT BEING HEROES?
YOU FORGET THAT I'M AN ACTIVE MEMBER OF THE SUPERMAN EMERGENCY SQUAD. I'VE HAD THE TRAINING NECCESSARY FOR THE JOB!
AND AS FOR YOU, WELL... YOU'RE YOUNG AND STRONG. YOU'LL BE ABLE TO HANDLE IT!
EVER SINCE NOR-KANN DIED, I'VE BEEN TAKING CARE OF THE NIGHTCAVE... EVEN FEEDING THE NIGHTWING AND FLAMEBIRD, THE KRYPTONIAN FOWL SUPERMAN MODELED THESE COSTUMES AFTER!
GET YOUR UNIFORM ON, AK! DON'T KEEP THE MONSTER WAITING!
I HAVE NO RIGHT TO PUT ON THIS COSTUME, VAN.
I WAS A CRIMINAL ON KRYPTON... I SPENT YEARS IN THE PHANTOM ZONE, PAYING FOR MY CRIME!
WHAT WOULD THE PEOPLE OF KANDOR SAY IF THEY FOUND OUT SUCH A MAN WAS THEIR HERO... FLAMEBIRD?
YOU SAID IT YOURSELF... YOU SPENT YEARS PAYING FOR YOUR CRIME... AND EVEN LONGER PROVING THAT YOU'RE A VALUABLE MEMBER OF SOCIETY!
AK... I WOULD BE PROUD TO HAVE YOU FIGHT BY MY SIDE!
NO FURTHER WORDS ARE SPOKEN BY THE TWO MEN... NO OTHER WORDS ARE NEEDED... AND WHERE VAN-ZEE AND AK-VAR FIRST ENTERED THE HIDDEN CAVE...
...NIGHTWING AND FLAMEBIRD EMERGE!
WHEW! THESE BELT-JETS ARE FANTASTIC!
I JUST HOPE THEY'RE FANTASTIC ENOUGH TO GET US BACK TO THE CITY IN TIME TO STOP THAT CREATURE!
6

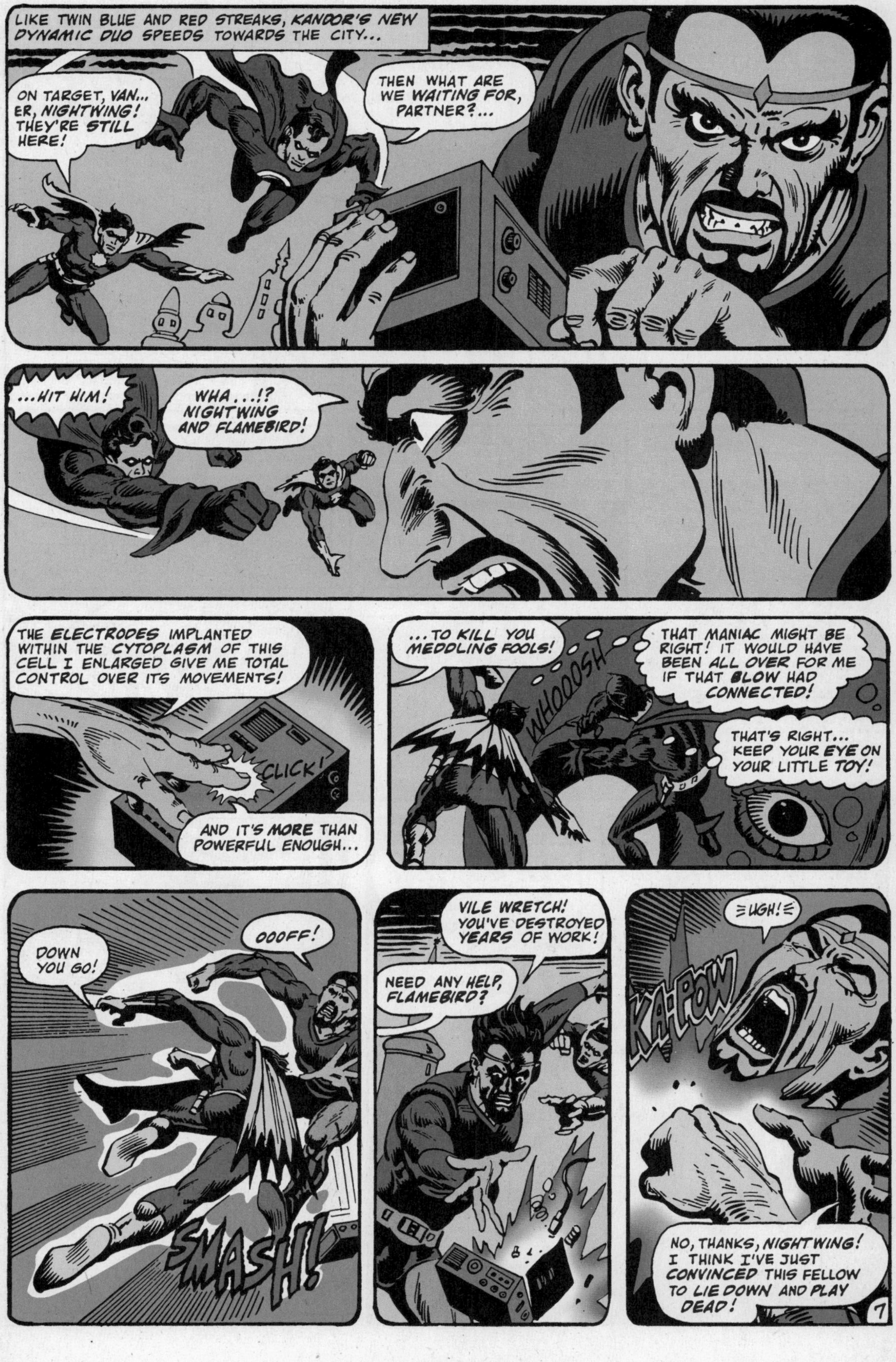
LIKE TWIN BLUE AND RED STREAKS, KANDOR'S NEW DYNAMIC DUO SPEEDS TOWARDS THE CITY...
ON TARGET, VAN... ER, NIGHTWING! THEY'RE STILL HERE!
THEN WHAT ARE WE WAITING FOR, PARTNER?...
...HIT HIM!
WHA...!? NIGHTWING AND FLAMEBIRD!
THE ELECTRODES IMPLANTED WITHIN THE CYTOPLASM OF THIS CELL I ENLARGED GIVE ME TOTAL CONTROL OVER ITS MOVEMENTS!
CLICK!
AND IT'S MORE THAN POWERFUL ENOUGH...
...TO KILL YOU MEDDLING FOOLS!
WHOOOSH
THAT MANIAC MIGHT BE RIGHT! IT WOULD HAVE BEEN ALL OVER FOR ME IF THAT BLOW HAD CONNECTED!
THAT'S RIGHT... KEEP YOUR EYE ON YOUR LITTLE TOY!
DOWN YOU GO!
OOOFF!
SMASH!
VILE WRETCH! YOU'VE DESTROYED YEARS OF WORK!
NEED ANY HELP, FLAMEBIRD?
UGH!
KA-POW
NO, THANKS, NIGHTWING! I THINK I'VE JUST CONVINCED THIS FELLOW TO LIE DOWN AND PLAY DEAD!
7

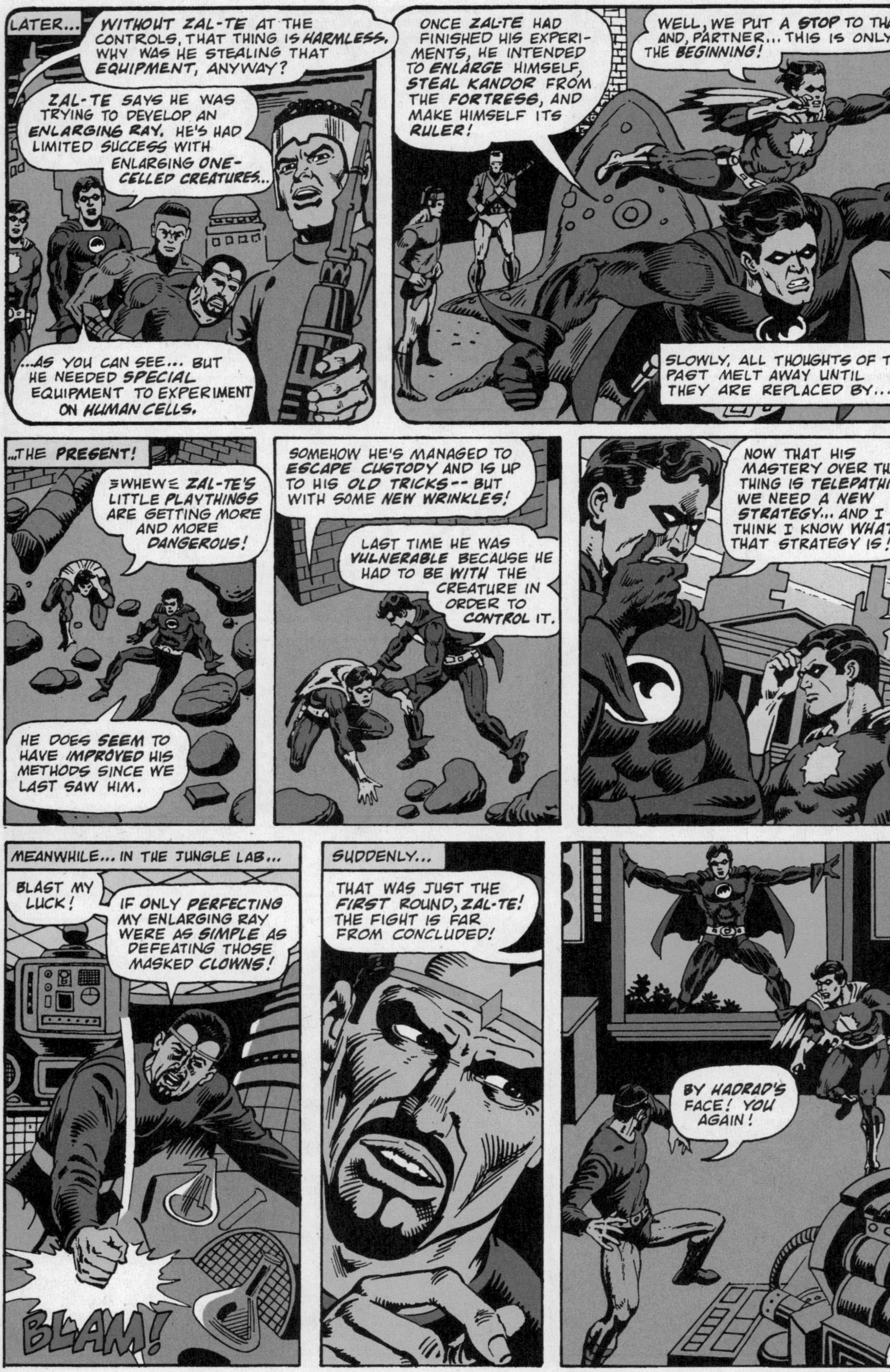
LATER...
WITHOUT ZAL-TE AT THE CONTROLS, THAT THING IS HARMLESS. WHY WAS HE STEALING THAT EQUIPMENT, ANYWAY?
ZAL-TE SAYS HE WAS TRYING TO DEVELOP AN ENLARGING RAY. HE'S HAD LIMITED SUCCESS WITH ENLARGING ONE-CELLED CREATURES...
...AS YOU CAN SEE... BUT HE NEEDED SPECIAL EQUIPMENT TO EXPERIMENT ON HUMAN CELLS.
ONCE ZAL-TE HAD FINISHED HIS EXPERIMENTS, HE INTENDED TO ENLARGE HIMSELF, STEAL KANDOR FROM THE FORTRESS, AND MAKE HIMSELF ITS RULER!
WELL, WE PUT A STOP TO THAT. AND, PARTNER... THIS IS ONLY THE BEGINNING!
SLOWLY, ALL THOUGHTS OF THE PAST MELT AWAY UNTIL THEY ARE REPLACED BY...
...THE PRESENT!
WHEW! ZAL-TE'S LITTLE PLAYTHINGS ARE GETTING MORE AND MORE DANGEROUS!
HE DOES SEEM TO HAVE IMPROVED HIS METHODS SINCE WE LAST SAW HIM.
SOMEHOW HE'S MANAGED TO ESCAPE CUSTODY AND IS UP TO HIS OLD TRICKS-- BUT WITH SOME NEW WRINKLES!
LAST TIME HE WAS VULNERABLE BECAUSE HE HAD TO BE WITH THE CREATURE IN ORDER TO CONTROL IT.
NOW THAT HIS MASTERY OVER THAT THING IS TELEPATHIC, WE NEED A NEW STRATEGY... AND I THINK I KNOW WHAT THAT STRATEGY IS!
MEANWHILE... IN THE JUNGLE LAB...
BLAST MY LUCK!
IF ONLY PERFECTING MY ENLARGING RAY WERE AS SIMPLE AS DEFEATING THOSE MASKED CLOWNS!
BLAM!
SUDDENLY...
THAT WAS JUST THE FIRST ROUND, ZAL-TE! THE FIGHT IS FAR FROM CONCLUDED!
BY HADRAD'S FACE! YOU AGAIN!
8

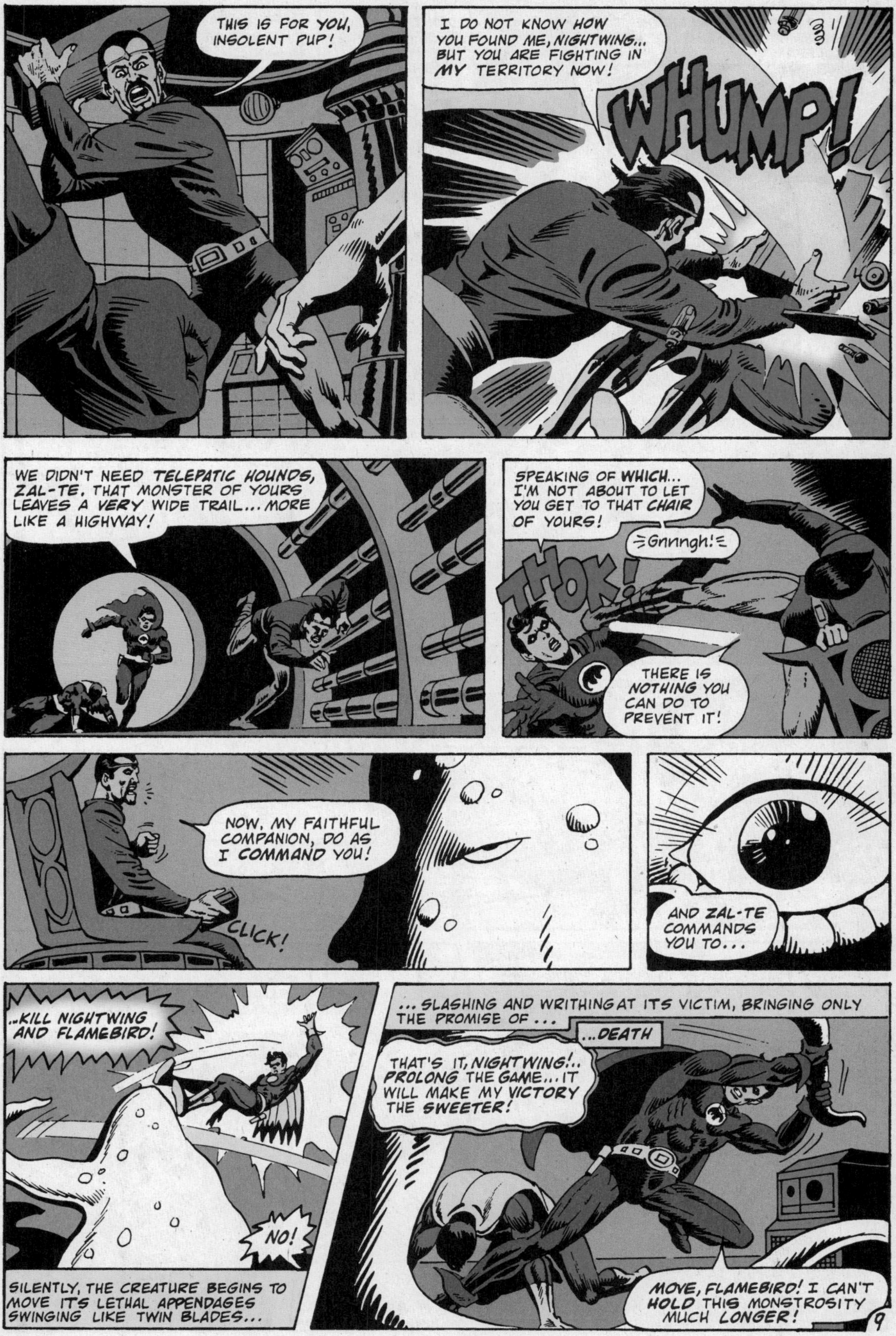

THIS IS FOR YOU, INSOLENT PUP!
I DO NOT KNOW HOW YOU FOUND ME, NIGHTWING... BUT YOU ARE FIGHTING IN MY TERRITORY NOW!
WHUMP!
WE DIDN'T NEED TELEPATIC HOUNDS, ZAL-TE. THAT MONSTER OF YOURS LEAVES A VERY WIDE TRAIL... MORE LIKE A HIGHWAY!
SPEAKING OF WHICH... I'M NOT ABOUT TO LET YOU GET TO THAT CHAIR OF YOURS!
Gnnngh!
THOK!
THERE IS NOTHING YOU CAN DO TO PREVENT IT!
NOW, MY FAITHFUL COMPANION, DO AS I COMMAND YOU!
CLICK!
AND ZAL-TE COMMANDS YOU TO...
..KILL NIGHTWING AND FLAMEBIRD!
NO!
SILENTLY, THE CREATURE BEGINS TO MOVE ITS LETHAL APPENDAGES SWINGING LIKE TWIN BLADES...
... SLASHING AND WRITHING AT ITS VICTIM, BRINGING ONLY THE PROMISE OF ...
...DEATH
THAT'S IT, NIGHTWING!.. PROLONG THE GAME... IT WILL MAKE MY VICTORY THE SWEETER!
MOVE, FLAMEBIRD! I CAN'T HOLD THIS MONSTROSITY MUCH LONGER!
9

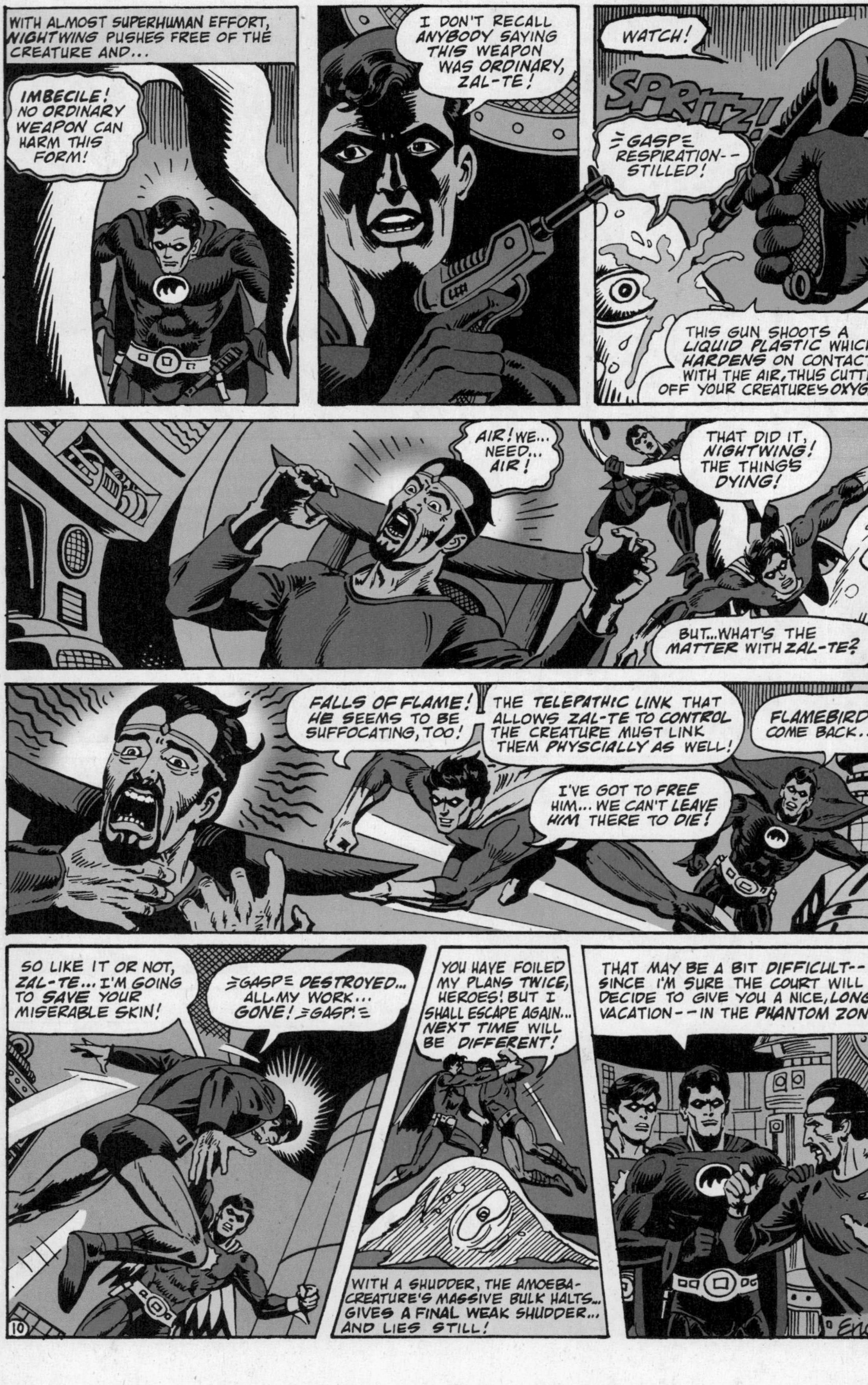
WITH ALMOST SUPERHUMAN EFFORT, NIGHTWING PUSHES FREE OF THE CREATURE AND...
IMBECILE! NO ORDINARY WEAPON CAN HARM THIS FORM!
I DON'T RECALL ANYBODY SAYING THIS WEAPON WAS ORDINARY, ZAL-TE!
WATCH!
SPRITZ!
=GASP= RESPIRATION--STILLED!
THIS GUN SHOOTS A LIQUID PLASTIC WHICH HARDENS ON CONTACT WITH THE AIR, THUS CUTTING OFF YOUR CREATURE'S OXYGEN!
AIR! WE... NEED... AIR!
THAT DID IT, NIGHTWING! THE THING'S DYING!
BUT...WHAT'S THE MATTER WITH ZAL-TE?
FALLS OF FLAME! HE SEEMS TO BE SUFFOCATING, TOO!
THE TELEPATHIC LINK THAT ALLOWS ZAL-TE TO CONTROL THE CREATURE MUST LINK THEM PHYSCIALLY AS WELL!
FLAMEBIRD! COME BACK...
I'VE GOT TO FREE HIM... WE CAN'T LEAVE HIM THERE TO DIE!
SO LIKE IT OR NOT, ZAL-TE... I'M GOING TO SAVE YOUR MISERABLE SKIN!
=GASP= DESTROYED... ALL MY WORK... GONE! =GASP!=
10
YOU HAVE FOILED MY PLANS TWICE, HEROES! BUT I SHALL ESCAPE AGAIN... NEXT TIME WILL BE DIFFERENT!
WITH A SHUDDER, THE AMOEBA-CREATURE'S MASSIVE BULK HALTS... GIVES A FINAL WEAK SHUDDER... AND LIES STILL!
THAT MAY BE A BIT DIFFICULT--SINCE I'M SURE THE COURT WILL DECIDE TO GIVE YOU A NICE, LONG VACATION--IN THE PHANTOM ZONE!
End

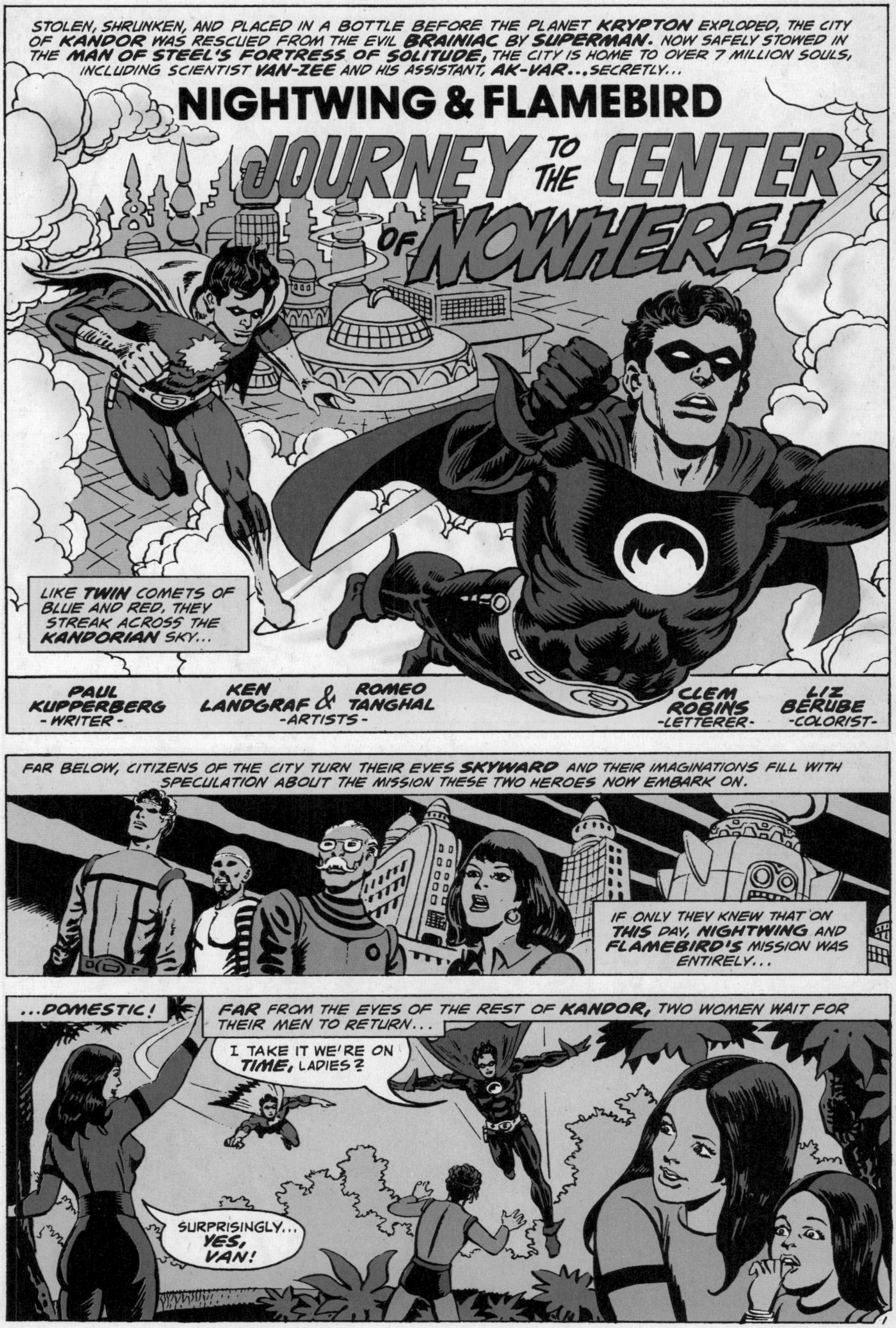
STOLEN, SHRUNKEN, AND PLACED IN A BOTTLE BEFORE THE PLANET KRYPTON EXPLODED, THE CITY OF KANDOR WAS RESCUED FROM THE EVIL BRAINIAC BY SUPERMAN. NOW SAFELY STOWED IN THE MAN OF STEEL'S FORTRESS OF SOLITUDE, THE CITY IS HOME TO OVER 7 MILLION SOULS, INCLUDING SCIENTIST VAN-ZEE AND HIS ASSISTANT, AK-VAR...SECRETLY...
NIGHTWING & FLAMEBIRD
JOURNEY TO THE CENTER OF NOWHERE!
LIKE TWIN COMETS OF BLUE AND RED, THEY STREAK ACROSS THE KANDORIAN SKY...
PAUL KUPPERBERG -WRITER-
KEN LANDGRAF & ROMEO TANGHAL -ARTISTS-
CLEM ROBINS -LETTERER-
LIZ BERUBE -COLORIST-
FAR BELOW, CITIZENS OF THE CITY TURN THEIR EYES SKYWARD AND THEIR IMAGINATIONS FILL WITH SPECULATION ABOUT THE MISSION THESE TWO HEROES NOW EMBARK ON.
IF ONLY THEY KNEW THAT ON THIS DAY, NIGHTWING AND FLAMEBIRD'S MISSION WAS ENTIRELY...
...DOMESTIC!
FAR FROM THE EYES OF THE REST OF KANDOR, TWO WOMEN WAIT FOR THEIR MEN TO RETURN...
I TAKE IT WE'RE ON TIME, LADIES?
SURPRISINGLY... YES, VAN!
1

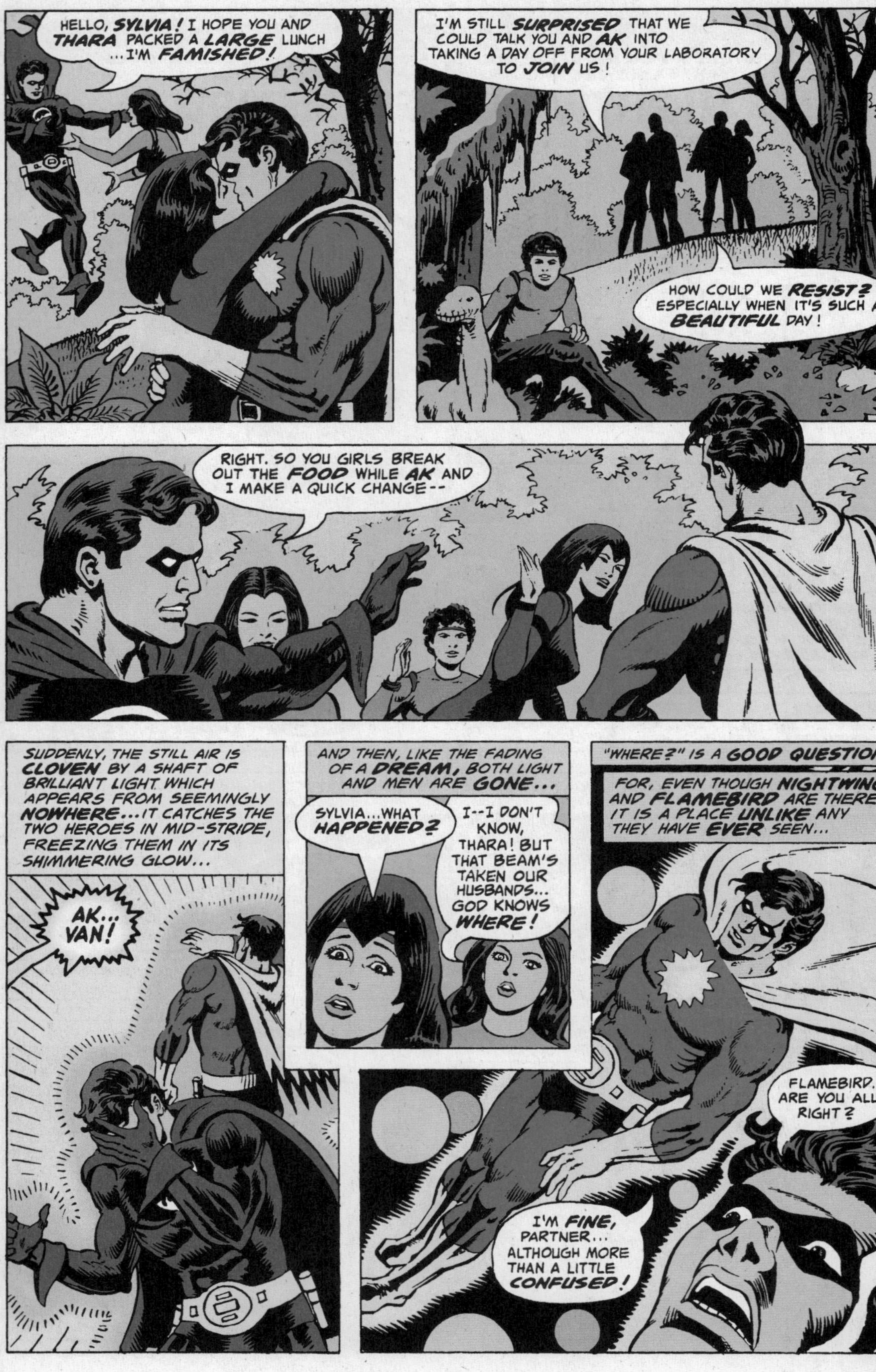

HELLO, SYLVIA! I HOPE YOU AND THARA PACKED A LARGE LUNCH ...I'M FAMISHED!
I'M STILL SURPRISED THAT WE COULD TALK YOU AND AK INTO TAKING A DAY OFF FROM YOUR LABORATORY TO JOIN US!
HOW COULD WE RESIST? ESPECIALLY WHEN IT'S SUCH A BEAUTIFUL DAY!
RIGHT. SO YOU GIRLS BREAK OUT THE FOOD WHILE AK AND I MAKE A QUICK CHANGE--
SUDDENLY, THE STILL AIR IS CLOVEN BY A SHAFT OF BRILLIANT LIGHT WHICH APPEARS FROM SEEMINGLY NOWHERE... IT CATCHES THE TWO HEROES IN MID-STRIDE, FREEZING THEM IN ITS SHIMMERING GLOW...
AK... VAN!
AND THEN, LIKE THE FADING OF A DREAM, BOTH LIGHT AND MEN ARE GONE...
SYLVIA... WHAT HAPPENED?
I--I DON'T KNOW, THARA! BUT THAT BEAM'S TAKEN OUR HUSBANDS... GOD KNOWS WHERE!
"WHERE?" IS A GOOD QUESTION!
FOR, EVEN THOUGH NIGHTWING AND FLAMEBIRD ARE THERE, IT IS A PLACE UNLIKE ANY THEY HAVE EVER SEEN...
FLAMEBIRD... ARE YOU ALL RIGHT?
I'M FINE, PARTNER... ALTHOUGH MORE THAN A LITTLE CONFUSED!
2

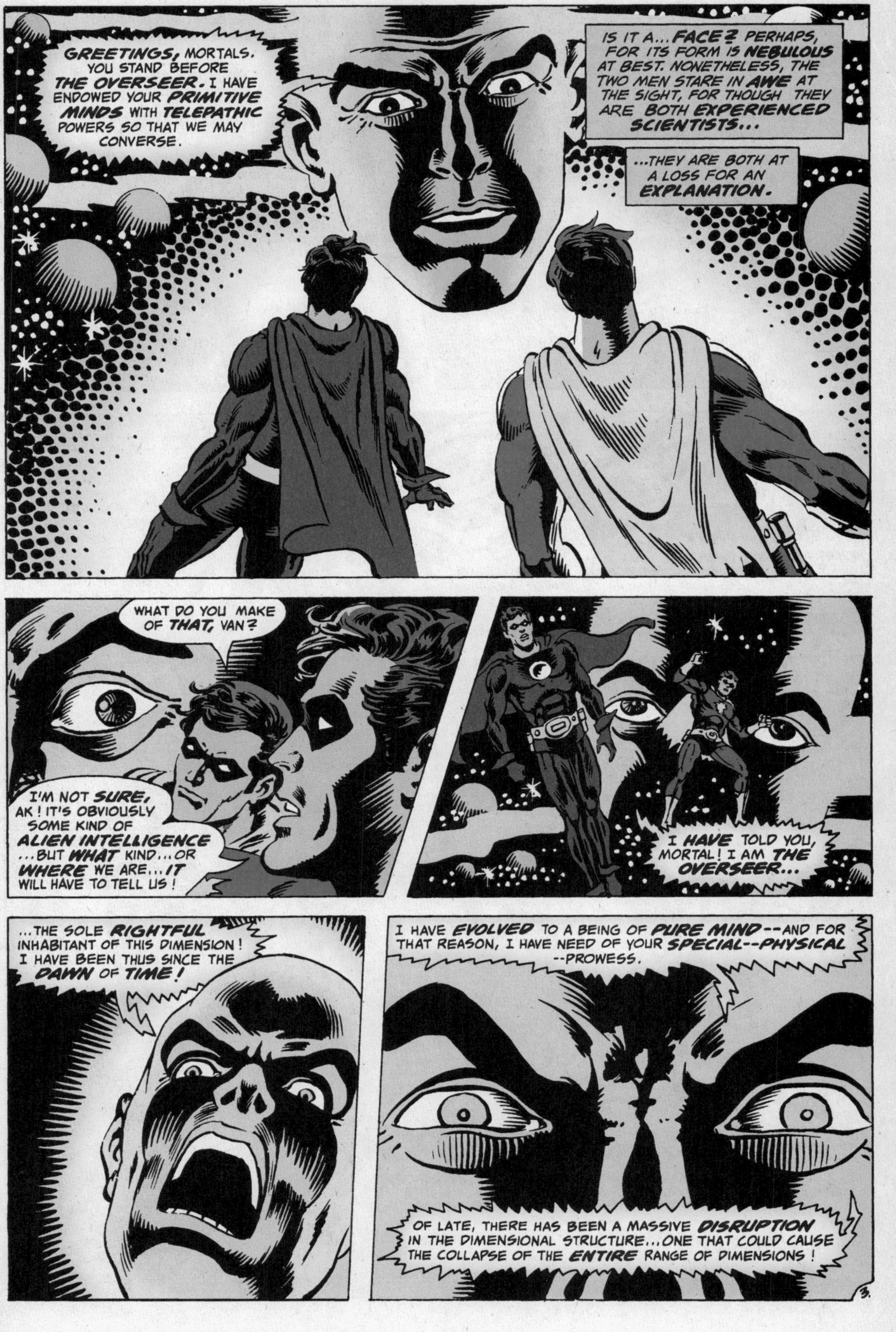
GREETINGS, MORTALS. YOU STAND BEFORE THE OVERSEER. I HAVE ENDOWED YOUR PRIMITIVE MINDS WITH TELEPATHIC POWERS SO THAT WE MAY CONVERSE.
IS IT A... FACE? PERHAPS, FOR ITS FORM IS NEBULOUS AT BEST. NONETHELESS, THE TWO MEN STARE IN AWE AT THE SIGHT, FOR THOUGH THEY ARE BOTH EXPERIENCED SCIENTISTS...
...THEY ARE BOTH AT A LOSS FOR AN EXPLANATION.
WHAT DO YOU MAKE OF THAT, VAN?
I'M NOT SURE, AK! IT'S OBVIOUSLY SOME KIND OF ALIEN INTELLIGENCE ...BUT WHAT KIND... OR WHERE WE ARE... IT WILL HAVE TO TELL US!
I HAVE TOLD YOU, MORTAL! I AM THE OVERSEER...
...THE SOLE RIGHTFUL INHABITANT OF THIS DIMENSION! I HAVE BEEN THUS SINCE THE DAWN OF TIME!
I HAVE EVOLVED TO A BEING OF PURE MIND--AND FOR THAT REASON, I HAVE NEED OF YOUR SPECIAL--PHYSICAL--PROWESS.
OF LATE, THERE HAS BEEN A MASSIVE DISRUPTION IN THE DIMENSIONAL STRUCTURE... ONE THAT COULD CAUSE THE COLLAPSE OF THE ENTIRE RANGE OF DIMENSIONS!
3.

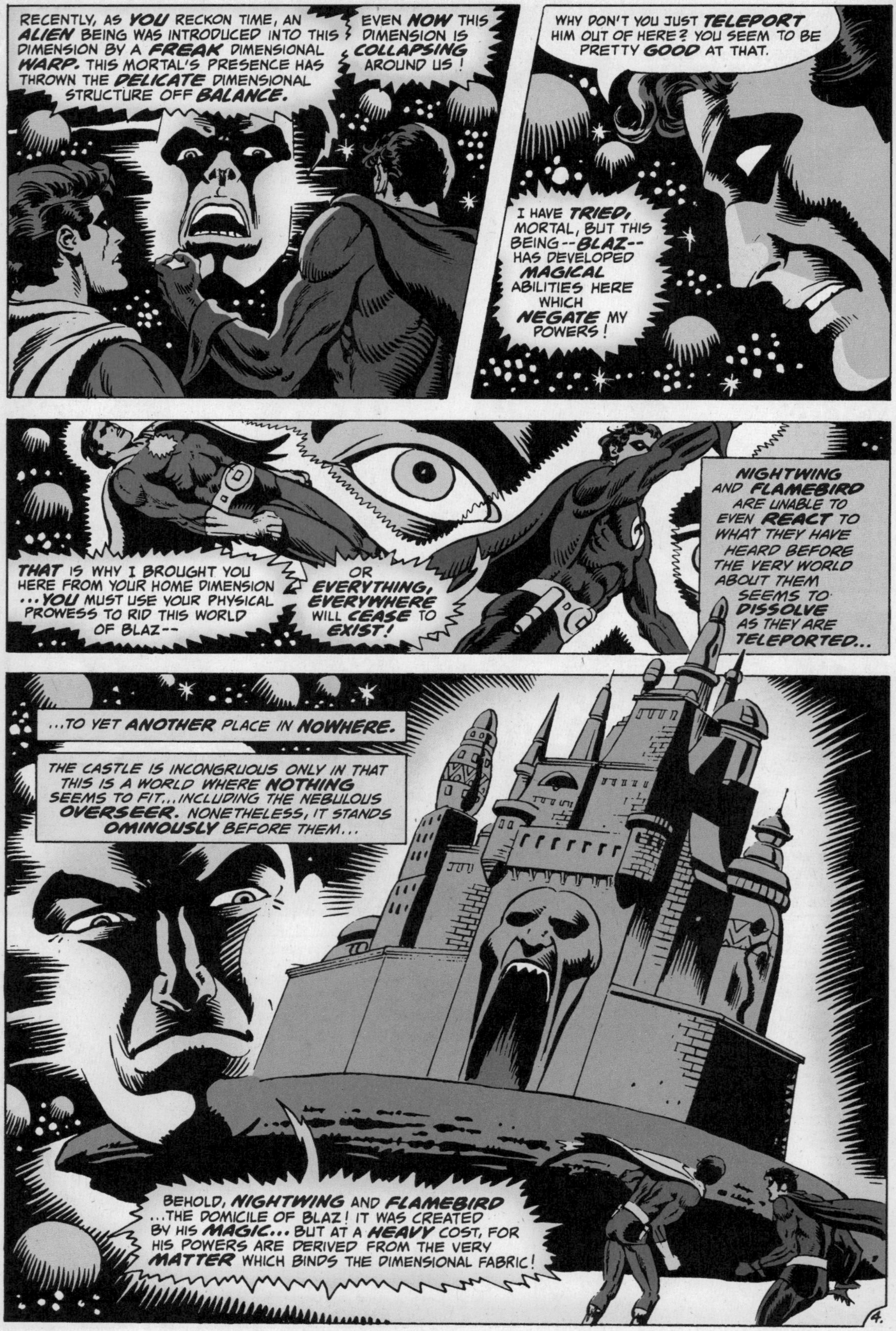
RECENTLY, AS YOU RECKON TIME, AN ALIEN BEING WAS INTRODUCED INTO THIS DIMENSION BY A FREAK DIMENSIONAL WARP. THIS MORTAL'S PRESENCE HAS THROWN THE DELICATE DIMENSIONAL STRUCTURE OFF BALANCE.
EVEN NOW THIS DIMENSION IS COLLAPSING AROUND US!
WHY DON'T YOU JUST TELEPORT HIM OUT OF HERE? YOU SEEM TO BE PRETTY GOOD AT THAT.
I HAVE TRIED, MORTAL, BUT THIS BEING--BLAZ--HAS DEVELOPED MAGICAL ABILITIES HERE WHICH NEGATE MY POWERS!
THAT IS WHY I BROUGHT YOU HERE FROM YOUR HOME DIMENSION ...YOU MUST USE YOUR PHYSICAL PROWESS TO RID THIS WORLD OF BLAZ--
OR EVERYTHING, EVERYWHERE WILL CEASE TO EXIST!
NIGHTWING AND FLAMEBIRD ARE UNABLE TO EVEN REACT TO WHAT THEY HAVE HEARD BEFORE THE VERY WORLD ABOUT THEM SEEMS TO DISSOLVE AS THEY ARE TELEPORTED...
...TO YET ANOTHER PLACE IN NOWHERE.
THE CASTLE IS INCONGRUOUS ONLY IN THAT THIS IS A WORLD WHERE NOTHING SEEMS TO FIT...INCLUDING THE NEBULOUS OVERSEER. NONETHELESS, IT STANDS OMINOUSLY BEFORE THEM...
BEHOLD, NIGHTWING AND FLAMEBIRD ...THE DOMICILE OF BLAZ! IT WAS CREATED BY HIS MAGIC... BUT AT A HEAVY COST, FOR HIS POWERS ARE DERIVED FROM THE VERY MATTER WHICH BINDS THE DIMENSIONAL FABRIC!
4.

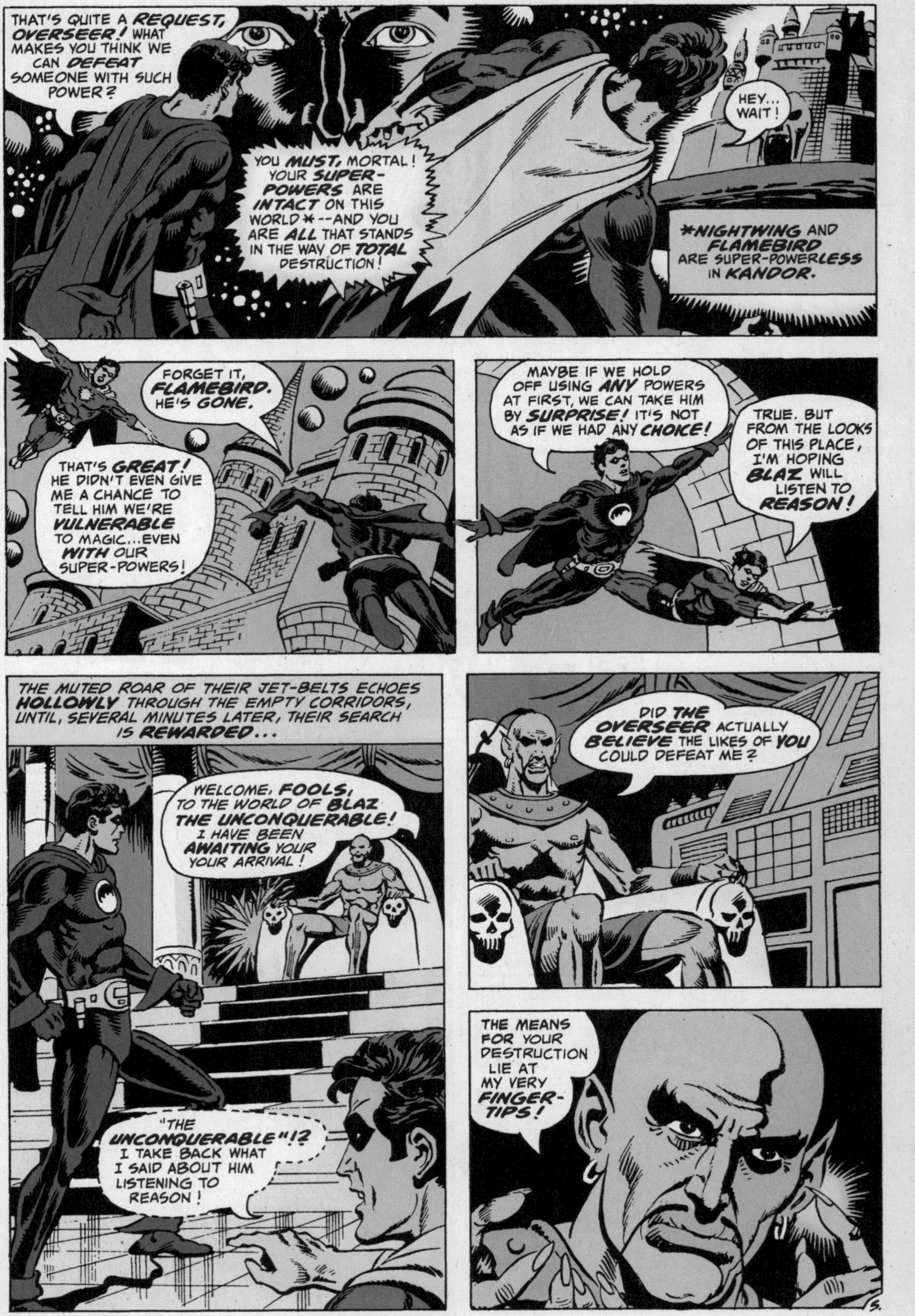
THAT'S QUITE A REQUEST, OVERSEER! WHAT MAKES YOU THINK WE CAN DEFEAT SOMEONE WITH SUCH POWER?
YOU MUST, MORTAL! YOUR SUPER-POWERS ARE INTACT ON THIS WORLD* --AND YOU ARE ALL THAT STANDS IN THE WAY OF TOTAL DESTRUCTION!
HEY... WAIT!
*NIGHTWING AND FLAMEBIRD ARE SUPER-POWERLESS IN KANDOR.
FORGET IT, FLAMEBIRD. HE'S GONE.
THAT'S GREAT! HE DIDN'T EVEN GIVE ME A CHANCE TO TELL HIM WE'RE VULNERABLE TO MAGIC...EVEN WITH OUR SUPER-POWERS!
MAYBE IF WE HOLD OFF USING ANY POWERS AT FIRST, WE CAN TAKE HIM BY SURPRISE! IT'S NOT AS IF WE HAD ANY CHOICE!
TRUE. BUT FROM THE LOOKS OF THIS PLACE, I'M HOPING BLAZ WILL LISTEN TO REASON!
THE MUTED ROAR OF THEIR JET-BELTS ECHOES HOLLOWLY THROUGH THE EMPTY CORRIDORS, UNTIL, SEVERAL MINUTES LATER, THEIR SEARCH IS REWARDED...
WELCOME, FOOLS, TO THE WORLD OF BLAZ THE UNCONQUERABLE! I HAVE BEEN AWAITING YOUR YOUR ARRIVAL!
"THE UNCONQUERABLE"!? I TAKE BACK WHAT I SAID ABOUT HIM LISTENING TO REASON!
DID THE OVERSEER ACTUALLY BELIEVE THE LIKES OF YOU COULD DEFEAT ME?
THE MEANS FOR YOUR DESTRUCTION LIE AT MY VERY FINGER-TIPS!

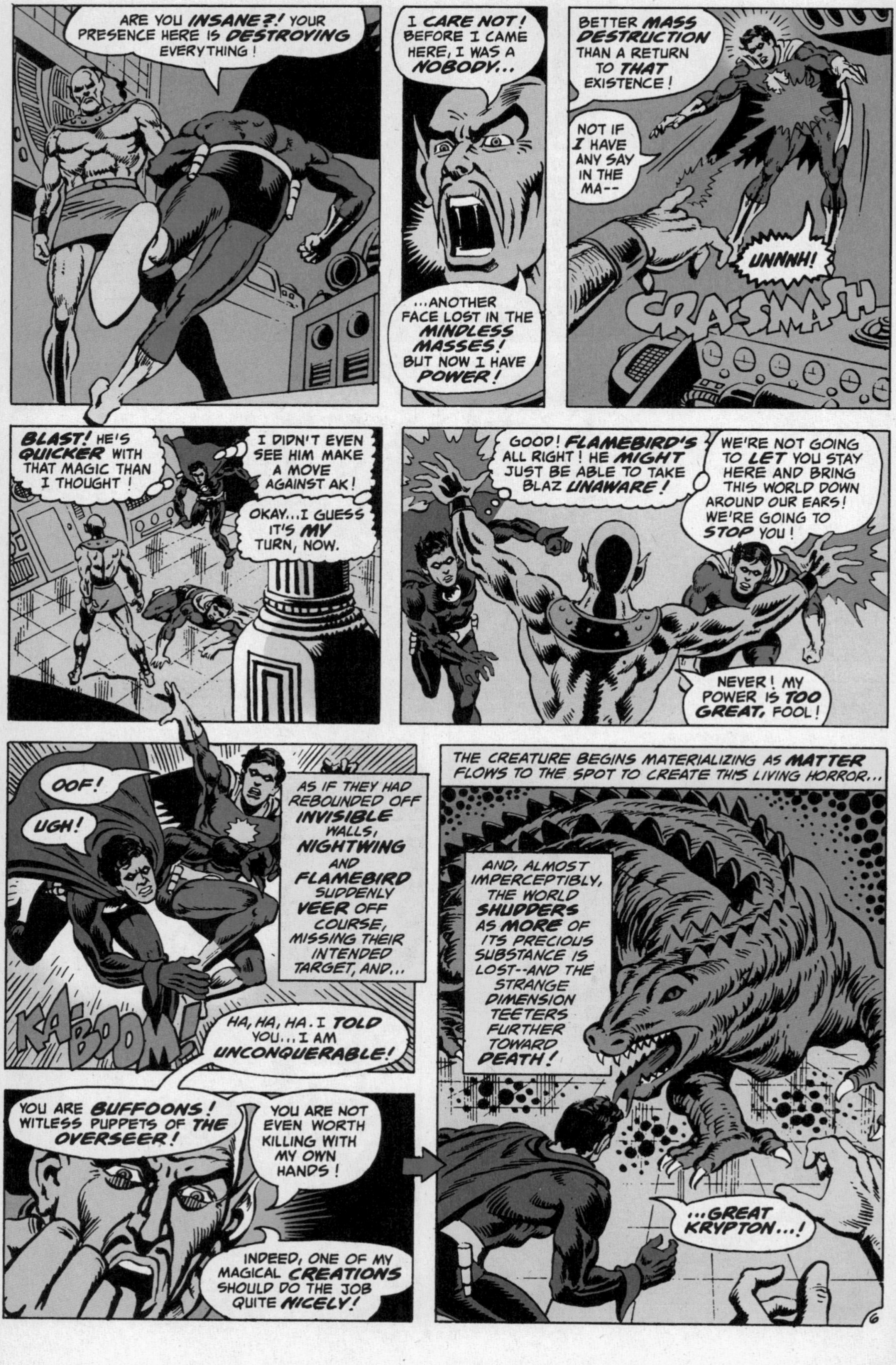
ARE YOU INSANE?! YOUR PRESENCE HERE IS DESTROYING EVERYTHING!
I CARE NOT! BEFORE I CAME HERE, I WAS A NOBODY...
...ANOTHER FACE LOST IN THE MINDLESS MASSES! BUT NOW I HAVE POWER!
BETTER MASS DESTRUCTION THAN A RETURN TO THAT EXISTENCE!
NOT IF I HAVE ANY SAY IN THE MA--
UNNNH!
CRA-SMASH
BLAST! HE'S QUICKER WITH THAT MAGIC THAN I THOUGHT!
I DIDN'T EVEN SEE HIM MAKE A MOVE AGAINST AK!
OKAY...I GUESS IT'S MY TURN, NOW.
GOOD! FLAMEBIRD'S ALL RIGHT! HE MIGHT JUST BE ABLE TO TAKE BLAZ UNAWARE!
WE'RE NOT GOING TO LET YOU STAY HERE AND BRING THIS WORLD DOWN AROUND OUR EARS! WE'RE GOING TO STOP YOU!
NEVER! MY POWER IS TOO GREAT, FOOL!
OOF!
UGH!
AS IF THEY HAD REBOUNDED OFF INVISIBLE WALLS, NIGHTWING AND FLAMEBIRD SUDDENLY VEER OFF COURSE, MISSING THEIR INTENDED TARGET, AND...
KA-BOOM!
HA, HA, HA. I TOLD YOU... I AM UNCONQUERABLE!
YOU ARE BUFFOONS! WITLESS PUPPETS OF THE OVERSEER!
YOU ARE NOT EVEN WORTH KILLING WITH MY OWN HANDS!
INDEED, ONE OF MY MAGICAL CREATIONS SHOULD DO THE JOB QUITE NICELY!
THE CREATURE BEGINS MATERIALIZING AS MATTER FLOWS TO THE SPOT TO CREATE THIS LIVING HORROR...
AND, ALMOST IMPERCEPTIBLY, THE WORLD SHUDDERS AS MORE OF ITS PRECIOUS SUBSTANCE IS LOST--AND THE STRANGE DIMENSION TEETERS FURTHER TOWARD DEATH!
...GREAT KRYPTON...!
6

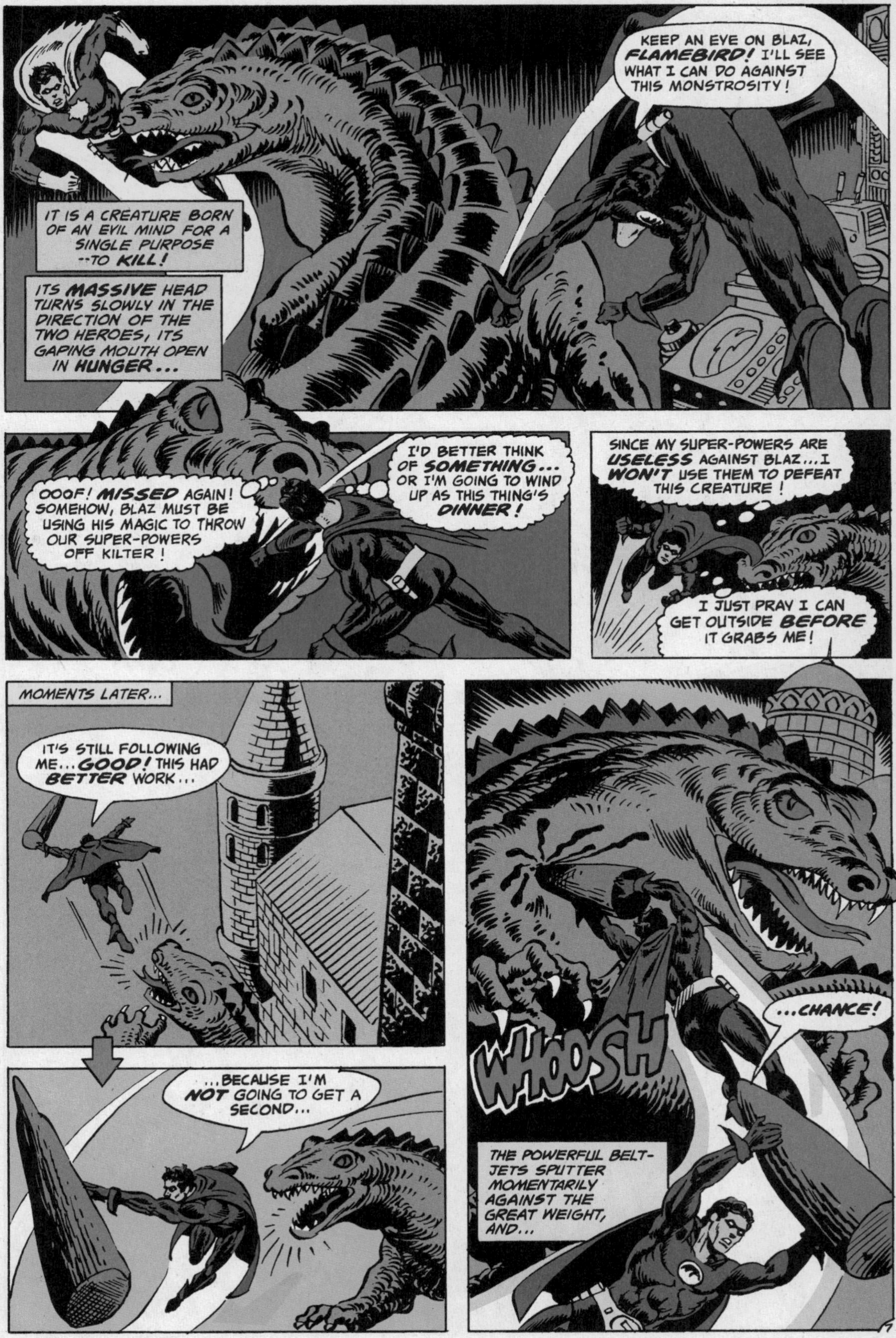
IT IS A CREATURE BORN OF AN EVIL MIND FOR A SINGLE PURPOSE --TO KILL!
ITS MASSIVE HEAD TURNS SLOWLY IN THE DIRECTION OF THE TWO HEROES, ITS GAPING MOUTH OPEN IN HUNGER...
KEEP AN EYE ON BLAZ, FLAMEBIRD! I'LL SEE WHAT I CAN DO AGAINST THIS MONSTROSITY!
OOOF! MISSED AGAIN! SOMEHOW, BLAZ MUST BE USING HIS MAGIC TO THROW OUR SUPER-POWERS OFF KILTER!
I'D BETTER THINK OF SOMETHING... OR I'M GOING TO WIND UP AS THIS THING'S DINNER!
SINCE MY SUPER-POWERS ARE USELESS AGAINST BLAZ... I WON'T USE THEM TO DEFEAT THIS CREATURE!
I JUST PRAY I CAN GET OUTSIDE BEFORE IT GRABS ME!
MOMENTS LATER...
IT'S STILL FOLLOWING ME... GOOD! THIS HAD BETTER WORK...
...BECAUSE I'M NOT GOING TO GET A SECOND...
WHOOSH
...CHANCE!
THE POWERFUL BELT-JETS SPUTTER MOMENTARILY AGAINST THE GREAT WEIGHT, AND...
7

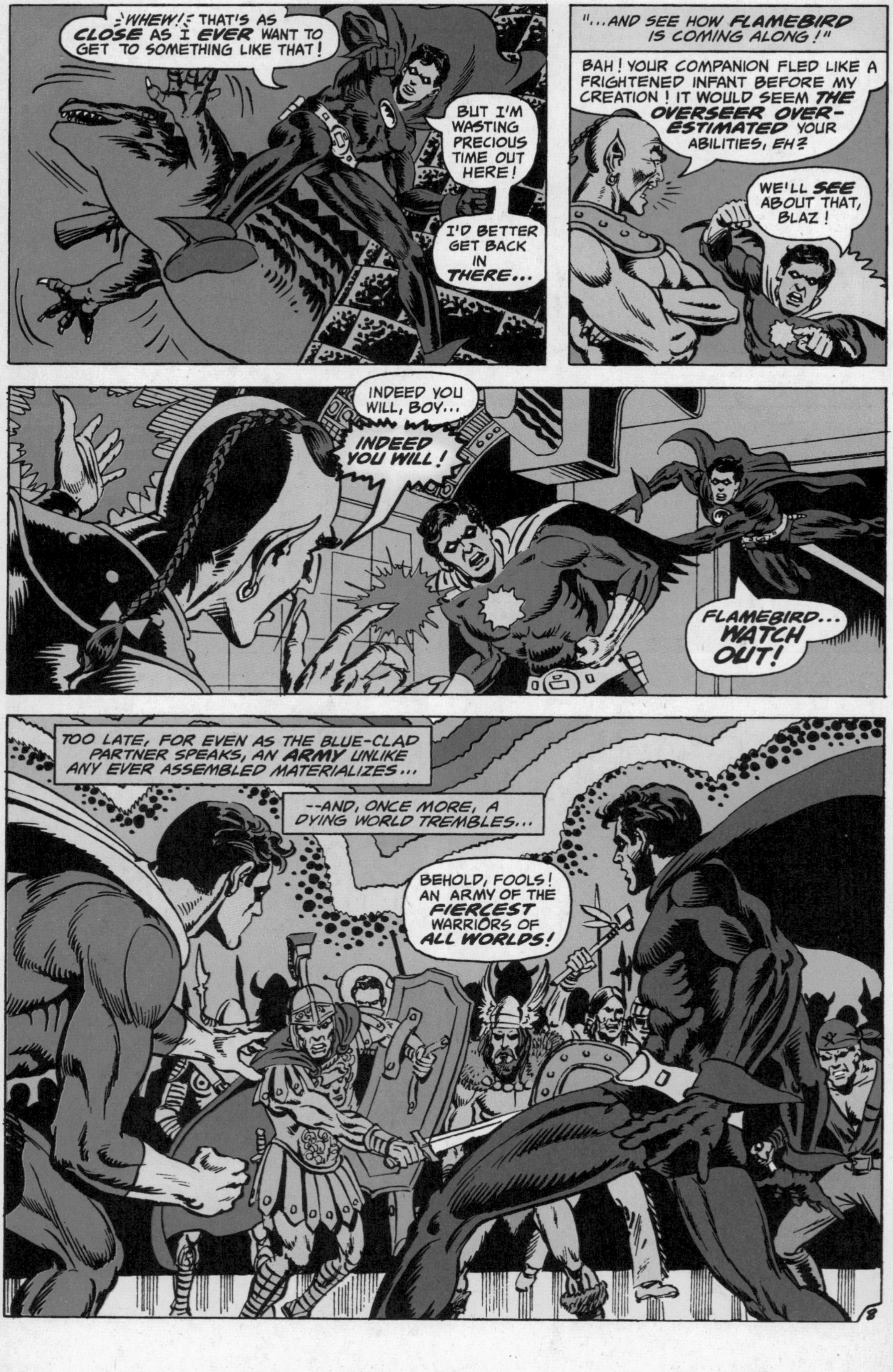
WHEW! THAT'S AS CLOSE AS I EVER WANT TO GET TO SOMETHING LIKE THAT!
BUT I'M WASTING PRECIOUS TIME OUT HERE!
I'D BETTER GET BACK IN THERE...
"...AND SEE HOW FLAMEBIRD IS COMING ALONG!"
BAH! YOUR COMPANION FLED LIKE A FRIGHTENED INFANT BEFORE MY CREATION! IT WOULD SEEM THE OVERSEER OVER-ESTIMATED YOUR ABILITIES, EH?
WE'LL SEE ABOUT THAT, BLAZ!
INDEED YOU WILL, BOY...
INDEED YOU WILL!
FLAMEBIRD... WATCH OUT!
TOO LATE, FOR EVEN AS THE BLUE-CLAD PARTNER SPEAKS, AN ARMY UNLIKE ANY EVER ASSEMBLED MATERIALIZES...
--AND, ONCE MORE, A DYING WORLD TREMBLES...
BEHOLD, FOOLS! AN ARMY OF THE FIERCEST WARRIORS OF ALL WORLDS!
8

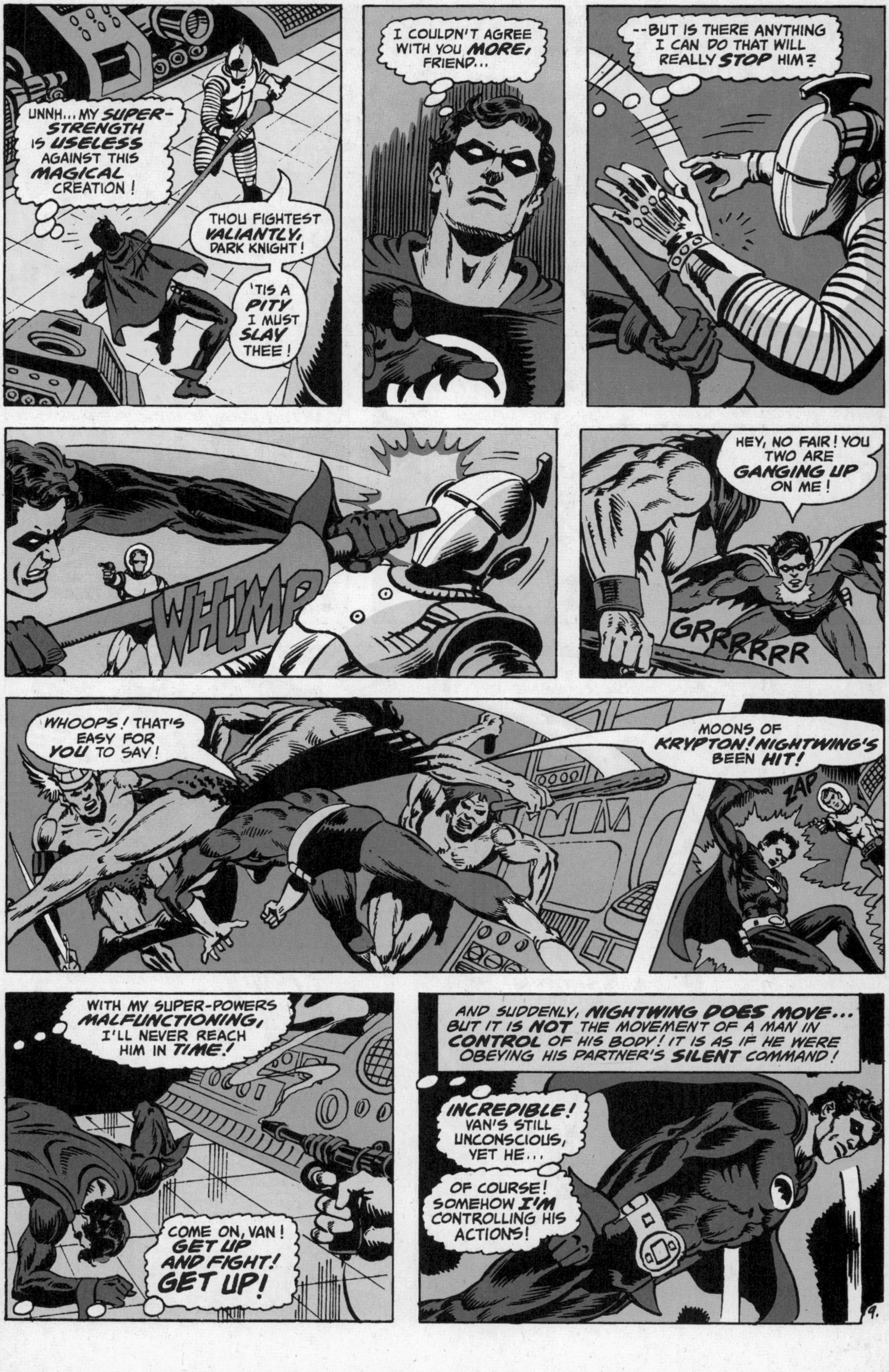
UNNH... MY SUPER-STRENGTH IS USELESS AGAINST THIS MAGICAL CREATION!
THOU FIGHTEST VALIANTLY, DARK KNIGHT!
'TIS A PITY I MUST SLAY THEE!
I COULDN'T AGREE WITH YOU MORE, FRIEND...
--BUT IS THERE ANYTHING I CAN DO THAT WILL REALLY STOP HIM?
WHUMP
HEY, NO FAIR! YOU TWO ARE GANGING UP ON ME!
GRRRRRRR
WHOOPS! THAT'S EASY FOR YOU TO SAY!
MOONS OF KRYPTON! NIGHTWING'S BEEN HIT!
ZAP
WITH MY SUPER-POWERS MALFUNCTIONING, I'LL NEVER REACH HIM IN TIME!
COME ON, VAN! GET UP AND FIGHT! GET UP!
AND SUDDENLY, NIGHTWING DOES MOVE... BUT IT IS NOT THE MOVEMENT OF A MAN IN CONTROL OF HIS BODY! IT IS AS IF HE WERE OBEYING HIS PARTNER'S SILENT COMMAND!
INCREDIBLE! VAN'S STILL UNCONSCIOUS, YET HE...
OF COURSE! SOMEHOW I'M CONTROLLING HIS ACTIONS!
9.

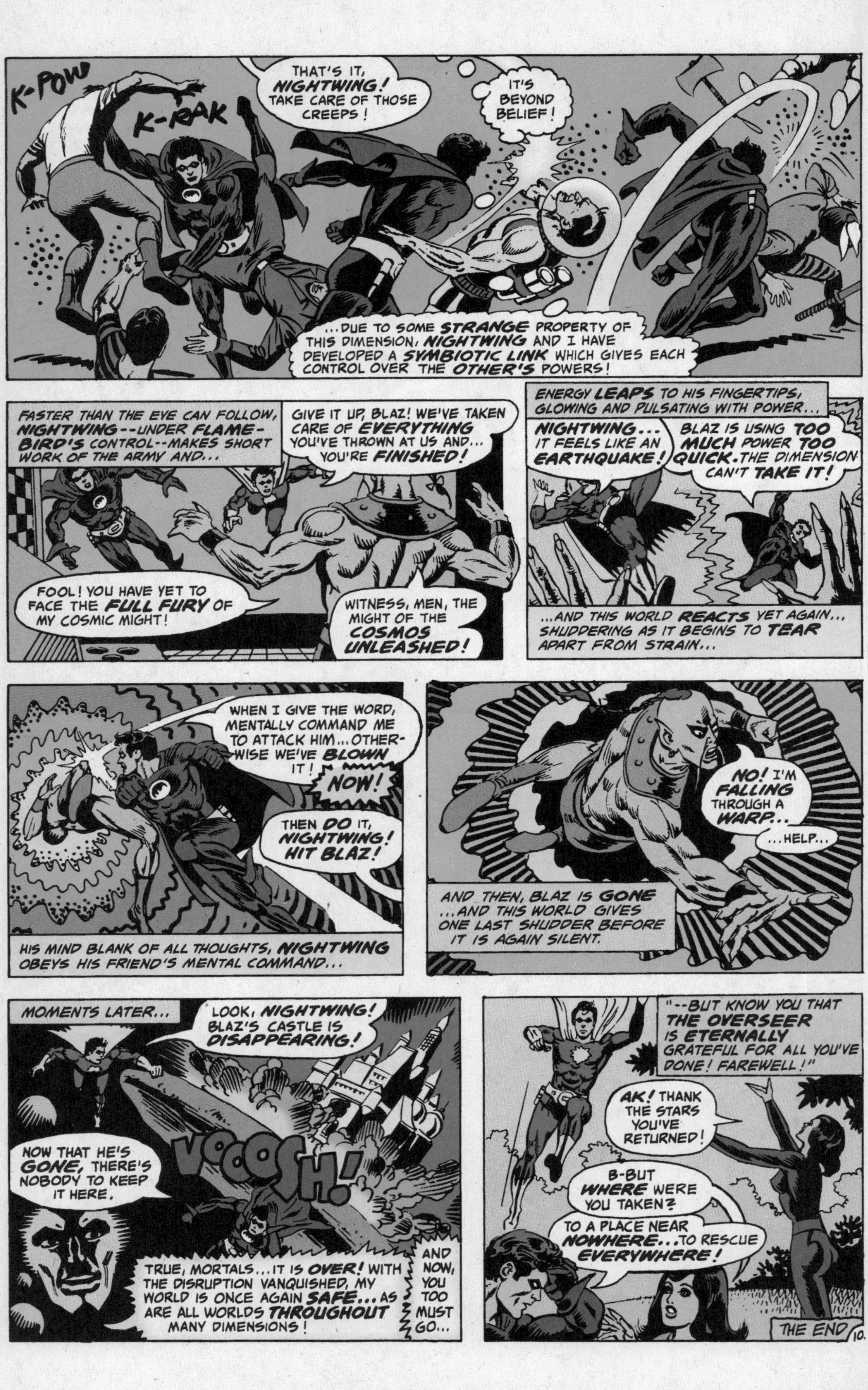
K-POW
K-RAK
THAT'S IT, NIGHTWING! TAKE CARE OF THOSE CREEPS!
IT'S BEYOND BELIEF!
...DUE TO SOME STRANGE PROPERTY OF THIS DIMENSION, NIGHTWING AND I HAVE DEVELOPED A SYMBIOTIC LINK WHICH GIVES EACH CONTROL OVER THE OTHER'S POWERS!
FASTER THAN THE EYE CAN FOLLOW, NIGHTWING--UNDER FLAME-BIRD'S CONTROL--MAKES SHORT WORK OF THE ARMY AND...
GIVE IT UP, BLAZ! WE'VE TAKEN CARE OF EVERYTHING YOU'VE THROWN AT US AND... YOU'RE FINISHED!
FOOL! YOU HAVE YET TO FACE THE FULL FURY OF MY COSMIC MIGHT!
WITNESS, MEN, THE MIGHT OF THE COSMOS UNLEASHED!
ENERGY LEAPS TO HIS FINGERTIPS, GLOWING AND PULSATING WITH POWER...
NIGHTWING... IT FEELS LIKE AN EARTHQUAKE!
BLAZ IS USING TOO MUCH POWER TOO QUICK. THE DIMENSION CAN'T TAKE IT!
...AND THIS WORLD REACTS YET AGAIN... SHUDDERING AS IT BEGINS TO TEAR APART FROM STRAIN...
WHEN I GIVE THE WORD, MENTALLY COMMAND ME TO ATTACK HIM... OTHER-WISE WE'VE BLOWN IT!
NOW!
THEN DO IT, NIGHTWING! HIT BLAZ!
HIS MIND BLANK OF ALL THOUGHTS, NIGHTWING OBEYS HIS FRIEND'S MENTAL COMMAND...
NO! I'M FALLING THROUGH A WARP...
...HELP...
AND THEN, BLAZ IS GONE ...AND THIS WORLD GIVES ONE LAST SHUDDER BEFORE IT IS AGAIN SILENT.
MOMENTS LATER...
LOOK, NIGHTWING! BLAZ'S CASTLE IS DISAPPEARING!
NOW THAT HE'S GONE, THERE'S NOBODY TO KEEP IT HERE.
VOOOSH!
TRUE, MORTALS... IT IS OVER! WITH THE DISRUPTION VANQUISHED, MY WORLD IS ONCE AGAIN SAFE... AS ARE ALL WORLDS THROUGHOUT MANY DIMENSIONS!
AND NOW, YOU TOO MUST GO...
"--BUT KNOW YOU THAT THE OVERSEER IS ETERNALLY GRATEFUL FOR ALL YOU'VE DONE! FAREWELL!"
AK! THANK THE STARS YOU'VE RETURNED!
B-BUT WHERE WERE YOU TAKEN?
TO A PLACE NEAR NOWHERE... TO RESCUE EVERYWHERE!
THE END
10.

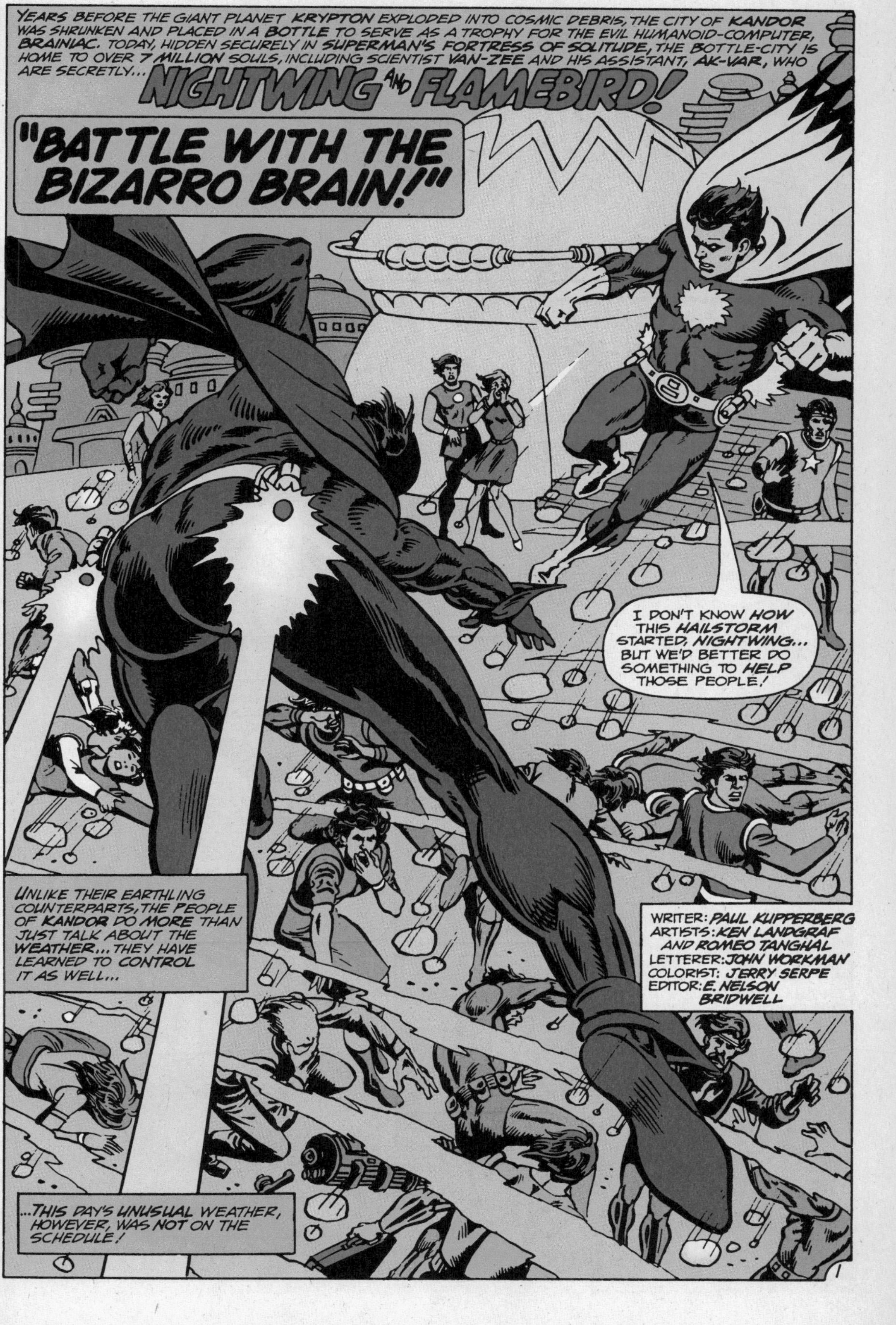
YEARS BEFORE THE GIANT PLANET KRYPTON EXPLODED INTO COSMIC DEBRIS, THE CITY OF KANDOR WAS SHRUNKEN AND PLACED IN A BOTTLE TO SERVE AS A TROPHY FOR THE EVIL HUMANOID-COMPUTER, BRAINIAC. TODAY, HIDDEN SECURELY IN SUPERMAN'S FORTRESS OF SOLITUDE, THE BOTTLE-CITY IS HOME TO OVER 7 MILLION SOULS, INCLUDING SCIENTIST VAN-ZEE AND HIS ASSISTANT, AK-VAR, WHO ARE SECRETLY...
NIGHTWING AND FLAMEBIRD!
"BATTLE WITH THE BIZARRO BRAIN!"
I DON'T KNOW HOW THIS HAILSTORM STARTED, NIGHTWING... BUT WE'D BETTER DO SOMETHING TO HELP THOSE PEOPLE!
UNLIKE THEIR EARTHLING COUNTERPARTS, THE PEOPLE OF KANDOR DO MORE THAN JUST TALK ABOUT THE WEATHER... THEY HAVE LEARNED TO CONTROL IT AS WELL...
WRITER: PAUL KUPPERBERG ARTISTS: KEN LANDGRAF AND ROMEO TANGHAL LETTERER: JOHN WORKMAN COLORIST: JERRY SERPE EDITOR: E. NELSON BRIDWELL
...THIS DAY'S UNUSUAL WEATHER, HOWEVER, WAS NOT ON THE SCHEDULE!
1

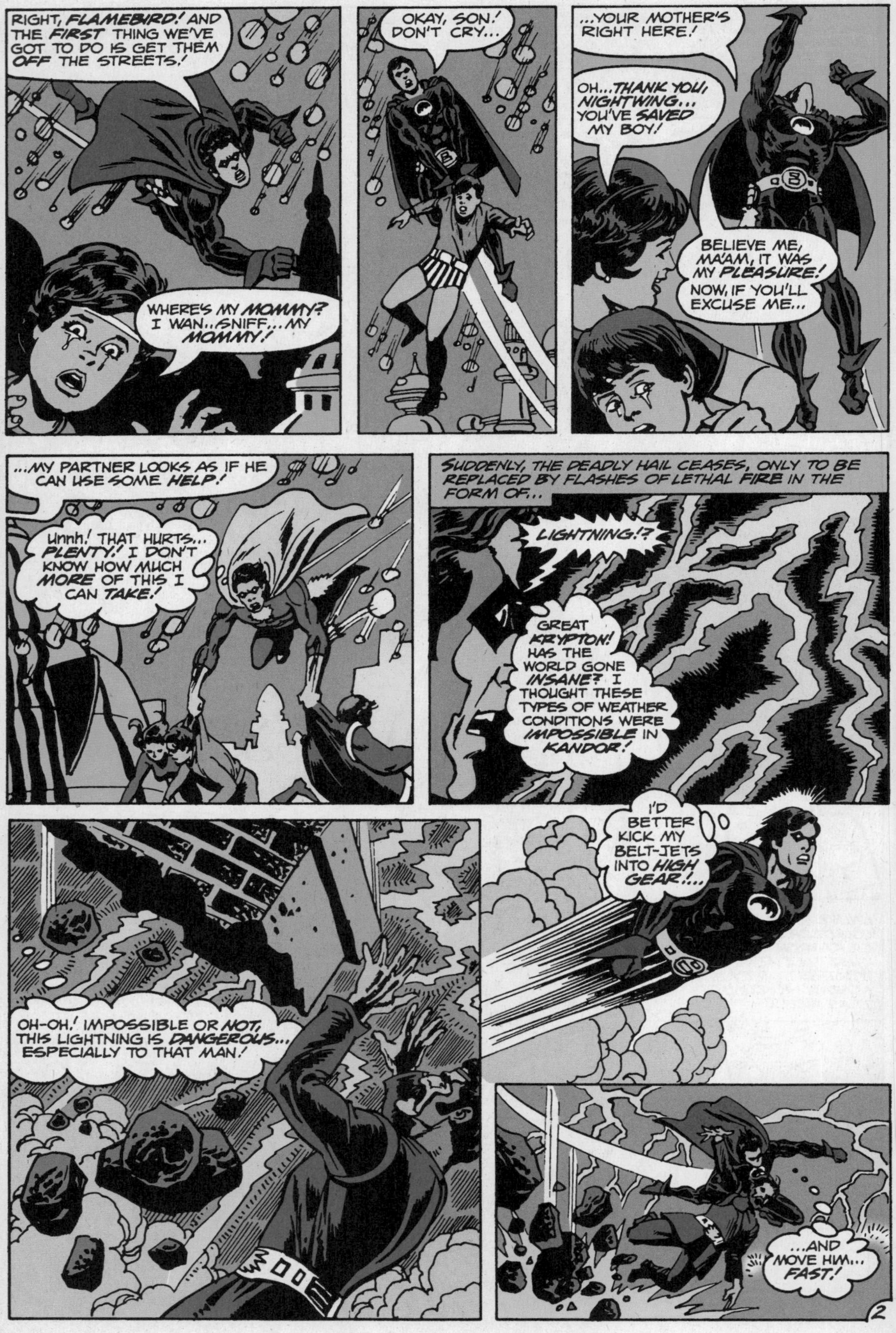

RIGHT, FLAMEBIRD! AND THE FIRST THING WE'VE GOT TO DO IS GET THEM OFF THE STREETS!
WHERE'S MY MOMMY? I WAN...SNIFF...MY MOMMY!
OKAY, SON! DON'T CRY...
...YOUR MOTHER'S RIGHT HERE!
OH...THANK YOU, NIGHTWING... YOU'VE SAVED MY BOY!
BELIEVE ME, MA'AM, IT WAS MY PLEASURE! NOW, IF YOU'LL EXCUSE ME...
...MY PARTNER LOOKS AS IF HE CAN USE SOME HELP!
Unnh! THAT HURTS... PLENTY! I DON'T KNOW HOW MUCH MORE OF THIS I CAN TAKE!
SUDDENLY, THE DEADLY HAIL CEASES, ONLY TO BE REPLACED BY FLASHES OF LETHAL FIRE IN THE FORM OF...
LIGHTNING!?
GREAT KRYPTON! HAS THE WORLD GONE INSANE? I THOUGHT THESE TYPES OF WEATHER CONDITIONS WERE IMPOSSIBLE IN KANDOR!
OH-OH! IMPOSSIBLE OR NOT, THIS LIGHTNING IS DANGEROUS... ESPECIALLY TO THAT MAN!
I'D BETTER KICK MY BELT-JETS INTO HIGH GEAR!...
...AND MOVE HIM... FAST!
2

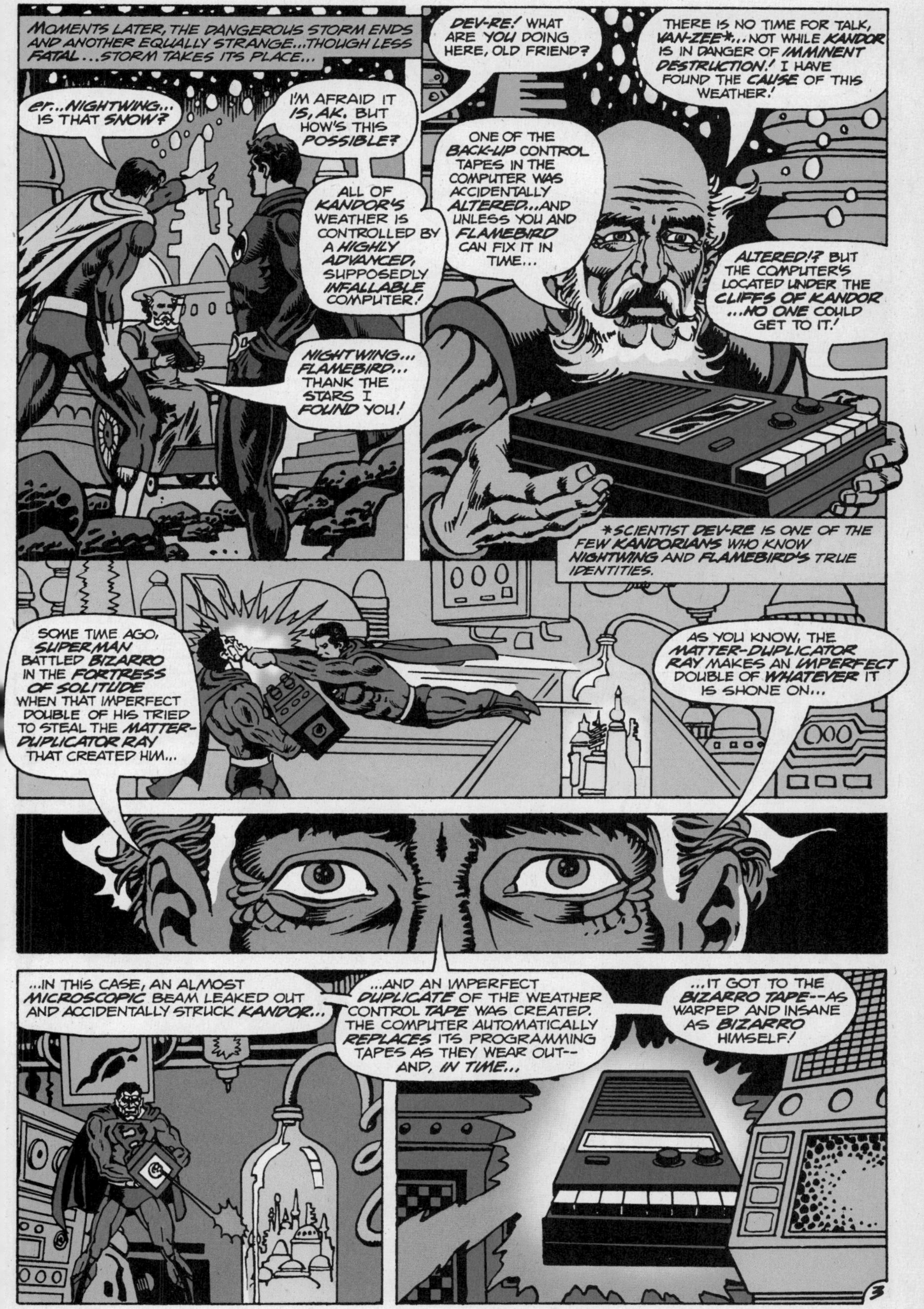
MOMENTS LATER, THE DANGEROUS STORM ENDS AND ANOTHER EQUALLY STRANGE...THOUGH LESS FATAL...STORM TAKES ITS PLACE...
er...NIGHTWING... IS THAT SNOW?
I'M AFRAID IT IS, AK. BUT HOW'S THIS POSSIBLE?
ALL OF KANDOR'S WEATHER IS CONTROLLED BY A HIGHLY ADVANCED, SUPPOSEDLY INFALLABLE COMPUTER!
NIGHTWING... FLAMEBIRD... THANK THE STARS I FOUND YOU!
DEV-RE! WHAT ARE YOU DOING HERE, OLD FRIEND?
THERE IS NO TIME FOR TALK, VAN-ZEE*... NOT WHILE KANDOR IS IN DANGER OF IMMINENT DESTRUCTION! I HAVE FOUND THE CAUSE OF THIS WEATHER!
ONE OF THE BACK-UP CONTROL TAPES IN THE COMPUTER WAS ACCIDENTALLY ALTERED...AND UNLESS YOU AND FLAMEBIRD CAN FIX IT IN TIME...
ALTERED!? BUT THE COMPUTER'S LOCATED UNDER THE CLIFFS OF KANDOR ...NO ONE COULD GET TO IT!
*SCIENTIST DEV-RE IS ONE OF THE FEW KANDORIANS WHO KNOW NIGHTWING AND FLAMEBIRD'S TRUE IDENTITIES.
SOME TIME AGO, SUPERMAN BATTLED BIZARRO IN THE FORTRESS OF SOLITUDE WHEN THAT IMPERFECT DOUBLE OF HIS TRIED TO STEAL THE MATTER-DUPLICATOR RAY THAT CREATED HIM...
AS YOU KNOW, THE MATTER-DUPLICATOR RAY MAKES AN IMPERFECT DOUBLE OF WHATEVER IT IS SHONE ON...
...IN THIS CASE, AN ALMOST MICROSCOPIC BEAM LEAKED OUT AND ACCIDENTALLY STRUCK KANDOR...
...AND AN IMPERFECT DUPLICATE OF THE WEATHER CONTROL TAPE WAS CREATED. THE COMPUTER AUTOMATICALLY REPLACES ITS PROGRAMMING TAPES AS THEY WEAR OUT--AND, IN TIME...
...IT GOT TO THE BIZARRO TAPE--AS WARPED AND INSANE AS BIZARRO HIMSELF!
3

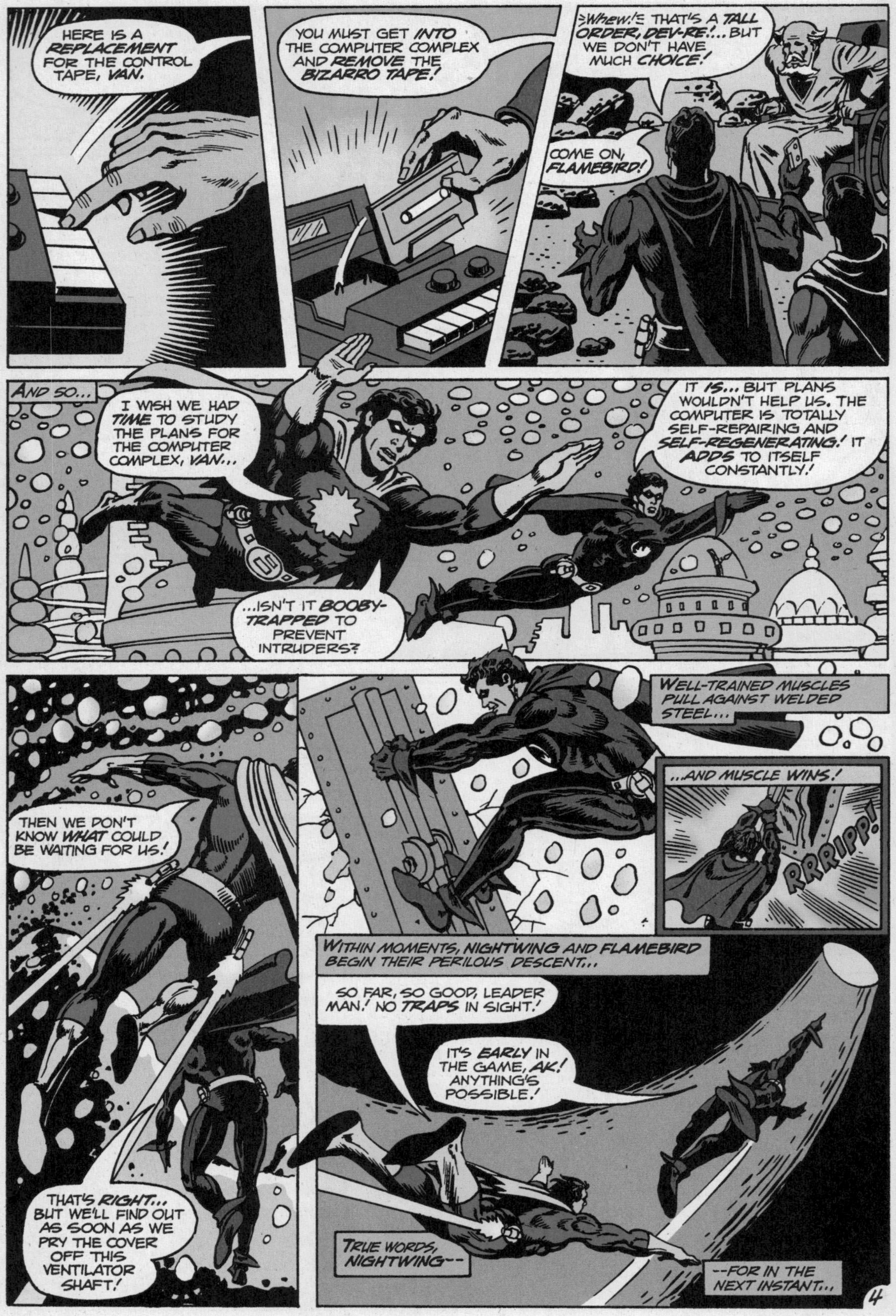

HERE IS A REPLACEMENT FOR THE CONTROL TAPE, VAN.
YOU MUST GET INTO THE COMPUTER COMPLEX AND REMOVE THE BIZARRO TAPE!
WHEW! THAT'S A TALL ORDER, DEV-RE!... BUT WE DON'T HAVE MUCH CHOICE!
COME ON, FLAMEBIRD!
AND SO...
I WISH WE HAD TIME TO STUDY THE PLANS FOR THE COMPUTER COMPLEX, VAN...
...ISN'T IT BOOBY-TRAPPED TO PREVENT INTRUDERS?
IT IS... BUT PLANS WOULDN'T HELP US. THE COMPUTER IS TOTALLY SELF-REPAIRING AND SELF-REGENERATING! IT ADDS TO ITSELF CONSTANTLY!
THEN WE DON'T KNOW WHAT COULD BE WAITING FOR US!
THAT'S RIGHT... BUT WE'LL FIND OUT AS SOON AS WE PRY THE COVER OFF THIS VENTILATOR SHAFT!
WELL-TRAINED MUSCLES PULL AGAINST WELDED STEEL...
...AND MUSCLE WINS!
RRRIPP!
WITHIN MOMENTS, NIGHTWING AND FLAMEBIRD BEGIN THEIR PERILOUS DESCENT...
SO FAR, SO GOOD, LEADER MAN! NO TRAPS IN SIGHT!
IT'S EARLY IN THE GAME, AK! ANYTHING'S POSSIBLE!
TRUE WORDS, NIGHTWING--
--FOR IN THE NEXT INSTANT...
4

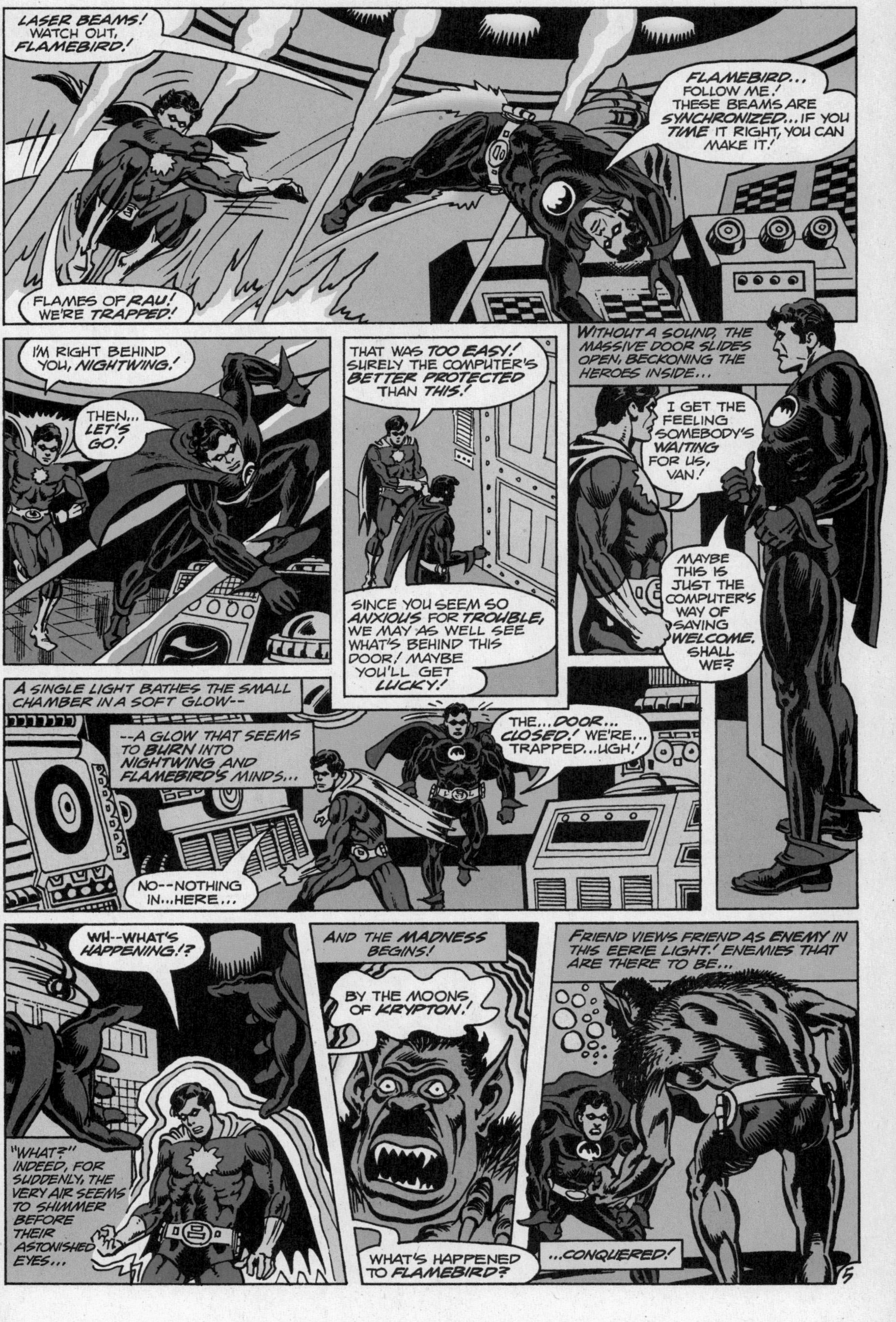

LASER BEAMS! WATCH OUT, FLAMEBIRD!
FLAMEBIRD... FOLLOW ME! THESE BEAMS ARE SYNCHRONIZED... IF YOU TIME IT RIGHT, YOU CAN MAKE IT!
FLAMES OF RAU! WE'RE TRAPPED!
I'M RIGHT BEHIND YOU, NIGHTWING!
THEN... LET'S GO!
THAT WAS TOO EASY! SURELY THE COMPUTER'S BETTER PROTECTED THAN THIS!
SINCE YOU SEEM SO ANXIOUS FOR TROUBLE, WE MAY AS WELL SEE WHAT'S BEHIND THIS DOOR! MAYBE YOU'LL GET LUCKY!
WITHOUT A SOUND, THE MASSIVE DOOR SLIDES OPEN, BECKONING THE HEROES INSIDE...
I GET THE FEELING SOMEBODY'S WAITING FOR US, VAN!
MAYBE THIS IS JUST THE COMPUTER'S WAY OF SAYING WELCOME. SHALL WE?
A SINGLE LIGHT BATHES THE SMALL CHAMBER IN A SOFT GLOW--
--A GLOW THAT SEEMS TO BURN INTO NIGHTWING AND FLAMEBIRD'S MINDS...
THE... DOOR... CLOSED! WE'RE... TRAPPED... UGH!
NO--NOTHING IN... HERE...
WH--WHAT'S HAPPENING!?
"WHAT?" INDEED, FOR SUDDENLY, THE VERY AIR SEEMS TO SHIMMER BEFORE THEIR ASTONISHED EYES...
AND THE MADNESS BEGINS!
BY THE MOONS OF KRYPTON!
WHAT'S HAPPENED TO FLAMEBIRD?
FRIEND VIEWS FRIEND AS ENEMY IN THIS EERIE LIGHT! ENEMIES THAT ARE THERE TO BE...
...CONQUERED!
5

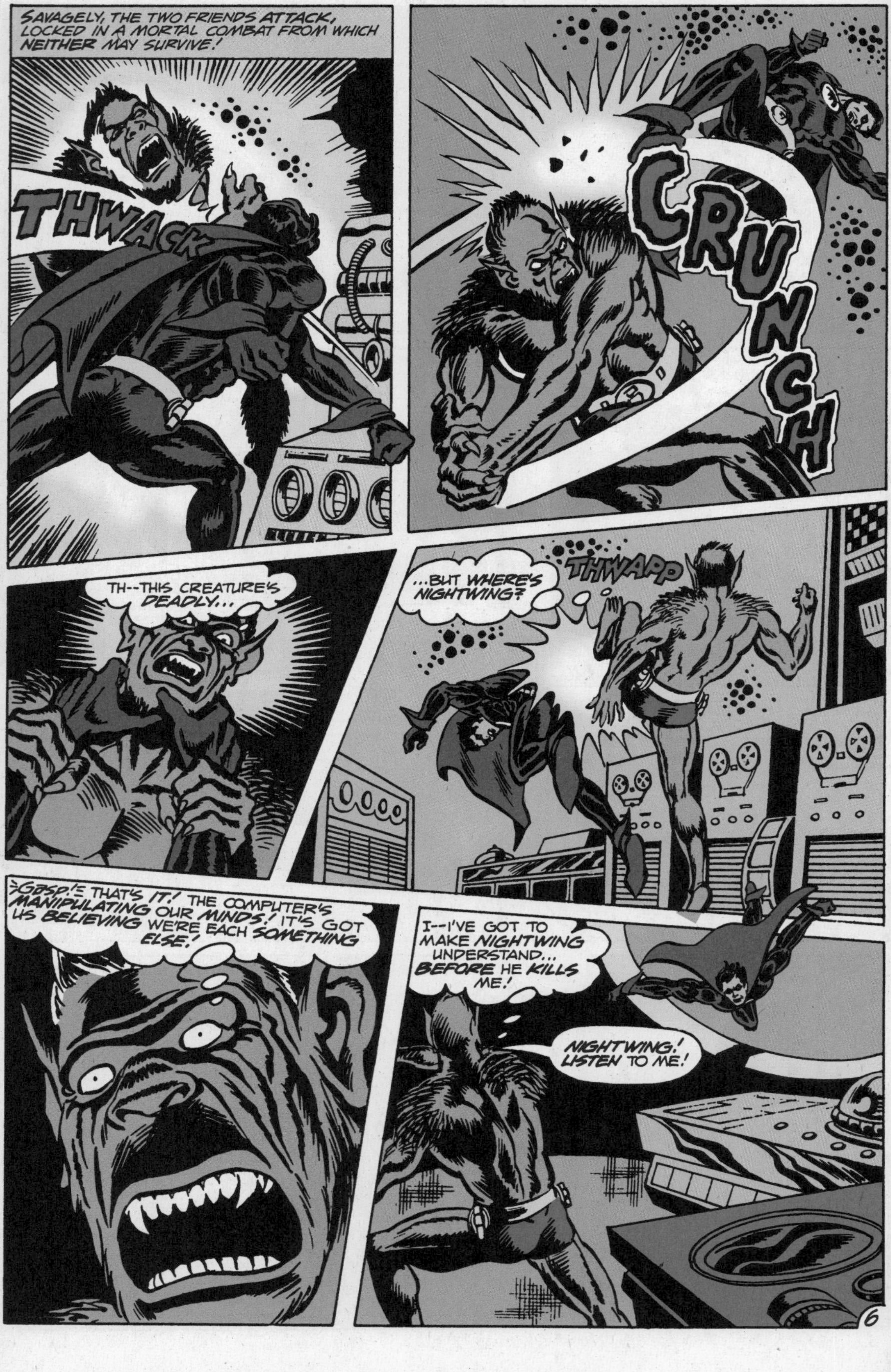

SAVAGELY, THE TWO FRIENDS ATTACK, LOCKED IN A MORTAL COMBAT FROM WHICH NEITHER MAY SURVIVE!
THWACK
CRUNCH
TH--THIS CREATURE'S DEADLY...
...BUT WHERE'S NIGHTWING?
THWAPP
GASP! THAT'S IT! THE COMPUTER'S MANIPULATING OUR MINDS! IT'S GOT US BELIEVING WE'RE EACH SOMETHING ELSE!
I--I'VE GOT TO MAKE NIGHTWING UNDERSTAND... BEFORE HE KILLS ME!
NIGHTWING! LISTEN TO ME!
6

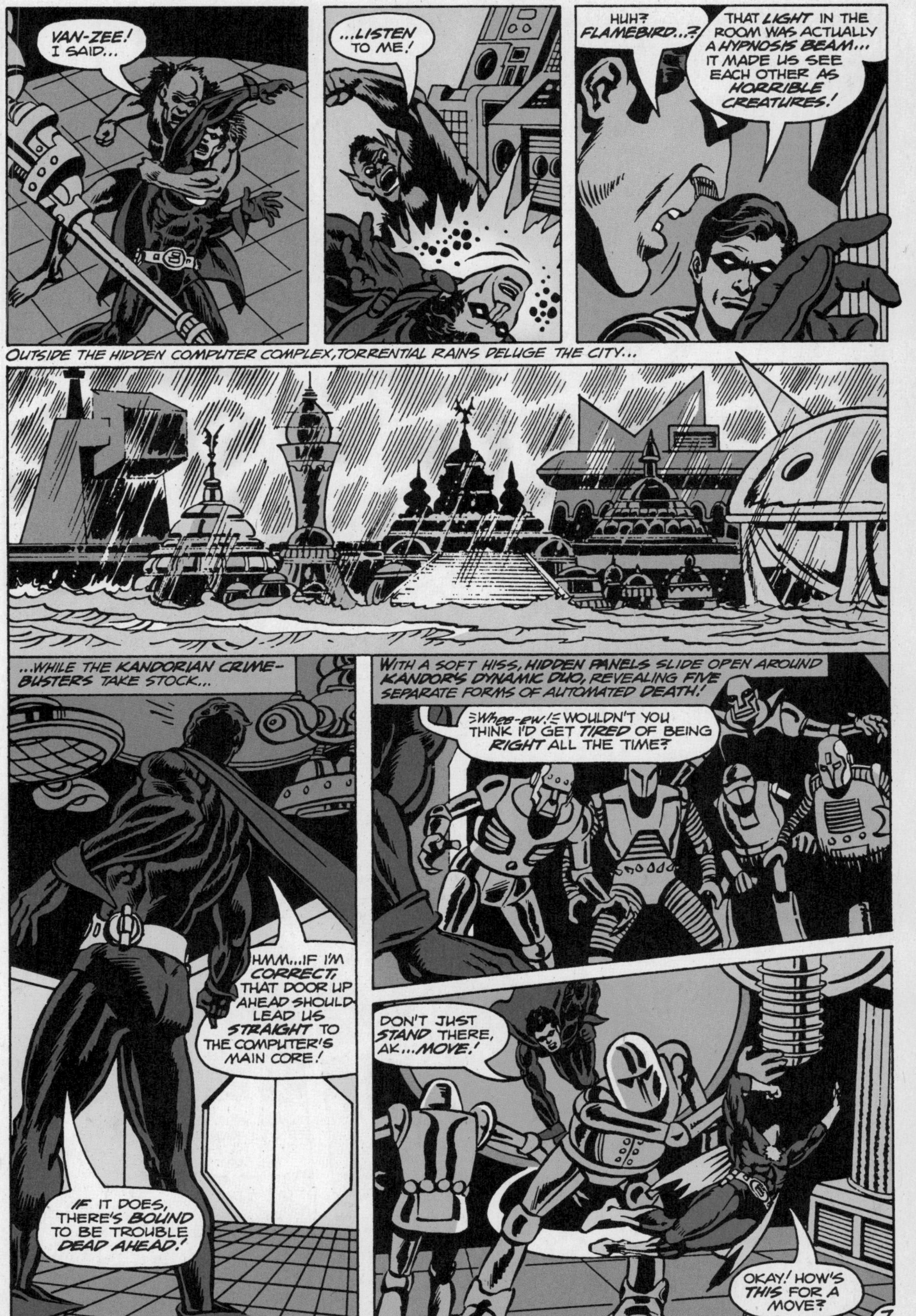
VAN-ZEE! I SAID...
...LISTEN TO ME!
HUH? FLAMEBIRD...?
THAT LIGHT IN THE ROOM WAS ACTUALLY A HYPNOSIS BEAM... IT MADE US SEE EACH OTHER AS HORRIBLE CREATURES!
OUTSIDE THE HIDDEN COMPUTER COMPLEX, TORRENTIAL RAINS DELUGE THE CITY...
...WHILE THE KANDORIAN CRIME-BUSTERS TAKE STOCK...
HMM...IF I'M CORRECT, THAT DOOR UP AHEAD SHOULD LEAD US STRAIGHT TO THE COMPUTER'S MAIN CORE!
IF IT DOES, THERE'S BOUND TO BE TROUBLE DEAD AHEAD!
WITH A SOFT HISS, HIDDEN PANELS SLIDE OPEN AROUND KANDOR'S DYNAMIC DUO, REVEALING FIVE SEPARATE FORMS OF AUTOMATED DEATH!
Whee-ew! WOULDN'T YOU THINK I'D GET TIRED OF BEING RIGHT ALL THE TIME?
DON'T JUST STAND THERE, AK...MOVE!
OKAY! HOW'S THIS FOR A MOVE?
7

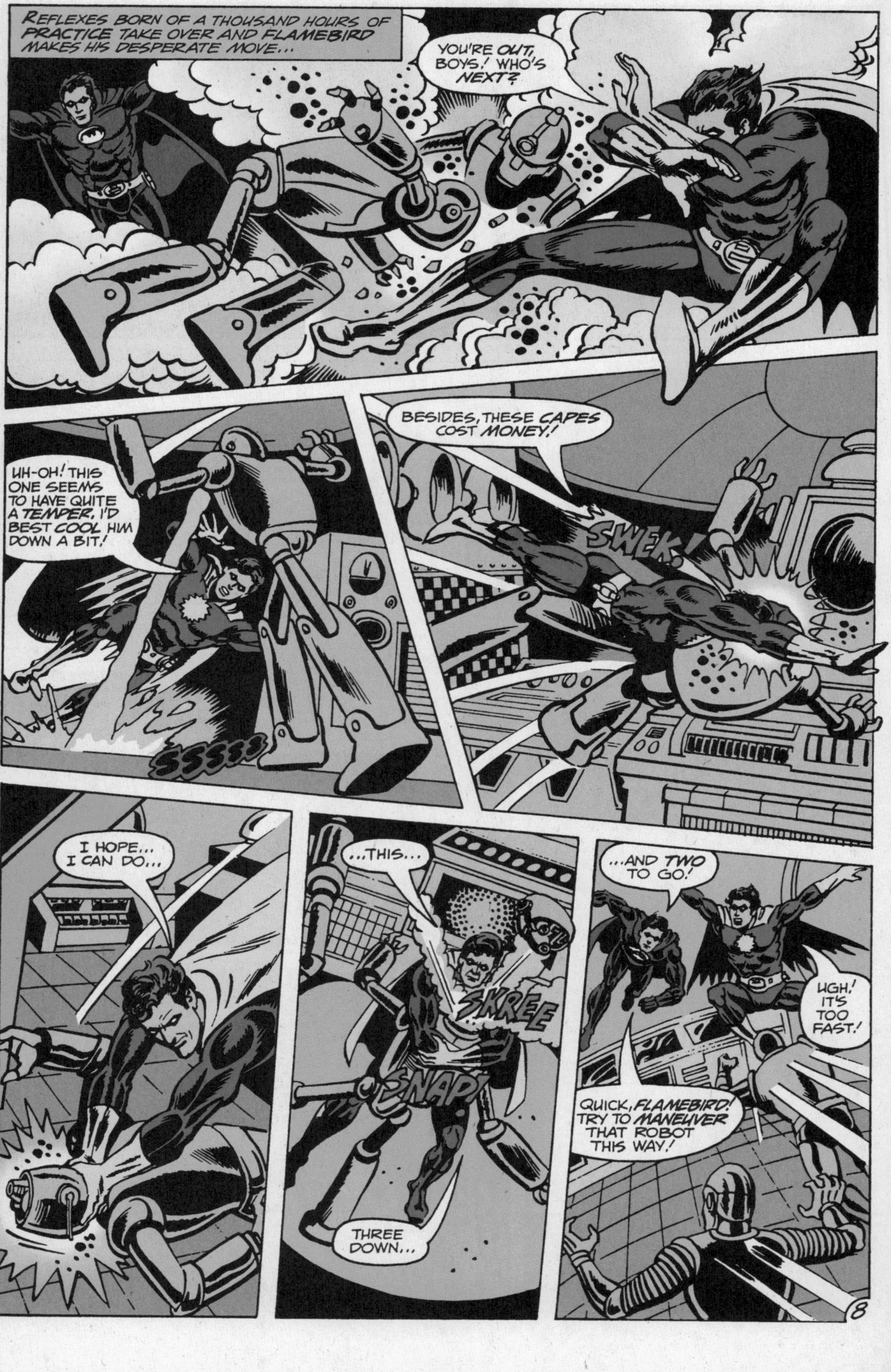
REFLEXES BORN OF A THOUSAND HOURS OF PRACTICE TAKE OVER AND FLAMEBIRD MAKES HIS DESPERATE MOVE...
YOU'RE OUT, BOYS! WHO'S NEXT?
UH-OH! THIS ONE SEEMS TO HAVE QUITE A TEMPER. I'D BEST COOL HIM DOWN A BIT!
SSSSS
BESIDES, THESE CAPES COST MONEY!
SWEK!
I HOPE... I CAN DO...
...THIS...
SKREE
SNAP
THREE DOWN...
...AND TWO TO GO!
UGH! IT'S TOO FAST!
QUICK, FLAMEBIRD! TRY TO MANEUVER THAT ROBOT THIS WAY!
8

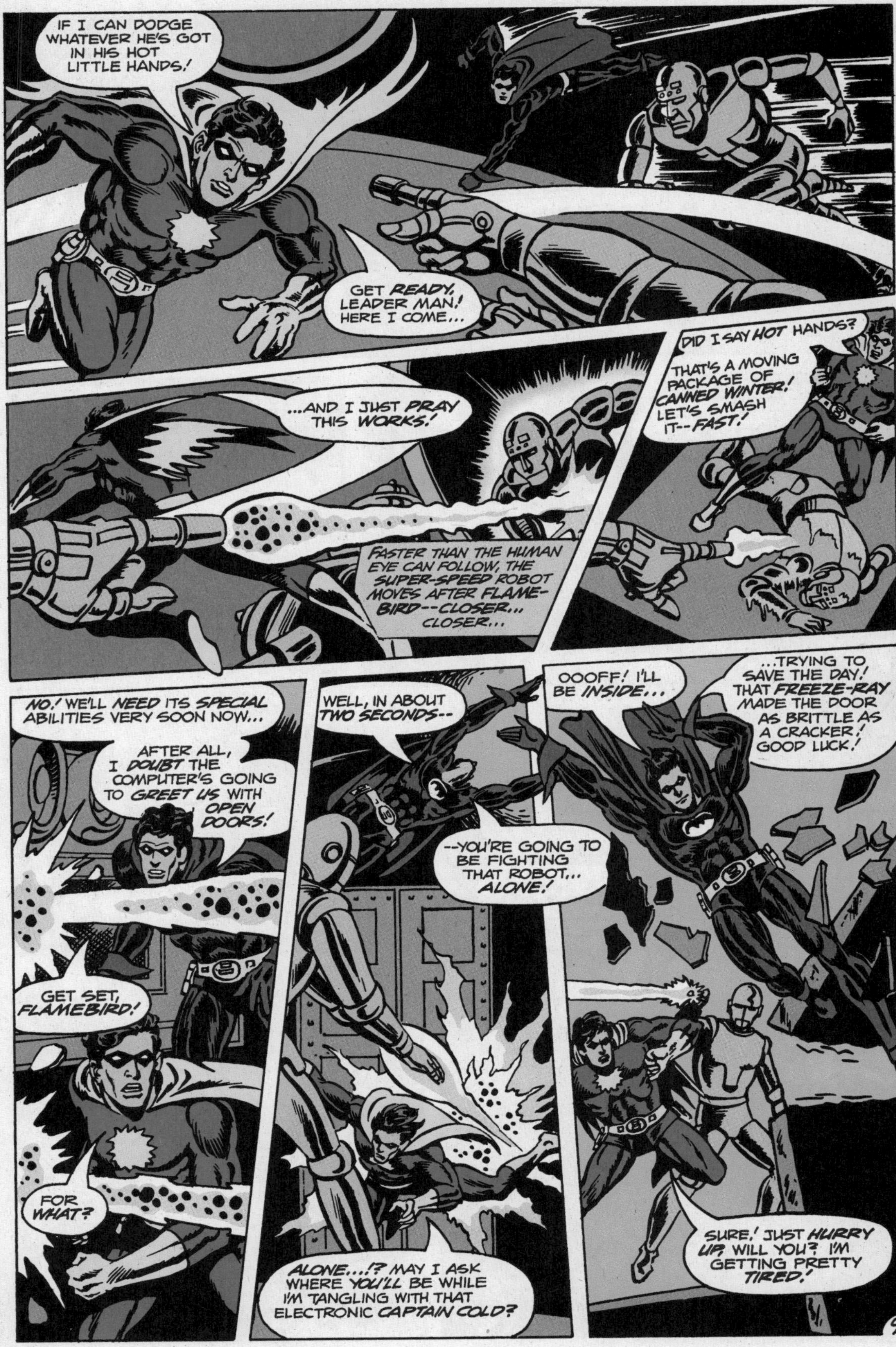
IF I CAN DODGE WHATEVER HE'S GOT IN HIS HOT LITTLE HANDS!
GET READY, LEADER MAN! HERE I COME...
...AND I JUST PRAY THIS WORKS!
FASTER THAN THE HUMAN EYE CAN FOLLOW, THE SUPER-SPEED ROBOT MOVES AFTER FLAME-BIRD--CLOSER... CLOSER...
DID I SAY HOT HANDS?
THAT'S A MOVING PACKAGE OF CANNED WINTER! LET'S SMASH IT--FAST!
NO! WE'LL NEED ITS SPECIAL ABILITIES VERY SOON NOW...
AFTER ALL, I DOUBT THE COMPUTER'S GOING TO GREET US WITH OPEN DOORS!
GET SET, FLAMEBIRD!
FOR WHAT?
WELL, IN ABOUT TWO SECONDS--
--YOU'RE GOING TO BE FIGHTING THAT ROBOT... ALONE!
ALONE...!? MAY I ASK WHERE YOU'LL BE WHILE I'M TANGLING WITH THAT ELECTRONIC CAPTAIN COLD?
OOOFF! I'LL BE INSIDE...
...TRYING TO SAVE THE DAY! THAT FREEZE-RAY MADE THE DOOR AS BRITTLE AS A CRACKER! GOOD LUCK!
SURE! JUST HURRY UP, WILL YOU? I'M GETTING PRETTY TIRED!
9

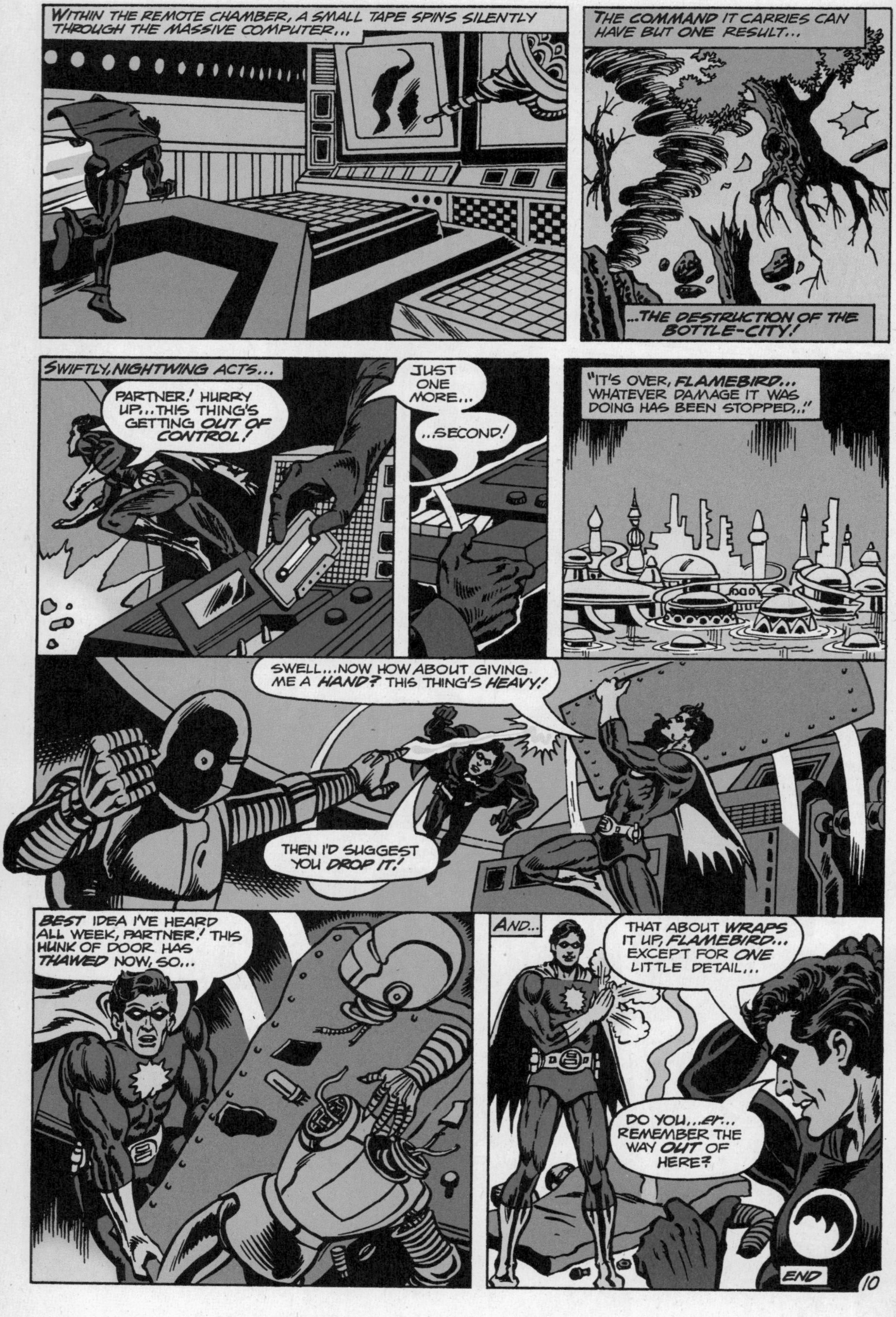
WITHIN THE REMOTE CHAMBER, A SMALL TAPE SPINS SILENTLY THROUGH THE MASSIVE COMPUTER...
THE COMMAND IT CARRIES CAN HAVE BUT ONE RESULT...
...THE DESTRUCTION OF THE BOTTLE-CITY!
SWIFTLY, NIGHTWING ACTS...
PARTNER! HURRY UP...THIS THING'S GETTING OUT OF CONTROL!
JUST ONE MORE...
...SECOND!
"IT'S OVER, FLAMEBIRD... WHATEVER DAMAGE IT WAS DOING HAS BEEN STOPPED..."
SWELL...NOW HOW ABOUT GIVING ME A HAND? THIS THING'S HEAVY!
THEN I'D SUGGEST YOU DROP IT!
BEST IDEA I'VE HEARD ALL WEEK, PARTNER! THIS HUNK OF DOOR HAS THAWED NOW, SO...
AND...
THAT ABOUT WRAPS IT UP, FLAMEBIRD... EXCEPT FOR ONE LITTLE DETAIL...
DO YOU...er... REMEMBER THE WAY OUT OF HERE?
END
10

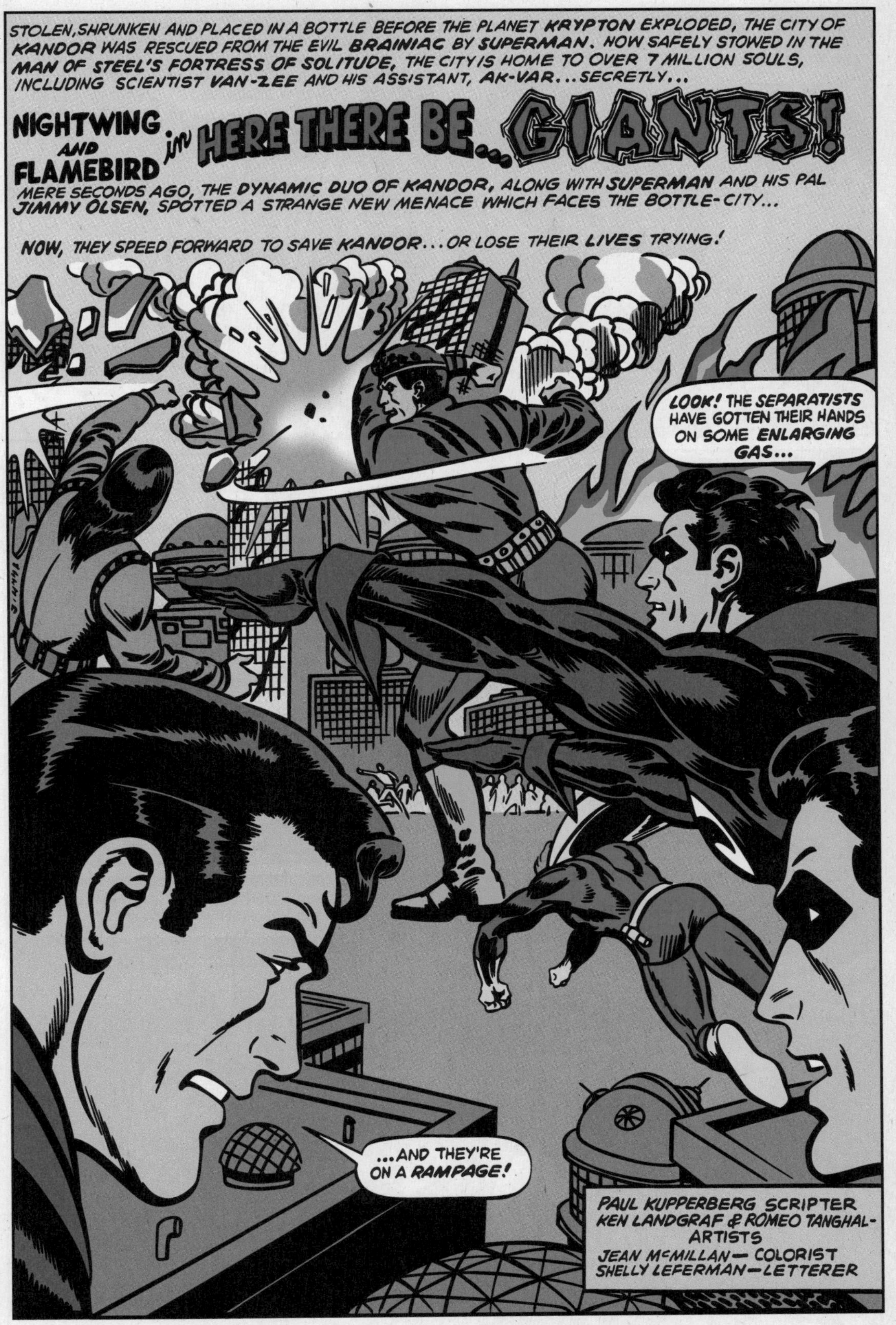
STOLEN, SHRUNKEN AND PLACED IN A BOTTLE BEFORE THE PLANET KRYPTON EXPLODED, THE CITY OF KANDOR WAS RESCUED FROM THE EVIL BRAINIAC BY SUPERMAN. NOW SAFELY STOWED IN THE MAN OF STEEL'S FORTRESS OF SOLITUDE, THE CITY IS HOME TO OVER 7 MILLION SOULS, INCLUDING SCIENTIST VAN-ZEE AND HIS ASSISTANT, AK-VAR... SECRETLY...
NIGHTWING AND FLAMEBIRD in HERE THERE BE... GIANTS!
MERE SECONDS AGO, THE DYNAMIC DUO OF KANDOR, ALONG WITH SUPERMAN AND HIS PAL JIMMY OLSEN, SPOTTED A STRANGE NEW MENACE WHICH FACES THE BOTTLE-CITY...
NOW, THEY SPEED FORWARD TO SAVE KANDOR... OR LOSE THEIR LIVES TRYING!
LOOK! THE SEPARATISTS HAVE GOTTEN THEIR HANDS ON SOME ENLARGING GAS...
...AND THEY'RE ON A RAMPAGE!
PAUL KUPPERBERG SCRIPTER
KEN LANDGRAF & ROMEO TANGHAL-ARTISTS
JEAN McMILLAN— COLORIST
SHELLY LEFERMAN—LETTERER

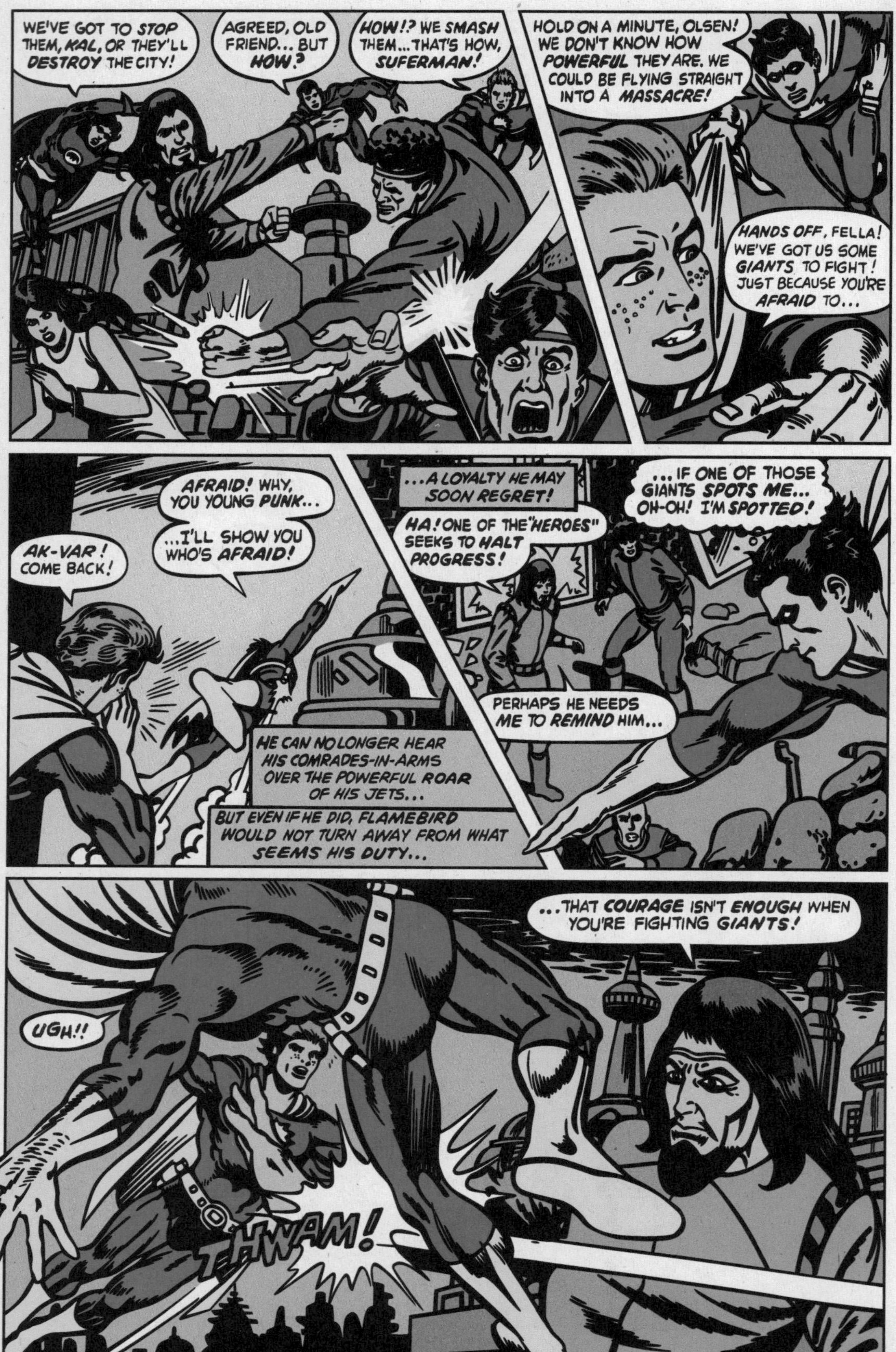
WE'VE GOT TO STOP THEM, KAL, OR THEY'LL DESTROY THE CITY!
AGREED, OLD FRIEND... BUT HOW?
HOW!? WE SMASH THEM... THAT'S HOW, SUPERMAN!
HOLD ON A MINUTE, OLSEN! WE DON'T KNOW HOW POWERFUL THEY ARE. WE COULD BE FLYING STRAIGHT INTO A MASSACRE!
HANDS OFF, FELLA! WE'VE GOT US SOME GIANTS TO FIGHT! JUST BECAUSE YOU'RE AFRAID TO...
AFRAID! WHY, YOU YOUNG PUNK...
...I'LL SHOW YOU WHO'S AFRAID!
AK-VAR! COME BACK!
HE CAN NO LONGER HEAR HIS COMRADES-IN-ARMS OVER THE POWERFUL ROAR OF HIS JETS...
BUT EVEN IF HE DID, FLAMEBIRD WOULD NOT TURN AWAY FROM WHAT SEEMS HIS DUTY...
...A LOYALTY HE MAY SOON REGRET!
HA! ONE OF THE "HEROES" SEEKS TO HALT PROGRESS!
...IF ONE OF THOSE GIANTS SPOTS ME... OH-OH! I'M SPOTTED!
PERHAPS HE NEEDS ME TO REMIND HIM...
...THAT COURAGE ISN'T ENOUGH WHEN YOU'RE FIGHTING GIANTS!
UGH!!
THWAM!

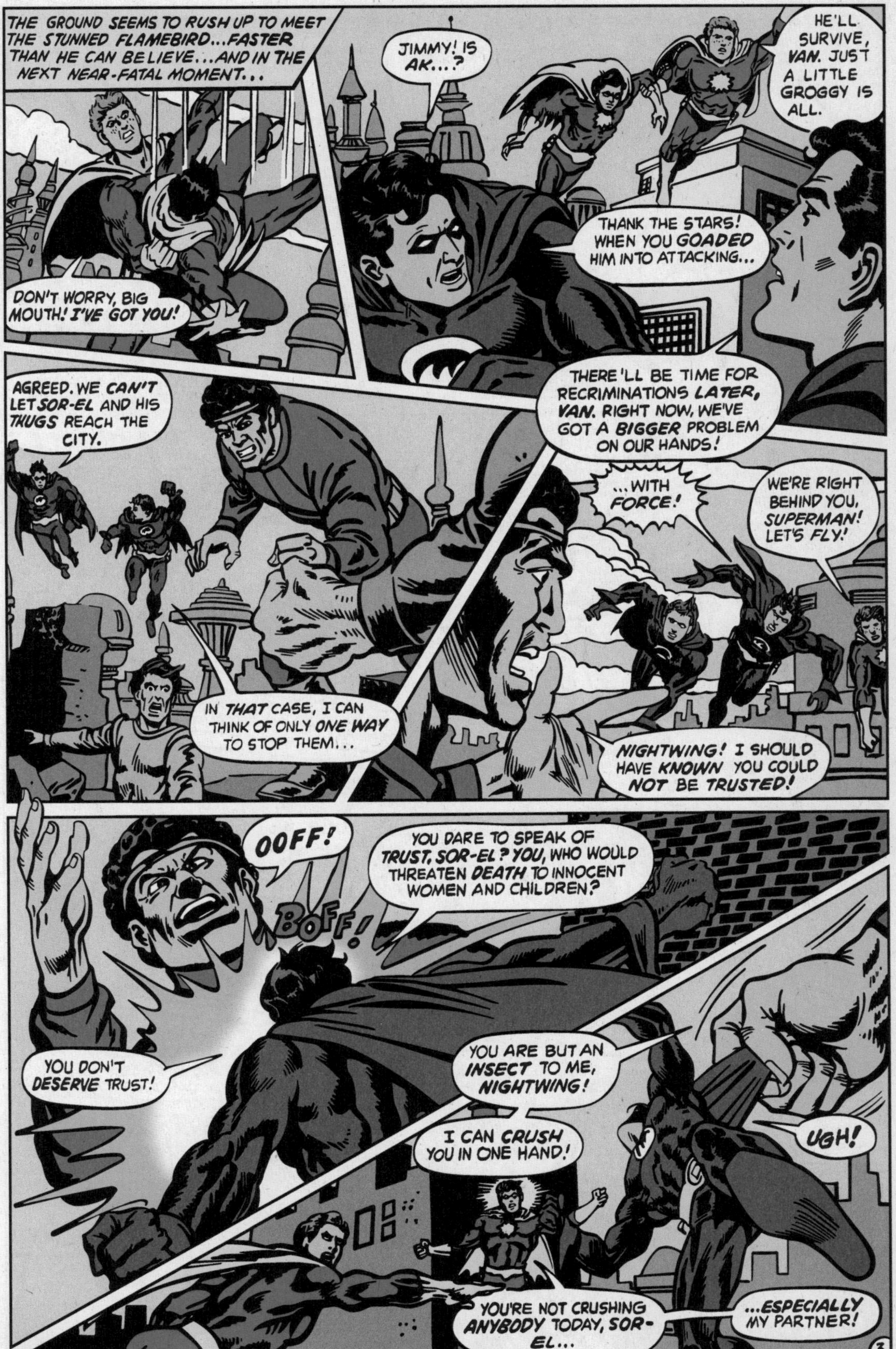
THE GROUND SEEMS TO RUSH UP TO MEET THE STUNNED FLAMEBIRD...FASTER THAN HE CAN BELIEVE...AND IN THE NEXT NEAR-FATAL MOMENT...
DON'T WORRY, BIG MOUTH! I'VE GOT YOU!
JIMMY! IS AK...?
HE'LL SURVIVE, VAN. JUST A LITTLE GROGGY IS ALL.
THANK THE STARS! WHEN YOU GOADED HIM INTO ATTACKING...
THERE'LL BE TIME FOR RECRIMINATIONS LATER, VAN. RIGHT NOW, WE'VE GOT A BIGGER PROBLEM ON OUR HANDS!
AGREED. WE CAN'T LET SOR-EL AND HIS THUGS REACH THE CITY.
IN THAT CASE, I CAN THINK OF ONLY ONE WAY TO STOP THEM...
...WITH FORCE!
WE'RE RIGHT BEHIND YOU, SUPERMAN! LET'S FLY!
NIGHTWING! I SHOULD HAVE KNOWN YOU COULD NOT BE TRUSTED!
OOFF!
BOFF!
YOU DARE TO SPEAK OF TRUST, SOR-EL? YOU, WHO WOULD THREATEN DEATH TO INNOCENT WOMEN AND CHILDREN?
YOU DON'T DESERVE TRUST!
YOU ARE BUT AN INSECT TO ME, NIGHTWING!
I CAN CRUSH YOU IN ONE HAND!
UGH!
YOU'RE NOT CRUSHING ANYBODY TODAY, SOR-EL...
...ESPECIALLY MY PARTNER!
3

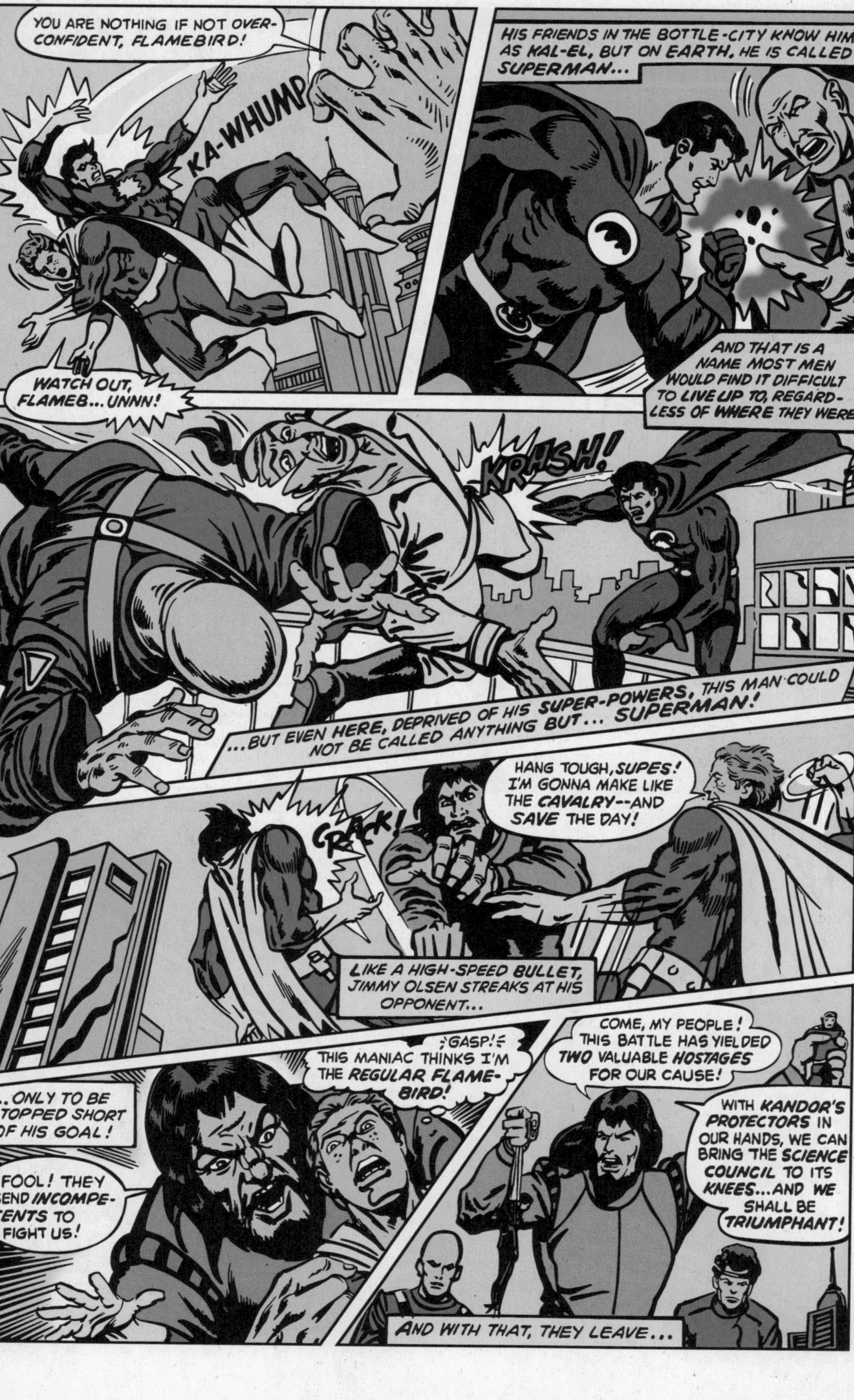
YOU ARE NOTHING IF NOT OVER-CONFIDENT, FLAMEBIRD!
KA-WHUMP
WATCH OUT, FLAMEB... UNNN!
HIS FRIENDS IN THE BOTTLE-CITY KNOW HIM AS KAL-EL, BUT ON EARTH, HE IS CALLED SUPERMAN...
AND THAT IS A NAME MOST MEN WOULD FIND IT DIFFICULT TO LIVE UP TO, REGARD-LESS OF WHERE THEY WERE
KRASH!
...BUT EVEN HERE, DEPRIVED OF HIS SUPER-POWERS, THIS MAN COULD NOT BE CALLED ANYTHING BUT... SUPERMAN!
HANG TOUGH, SUPES! I'M GONNA MAKE LIKE THE CAVALRY--AND SAVE THE DAY!
CRACK!
LIKE A HIGH-SPEED BULLET, JIMMY OLSEN STREAKS AT HIS OPPONENT...
...ONLY TO BE STOPPED SHORT OF HIS GOAL!
;GASP!; THIS MANIAC THINKS I'M THE REGULAR FLAME-BIRD!
FOOL! THEY SEND INCOMPE-TENTS TO FIGHT US!
COME, MY PEOPLE! THIS BATTLE HAS YIELDED TWO VALUABLE HOSTAGES FOR OUR CAUSE!
WITH KANDOR'S PROTECTORS IN OUR HANDS, WE CAN BRING THE SCIENCE COUNCIL TO ITS KNEES...AND WE SHALL BE TRIUMPHANT!
AND WITH THAT, THEY LEAVE...

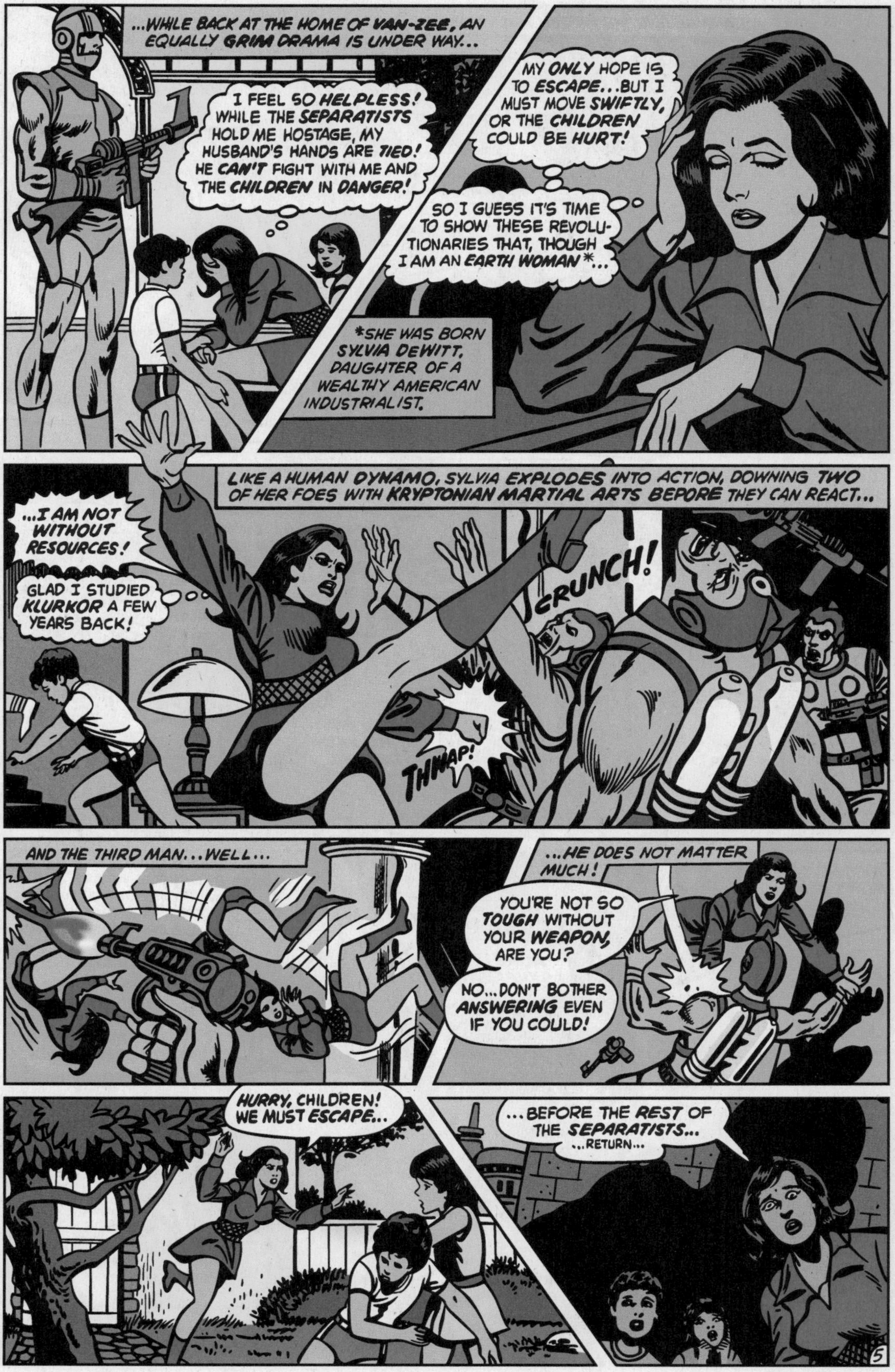
...WHILE BACK AT THE HOME OF VAN-ZEE, AN EQUALLY GRIM DRAMA IS UNDER WAY...
I FEEL SO HELPLESS! WHILE THE SEPARATISTS HOLD ME HOSTAGE, MY HUSBAND'S HANDS ARE TIED! HE CAN'T FIGHT WITH ME AND THE CHILDREN IN DANGER!
MY ONLY HOPE IS TO ESCAPE...BUT I MUST MOVE SWIFTLY, OR THE CHILDREN COULD BE HURT!
SO I GUESS IT'S TIME TO SHOW THESE REVOLUTIONARIES THAT, THOUGH I AM AN EARTH WOMAN*...
*SHE WAS BORN SYLVIA DEWITT, DAUGHTER OF A WEALTHY AMERICAN INDUSTRIALIST.
LIKE A HUMAN DYNAMO, SYLVIA EXPLODES INTO ACTION, DOWNING TWO OF HER FOES WITH KRYPTONIAN MARTIAL ARTS BEFORE THEY CAN REACT...
...I AM NOT WITHOUT RESOURCES!
GLAD I STUDIED KLURKOR A FEW YEARS BACK!
CRUNCH!
THWAP!
AND THE THIRD MAN...WELL...
...HE DOES NOT MATTER MUCH!
YOU'RE NOT SO TOUGH WITHOUT YOUR WEAPON, ARE YOU?
NO...DON'T BOTHER ANSWERING EVEN IF YOU COULD!
HURRY, CHILDREN! WE MUST ESCAPE...
...BEFORE THE REST OF THE SEPARATISTS... ...RETURN...
5

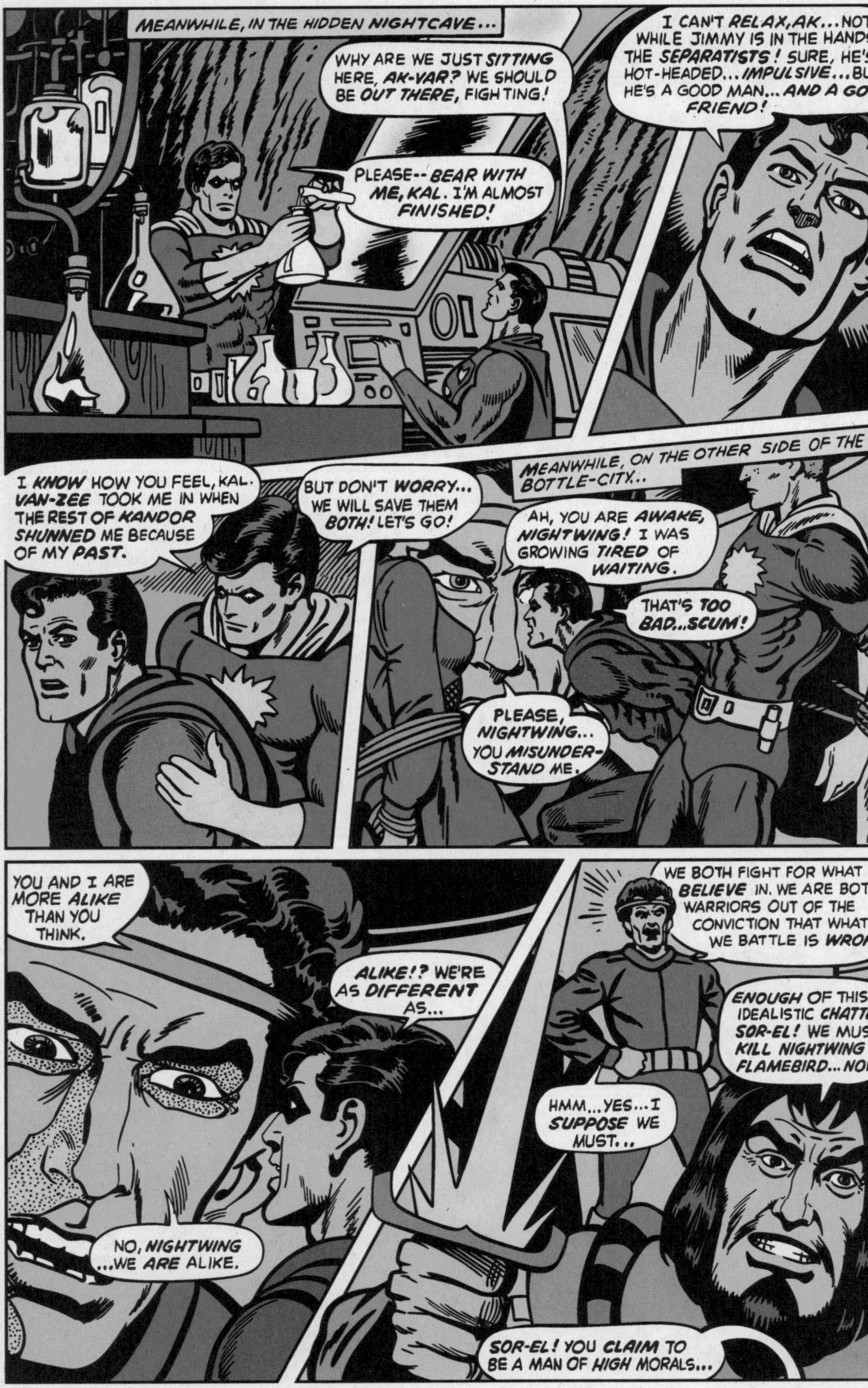
MEANWHILE, IN THE HIDDEN NIGHTCAVE...
WHY ARE WE JUST SITTING HERE, AK-VAR? WE SHOULD BE OUT THERE, FIGHTING!
PLEASE--BEAR WITH ME, KAL. I'M ALMOST FINISHED!
I CAN'T RELAX, AK...NOT WHILE JIMMY IS IN THE HANDS OF THE SEPARATISTS! SURE, HE'S HOT-HEADED...IMPULSIVE...BUT HE'S A GOOD MAN...AND A GOOD FRIEND!
I KNOW HOW YOU FEEL, KAL. VAN-ZEE TOOK ME IN WHEN THE REST OF KANDOR SHUNNED ME BECAUSE OF MY PAST.
BUT DON'T WORRY... WE WILL SAVE THEM BOTH! LET'S GO!
MEANWHILE, ON THE OTHER SIDE OF THE BOTTLE-CITY...
AH, YOU ARE AWAKE, NIGHTWING! I WAS GROWING TIRED OF WAITING.
THAT'S TOO BAD...SCUM!
PLEASE, NIGHTWING... YOU MISUNDER-STAND ME.
YOU AND I ARE MORE ALIKE THAN YOU THINK.
ALIKE!? WE'RE AS DIFFERENT AS...
NO, NIGHTWING ...WE ARE ALIKE.
WE BOTH FIGHT FOR WHAT BELIEVE IN. WE ARE BOTH WARRIORS OUT OF THE CONVICTION THAT WHAT WE BATTLE IS WRONG.
ENOUGH OF THIS IDEALISTIC CHATTER SOR-EL! WE MUST KILL NIGHTWING FLAMEBIRD...NOW!
HMM...YES...I SUPPOSE WE MUST...
SOR-EL! YOU CLAIM TO BE A MAN OF HIGH MORALS...

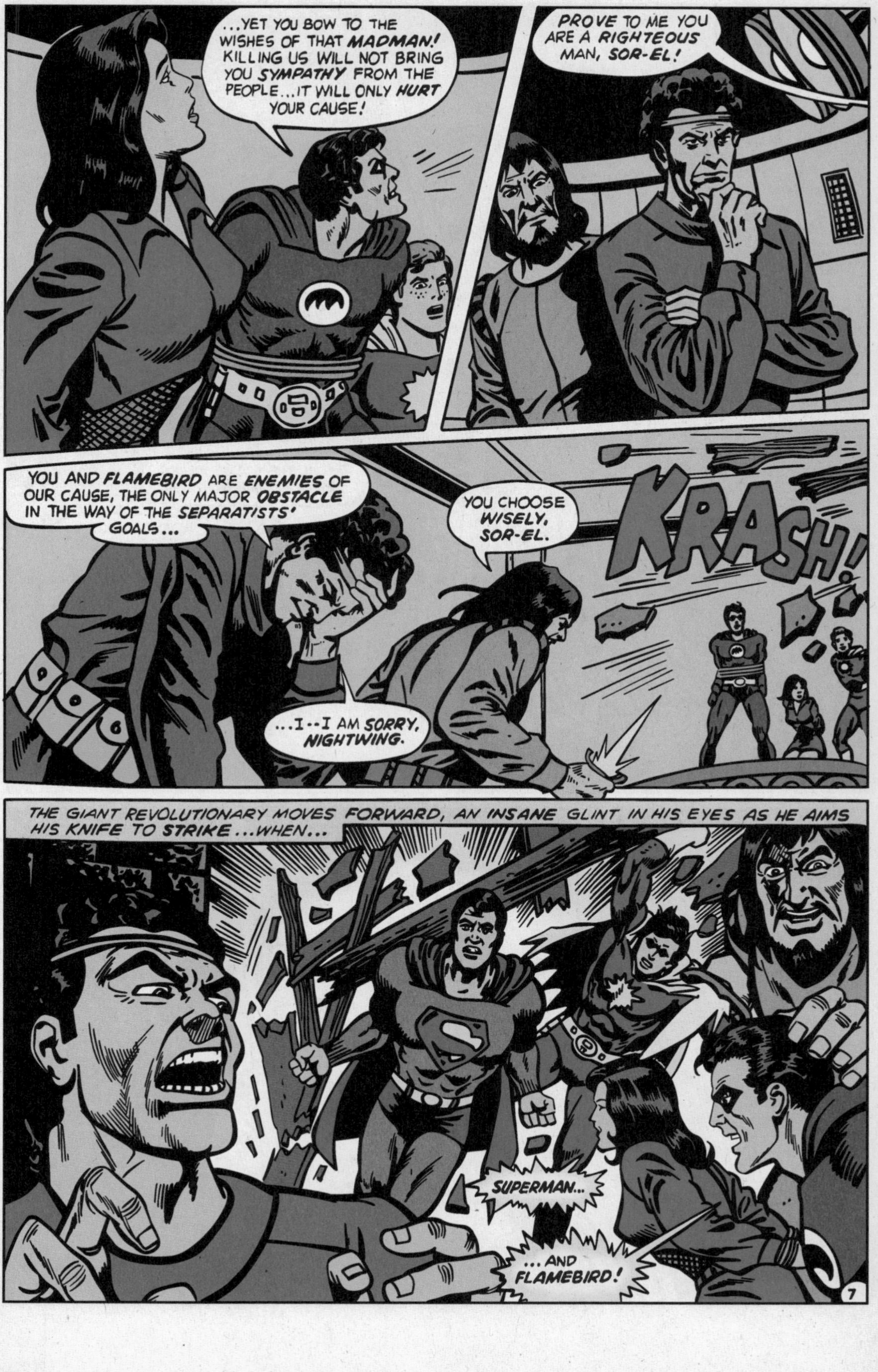

...YET YOU BOW TO THE WISHES OF THAT MADMAN! KILLING US WILL NOT BRING YOU SYMPATHY FROM THE PEOPLE...IT WILL ONLY HURT YOUR CAUSE!
PROVE TO ME YOU ARE A RIGHTEOUS MAN, SOR-EL!
YOU AND FLAMEBIRD ARE ENEMIES OF OUR CAUSE, THE ONLY MAJOR OBSTACLE IN THE WAY OF THE SEPARATISTS' GOALS...
...I--I AM SORRY, NIGHTWING.
YOU CHOOSE WISELY, SOR-EL.
KRASH!
THE GIANT REVOLUTIONARY MOVES FORWARD, AN INSANE GLINT IN HIS EYES AS HE AIMS HIS KNIFE TO STRIKE...WHEN...
SUPERMAN...
...AND FLAMEBIRD!
7

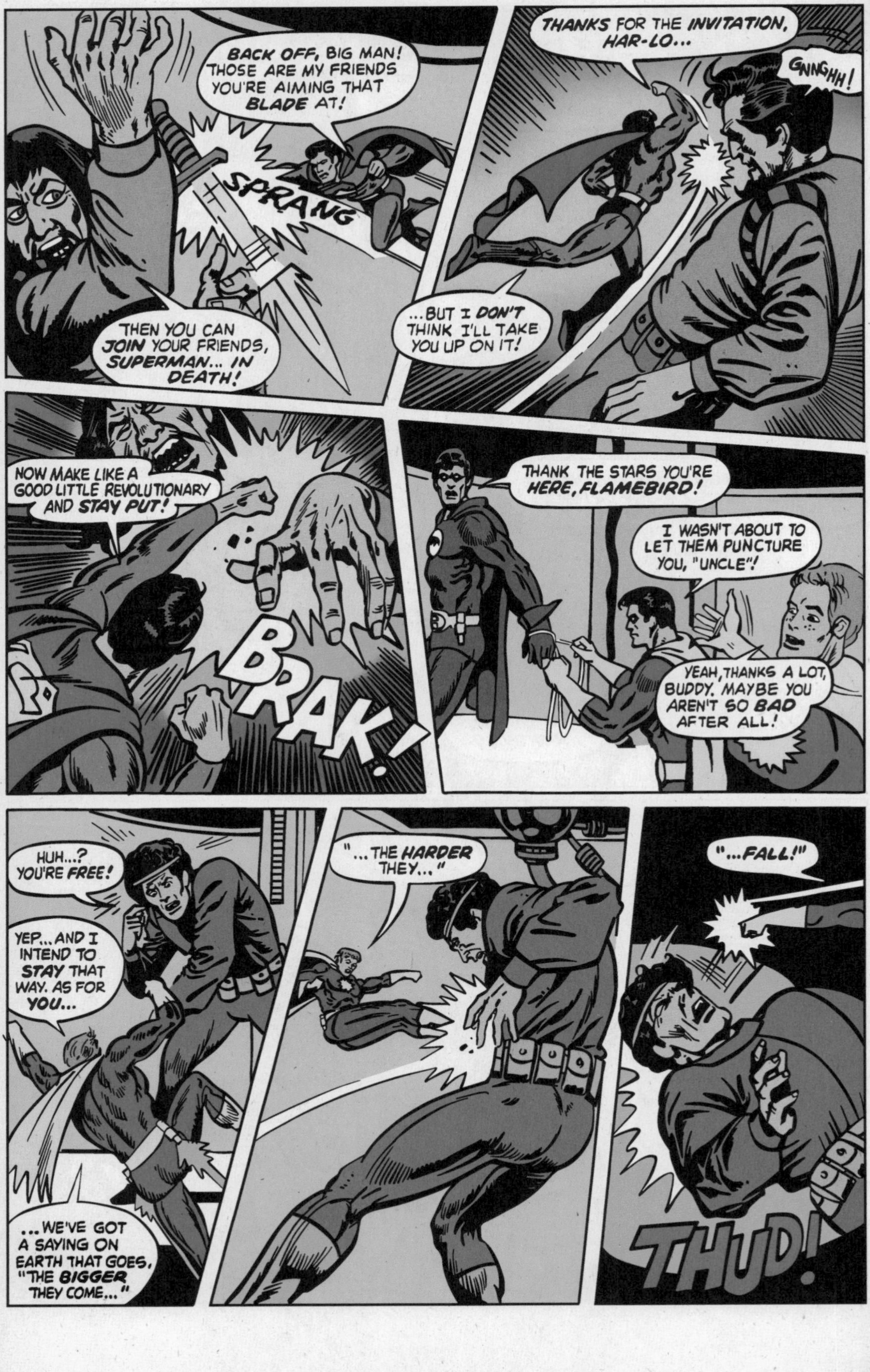
BACK OFF, BIG MAN! THOSE ARE MY FRIENDS YOU'RE AIMING THAT BLADE AT!
SPRANG
THEN YOU CAN JOIN YOUR FRIENDS, SUPERMAN... IN DEATH!
THANKS FOR THE INVITATION, HAR-LO...
GNNGHH!
...BUT I DON'T THINK I'LL TAKE YOU UP ON IT!
NOW MAKE LIKE A GOOD LITTLE REVOLUTIONARY AND STAY PUT!
BRAK!
THANK THE STARS YOU'RE HERE, FLAMEBIRD!
I WASN'T ABOUT TO LET THEM PUNCTURE YOU, "UNCLE"!
YEAH, THANKS A LOT, BUDDY. MAYBE YOU AREN'T SO BAD AFTER ALL!
HUH...? YOU'RE FREE!
YEP... AND I INTEND TO STAY THAT WAY. AS FOR YOU...
...WE'VE GOT A SAYING ON EARTH THAT GOES, "THE BIGGER THEY COME..."
"...THE HARDER THEY..."
"...FALL!"
THUD!

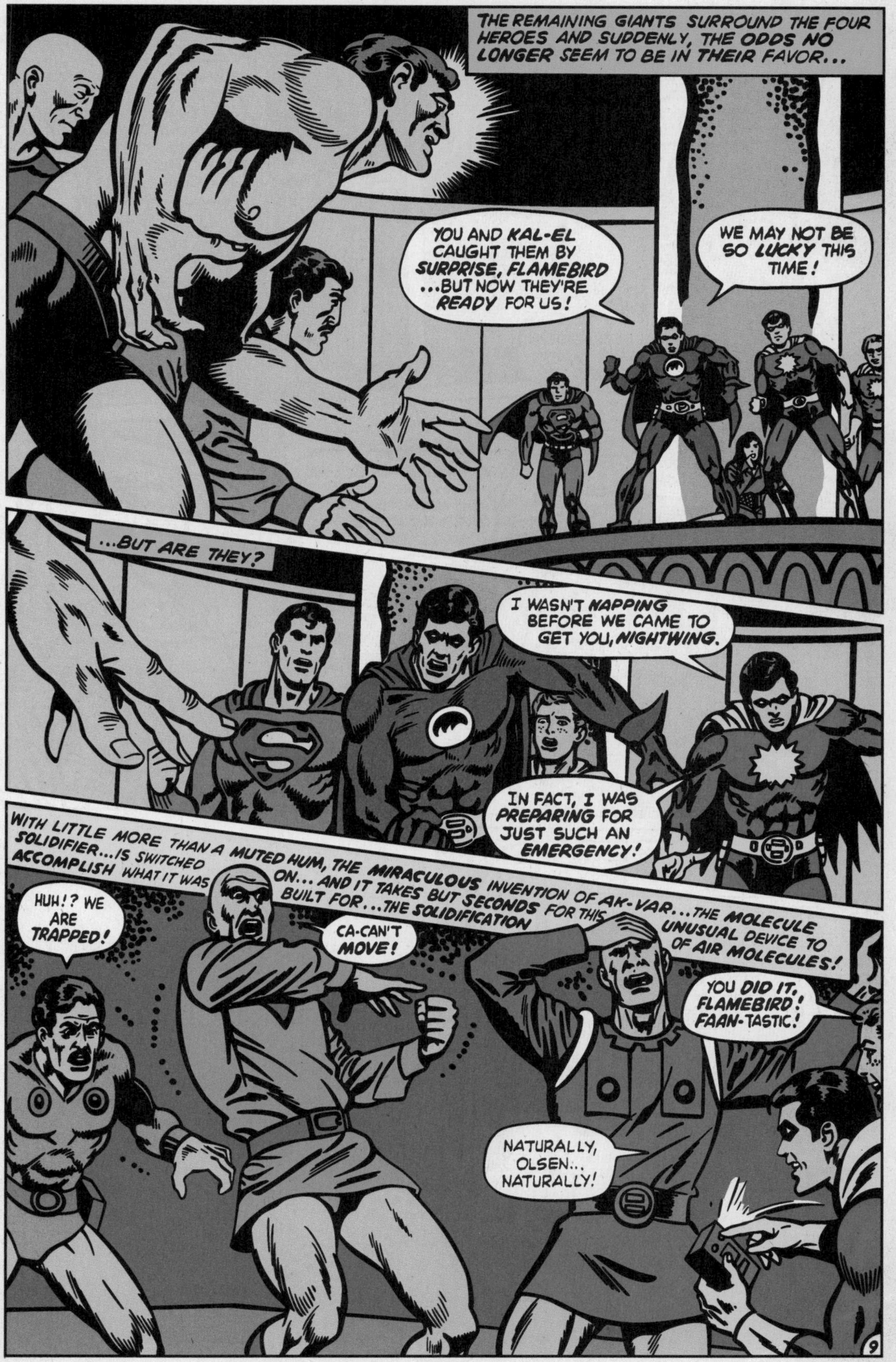
THE REMAINING GIANTS SURROUND THE FOUR HEROES AND SUDDENLY, THE ODDS NO LONGER SEEM TO BE IN THEIR FAVOR...
YOU AND KAL-EL CAUGHT THEM BY SURPRISE, FLAMEBIRD ...BUT NOW THEY'RE READY FOR US!
WE MAY NOT BE SO LUCKY THIS TIME!
...BUT ARE THEY?
I WASN'T NAPPING BEFORE WE CAME TO GET YOU, NIGHTWING.
IN FACT, I WAS PREPARING FOR JUST SUCH AN EMERGENCY!
WITH LITTLE MORE THAN A MUTED HUM, THE MIRACULOUS INVENTION OF AK-VAR...THE MOLECULE SOLIDIFIER...IS SWITCHED ON... AND IT TAKES BUT SECONDS FOR THIS UNUSUAL DEVICE TO ACCOMPLISH WHAT IT WAS BUILT FOR...THE SOLIDIFICATION OF AIR MOLECULES!
HUH!? WE ARE TRAPPED!
CA-CAN'T MOVE!
YOU DID IT, FLAMEBIRD! FAAN-TASTIC!
NATURALLY, OLSEN... NATURALLY!
9

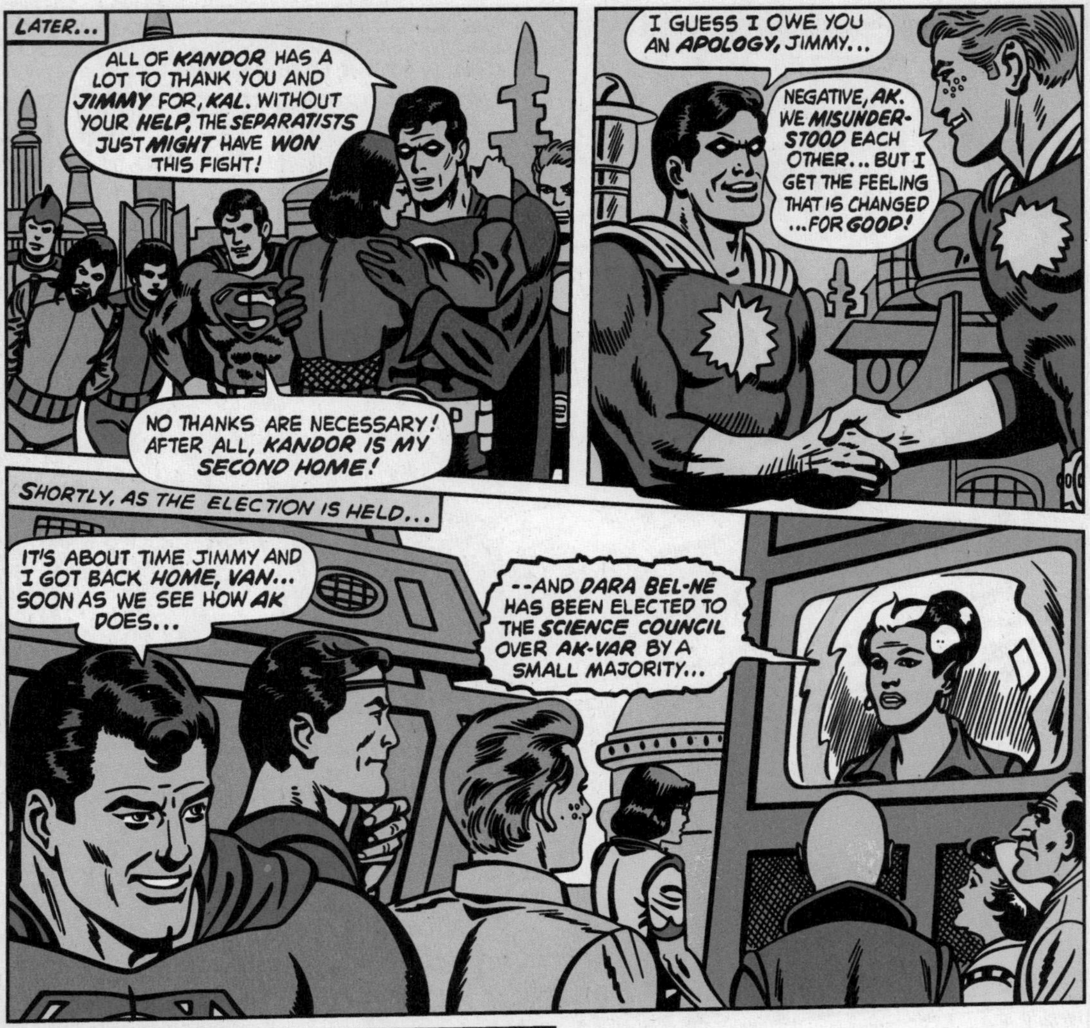
LATER...
ALL OF KANDOR HAS A LOT TO THANK YOU AND JIMMY FOR, KAL. WITHOUT YOUR HELP, THE SEPARATISTS JUST MIGHT HAVE WON THIS FIGHT!
NO THANKS ARE NECESSARY! AFTER ALL, KANDOR IS MY SECOND HOME!
I GUESS I OWE YOU AN APOLOGY, JIMMY...
NEGATIVE, AK. WE MISUNDERSTOOD EACH OTHER... BUT I GET THE FEELING THAT IS CHANGED ...FOR GOOD!
SHORTLY, AS THE ELECTION IS HELD...
IT'S ABOUT TIME JIMMY AND I GOT BACK HOME, VAN... SOON AS WE SEE HOW AK DOES...
--AND DARA BEL-NE HAS BEEN ELECTED TO THE SCIENCE COUNCIL OVER AK-VAR BY A SMALL MAJORITY...

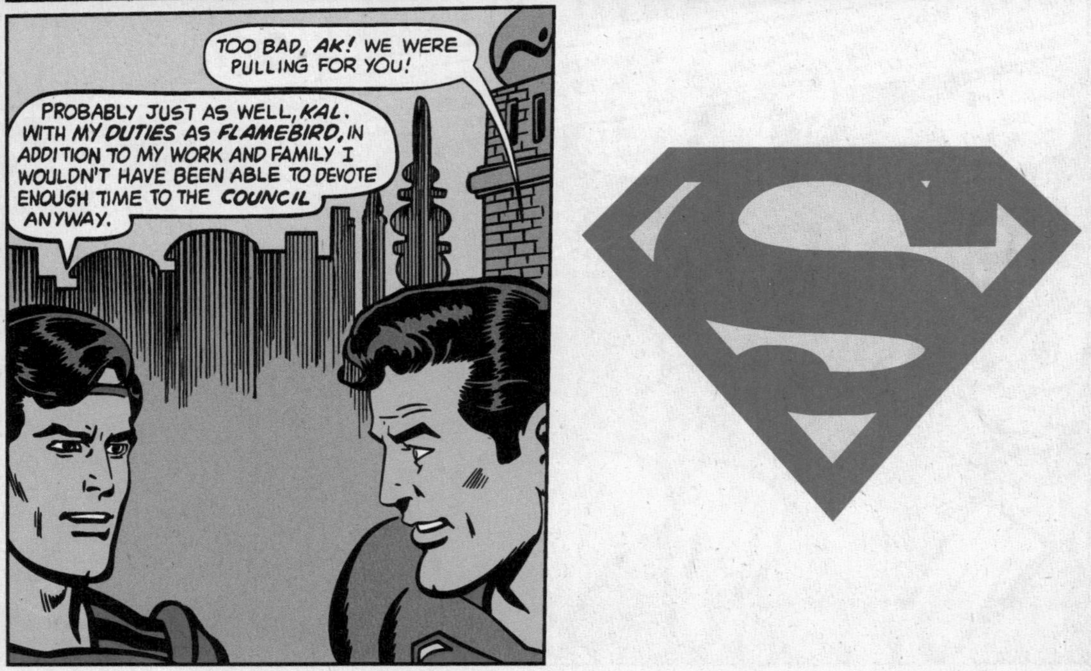
TOO BAD, AK! WE WERE PULLING FOR YOU!
PROBABLY JUST AS WELL, KAL. WITH MY DUTIES AS FLAMEBIRD, IN ADDITION TO MY WORK AND FAMILY I WOULDN'T HAVE BEEN ABLE TO DEVOTE ENOUGH TIME TO THE COUNCIL ANYWAY.

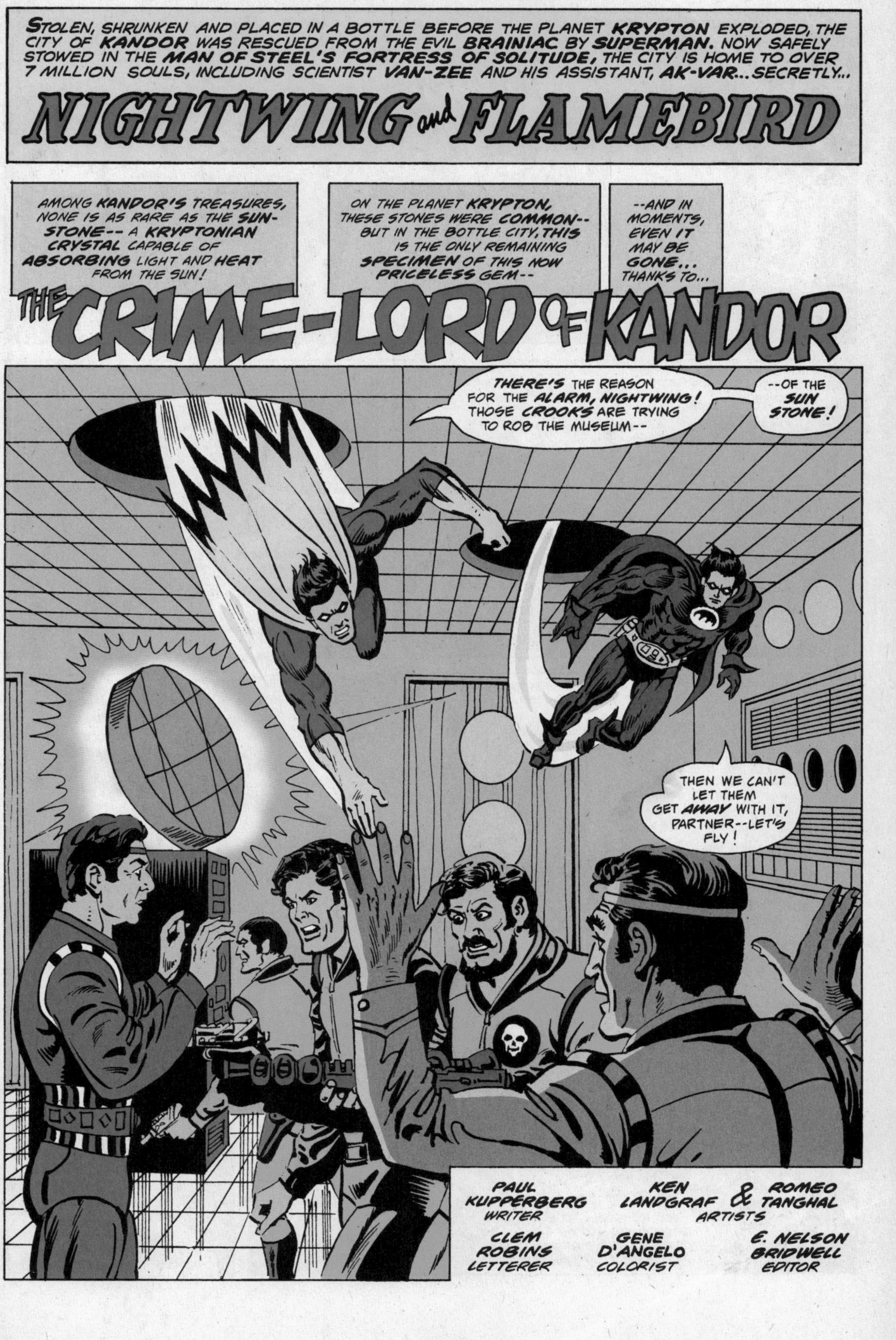
STOLEN, SHRUNKEN AND PLACED IN A BOTTLE BEFORE THE PLANET KRYPTON EXPLODED, THE CITY OF KANDOR WAS RESCUED FROM THE EVIL BRAINIAC BY SUPERMAN. NOW SAFELY STOWED IN THE MAN OF STEEL'S FORTRESS OF SOLITUDE, THE CITY IS HOME TO OVER 7 MILLION SOULS, INCLUDING SCIENTIST VAN-ZEE AND HIS ASSISTANT, AK-VAR... SECRETLY...
NIGHTWING and FLAMEBIRD
AMONG KANDOR'S TREASURES, NONE IS AS RARE AS THE SUN-STONE-- A KRYPTONIAN CRYSTAL CAPABLE OF ABSORBING LIGHT AND HEAT FROM THE SUN!
ON THE PLANET KRYPTON, THESE STONES WERE COMMON-- BUT IN THE BOTTLE CITY, THIS IS THE ONLY REMAINING SPECIMEN OF THIS NOW PRICELESS GEM--
--AND IN MOMENTS, EVEN IT MAY BE GONE... THANKS TO...
THE CRIME-LORD OF KANDOR
THERE'S THE REASON FOR THE ALARM, NIGHTWING! THOSE CROOKS ARE TRYING TO ROB THE MUSEUM--
--OF THE SUN STONE!
THEN WE CAN'T LET THEM GET AWAY WITH IT, PARTNER--LET'S FLY!
PAUL KUPPERBERG WRITER
KEN LANDGRAF & ROMEO TANGHAL ARTISTS
CLEM ROBINS LETTERER
GENE D'ANGELO COLORIST
E. NELSON BRIDWELL EDITOR

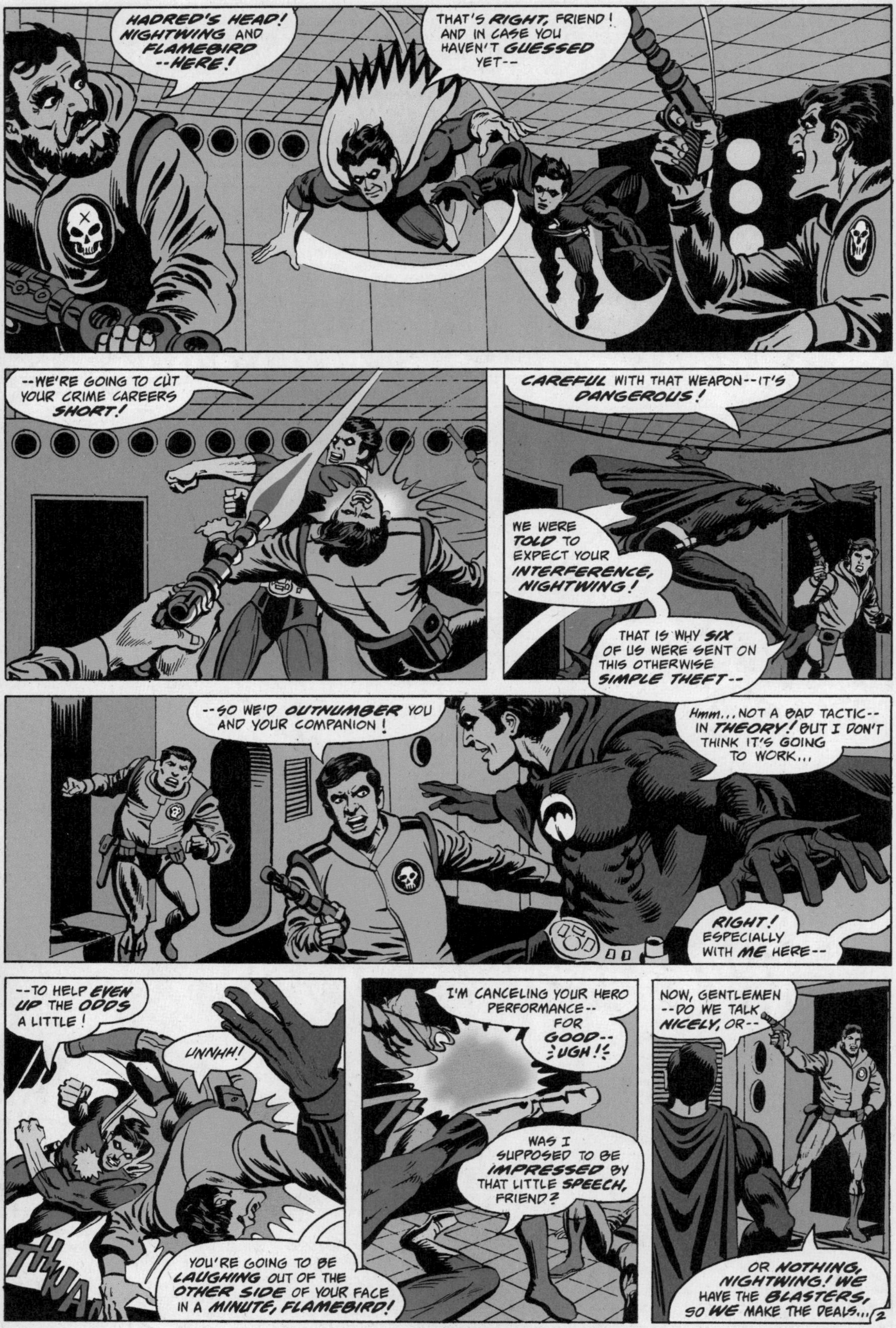
HADRED'S HEAD! NIGHTWING AND FLAMEBIRD --HERE!
THAT'S RIGHT, FRIEND! AND IN CASE YOU HAVEN'T GUESSED YET--
--WE'RE GOING TO CUT YOUR CRIME CAREERS SHORT!
CAREFUL WITH THAT WEAPON--IT'S DANGEROUS!
WE WERE TOLD TO EXPECT YOUR INTERFERENCE, NIGHTWING!
THAT IS WHY SIX OF US WERE SENT ON THIS OTHERWISE SIMPLE THEFT--
--SO WE'D OUTNUMBER YOU AND YOUR COMPANION!
Hmm... NOT A BAD TACTIC--IN THEORY! BUT I DON'T THINK IT'S GOING TO WORK...
RIGHT! ESPECIALLY WITH ME HERE--
--TO HELP EVEN UP THE ODDS A LITTLE!
UNNHH!
THWAM
YOU'RE GOING TO BE LAUGHING OUT OF THE OTHER SIDE OF YOUR FACE IN A MINUTE, FLAMEBIRD!
I'M CANCELING YOUR HERO PERFORMANCE-- FOR GOOD-- UGH!!
WAS I SUPPOSED TO BE IMPRESSED BY THAT LITTLE SPEECH, FRIEND?
NOW, GENTLEMEN --DO WE TALK NICELY, OR--
OR NOTHING, NIGHTWING! WE HAVE THE BLASTERS, SO WE MAKE THE DEALS...
2

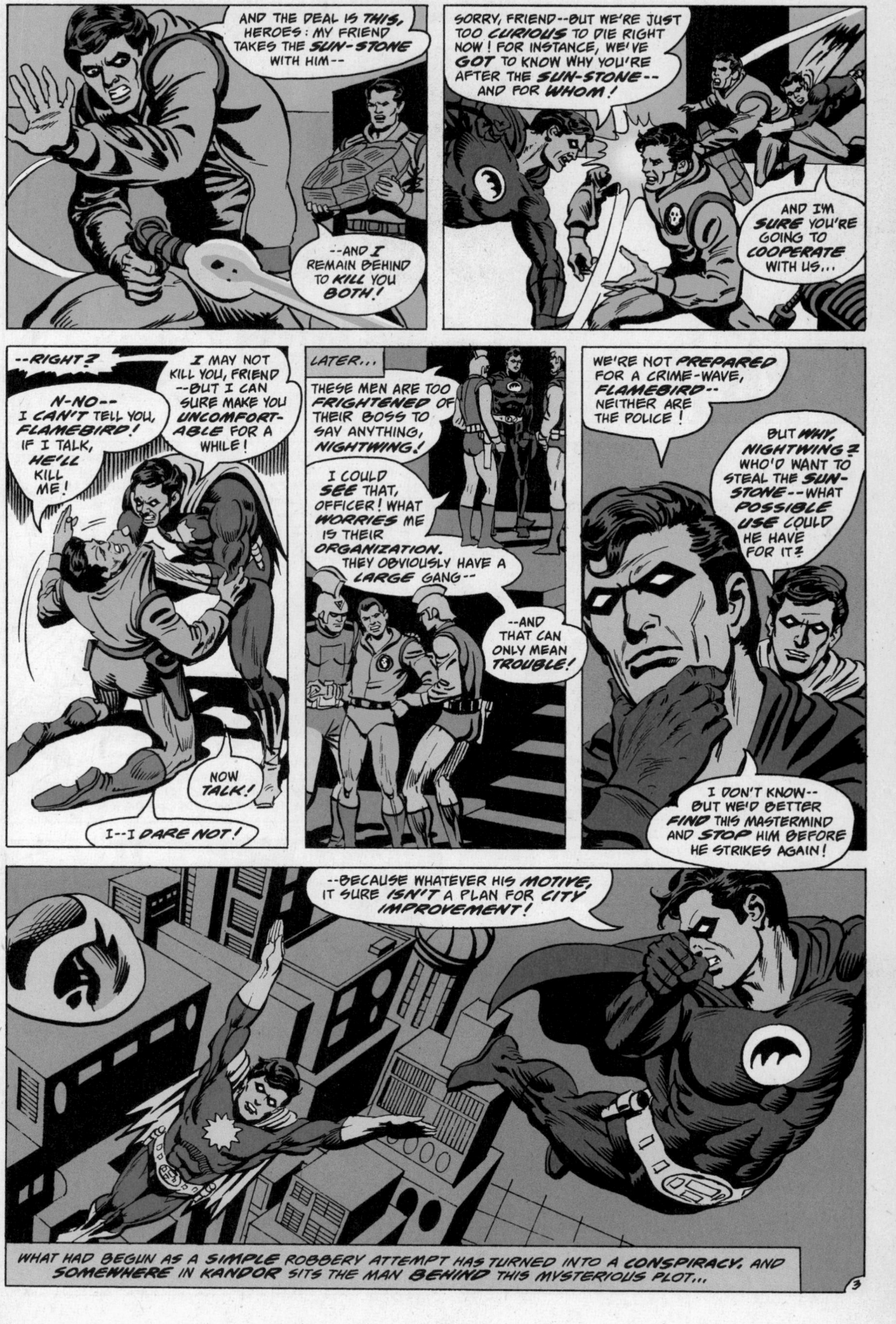
AND THE DEAL IS THIS, HEROES: MY FRIEND TAKES THE SUN-STONE WITH HIM--
--AND I REMAIN BEHIND TO KILL YOU BOTH!
SORRY, FRIEND--BUT WE'RE JUST TOO CURIOUS TO DIE RIGHT NOW! FOR INSTANCE, WE'VE GOT TO KNOW WHY YOU'RE AFTER THE SUN-STONE-- AND FOR WHOM!
AND I'M SURE YOU'RE GOING TO COOPERATE WITH US...
--RIGHT?
N-NO-- I CAN'T TELL YOU, FLAMEBIRD! IF I TALK, HE'LL KILL ME!
I MAY NOT KILL YOU, FRIEND --BUT I CAN SURE MAKE YOU UNCOMFORTABLE FOR A WHILE!
NOW TALK!
I--I DARE NOT!
LATER...
THESE MEN ARE TOO FRIGHTENED OF THEIR BOSS TO SAY ANYTHING, NIGHTWING!
I COULD SEE THAT, OFFICER! WHAT WORRIES ME IS THEIR ORGANIZATION. THEY OBVIOUSLY HAVE A LARGE GANG--
--AND THAT CAN ONLY MEAN TROUBLE!
WE'RE NOT PREPARED FOR A CRIME-WAVE, FLAMEBIRD-- NEITHER ARE THE POLICE!
BUT WHY, NIGHTWING? WHO'D WANT TO STEAL THE SUN-STONE--WHAT POSSIBLE USE COULD HE HAVE FOR IT?
I DON'T KNOW-- BUT WE'D BETTER FIND THIS MASTERMIND AND STOP HIM BEFORE HE STRIKES AGAIN!
--BECAUSE WHATEVER HIS MOTIVE, IT SURE ISN'T A PLAN FOR CITY IMPROVEMENT!
WHAT HAD BEGUN AS A SIMPLE ROBBERY ATTEMPT HAS TURNED INTO A CONSPIRACY. AND SOMEWHERE IN KANDOR SITS THE MAN BEHIND THIS MYSTERIOUS PLOT...
3

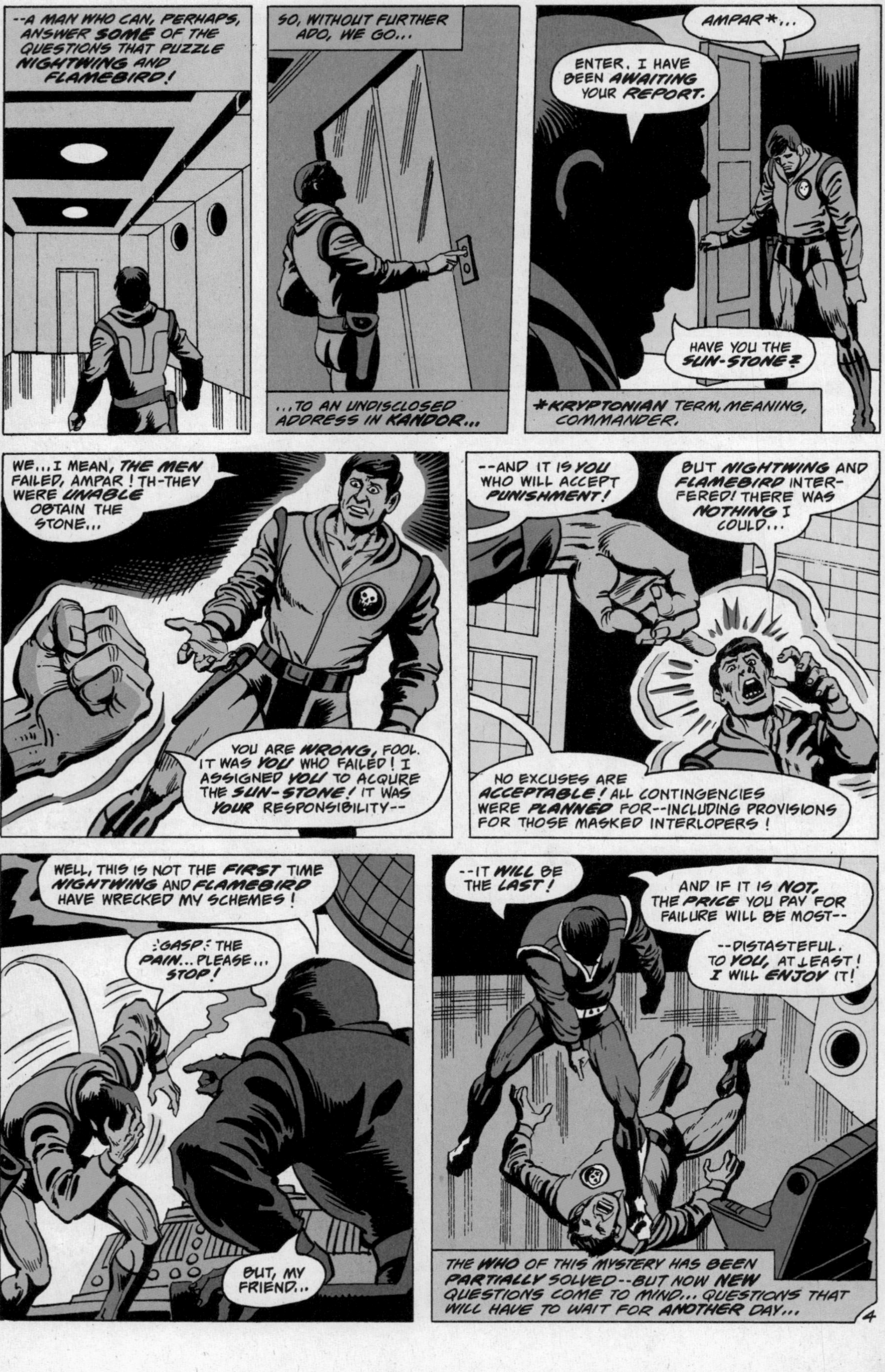
--A MAN WHO CAN, PERHAPS, ANSWER SOME OF THE QUESTIONS THAT PUZZLE NIGHTWING AND FLAMEBIRD!
SO, WITHOUT FURTHER ADO, WE GO...
...TO AN UNDISCLOSED ADDRESS IN KANDOR...
AMPAR*...
ENTER. I HAVE BEEN AWAITING YOUR REPORT.
HAVE YOU THE SUN-STONE?
*KRYPTONIAN TERM, MEANING, COMMANDER.
WE...I MEAN, THE MEN FAILED, AMPAR! TH-THEY WERE UNABLE OBTAIN THE STONE...
YOU ARE WRONG, FOOL. IT WAS YOU WHO FAILED! I ASSIGNED YOU TO ACQURE THE SUN-STONE! IT WAS YOUR RESPONSIBILITY--
--AND IT IS YOU WHO WILL ACCEPT PUNISHMENT!
BUT NIGHTWING AND FLAMEBIRD INTERFERED! THERE WAS NOTHING I COULD...
NO EXCUSES ARE ACCEPTABLE! ALL CONTINGENCIES WERE PLANNED FOR--INCLUDING PROVISIONS FOR THOSE MASKED INTERLOPERS!
WELL, THIS IS NOT THE FIRST TIME NIGHTWING AND FLAMEBIRD HAVE WRECKED MY SCHEMES!
GASP THE PAIN... PLEASE... STOP!
BUT, MY FRIEND...
--IT WILL BE THE LAST!
AND IF IT IS NOT, THE PRICE YOU PAY FOR FAILURE WILL BE MOST--
--DISTASTEFUL. TO YOU, AT LEAST! I WILL ENJOY IT!
THE WHO OF THIS MYSTERY HAS BEEN PARTIALLY SOLVED--BUT NOW NEW QUESTIONS COME TO MIND... QUESTIONS THAT WILL HAVE TO WAIT FOR ANOTHER DAY...
4

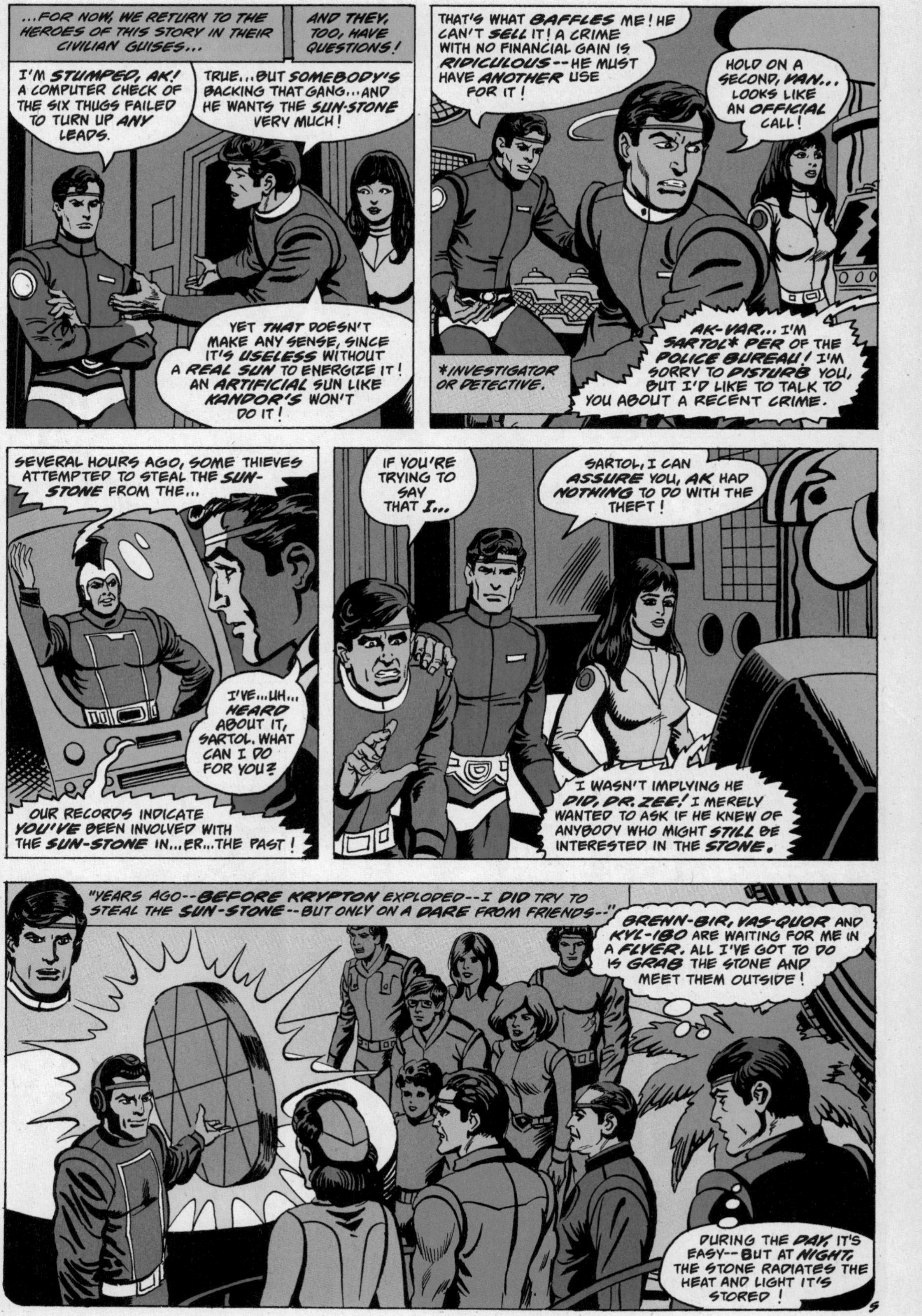
...FOR NOW, WE RETURN TO THE HEROES OF THIS STORY IN THEIR CIVILIAN GUISES...
AND THEY, TOO, HAVE QUESTIONS!
I'M STUMPED, AK! A COMPUTER CHECK OF THE SIX THUGS FAILED TO TURN UP ANY LEADS.
TRUE...BUT SOMEBODY'S BACKING THAT GANG...AND HE WANTS THE SUN-STONE VERY MUCH!
YET THAT DOESN'T MAKE ANY SENSE, SINCE IT'S USELESS WITHOUT A REAL SUN TO ENERGIZE IT! AN ARTIFICIAL SUN LIKE KANDOR'S WON'T DO IT!
THAT'S WHAT BAFFLES ME! HE CAN'T SELL IT! A CRIME WITH NO FINANCIAL GAIN IS RIDICULOUS--HE MUST HAVE ANOTHER USE FOR IT!
HOLD ON A SECOND, VAN... LOOKS LIKE AN OFFICIAL CALL!
AK-VAR... I'M SARTOL* PER OF THE POLICE BUREAU! I'M SORRY TO DISTURB YOU, BUT I'D LIKE TO TALK TO YOU ABOUT A RECENT CRIME.
*INVESTIGATOR OR DETECTIVE.
SEVERAL HOURS AGO, SOME THIEVES ATTEMPTED TO STEAL THE SUN-STONE FROM THE...
I'VE...UH... HEARD ABOUT IT, SARTOL. WHAT CAN I DO FOR YOU?
OUR RECORDS INDICATE YOU'VE BEEN INVOLVED WITH THE SUN-STONE IN...ER...THE PAST!
IF YOU'RE TRYING TO SAY THAT I...
SARTOL, I CAN ASSURE YOU, AK HAD NOTHING TO DO WITH THE THEFT!
I WASN'T IMPLYING HE DID, DR. ZEE! I MERELY WANTED TO ASK IF HE KNEW OF ANYBODY WHO MIGHT STILL BE INTERESTED IN THE STONE.
"YEARS AGO--BEFORE KRYPTON EXPLODED--I DID TRY TO STEAL THE SUN-STONE--BUT ONLY ON A DARE FROM FRIENDS--"
BRENN-BIR, VAS-QUOR AND KYL-IBO ARE WAITING FOR ME IN A FLYER. ALL I'VE GOT TO DO IS GRAB THE STONE AND MEET THEM OUTSIDE!
DURING THE DAY, IT'S EASY--BUT AT NIGHT, THE STONE RADIATES THE HEAT AND LIGHT IT'S STORED!
5

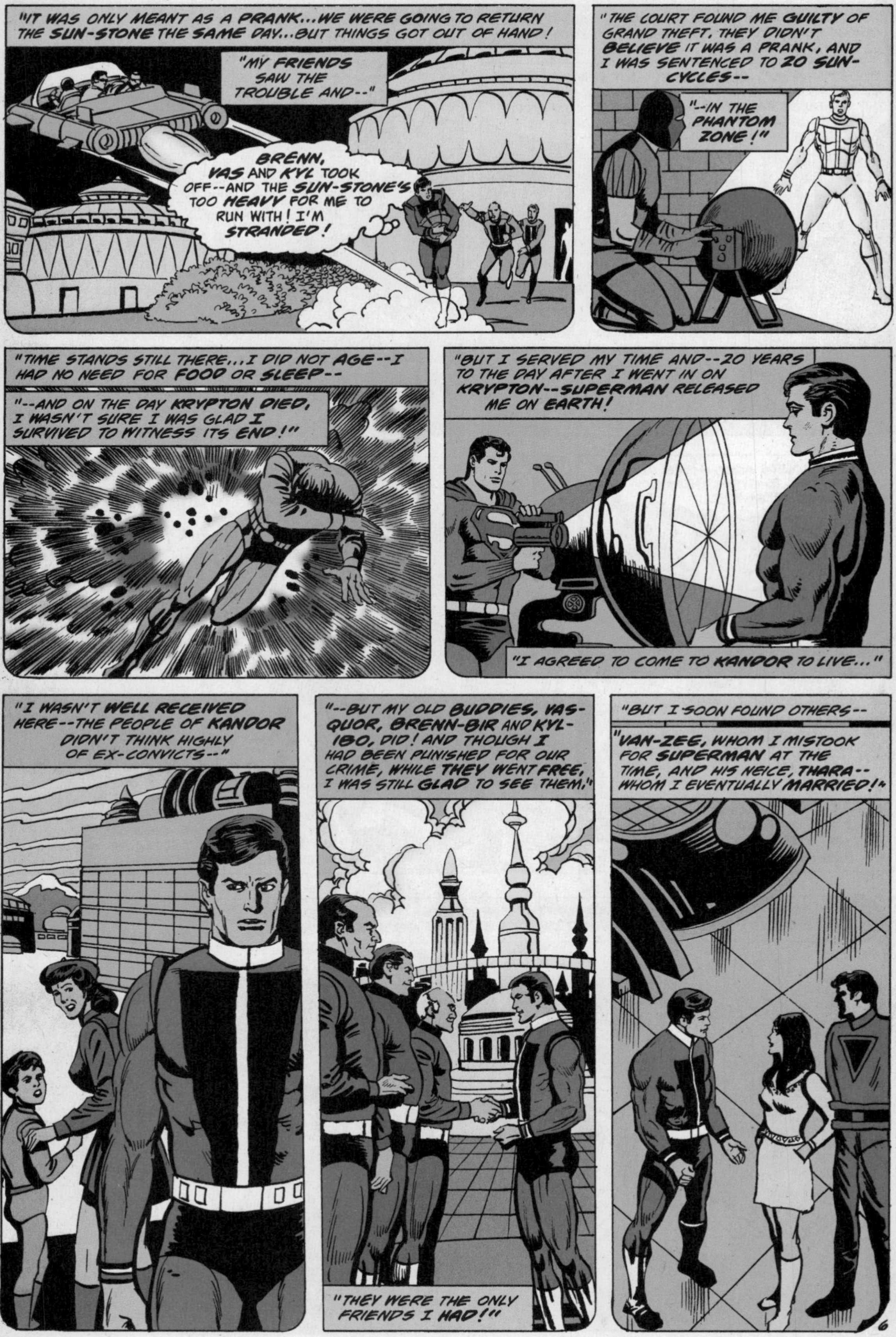
"IT WAS ONLY MEANT AS A PRANK... WE WERE GOING TO RETURN THE SUN-STONE THE SAME DAY... BUT THINGS GOT OUT OF HAND!
"MY FRIENDS SAW THE TROUBLE AND--"
BRENN, VAS AND KYL TOOK OFF--AND THE SUN-STONE'S TOO HEAVY FOR ME TO RUN WITH! I'M STRANDED!
"THE COURT FOUND ME GUILTY OF GRAND THEFT. THEY DIDN'T BELIEVE IT WAS A PRANK, AND I WAS SENTENCED TO 20 SUN-CYCLES--
"--IN THE PHANTOM ZONE!"
"TIME STANDS STILL THERE... I DID NOT AGE--I HAD NO NEED FOR FOOD OR SLEEP--
"--AND ON THE DAY KRYPTON DIED, I WASN'T SURE I WAS GLAD I SURVIVED TO WITNESS ITS END!"
"BUT I SERVED MY TIME AND--20 YEARS TO THE DAY AFTER I WENT IN ON KRYPTON--SUPERMAN RELEASED ME ON EARTH!
"I AGREED TO COME TO KANDOR TO LIVE..."
"I WASN'T WELL RECEIVED HERE--THE PEOPLE OF KANDOR DIDN'T THINK HIGHLY OF EX-CONVICTS--"
"--BUT MY OLD BUDDIES, VAS-QUOR, BRENN-BIR AND KYL-IBO, DID! AND THOUGH I HAD BEEN PUNISHED FOR OUR CRIME, WHILE THEY WENT FREE, I WAS STILL GLAD TO SEE THEM."
"THEY WERE THE ONLY FRIENDS I HAD!"
"BUT I SOON FOUND OTHERS--
"VAN-ZEE, WHOM I MISTOOK FOR SUPERMAN AT THE TIME, AND HIS NEICE, THARA--WHOM I EVENTUALLY MARRIED!"
6

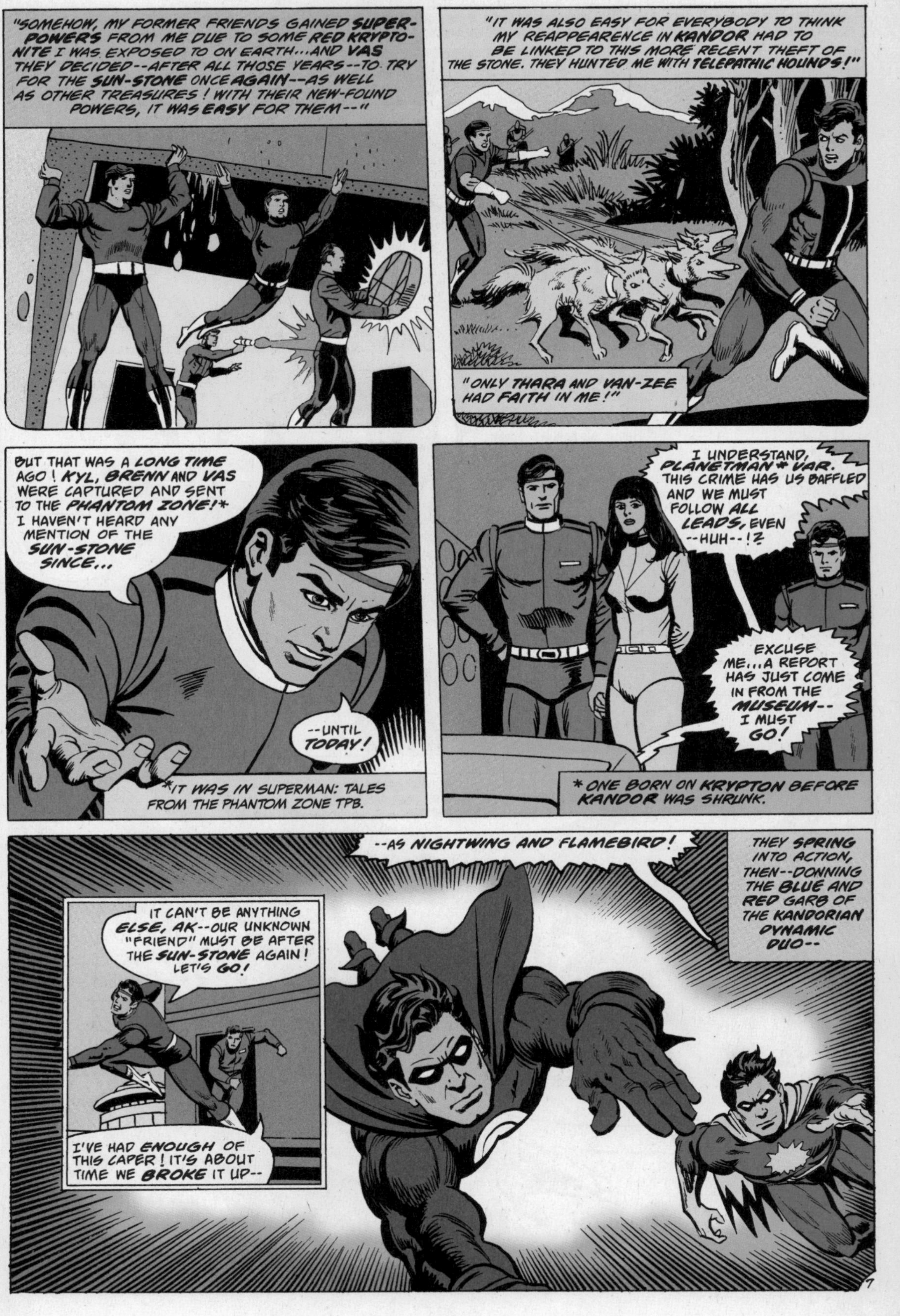
"SOMEHOW, MY FORMER FRIENDS GAINED SUPER-POWERS FROM ME DUE TO SOME RED KRYPTONITE I WAS EXPOSED TO ON EARTH...AND VAS THEY DECIDED--AFTER ALL THOSE YEARS--TO TRY FOR THE SUN-STONE ONCE AGAIN--AS WELL AS OTHER TREASURES! WITH THEIR NEW-FOUND POWERS, IT WAS EASY FOR THEM--"
"IT WAS ALSO EASY FOR EVERYBODY TO THINK MY REAPPEARENCE IN KANDOR HAD TO BE LINKED TO THIS MORE RECENT THEFT OF THE STONE. THEY HUNTED ME WITH TELEPATHIC HOUNDS!"
"ONLY THARA AND VAN-ZEE HAD FAITH IN ME!"
BUT THAT WAS A LONG TIME AGO! KYL, BRENN AND VAS WERE CAPTURED AND SENT TO THE PHANTOM ZONE!* I HAVEN'T HEARD ANY MENTION OF THE SUN-STONE SINCE...
--UNTIL TODAY!
*IT WAS IN SUPERMAN: TALES FROM THE PHANTOM ZONE TPB.
I UNDERSTAND, PLANETMAN* VAR. THIS CRIME HAS US BAFFLED AND WE MUST FOLLOW ALL LEADS, EVEN --HUH--!?
EXCUSE ME...A REPORT HAS JUST COME IN FROM THE MUSEUM-- I MUST GO!
* ONE BORN ON KRYPTON BEFORE KANDOR WAS SHRUNK.
IT CAN'T BE ANYTHING ELSE, AK--OUR UNKNOWN "FRIEND" MUST BE AFTER THE SUN-STONE AGAIN! LET'S GO!
I'VE HAD ENOUGH OF THIS CAPER! IT'S ABOUT TIME WE BROKE IT UP--
THEY SPRING INTO ACTION, THEN--DONNING THE BLUE AND RED GARB OF THE KANDORIAN DYNAMIC DUO--
--AS NIGHTWING AND FLAMEBIRD!
7

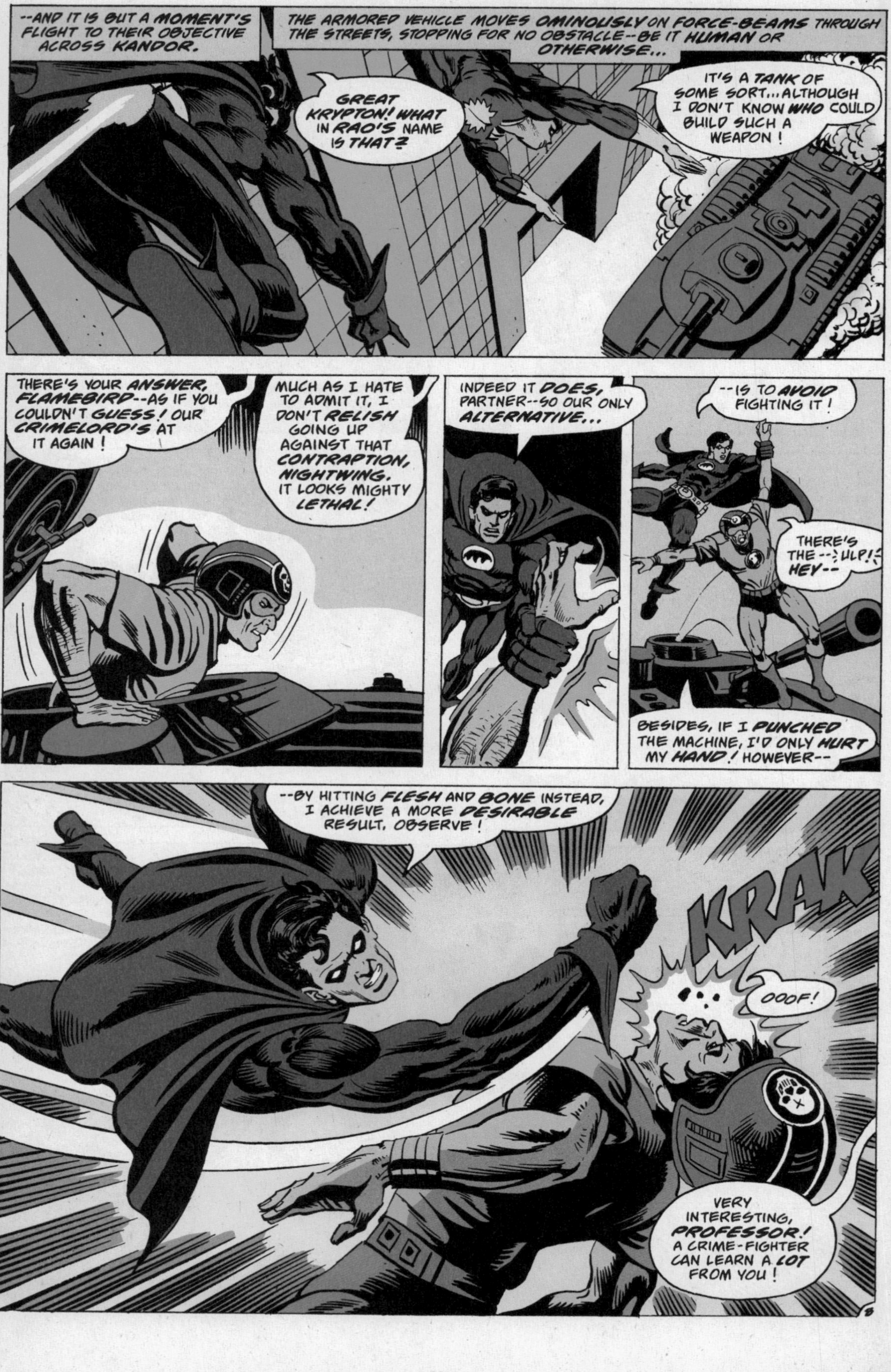
--AND IT IS BUT A MOMENT'S FLIGHT TO THEIR OBJECTIVE ACROSS KANDOR.
THE ARMORED VEHICLE MOVES OMINOUSLY ON FORCE-BEAMS THROUGH THE STREETS, STOPPING FOR NO OBSTACLE--BE IT HUMAN OR OTHERWISE...
GREAT KRYPTON! WHAT IN RAO'S NAME IS THAT?
IT'S A TANK OF SOME SORT... ALTHOUGH I DON'T KNOW WHO COULD BUILD SUCH A WEAPON!
THERE'S YOUR ANSWER, FLAMEBIRD--AS IF YOU COULDN'T GUESS! OUR CRIMELORD'S AT IT AGAIN!
MUCH AS I HATE TO ADMIT IT, I DON'T RELISH GOING UP AGAINST THAT CONTRAPTION, NIGHTWING. IT LOOKS MIGHTY LETHAL!
INDEED IT DOES, PARTNER--SO OUR ONLY ALTERNATIVE...
--IS TO AVOID FIGHTING IT!
THERE'S THE-- ULP! HEY--
BESIDES, IF I PUNCHED THE MACHINE, I'D ONLY HURT MY HAND! HOWEVER--
--BY HITTING FLESH AND BONE INSTEAD, I ACHIEVE A MORE DESIRABLE RESULT. OBSERVE!
KRAK
OOOF!
VERY INTERESTING, PROFESSOR! A CRIME-FIGHTER CAN LEARN A LOT FROM YOU!
8

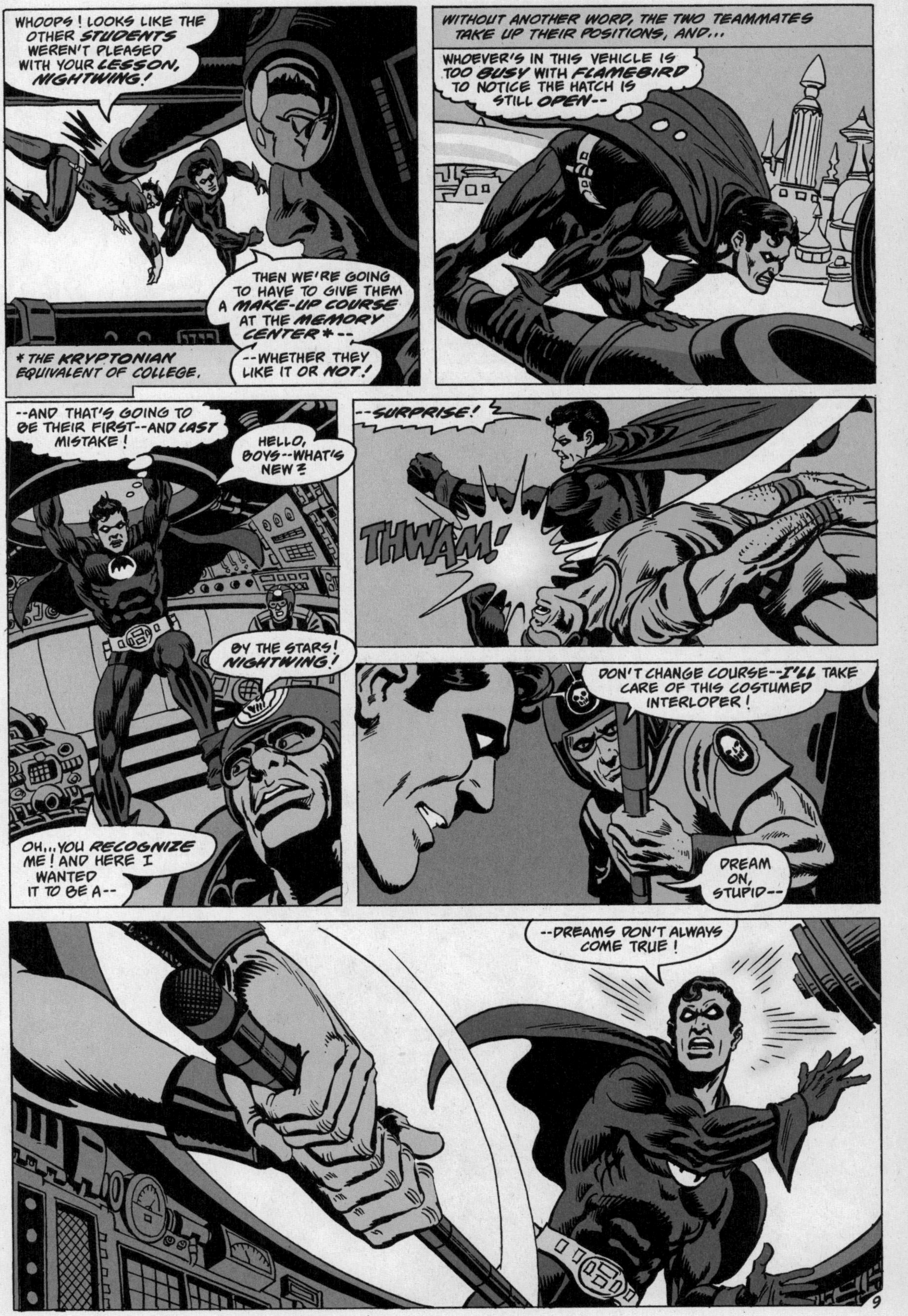

WHOOPS! LOOKS LIKE THE OTHER STUDENTS WEREN'T PLEASED WITH YOUR LESSON, NIGHTWING!
THEN WE'RE GOING TO HAVE TO GIVE THEM A MAKE-UP COURSE AT THE MEMORY CENTER* --
--WHETHER THEY LIKE IT OR NOT!
* THE KRYPTONIAN EQUIVALENT OF COLLEGE.
WITHOUT ANOTHER WORD, THE TWO TEAMMATES TAKE UP THEIR POSITIONS, AND...
WHOEVER'S IN THIS VEHICLE IS TOO BUSY WITH FLAMEBIRD TO NOTICE THE HATCH IS STILL OPEN--
--AND THAT'S GOING TO BE THEIR FIRST--AND LAST MISTAKE!
HELLO, BOYS--WHAT'S NEW?
BY THE STARS! NIGHTWING!
OH... YOU RECOGNIZE ME! AND HERE I WANTED IT TO BE A--
--SURPRISE!
THWAM!
DON'T CHANGE COURSE--I'LL TAKE CARE OF THIS COSTUMED INTERLOPER!
DREAM ON, STUPID--
--DREAMS DON'T ALWAYS COME TRUE!
9

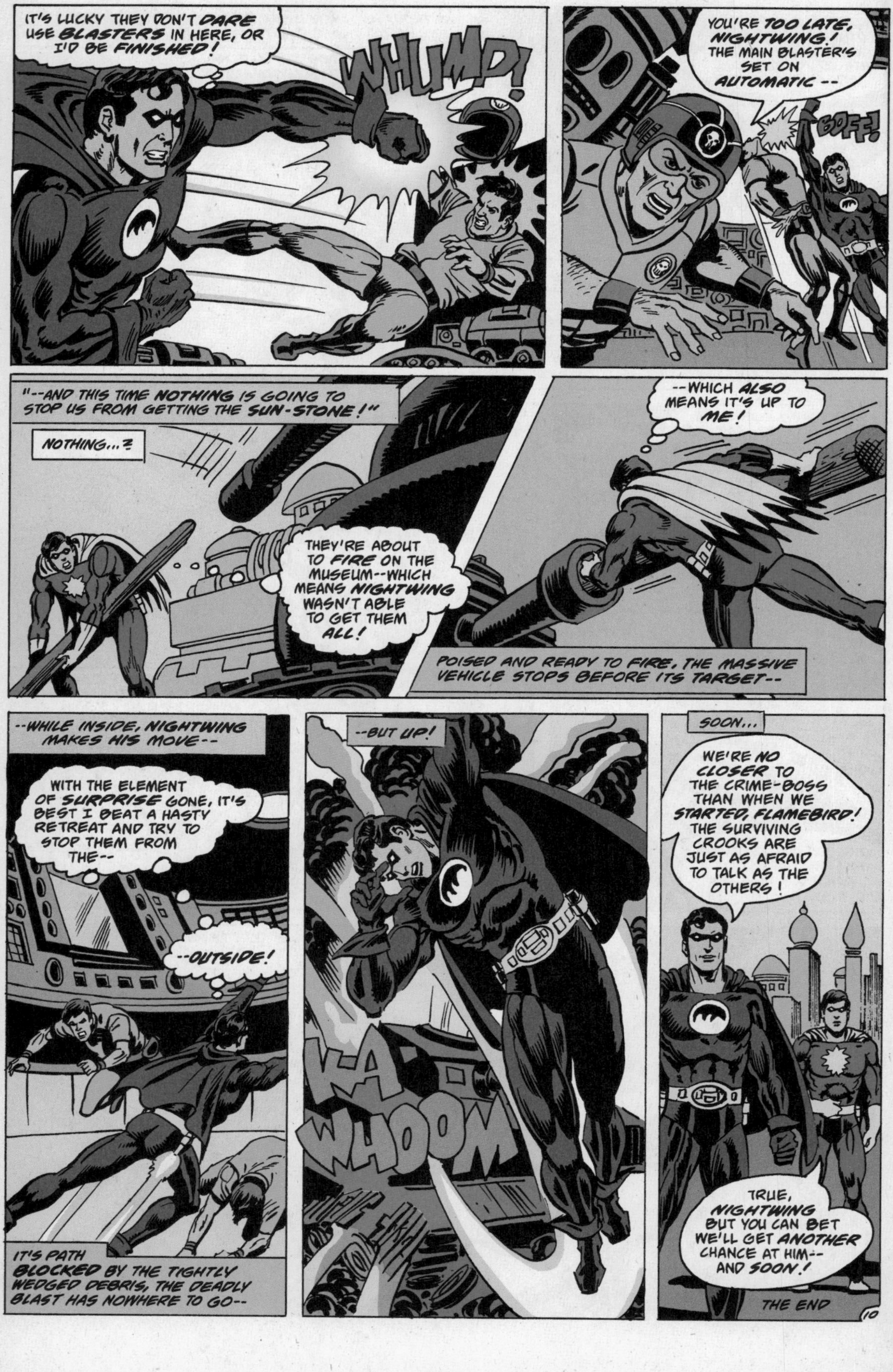
IT'S LUCKY THEY DON'T DARE USE BLASTERS IN HERE, OR I'D BE FINISHED!
WHUMP!
YOU'RE TOO LATE, NIGHTWING! THE MAIN BLASTER'S SET ON AUTOMATIC --
BOFF!
"--AND THIS TIME NOTHING IS GOING TO STOP US FROM GETTING THE SUN-STONE!"
NOTHING...?
THEY'RE ABOUT TO FIRE ON THE MUSEUM--WHICH MEANS NIGHTWING WASN'T ABLE TO GET THEM ALL!
--WHICH ALSO MEANS IT'S UP TO ME!
POISED AND READY TO FIRE, THE MASSIVE VEHICLE STOPS BEFORE ITS TARGET--
--WHILE INSIDE, NIGHTWING MAKES HIS MOVE--
WITH THE ELEMENT OF SURPRISE GONE, IT'S BEST I BEAT A HASTY RETREAT AND TRY TO STOP THEM FROM THE--
--OUTSIDE!
IT'S PATH BLOCKED BY THE TIGHTLY WEDGED DEBRIS, THE DEADLY BLAST HAS NOWHERE TO GO--
--BUT UP!
KA WHOOM
SOON...
WE'RE NO CLOSER TO THE CRIME-BOSS THAN WHEN WE STARTED, FLAMEBIRD! THE SURVIVING CROOKS ARE JUST AS AFRAID TO TALK AS THE OTHERS!
TRUE, NIGHTWING BUT YOU CAN BET WE'LL GET ANOTHER CHANCE AT HIM--AND SOON!
THE END
10

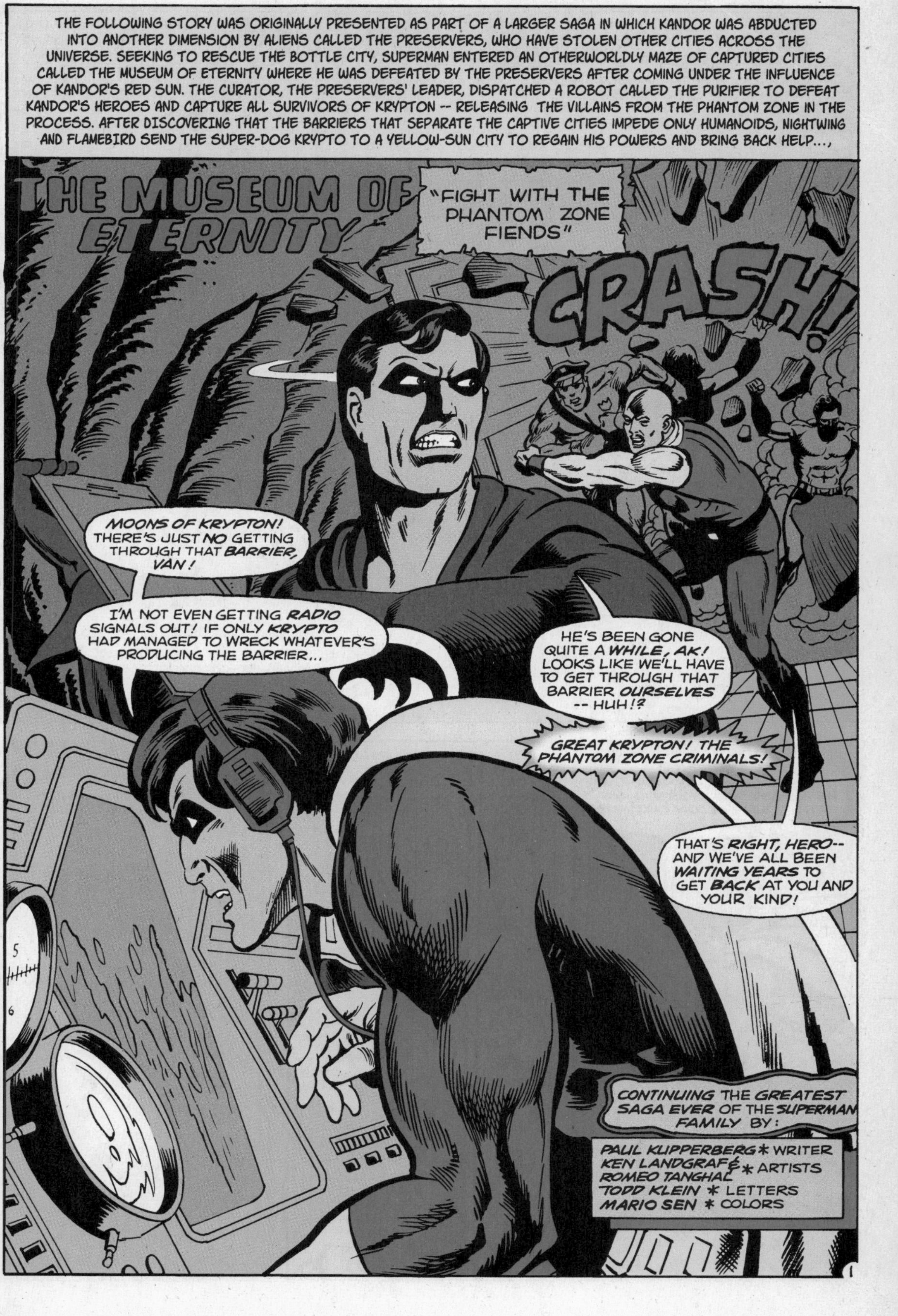
THE FOLLOWING STORY WAS ORIGINALLY PRESENTED AS PART OF A LARGER SAGA IN WHICH KANDOR WAS ABDUCTED INTO ANOTHER DIMENSION BY ALIENS CALLED THE PRESERVERS, WHO HAVE STOLEN OTHER CITIES ACROSS THE UNIVERSE. SEEKING TO RESCUE THE BOTTLE CITY, SUPERMAN ENTERED AN OTHERWORLDLY MAZE OF CAPTURED CITIES CALLED THE MUSEUM OF ETERNITY WHERE HE WAS DEFEATED BY THE PRESERVERS AFTER COMING UNDER THE INFLUENCE OF KANDOR'S RED SUN. THE CURATOR, THE PRESERVERS' LEADER, DISPATCHED A ROBOT CALLED THE PURIFIER TO DEFEAT KANDOR'S HEROES AND CAPTURE ALL SURVIVORS OF KRYPTON -- RELEASING THE VILLAINS FROM THE PHANTOM ZONE IN THE PROCESS. AFTER DISCOVERING THAT THE BARRIERS THAT SEPARATE THE CAPTIVE CITIES IMPEDE ONLY HUMANOIDS, NIGHTWING AND FLAMEBIRD SEND THE SUPER-DOG KRYPTO TO A YELLOW-SUN CITY TO REGAIN HIS POWERS AND BRING BACK HELP...,
THE MUSEUM OF ETERNITY
"FIGHT WITH THE PHANTOM ZONE FIENDS"
CRASH!
MOONS OF KRYPTON! THERE'S JUST NO GETTING THROUGH THAT BARRIER, VAN!
I'M NOT EVEN GETTING RADIO SIGNALS OUT! IF ONLY KRYPTO HAD MANAGED TO WRECK WHATEVER'S PRODUCING THE BARRIER...
HE'S BEEN GONE QUITE A WHILE, AK! LOOKS LIKE WE'LL HAVE TO GET THROUGH THAT BARRIER OURSELVES -- HUH!?
GREAT KRYPTON! THE PHANTOM ZONE CRIMINALS!
THAT'S RIGHT, HERO-- AND WE'VE ALL BEEN WAITING YEARS TO GET BACK AT YOU AND YOUR KIND!
CONTINUING THE GREATEST SAGA EVER OF THE SUPERMAN FAMILY BY:
PAUL KUPPERBERG * WRITER
KEN LANDGRAF & ROMEO TANGHAL * ARTISTS
TODD KLEIN * LETTERS
MARIO SEN * COLORS
1

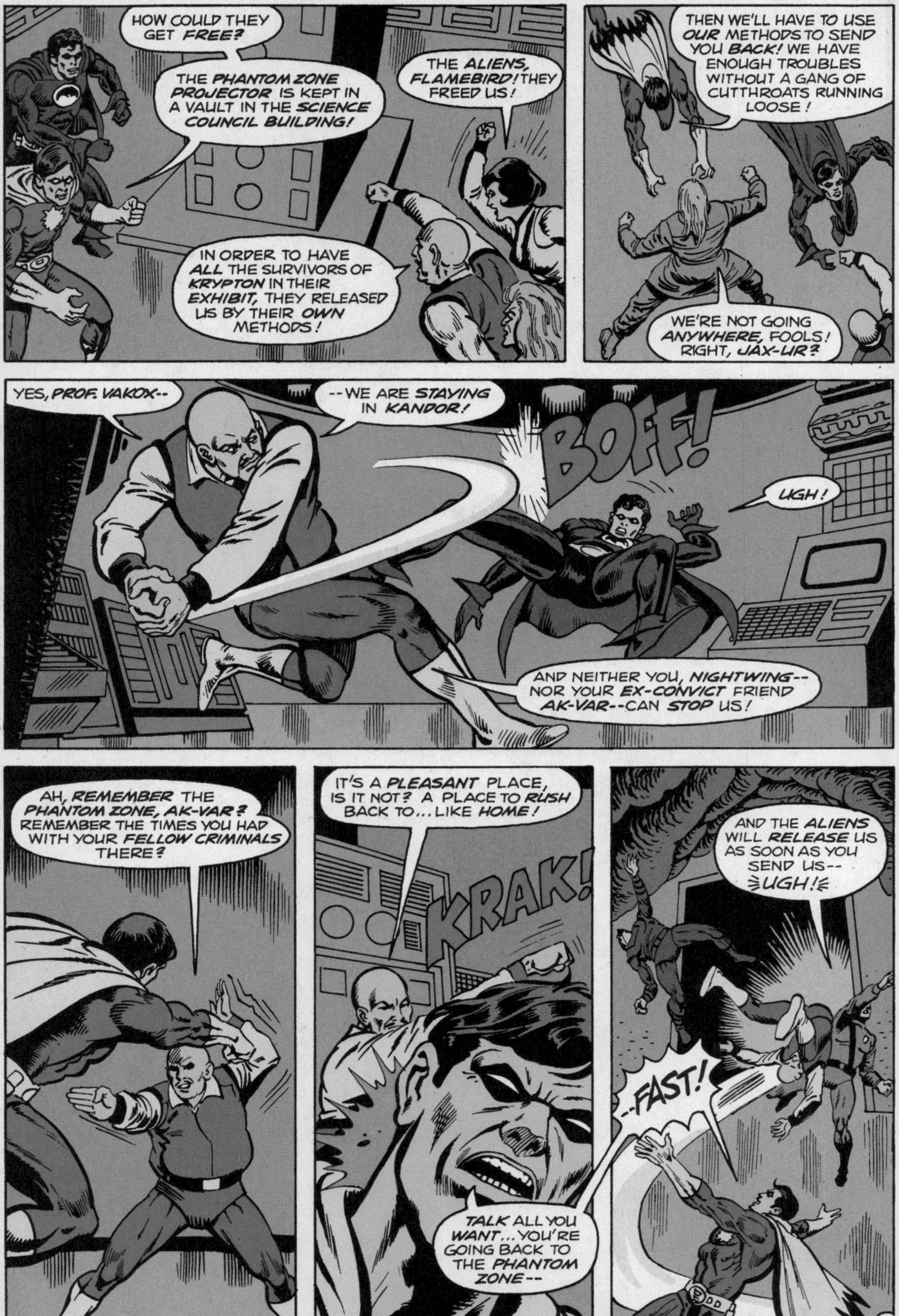
HOW COULD THEY GET FREE?
THE PHANTOM ZONE PROJECTOR IS KEPT IN A VAULT IN THE SCIENCE COUNCIL BUILDING!
THE ALIENS, FLAMEBIRD! THEY FREED US!
IN ORDER TO HAVE ALL THE SURVIVORS OF KRYPTON IN THEIR EXHIBIT, THEY RELEASED US BY THEIR OWN METHODS!
THEN WE'LL HAVE TO USE OUR METHODS TO SEND YOU BACK! WE HAVE ENOUGH TROUBLES WITHOUT A GANG OF CUTTHROATS RUNNING LOOSE!
WE'RE NOT GOING ANYWHERE, FOOLS! RIGHT, JAX-UR?
YES, PROF. VAKOX--
--WE ARE STAYING IN KANDOR!
BOFF!
UGH!
AND NEITHER YOU, NIGHTWING-- NOR YOUR EX-CONVICT FRIEND AK-VAR--CAN STOP US!
AH, REMEMBER THE PHANTOM ZONE, AK-VAR? REMEMBER THE TIMES YOU HAD WITH YOUR FELLOW CRIMINALS THERE?
IT'S A PLEASANT PLACE, IS IT NOT? A PLACE TO RUSH BACK TO... LIKE HOME!
KRAK!
TALK ALL YOU WANT... YOU'RE GOING BACK TO THE PHANTOM ZONE--
AND THE ALIENS WILL RELEASE US AS SOON AS YOU SEND US-- UGH!
--FAST!
2

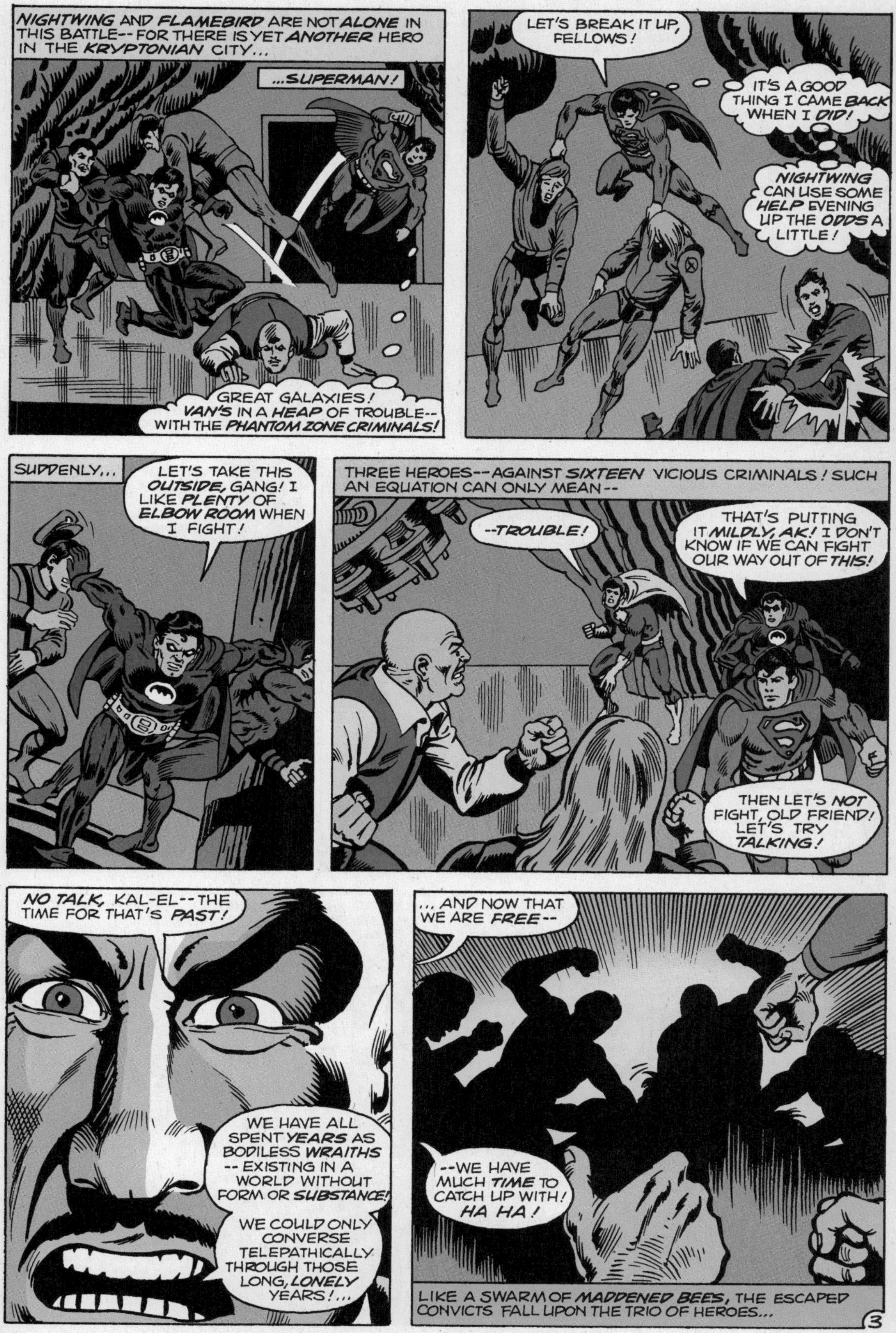
NIGHTWING AND FLAMEBIRD ARE NOT ALONE IN THIS BATTLE-- FOR THERE IS YET ANOTHER HERO IN THE KRYPTONIAN CITY...
...SUPERMAN!
GREAT GALAXIES! VAN'S IN A HEAP OF TROUBLE-- WITH THE PHANTOM ZONE CRIMINALS!
LET'S BREAK IT UP, FELLOWS!
IT'S A GOOD THING I CAME BACK WHEN I DID!
NIGHTWING CAN USE SOME HELP EVENING UP THE ODDS A LITTLE!
SUDDENLY,...
LET'S TAKE THIS OUTSIDE, GANG! I LIKE PLENTY OF ELBOW ROOM WHEN I FIGHT!
THREE HEROES--AGAINST SIXTEEN VICIOUS CRIMINALS! SUCH AN EQUATION CAN ONLY MEAN--
--TROUBLE!
THAT'S PUTTING IT MILDLY, AK! I DON'T KNOW IF WE CAN FIGHT OUR WAY OUT OF THIS!
THEN LET'S NOT FIGHT, OLD FRIEND! LET'S TRY TALKING!
NO TALK, KAL-EL--THE TIME FOR THAT'S PAST!
WE HAVE ALL SPENT YEARS AS BODILESS WRAITHS -- EXISTING IN A WORLD WITHOUT FORM OR SUBSTANCE!
WE COULD ONLY CONVERSE TELEPATHICALLY THROUGH THOSE LONG, LONELY YEARS!...
...AND NOW THAT WE ARE FREE--
--WE HAVE MUCH TIME TO CATCH UP WITH! HA HA!
LIKE A SWARM OF MADDENED BEES, THE ESCAPED CONVICTS FALL UPON THE TRIO OF HEROES...
3

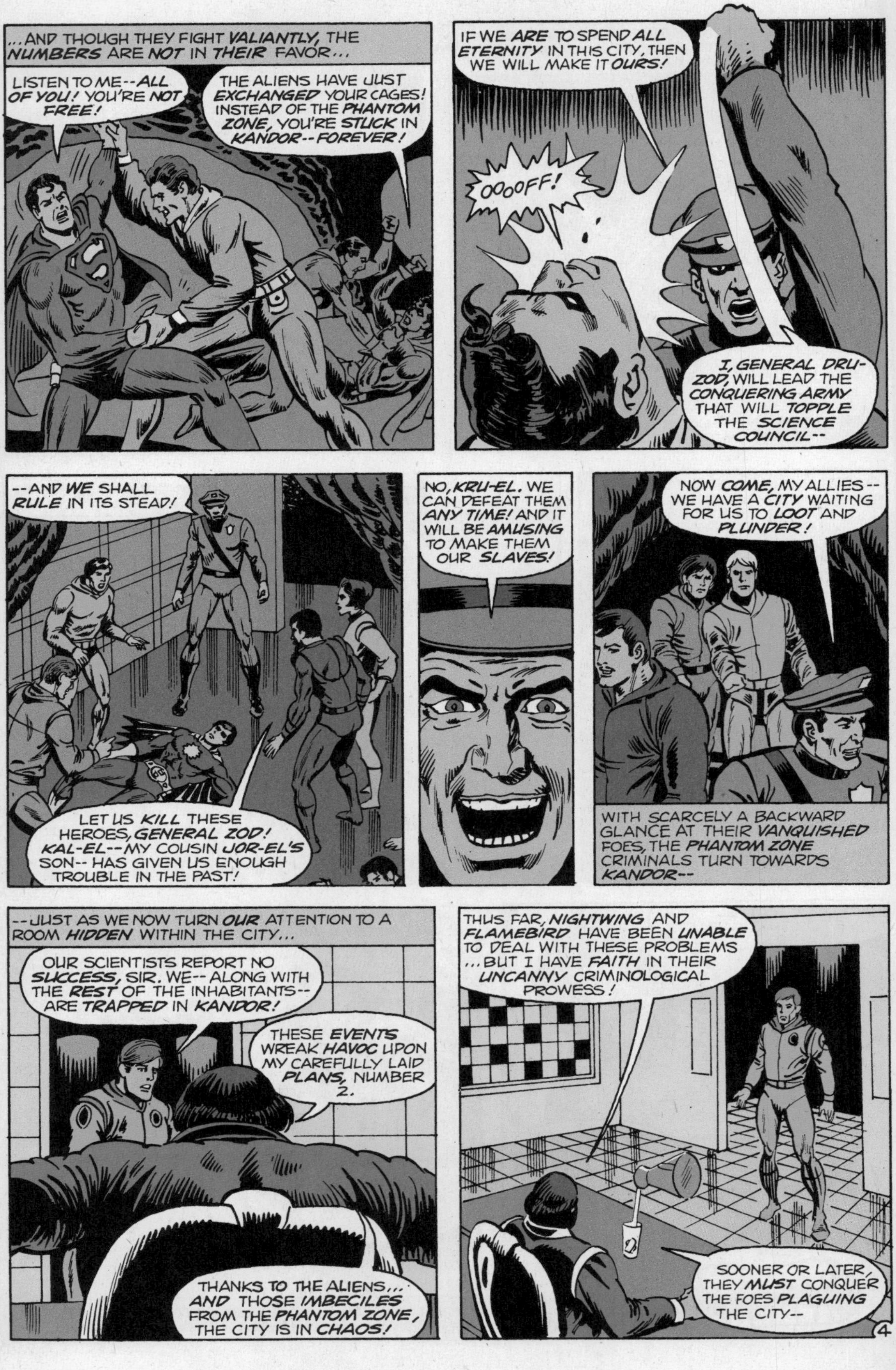
...AND THOUGH THEY FIGHT VALIANTLY, THE NUMBERS ARE NOT IN THEIR FAVOR...
LISTEN TO ME--ALL OF YOU! YOU'RE NOT FREE!
THE ALIENS HAVE JUST EXCHANGED YOUR CAGES! INSTEAD OF THE PHANTOM ZONE, YOU'RE STUCK IN KANDOR--FOREVER!
IF WE ARE TO SPEND ALL ETERNITY IN THIS CITY, THEN WE WILL MAKE IT OURS!
OOOOFF!
I, GENERAL DRU-ZOD, WILL LEAD THE CONQUERING ARMY THAT WILL TOPPLE THE SCIENCE COUNCIL--
--AND WE SHALL RULE IN ITS STEAD!
LET US KILL THESE HEROES, GENERAL ZOD! KAL-EL--MY COUSIN JOR-EL'S SON--HAS GIVEN US ENOUGH TROUBLE IN THE PAST!
NO, KRU-EL. WE CAN DEFEAT THEM ANY TIME! AND IT WILL BE AMUSING TO MAKE THEM OUR SLAVES!
NOW COME, MY ALLIES--WE HAVE A CITY WAITING FOR US TO LOOT AND PLUNDER!
WITH SCARCELY A BACKWARD GLANCE AT THEIR VANQUISHED FOES, THE PHANTOM ZONE CRIMINALS TURN TOWARDS KANDOR--
--JUST AS WE NOW TURN OUR ATTENTION TO A ROOM HIDDEN WITHIN THE CITY...
OUR SCIENTISTS REPORT NO SUCCESS, SIR. WE--ALONG WITH THE REST OF THE INHABITANTS--ARE TRAPPED IN KANDOR!
THESE EVENTS WREAK HAVOC UPON MY CAREFULLY LAID PLANS, NUMBER 2.
THANKS TO THE ALIENS... AND THOSE IMBECILES FROM THE PHANTOM ZONE, THE CITY IS IN CHAOS!
THUS FAR, NIGHTWING AND FLAMEBIRD HAVE BEEN UNABLE TO DEAL WITH THESE PROBLEMS ...BUT I HAVE FAITH IN THEIR UNCANNY CRIMINOLOGICAL PROWESS!
SOONER OR LATER, THEY MUST CONQUER THE FOES PLAGUING THE CITY--
4

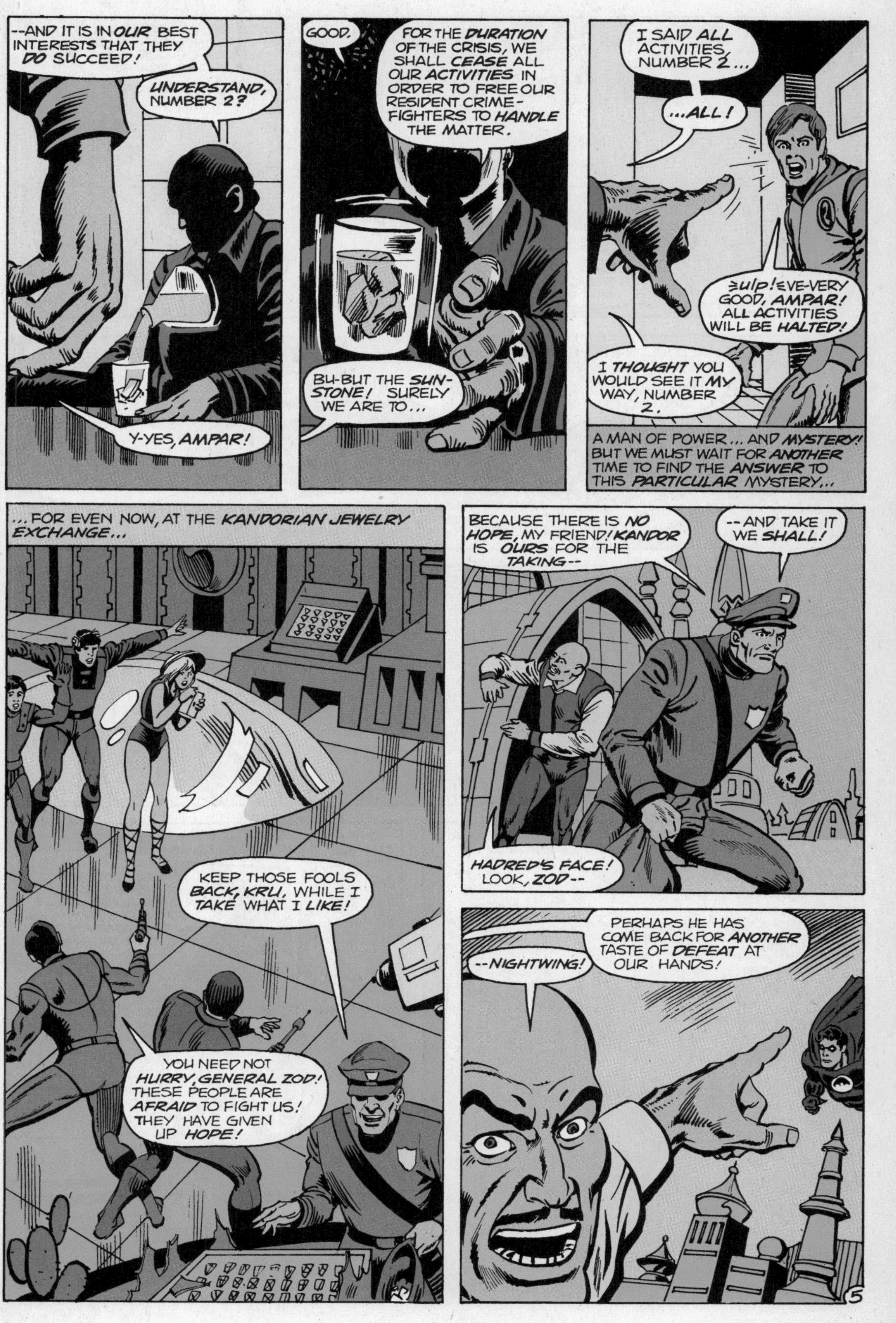
--AND IT IS IN OUR BEST INTERESTS THAT THEY DO SUCCEED!
UNDERSTAND, NUMBER 2?
Y-YES, AMPAR!
GOOD.
FOR THE DURATION OF THE CRISIS, WE SHALL CEASE ALL OUR ACTIVITIES IN ORDER TO FREE OUR RESIDENT CRIME-FIGHTERS TO HANDLE THE MATTER.
BU-BUT THE SUN-STONE! SURELY WE ARE TO...
I SAID ALL ACTIVITIES, NUMBER 2...
...ALL!
gulp! EVE-VERY GOOD, AMPAR! ALL ACTIVITIES WILL BE HALTED!
I THOUGHT YOU WOULD SEE IT MY WAY, NUMBER 2.
A MAN OF POWER... AND MYSTERY! BUT WE MUST WAIT FOR ANOTHER TIME TO FIND THE ANSWER TO THIS PARTICULAR MYSTERY...
...FOR EVEN NOW, AT THE KANDORIAN JEWELRY EXCHANGE...
KEEP THOSE FOOLS BACK, KRU, WHILE I TAKE WHAT I LIKE!
YOU NEED NOT HURRY, GENERAL ZOD! THESE PEOPLE ARE AFRAID TO FIGHT US! THEY HAVE GIVEN UP HOPE!
BECAUSE THERE IS NO HOPE, MY FRIEND! KANDOR IS OURS FOR THE TAKING--
--AND TAKE IT WE SHALL!
HADRED'S FACE! LOOK, ZOD--
--NIGHTWING!
PERHAPS HE HAS COME BACK FOR ANOTHER TASTE OF DEFEAT AT OUR HANDS!
5

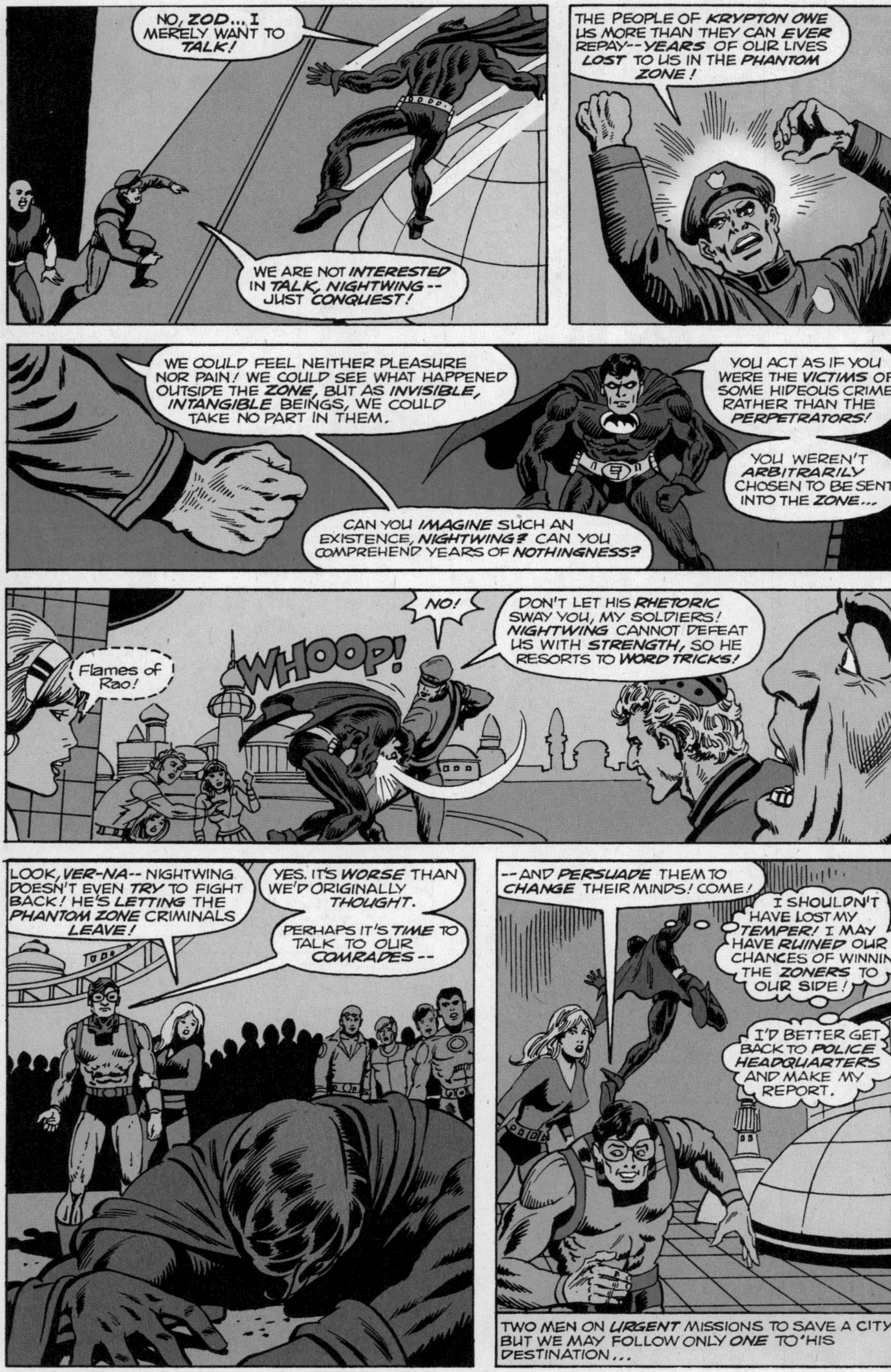
NO, ZOD... I MERELY WANT TO TALK!
WE ARE NOT INTERESTED IN TALK, NIGHTWING -- JUST CONQUEST!
THE PEOPLE OF KRYPTON OWE US MORE THAN THEY CAN EVER REPAY--YEARS OF OUR LIVES LOST TO US IN THE PHANTOM ZONE!
WE COULD FEEL NEITHER PLEASURE NOR PAIN! WE COULD SEE WHAT HAPPENED OUTSIDE THE ZONE, BUT AS INVISIBLE, INTANGIBLE BEINGS, WE COULD TAKE NO PART IN THEM.
CAN YOU IMAGINE SUCH AN EXISTENCE, NIGHTWING? CAN YOU COMPREHEND YEARS OF NOTHINGNESS?
YOU ACT AS IF YOU WERE THE VICTIMS OF SOME HIDEOUS CRIME RATHER THAN THE PERPETRATORS!
YOU WEREN'T ARBITRARILY CHOSEN TO BE SENT INTO THE ZONE...
Flames of Rao!
WHOOP!
NO!
DON'T LET HIS RHETORIC SWAY YOU, MY SOLDIERS! NIGHTWING CANNOT DEFEAT US WITH STRENGTH, SO HE RESORTS TO WORD TRICKS!
LOOK, VER-NA-- NIGHTWING DOESN'T EVEN TRY TO FIGHT BACK! HE'S LETTING THE PHANTOM ZONE CRIMINALS LEAVE!
YES. IT'S WORSE THAN WE'D ORIGINALLY THOUGHT.
PERHAPS IT'S TIME TO TALK TO OUR COMRADES --
--AND PERSUADE THEM TO CHANGE THEIR MINDS! COME!
I SHOULDN'T HAVE LOST MY TEMPER! I MAY HAVE RUINED OUR CHANCES OF WINNING THE ZONERS TO OUR SIDE!
I'D BETTER GET BACK TO POLICE HEADQUARTERS AND MAKE MY REPORT.
TWO MEN ON URGENT MISSIONS TO SAVE A CITY! BUT WE MAY FOLLOW ONLY ONE TO HIS DESTINATION...
6

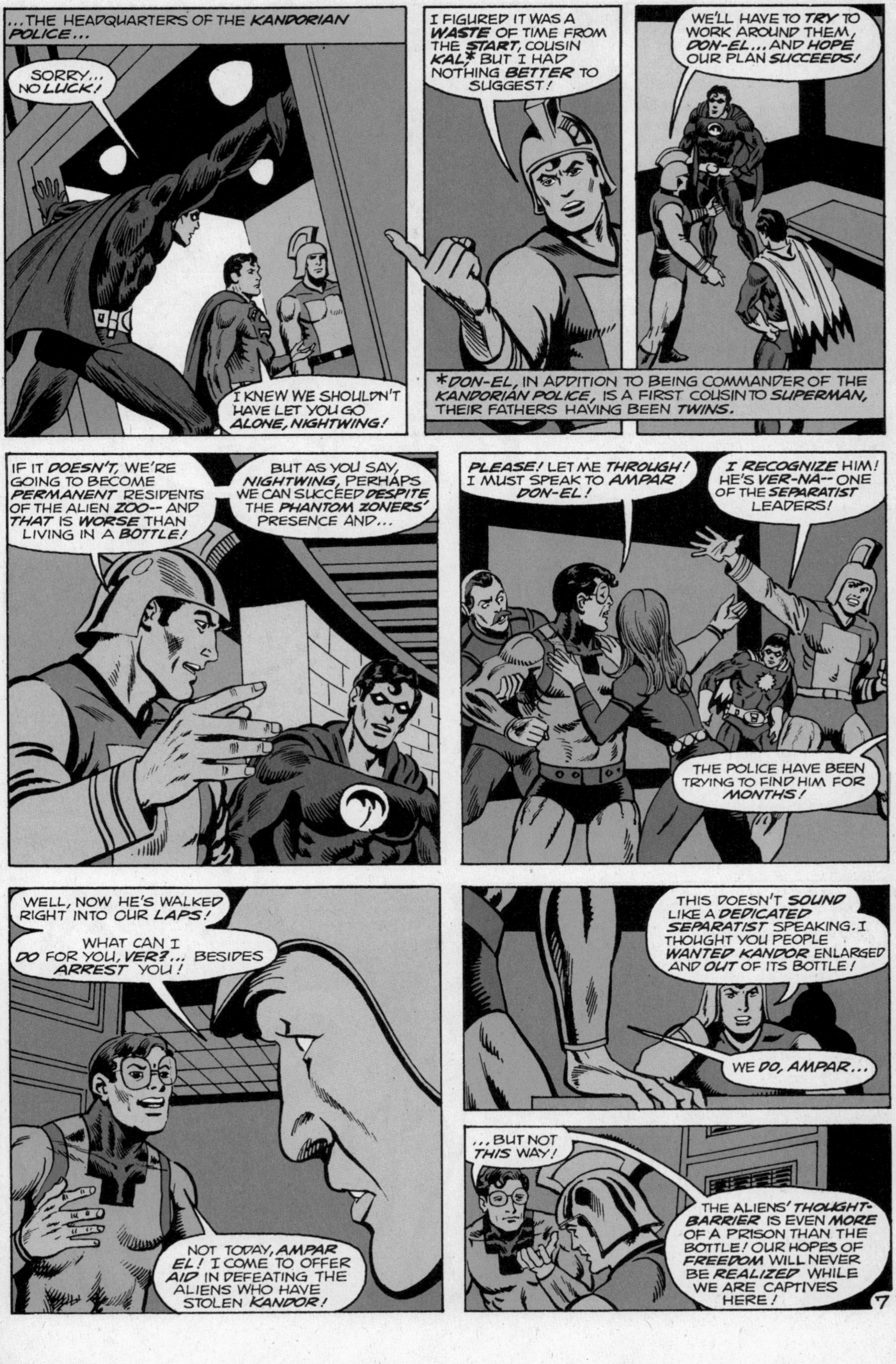
...THE HEADQUARTERS OF THE KANDORIAN POLICE...
SORRY... NO LUCK!
I KNEW WE SHOULDN'T HAVE LET YOU GO ALONE, NIGHTWING!
I FIGURED IT WAS A WASTE OF TIME FROM THE START, COUSIN KAL!* BUT I HAD NOTHING BETTER TO SUGGEST!
WE'LL HAVE TO TRY TO WORK AROUND THEM, DON-EL... AND HOPE OUR PLAN SUCCEEDS!
*DON-EL, IN ADDITION TO BEING COMMANDER OF THE KANDORIAN POLICE, IS A FIRST COUSIN TO SUPERMAN, THEIR FATHERS HAVING BEEN TWINS.
IF IT DOESN'T, WE'RE GOING TO BECOME PERMANENT RESIDENTS OF THE ALIEN ZOO-- AND THAT IS WORSE THAN LIVING IN A BOTTLE!
BUT AS YOU SAY, NIGHTWING, PERHAPS WE CAN SUCCEED DESPITE THE PHANTOM ZONERS' PRESENCE AND...
PLEASE! LET ME THROUGH! I MUST SPEAK TO AMPAR DON-EL!
I RECOGNIZE HIM! HE'S VER-NA-- ONE OF THE SEPARATIST LEADERS!
THE POLICE HAVE BEEN TRYING TO FIND HIM FOR MONTHS!
WELL, NOW HE'S WALKED RIGHT INTO OUR LAPS!
WHAT CAN I DO FOR YOU, VER?... BESIDES ARREST YOU!
NOT TODAY, AMPAR EL! I COME TO OFFER AID IN DEFEATING THE ALIENS WHO HAVE STOLEN KANDOR!
THIS DOESN'T SOUND LIKE A DEDICATED SEPARATIST SPEAKING. I THOUGHT YOU PEOPLE WANTED KANDOR ENLARGED AND OUT OF ITS BOTTLE!
WE DO, AMPAR...
...BUT NOT THIS WAY!
THE ALIENS' THOUGHT-BARRIER IS EVEN MORE OF A PRISON THAN THE BOTTLE! OUR HOPES OF FREEDOM WILL NEVER BE REALIZED WHILE WE ARE CAPTIVES HERE!
7

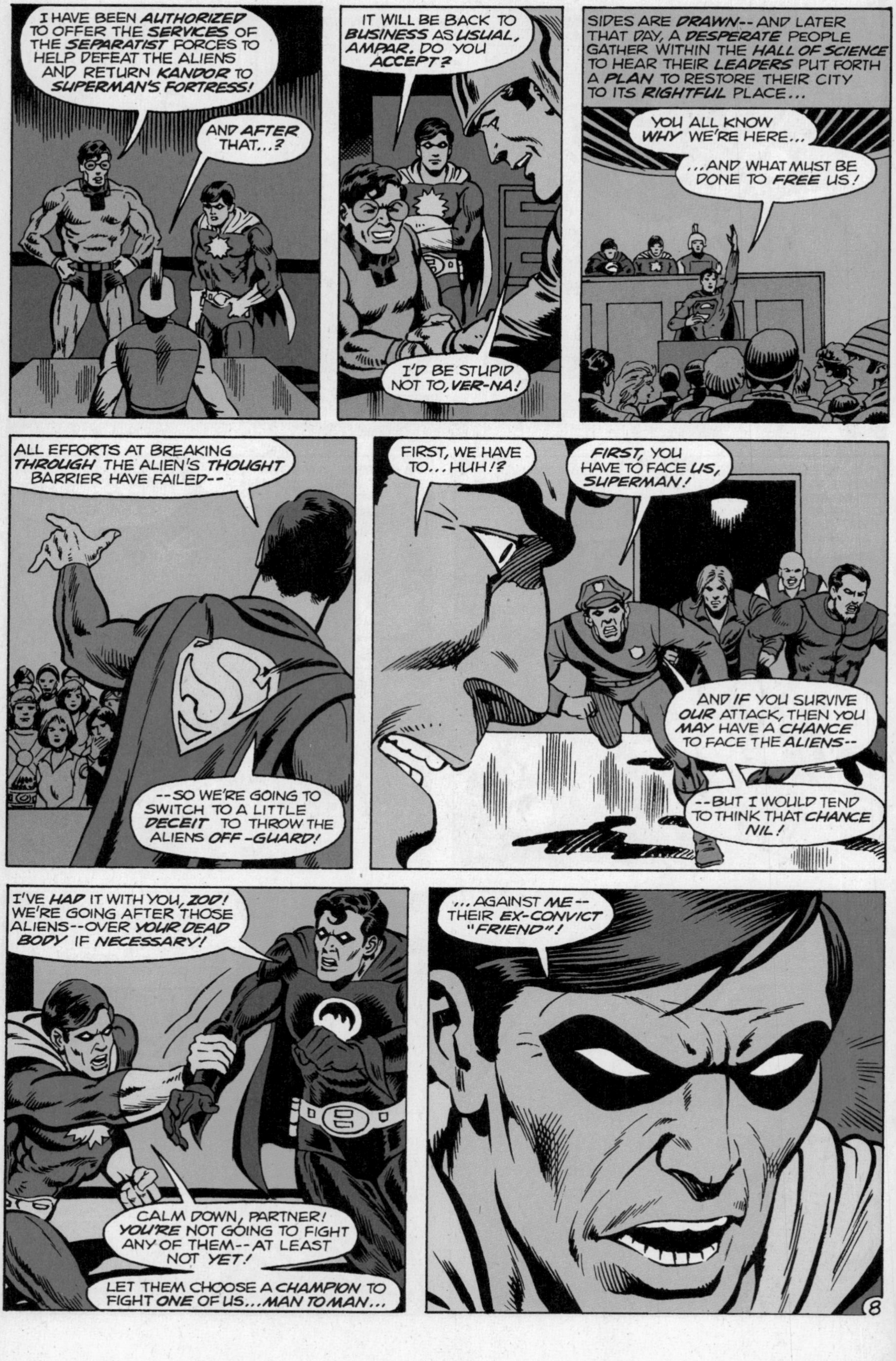

I HAVE BEEN AUTHORIZED TO OFFER THE SERVICES OF THE SEPARATIST FORCES TO HELP DEFEAT THE ALIENS AND RETURN KANDOR TO SUPERMAN'S FORTRESS!
AND AFTER THAT...?
IT WILL BE BACK TO BUSINESS AS USUAL, AMPAR. DO YOU ACCEPT?
I'D BE STUPID NOT TO, VER-NA!
SIDES ARE DRAWN-- AND LATER THAT DAY, A DESPERATE PEOPLE GATHER WITHIN THE HALL OF SCIENCE TO HEAR THEIR LEADERS PUT FORTH A PLAN TO RESTORE THEIR CITY TO ITS RIGHTFUL PLACE...
YOU ALL KNOW WHY WE'RE HERE...
...AND WHAT MUST BE DONE TO FREE US!
ALL EFFORTS AT BREAKING THROUGH THE ALIEN'S THOUGHT BARRIER HAVE FAILED--
--SO WE'RE GOING TO SWITCH TO A LITTLE DECEIT TO THROW THE ALIENS OFF-GUARD!
FIRST, WE HAVE TO... HUH!?
FIRST, YOU HAVE TO FACE US, SUPERMAN!
AND IF YOU SURVIVE OUR ATTACK, THEN YOU MAY HAVE A CHANCE TO FACE THE ALIENS--
--BUT I WOULD TEND TO THINK THAT CHANCE NIL!
I'VE HAD IT WITH YOU, ZOD! WE'RE GOING AFTER THOSE ALIENS--OVER YOUR DEAD BODY IF NECESSARY!
CALM DOWN, PARTNER! YOU'RE NOT GOING TO FIGHT ANY OF THEM--AT LEAST NOT YET!
LET THEM CHOOSE A CHAMPION TO FIGHT ONE OF US...MAN TO MAN...
...AGAINST ME-- THEIR EX-CONVICT "FRIEND"!
8

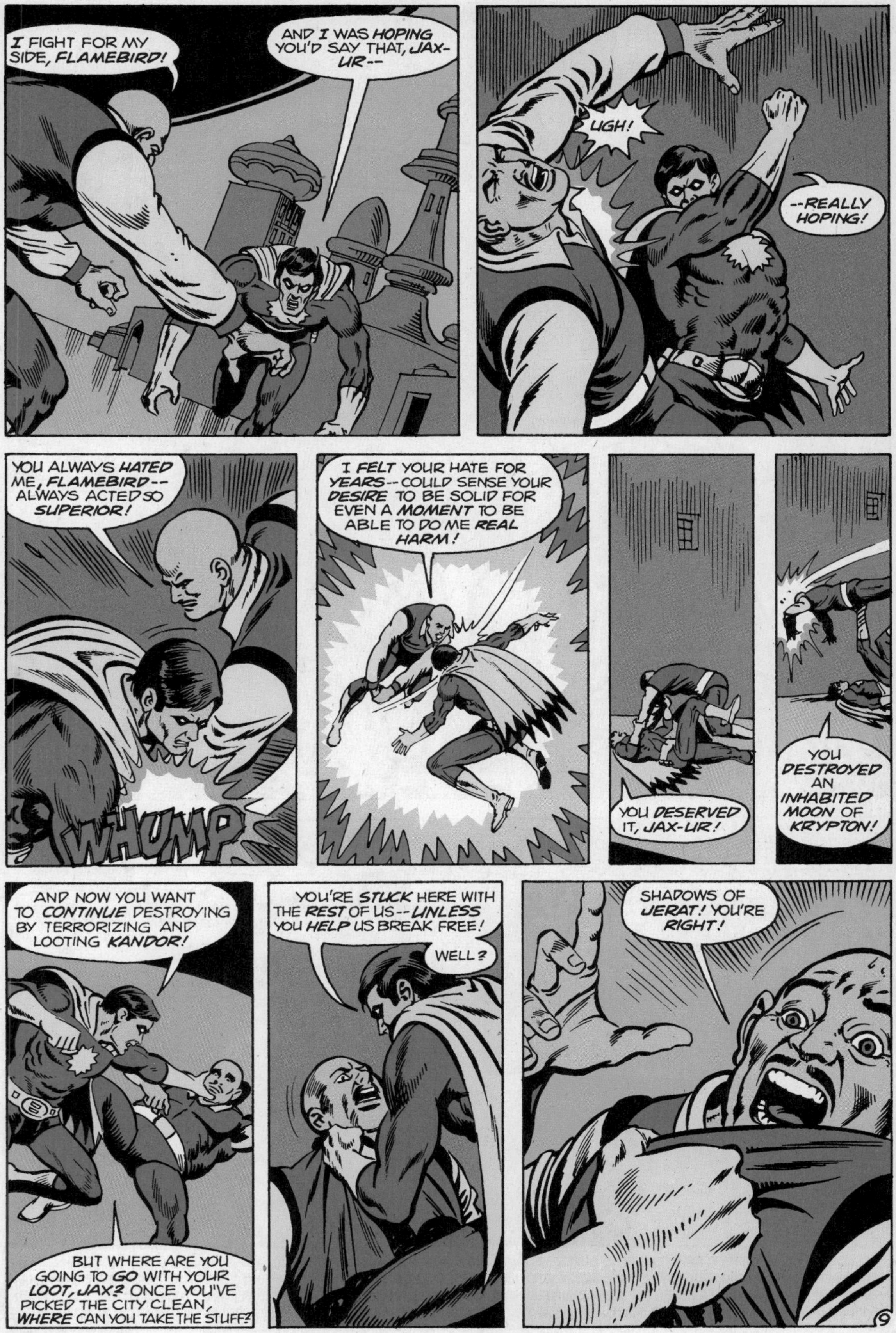
I FIGHT FOR MY SIDE, FLAMEBIRD!
AND I WAS HOPING YOU'D SAY THAT, JAX-UR--
UGH!
--REALLY HOPING!
YOU ALWAYS HATED ME, FLAMEBIRD-- ALWAYS ACTED SO SUPERIOR!
WHUMP
I FELT YOUR HATE FOR YEARS--COULD SENSE YOUR DESIRE TO BE SOLID FOR EVEN A MOMENT TO BE ABLE TO DO ME REAL HARM!
YOU DESERVED IT, JAX-UR!
YOU DESTROYED AN INHABITED MOON OF KRYPTON!
AND NOW YOU WANT TO CONTINUE DESTROYING BY TERRORIZING AND LOOTING KANDOR!
BUT WHERE ARE YOU GOING TO GO WITH YOUR LOOT, JAX? ONCE YOU'VE PICKED THE CITY CLEAN, WHERE CAN YOU TAKE THE STUFF?
YOU'RE STUCK HERE WITH THE REST OF US--UNLESS YOU HELP US BREAK FREE!
WELL?
SHADOWS OF JERAT! YOU'RE RIGHT!
9

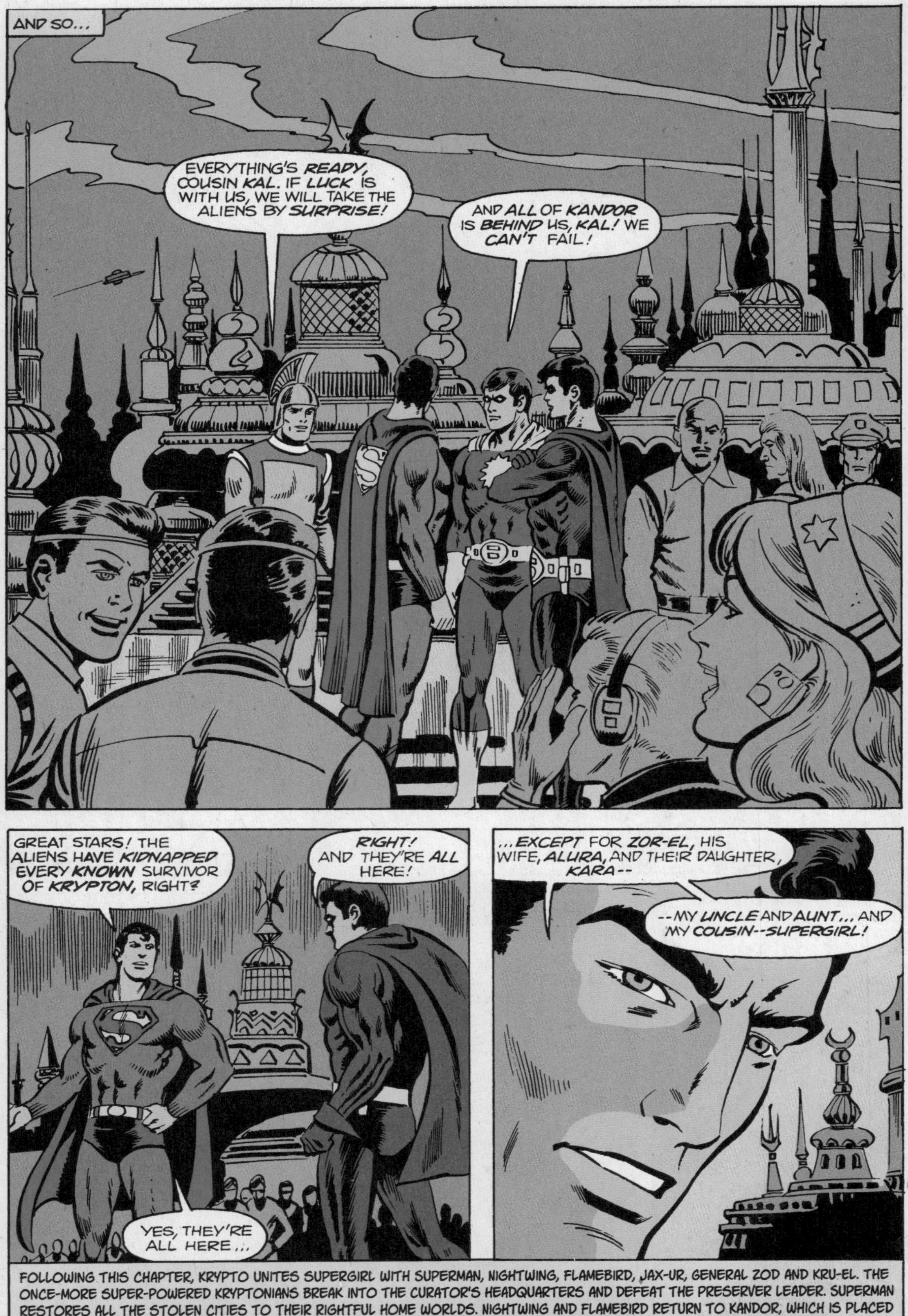
AND SO...
EVERYTHING'S READY, COUSIN KAL. IF LUCK IS WITH US, WE WILL TAKE THE ALIENS BY SURPRISE!
AND ALL OF KANDOR IS BEHIND US, KAL! WE CAN'T FAIL!
GREAT STARS! THE ALIENS HAVE KIDNAPPED EVERY KNOWN SURVIVOR OF KRYPTON, RIGHT?
RIGHT! AND THEY'RE ALL HERE!
YES, THEY'RE ALL HERE...
...EXCEPT FOR ZOR-EL, HIS WIFE, ALURA, AND THEIR DAUGHTER, KARA--
--MY UNCLE AND AUNT... AND MY COUSIN--SUPERGIRL!
FOLLOWING THIS CHAPTER, KRYPTO UNITES SUPERGIRL WITH SUPERMAN, NIGHTWING, FLAMEBIRD, JAX-UR, GENERAL ZOD AND KRU-EL. THE ONCE-MORE SUPER-POWERED KRYPTONIANS BREAK INTO THE CURATOR'S HEADQUARTERS AND DEFEAT THE PRESERVER LEADER. SUPERMAN RESTORES ALL THE STOLEN CITIES TO THEIR RIGHTFUL HOME WORLDS. NIGHTWING AND FLAMEBIRD RETURN TO KANDOR, WHICH IS PLACED SAFELY BACK IN THE FORTRESS OF SOLITUDE, WHILE THE KRYPTONIAN CRIMINALS RESUME THEIR EXILE IN THE PHANTOM ZONE.
10

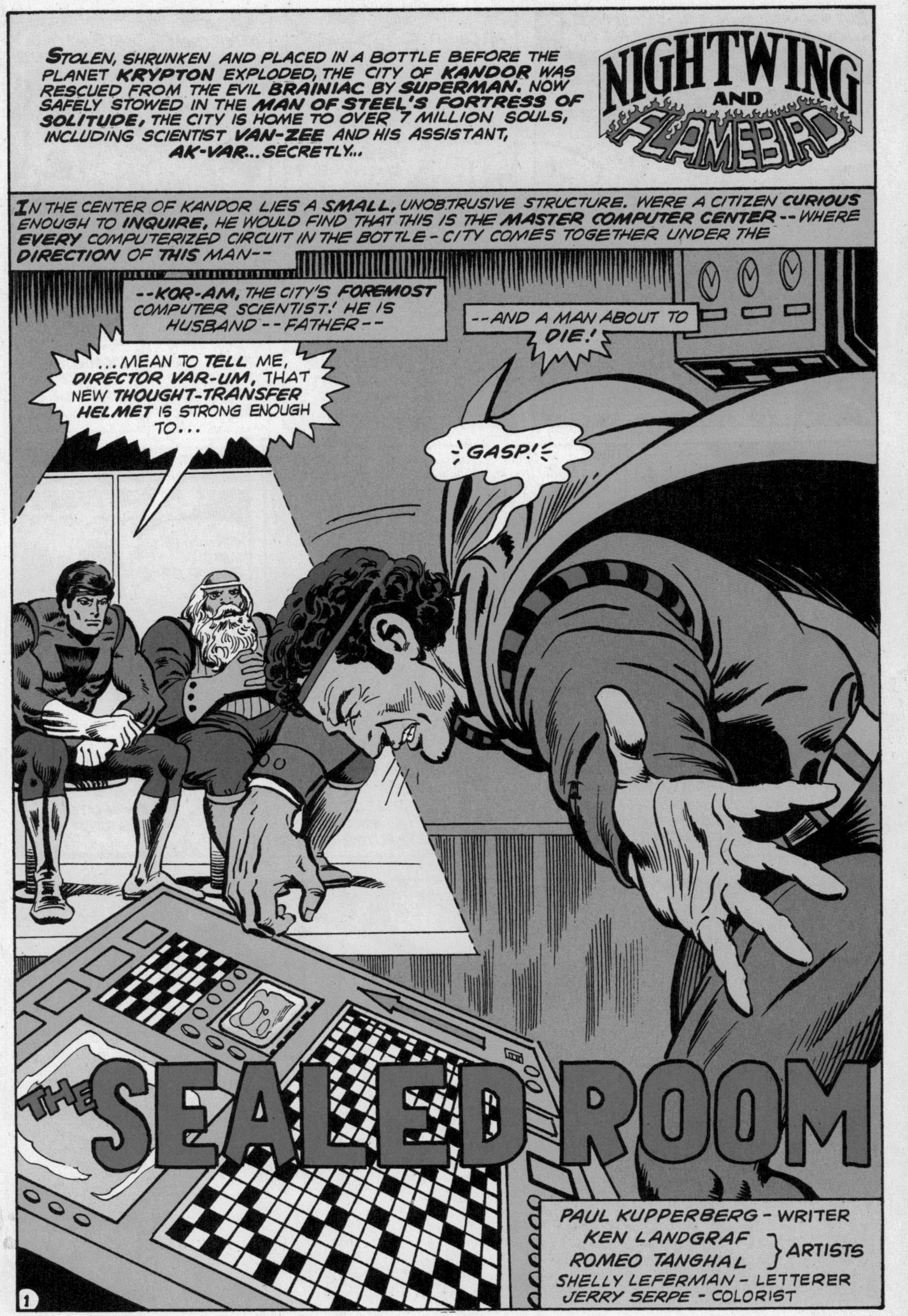
STOLEN, SHRUNKEN AND PLACED IN A BOTTLE BEFORE THE PLANET KRYPTON EXPLODED, THE CITY OF KANDOR WAS RESCUED FROM THE EVIL BRAINIAC BY SUPERMAN. NOW SAFELY STOWED IN THE MAN OF STEEL'S FORTRESS OF SOLITUDE, THE CITY IS HOME TO OVER 7 MILLION SOULS, INCLUDING SCIENTIST VAN-ZEE AND HIS ASSISTANT, AK-VAR... SECRETLY...
NIGHTWING AND FLAMEBIRD
IN THE CENTER OF KANDOR LIES A SMALL, UNOBTRUSIVE STRUCTURE. WERE A CITIZEN CURIOUS ENOUGH TO INQUIRE, HE WOULD FIND THAT THIS IS THE MASTER COMPUTER CENTER -- WHERE EVERY COMPUTERIZED CIRCUIT IN THE BOTTLE-CITY COMES TOGETHER UNDER THE DIRECTION OF THIS MAN--
--KOR-AM, THE CITY'S FOREMOST COMPUTER SCIENTIST! HE IS HUSBAND -- FATHER --
--AND A MAN ABOUT TO DIE!
...MEAN TO TELL ME, DIRECTOR VAR-UM, THAT NEW THOUGHT-TRANSFER HELMET IS STRONG ENOUGH TO...
GASP!
THE SEALED ROOM
PAUL KUPPERBERG - WRITER
KEN LANDGRAF
ROMEO TANGHAL
ARTISTS
SHELLY LEFERMAN - LETTERER
JERRY SERPE - COLORIST
1

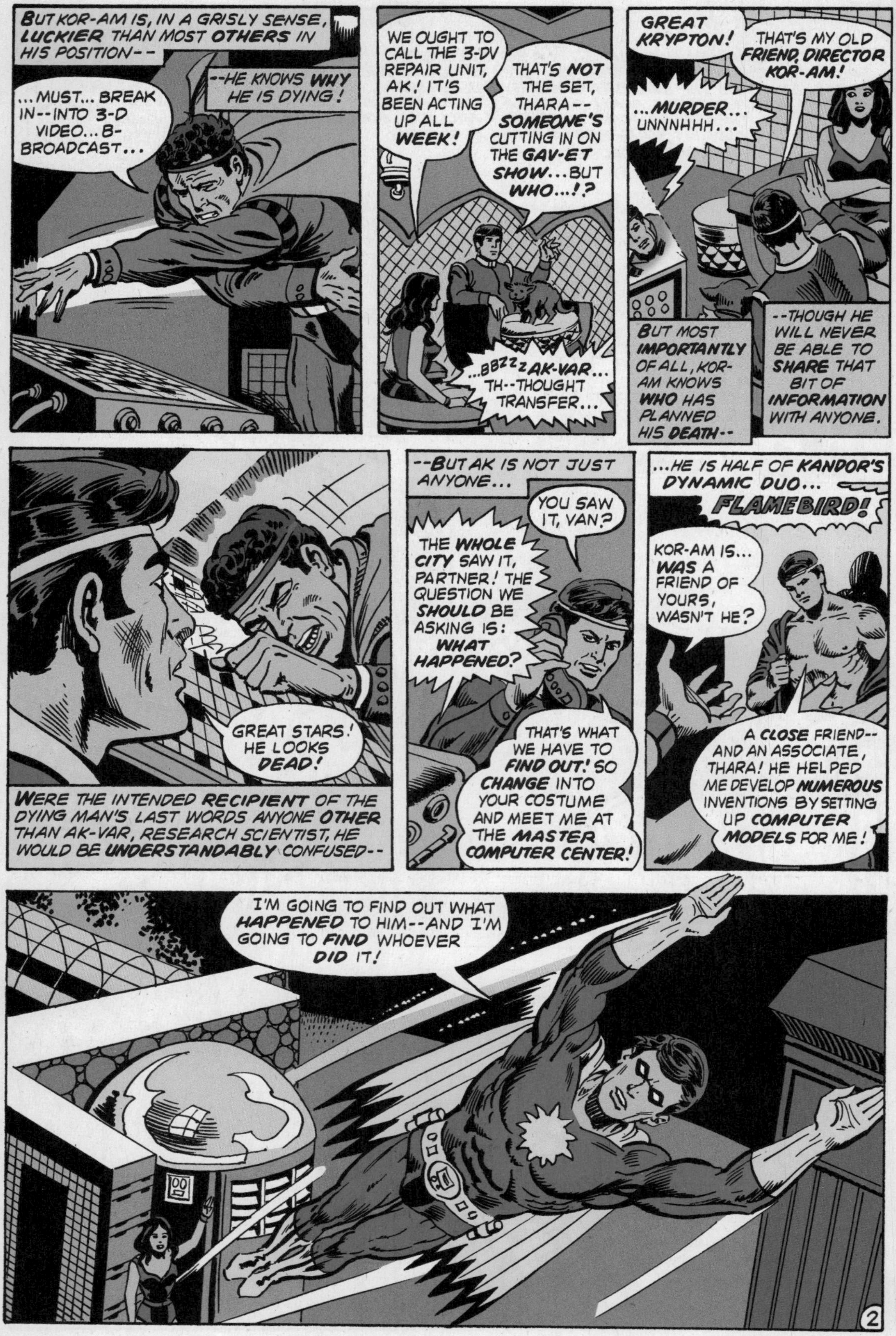
BUT KOR-AM IS, IN A GRISLY SENSE, LUCKIER THAN MOST OTHERS IN HIS POSITION--
--HE KNOWS WHY HE IS DYING!
...MUST... BREAK IN--INTO 3-D VIDEO... B-BROADCAST...
WE OUGHT TO CALL THE 3-DV REPAIR UNIT, AK! IT'S BEEN ACTING UP ALL WEEK!
THAT'S NOT THE SET, THARA--SOMEONE'S CUTTING IN ON THE GAV-ET SHOW...BUT WHO...!?
...BBZZZ AK-VAR... TH--THOUGHT TRANSFER...
GREAT KRYPTON!
THAT'S MY OLD FRIEND, DIRECTOR KOR-AM!
...MURDER... UNNNHHH...
BUT MOST IMPORTANTLY OF ALL, KOR-AM KNOWS WHO HAS PLANNED HIS DEATH--
--THOUGH HE WILL NEVER BE ABLE TO SHARE THAT BIT OF INFORMATION WITH ANYONE.
GREAT STARS! HE LOOKS DEAD!
WERE THE INTENDED RECIPIENT OF THE DYING MAN'S LAST WORDS ANYONE OTHER THAN AK-VAR, RESEARCH SCIENTIST, HE WOULD BE UNDERSTANDABLY CONFUSED--
--BUT AK IS NOT JUST ANYONE...
YOU SAW IT, VAN?
THE WHOLE CITY SAW IT, PARTNER! THE QUESTION WE SHOULD BE ASKING IS: WHAT HAPPENED?
THAT'S WHAT WE HAVE TO FIND OUT! SO CHANGE INTO YOUR COSTUME AND MEET ME AT THE MASTER COMPUTER CENTER!
...HE IS HALF OF KANDOR'S DYNAMIC DUO... FLAMEBIRD!
KOR-AM IS... WAS A FRIEND OF YOURS, WASN'T HE?
A CLOSE FRIEND--AND AN ASSOCIATE, THARA! HE HELPED ME DEVELOP NUMEROUS INVENTIONS BY SETTING UP COMPUTER MODELS FOR ME!
I'M GOING TO FIND OUT WHAT HAPPENED TO HIM--AND I'M GOING TO FIND WHOEVER DID IT!
2

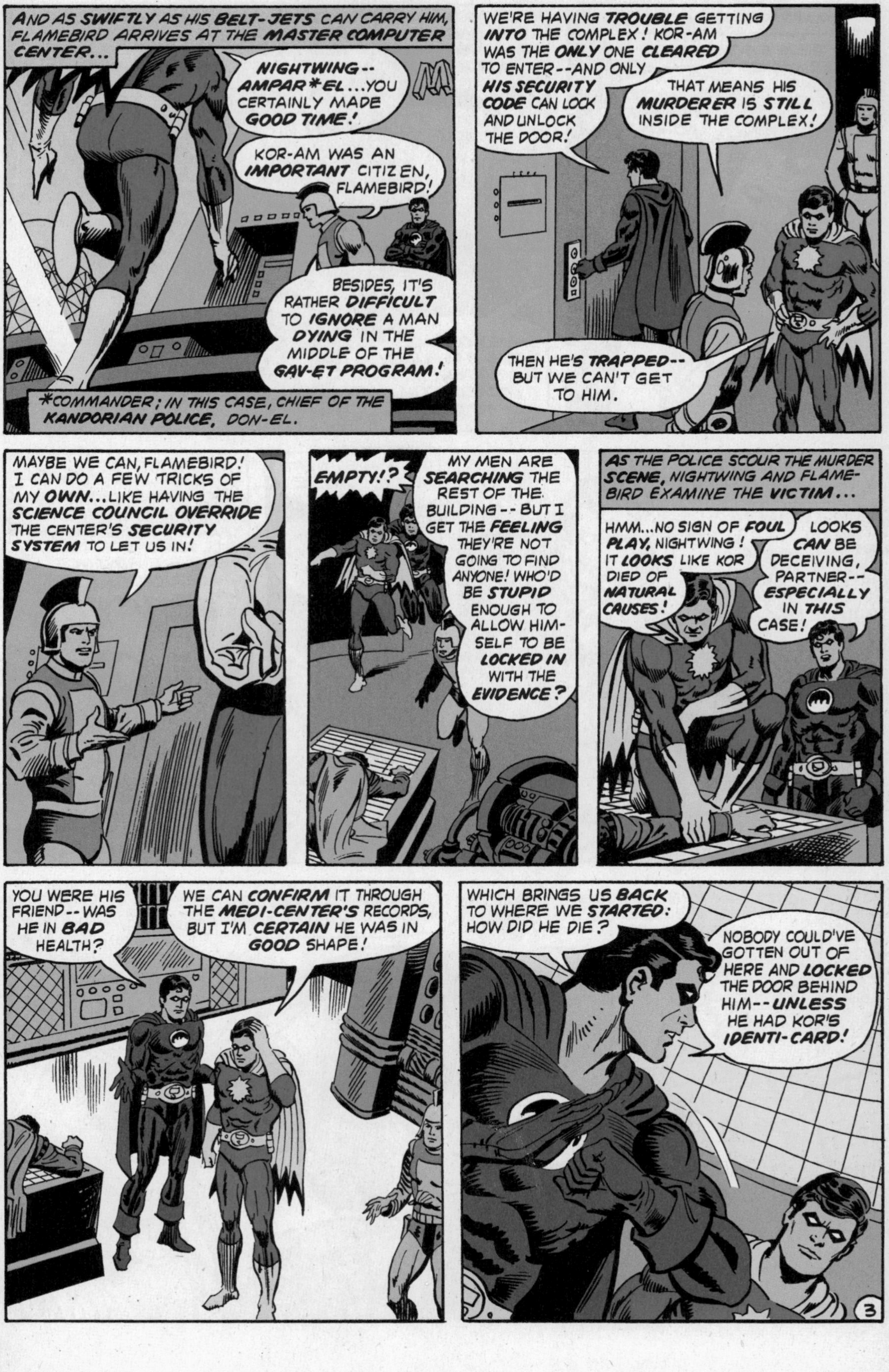
AND AS SWIFTLY AS HIS BELT-JETS CAN CARRY HIM, FLAMEBIRD ARRIVES AT THE MASTER COMPUTER CENTER...
NIGHTWING--AMPAR*EL...YOU CERTAINLY MADE GOOD TIME!
KOR-AM WAS AN IMPORTANT CITIZEN, FLAMEBIRD!
BESIDES, IT'S RATHER DIFFICULT TO IGNORE A MAN DYING IN THE MIDDLE OF THE GAV-ET PROGRAM!
*COMMANDER; IN THIS CASE, CHIEF OF THE KANDORIAN POLICE, DON-EL.
WE'RE HAVING TROUBLE GETTING INTO THE COMPLEX! KOR-AM WAS THE ONLY ONE CLEARED TO ENTER--AND ONLY HIS SECURITY CODE CAN LOCK AND UNLOCK THE DOOR!
THAT MEANS HIS MURDERER IS STILL INSIDE THE COMPLEX!
THEN HE'S TRAPPED--BUT WE CAN'T GET TO HIM.
MAYBE WE CAN, FLAMEBIRD! I CAN DO A FEW TRICKS OF MY OWN...LIKE HAVING THE SCIENCE COUNCIL OVERRIDE THE CENTER'S SECURITY SYSTEM TO LET US IN!
EMPTY!?
MY MEN ARE SEARCHING THE REST OF THE BUILDING--BUT I GET THE FEELING THEY'RE NOT GOING TO FIND ANYONE! WHO'D BE STUPID ENOUGH TO ALLOW HIMSELF TO BE LOCKED IN WITH THE EVIDENCE?
AS THE POLICE SCOUR THE MURDER SCENE, NIGHTWING AND FLAMEBIRD EXAMINE THE VICTIM...
HMM...NO SIGN OF FOUL PLAY, NIGHTWING! IT LOOKS LIKE KOR DIED OF NATURAL CAUSES!
LOOKS CAN BE DECEIVING, PARTNER--ESPECIALLY IN THIS CASE!
YOU WERE HIS FRIEND--WAS HE IN BAD HEALTH?
WE CAN CONFIRM IT THROUGH THE MEDI-CENTER'S RECORDS, BUT I'M CERTAIN HE WAS IN GOOD SHAPE!
WHICH BRINGS US BACK TO WHERE WE STARTED: HOW DID HE DIE?
NOBODY COULD'VE GOTTEN OUT OF HERE AND LOCKED THE DOOR BEHIND HIM--UNLESS HE HAD KOR'S IDENTI-CARD!
3

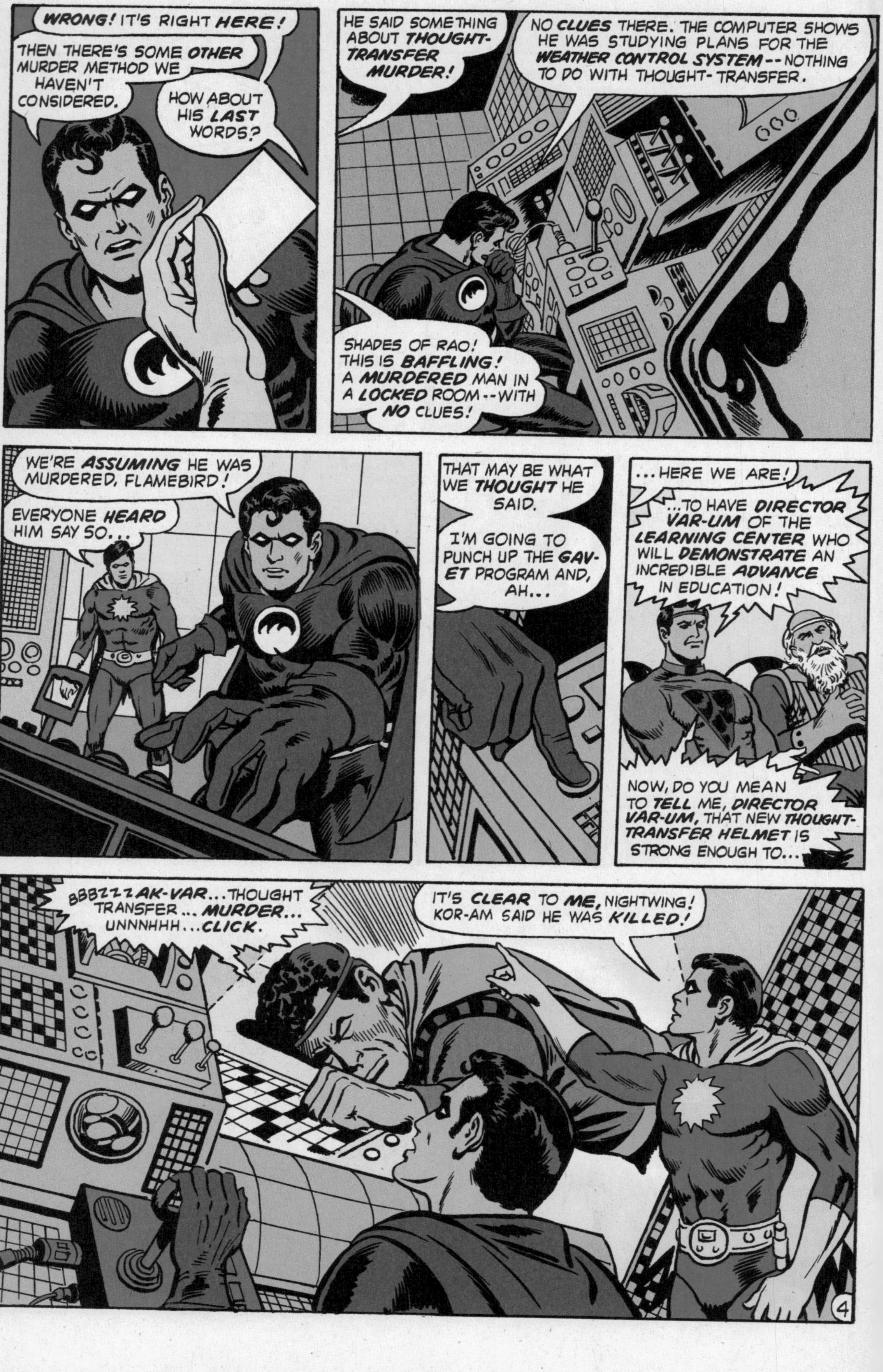

WRONG! IT'S RIGHT HERE!
THEN THERE'S SOME OTHER MURDER METHOD WE HAVEN'T CONSIDERED.
HOW ABOUT HIS LAST WORDS?
HE SAID SOMETHING ABOUT THOUGHT-TRANSFER MURDER!
NO CLUES THERE. THE COMPUTER SHOWS HE WAS STUDYING PLANS FOR THE WEATHER CONTROL SYSTEM -- NOTHING TO DO WITH THOUGHT-TRANSFER.
SHADES OF RAO! THIS IS BAFFLING! A MURDERED MAN IN A LOCKED ROOM -- WITH NO CLUES!
WE'RE ASSUMING HE WAS MURDERED, FLAMEBIRD!
EVERYONE HEARD HIM SAY SO...
THAT MAY BE WHAT WE THOUGHT HE SAID.
I'M GOING TO PUNCH UP THE GAV-ET PROGRAM AND, AH...
... HERE WE ARE!
...TO HAVE DIRECTOR VAR-UM OF THE LEARNING CENTER WHO WILL DEMONSTRATE AN INCREDIBLE ADVANCE IN EDUCATION!
NOW, DO YOU MEAN TO TELL ME, DIRECTOR VAR-UM, THAT NEW THOUGHT-TRANSFER HELMET IS STRONG ENOUGH TO...
BBBZZZAK-VAR... THOUGHT TRANSFER... MURDER... UNNNHHH... CLICK.
IT'S CLEAR TO ME, NIGHTWING! KOR-AM SAID HE WAS KILLED!
4

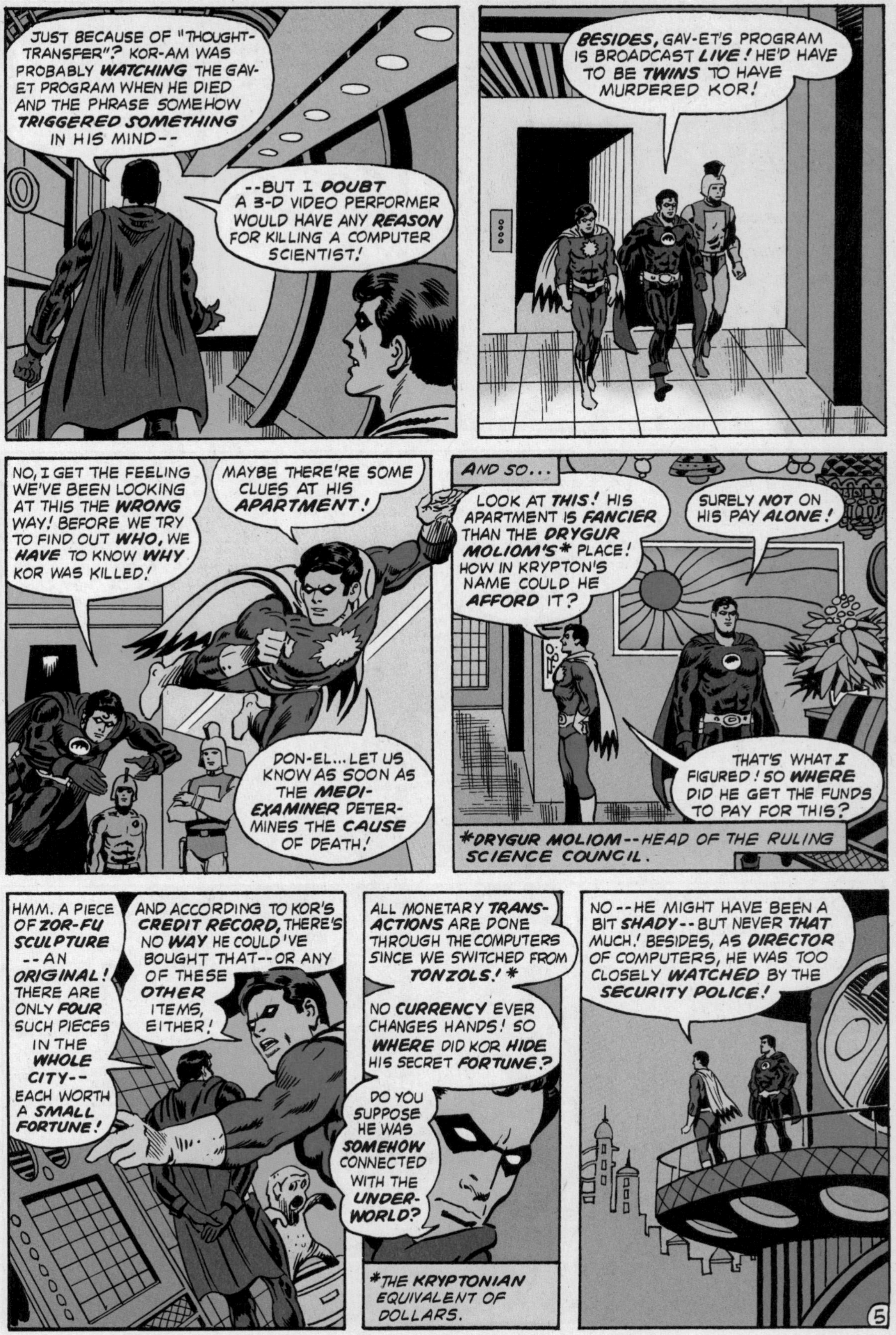
JUST BECAUSE OF "THOUGHT-TRANSFER"? KOR-AM WAS PROBABLY WATCHING THE GAV-ET PROGRAM WHEN HE DIED AND THE PHRASE SOMEHOW TRIGGERED SOMETHING IN HIS MIND--
--BUT I DOUBT A 3-D VIDEO PERFORMER WOULD HAVE ANY REASON FOR KILLING A COMPUTER SCIENTIST!
BESIDES, GAV-ET'S PROGRAM IS BROADCAST LIVE! HE'D HAVE TO BE TWINS TO HAVE MURDERED KOR!
NO, I GET THE FEELING WE'VE BEEN LOOKING AT THIS THE WRONG WAY! BEFORE WE TRY TO FIND OUT WHO, WE HAVE TO KNOW WHY KOR WAS KILLED!
MAYBE THERE'RE SOME CLUES AT HIS APARTMENT!
DON-EL...LET US KNOW AS SOON AS THE MEDI-EXAMINER DETERMINES THE CAUSE OF DEATH!
AND SO...
LOOK AT THIS! HIS APARTMENT IS FANCIER THAN THE DRYGUR MOLIOM'S* PLACE! HOW IN KRYPTON'S NAME COULD HE AFFORD IT?
SURELY NOT ON HIS PAY ALONE!
THAT'S WHAT I FIGURED! SO WHERE DID HE GET THE FUNDS TO PAY FOR THIS?
*DRYGUR MOLIOM--HEAD OF THE RULING SCIENCE COUNCIL.
HMM. A PIECE OF ZOR-FU SCULPTURE --AN ORIGINAL! THERE ARE ONLY FOUR SUCH PIECES IN THE WHOLE CITY--EACH WORTH A SMALL FORTUNE!
AND ACCORDING TO KOR'S CREDIT RECORD, THERE'S NO WAY HE COULD'VE BOUGHT THAT--OR ANY OF THESE OTHER ITEMS, EITHER!
ALL MONETARY TRANSACTIONS ARE DONE THROUGH THE COMPUTERS SINCE WE SWITCHED FROM TONZOLS!*
NO CURRENCY EVER CHANGES HANDS! SO WHERE DID KOR HIDE HIS SECRET FORTUNE?
DO YOU SUPPOSE HE WAS SOMEHOW CONNECTED WITH THE UNDERWORLD?
*THE KRYPTONIAN EQUIVALENT OF DOLLARS.
NO--HE MIGHT HAVE BEEN A BIT SHADY--BUT NEVER THAT MUCH! BESIDES, AS DIRECTOR OF COMPUTERS, HE WAS TOO CLOSELY WATCHED BY THE SECURITY POLICE!
5

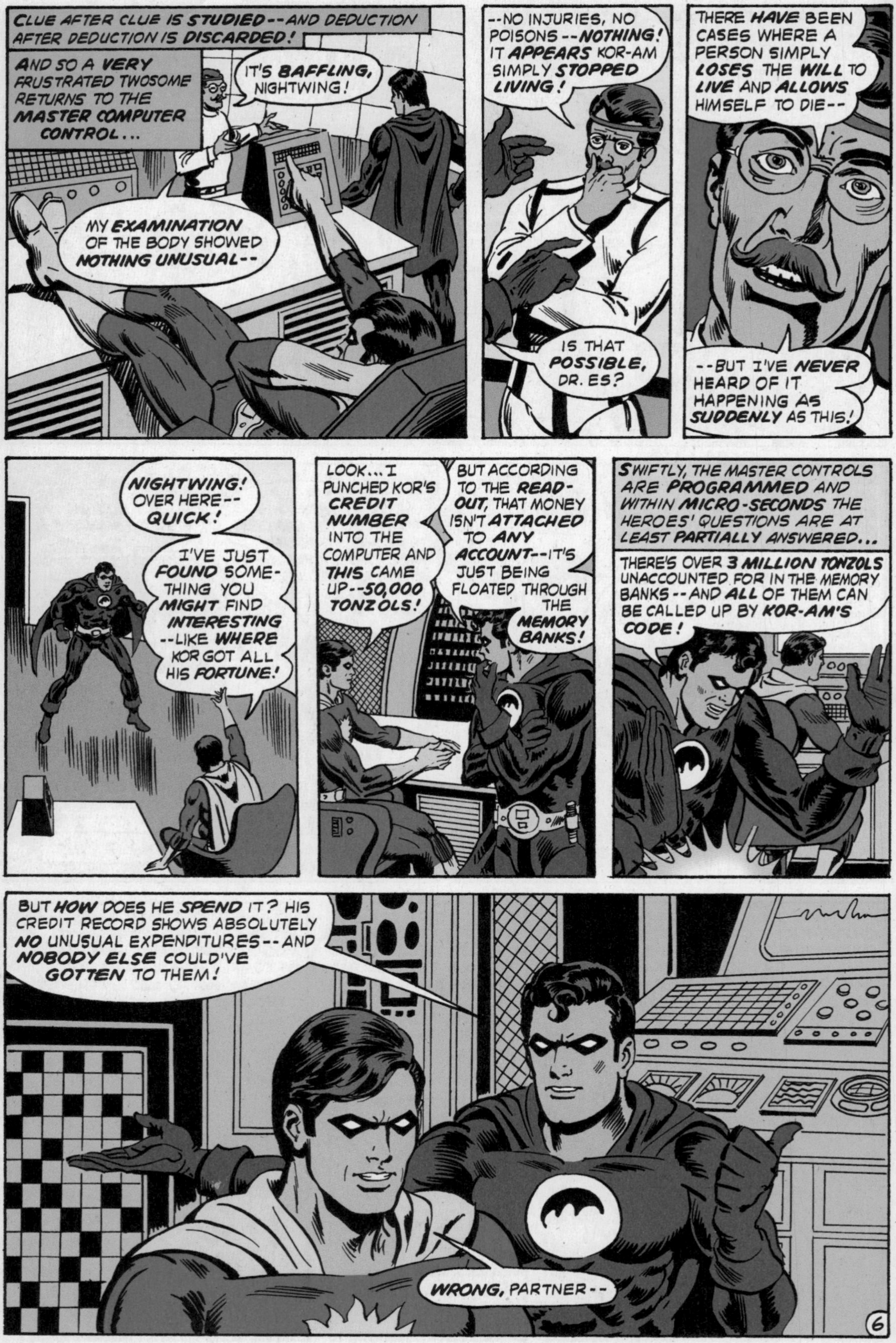
CLUE AFTER CLUE IS STUDIED--AND DEDUCTION AFTER DEDUCTION IS DISCARDED!
AND SO A VERY FRUSTRATED TWOSOME RETURNS TO THE MASTER COMPUTER CONTROL...
IT'S BAFFLING, NIGHTWING!
MY EXAMINATION OF THE BODY SHOWED NOTHING UNUSUAL--
--NO INJURIES, NO POISONS--NOTHING! IT APPEARS KOR-AM SIMPLY STOPPED LIVING!
IS THAT POSSIBLE, DR. ES?
THERE HAVE BEEN CASES WHERE A PERSON SIMPLY LOSES THE WILL TO LIVE AND ALLOWS HIMSELF TO DIE--
--BUT I'VE NEVER HEARD OF IT HAPPENING AS SUDDENLY AS THIS!
NIGHTWING! OVER HERE--QUICK!
I'VE JUST FOUND SOMETHING YOU MIGHT FIND INTERESTING--LIKE WHERE KOR GOT ALL HIS FORTUNE!
LOOK...I PUNCHED KOR'S CREDIT NUMBER INTO THE COMPUTER AND THIS CAME UP--50,000 TONZOLS!
BUT ACCORDING TO THE READ-OUT, THAT MONEY ISN'T ATTACHED TO ANY ACCOUNT--IT'S JUST BEING FLOATED THROUGH THE MEMORY BANKS!
SWIFTLY, THE MASTER CONTROLS ARE PROGRAMMED AND WITHIN MICRO-SECONDS THE HEROES' QUESTIONS ARE AT LEAST PARTIALLY ANSWERED...
THERE'S OVER 3 MILLION TONZOLS UNACCOUNTED FOR IN THE MEMORY BANKS--AND ALL OF THEM CAN BE CALLED UP BY KOR-AM'S CODE!
BUT HOW DOES HE SPEND IT? HIS CREDIT RECORD SHOWS ABSOLUTELY NO UNUSUAL EXPENDITURES--AND NOBODY ELSE COULD'VE GOTTEN TO THEM!
WRONG, PARTNER--
6

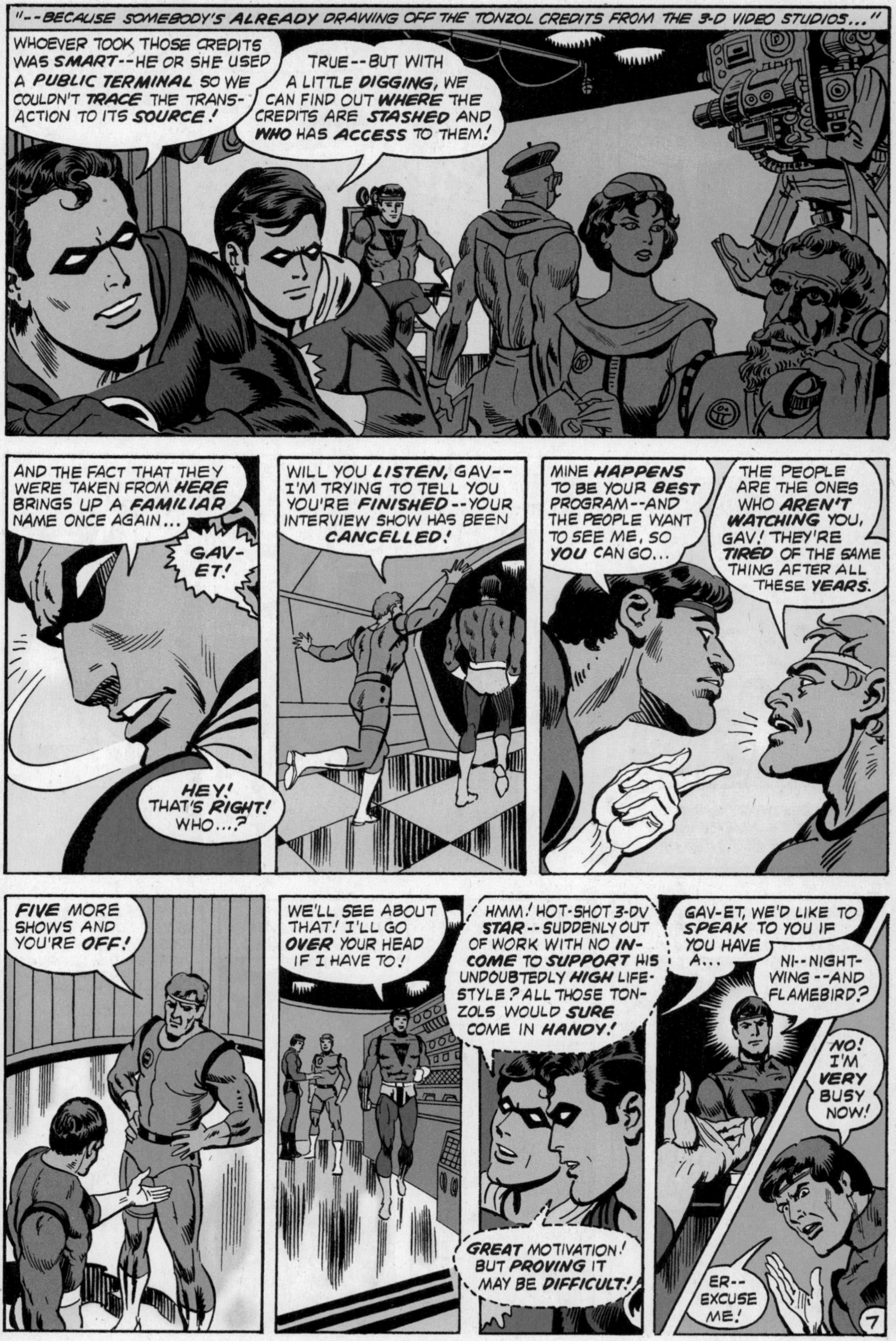
"--BECAUSE SOMEBODY'S ALREADY DRAWING OFF THE TONZOL CREDITS FROM THE 3-D VIDEO STUDIOS..."
WHOEVER TOOK THOSE CREDITS WAS SMART--HE OR SHE USED A PUBLIC TERMINAL SO WE COULDN'T TRACE THE TRANSACTION TO ITS SOURCE!
TRUE--BUT WITH A LITTLE DIGGING, WE CAN FIND OUT WHERE THE CREDITS ARE STASHED AND WHO HAS ACCESS TO THEM!
AND THE FACT THAT THEY WERE TAKEN FROM HERE BRINGS UP A FAMILIAR NAME ONCE AGAIN...
GAV-ET!
HEY! THAT'S RIGHT! WHO...?
WILL YOU LISTEN, GAV--I'M TRYING TO TELL YOU YOU'RE FINISHED--YOUR INTERVIEW SHOW HAS BEEN CANCELLED!
MINE HAPPENS TO BE YOUR BEST PROGRAM--AND THE PEOPLE WANT TO SEE ME, SO YOU CAN GO...
THE PEOPLE ARE THE ONES WHO AREN'T WATCHING YOU, GAV! THEY'RE TIRED OF THE SAME THING AFTER ALL THESE YEARS.
FIVE MORE SHOWS AND YOU'RE OFF!
WE'LL SEE ABOUT THAT! I'LL GO OVER YOUR HEAD IF I HAVE TO!
HMM! HOT-SHOT 3-DV STAR--SUDDENLY OUT OF WORK WITH NO INCOME TO SUPPORT HIS UNDOUBTEDLY HIGH LIFE-STYLE? ALL THOSE TONZOLS WOULD SURE COME IN HANDY!
GREAT MOTIVATION! BUT PROVING IT MAY BE DIFFICULT!
GAV-ET, WE'D LIKE TO SPEAK TO YOU IF YOU HAVE A...
NI--NIGHTWING--AND FLAMEBIRD?
NO! I'M VERY BUSY NOW!
ER--EXCUSE ME!
7

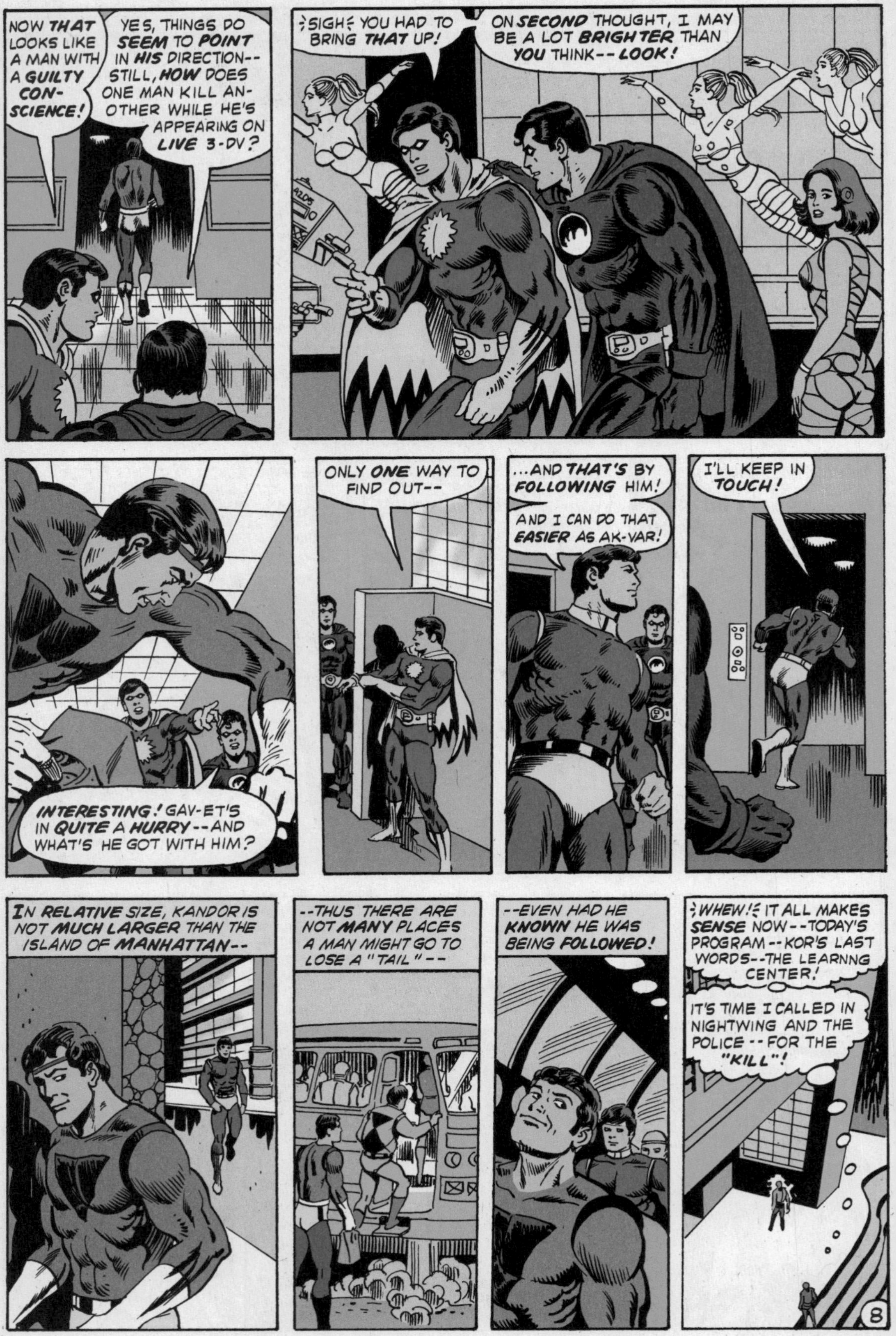

NOW THAT LOOKS LIKE A MAN WITH A GUILTY CON-SCIENCE!
YES, THINGS DO SEEM TO POINT IN HIS DIRECTION--STILL, HOW DOES ONE MAN KILL AN-OTHER WHILE HE'S APPEARING ON LIVE 3-DV?
-SIGH- YOU HAD TO BRING THAT UP!
ON SECOND THOUGHT, I MAY BE A LOT BRIGHTER THAN YOU THINK--LOOK!
INTERESTING! GAV-ET'S IN QUITE A HURRY--AND WHAT'S HE GOT WITH HIM?
ONLY ONE WAY TO FIND OUT--
...AND THAT'S BY FOLLOWING HIM!
AND I CAN DO THAT EASIER AS AK-VAR!
I'LL KEEP IN TOUCH!
IN RELATIVE SIZE, KANDOR IS NOT MUCH LARGER THAN THE ISLAND OF MANHATTAN--
--THUS THERE ARE NOT MANY PLACES A MAN MIGHT GO TO LOSE A "TAIL"--
--EVEN HAD HE KNOWN HE WAS BEING FOLLOWED!
-WHEW!- IT ALL MAKES SENSE NOW--TODAY'S PROGRAM--KOR'S LAST WORDS--THE LEARNNG CENTER!
IT'S TIME I CALLED IN NIGHTWING AND THE POLICE--FOR THE "KILL"!
8

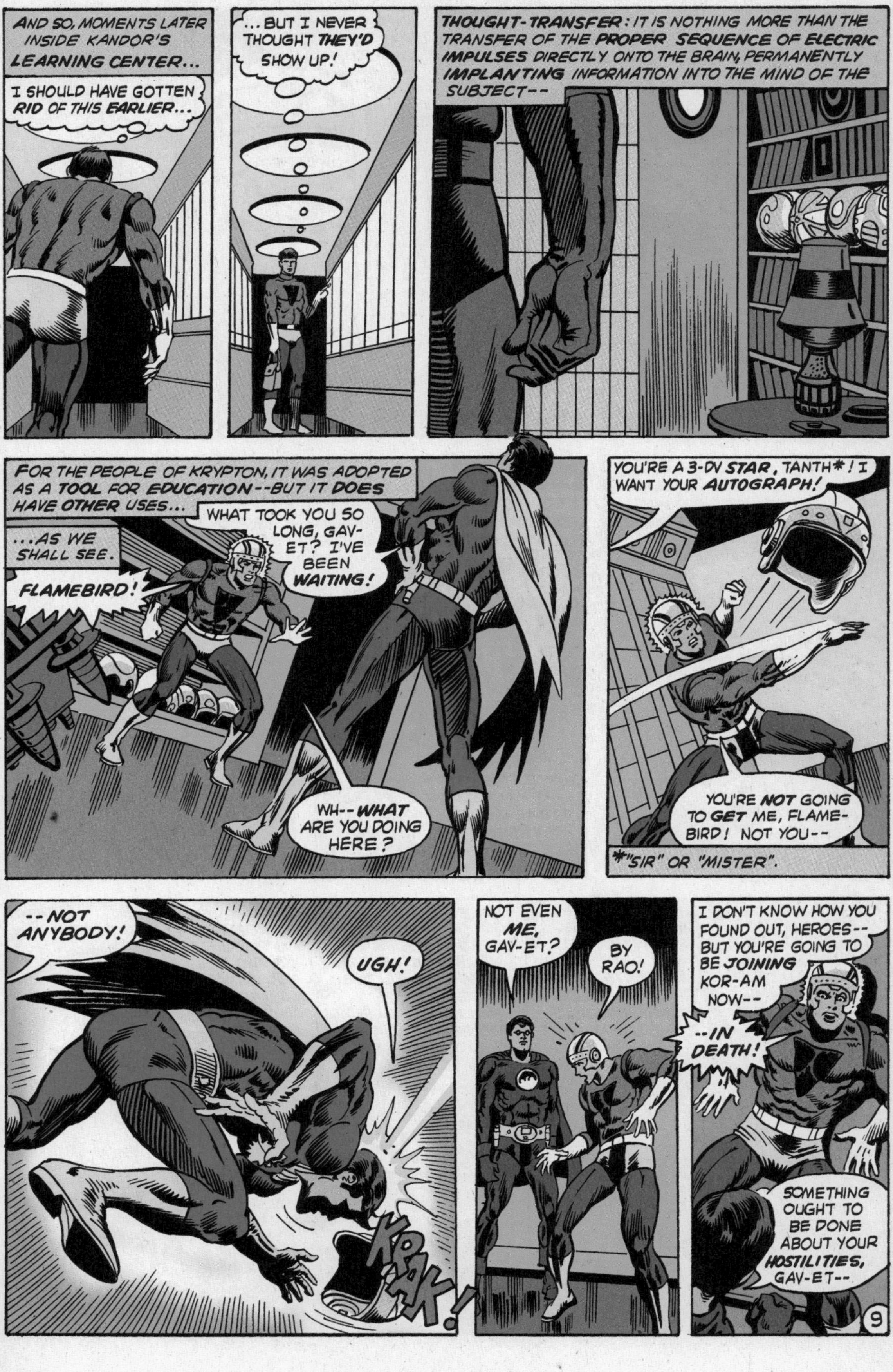
AND SO, MOMENTS LATER INSIDE KANDOR'S LEARNING CENTER...
I SHOULD HAVE GOTTEN RID OF THIS EARLIER...
...BUT I NEVER THOUGHT THEY'D SHOW UP!
THOUGHT-TRANSFER: IT IS NOTHING MORE THAN THE TRANSFER OF THE PROPER SEQUENCE OF ELECTRIC IMPULSES DIRECTLY ONTO THE BRAIN, PERMANENTLY IMPLANTING INFORMATION INTO THE MIND OF THE SUBJECT--
FOR THE PEOPLE OF KRYPTON, IT WAS ADOPTED AS A TOOL FOR EDUCATION--BUT IT DOES HAVE OTHER USES...
...AS WE SHALL SEE.
WHAT TOOK YOU SO LONG, GAV-ET? I'VE BEEN WAITING!
FLAMEBIRD!
WH--WHAT ARE YOU DOING HERE?
YOU'RE A 3-DV STAR, TANTH*! I WANT YOUR AUTOGRAPH!
YOU'RE NOT GOING TO GET ME, FLAME-BIRD! NOT YOU--
*"SIR" OR "MISTER".
--NOT ANYBODY!
UGH!
KRAK!
NOT EVEN ME, GAV-ET?
BY RAO!
I DON'T KNOW HOW YOU FOUND OUT, HEROES--BUT YOU'RE GOING TO BE JOINING KOR-AM NOW--
--IN DEATH!
SOMETHING OUGHT TO BE DONE ABOUT YOUR HOSTILITIES, GAV-ET--
9

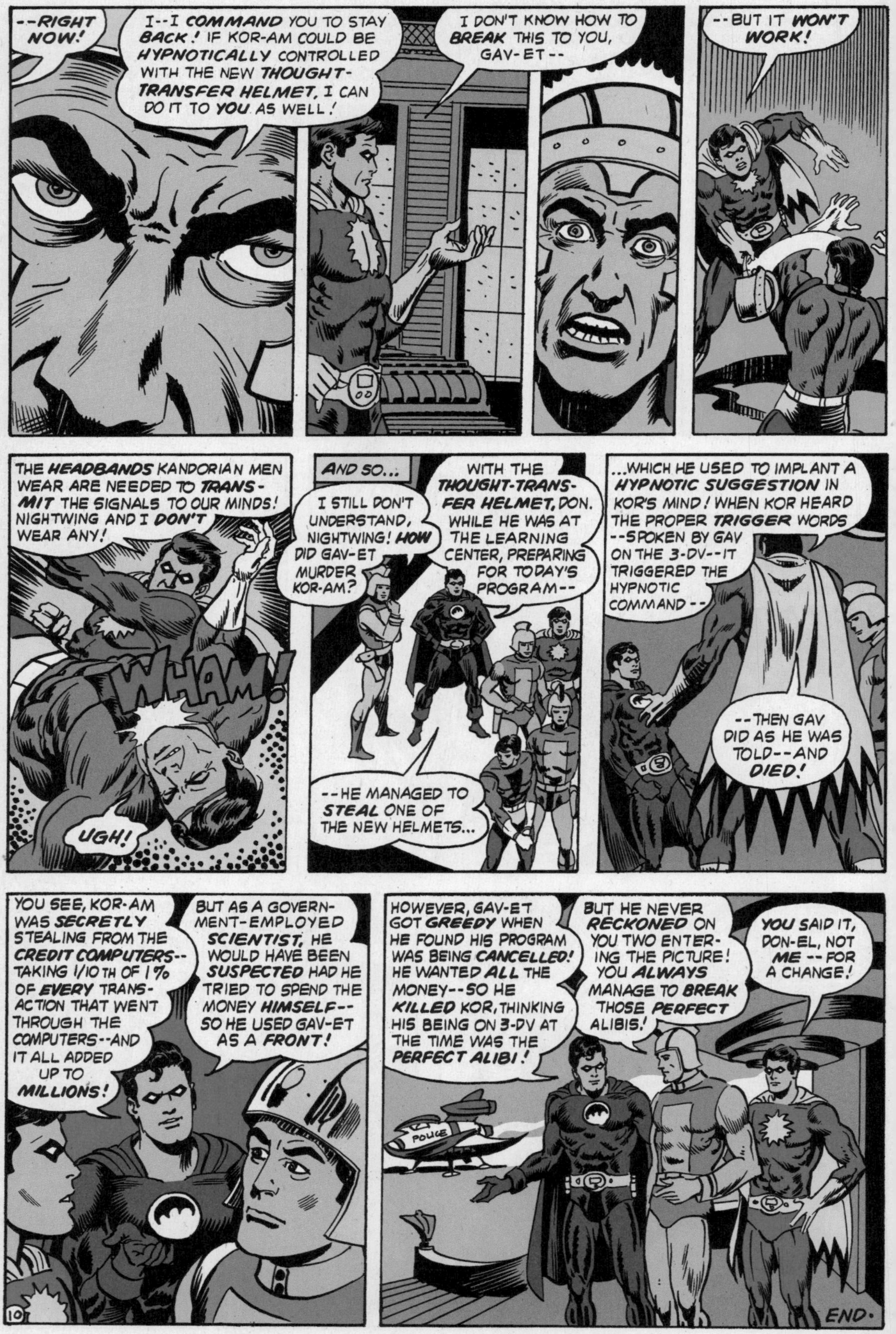
--RIGHT NOW!
I--I COMMAND YOU TO STAY BACK! IF KOR-AM COULD BE HYPNOTICALLY CONTROLLED WITH THE NEW THOUGHT-TRANSFER HELMET, I CAN DO IT TO YOU AS WELL!
I DON'T KNOW HOW TO BREAK THIS TO YOU, GAV-ET--
--BUT IT WON'T WORK!
THE HEADBANDS KANDORIAN MEN WEAR ARE NEEDED TO TRANSMIT THE SIGNALS TO OUR MINDS! NIGHTWING AND I DON'T WEAR ANY!
WHAM!
UGH!
AND SO...
I STILL DON'T UNDERSTAND, NIGHTWING! HOW DID GAV-ET MURDER KOR-AM?
WITH THE THOUGHT-TRANSFER HELMET, DON. WHILE HE WAS AT THE LEARNING CENTER, PREPARING FOR TODAY'S PROGRAM--
--HE MANAGED TO STEAL ONE OF THE NEW HELMETS...
...WHICH HE USED TO IMPLANT A HYPNOTIC SUGGESTION IN KOR'S MIND! WHEN KOR HEARD THE PROPER TRIGGER WORDS --SPOKEN BY GAV ON THE 3-DV--IT TRIGGERED THE HYPNOTIC COMMAND--
--THEN GAV DID AS HE WAS TOLD--AND DIED!
YOU SEE, KOR-AM WAS SECRETLY STEALING FROM THE CREDIT COMPUTERS--TAKING 1/10TH OF 1% OF EVERY TRANSACTION THAT WENT THROUGH THE COMPUTERS--AND IT ALL ADDED UP TO MILLIONS!
BUT AS A GOVERNMENT-EMPLOYED SCIENTIST, HE WOULD HAVE BEEN SUSPECTED HAD HE TRIED TO SPEND THE MONEY HIMSELF--SO HE USED GAV-ET AS A FRONT!
10
HOWEVER, GAV-ET GOT GREEDY WHEN HE FOUND HIS PROGRAM WAS BEING CANCELLED! HE WANTED ALL THE MONEY--SO HE KILLED KOR, THINKING HIS BEING ON 3-DV AT THE TIME WAS THE PERFECT ALIBI!
BUT HE NEVER RECKONED ON YOU TWO ENTERING THE PICTURE! YOU ALWAYS MANAGE TO BREAK THOSE PERFECT ALIBIS!
YOU SAID IT, DON-EL, NOT ME --FOR A CHANGE!
POLICE
END.

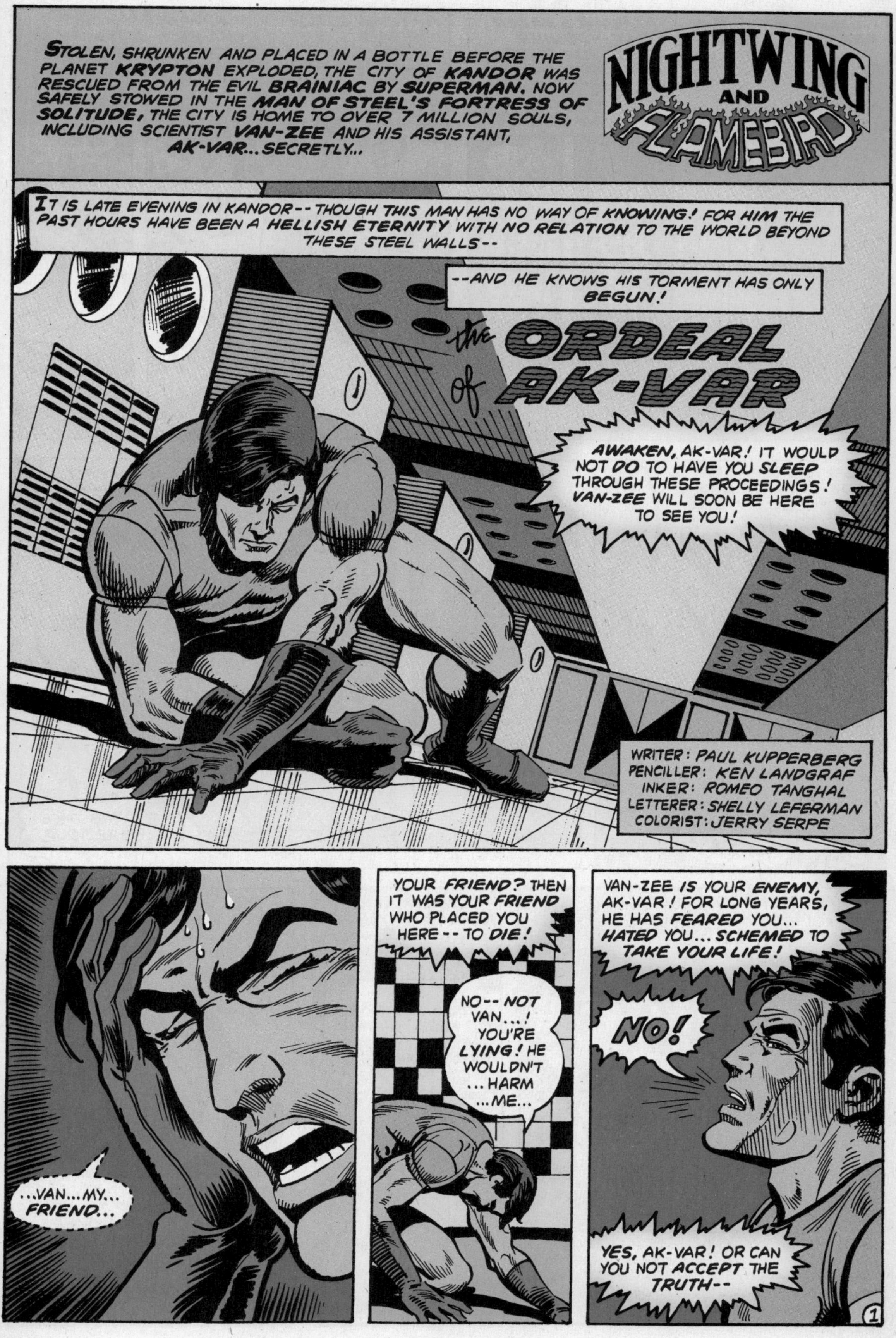
STOLEN, SHRUNKEN AND PLACED IN A BOTTLE BEFORE THE PLANET KRYPTON EXPLODED, THE CITY OF KANDOR WAS RESCUED FROM THE EVIL BRAINIAC BY SUPERMAN. NOW SAFELY STOWED IN THE MAN OF STEEL'S FORTRESS OF SOLITUDE, THE CITY IS HOME TO OVER 7 MILLION SOULS, INCLUDING SCIENTIST VAN-ZEE AND HIS ASSISTANT, AK-VAR... SECRETLY...
NIGHTWING AND FLAMEBIRD
IT IS LATE EVENING IN KANDOR-- THOUGH THIS MAN HAS NO WAY OF KNOWING! FOR HIM THE PAST HOURS HAVE BEEN A HELLISH ETERNITY WITH NO RELATION TO THE WORLD BEYOND THESE STEEL WALLS--
--AND HE KNOWS HIS TORMENT HAS ONLY BEGUN!
the ORDEAL of AK-VAR
AWAKEN, AK-VAR! IT WOULD NOT DO TO HAVE YOU SLEEP THROUGH THESE PROCEEDINGS! VAN-ZEE WILL SOON BE HERE TO SEE YOU!
WRITER: PAUL KUPPERBERG
PENCILLER: KEN LANDGRAF
INKER: ROMEO TANGHAL
LETTERER: SHELLY LEFERMAN
COLORIST: JERRY SERPE
...VAN... MY... FRIEND...
YOUR FRIEND? THEN IT WAS YOUR FRIEND WHO PLACED YOU HERE -- TO DIE!
NO -- NOT VAN...! YOU'RE LYING! HE WOULDN'T ... HARM ... ME...
VAN-ZEE IS YOUR ENEMY, AK-VAR! FOR LONG YEARS, HE HAS FEARED YOU... HATED YOU... SCHEMED TO TAKE YOUR LIFE!
NO!
YES, AK-VAR! OR CAN YOU NOT ACCEPT THE TRUTH--
1

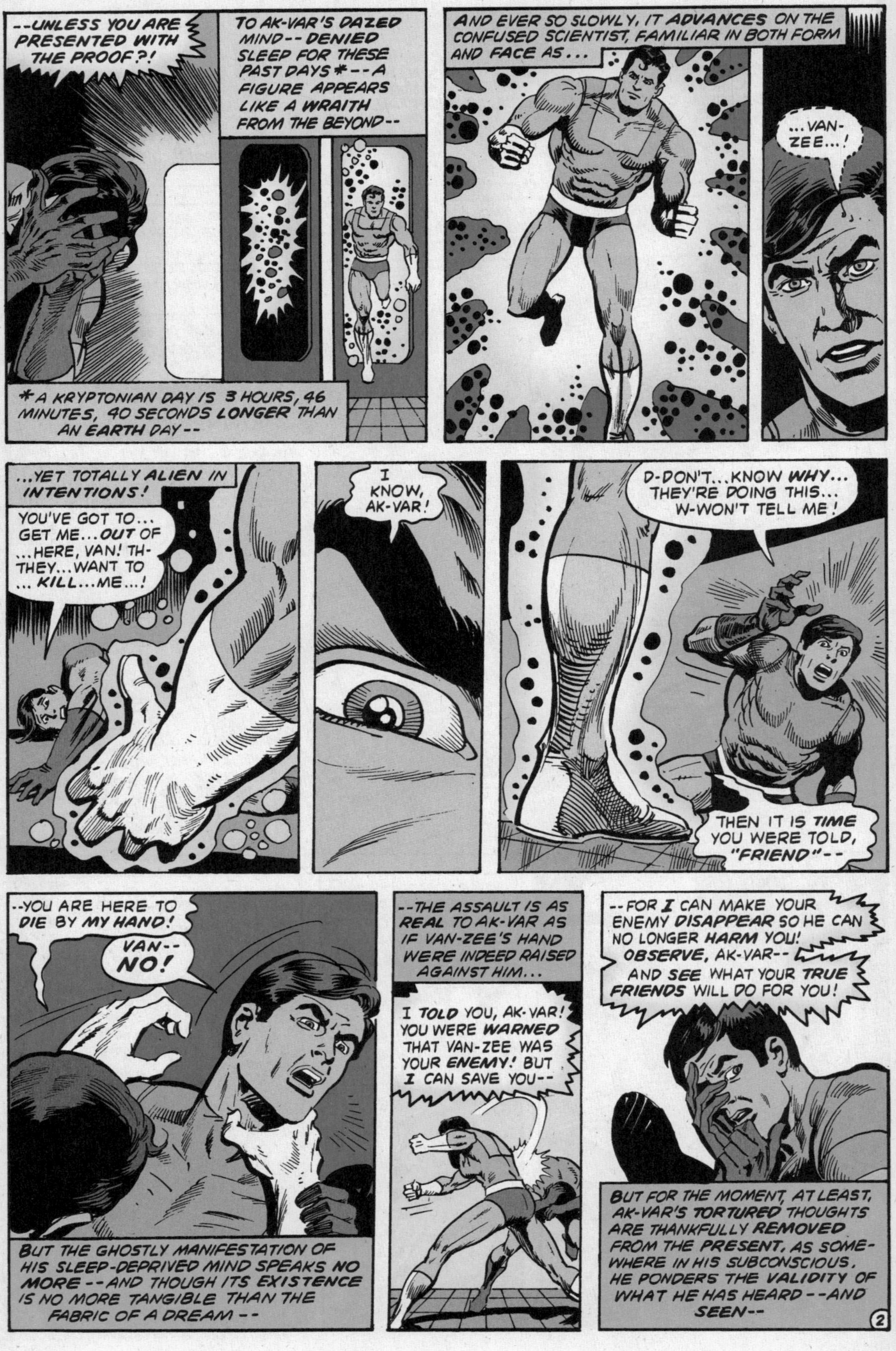
--UNLESS YOU ARE PRESENTED WITH THE PROOF?!
TO AK-VAR'S DAZED MIND--DENIED SLEEP FOR THESE PAST DAYS*--A FIGURE APPEARS LIKE A WRAITH FROM THE BEYOND--
*A KRYPTONIAN DAY IS 3 HOURS, 46 MINUTES, 40 SECONDS LONGER THAN AN EARTH DAY--
AND EVER SO SLOWLY, IT ADVANCES ON THE CONFUSED SCIENTIST, FAMILIAR IN BOTH FORM AND FACE AS...
...VAN-ZEE...!
...YET TOTALLY ALIEN IN INTENTIONS!
YOU'VE GOT TO... GET ME...OUT OF ...HERE, VAN! TH-THEY...WANT TO ...KILL...ME...!
I KNOW, AK-VAR!
D-DON'T...KNOW WHY... THEY'RE DOING THIS... W-WON'T TELL ME!
THEN IT IS TIME YOU WERE TOLD, "FRIEND"--
--YOU ARE HERE TO DIE BY MY HAND!
VAN--NO!
BUT THE GHOSTLY MANIFESTATION OF HIS SLEEP-DEPRIVED MIND SPEAKS NO MORE--AND THOUGH ITS EXISTENCE IS NO MORE TANGIBLE THAN THE FABRIC OF A DREAM--
--THE ASSAULT IS AS REAL TO AK-VAR AS IF VAN-ZEE'S HAND WERE INDEED RAISED AGAINST HIM...
I TOLD YOU, AK-VAR! YOU WERE WARNED THAT VAN-ZEE WAS YOUR ENEMY! BUT I CAN SAVE YOU--
--FOR I CAN MAKE YOUR ENEMY DISAPPEAR SO HE CAN NO LONGER HARM YOU! OBSERVE, AK-VAR--
AND SEE WHAT YOUR TRUE FRIENDS WILL DO FOR YOU!
BUT FOR THE MOMENT, AT LEAST, AK-VAR'S TORTURED THOUGHTS ARE THANKFULLY REMOVED FROM THE PRESENT, AS SOMEWHERE IN HIS SUBCONSCIOUS, HE PONDERS THE VALIDITY OF WHAT HE HAS HEARD--AND SEEN--
2

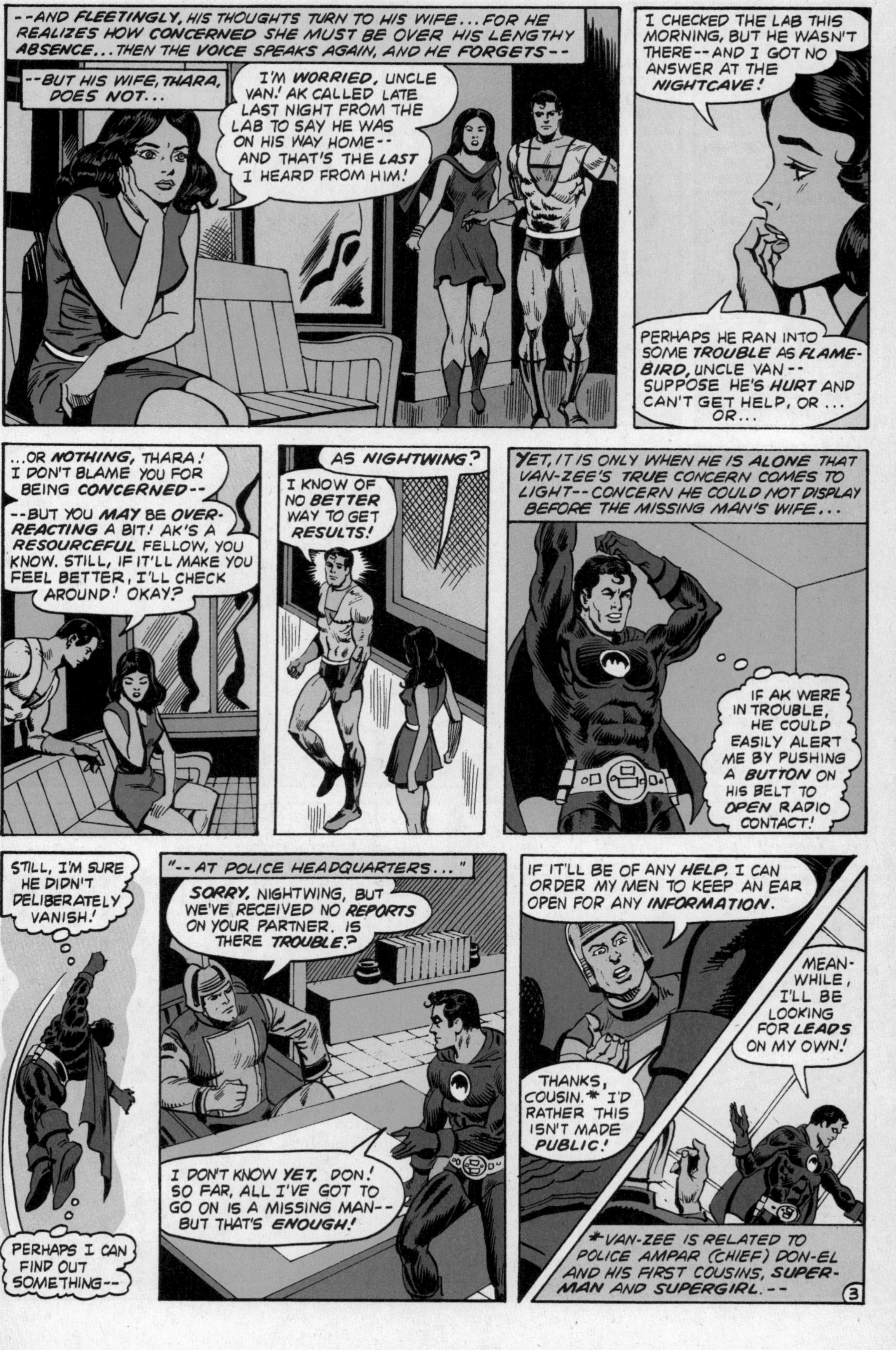
--AND FLEETINGLY, HIS THOUGHTS TURN TO HIS WIFE... FOR HE REALIZES HOW CONCERNED SHE MUST BE OVER HIS LENGTHY ABSENCE... THEN THE VOICE SPEAKS AGAIN, AND HE FORGETS--
--BUT HIS WIFE, THARA, DOES NOT...
I'M WORRIED, UNCLE VAN! AK CALLED LATE LAST NIGHT FROM THE LAB TO SAY HE WAS ON HIS WAY HOME-- AND THAT'S THE LAST I HEARD FROM HIM!
I CHECKED THE LAB THIS MORNING, BUT HE WASN'T THERE--AND I GOT NO ANSWER AT THE NIGHTCAVE!
PERHAPS HE RAN INTO SOME TROUBLE AS FLAME-BIRD, UNCLE VAN-- SUPPOSE HE'S HURT AND CAN'T GET HELP, OR ... OR...
...OR NOTHING, THARA! I DON'T BLAME YOU FOR BEING CONCERNED--
--BUT YOU MAY BE OVER-REACTING A BIT! AK'S A RESOURCEFUL FELLOW, YOU KNOW. STILL, IF IT'LL MAKE YOU FEEL BETTER, I'LL CHECK AROUND! OKAY?
AS NIGHTWING?
I KNOW OF NO BETTER WAY TO GET RESULTS!
YET, IT IS ONLY WHEN HE IS ALONE THAT VAN-ZEE'S TRUE CONCERN COMES TO LIGHT--CONCERN HE COULD NOT DISPLAY BEFORE THE MISSING MAN'S WIFE...
IF AK WERE IN TROUBLE, HE COULD EASILY ALERT ME BY PUSHING A BUTTON ON HIS BELT TO OPEN RADIO CONTACT!
STILL, I'M SURE HE DIDN'T DELIBERATELY VANISH!
PERHAPS I CAN FIND OUT SOMETHING--
"--AT POLICE HEADQUARTERS..."
SORRY, NIGHTWING, BUT WE'VE RECEIVED NO REPORTS ON YOUR PARTNER. IS THERE TROUBLE?
I DON'T KNOW YET, DON! SO FAR, ALL I'VE GOT TO GO ON IS A MISSING MAN-- BUT THAT'S ENOUGH!
IF IT'LL BE OF ANY HELP, I CAN ORDER MY MEN TO KEEP AN EAR OPEN FOR ANY INFORMATION.
MEAN-WHILE, I'LL BE LOOKING FOR LEADS ON MY OWN!
THANKS, COUSIN.* I'D RATHER THIS ISN'T MADE PUBLIC!
*VAN-ZEE IS RELATED TO POLICE AMPAR (CHIEF) DON-EL AND HIS FIRST COUSINS, SUPER-MAN AND SUPERGIRL.--
3

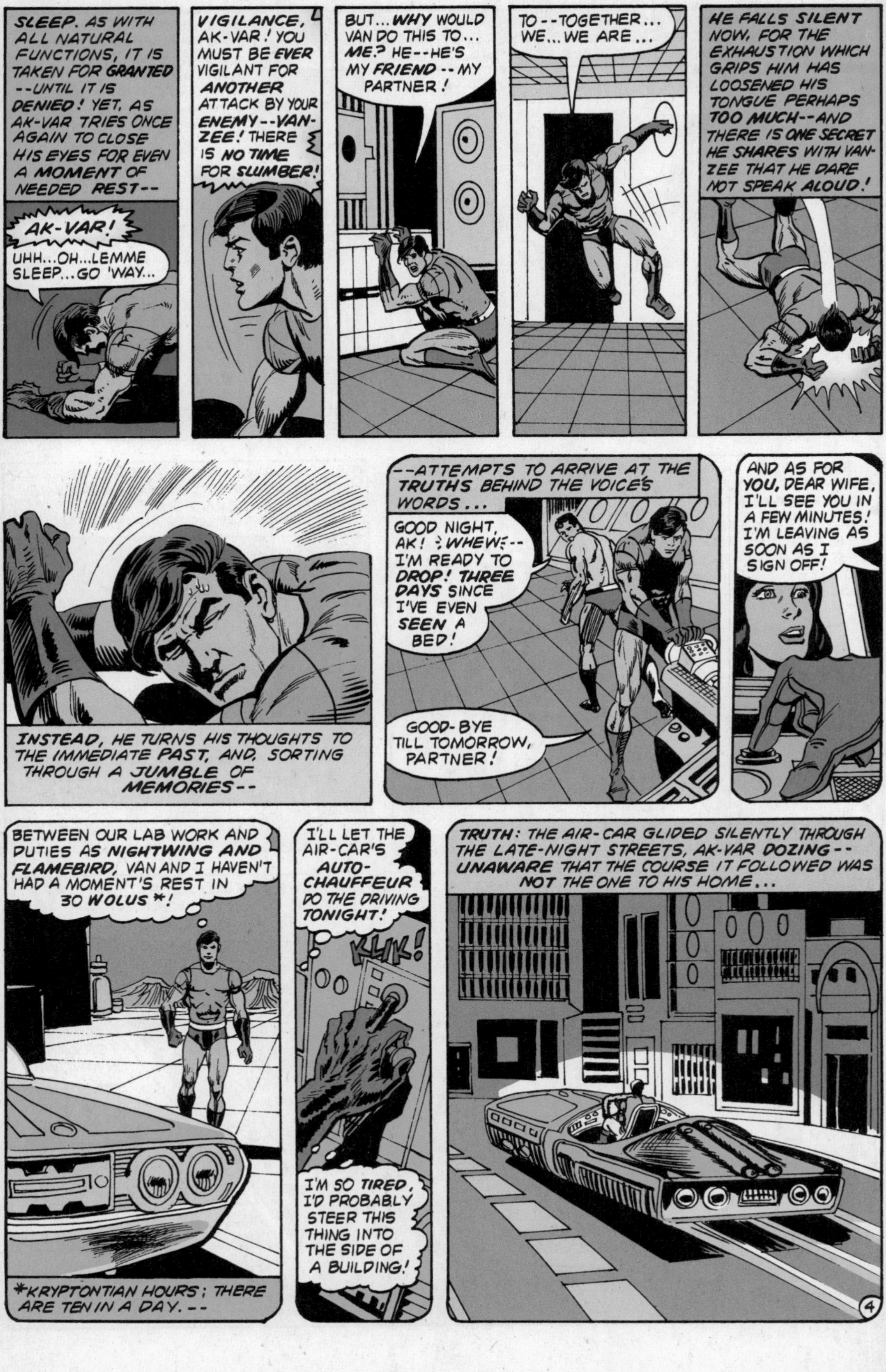
SLEEP. AS WITH ALL NATURAL FUNCTIONS, IT IS TAKEN FOR GRANTED --UNTIL IT IS DENIED! YET, AS AK-VAR TRIES ONCE AGAIN TO CLOSE HIS EYES FOR EVEN A MOMENT OF NEEDED REST--
AK-VAR!
UHH...OH...LEMME SLEEP...GO 'WAY...
VIGILANCE, AK-VAR! YOU MUST BE EVER VIGILANT FOR ANOTHER ATTACK BY YOUR ENEMY--VAN-ZEE! THERE IS NO TIME FOR SLUMBER!
BUT...WHY WOULD VAN DO THIS TO... ME? HE--HE'S MY FRIEND--MY PARTNER!
TO--TOGETHER... WE...WE ARE...
HE FALLS SILENT NOW, FOR THE EXHAUSTION WHICH GRIPS HIM HAS LOOSENED HIS TONGUE PERHAPS TOO MUCH--AND THERE IS ONE SECRET HE SHARES WITH VAN-ZEE THAT HE DARE NOT SPEAK ALOUD!
INSTEAD, HE TURNS HIS THOUGHTS TO THE IMMEDIATE PAST, AND, SORTING THROUGH A JUMBLE OF MEMORIES--
--ATTEMPTS TO ARRIVE AT THE TRUTHS BEHIND THE VOICE'S WORDS...
GOOD NIGHT, AK! WHEW--I'M READY TO DROP! THREE DAYS SINCE I'VE EVEN SEEN A BED!
GOOD-BYE TILL TOMORROW, PARTNER!
AND AS FOR YOU, DEAR WIFE, I'LL SEE YOU IN A FEW MINUTES! I'M LEAVING AS SOON AS I SIGN OFF!
BETWEEN OUR LAB WORK AND DUTIES AS NIGHTWING AND FLAMEBIRD, VAN AND I HAVEN'T HAD A MOMENT'S REST IN 30 WOLUS*!
*KRYPTONTIAN HOURS; THERE ARE TEN IN A DAY.--
I'LL LET THE AIR-CAR'S AUTO-CHAUFFEUR DO THE DRIVING TONIGHT!
KLIK!
I'M SO TIRED, I'D PROBABLY STEER THIS THING INTO THE SIDE OF A BUILDING!
TRUTH: THE AIR-CAR GLIDED SILENTLY THROUGH THE LATE-NIGHT STREETS, AK-VAR DOZING--UNAWARE THAT THE COURSE IT FOLLOWED WAS NOT THE ONE TO HIS HOME...
4

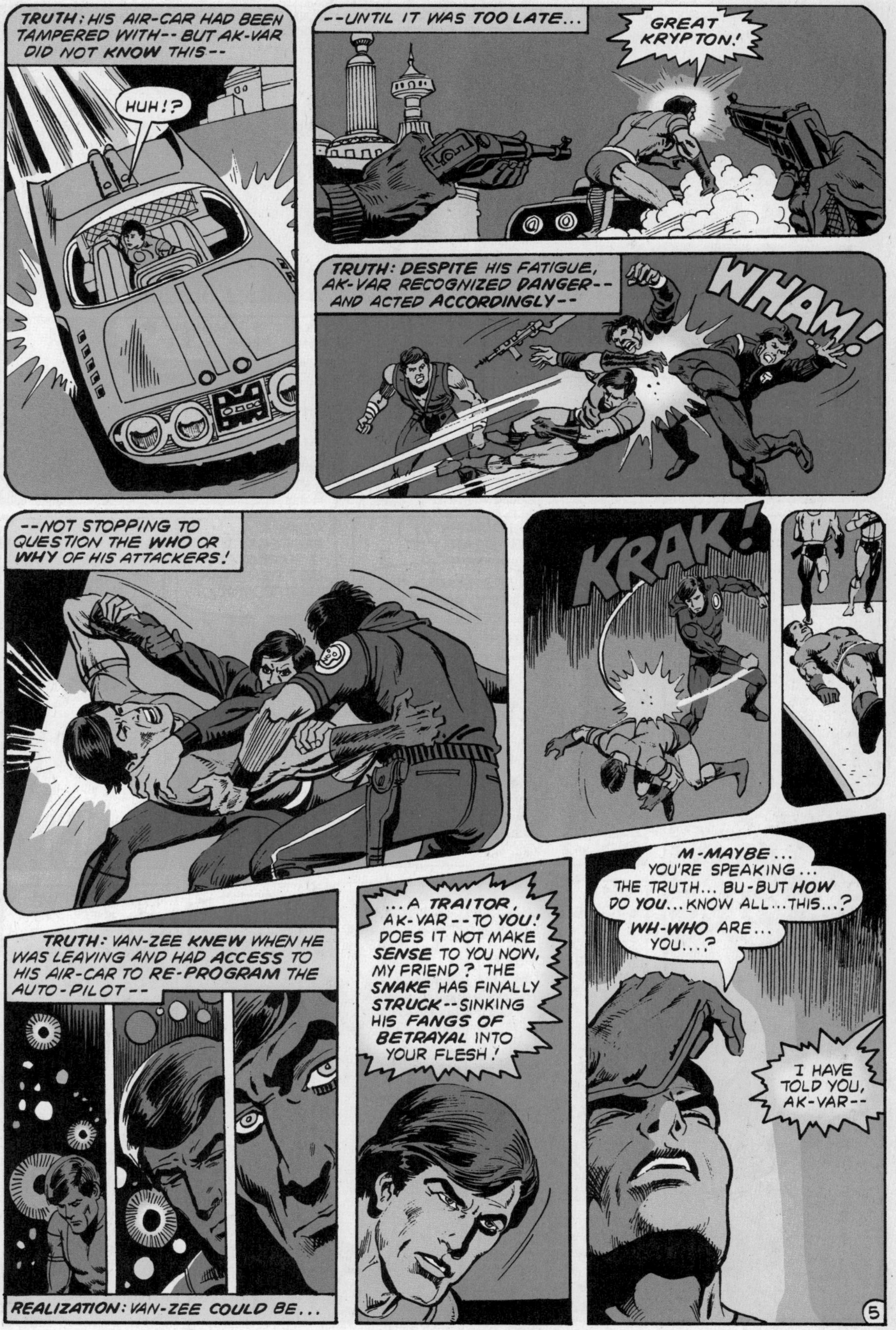
TRUTH: HIS AIR-CAR HAD BEEN TAMPERED WITH-- BUT AK-VAR DID NOT KNOW THIS--
HUH!?
--UNTIL IT WAS TOO LATE...
GREAT KRYPTON!
TRUTH: DESPITE HIS FATIGUE, AK-VAR RECOGNIZED DANGER-- AND ACTED ACCORDINGLY--
WHAM!
--NOT STOPPING TO QUESTION THE WHO OR WHY OF HIS ATTACKERS!
KRAK!
TRUTH: VAN-ZEE KNEW WHEN HE WAS LEAVING AND HAD ACCESS TO HIS AIR-CAR TO RE-PROGRAM THE AUTO-PILOT--
REALIZATION: VAN-ZEE COULD BE...
...A TRAITOR, AK-VAR--TO YOU! DOES IT NOT MAKE SENSE TO YOU NOW, MY FRIEND? THE SNAKE HAS FINALLY STRUCK--SINKING HIS FANGS OF BETRAYAL INTO YOUR FLESH!
M-MAYBE... YOU'RE SPEAKING... THE TRUTH... BU-BUT HOW DO YOU... KNOW ALL... THIS...? WH-WHO ARE... YOU...?
I HAVE TOLD YOU, AK-VAR--
5

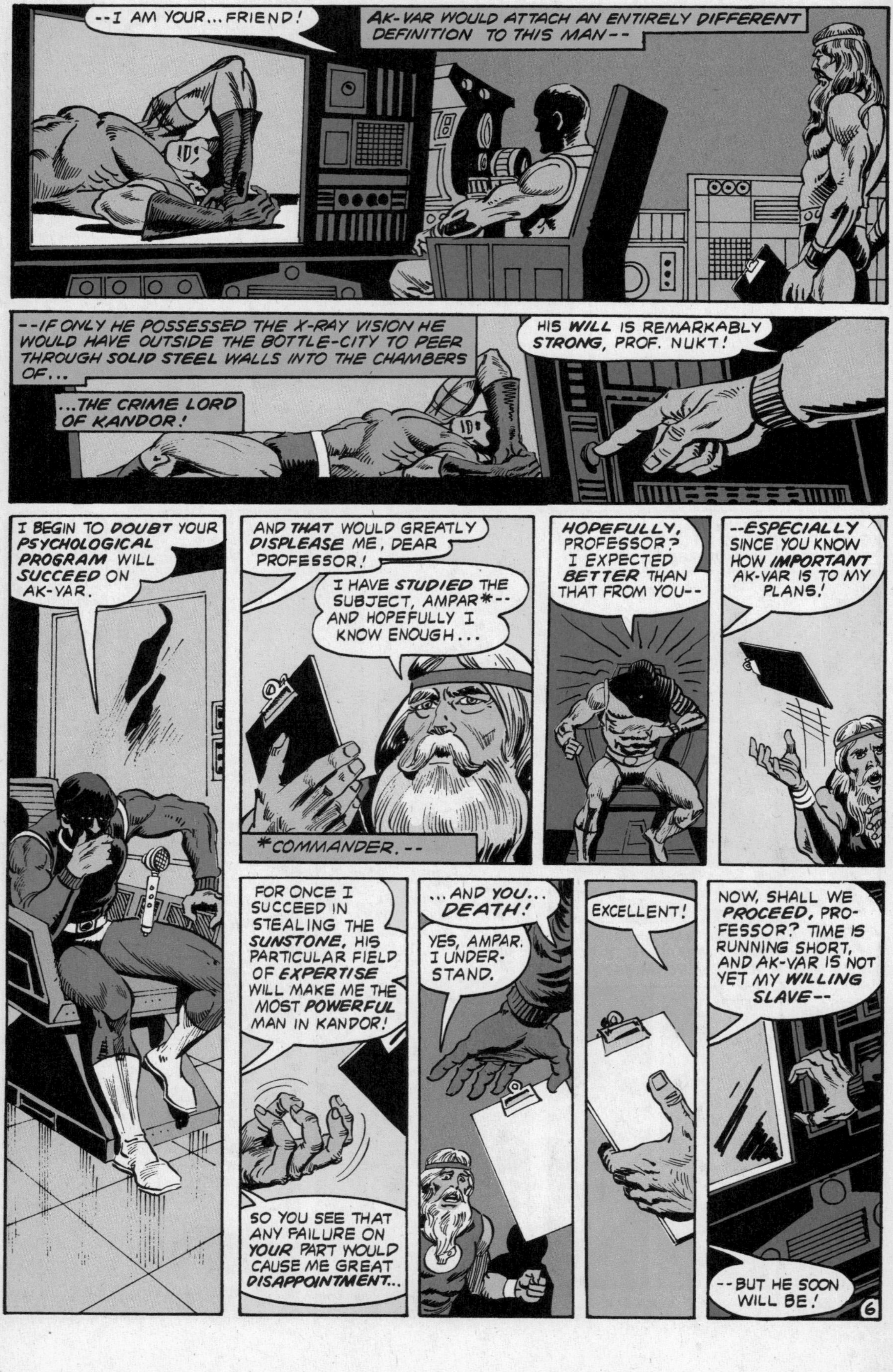
--I AM YOUR... FRIEND!
AK-VAR WOULD ATTACH AN ENTIRELY DIFFERENT DEFINITION TO THIS MAN--
--IF ONLY HE POSSESSED THE X-RAY VISION HE WOULD HAVE OUTSIDE THE BOTTLE-CITY TO PEER THROUGH SOLID STEEL WALLS INTO THE CHAMBERS OF...
...THE CRIME LORD OF KANDOR!
HIS WILL IS REMARKABLY STRONG, PROF. NUKT!
I BEGIN TO DOUBT YOUR PSYCHOLOGICAL PROGRAM WILL SUCCEED ON AK-VAR.
AND THAT WOULD GREATLY DISPLEASE ME, DEAR PROFESSOR!
I HAVE STUDIED THE SUBJECT, AMPAR*-- AND HOPEFULLY I KNOW ENOUGH...
*COMMANDER.--
HOPEFULLY, PROFESSOR? I EXPECTED BETTER THAN THAT FROM YOU--
--ESPECIALLY SINCE YOU KNOW HOW IMPORTANT AK-VAR IS TO MY PLANS!
FOR ONCE I SUCCEED IN STEALING THE SUNSTONE, HIS PARTICULAR FIELD OF EXPERTISE WILL MAKE ME THE MOST POWERFUL MAN IN KANDOR!
SO YOU SEE THAT ANY FAILURE ON YOUR PART WOULD CAUSE ME GREAT DISAPPOINTMENT...
...AND YOU... DEATH!
YES, AMPAR. I UNDER-STAND.
EXCELLENT!
NOW, SHALL WE PROCEED, PRO-FESSOR? TIME IS RUNNING SHORT, AND AK-VAR IS NOT YET MY WILLING SLAVE--
--BUT HE SOON WILL BE!
6

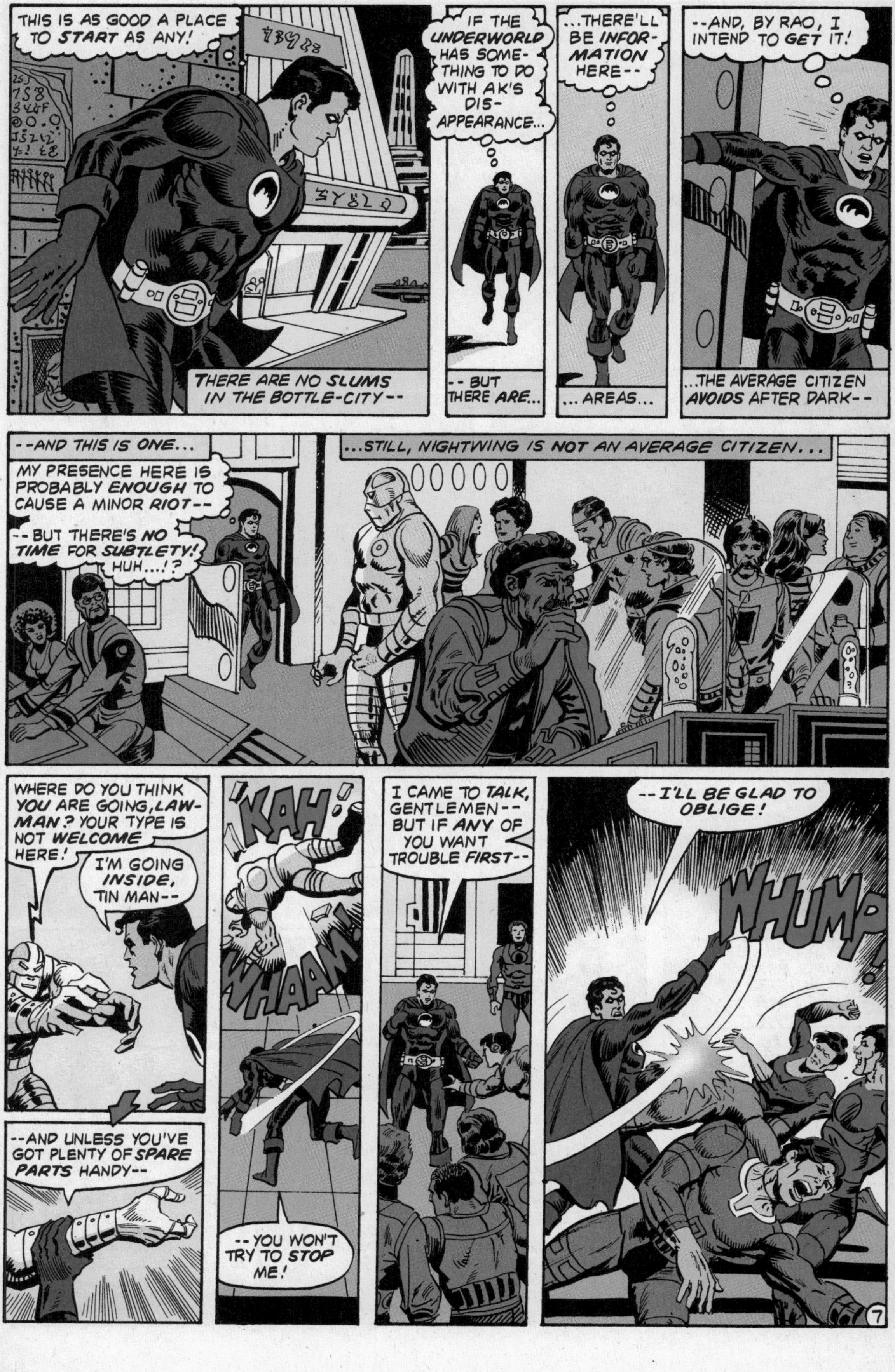
THIS IS AS GOOD A PLACE TO START AS ANY!
THERE ARE NO SLUMS IN THE BOTTLE-CITY--
IF THE UNDERWORLD HAS SOMETHING TO DO WITH AK'S DISAPPEARANCE...
-- BUT THERE ARE...
...THERE'LL BE INFORMATION HERE--
...AREAS...
--AND, BY RAO, I INTEND TO GET IT!
...THE AVERAGE CITIZEN AVOIDS AFTER DARK--
--AND THIS IS ONE...
MY PRESENCE HERE IS PROBABLY ENOUGH TO CAUSE A MINOR RIOT--
-- BUT THERE'S NO TIME FOR SUBTLETY!
...STILL, NIGHTWING IS NOT AN AVERAGE CITIZEN...
HUH...!?
WHERE DO YOU THINK YOU ARE GOING, LAWMAN? YOUR TYPE IS NOT WELCOME HERE!
I'M GOING INSIDE, TIN MAN--
--AND UNLESS YOU'VE GOT PLENTY OF SPARE PARTS HANDY--
KAH
WHAAM!
--YOU WON'T TRY TO STOP ME!
I CAME TO TALK, GENTLEMEN-- BUT IF ANY OF YOU WANT TROUBLE FIRST--
--I'LL BE GLAD TO OBLIGE!
WHUMP!
7

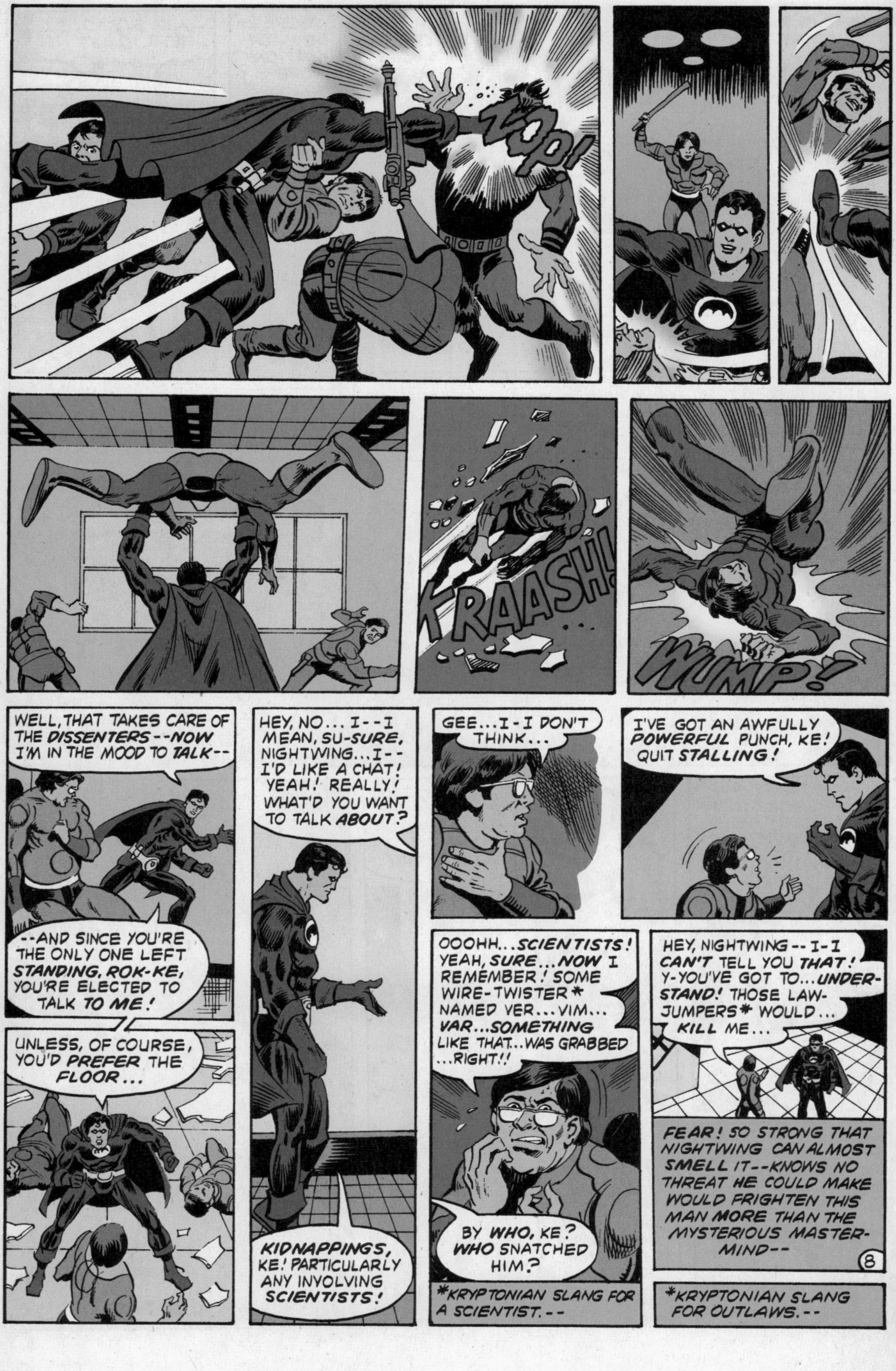

ZOP!
KRAASH!
WUMP!
WELL, THAT TAKES CARE OF THE DISSENTERS--NOW I'M IN THE MOOD TO TALK--
--AND SINCE YOU'RE THE ONLY ONE LEFT STANDING, ROK-KE, YOU'RE ELECTED TO TALK TO ME!
UNLESS, OF COURSE, YOU'D PREFER THE FLOOR...
HEY, NO... I--I MEAN, SU-SURE, NIGHTWING...I--I'D LIKE A CHAT! YEAH! REALLY! WHAT'D YOU WANT TO TALK ABOUT?
KIDNAPPINGS, KE! PARTICULARLY ANY INVOLVING SCIENTISTS!
GEE...I-I DON'T THINK...
I'VE GOT AN AWFULLY POWERFUL PUNCH, KE! QUIT STALLING!
OOOHH...SCIENTISTS! YEAH, SURE...NOW I REMEMBER! SOME WIRE-TWISTER* NAMED VER...VIM...VAR...SOMETHING LIKE THAT...WAS GRABBED ...RIGHT!!
BY WHO, KE? WHO SNATCHED HIM?
*KRYPTONIAN SLANG FOR A SCIENTIST.--
HEY, NIGHTWING--I-I CAN'T TELL YOU THAT! Y-YOU'VE GOT TO...UNDERSTAND! THOSE LAW-JUMPERS* WOULD... KILL ME...
FEAR! SO STRONG THAT NIGHTWING CAN ALMOST SMELL IT--KNOWS NO THREAT HE COULD MAKE WOULD FRIGHTEN THIS MAN MORE THAN THE MYSTERIOUS MASTER-MIND--
8
*KRYPTONIAN SLANG FOR OUTLAWS.--

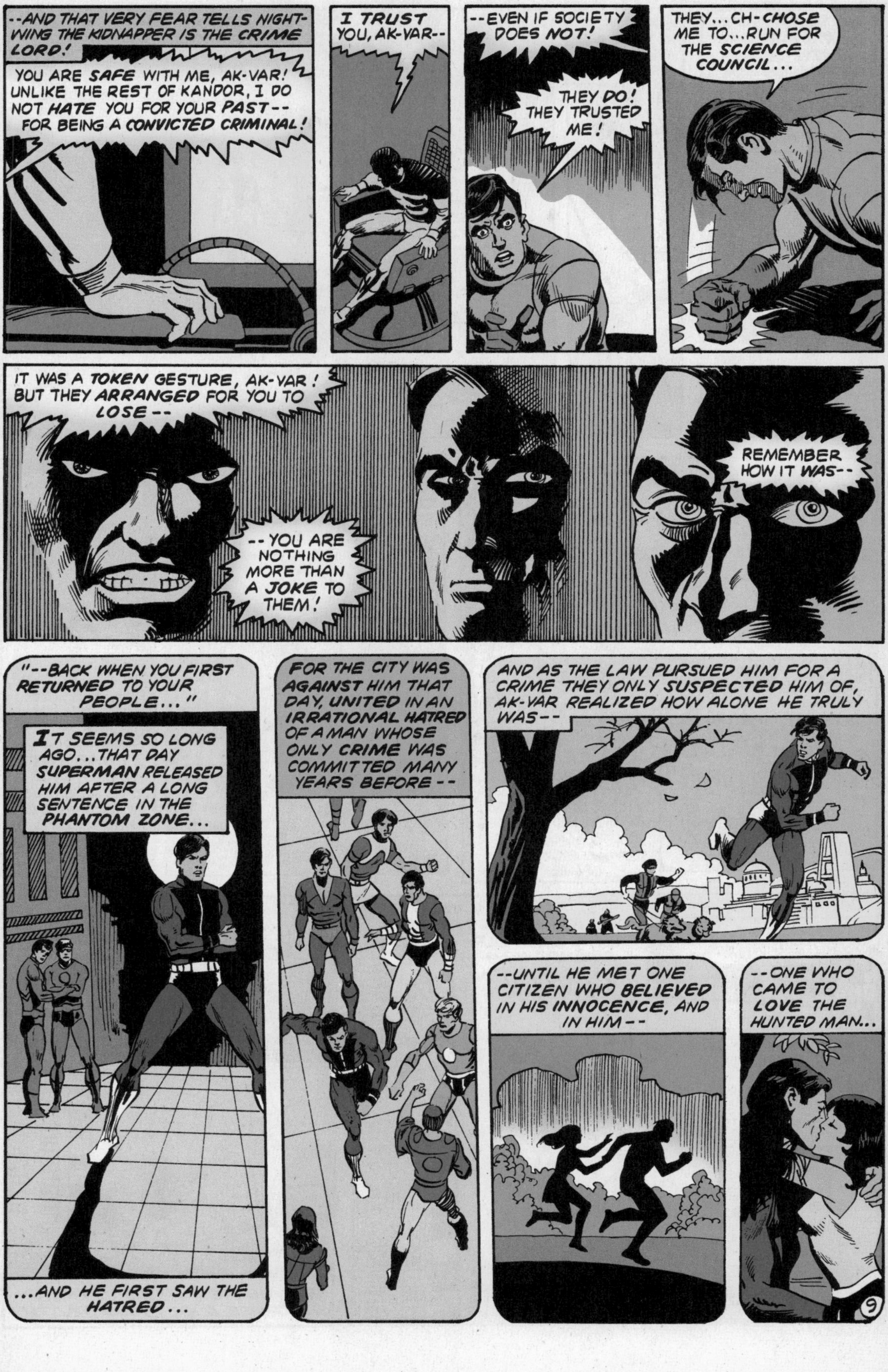
--AND THAT VERY FEAR TELLS NIGHTWING THE KIDNAPPER IS THE CRIME LORD!
YOU ARE SAFE WITH ME, AK-VAR! UNLIKE THE REST OF KANDOR, I DO NOT HATE YOU FOR YOUR PAST-- FOR BEING A CONVICTED CRIMINAL!
I TRUST YOU, AK-VAR--
--EVEN IF SOCIETY DOES NOT!
THEY DO! THEY TRUSTED ME!
THEY...CH-CHOSE ME TO...RUN FOR THE SCIENCE COUNCIL...
IT WAS A TOKEN GESTURE, AK-VAR! BUT THEY ARRANGED FOR YOU TO LOSE--
--YOU ARE NOTHING MORE THAN A JOKE TO THEM!
REMEMBER HOW IT WAS--
"--BACK WHEN YOU FIRST RETURNED TO YOUR PEOPLE..."
IT SEEMS SO LONG AGO...THAT DAY SUPERMAN RELEASED HIM AFTER A LONG SENTENCE IN THE PHANTOM ZONE...
...AND HE FIRST SAW THE HATRED...
FOR THE CITY WAS AGAINST HIM THAT DAY, UNITED IN AN IRRATIONAL HATRED OF A MAN WHOSE ONLY CRIME WAS COMMITTED MANY YEARS BEFORE--
AND AS THE LAW PURSUED HIM FOR A CRIME THEY ONLY SUSPECTED HIM OF, AK-VAR REALIZED HOW ALONE HE TRULY WAS--
--UNTIL HE MET ONE CITIZEN WHO BELIEVED IN HIS INNOCENCE, AND IN HIM--
--ONE WHO CAME TO LOVE THE HUNTED MAN...
9

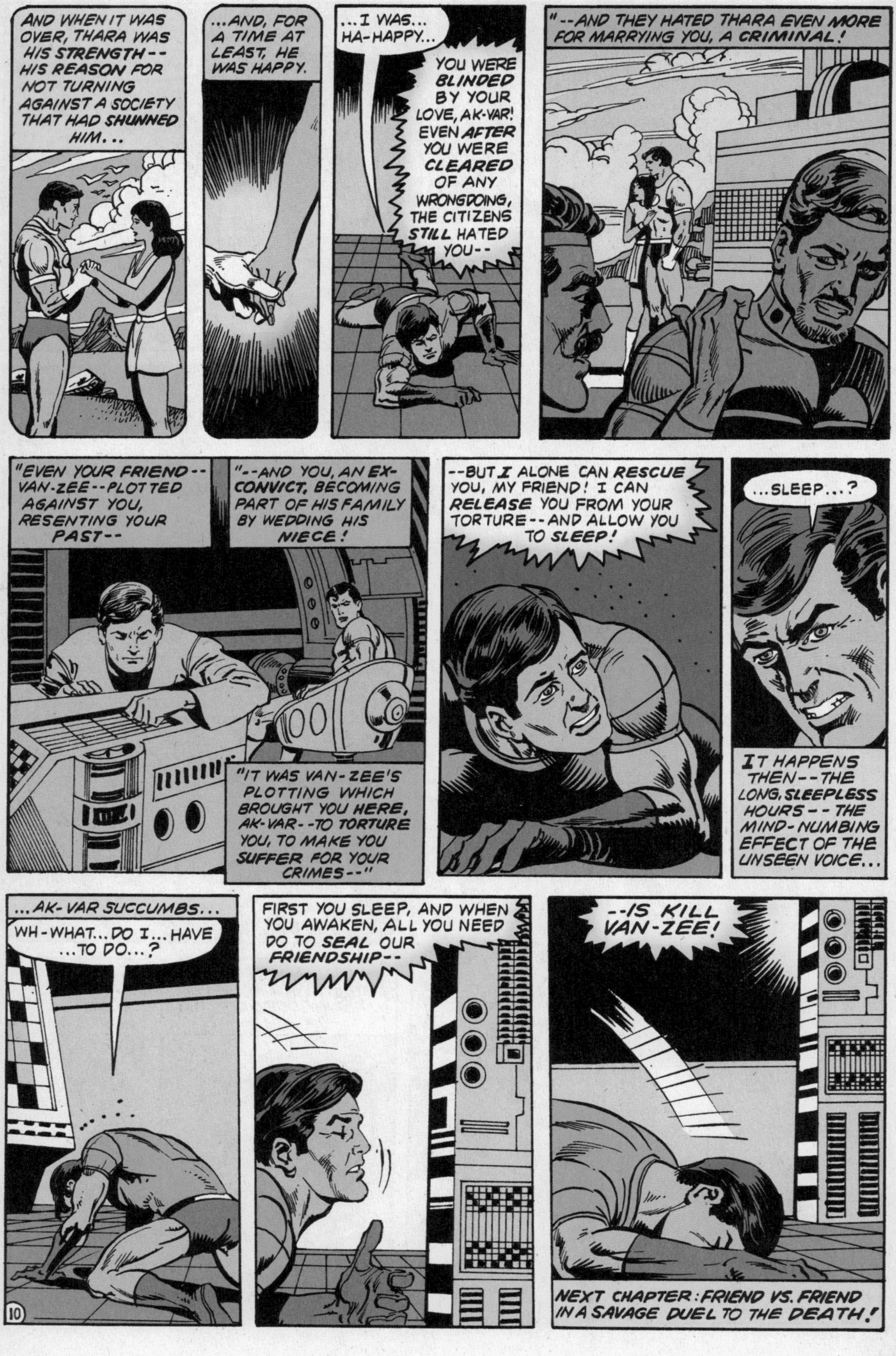
AND WHEN IT WAS OVER, THARA WAS HIS STRENGTH-- HIS REASON FOR NOT TURNING AGAINST A SOCIETY THAT HAD SHUNNED HIM...
...AND, FOR A TIME AT LEAST, HE WAS HAPPY.
...I WAS... HA-HAPPY...
YOU WERE BLINDED BY YOUR LOVE, AK-VAR! EVEN AFTER YOU WERE CLEARED OF ANY WRONGDOING, THE CITIZENS STILL HATED YOU--
"--AND THEY HATED THARA EVEN MORE FOR MARRYING YOU, A CRIMINAL!
"EVEN YOUR FRIEND-- VAN-ZEE--PLOTTED AGAINST YOU, RESENTING YOUR PAST--
"--AND YOU, AN EX-CONVICT, BECOMING PART OF HIS FAMILY BY WEDDING HIS NIECE!
"IT WAS VAN-ZEE'S PLOTTING WHICH BROUGHT YOU HERE, AK-VAR--TO TORTURE YOU, TO MAKE YOU SUFFER FOR YOUR CRIMES--"
--BUT I ALONE CAN RESCUE YOU, MY FRIEND! I CAN RELEASE YOU FROM YOUR TORTURE--AND ALLOW YOU TO SLEEP!
...SLEEP...?
IT HAPPENS THEN--THE LONG, SLEEPLESS HOURS--THE MIND-NUMBING EFFECT OF THE UNSEEN VOICE...
...AK-VAR SUCCUMBS...
WH-WHAT...DO I...HAVE ...TO DO...?
FIRST YOU SLEEP, AND WHEN YOU AWAKEN, ALL YOU NEED DO TO SEAL OUR FRIENDSHIP--
--IS KILL VAN-ZEE!
10
NEXT CHAPTER: FRIEND VS. FRIEND IN A SAVAGE DUEL TO THE DEATH!

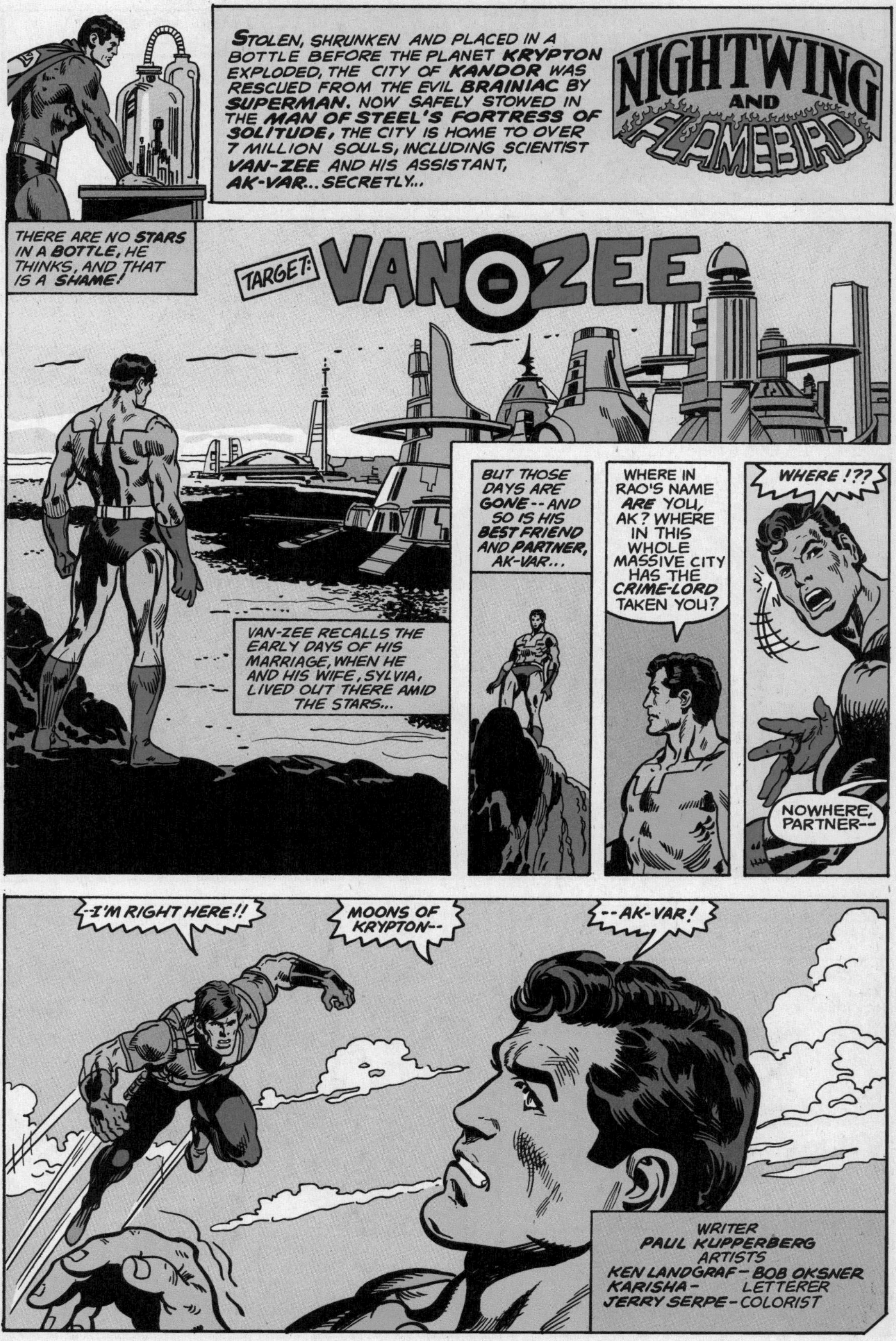

STOLEN, SHRUNKEN AND PLACED IN A BOTTLE BEFORE THE PLANET KRYPTON EXPLODED, THE CITY OF KANDOR WAS RESCUED FROM THE EVIL BRAINIAC BY SUPERMAN. NOW SAFELY STOWED IN THE MAN OF STEEL'S FORTRESS OF SOLITUDE, THE CITY IS HOME TO OVER 7 MILLION SOULS, INCLUDING SCIENTIST VAN-ZEE AND HIS ASSISTANT, AK-VAR... SECRETLY...
NIGHTWING AND FLAMEBIRD
THERE ARE NO STARS IN A BOTTLE, HE THINKS, AND THAT IS A SHAME!
TARGET: VAN-ZEE
VAN-ZEE RECALLS THE EARLY DAYS OF HIS MARRIAGE, WHEN HE AND HIS WIFE, SYLVIA, LIVED OUT THERE AMID THE STARS...
BUT THOSE DAYS ARE GONE -- AND SO IS HIS BEST FRIEND AND PARTNER, AK-VAR...
WHERE IN RAO'S NAME ARE YOU, AK? WHERE IN THIS WHOLE MASSIVE CITY HAS THE CRIME-LORD TAKEN YOU?
WHERE !??
NOWHERE, PARTNER--
--I'M RIGHT HERE!!
MOONS OF KRYPTON--
--AK-VAR!
WRITER PAUL KUPPERBERG
ARTISTS KEN LANDGRAF - BOB OKSNER
KARISHA - LETTERER
JERRY SERPE - COLORIST

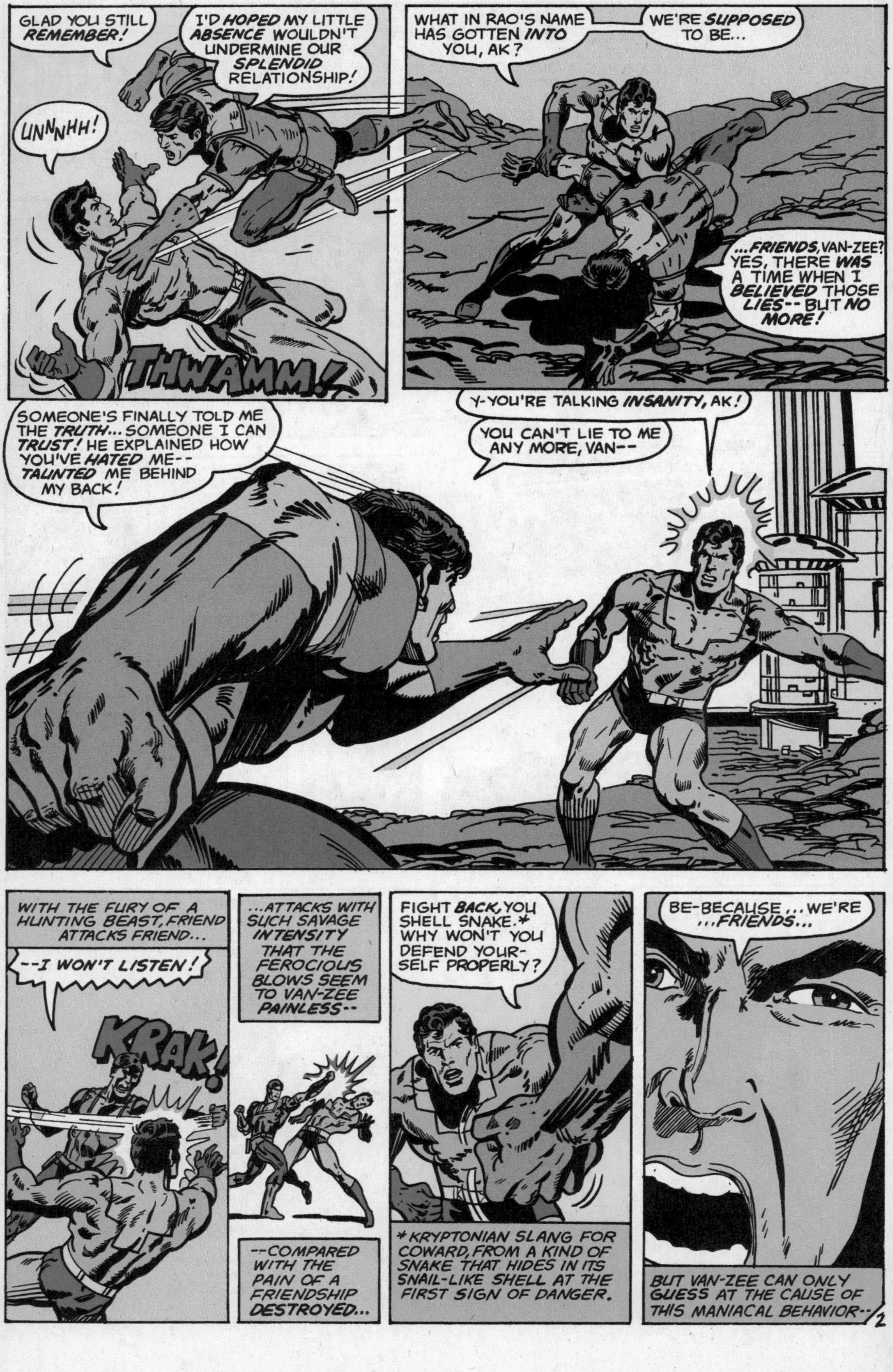
GLAD YOU STILL REMEMBER!
I'D HOPED MY LITTLE ABSENCE WOULDN'T UNDERMINE OUR SPLENDID RELATIONSHIP!
UNNNHH!
THWAMM!
WHAT IN RAO'S NAME HAS GOTTEN INTO YOU, AK?
WE'RE SUPPOSED TO BE...
...FRIENDS, VAN-ZEE? YES, THERE WAS A TIME WHEN I BELIEVED THOSE LIES-- BUT NO MORE!
SOMEONE'S FINALLY TOLD ME THE TRUTH... SOMEONE I CAN TRUST! HE EXPLAINED HOW YOU'VE HATED ME-- TAUNTED ME BEHIND MY BACK!
Y-YOU'RE TALKING INSANITY, AK!
YOU CAN'T LIE TO ME ANY MORE, VAN--
WITH THE FURY OF A HUNTING BEAST, FRIEND ATTACKS FRIEND...
--I WON'T LISTEN!
KRAK!
...ATTACKS WITH SUCH SAVAGE INTENSITY THAT THE FEROCIOUS BLOWS SEEM TO VAN-ZEE PAINLESS--
--COMPARED WITH THE PAIN OF A FRIENDSHIP DESTROYED...
FIGHT BACK, YOU SHELL SNAKE.* WHY WON'T YOU DEFEND YOURSELF PROPERLY?
*KRYPTONIAN SLANG FOR COWARD, FROM A KIND OF SNAKE THAT HIDES IN ITS SNAIL-LIKE SHELL AT THE FIRST SIGN OF DANGER.
BE-BECAUSE... WE'RE ...FRIENDS...
BUT VAN-ZEE CAN ONLY GUESS AT THE CAUSE OF THIS MANIACAL BEHAVIOR--
2

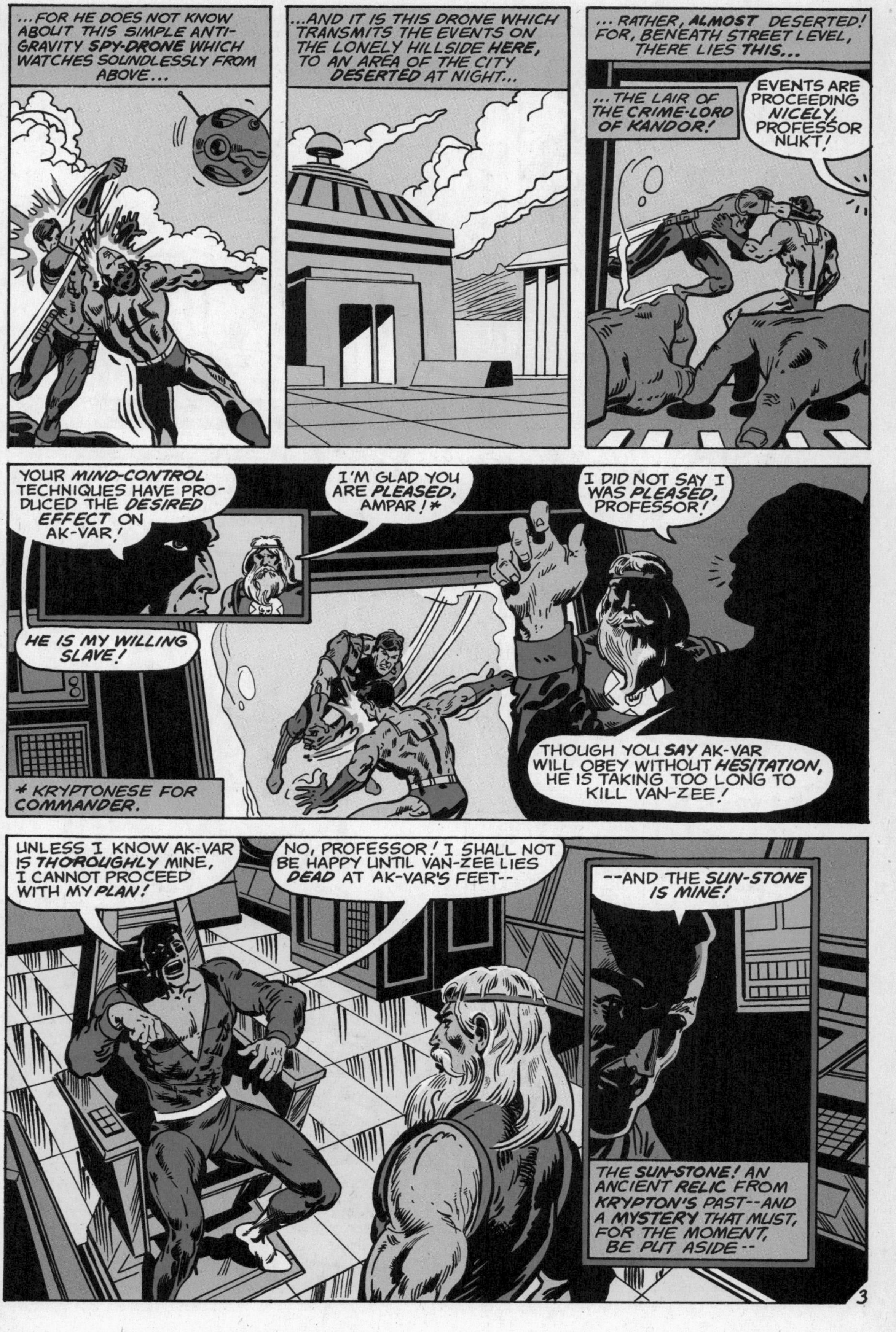
...FOR HE DOES NOT KNOW ABOUT THIS SIMPLE ANTI-GRAVITY SPY-DRONE WHICH WATCHES SOUNDLESSLY FROM ABOVE...
...AND IT IS THIS DRONE WHICH TRANSMITS THE EVENTS ON THE LONELY HILLSIDE HERE, TO AN AREA OF THE CITY DESERTED AT NIGHT...
...RATHER, ALMOST DESERTED! FOR, BENEATH STREET LEVEL, THERE LIES THIS...
...THE LAIR OF THE CRIME-LORD OF KANDOR!
EVENTS ARE PROCEEDING NICELY, PROFESSOR NUKT!
YOUR MIND-CONTROL TECHNIQUES HAVE PRODUCED THE DESIRED EFFECT ON AK-VAR!
I'M GLAD YOU ARE PLEASED, AMPAR!*
I DID NOT SAY I WAS PLEASED, PROFESSOR!
HE IS MY WILLING SLAVE!
THOUGH YOU SAY AK-VAR WILL OBEY WITHOUT HESITATION, HE IS TAKING TOO LONG TO KILL VAN-ZEE!
* KRYPTONESE FOR COMMANDER.
UNLESS I KNOW AK-VAR IS THOROUGHLY MINE, I CANNOT PROCEED WITH MY PLAN!
NO, PROFESSOR! I SHALL NOT BE HAPPY UNTIL VAN-ZEE LIES DEAD AT AK-VAR'S FEET--
--AND THE SUN-STONE IS MINE!
THE SUN-STONE! AN ANCIENT RELIC FROM KRYPTON'S PAST--AND A MYSTERY THAT MUST, FOR THE MOMENT, BE PUT ASIDE--
3

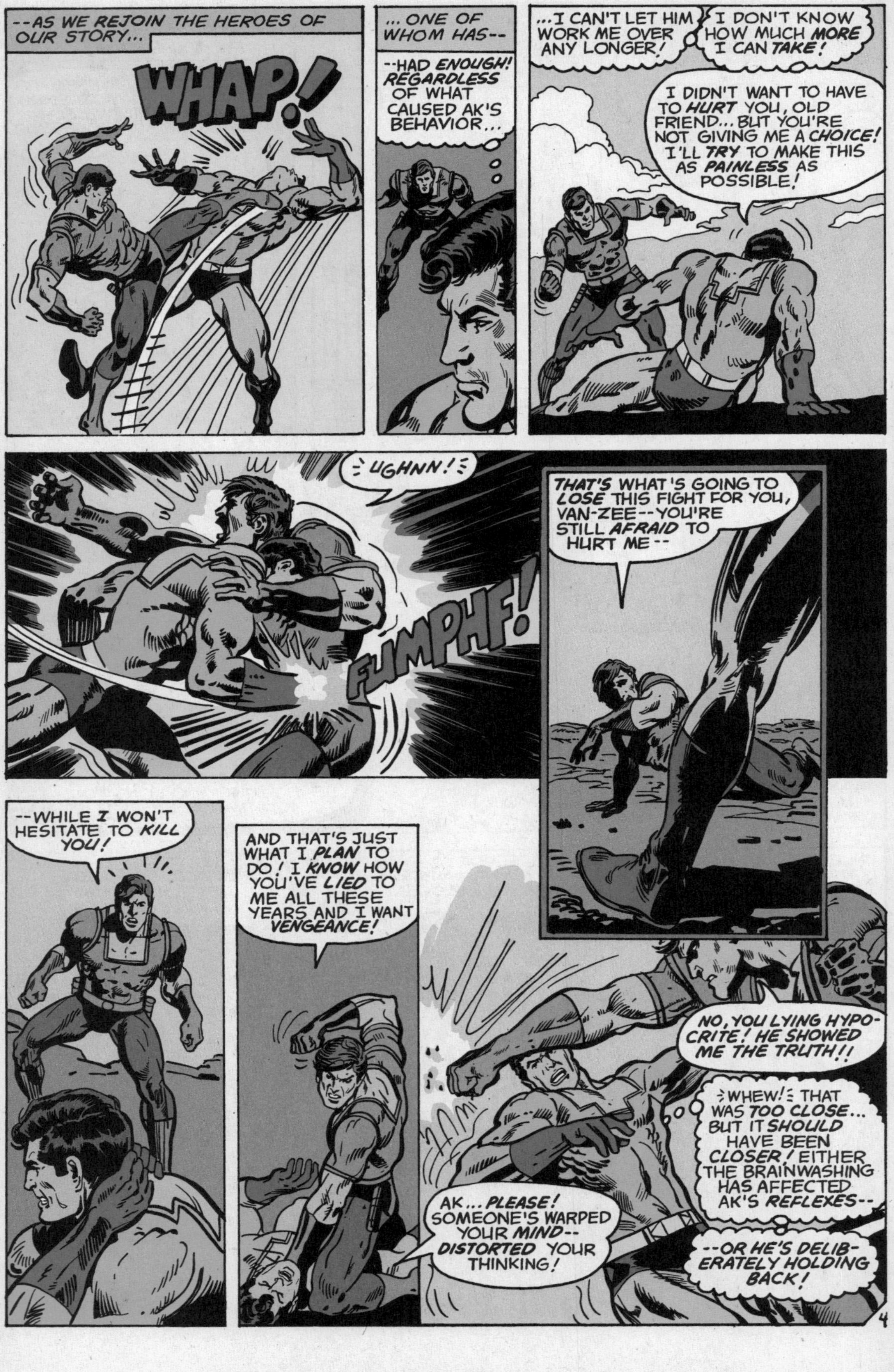
--AS WE REJOIN THE HEROES OF OUR STORY...
WHAP!
...ONE OF WHOM HAS--
--HAD ENOUGH! REGARDLESS OF WHAT CAUSED AK'S BEHAVIOR...
...I CAN'T LET HIM WORK ME OVER ANY LONGER!
I DON'T KNOW HOW MUCH MORE I CAN TAKE!
I DIDN'T WANT TO HAVE TO HURT YOU, OLD FRIEND... BUT YOU'RE NOT GIVING ME A CHOICE! I'LL TRY TO MAKE THIS AS PAINLESS AS POSSIBLE!
UGHNN!
FUMPHF!
THAT'S WHAT'S GOING TO LOSE THIS FIGHT FOR YOU, VAN-ZEE--YOU'RE STILL AFRAID TO HURT ME--
--WHILE I WON'T HESITATE TO KILL YOU!
AND THAT'S JUST WHAT I PLAN TO DO! I KNOW HOW YOU'VE LIED TO ME ALL THESE YEARS AND I WANT VENGEANCE!
NO, YOU LYING HYPOCRITE! HE SHOWED ME THE TRUTH!!
AK... PLEASE! SOMEONE'S WARPED YOUR MIND--DISTORTED YOUR THINKING!
WHEW! THAT WAS TOO CLOSE... BUT IT SHOULD HAVE BEEN CLOSER! EITHER THE BRAINWASHING HAS AFFECTED AK'S REFLEXES--
--OR HE'S DELIBERATELY HOLDING BACK!
4

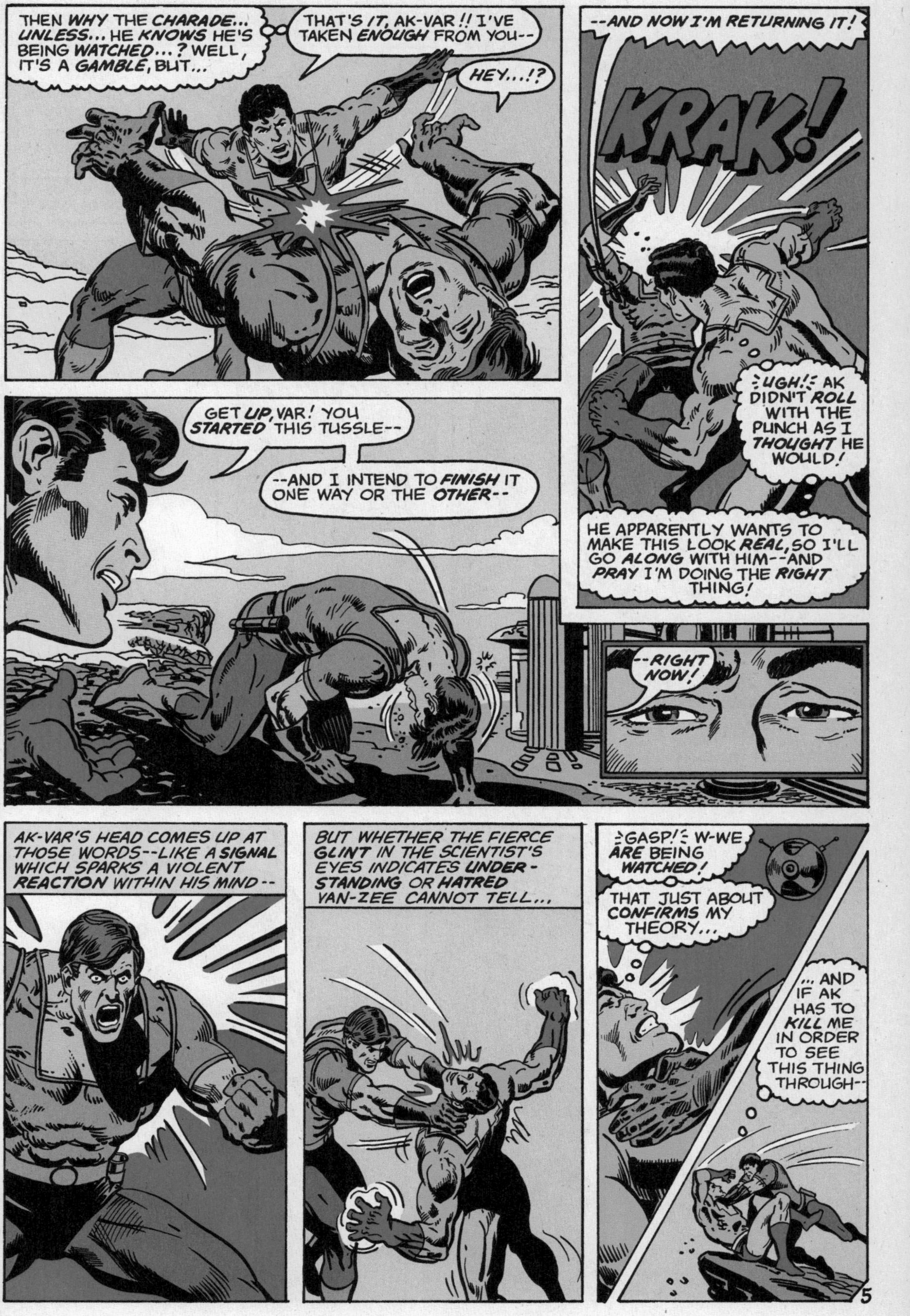
THEN WHY THE CHARADE... UNLESS... HE KNOWS HE'S BEING WATCHED...? WELL, IT'S A GAMBLE, BUT...
THAT'S IT, AK-VAR!! I'VE TAKEN ENOUGH FROM YOU--
HEY...!?
--AND NOW I'M RETURNING IT!
KRAK!
UGH! AK DIDN'T ROLL WITH THE PUNCH AS I THOUGHT HE WOULD!
HE APPARENTLY WANTS TO MAKE THIS LOOK REAL, SO I'LL GO ALONG WITH HIM--AND PRAY I'M DOING THE RIGHT THING!
GET UP, VAR! YOU STARTED THIS TUSSLE--
--AND I INTEND TO FINISH IT ONE WAY OR THE OTHER--
--RIGHT NOW!
AK-VAR'S HEAD COMES UP AT THOSE WORDS--LIKE A SIGNAL WHICH SPARKS A VIOLENT REACTION WITHIN HIS MIND--
BUT WHETHER THE FIERCE GLINT IN THE SCIENTIST'S EYES INDICATES UNDER-STANDING OR HATRED VAN-ZEE CANNOT TELL...
GASP! W-WE ARE BEING WATCHED!
THAT JUST ABOUT CONFIRMS MY THEORY...
...AND IF AK HAS TO KILL ME IN ORDER TO SEE THIS THING THROUGH--
5

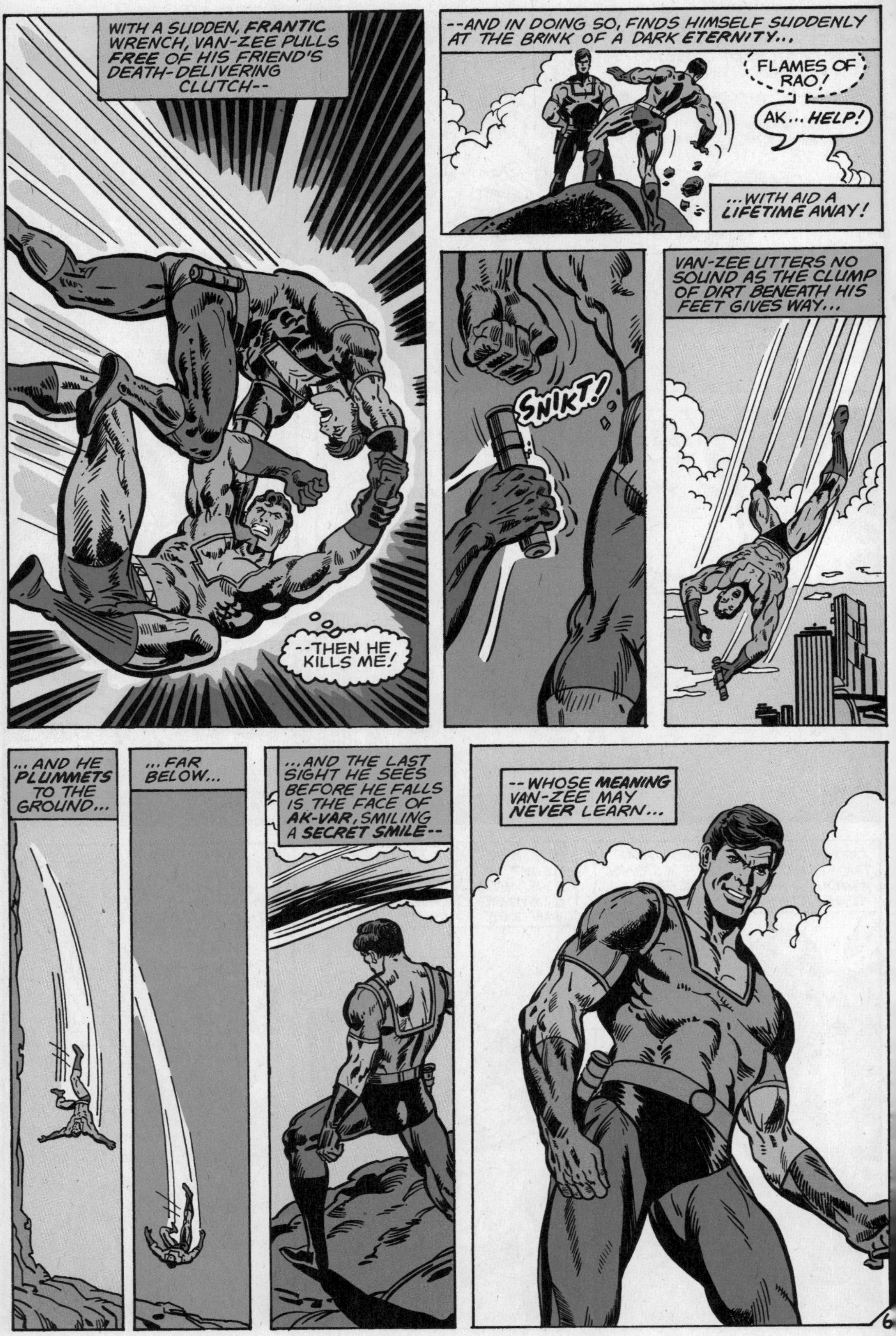
WITH A SUDDEN, FRANTIC WRENCH, VAN-ZEE PULLS FREE OF HIS FRIEND'S DEATH-DELIVERING CLUTCH--
--THEN HE KILLS ME!
--AND IN DOING SO, FINDS HIMSELF SUDDENLY AT THE BRINK OF A DARK ETERNITY...
FLAMES OF RAO!
AK... HELP!
...WITH AID A LIFETIME AWAY!
SNIKT!
VAN-ZEE UTTERS NO SOUND AS THE CLUMP OF DIRT BENEATH HIS FEET GIVES WAY...
...AND HE PLUMMETS TO THE GROUND...
...FAR BELOW...
...AND THE LAST SIGHT HE SEES BEFORE HE FALLS IS THE FACE OF AK-VAR, SMILING A SECRET SMILE--
--WHOSE MEANING VAN-ZEE MAY NEVER LEARN...
6

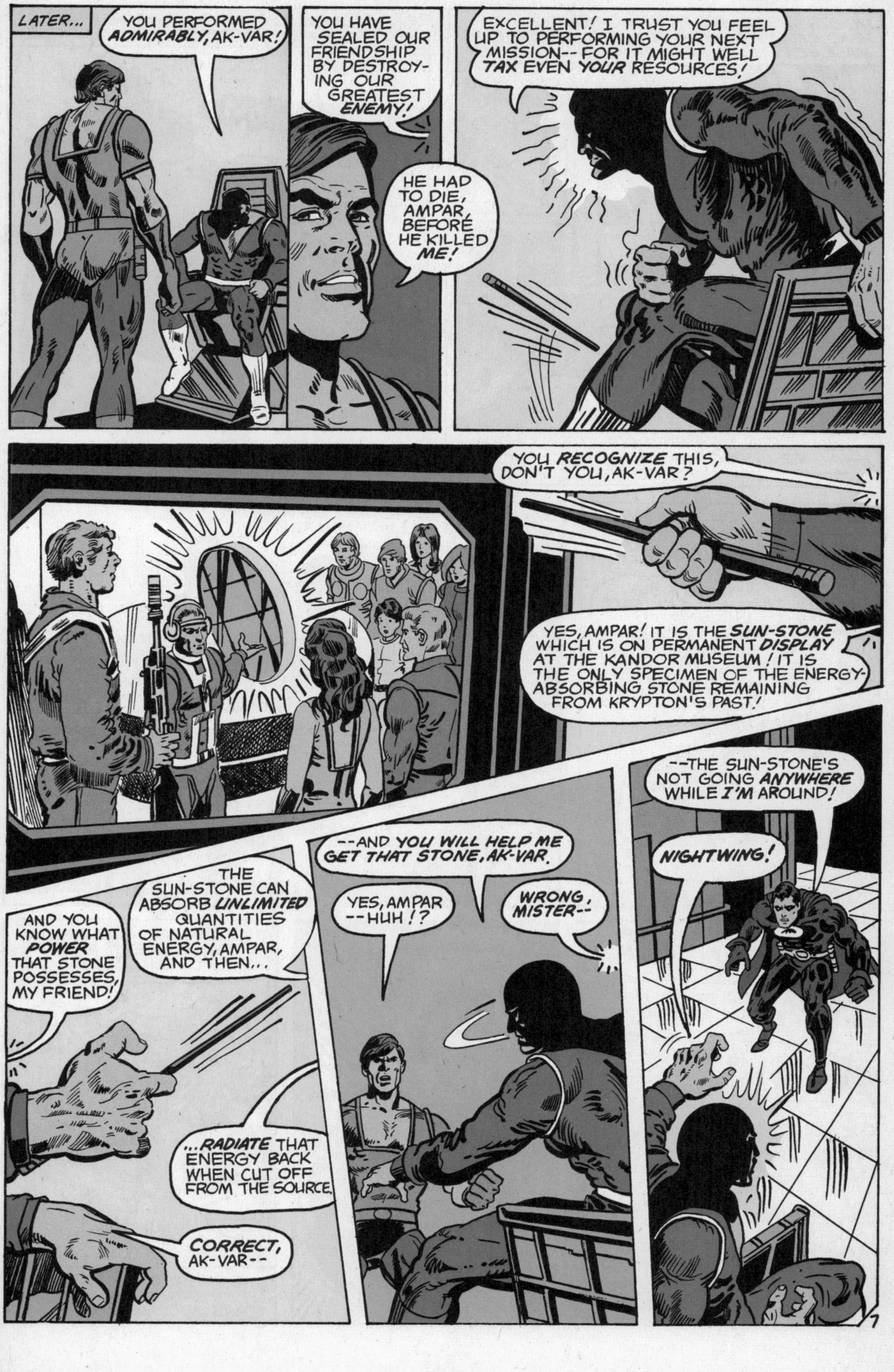
LATER...
YOU PERFORMED ADMIRABLY, AK-VAR!
YOU HAVE SEALED OUR FRIENDSHIP BY DESTROYING OUR GREATEST ENEMY!
HE HAD TO DIE, AMPAR, BEFORE HE KILLED ME!
EXCELLENT! I TRUST YOU FEEL UP TO PERFORMING YOUR NEXT MISSION-- FOR IT MIGHT WELL TAX EVEN YOUR RESOURCES!
YOU RECOGNIZE THIS, DON'T YOU, AK-VAR?
YES, AMPAR! IT IS THE SUN-STONE WHICH IS ON PERMANENT DISPLAY AT THE KANDOR MUSEUM! IT IS THE ONLY SPECIMEN OF THE ENERGY-ABSORBING STONE REMAINING FROM KRYPTON'S PAST!
AND YOU KNOW WHAT POWER THAT STONE POSSESSES, MY FRIEND!
THE SUN-STONE CAN ABSORB UNLIMITED QUANTITIES OF NATURAL ENERGY, AMPAR, AND THEN...
...RADIATE THAT ENERGY BACK WHEN CUT OFF FROM THE SOURCE.
CORRECT, AK-VAR--
--AND YOU WILL HELP ME GET THAT STONE, AK-VAR.
YES, AMPAR --HUH!?
WRONG, MISTER--
--THE SUN-STONE'S NOT GOING ANYWHERE WHILE I'M AROUND!
NIGHTWING!
7

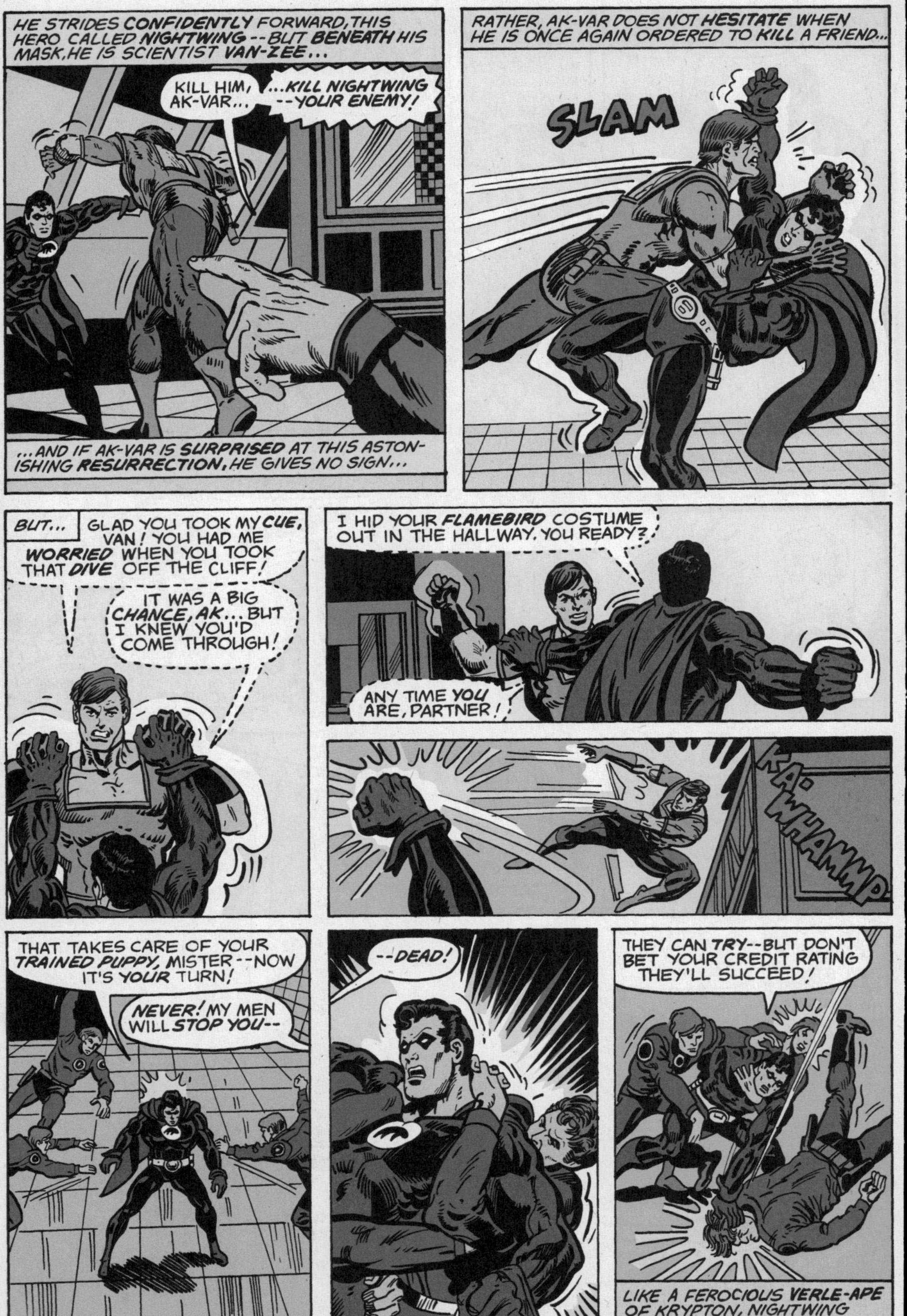

HE STRIDES CONFIDENTLY FORWARD, THIS HERO CALLED NIGHTWING -- BUT BENEATH HIS MASK, HE IS SCIENTIST VAN-ZEE...
KILL HIM, AK-VAR...
...KILL NIGHTWING -- YOUR ENEMY!
...AND IF AK-VAR IS SURPRISED AT THIS ASTONISHING RESURRECTION, HE GIVES NO SIGN...
RATHER, AK-VAR DOES NOT HESITATE WHEN HE IS ONCE AGAIN ORDERED TO KILL A FRIEND...
SLAM
BUT...
GLAD YOU TOOK MY CUE, VAN! YOU HAD ME WORRIED WHEN YOU TOOK THAT DIVE OFF THE CLIFF!
IT WAS A BIG CHANCE, AK... BUT I KNEW YOU'D COME THROUGH!
I HID YOUR FLAMEBIRD COSTUME OUT IN THE HALLWAY. YOU READY?
ANY TIME YOU ARE, PARTNER!
KA-WHAMMP
THAT TAKES CARE OF YOUR TRAINED PUPPY, MISTER -- NOW IT'S YOUR TURN!
NEVER! MY MEN WILL STOP YOU--
--DEAD!
THEY CAN TRY -- BUT DON'T BET YOUR CREDIT RATING THEY'LL SUCCEED!
LIKE A FEROCIOUS VERLE-APE OF KRYPTON, NIGHTWING TEARS INTO HIS FOES--
8

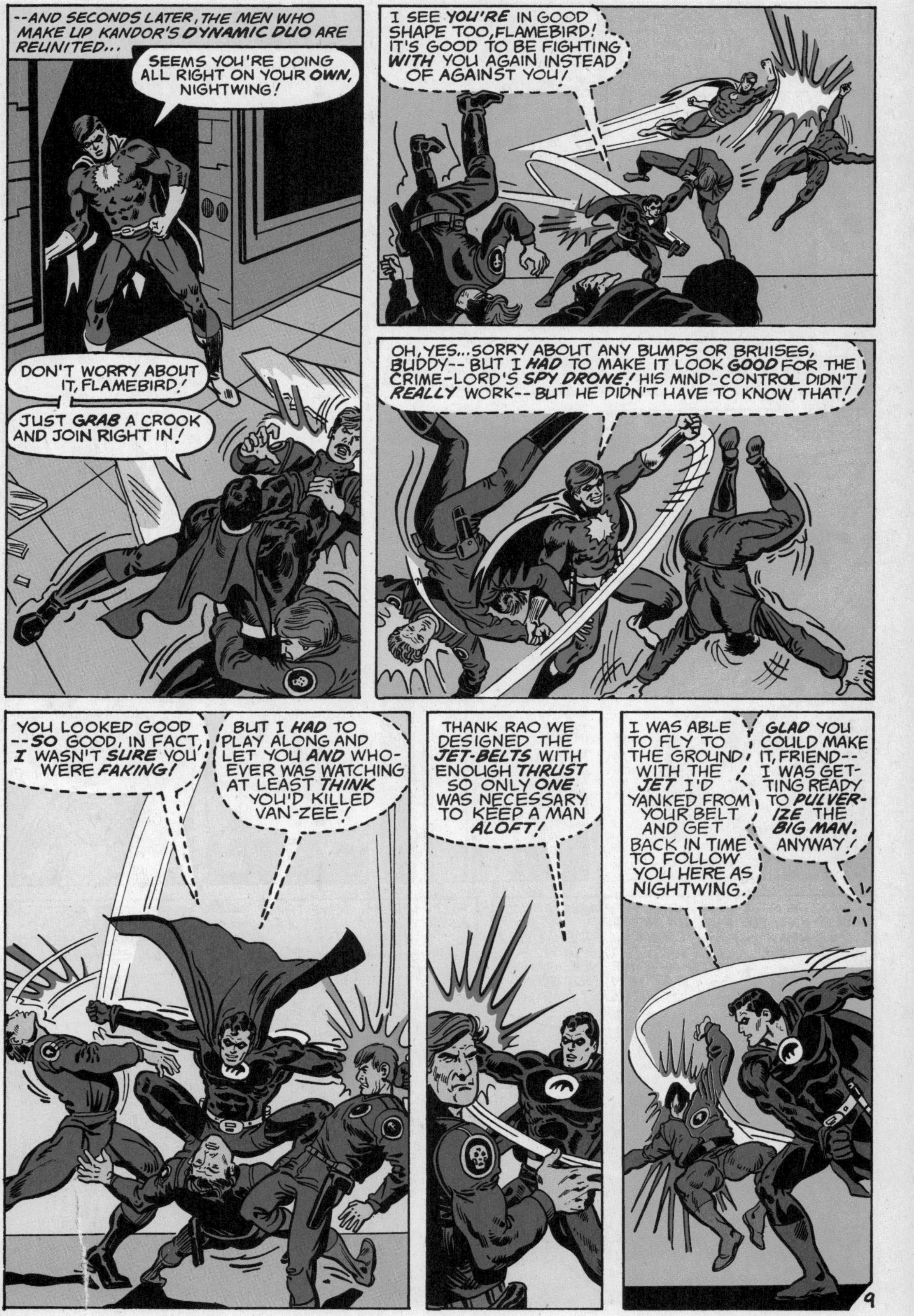
--AND SECONDS LATER, THE MEN WHO MAKE UP KANDOR'S DYNAMIC DUO ARE REUNITED...
SEEMS YOU'RE DOING ALL RIGHT ON YOUR OWN, NIGHTWING!
I SEE YOU'RE IN GOOD SHAPE TOO, FLAMEBIRD! IT'S GOOD TO BE FIGHTING WITH YOU AGAIN INSTEAD OF AGAINST YOU!
DON'T WORRY ABOUT IT, FLAMEBIRD!
JUST GRAB A CROOK AND JOIN RIGHT IN!
OH, YES... SORRY ABOUT ANY BUMPS OR BRUISES, BUDDY-- BUT I HAD TO MAKE IT LOOK GOOD FOR THE CRIME-LORD'S SPY DRONE! HIS MIND-CONTROL DIDN'T REALLY WORK-- BUT HE DIDN'T HAVE TO KNOW THAT!
YOU LOOKED GOOD --SO GOOD, IN FACT, I WASN'T SURE YOU WERE FAKING!
BUT I HAD TO PLAY ALONG AND LET YOU AND WHO-EVER WAS WATCHING AT LEAST THINK YOU'D KILLED VAN-ZEE!
THANK RAO WE DESIGNED THE JET-BELTS WITH ENOUGH THRUST SO ONLY ONE WAS NECESSARY TO KEEP A MAN ALOFT!
I WAS ABLE TO FLY TO THE GROUND WITH THE JET I'D YANKED FROM YOUR BELT AND GET BACK IN TIME TO FOLLOW YOU HERE AS NIGHTWING.
GLAD YOU COULD MAKE IT, FRIEND-- I WAS GETTING READY TO PULVERIZE THE BIG MAN, ANYWAY!
9

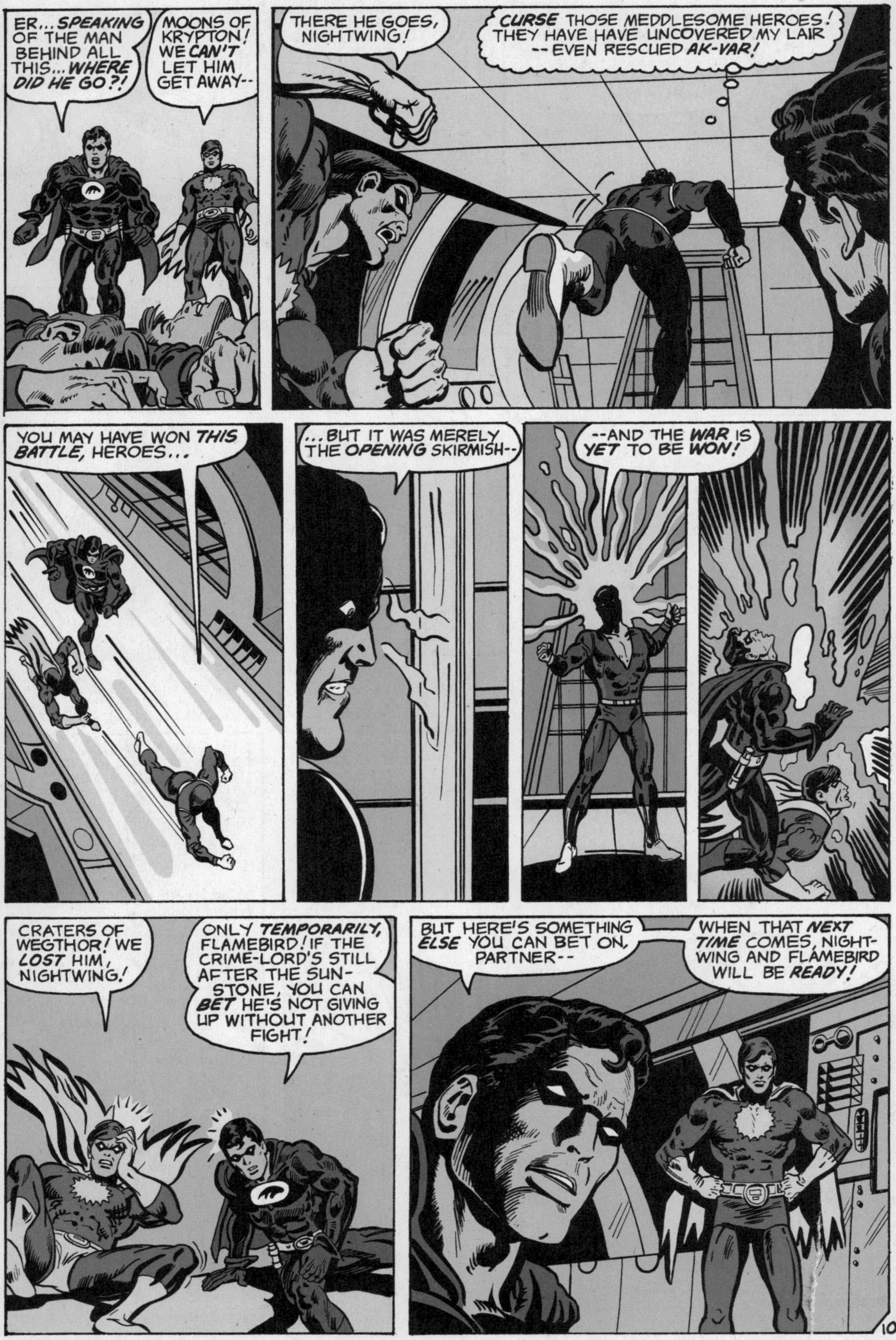

ER... SPEAKING OF THE MAN BEHIND ALL THIS... WHERE DID HE GO?!
MOONS OF KRYPTON! WE CAN'T LET HIM GET AWAY--
THERE HE GOES, NIGHTWING!
CURSE THOSE MEDDLESOME HEROES! THEY HAVE HAVE UNCOVERED MY LAIR -- EVEN RESCUED AK-VAR!
YOU MAY HAVE WON THIS BATTLE, HEROES...
...BUT IT WAS MERELY THE OPENING SKIRMISH--
--AND THE WAR IS YET TO BE WON!
CRATERS OF WEGTHOR! WE LOST HIM, NIGHTWING!
ONLY TEMPORARILY, FLAMEBIRD! IF THE CRIME-LORD'S STILL AFTER THE SUN-STONE, YOU CAN BET HE'S NOT GIVING UP WITHOUT ANOTHER FIGHT!
BUT HERE'S SOMETHING ELSE YOU CAN BET ON, PARTNER--
WHEN THAT NEXT TIME COMES, NIGHT-WING AND FLAMEBIRD WILL BE READY!
10

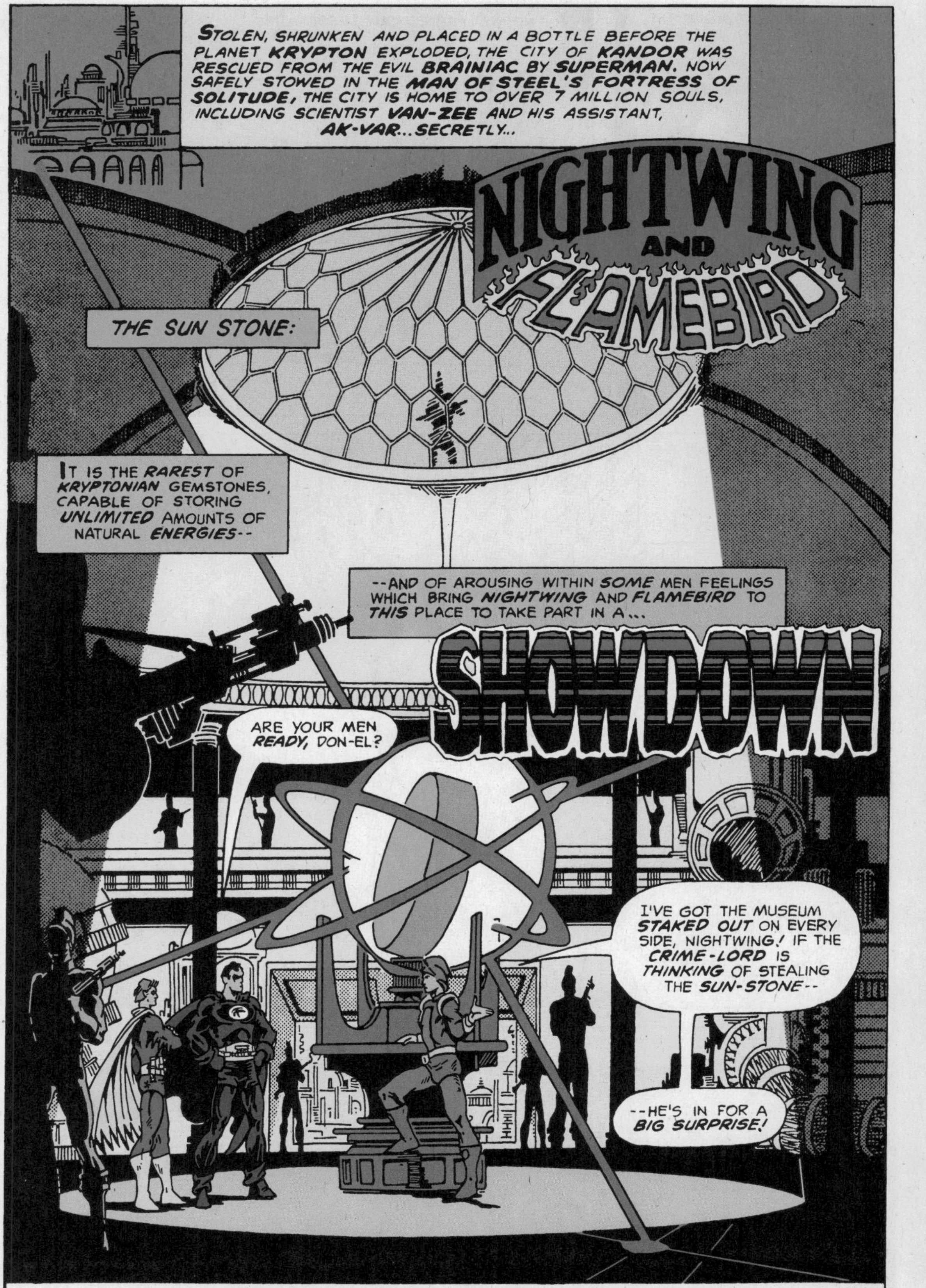
STOLEN, SHRUNKEN AND PLACED IN A BOTTLE BEFORE THE PLANET KRYPTON EXPLODED, THE CITY OF KANDOR WAS RESCUED FROM THE EVIL BRAINIAC BY SUPERMAN. NOW SAFELY STOWED IN THE MAN OF STEEL'S FORTRESS OF SOLITUDE, THE CITY IS HOME TO OVER 7 MILLION SOULS, INCLUDING SCIENTIST VAN-ZEE AND HIS ASSISTANT, AK-VAR...SECRETLY...
NIGHTWING AND FLAMEBIRD
THE SUN STONE:
IT IS THE RAREST OF KRYPTONIAN GEMSTONES, CAPABLE OF STORING UNLIMITED AMOUNTS OF NATURAL ENERGIES--
--AND OF AROUSING WITHIN SOME MEN FEELINGS WHICH BRING NIGHTWING AND FLAMEBIRD TO THIS PLACE TO TAKE PART IN A...
SHOWDOWN
ARE YOUR MEN READY, DON-EL?
I'VE GOT THE MUSEUM STAKED OUT ON EVERY SIDE, NIGHTWING! IF THE CRIME-LORD IS THINKING OF STEALING THE SUN-STONE--
--HE'S IN FOR A BIG SURPRISE!
PAUL KUPPERBERG – WRITER • MARSHALL ROGERS – ARTIST
BEN ODA – LETTERER • JERRY SERPE – COLORIST

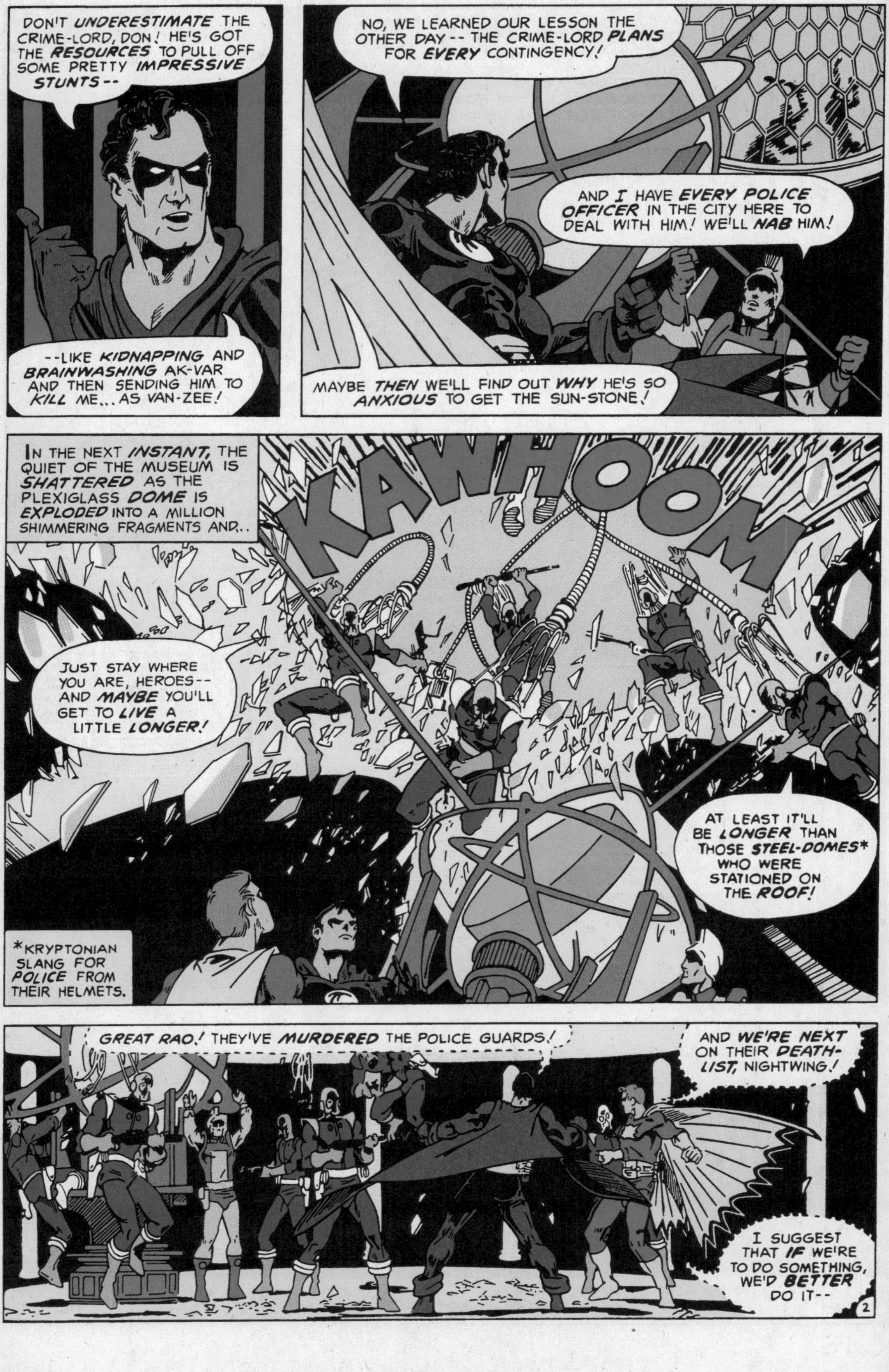
DON'T UNDERESTIMATE THE CRIME-LORD, DON! HE'S GOT THE RESOURCES TO PULL OFF SOME PRETTY IMPRESSIVE STUNTS--
--LIKE KIDNAPPING AND BRAINWASHING AK-VAR AND THEN SENDING HIM TO KILL ME... AS VAN-ZEE!
NO, WE LEARNED OUR LESSON THE OTHER DAY -- THE CRIME-LORD PLANS FOR EVERY CONTINGENCY!
AND I HAVE EVERY POLICE OFFICER IN THE CITY HERE TO DEAL WITH HIM! WE'LL NAB HIM!
MAYBE THEN WE'LL FIND OUT WHY HE'S SO ANXIOUS TO GET THE SUN-STONE!
IN THE NEXT INSTANT, THE QUIET OF THE MUSEUM IS SHATTERED AS THE PLEXIGLASS DOME IS EXPLODED INTO A MILLION SHIMMERING FRAGMENTS AND..
KAWHOOM
JUST STAY WHERE YOU ARE, HEROES-- AND MAYBE YOU'LL GET TO LIVE A LITTLE LONGER!
AT LEAST IT'LL BE LONGER THAN THOSE STEEL-DOMES* WHO WERE STATIONED ON THE ROOF!
*KRYPTONIAN SLANG FOR POLICE FROM THEIR HELMETS.
GREAT RAO! THEY'VE MURDERED THE POLICE GUARDS!
AND WE'RE NEXT ON THEIR DEATH-LIST, NIGHTWING!
I SUGGEST THAT IF WE'RE TO DO SOMETHING, WE'D BETTER DO IT--
2

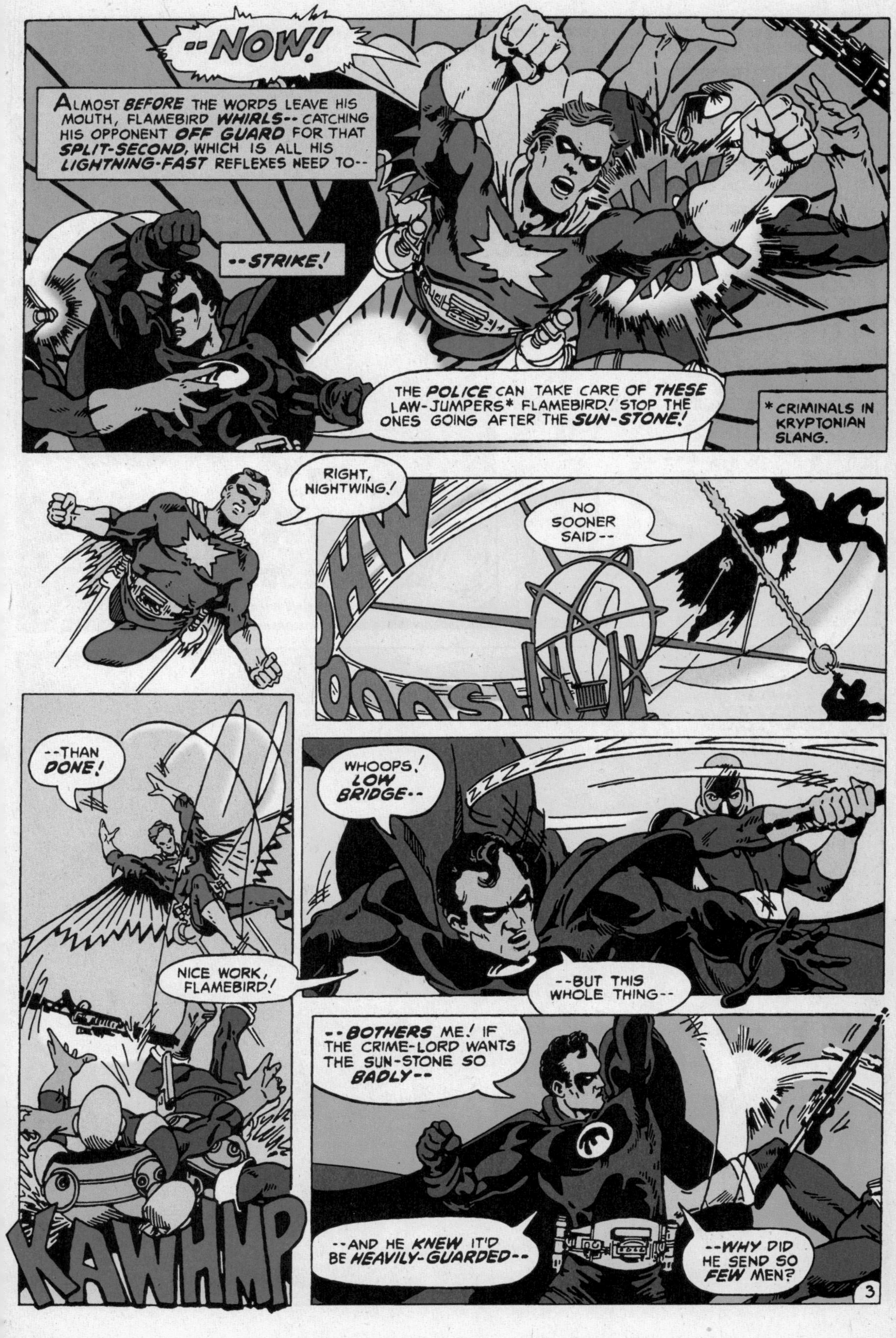
--NOW!
ALMOST BEFORE THE WORDS LEAVE HIS MOUTH, FLAMEBIRD WHIRLS-- CATCHING HIS OPPONENT OFF GUARD FOR THAT SPLIT-SECOND, WHICH IS ALL HIS LIGHTNING-FAST REFLEXES NEED TO--
--STRIKE!
THE POLICE CAN TAKE CARE OF THESE LAW-JUMPERS* FLAMEBIRD! STOP THE ONES GOING AFTER THE SUN-STONE!
*CRIMINALS IN KRYPTONIAN SLANG.
RIGHT, NIGHTWING!
NO SOONER SAID--
WHOOSH
--THAN DONE!
WHOOPS! LOW BRIDGE--
NICE WORK, FLAMEBIRD!
--BUT THIS WHOLE THING--
KAWHMP
--BOTHERS ME! IF THE CRIME-LORD WANTS THE SUN-STONE SO BADLY--
--AND HE KNEW IT'D BE HEAVILY-GUARDED--
--WHY DID HE SEND SO FEW MEN?
3

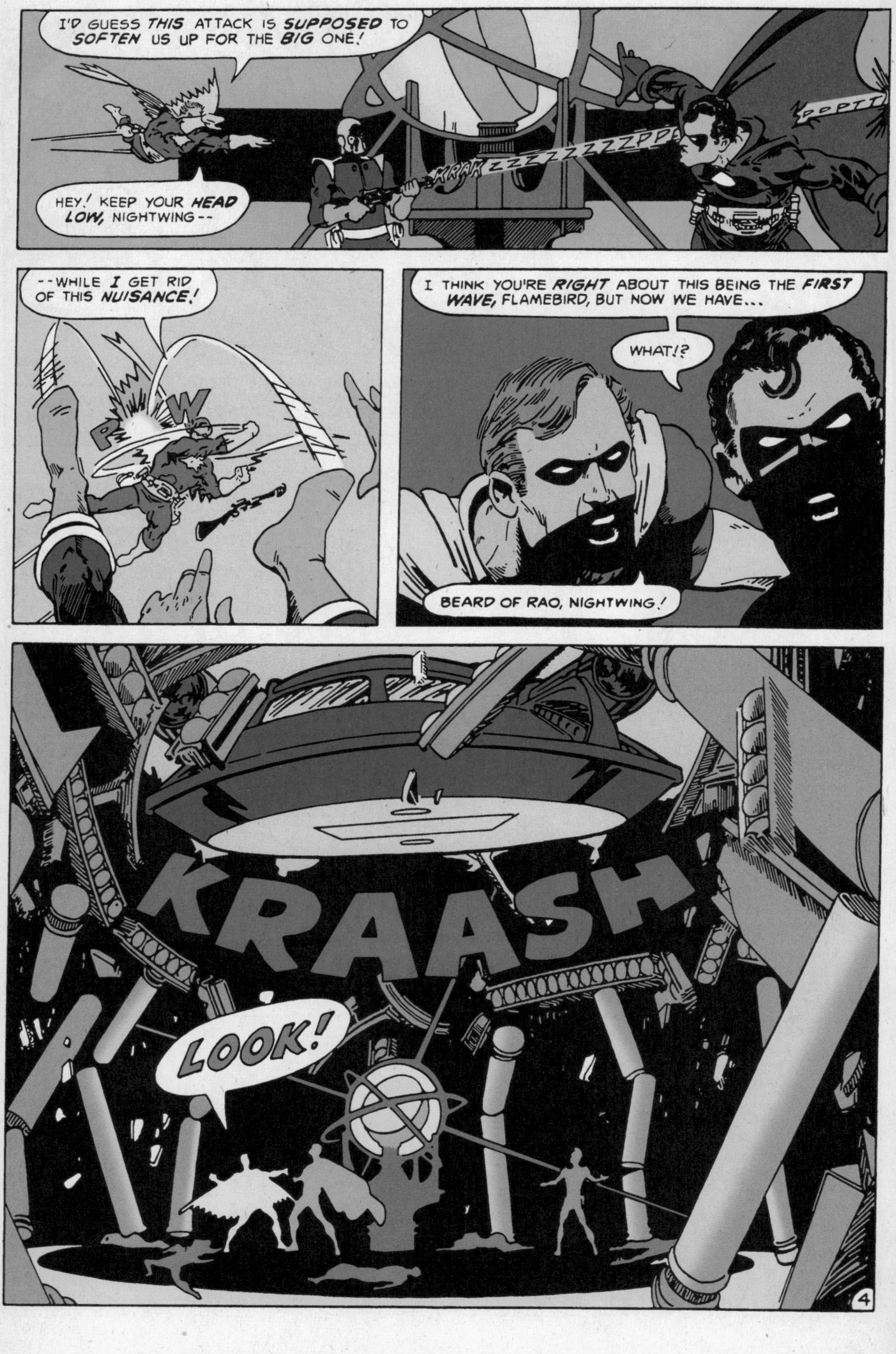
I'D GUESS THIS ATTACK IS SUPPOSED TO SOFTEN US UP FOR THE BIG ONE!
HEY! KEEP YOUR HEAD LOW, NIGHTWING--
KRAK ZZZZZZZZZZZPPP
PPPTTT
--WHILE I GET RID OF THIS NUISANCE!
POW
I THINK YOU'RE RIGHT ABOUT THIS BEING THE FIRST WAVE, FLAMEBIRD, BUT NOW WE HAVE...
WHAT!?
BEARD OF RAO, NIGHTWING!
KRAASH
LOOK!
4

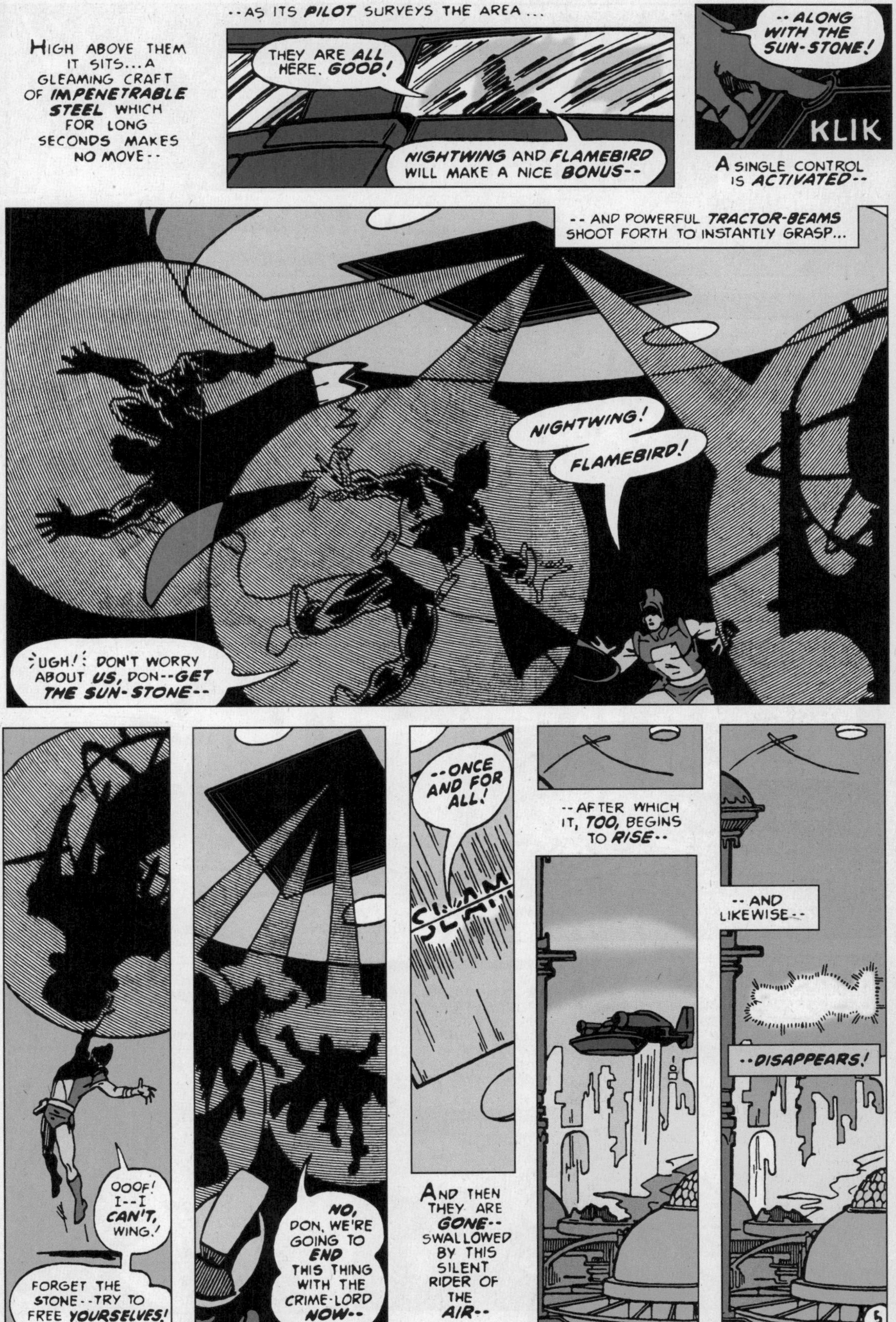

HIGH ABOVE THEM IT SITS... A GLEAMING CRAFT OF IMPENETRABLE STEEL WHICH FOR LONG SECONDS MAKES NO MOVE--
--AS ITS PILOT SURVEYS THE AREA...
THEY ARE ALL HERE. GOOD!
NIGHTWING AND FLAMEBIRD WILL MAKE A NICE BONUS--
--ALONG WITH THE SUN-STONE!
KLIK
A SINGLE CONTROL IS ACTIVATED--
--AND POWERFUL TRACTOR-BEAMS SHOOT FORTH TO INSTANTLY GRASP...
NIGHTWING!
FLAMEBIRD!
UGH! DON'T WORRY ABOUT US, DON--GET THE SUN-STONE--
OOOF! I--I CAN'T, WING!
FORGET THE STONE--TRY TO FREE YOURSELVES!
NO, DON, WE'RE GOING TO END THIS THING WITH THE CRIME-LORD NOW--
--ONCE AND FOR ALL!
AND THEN THEY ARE GONE--SWALLOWED BY THIS SILENT RIDER OF THE AIR--
--AFTER WHICH IT, TOO, BEGINS TO RISE--
--AND LIKEWISE--
--DISAPPEARS!

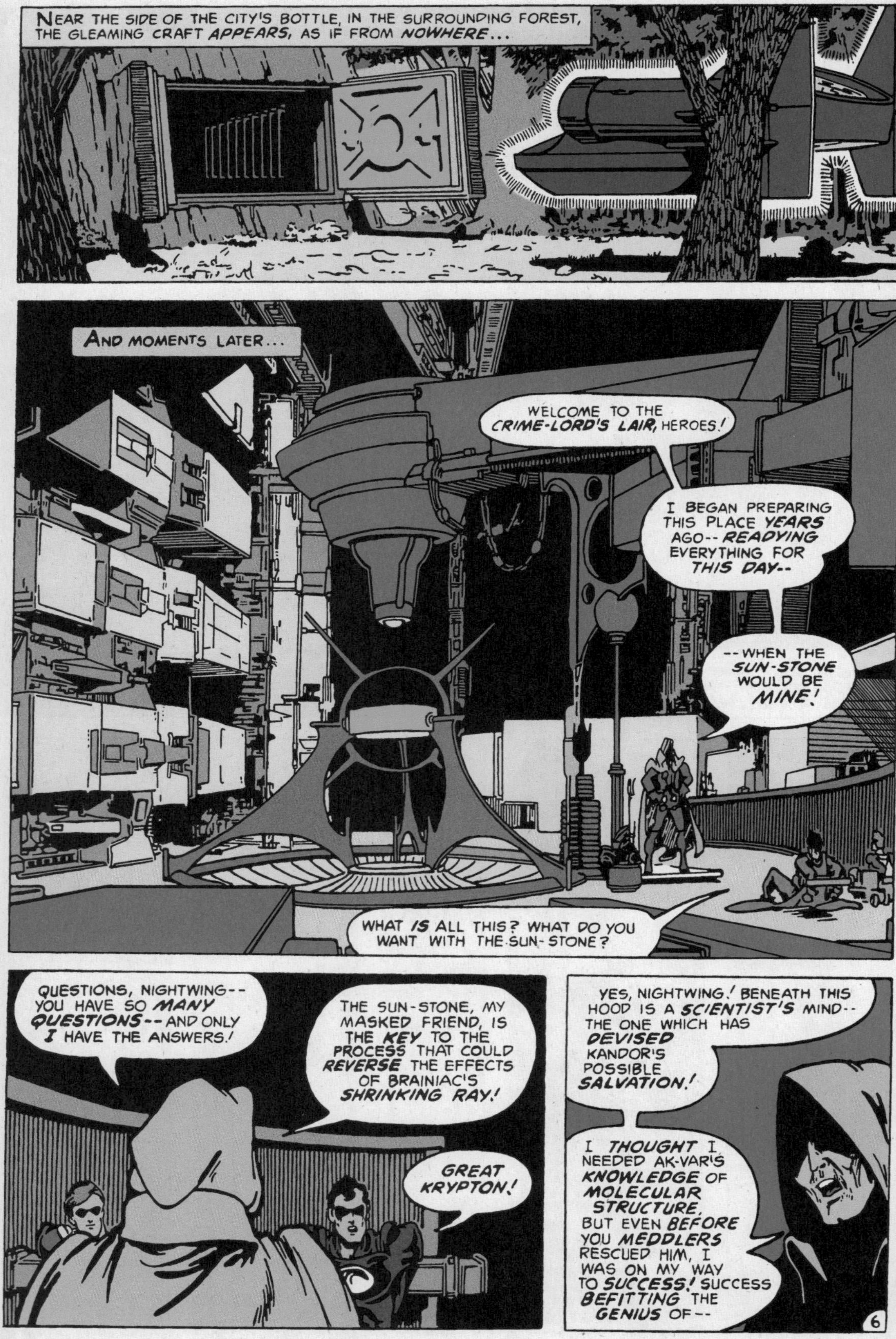
NEAR THE SIDE OF THE CITY'S BOTTLE, IN THE SURROUNDING FOREST, THE GLEAMING CRAFT APPEARS, AS IF FROM NOWHERE...
AND MOMENTS LATER...
WELCOME TO THE CRIME-LORD'S LAIR, HEROES!
I BEGAN PREPARING THIS PLACE YEARS AGO-- READYING EVERYTHING FOR THIS DAY--
--WHEN THE SUN-STONE WOULD BE MINE!
WHAT IS ALL THIS? WHAT DO YOU WANT WITH THE SUN-STONE?
QUESTIONS, NIGHTWING-- YOU HAVE SO MANY QUESTIONS-- AND ONLY I HAVE THE ANSWERS!
THE SUN-STONE, MY MASKED FRIEND, IS THE KEY TO THE PROCESS THAT COULD REVERSE THE EFFECTS OF BRAINIAC'S SHRINKING RAY!
GREAT KRYPTON!
YES, NIGHTWING! BENEATH THIS HOOD IS A SCIENTIST'S MIND-- THE ONE WHICH HAS DEVISED KANDOR'S POSSIBLE SALVATION!
I THOUGHT I NEEDED AK-VAR'S KNOWLEDGE OF MOLECULAR STRUCTURE, BUT EVEN BEFORE YOU MEDDLERS RESCUED HIM, I WAS ON MY WAY TO SUCCESS! SUCCESS BEFITTING THE GENIUS OF--
6

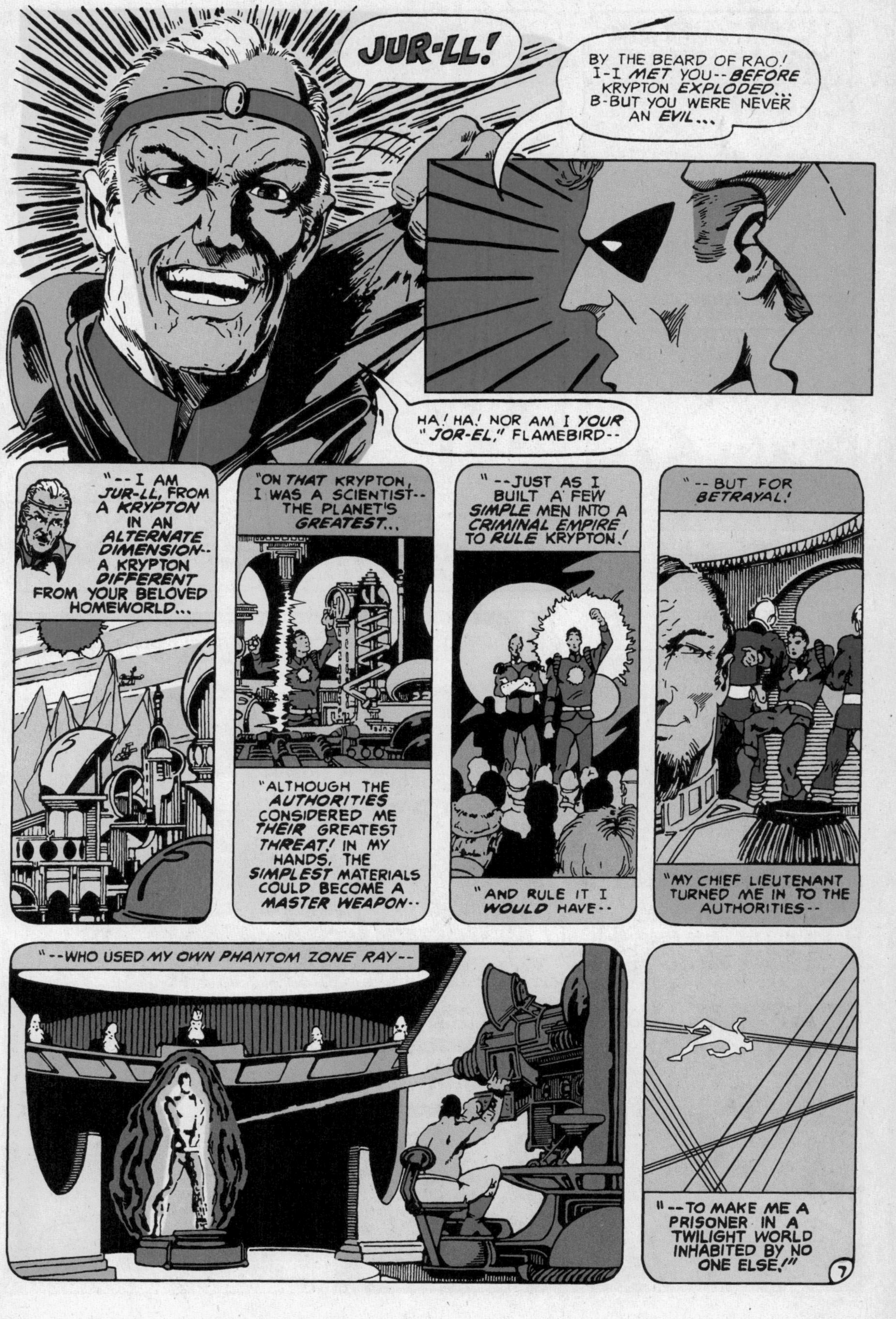
JUR-LL!
BY THE BEARD OF RAO! I-I MET YOU--BEFORE KRYPTON EXPLODED... B-BUT YOU WERE NEVER AN EVIL...
HA! HA! NOR AM I YOUR "JOR-EL," FLAMEBIRD--
"--I AM JUR-LL, FROM A KRYPTON IN AN ALTERNATE DIMENSION--A KRYPTON DIFFERENT FROM YOUR BELOVED HOMEWORLD...
"ON THAT KRYPTON, I WAS A SCIENTIST--THE PLANET'S GREATEST...
"ALTHOUGH THE AUTHORITIES CONSIDERED ME THEIR GREATEST THREAT! IN MY HANDS, THE SIMPLEST MATERIALS COULD BECOME A MASTER WEAPON--
"--JUST AS I BUILT A FEW SIMPLE MEN INTO A CRIMINAL EMPIRE TO RULE KRYPTON!
"AND RULE IT I WOULD HAVE--
"--BUT FOR BETRAYAL!
"MY CHIEF LIEUTENANT TURNED ME IN TO THE AUTHORITIES--
"--WHO USED MY OWN PHANTOM ZONE RAY--
"--TO MAKE ME A PRISONER IN A TWILIGHT WORLD INHABITED BY NO ONE ELSE!"
7

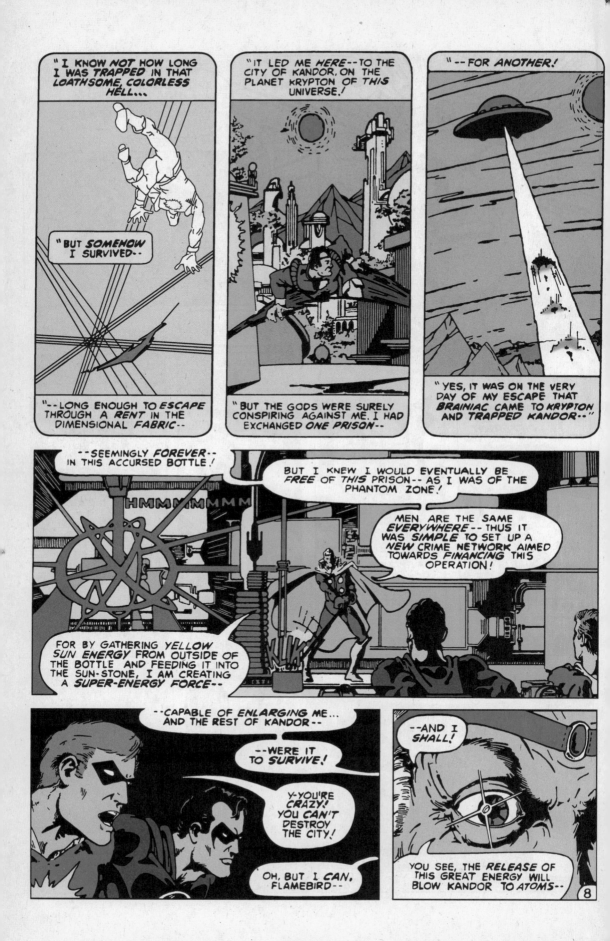

"I KNOW *NOT* HOW LONG I WAS *TRAPPED* IN THAT *LOATHSOME, COLORLESS HELL...*"

"BUT *SOMEHOW* I SURVIVED--"

"--LONG ENOUGH TO *ESCAPE* THROUGH A *RENT* IN THE DIMENSIONAL *FABRIC*--"

"IT LED ME *HERE*--TO THE CITY OF KANDOR, ON THE PLANET KRYPTON OF *THIS* UNIVERSE!"

"BUT THE GODS WERE SURELY CONSPIRING AGAINST ME. I HAD EXCHANGED *ONE* PRISON--"

"-- FOR *ANOTHER!*"

"YES, IT WAS ON THE VERY DAY OF MY ESCAPE THAT *BRAINIAC* CAME TO *KRYPTON* AND *TRAPPED KANDOR*--"

"--SEEMINGLY *FOREVER*-- IN THIS ACCURSED BOTTLE!"

HMMMMMMMM

BUT I KNEW I WOULD EVENTUALLY BE *FREE* OF *THIS* PRISON-- AS I WAS OF THE *PHANTOM ZONE!*

MEN ARE THE SAME *EVERYWHERE*-- THUS IT WAS *SIMPLE* TO SET UP A *NEW* CRIME NETWORK AIMED TOWARDS *FINANCING* THIS OPERATION!

FOR BY GATHERING *YELLOW SUN ENERGY* FROM OUTSIDE OF THE BOTTLE AND FEEDING IT INTO THE *SUN-STONE,* I AM CREATING A *SUPER-ENERGY FORCE*--

--CAPABLE OF *ENLARGING* ME... AND THE REST OF KANDOR--

--WERE IT TO *SURVIVE!*

Y-YOU'RE *CRAZY!* YOU *CAN'T* DESTROY THE CITY!

OH, BUT I *CAN,* FLAMEBIRD--

--AND I *SHALL!*

YOU SEE, THE *RELEASE* OF THIS GREAT ENERGY WILL BLOW KANDOR TO *ATOMS*--

8

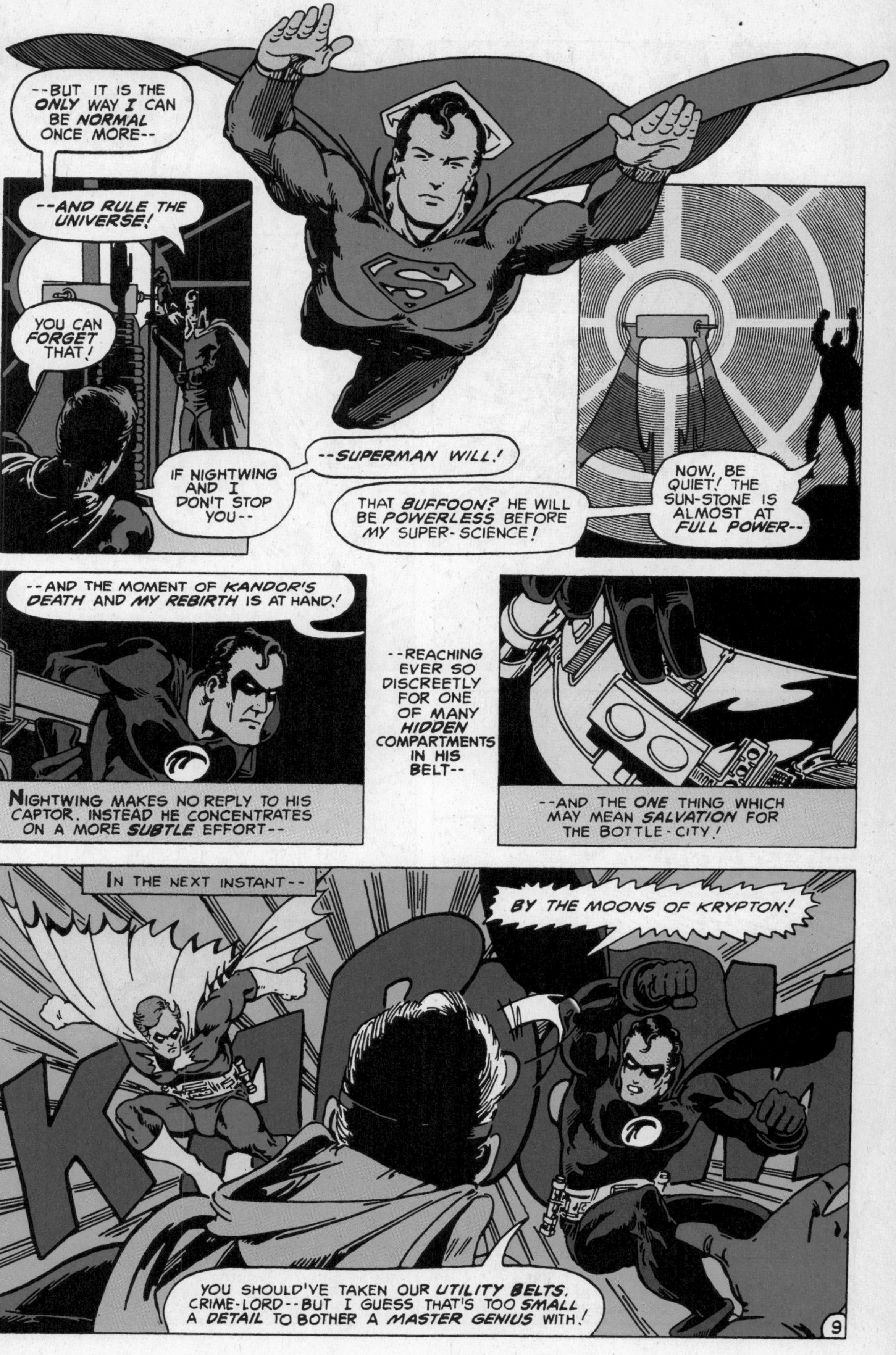
--BUT IT IS THE ONLY WAY I CAN BE NORMAL ONCE MORE--
--AND RULE THE UNIVERSE!
YOU CAN FORGET THAT!
IF NIGHTWING AND I DON'T STOP YOU--
--SUPERMAN WILL!
THAT BUFFOON? HE WILL BE POWERLESS BEFORE MY SUPER-SCIENCE!
NOW, BE QUIET! THE SUN-STONE IS ALMOST AT FULL POWER--
--AND THE MOMENT OF KANDOR'S DEATH AND MY REBIRTH IS AT HAND!
NIGHTWING MAKES NO REPLY TO HIS CAPTOR. INSTEAD HE CONCENTRATES ON A MORE SUBTLE EFFORT--
--REACHING EVER SO DISCREETLY FOR ONE OF MANY HIDDEN COMPARTMENTS IN HIS BELT--
--AND THE ONE THING WHICH MAY MEAN SALVATION FOR THE BOTTLE-CITY!
IN THE NEXT INSTANT--
BY THE MOONS OF KRYPTON!
YOU SHOULD'VE TAKEN OUR UTILITY BELTS, CRIME-LORD--BUT I GUESS THAT'S TOO SMALL A DETAIL TO BOTHER A MASTER GENIUS WITH!
9

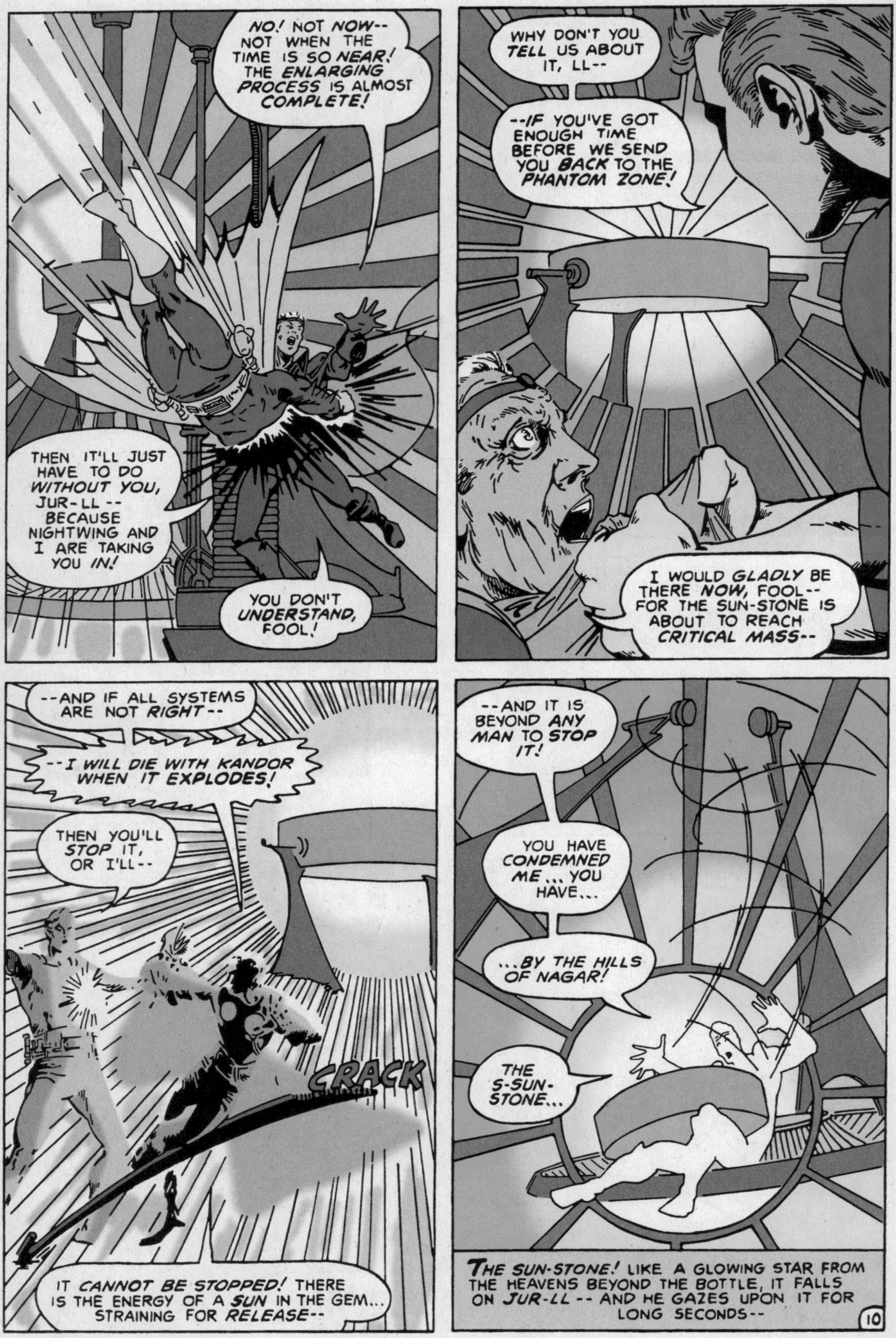
NO! NOT NOW-- NOT WHEN THE TIME IS SO NEAR! THE ENLARGING PROCESS IS ALMOST COMPLETE!
THEN IT'LL JUST HAVE TO DO WITHOUT YOU, JUR-LL -- BECAUSE NIGHTWING AND I ARE TAKING YOU IN!
YOU DON'T UNDERSTAND, FOOL!
WHY DON'T YOU TELL US ABOUT IT, LL--
--IF YOU'VE GOT ENOUGH TIME BEFORE WE SEND YOU BACK TO THE PHANTOM ZONE!
I WOULD GLADLY BE THERE NOW, FOOL-- FOR THE SUN-STONE IS ABOUT TO REACH CRITICAL MASS--
--AND IF ALL SYSTEMS ARE NOT RIGHT--
--I WILL DIE WITH KANDOR WHEN IT EXPLODES!
THEN YOU'LL STOP IT, OR I'LL--
CRACK
IT CANNOT BE STOPPED! THERE IS THE ENERGY OF A SUN IN THE GEM... STRAINING FOR RELEASE--
--AND IT IS BEYOND ANY MAN TO STOP IT!
YOU HAVE CONDEMNED ME... YOU HAVE...
...BY THE HILLS OF NAGAR!
THE S-SUN-STONE...
THE SUN-STONE! LIKE A GLOWING STAR FROM THE HEAVENS BEYOND THE BOTTLE, IT FALLS ON JUR-LL -- AND HE GAZES UPON IT FOR LONG SECONDS--
10

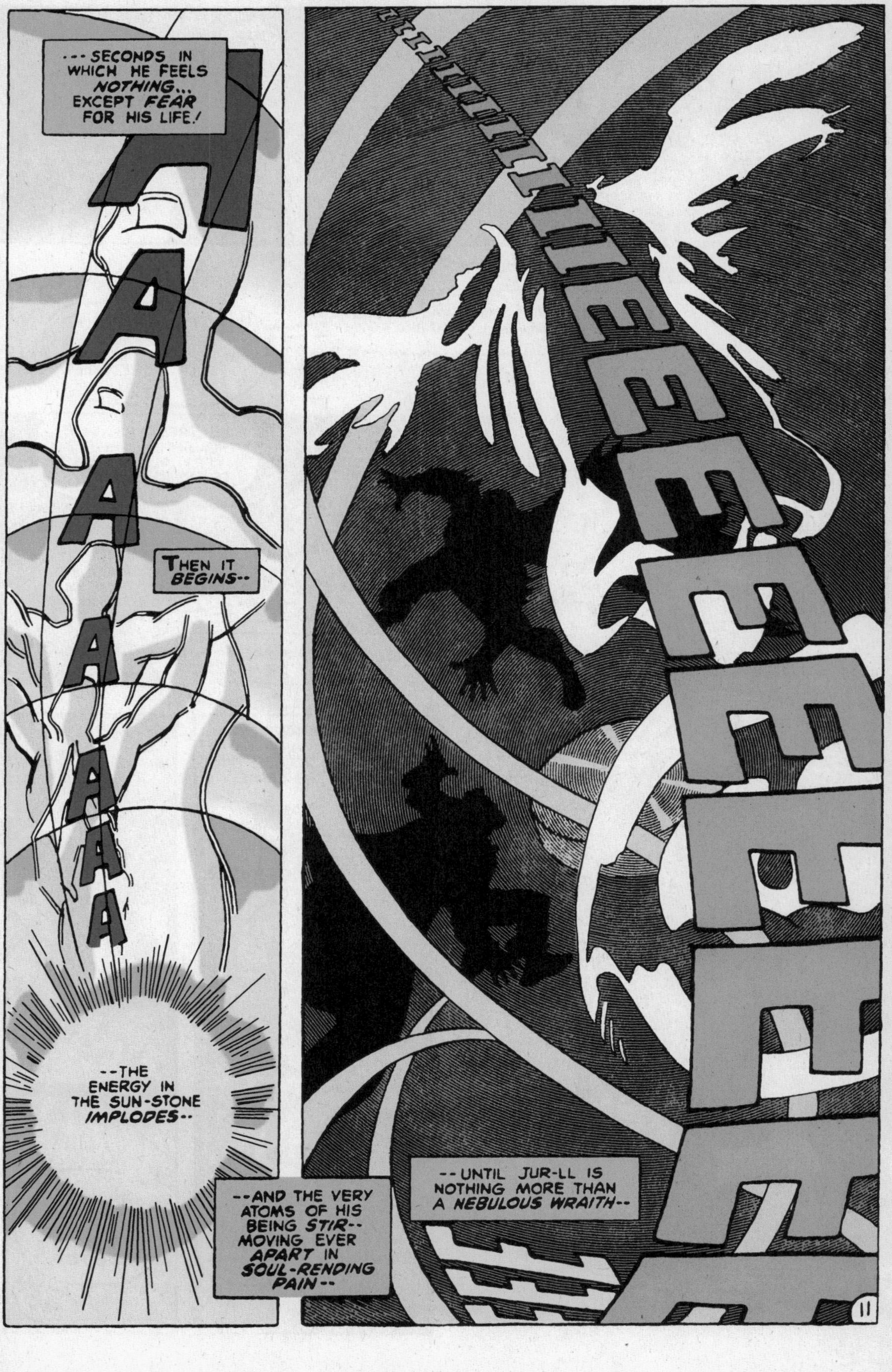
--- SECONDS IN WHICH HE FEELS NOTHING... EXCEPT FEAR FOR HIS LIFE!
THEN IT BEGINS--
--THE ENERGY IN THE SUN-STONE IMPLODES--
--AND THE VERY ATOMS OF HIS BEING STIR-- MOVING EVER APART IN SOUL-RENDING PAIN--
--UNTIL JUR-LL IS NOTHING MORE THAN A NEBULOUS WRAITH--

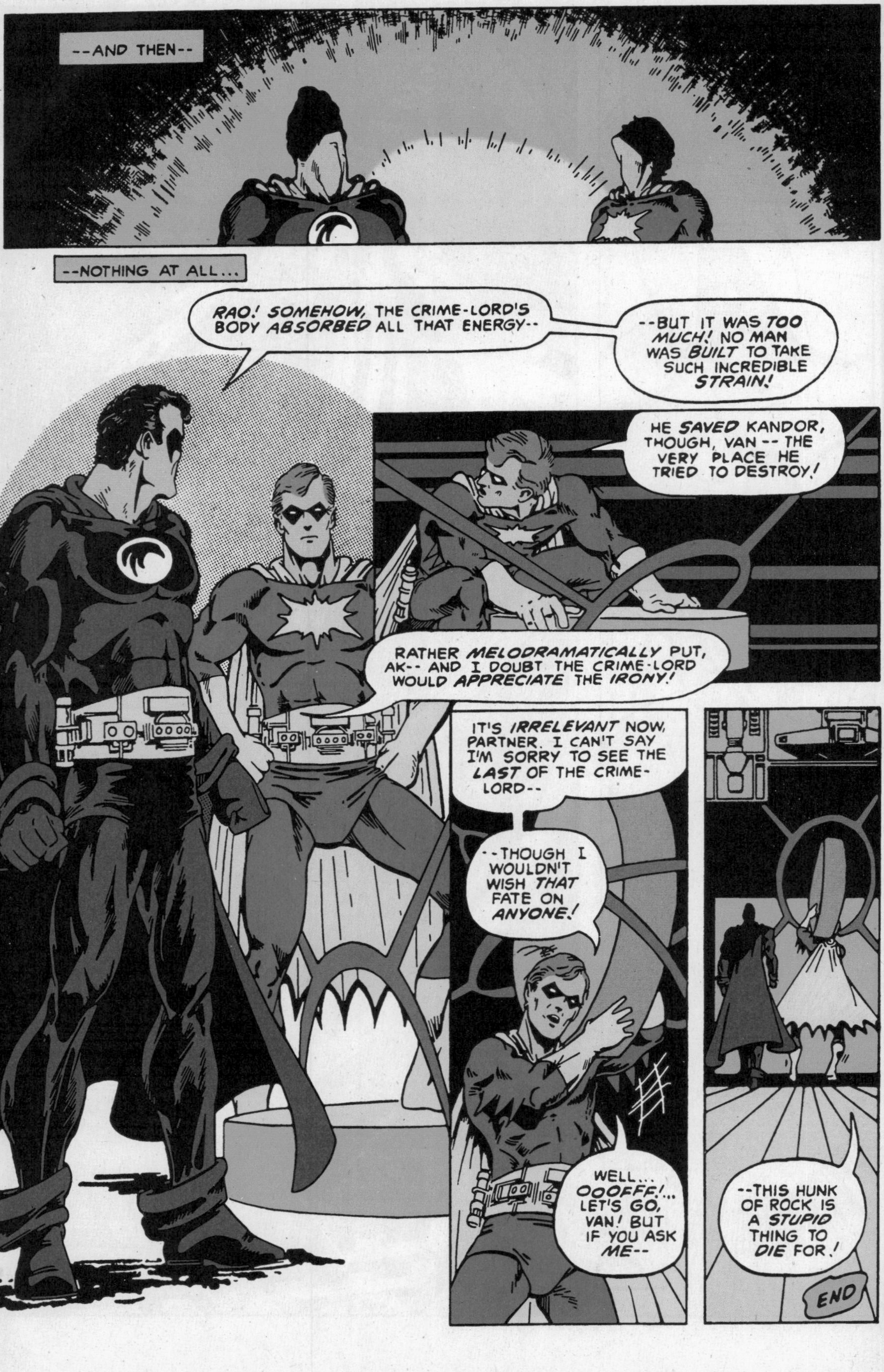
--AND THEN--
--NOTHING AT ALL...
RAO! SOMEHOW, THE CRIME-LORD'S BODY ABSORBED ALL THAT ENERGY--
--BUT IT WAS TOO MUCH! NO MAN WAS BUILT TO TAKE SUCH INCREDIBLE STRAIN!
HE SAVED KANDOR, THOUGH, VAN -- THE VERY PLACE HE TRIED TO DESTROY!
RATHER MELODRAMATICALLY PUT, AK-- AND I DOUBT THE CRIME-LORD WOULD APPRECIATE THE IRONY!
IT'S IRRELEVANT NOW, PARTNER. I CAN'T SAY I'M SORRY TO SEE THE LAST OF THE CRIME-LORD--
--THOUGH I WOULDN'T WISH THAT FATE ON ANYONE!
WELL... OOOFFF!... LET'S GO, VAN! BUT IF YOU ASK ME--
--THIS HUNK OF ROCK IS A STUPID THING TO DIE FOR!
END

BASIC SKILLS

Electronics

Tom Duncan

JOHN MURRAY

Other books in the Basic Skills series:

English by Paul Groves and Nigel Grimshaw
with *Teachers' Resource Book*

Arithmetic by John Deft
with *Teachers' Resource Book*

Health, Hygiene and Safety by Di Barton and
Wilf Stout

Science by Peter Leckstein

Geography by Sally Naish and
Katherine Goldsmith
with Teachers' Resource Book

© Tom Duncan 1988

First published 1988 by
John Murray (Publishers) Ltd
50 Albemarle Street, London W1X 4BD

Reprinted 1990, 1992, 1994, 1995, 1997, 1998 (twice)

Printed in Great Britain at
Athenæum Press Ltd, Gateshead, Tyne & Wear

**A CIP record for this book is available from
the British Library.**

ISBN 0 7195 4449 1

About this Book

This book is intended for all who want to gain a knowledge and understanding of some of the basic principles of electronics. It is suitable for anyone taking an introductory course in electronics, at school, college or by study at home. In particular, those working for the Associated Examining Board's *Basic Test (Specialist) in Electronics* will find it meets their needs. The ultimate aim may be to enter an electronics-related industry by direct employment or through a training scheme or after further education.

In **Part 1** the facts are explained in a straightforward way and questions (with answers at the end of the book) are included for assessing progress.

Part 2 provides a course of practical work in the form of experiments and projects. The experiments offer an opportunity to become familiar with some basic components before they are met in the projects. The latter involve assembling and investigating simple electronic systems that do something. The no-soldering S-DeC method of construction is employed. It is described in the section on *Building circuits*, along with the matrix board and stripboard methods which are suitable alternatives and may be preferred. Instructions for soldering are also given, should stripboard be used. More projects of a similar nature may be found in *Adventures with Electronics* by the same author.*

* ISBN 0 7195 3554 9, John Murray

Contents

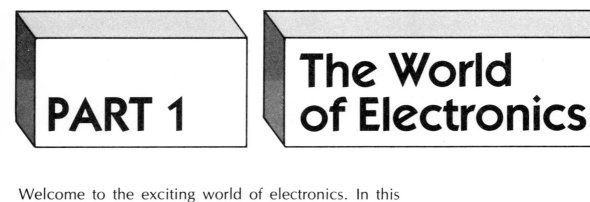

PART 1

The World of Electronics

Welcome to the exciting world of electronics. In this 'high-tech' age more and more people are finding they need to explore it. Not only is the electronics industry itself expanding but other, older industries are becoming increasingly dependent on electronic equipment. People with a knowledge of the subject are in demand.

The photographs show some systems which use electronics and may be familiar to you. Identify each one.

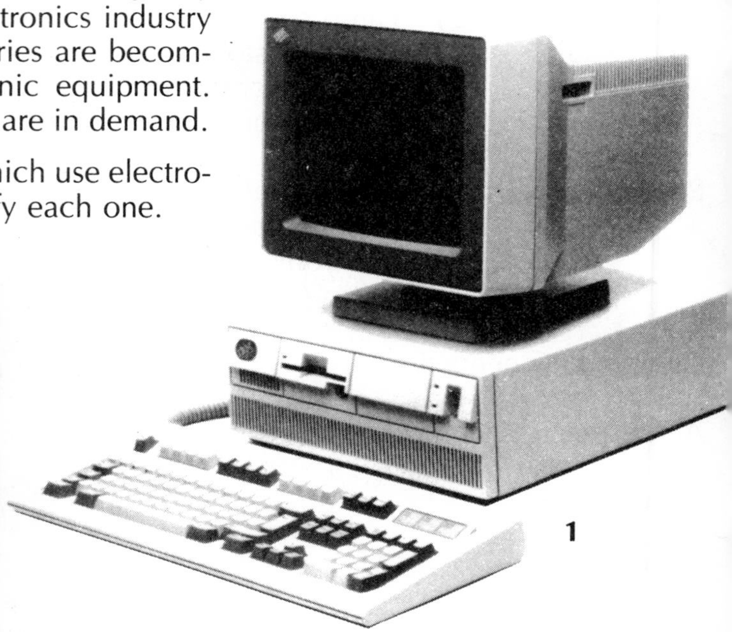

1

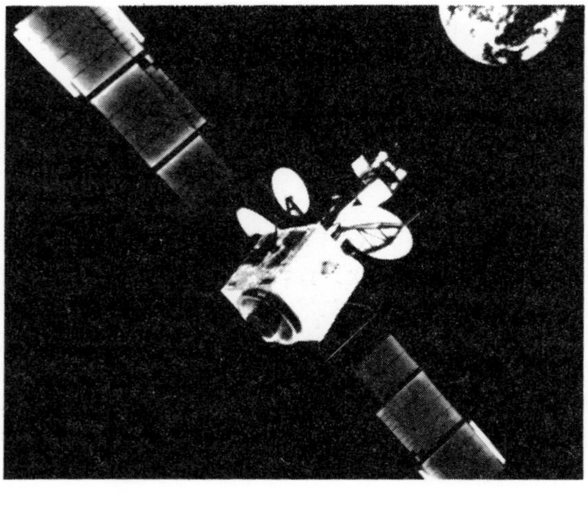

2

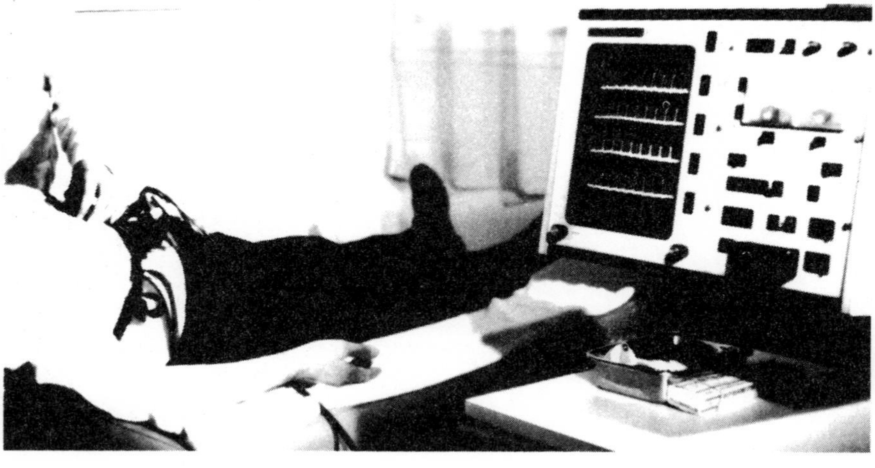

3

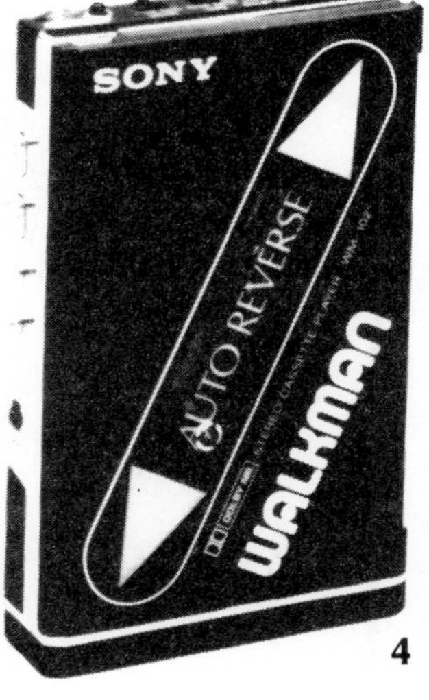
SONY
AUTO REVERSE
WALKMAN

4

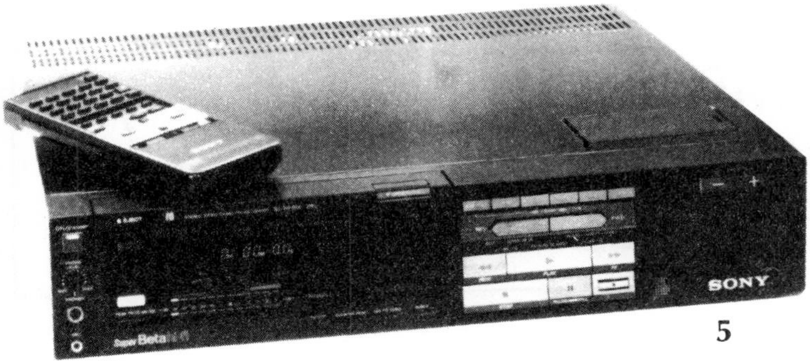
SONY
Beta

5

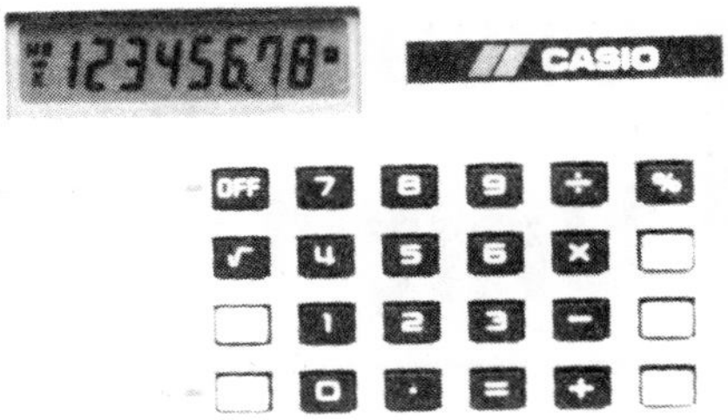
12345678
CASIO
OFF
7
8
9
÷
%
√
4
5
6
×
1
2
3
−
0
·
=
+

6

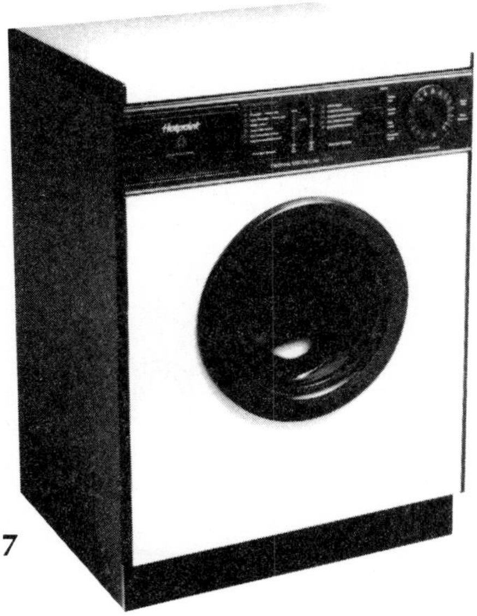

7

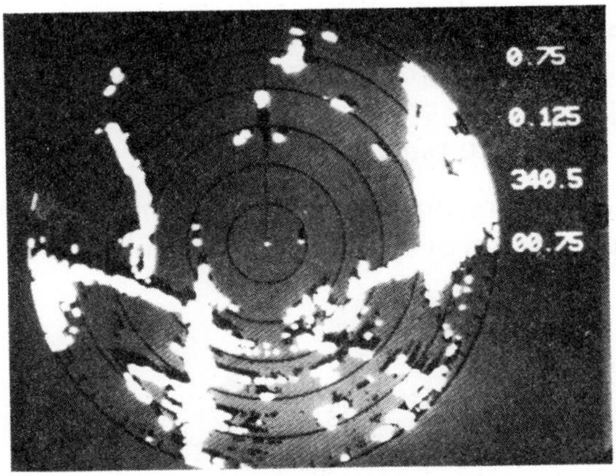
0.75
0.125
340.5
00.75

8

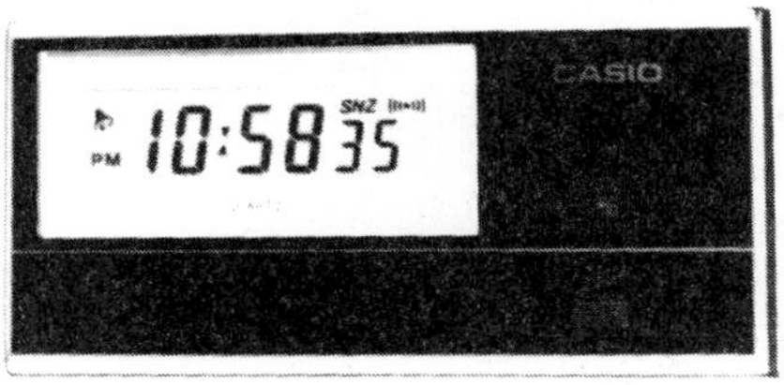
CASIO
PM
10:58 35
SNZ

9

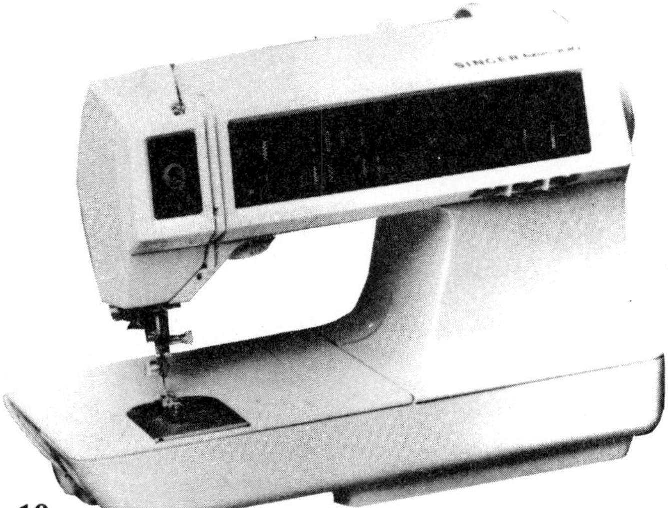

10

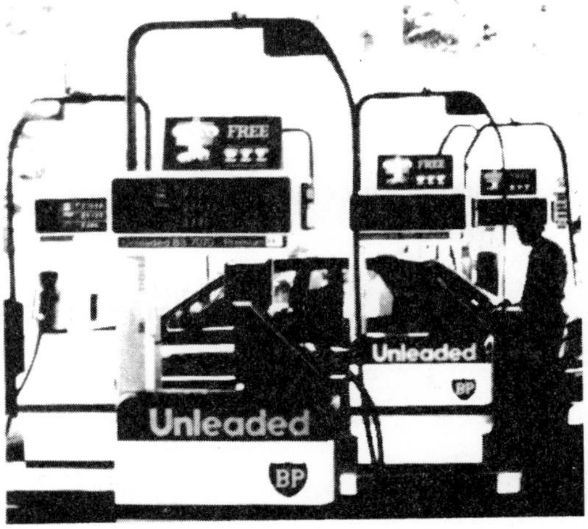
FREE
Unleaded
BP
Unleaded
BP

11

CIRCUITS AND COMPONENTS

Unit 1   Circuit Diagrams

Electronic circuits consist of **components** (parts) such as lamps, resistors and transistors, connected to an **electrical supply**, e.g. a battery. The connections are wires or strips of materials that are good **electrical conductors**, like copper. The connections and components must make a **complete path**, i.e. a circuit.

Circuits are represented by diagrams in which each part is shown by a sign or **symbol**. A few symbols are shown in Fig. 1.1.

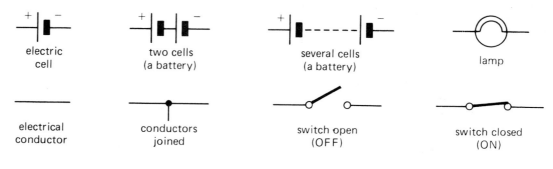

electric cell	two cells (a battery)	several cells (a battery)	lamp
electrical conductor	conductors joined	switch open (OFF)	switch closed (ON)

Figure 1.1

Questions

1 In the simple circuit diagram of Fig. 1.2, what are A, B, C and D?

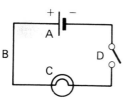

Figure 1.2

2 The circuit in Fig. 1.3 shows the lamps L_1 and L_2 connected in **series** (that is, one after the other) with a cell and a closed switch. What happens to L_1 if L_2 fails?

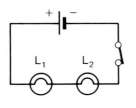

Figure 1.3

3 In Fig. 1.4 lamps L_1 and L_2 are connected in **parallel** (that is, side by side) and both are controlled by the same switch.
   (a) What happens this time to L_1 if L_2 fails?
   (b) Redraw the circuit so that each lamp has a separate switch.

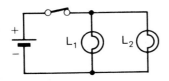

Figure 1.4

4 In Fig. 1.5, one lamp fails in each circuit. In which circuit, A, B or C, will
   (a) one lamp go out
   (b) two lamps go out
   (c) four lamps go out?

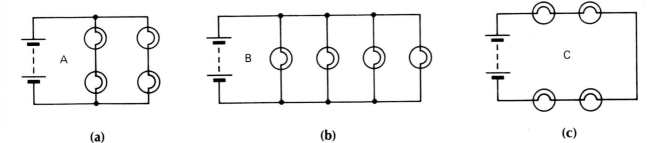

(a)   (b)   (c)

Figure 1.5

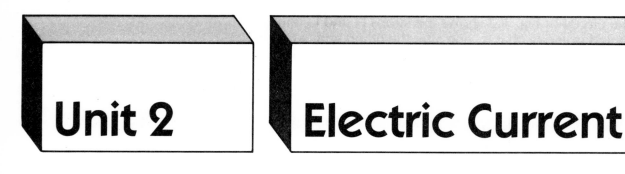

Unit 2 Electric Current

What is it?

An atom consists of a tiny core or **nucleus** with a positive (+) electric charge, surrounded by **electrons** which have an equal negative (−) electric charge, Fig. 2.1. The atom as a whole is electrically **neutral** because the + and − charges cancel.

electrons (−)
nucleus (+)

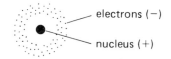

Figure 2.1

In an electrical conductor, some electrons are only loosely attached to their atoms. When the conductor is part of a circuit connected to a battery, the battery forces these electrons to move through the conductor in the direction from the battery's negative (−) terminal towards its positive (+) terminal, Fig. 2.2. This **flow of electrons** is an electric **current**.

electron
battery terminals
metal
−
+
battery

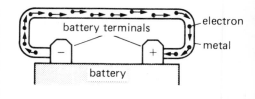

Figure 2.2

Direction of current

Before the electron was discovered scientists thought of current as positive charge moving from a battery's + terminal round the circuit to its − terminal. The choice has been kept and arrows on circuit diagrams show the direction of what is called the **conventional current**, Fig. 2.3. It is the direction in which + charges would move.

+
conventional current

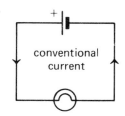

Figure 2.3

The ampere and ammeters

Current (symbol I) is measured in **amperes** (shortened to A) by an **ammeter**. The current through a large flashlamp bulb is about 0.5 A and through a car headlamp 3 to 4 A.

An ammeter is shown in Fig. 2.4(a), with its circuit symbol in (b). One terminal is marked + (or coloured red) and this is the one the conventional current must enter, that is, *the + terminal must lead to the + terminal of the*

+
1 A D.C.
maximum
A

(a)

+
A

(b)

Figure 2.4

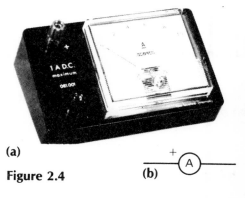

battery. Otherwise the pointer on the ammeter is deflected in the wrong direction and the ammeter may be damaged.

The **milliampere** (mA) is a smaller unit of current, much used in electronics.

$$1\text{ mA} = \frac{1}{1000}\text{ A} \qquad \text{or} \qquad 1000\text{ mA} = 1\text{ A}$$

Current is not used up in a circuit

To measure a current the circuit has to be broken and the ammeter connected in the gap, i.e. in **series**.

(A) Series circuit In Fig. 2.5(a) lamps L_1 and L_2 are in series. The readings on ammeters (A_1), (A_2) and (A_3) are equal and show that **the current is the same** at all parts of the circuit.

(B) Parallel circuit In Fig. 2.5(b) L_1 and L_2 are in parallel and there are alternative paths for the main current I which splits into I_1 and I_2. The readings on ammeters (A_1), (A_2) and (A_3) show that

$$I = I_1 + I_2$$

For example if $I_1 = 0.1$ A and $I_2 = 0.3$ A, then $I = 0.4$ A. **Current is not used up**.

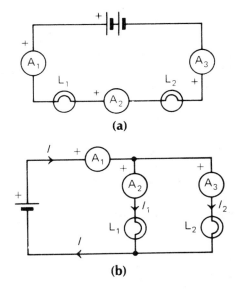

A1
A2
A3
L1
L2
(a)
I
A1
A2
A3
I1
I2
L1
L2
(b)

Figure 2.5

Direct current

In a **direct current** (**d.c.**) electrons flow in one direction only. A battery produces d.c.

The **waveform** of a current is a graph whose shape shows how the value of the current changes with time. Those in Fig. 2.6(a) and (b) are for steady and varying d.c.

current
steady d.c.
0
time
current
varying d.c.
0
time

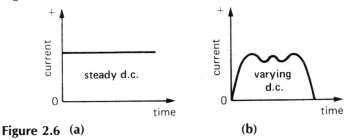

Figure 2.6 (a) (b)

Alternating current

In an **alternating current** (**a.c.**) the direction of electron flow reverses regularly. An alternator (in a car or power station) produces a.c. In the a.c. waveform of Fig. 2.7 the current rises from zero to a maximum in one direction (+), falls to zero again before becoming a maximum in the opposite direction (−) and then rises to zero once more and so on. The circuit symbol for a.c. is ∿

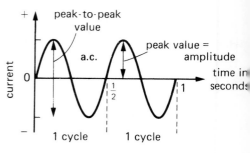

The pointer of a d.c. ammeter is deflected one way by d.c., Fig. 2.8(a); a.c. makes it move to and fro about the scale zero if the direction changes are slow enough, Fig. 2.8(b). If they are too fast no deflection occurs.

Electric heaters and lamps work off either a.c. or d.c., but most electronic systems require d.c.

+
−
0
current
peak-to-peak value
a.c.
peak value = amplitude
time in seconds
$\frac{1}{2}$
1
1 cycle
1 cycle

Figure 2.7

1
0
1
+
d.c.
(a)
a.c.
(b)

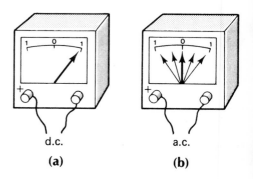

Figure 2.8

Frequency of a.c.

The **frequency** of a.c. is the number of complete **cycles** or alternations made in 1 second. The unit of frequency is the **hertz** (Hz). The a.c. in Fig. 2.7 makes 2 cycles in 1 second, that is, its frequency is 2 Hz. Its **period**, the time for 1 cycle, is $\frac{1}{2}$ second (0.5 s). The frequency of the mains electricity supply in the U.K. is 50 Hz.

Larger units are the kilohertz (kHz) and the megahertz (MHz).

$$1\ \text{kHz} = 1000\ \text{Hz} \qquad 1\ \text{MHz} = 1\,000\,000\ \text{Hz}$$

Audio frequency (**a.f.**) currents have frequencies from 20 Hz or so to about 20 kHz. They produce an audible sound in a loudspeaker.

Radio frequency (**r.f.**) currents have frequencies above 20 kHz. They produce radio waves from an aerial.

Electronic circuits called **oscillators** can generate a.f. and r.f. currents.

Static electric charges

Electric charges that do not move, called **static** charges, can be produced on plastics. Such materials are electrical **insulators**. For example, when a polythene strip is rubbed with a cloth, electrons pass from the cloth to the polythene. The cloth is left with a + charge because its atoms have lost electrons, while the polythene gets a − charge because it gains electrons (which have a − charge), Fig. 2.9.

cloth
rub
polythene
++++
positively charged cloth
negatively charged polythene
− − − −

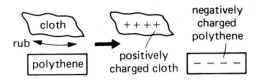

Figure 2.9

Static charges cause sparks and crackles. A nylon garment may become charged as you take it off, through 'rubbing'. It can be shown that

> **like charges** (+ and +, − and −) **repel**
>
> **unlike charges** (+ and −) **attract**

Questions

1 (a) In Fig. 2.5(a), page 11, Ⓐ$_1$ reads 0.2 A. What are the readings on Ⓐ$_2$ and Ⓐ$_3$?

(b) In Fig. 2.5(b) Ⓐ$_2$ reads 0.3 A and Ⓐ$_3$ reads 0.2 A. What does Ⓐ$_1$ read?

2 If the lamps are exactly the same in Fig. 2.5(b), page 11, what do Ⓐ$_2$ and Ⓐ$_3$ read if Ⓐ$_1$ now reads 0.4 A?

3 (a) In Fig. 2.10 Ⓐ$_2$ reads 0.3 A. What do Ⓐ$_1$ and Ⓐ$_3$ read?

(b) Copy Fig. 2.10 and mark the + terminals on Ⓐ$_1$, Ⓐ$_2$ and Ⓐ$_3$ for correct connections.

+
A1
+
A3
A2

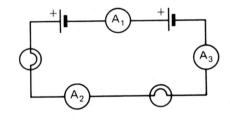

Figure 2.10

4 (a) Does the waveform in Fig. 2.11 represent d.c. or a.c.? Explain your answer.

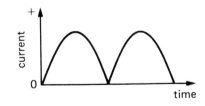

+
current
0
time

Figure 2.11

+
current
0
−
0.2
time in seconds

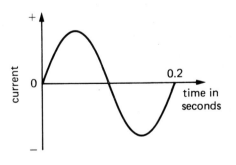

Figure 2.12

(b) What is **(i)** the period **(ii)** the frequency of the a.c. in Fig. 2.12?

5 (a) What are the following currents in mA: **(i)** 1 A **(ii)** 0.5 A **(iii)** 0.02 A?

(b) What are the following currents in A: **(i)** 1500 mA **(ii)** 300 mA **(iii)** 60 mA?

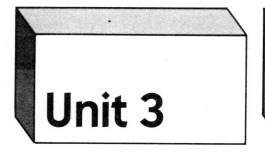

Unit 3 Voltage

About voltage

Voltage (symbol *V*) **causes current**. The voltage of a cell, a battery or a generator is what forces the electrons round a circuit.

It is also called **potential difference** (**p.d.**). It is measured in **volts** (V) by a **voltmeter**.

The voltage of a carbon–zinc or dry cell, Fig. 3.1(a), is 1.5 V. Two cells connected in series, that is + terminal of one to − terminal of next, Fig. 3.1(c), have a voltage of 2 × 1.5 V = 3 V. In a 9 V battery, Fig. 3.1(b), six 1.5 V cells are connected in series. How many are in series in a 4.5 V battery?

The mains supply, which is a.c., has a voltage of 240 V in many countries including the U.K. (The 'peak' value, see Fig. 2.7, is 340 V. 240 V is the 'heating and lighting' or 'equivalent d.c.' value.)

EVER READY
SILVER SEAL
R20S
EVER READY
SILVER SEAL
PP3
1.5 V 1.5 V
+ − + −
+
3 V
−
(a) (b) (c)

Figure 3.1

Voltmeters

A **voltmeter** is shown in Fig. 3.2(a), with its circuit symbol in (b). Like an ammeter, its + terminal (often coloured red) must lead to the + terminal of the voltage supply being measured, as in Fig. 3.2(c), otherwise it may be damaged.

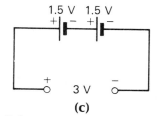

+
5 V D.C.
0 1 2 3 4 5
V
+
V
+
+
V
(a) (b) (c)

Figure 3.2

Voltage <u>is</u> used up in a circuit

If there is current through any component of a circuit, there must be a **voltage drop** across that component. The drop is measured by connecting a voltmeter across the component, i.e. in **parallel** with it. (Remember an ammeter is connected in series to measure current in any part.)

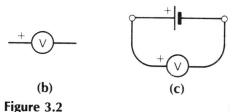

(A) Series circuits In Fig. 3.3(a), $\bigvee$ measures the voltage drop across L_1, which equals the supply voltage of 1.5 V, since the **voltage drops across connecting leads can usually be ignored**.

In (b), $\bigvee$ measures the voltage drop across L_2, which is half the supply voltage of 3 V if L_2 and L_3 are identical lamps, i.e. 1.5 V.

In (c), $\bigvee$ measures the voltage drop across L_3, which is 1.5 V if L_2 and L_3 are identical lamps.

In (d), $\bigvee$ measures the voltage drop across L_2 and L_3 in series, which is the supply voltage of 3 V.

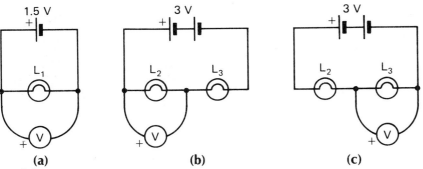

(a)   **(b)**   **(c)**   **(d)**

Figure 3.3

The supply voltage is used up round a circuit and measurements show that

> **supply voltage = sum of all the voltage drops round the circuit**

For example, in Fig. 3.4, $\bigvee_1$ reads 2 V, $\bigvee_2$ reads 3 V and $\bigvee_3$ reads 4 V. The supply voltage = $(2 + 3 + 4)$ V = 9 V = all the voltage drops added together.

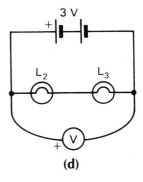

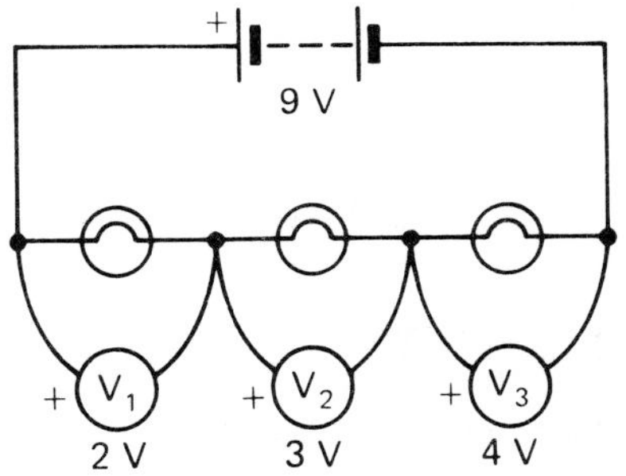

Figure 3.4

(B) Parallel circuits In Fig. 3.5, L_1 and L_2 are in parallel across the supply. The **voltage across each is the same** and equal to the supply voltage, even if the lamps are not identical. That is $V_1 = V_2 = 1.5$ V.

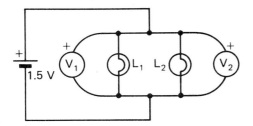

Figure 3.5

Questions

1 What are the voltages of the batteries of 1.5 V cells connected as in Fig. 3.6(a), (b) and (c)?

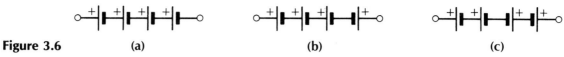

Figure 3.6   (a)   (b)   (c)

2 Three voltmeters (V), (V_1), (V_2) are connected as in Fig. 3.7.
   (a) If (V) reads 9 V and (V_1) reads 6 V, what does (V_2) read?
   (b) Copy Fig. 3.7 and mark the + terminals of the voltmeters for correct connection.

3 The table gives the voltmeter readings that were obtained with the circuit of Fig. 3.7 when different batteries were used. What are the values of x, y and z?

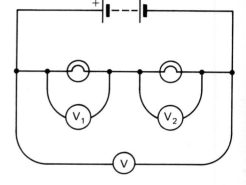

Figure 3.7

Readings in volts		
V	V_1	V_2
x	12	6
6	4	y
12	z	4

⌧ The experiment on *Lamp circuits* (Unit 21) may be done now. Read the section on *Building circuits* (pages 76–81) first.

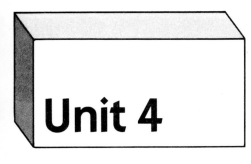

Unit 4 Resistors

About resistance

Electrons move more easily through some conductors than others. Opposition to current is called **resistance**. A short thick wire has less resistance than a long thin one of the same material.

The smaller the resistance of the conductor, the greater the current caused by a certain voltage, Fig. 4.1. We use this fact to measure resistance.

short
thick
wire
large current
small resistance
small current
long
thin
wire
large resistance

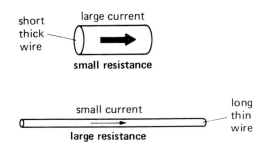

Figure 4.1

If the current through a conductor is I when the voltage drop across it is V, its resistance R is given by the equation

$$R = \frac{V}{I}$$

This is a reasonable way to measure R since the smaller I is for a certain V, the greater is R. If V is in volts and I in amperes, then R is in **ohms** (symbol Ω, pronounced ómegà).

For example, if $I = 2$ A when $V = 6$ V, *then* $R = 6\ \text{V}/2\ \text{A} = 3\ \Omega$.

But if $I = 1$ A when $V = 6$ V then $R = 6\ \text{V}/1\ \text{A} = 6\ \Omega$.

That is, R is greater because I is smaller.

Circuit calculations

Sometimes R is known and we have to calculate V or I. The equation for R can be rearranged so that

(1) V can be found when R and I are known, using the equation

$$\boxed{V = I \times R}$$

(2) I can be found when R and V are known, using the equation

$$\boxed{I = \frac{V}{R}}$$

The triangle in Fig. 4.2(a) is an aid to remembering the three equations. To use it, cover the quantity you want with your finger, then what you still see is what the quantity equals.

For instance, covering I leaves $\dfrac{V}{R}$, Fig. 4.2(b), and covering V gives $I \times R$, Fig. 4.2(c).

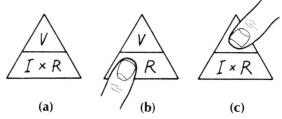

(a)　　　　(b)　　　　(c)

Figure 4.2

Worked examples

1 Find the voltage across a wire of resistance $10\,\Omega$ carrying a current of $0.5\,\text{A}$.

$R = 10\,\Omega$, $I = 0.5\,\text{A}$, $V = ?$
$V = I \times R = 0.5 \times 10 = 5\,\text{V}$

2 Calculate the current through a wire of resistance $3\,\Omega$ when there is a voltage drop of $9\,\text{V}$ across it.

$R = 3\,\Omega$, $V = 9\,\text{V}$, $I = ?$
$$I = \frac{V}{R} = \frac{9}{3} = 3\,\text{A}$$

Units

Two larger units of resistance are the **kilohm** (kΩ) and the **megohm** (MΩ).

$$1\,k\Omega = 1000\,\Omega \qquad 1\,M\Omega = 1\,000\,000\,\Omega$$

In electronics I is often in mA and R in kΩ. Using these units V is still in volts. For example if

(a) $I = 2\,mA$ and $R = 10\,k\Omega$, then $V = I \times R = 2 \times 10 = 20\,V$
(b) $I = 2\,mA$ and $V = 4\,V$, then $R = V/I = 4/2 = 2\,k\Omega$
(c) $R = 2\,k\Omega$ and $V = 6\,V$, then $I = V/R = 6/2 = 3\,mA$.

Fixed resistors

Resistors are conductors that are specially made to have resistance so that they reduce the current to a desired value in a circuit. Fixed resistors have fixed values of resistance which range from a few ohms to millions of ohms. One is shown in Fig. 4.3(a), with its symbol in (b). The three bands round it are coloured. Each colour stands for a number and together they give the resistance in ohms.

The table in Fig. 4.4(a) gives the colour code values.

To read a resistance, start at the first band, which is nearest one end. (Sometimes there is a fourth band of gold or silver near the other end. This is not used for calculating the value, but gives the accuracy of the resistor.)

The *1st band* gives the first number, the *2nd band* gives the second number and the *3rd band* tells how many 0's come after the first two numbers. Study the examples given in Fig. 4.4(b).

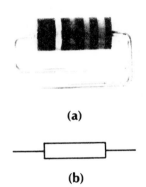

(a)

(b)

Figure 4.3

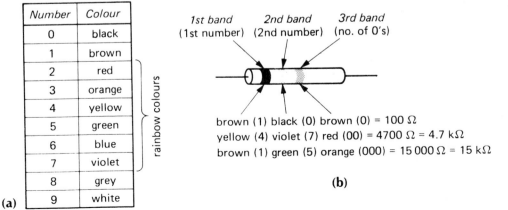

Number	Colour
0	black
1	brown
2	red
3	orange
4	yellow
5	green
6	blue
7	violet
8	grey
9	white

rainbow colours

1st band (1st number) 2nd band (2nd number) 3rd band (no. of 0's)

brown (1) black (0) brown (0) = 100 Ω
yellow (4) violet (7) red (00) = 4700 Ω = 4.7 kΩ
brown (1) green (5) orange (000) = 15 000 Ω = 15 kΩ

(b)

Figure 4.4 **(a)**

Variable resistors

Variable resistors are used in electronics as volume and other controls. One is shown in Fig. 4.5(a), with its symbol in (b). It has three terminals but when used to change the current in a circuit only one end terminal and the central terminal are connected. Rotating the spindle varies the resistance.

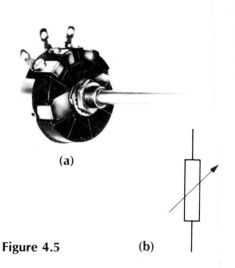

(a) (b)

Figure 4.5

Power rating of a resistor

When current passes through a resistor heat is produced. The larger the current, the hotter the resistor becomes. Overheating causes damage, so for every resistor there is a limit to the amount of heat that can be generated in it per second. This maximum safe rate of heat production is called the **power rating** of the resistor and should not be exceeded. In general the larger the physicial size of a resistor the greater is its rating.

The power P that is generated (dissipated as heat) in a resistor carrying a current I when there is a voltage V across it can be calculated from

$$\boxed{P = V \times I}$$

where P is in watts (W) if V is in volts (V) and I is in amperes (A), Fig. 4.6.

V
I
I

Figure 4.6

For example, if $V = 2\,\text{V}$ and $I = 0.5\,\text{A}$, then $P = 2 \times 0.5 = 1\,\text{W}$.

If I is in mA and V in volts, P is in **milliwatts** (mW) where $1000\,\text{mW} = 1\,\text{W}$, e.g. if $I = 5\,\text{mA}$ and $V = 10\,\text{V}$, then $P = 5 \times 10 = 50\,\text{mW}$ $(= 50/1000\,\text{W} = 0.05\,\text{W})$.

In most electronic circuits resistors with 0.25 or 0.5 W ratings are adequate.

Resistors in series

For Fig. 4.7 we can say

I
R1
R2
I
V1
V2
V

Figure 4.7

(1) I is the same in R_1 and R_2,

(2) $V = V_1 + V_2$ where $V_1 = IR_1$ and $V_2 = IR_2$

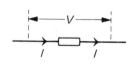

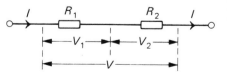

(3) the total resistance $R = R_1 + R_2$, therefore if $R_1 = 1\,\Omega$ and $R_2 = 2\,\Omega$, then $R = 1 + 2 = 3\,\Omega$.

Resistors in parallel

For Fig. 4.8 we can say

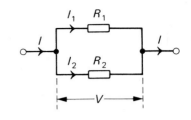

(1) $I = I_1 + I_2$ and I_1 and I_2 split so that if R_1 is *twice* R_2, then I_1 is *half* I_2.

For example, if $I = 3$ A, $R_1 = 2\Omega$ and $R_2 = 1\Omega$, then $I_1 = 1$ A and $I_2 = 2$ A (since $I = I_1 + I_2 = 1 + 2 = 3$ A).

(2) V is the same across R_1 and R_2, i.e. $V = I_1R_1 = I_2R_2$.

(3) the total resistance R is *less* than either R_1 or R_2 and if $R_1 = R_2$ then $R = R_1/2 = R_2/2$.

For example, if $R_1 = R_2 = 4\Omega$, then $R = 4/2 = 2\Omega$.

I_1
R_1
I
I
I_2
R_2
V

Figure 4.8

Worked example

For the circuits in Fig. 4.9(a), (b) what is

(i) the current in the 2Ω resistor
(ii) the current in the 4Ω resistor
(iii) the voltage across the 2Ω resistor
(iv) the voltage across the 4Ω resistor
(v) the supply voltage?

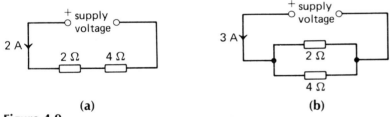

+ supply voltage
2 A
2 Ω
4 Ω
(a)
+ supply voltage
3 A
2 Ω
4 Ω
(b)

Figure 4.9

(a) **(i)** 2 A **(ii)** 2 A **(iii)** $2\text{ A} \times 2\Omega = 4$ V
(iv) $2\text{ A} \times 4\Omega = 8$ V **(v)** $4\text{ V} + 8\text{ V} = 12$ V
(b) **(i)** 2 A **(ii)** 1 A **(iii)** $2\text{ A} \times 2\Omega = 4$ V
(iv) $1\text{ A} \times 4\Omega = 4$ V **(v)** 4 V

Questions

1 **(a)** What will the ammeter Ⓐ read in Fig. 4.10?
(b) What is the voltage drop across the 5Ω resistor if Ⓐ has negligible resistance?
(c) Redraw the circuit with a voltmeter Ⓥ connected to measure the voltage drop across the resistor; mark its + terminal.

+
+
A
10 V
5 Ω

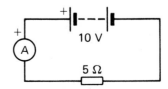

Figure 4.10

2 (a) What is the resistance of a lamp when a voltage of 12 V across it causes a current of 4 A?

(b) Calculate the voltage across a 10 Ω resistor carrying a current of 2 A.

3 In the circuit of Fig. 4.11 calculate

(a) V if $I = 5$ mA and $R = 2$ kΩ

(b) R if $V = 12$ V and $I = 3$ mA

(c) I if $V = 10$ V and $R = 5$ kΩ

(d) the power P dissipated in R in (b).

+
V
I
R

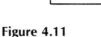

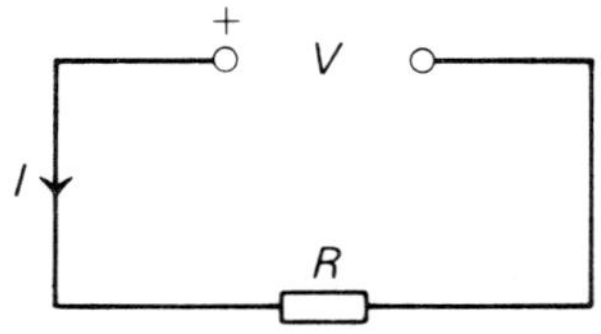

Figure 4.11

4 Using the colour code table (page 19) state the value of the resistors in Fig. 4.12(a), (b).

black
brown
red
violet
yellow
orange

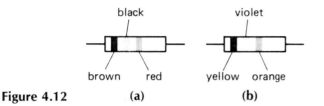

Figure 4.12 **(a)** **(b)**

5 What are the colours of the 1st, 2nd and 3rd bands on a resistor of value

(a) 10 Ω **(b)** 150 Ω **(c)** 3.9 kΩ **(d)** 10 kΩ **(e)** 330 kΩ **(f)** 1 MΩ?

6 In the circuit of Fig. 4.13 what is

(a) the current in the 3 Ω resistor

(b) the current in the 6 Ω resistor

(c) the voltage across the 3 Ω resistor

(d) the voltage across the 6 Ω resistor

(e) the supply voltage?

+ supply
voltage
1 A
3 Ω
6 Ω

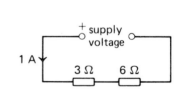

Figure 4.13

7 Repeat Question 6 for the circuit in Fig. 4.14.

+ supply
voltage
6 A
3 Ω
6 Ω

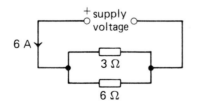

Figure 4.14

8 Draw a diagram to show how you would connect two 10Ω resistors to give a total resistance of 5 Ω.

[*] The experiment *What resistors do* (Unit 22) may be done now.

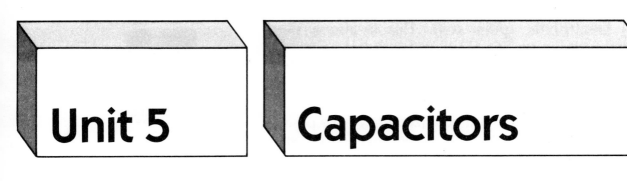

Unit 5 Capacitors

About capacitors

A capacitor **stores electric charge** in the form of electrons.

(A) Construction The simplest capacitor is constructed of two metal plates (conductors) separated by an insulating material (a non-conductor) called the **dielectric**, Fig. 5.1(a). Its circuit symbol is shown in (b).

connecting lead
metal plate
dielectric
(a)
metal plate
connecting lead
(b)

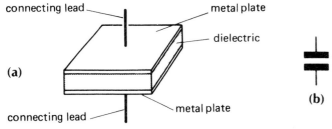

Figure 5.1

(B) Capacitance The more charge a capacitor can store, the greater is its capacitance (C). The capacitance is large when the plates have a large area and are close together. Capacitance is measured in **farads** (F) but smaller units such as the **microfarad** (μF), the **nanofarad** (nF) and the **picofarad** (pF) are more convenient.

1 000 000 μF = 1 F 1000 nF = 1 μF 1000 pF = 1 nF

(C) Working voltage (WV) This is the maximum voltage (d.c. or peak a.c.) a capacitor can withstand across its plates before the dielectric breaks down. It is often marked on it, e.g. 30 WV.

Types of capacitor

(A) Fixed These have a fixed value of capacitance (up to about 1 μF). They are named by their type of dielectric, e.g. polyester, mica, ceramic, shown in Fig. 5.2(a), (b), (c) respectively. They can be connected either way round.

(a)
(b)
(c)

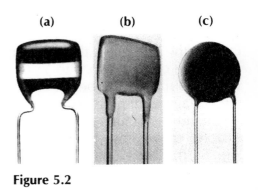

Figure 5.2

(B) Electrolytic (polarized) This is also a fixed-value type (up to 100 000 μF or so). It has a very thin dielectric layer of aluminium oxide between two strips of aluminium foil. This 'sandwich' is rolled into a cylinder, Fig. 5.3, to give a compact, high-value capacitor.

+

Figure 5.3 (a) (b)

Electrolytic capacitors are polarized (they have positive and negative parts) so must be connected into a circuit so that their + connection leads to the + of the voltage supply.

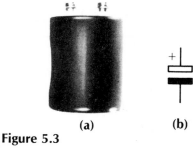

(C) Variable These have two sets of parallel metal plates separated by air as the dielectric. Each set consists of several plates joined together to give, in effect, one large plate, Fig. 5.4. One set is fixed, the other can be rotated to vary the area of overlap of the plates, thus altering the capacitance (up to 500 pF). This type is used to tune a radio receiver.

moving
plates
fixed
plates

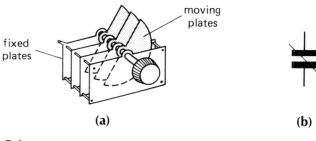

(a) (b)

Figure 5.4

Charging a capacitor

When the capacitor in Fig. 5.5(a) is connected to the battery, the + of the battery attracts electrons (since they have a negative charge) from plate X and the − of the battery repels electrons to plate Y. A positive charge builds up on plate X (since it loses electrons) and an equal negative charge builds up on Y (since it gains electrons).

During the charging, there is a brief flow of electrons round the circuit from X to Y. Charging stops when the voltage built up between X and Y equals (and opposes) the voltage of the battery.

Charging occurs almost immediately, but can be slowed down by having a resistor in the circuit, Fig. 5.5(b). The graph in Fig. 5.5(c) shows how the charge and voltage build up with time.

metal plate Y
metal plate X
electrons
electrons
+
−
dielectric
battery

(a)

+
C
R

(b)

voltage
or
charge
charging
0
time

(c)

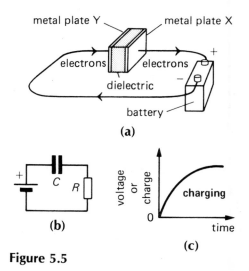

Figure 5.5

Discharging a capacitor

A capacitor can store a charge for a long time after the battery is removed. Eventually it leaks through the dielectric and the capacitor is then discharged. The discharge can be speeded up by connecting a conductor across its leads (*but see* Unit 19) or slowed down by discharging through a resistor as in Fig. 5.6(a). Fig. 5.6(b) shows the discharge–time graph.

C
R
voltage
or
charge
discharging
0
time

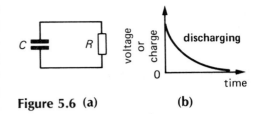

Figure 5.6 (a) **(b)**

Capacitors block d.c. and pass a.c.

(A) d.c. In Fig. 5.7(a) the supply is d.c. Initially there is a brief flow of electrons, i.e. momentary current, which charges C, then it stops. The lamp does not light, showing that a **capacitor blocks d.c.**

1000 μF
+
C
2 V
d.c.
1.25 V
1000 μF
+
C
2 V
a.c.
~
1.25 V

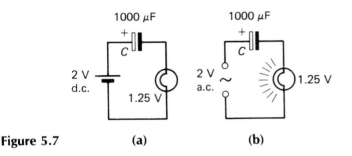

Figure 5.7 **(a)** **(b)**

(B) a.c. In Fig. 5.7(b) the supply is a.c. and the lamp lights, showing that a **capacitor passes a.c.** In fact, no current actually passes *through* C since its plates are separated by an insulator. But it *seems* to do so because electrons flow on and off the plates as the direction of the a.c. reverses (causing C to charge and discharge).

Questions

1 **(a)** What does it mean if a capacitor is marked 0.1 μF 25 WV?

(b) Why should a capacitor with a working voltage of 250 V not be used on a 240 V a.c. supply?

2 Arrange the following capacitances in order of increasing value: 100 pF, 4.7 μF, 2.2 nF.

3 If you wanted to stop d.c. passing through a component but allow a.c. to pass, what would you do?

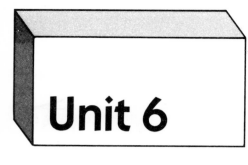

Unit 6 Transformers

About transformers

A transformer changes (transforms) **alternating** voltages and currents to higher or lower values. A **step-up** transformer increases the voltage but the current is decreased. A **step-down** transformer decreases the voltage but the current is increased.

A transformer consists of two coils of wire called the **primary** and the **secondary** windings which are not connected to one another electrically. The coils are wound on a core of soft-iron sheets, either one on top of the other as in Fig. 6.1(a), or side-by-side as in Fig. 6.1(b).

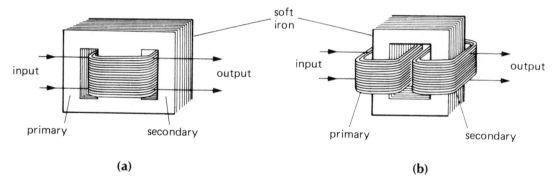

soft
iron
input
output
primary
secondary
(a)
input
output
primary
secondary
(b)

Figure 6.1

An alternating voltage applied to the primary (the **input**) produces a larger (step-up) or smaller (step-down) alternating voltage in the secondary (the **output**). In neither case can the power output be greater than the power input. $(V \times I)_{\text{secondary}}$ is less than but approximately equal to $(V \times I)_{\text{primary}}$.

The symbols for step-up and step-down transformers are shown in Fig. 6.2(a), (b).

STEP-UP
STEP-DOWN
primary
secondary
primary
secondary
(a)
(b)

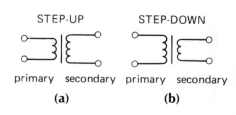

Figure 6.2

Turns ratio

The ratio of the input voltage to the primary, to the output voltage from the secondary, approximately equals the **turns ratio** of the windings. That is

$$\frac{\text{primary voltage}}{\text{secondary voltage}} = \frac{\text{primary turns}}{\text{secondary turns}}$$

In symbols

$$\frac{V_p}{V_s} = \frac{N_p}{N_s}$$

For example, in a step-up transformer, if $N_p = 1000$ turns and $N_s = 2000$ turns, $N_p/N_s = 1000/2000 = 1$ to 2, and V_s will be *twice* V_p. Therefore if $V_p = 12\,V$, $V_s = 24\,V$, but the secondary (output) current will be about *half* the primary (input) current.

In a step-down transformer, if $N_p = 1000$ turns and $N_s = 500$ turns, $N_p/N_s = 1000/500 = 2$ to 1 and V_s will be *half* V_p. Therefore if $V_p = 12\,V$, $V_s = 6\,V$ but the secondary current will be about *twice* the primary current.

Worked example

A transformer steps down the mains supply from 240 V to 12 V to light a lamp, Fig. 6.3.

(a) What is the turns ratio of the transformer windings?

(b) How many turns are on the primary if the secondary has 100 turns?

(c) Estimate the current in the primary if the current in the lamp is 2A.

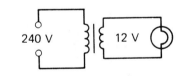

Figure 6.3

Answers

(a) Primary voltage $= V_p = 240\,V$, secondary voltage $= V_s = 12\,V$.

$$\text{Turns ratio} = \frac{N_p}{N_s} = \frac{V_p}{V_s} = \frac{240}{12} = \frac{20}{1} \quad \text{(step-down)}.$$

N_p is 20 times greater than N_s, i.e. $N_p = 20\,N_s$.

(b) Secondary turns $= N_s = 100$.
From (a), $N_p = 20\,N_s = 20 \times 100 = 2000$ turns.

(c) The voltage is stepped down 20 times, therefore the current is stepped up about 20 times. Secondary current = 2 A, so

$$\text{primary current} = \frac{1}{20} \times 2A = \frac{1}{10} = 0.1\,A \text{ (approximately)}$$

Types of transformer

(A) Mains This type, Fig. 6.4(a), is used to change the mains voltage (240 V in the U.K.) to a lower or higher voltage in a power supply unit.

(B) Audio An amplifier is matched to a microphone or loudspeaker with this type, Fig. 6.4(b).

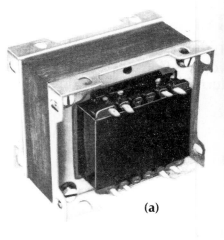

(a)

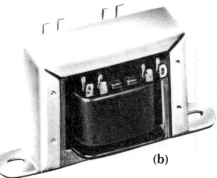

(b)

Questions

1 What is the turns ratio of a transformer in which
   (a) $N_p = 200$ and $N_s = 400$ **(b)** $N_p = 600$ and $N_s = 300$
   (c) $V_p = 1\,V$ and $V_s = 4\,V$ **(d)** $V_p = 10\,V$ and $V_s = 2\,V$?

2 What is the value of
   (a) V_s in Fig. 6.5(a) **(b)** V_p in Fig. 6.5(b)
   (c) N_s in Fig. 6.5(c) **(d)** N_p in Fig. 6.5(d)?

Figure 6.4

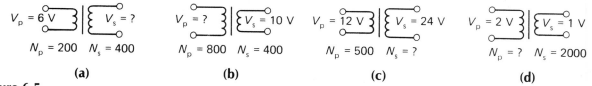

$V_p = 6\,V$ $V_s = ?$

$N_p = 200$ $N_s = 400$

(a)

$V_p = ?$ $V_s = 10\,V$

$N_p = 800$ $N_s = 400$

(b)

$V_p = 12\,V$ $V_s = 24\,V$

$N_p = 500$ $N_s = ?$

(c)

$V_p = 2\,V$ $V_s = 1\,V$

$N_p = ?$ $N_s = 2000$

(d)

Figure 6.5

3 On a 240 V a.c. supply a transformer takes 200 mA. What is the *maximum* current it can deliver from its secondary winding if the output voltage is 480 V?

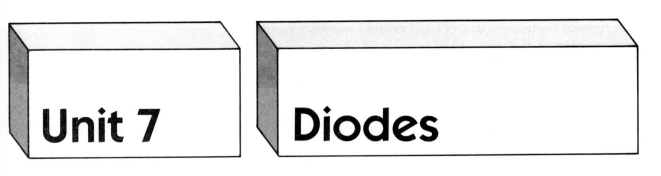

Unit 7 Diodes

What a diode does

A diode allows current to pass through it in one direction only. One is shown in Fig. 7.1, with its symbol. The lead nearest the band is called the **cathode** and the one at the other end is the **anode**.

The diode conducts when the anode goes to the + terminal of the voltage supply and the cathode to the − terminal, Fig. 7.2(a). It is then **forward biased** and conventional current passes in the direction of the arrow on its symbol. If the connections are the other way round, it does not conduct and is said to be **reverse biased**, Fig. 7.2(b).

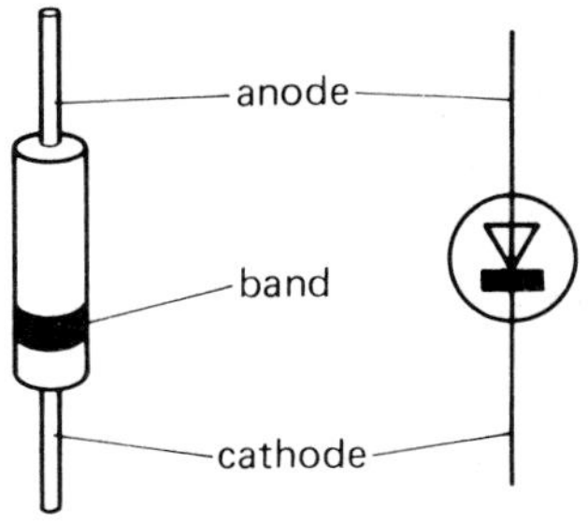

anode
band
cathode

Figure 7.1

current passes
anode
+
FORWARD BIAS
cathode
(a)
no current
cathode
+
REVERSE BIAS
anode
(b)

Figure 7.2

Diodes are made from **semiconductors** such as silicon and germanium.

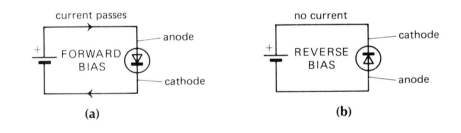

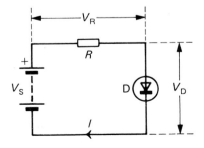

Diode behaviour

(A) Forward bias If the current through a forward-biased diode is too large, it will overheat and may break and melt. To prevent this, a **safety resistor** is included in **series** in the circuit, Fig. 7.3, to use up the excess supply voltage which is causing the large current.

V_R
R
+
V_S
D
V_D
I

Figure 7.3

The resistor limits the current to its correct working value if its resistance R is such that

voltage across $R\,(V_R)$ = supply voltage (V_s) − voltage across diode (V_D)

For example, if $V_S = 3\,\text{V}$ and $V_D = 1\,\text{V}$, then $V_R = V_S - V_D = 3\,\text{V} - 1\,\text{V} = 2\,\text{V}$; that is, of the 3 V supplied, 2 V is dropped across R and 1 V across D.

If the diode current $I = 1\,\text{A}$, we have

$$R = \frac{V_R}{I} = \frac{V_S - V_D}{I} = \frac{2\,\text{V}}{1\,\text{A}} = 2\,\Omega$$

(B) Reverse bias If too great a reverse bias voltage is applied to a diode (e.g. 50 V), it conducts suddenly in the wrong direction and may break down.

The graph in Fig. 7.4 sums up the behaviour of a diode.

V_F = forward voltage
V_R = reverse voltage
I_F = forward current
I_R = reverse current
I_F
V_R
V_F
0
0.6 V
(silicon)
breakdown
I_R
NOT TO SCALE

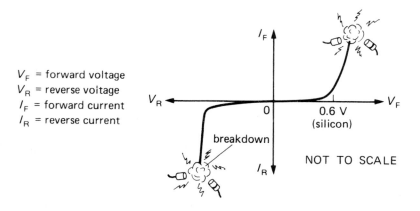

Figure 7.4

Diode as a rectifier

Many electronic systems require a d.c. supply. Batteries are suitable for portable equipment but, in general, **power supply units** operated from the a.c. mains are used. These often contain a transformer to step down the mains from 240 V to a much lower voltage, which is then changed to d.c., i.e. **rectified**, by one or more diodes.

In the single-diode rectifier circuit of Fig. 7.5, the **load** (an electronic system such as a radio, TV set or computer) is represented by a resistor.

positive
half-cycle
negative
half-cycle
a.c.
input
load
varying d.c.
output
positive
half-cycles
only

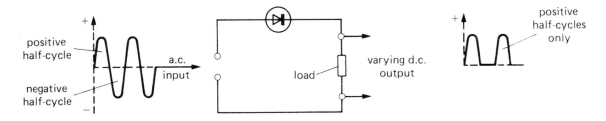

Figure 7.5

The positive half-cycles of the a.c. input (from the secondary of a step-down transformer) forward bias the diode which conducts, producing positive half-cycles of current. The negative half-cycles of the input reverse bias the diode and no current passes.

The output across the load is a varying but direct (one-way) voltage, that is, d.c., consisting of only the positive half-cycles of the a.c. input.

Light-emitting diode (LED)

(A) What it does An LED, shown in Fig. 7.6 with its symbol, is a diode made from the semiconductor gallium arsenide phosphide. When forward biased it conducts and **emits light**, red, green or yellow depending on its composition. No conduction or emission of light occurs for reverse bias which, if it exceeds 5 V, may damage the LED.

coloured
plastic
case
flat
edge is
nearest
cathode
anode
anode
cathode

Figure 7.6

(B) Series resistor As for an ordinary diode, a resistor R has to be connected in series with an LED to limit the current, Fig. 7.7, otherwise it could be destroyed. The forward voltage drop V_{LED} across an LED is about 2 V (compared with 1 V for an ordinary diode) and a typical current $I = 10\,mA = 0.01\,A$. The value of R depends on the supply voltage V_S and must be such that $V_R = V_S - V_{LED}$. It is given, as before, by

$$R = \frac{V_R}{I} = \frac{V_S - V_{LED}}{I}$$

For example, if $V_S = 5\,V$ then $R = (5\,V - 2\,V)/0.01\,A = 3\,V/0.01\,A = 300\,\Omega$. Note that of the 5 V supplied, 3 V is dropped across R and 2 V across the LED.

V_R
R
+
V_S
I
V_{LED}

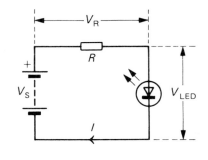

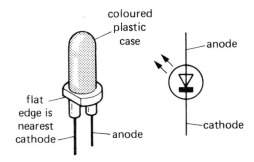

Figure 7.7

(C) Uses LEDs are used as indicator lamps in radio receivers and other electronic equipment. Many calculators, clocks, cash registers and measuring instruments have seven-segment red or green numerical displays, Fig. 7.8(a). Each segment is an LED and, depending on which segments have a voltage across them, the display lights up the numbers 0 to 9, as in Fig. 7.8(b).

The advantages of LEDs over ordinary lamps are their small size, reliability, long life, fast response and modest current requirements.

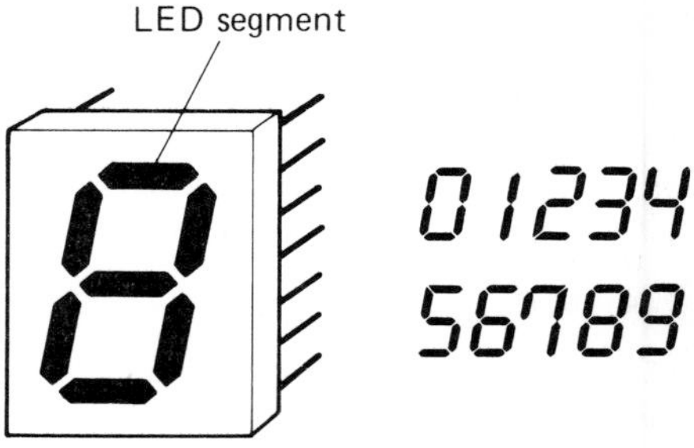

LED segment
01234
56789
(a) (b)

Figure 7.8

Zener diode

(A) What it does A Zener diode is shown in Fig. 7.9, with its symbol. It behaves like a normal silicon diode but when reverse biased, it breaks down at a particular voltage, called its **breakdown** or **Zener voltage**. This ranges from about 2 to 200 V, depending on the diode's composition.

At its Zener voltage (V_Z), a Zener diode suddenly conducts but the voltage across it (i.e. V_Z) remains constant for a wide range of reverse currents. To limit the reverse current and prevent overheating, a suitable resistor must always be joined in series with the diode.

anode
cathode
(a)

(b)

Figure 7.9

(B) Voltage regulation Zener diodes are used to regulate or stabilize (i.e. keep steady) the output voltage from a power supply unit or a battery. In an unregulated power supply the output voltage falls if the output current rises and this may upset the working of the electronic system being supplied, i.e. the load.

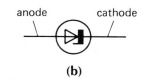

In the regulating circuit of Fig. 7.10, the Zener diode is reverse biased and in parallel with the load. The input voltage V_i to the circuit is greater than the output voltage V_o that is developed across the load and is taken from an unregulated supply, e.g. a battery.

V_R
+
−
I
R
I_Z
I_L
cathode
anode
load
V_i
$V_o = V_Z$

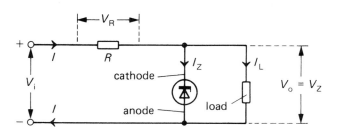

Figure 7.10

If I_Z and I_L are the currents in the diode and load respectively, the total current supplied, I, is given by

$$I = I_Z + I_L$$

If I_L rises (or falls), I_Z is found to fall (or rise) by the *same* amount, so keeping I and therefore V_o ($= V_Z$) constant. This happens because, even with different currents (reverse) through it, a Zener diode at breakdown has a constant voltage across it.

The **series resistor** in a regulating circuit should have a resistance R which is such that $V_R = V_i - V_Z$. It is given by

$$R = \frac{V_R}{I} = \frac{V_i - V_Z}{I}$$

In Fig. 7.10 if $V_i = 9\,V$, $V_o = V_Z = 5V$, $I_L = 40\,mA$ and $I_Z = 10\,mA$, then

$$I = I_Z + I_L = 10 + 40 = 50\,mA = 0.05\,A$$
$$R = V_R/I = (V_i - V_Z)/I = (9\,V - 5\,V)/0.05\,A$$
$$= 4\,V/0.05\,A = 80\Omega$$

$P_Z = $ power dissipated in diode $= V_Z \times I_Z = 5\,V \times 10\,mA = 50\,mW = 0.05\,W$

Note that if the load is disconnected, $I_L = 0$ and $I_Z = 50\,mA$ making $P_Z = 5\,V \times 50\,mA = 250\,mW = 0.25\,W$. The diode should therefore be rated for 0.25 W at least, to carry 50 mA safely.

$P_L = $ power dissipated in load $= V_o \times I_L = 5\,V \times 40\,mA = 200\,mW = 0.2\,W$

$P_R = $ power dissipated in $R = V_R \times I = 4\,V \times 50\,mA = 200\,mW = 0.2\,W$

$P_S = $ total power taken from supply $= P_Z + P_L + P_R = 0.05 + 0.2 + 0.2 = 0.45\,W$

Questions

1 Which lamp lights in the circuit of Fig. 7.11?

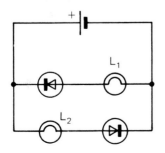

Figure 7.11

2 The voltage drop across a forward biased diode is 1 V when the current through it is 1 A on a 6 V supply, Fig. 7.12. What is

(a) the voltage drop across the safety resistor R
(b) the current through R
(c) the value of R
(d) the power dissipated in R
(e) the power dissipated in the diode
(f) the power taken from the supply?

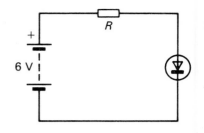

Figure 7.12

3 In Fig. 7.13 the LED is bright when the current through it is 10 mA and the voltage across it is 2 V. Calculate the value of the protective resistor R if the supply is 9 V.

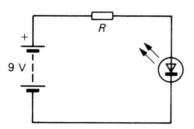

Figure 7.13

4 In Fig. 7.10 (page 32) the Zener diode has a breakdown voltage of 3 V. If the input voltage $V_i = 7$ V, what is

(a) the output voltage V_o
(b) the voltage V_R across R
(c) the current I if $I_Z = 5$ mA and $I_L = 35$ mA
(d) the value of R
(e) the power dissipated in the diode?

5 In Fig. 7.10 (page 32) if $V_i = 8$ V, $V_o = 3$ V and R = 50 Ω, what is the value of
(a) I (b) I_L if $I_Z = 20$ mA?

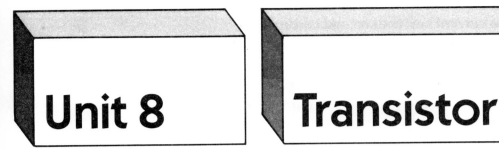

Unit 8 Transistor

What a transistor does

There are different types of transistor but all have three leads, called the **collector** (C), the **base** (B) and the **emitter** (E). The one shown in Fig. 8.1 is an 'npn' type in which the collector and base must go to battery + and the emitter to battery −.

(a)

C
B
E

(b)

Figure 8.1

For a 'pnp' type the arrow on the symbol and the battery connections are reversed.

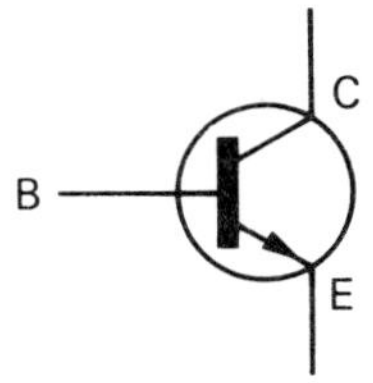

There are two current paths through a transistor. In an npn type **base current** enters by the base and the **collector current** by the collector. Both leave by the emitter. The circuit in Fig. 8.2 can be used to show what a transistor does.

When switch S is **open**, *the base current is zero* and neither L_1 nor L_2 light up, showing that the *collector current is also zero* even though the battery is correctly connected across the collector–emitter path.

S
base current
collector current
L_1
L_2
+
6–9 V
−
C
R
B
2N3053
collector current + base current
E
R = 10 kΩ
L_1 = L_2 = 6 V 60 mA

Figure 8.2

When S is **closed**, the base is connected through R to battery + and L_2 lights up but not L_1. This shows there is now *collector current* (which passes through L_2) and that it is *much greater than the base current* (which passes through L_1, but is too small to light it).

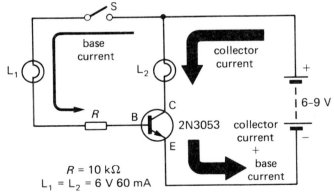

In a transistor the base current switches on and controls the much greater collector current.

Two further points to note are

(1) R must be in the circuit *to limit the base current*, otherwise it causes an excessive collector current which destroys the transistor by overheating, and

(2) the collector and base current paths have a common connection at the emitter and the transistor is said to be in **common–emitter connection**.

Transistor as a current amplifier

If we think of the base current I_B as the **input** to a transistor and the collector current I_C as the **output** from it, then the transistor acts as a **current amplifier** since I_C is greater than I_B.

I_C is 10 to 1000 times greater than I_B depending on the type of transistor. The **current gain** is an important property of a transistor given by

$$\text{current gain} = \frac{I_C}{I_B}$$

For example, if $I_C = 50\,\text{mA}$ and $I_B = 0.5\,\text{mA}$, current gain $= 50/0.5 = 100$.

Transistor as a switch

Transistors are used as very fast-acting electrical switches in digital watches, pocket calculators, computers and other electronic systems. Their action arises from the fact the collector current is switched on and off, and controlled by the base current. When used in circuits containing components such as light-dependent resistors (LDRs), thermistors and microphones, they respond to changes of light strength, temperature and sound level and can operate as alarms.

(A) Basic switching circuit, Fig. 8.3   When the resistance of the variable resistor VR is reduced from its maximum value, the base current increases until it switches on and produces a collector current that is large enough to light L. R is included in the base circuit to protect the transistor when VR is zero.

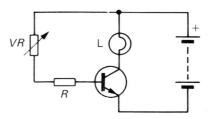

Figure 8.3

(B) Temperature-operated switch, Fig. 8.4 The thermistor TH (see page 41) acts as a variable resistor whose resistance decreases when its temperature rises. This allows the base current to increase and switch on the transistor, so lighting L. The circuit could form the basis of a high-temperature warning device, e.g. a fire alarm.

TH
L
R
+

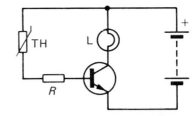

Figure 8.4

(C) Light-operated switch, Fig. 8.5 The resistance of the light-dependent resistor LDR (see page 41) decreases when it is illuminated. In the dark the LDR has a very high resistance. It is not until light falls on it that the base current is sufficient to switch on the transistor. The collector current, which is too small to ring the bell directly, goes through the relay coil (see page 43). This causes the relay contacts to close, enabling the bell to obtain from the battery the larger current it needs.

relay
LDR
R
electric
bell
+

Figure 8.5

The circuit could be used as an early-morning alarm or to give warning of the entry into another room at night of a burglar who has switched on a light.

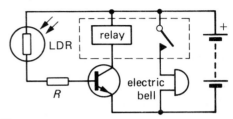

Questions

1 In the labelled circuit of Fig. 8.6 which path through the transistor is taken by
(a) the base current
(b) the collector current?

A
C
B
E
+

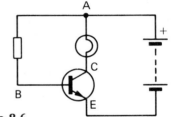

Figure 8.6

2 In which circuit(s) in Fig. 8.7 will L light up (if *R* is not too large)?

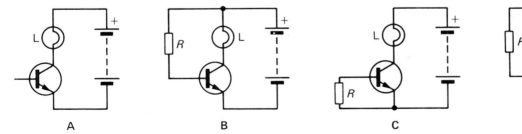

L
R
+
A
B
C
D

Figure 8.7

3 What is the current gain of a transistor in which a base current of 1 mA causes a collector current of 200 mA?

[*] The experiments on *Diodes, thermistors, LDRs* and *What a transistor does* (Units 23 and 24) and the projects *Parking light, Flashing lamp* and *Electronic organ* (Units 25, 26 and 27) may be done now.

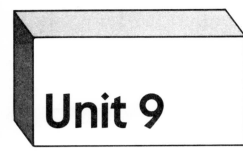

Unit 9 Integrated Circuits

What are they?

Integrated circuits (ICs) are densely populated electronic circuits which are much smaller, much cheaper to make and much less likely to fail than circuits built from discrete (separate) components. They may contain thousands of transistors and often diodes, resistors and small capacitors. All are made at the same time on a tiny 'chip' of silicon, no more than 5 mm square and 0.5 mm thick and connected together by thin aluminium strips.

ICs have made possible digital watches, pocket calculators, video games, microcomputers and many other sophisticated electronic systems. One is shown in Fig. 9.1(a) in its protective plastic case (its package) which has been partly removed in Fig. 9.1(b) to show the leads radiating from the 'chip' to the pins that enable it to communicate with the outside world. This type of package is the dual-in-line (d.i.l.) arrangement with the pins (from 6 to 64 in number but often 14 or 16) 0.1 inch apart, in two lines on either side of the case.

13-200-5
Δ8642

(a)

'chip'
plastic case
connection from 'chip' to pin
metal pin
notch
small dot
0.1 inch
pin 1

(b)

Figure 9.1

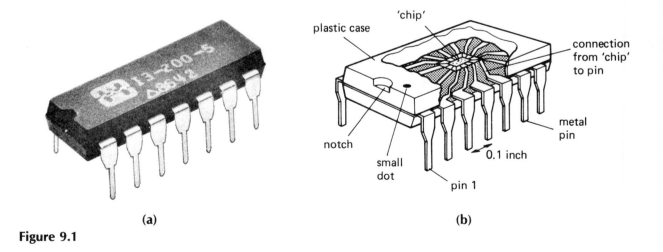

Types of IC

There are two broad groups.

(A) Digital ICs These contain **switching-type** circuits handling voltage pulses which have only **one of two levels**, Fig. 9.2. That is, their inputs and outputs are either 'high' (e.g. near the supply voltage, which is often 5 V) or 'low' (e.g. near 0 V). They include logic gates (see page 45), memories, microprocessors and many other kinds of chip.

digital signal
pulse
'high'
voltage
'low'
0
time

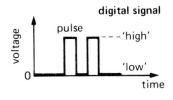

Figure 9.2

(B) Linear or analogue ICs These include **amplifier-type** circuits of many kinds for both audio and radio frequencies. They handle voltages that vary smoothly and continuously over a **range of values**, Fig. 9.3.

analogue signal
+
voltage
0
time
−

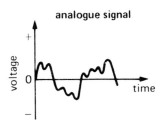

Figure 9.3

[*] The project *'Chip' radio* (Unit 28) may be done now.

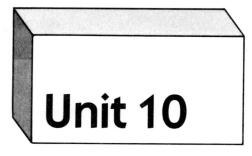

Unit 10 Transducers

About transducers

Transducers change energy from one form to another. In electronic systems **input transducers** *supply* the system with electrical energy by converting some other form into it; **output transducers** change the electrical energy they *receive* from the system into another form. Both types enable the system to communicate with the outside world. Some examples are given in Fig. 10.1.

| INPUT TRANSDUCER e.g. microphone, pick-up, thermistor, light dependent resistor (LDR), keyboard | electrical energy | ELECTRONIC SYSTEM e.g. radio, record player, TV, computer | electrical energy | OUTPUT TRANSDUCER e.g. loudspeaker, relay, motor, lamp, heater, LED, cathode ray tube |

Figure 10.1

Input transducers

(A) Microphone A microphone changes sound energy into electrical energy. Sound waves falling on it make a flexible foil, called the diaphragm, vibrate backwards and forwards. This movement produces a varying electric current in a way that depends on the type of microphone. The popular moving-coil type is shown in Fig. 10.2(a), and the capacitor-type tie model, which is used for broadcasting and concerts, in Fig. 10.2(b). The microphone symbol is given in Fig. 10.2(c).

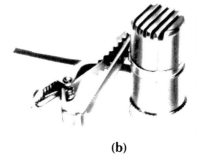

(b)

(a)

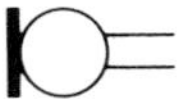

(c)

Figure 10.2

(B) Pick-up The pick-up for a conventional record player consists of a stylus and a cartridge, Fig. 10.3(a). When the turntable revolves, the stylus is made to vibrate as it follows the wavy shape of the sides of the groove of the record which stores the sound. The vibration (i.e. mechanical energy) is changed into a voltage by the cartridge. Overall, sound is converted into electrical energy.

cartridge
stylus
groove
on
record

(a) (b)

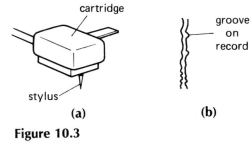

Figure 10.3

(C) Thermistor The use of a thermistor as a transducer (in, for example, Fig. 8.4) to change heat energy into electrical energy depends on the fact that the resistance of the commonest type *decreases* considerably when its temperature *rises*. One is shown in Fig. 10.4.

(a) (b)

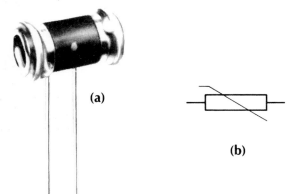

Figure 10.4

(D) Light-dependent resistor (LDR) The resistance of an LDR decreases when it is illuminated, enabling it to change light into electrical energy (as in Fig. 8.5). One is shown in Fig. 10.5. It is also called a photoconductive cell or **photocell**.

(a) (b)

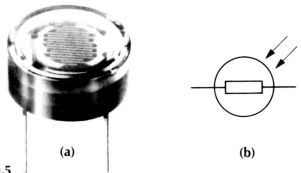

Figure 10.5

[*] The experiment on *Diodes, thermistors, LDRs* (Unit 23) should be done now if you have not already done it.

(E) Switches When a switch is operated and completes a circuit, we can look upon the mechanical energy supplied by the person operating it as causing the production of electrical energy in the circuit. It is a kind of input transducer.

Four of the many types of switch used in electronics are shown with their symbols in Fig. 10.6(a), (b), (c), (d).

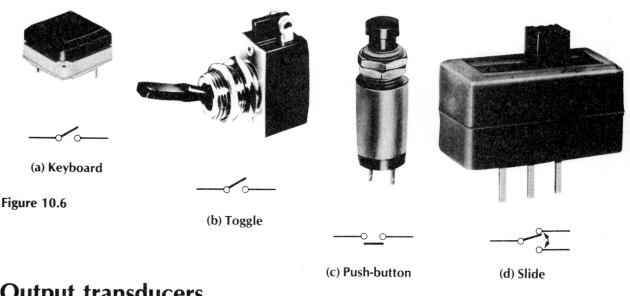

(a) Keyboard

Figure 10.6

(b) Toggle

(c) Push-button

(d) Slide

Output transducers

(A) Loudspeaker A loudspeaker changes electrical energy into sound. A moving-coil type is similar to a moving-coil microphone, and can be used as a microphone. A speaker and its symbol are shown in Fig. 10.7(a), (b).

(a)

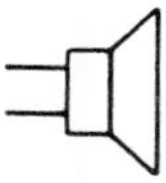

(b)

Figure 10.7

(B) Solenoid A solenoid is a coil of wire, Fig. 10.8(a), which becomes a temporary magnet *while* current is passing through it. Its magnetism is much greater if it is wound on a core of a magnetic material such as soft iron or ferrite, Fig. 10.8(b). Any object near it which is made of magnetic material moves towards it, that is, it changes electrical energy to mechanical energy.

coil
core
symbol
(a)
symbol
(b)

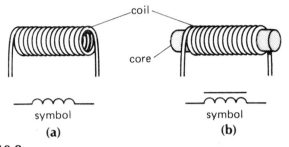

Figure 10.8

(C) Relay This is an electrically operated switch in which a small current passes through a coil and magnetizes it. The coil then pulls one switch contact against (or away from) another. It changes electrical energy into mechanical energy (movement) and is useful if we want a small current in one circuit to control another circuit containing a device which needs a large current, such as a lamp, an electric motor or an electric bell (as in Fig. 8.5).

A relay and its symbol are shown in Fig. 10.9(a), (b).

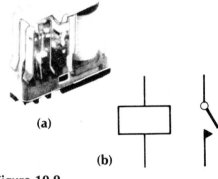

(a)
(b)

Figure 10.9

(D) Electric motor Electric motors cause rotation, changing electrical energy into mechanical energy. Large ones can drive electric trains and operate lifts. Smaller ones are used as car starter-motors and in many domestic appliances such as vacuum cleaners, washing machines and refrigerators. One of the newest uses is in robots where 'stepper' motors, driven by pulses of current, turn the robot arm a small fixed amount per pulse. A small motor is shown in Fig. 10.10, with its symbol.

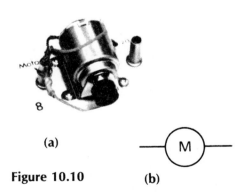

(a)
M
(b)

Figure 10.10

(E) Lamps These convert electrical energy into light. In an ordinary **filament** lamp, only about 2% of the electrical energy is changed to light, the rest becomes unwanted heat. For a **fluorescent** lamp the value is 10 to 12% (and the lamp lasts 3 to 4 times longer). An **LED** (see page 31) changes electrical energy *directly* to light and is more efficient than other light sources.

(F) Heaters An electric heater is designed to produce heat from electrical energy. The elements in **radiant** electric fires are at red heat (about 900 °C) and the radiation emitted is directed into the room by polished reflectors. In **convector** types the elements are below red heat (about 450 °C) and heat air which is drawn through the heater by natural or forced convection. In **storage** heaters the elements heat fire-clay bricks during the night using off-peak electricity. Next day these cool down, giving off the stored heat.

Questions

1 Identify the transducers represented by the symbols in Fig. 10.11(a) to (h). What does each transducer do?

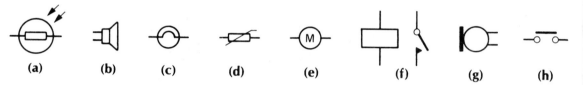

(a)   (b)   (c)   (d)   (e)   (f)   (g)   (h)

Figure 10.11

2 What is the difference in terms of the **forms** of energy involved, between input and output transducers used in electronic systems?

3 L is just alight in the circuits of Fig. 10.12(a), (b). Does it get brighter or dimmer in
(a) if the thermistor is heated
(b) if the LDR is screened from the daylight?

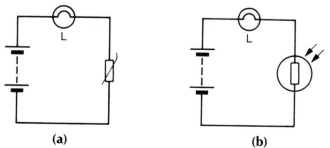

(a)   (b)

Figure 10.12

4 Name six domestic/everyday appliances which contain an electric motor (excluding those mentioned in this Unit).

ELECTRONIC SYSTEMS

Unit 11 Logic Systems

Logic gates

Logic gates are electronically controlled switching-type circuits in which the output and input voltages are either 'high', e.g. + 5 V, or 'low', e.g. 0 V (see page 39). The voltage levels 'high' and 'low' are represented by the digits 1 and 0 respectively. Digital ICs used in calculators and computers contain large numbers of logic gates.

A logic gate 'opens' and gives a 'high' output depending on the combination of signals at its input, of which there is usually more than one. There are various types of logic gate. The behaviour of each is summed up by a **truth table** which shows in terms of 1s ('high') and 0s ('low') what the output is for all possible inputs.

Truth tables can be found using the apparatus of Fig. 11.1 in which the logic gate, in IC form, is mounted on a board with sockets for the power supply, for the inputs A and B and for the output Q.

+ 5 V
power supply
0 V
+ 5 V
logic gate IC
A
B
0 V
Q
0 V
L.E.D. indicator

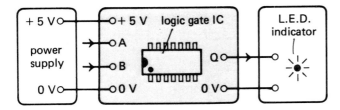

Figure 11.1

If an input is connected to +5 V on the power supply, it is 'high' (1), and if it is connected to 0 V, it is 'low' (0). The output is 'high' (1) if the LED lights up and 'low' (0) if it doesn't.

(A) NOT gate or inverter This is the simplest gate, with one input and one output. It produces a 'high' output if the input is 'low', i.e. NOT 'high', and vice versa. Whatever the input, the gate inverts it, that is, it turns a 1 to a 0 and a 0 to a 1. The British and American symbols and the truth table are given in Fig. 11.2.

NOT gate
British
1
input
output
American
input
output

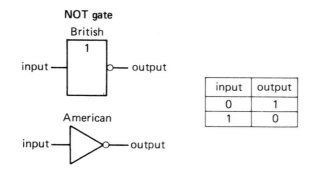

input	output
0	1
1	0

Figure 11.2

(B) OR and NOR gates These have two (or more) inputs A and B, and one output Q. Their symbols and truth tables for the four possible input combinations are shown in Figs. 11.3 and 11.4.

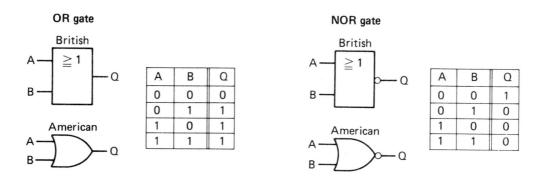

OR gate
British
A
B
≧1
Q
American
A
B
Q

A	B	Q
0	0	0
0	1	1
1	0	1
1	1	1

Figure 11.3

NOR gate
British
A
B
≧1
Q
American
A
B
Q

A	B	Q
0	0	1
0	1	0
1	0	0
1	1	0

Figure 11.4

Try to remember:

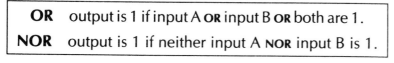

OR output is 1 if input A OR input B OR both are 1.

NOR output is 1 if neither input A NOR input B is 1.

(C) AND and NAND gates Their symbols and truth tables are given in Figs. 11.5 and 11.6.

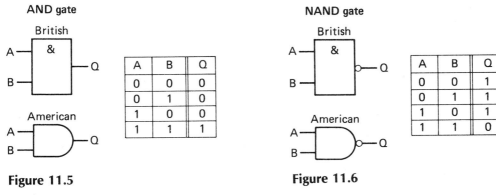

AND gate

British
&
A
B
Q
American
A
B
Q

A	B	Q
0	0	0
0	1	0
1	0	0
1	1	1

Figure 11.5

NAND gate

British
&
A
B
Q
American
A
B
Q

A	B	Q
0	0	1
0	1	1
1	0	1
1	1	0

Figure 11.6

Try to remember:

> **AND** output is 1 if input A **AND** input B are both 1.
>
> **NAND** output is 1 if input A **AND** input B are **NOT** both 1.

Note that the outputs of the NOR and NAND gates are the opposite of the OR and AND gates respectively. They have a small circle at the outputs of their symbols to show this.

Combinations of logic gates

When gates are combined to produce more complex logic circuits the final output can be worked out by producing a truth table. For example, the logic circuit of the three gates connected as in Fig. 11.7 has the truth table shown.

A
B
&
C
1
D
≥1
Q
A
B
C
D
Q

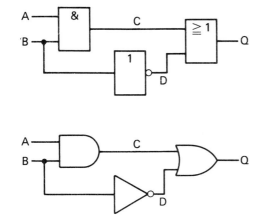

A	B	C	D	Q
0	0	0	1	1
0	1	0	0	0
1	0	0	1	1
1	1	1	0	1

Figure 11.7

The AND gate output C is 1 only when inputs A and B are both 1.

The NOT gate output D is 1 only when B is 0.

The OR gate output Q is 1 when either C or D or both are 1s, i.e. it is 1 except when A is 0 and B is 1.

Questions

1 What do the symbols in Fig. 11.8(a) to (e) represent?

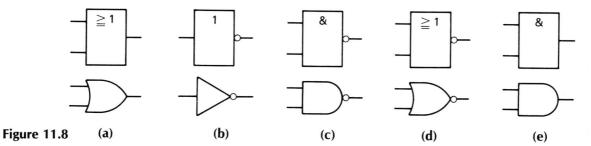

Figure 11.8 **(a)** **(b)** **(c)** **(d)** **(e)**

2 Draw up truth tables for the logic circuits in Fig. 11.9(a), (b), (c). Those in (a) and (b) can be replaced by one gate: name it in each case.

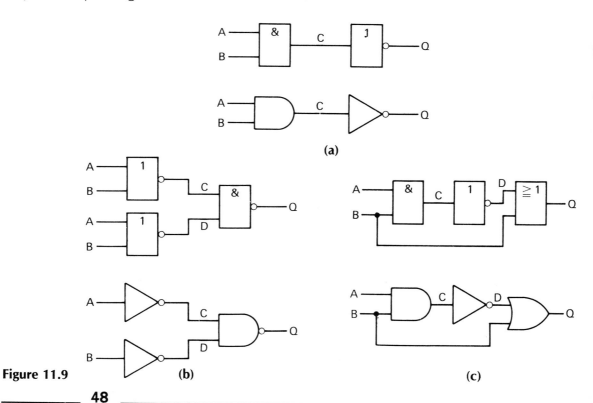

Figure 11.9 **(b)** **(c)**

3 Identify each of the gates A, B, C and D whose truth tables are given in Fig. 11.10.

inputs		outputs A	outputs B	outputs C	outputs D
0	0	0	0	1	1
0	1	0	1	1	0
1	0	0	1	1	0
1	1	1	1	0	0

Figure 11.10

4 Combinations of switches can act as logic gates. Which type are those in Fig. 11.11(a) and (b)? (Treat A and B as inputs and Q as the output.)

A
B
Q
(a)
A
B
Q
(b)

Figure 11.11

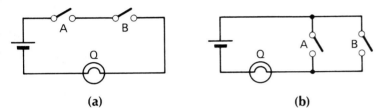

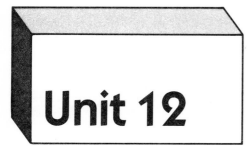

Unit 12 Microcomputer Systems

Computer building blocks

All computers contain the building blocks, called **hardware**, shown in Fig. 12.1.

ADDRESS BUS (one-way)
CPU
ROM
RAM
INPUT
OUTPUT
DATA BUS (two-way)
CONTROL BUS (one-way)

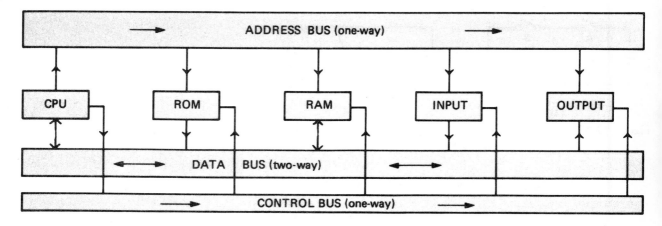

Figure 12.1

(A) Central processing unit (CPU) The CPU organizes and controls all the arithmetic and logic operations the computer can perform. It is sometimes called the 'brain' of the computer and consists of a complex combination of logic gates. It interprets and obeys a sequence of instructions called the **program**. In a microcomputer the CPU is a **microprocessor**, in the form of a single IC.

(B) Memory The memory stores (i) the **program** (called **software**) which tells the CPU what to do and (ii) the **data** or information processed during the running of the program.

A **ROM** or **Read Only Memory** is an IC used to store the program because its contents have only to be 'read' by the CPU and are not lost when the computer is switched off, i.e. it is a permanent store.

A **RAM** or **Random Access Memory** is an IC used to store the data. It not only allows data to be 'read' but it can also have new data 'written' in. Its contents are lost when the computer is switched off, i.e. it is a temporary store.

(C) Input and output (I/O) These allow the computer to communicate with the outside world. Their form depends on what the computer is being used for. Often the input is provided by a keyboard like that on a typewriter but with extra 'command' keys, and the output may be supplied to a printer or a visual display unit (**VDU**), Fig. 12.2.

Figure 12.2

(D) Interfaces The input to a CPU must consist of **digital** signals (like those in Fig. 9.2, page 39) as they are from a keyboard. Those from a thermistor or an LDR are analogue signals (Fig. 9.3) and must be changed to digital ones by an **interfacing circuit** called an 'analogue-to-digital converter'.

The output from a CPU is digital, so if the output device being supplied requires analogue signals, a digital-to-analogue interfacing circuit is needed.

(E) Buses The CPU is connected to other parts by three sets of wires, called **buses** because they 'transport' information in the form of digital signals. The **address bus**

carries signals from the CPU which enables it to find data stored in a particular location of the memory. The **data bus** allows the two-way passage of data between the CPU and other parts. The **control bus** transmits timing and control signals which keep the various parts working in step.

In diagrams each bus is represented by one broad line; in practice it may consist of 8, 16 or 32 separate lines. The arrows in Fig. 12.1 show the directions in which data passes in the different buses.

Uses of microprocessors

Microprocessors can be programmed to do tasks other than that of acting as a CPU in a microcomputer. In the past, some of these tasks have been done by complex, specially designed circuits. If the required program is stored in a ROM, the microprocessor carries out just one task when it is switched on, so long as no provision has been made for reprogramming in its design. It is often much cheaper to do this than to have a purpose-built system, even if all the facilities available on the micro-processor are not used.

This approach has been adopted in pocket calculators, washing machines, cash registers, sewing machines, petrol pumps, video games, traffic lights and industrial robots (Fig. 12.3).

Figure 12.3

Microprocessors are also being used in cars to replace a number of devices. Advantages gained are saving of space, longer life, cheapness, easier replacement and ability to perform a wider range of jobs (e.g. controlling engine efficiency, checking tyre pressures and condition of light bulbs). One disadvantage is that more than one system in the car would fail if it went wrong.

Questions

1 (a) What kind of signals (digital or analogue) must pass between a CPU and its inputs and outputs?
   (b) Why are interfacing circuits required?
2 (a) Name **two** types of memory used in computers.
   (b) State **two** ways in which they differ.
   (c) Which type stores **(i)** the program **(ii)** data?

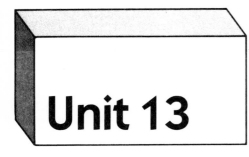

Unit 13 Audio Systems

An audio system reproduces and amplifies sound. It handles alternating voltages and currents which have frequencies from about 20 Hz to 20 000 Hz (20 kHz) or so, that is, in the audio frequency (a.f.) range (see p. 12). Electrical signals with these frequencies produce sound when fed to a loudspeaker.

The block diagram for an audio system is shown in Fig. 13.1. It has three main parts—an input transducer, an audio amplifier and an output transducer.

AUDIO AMPLIFIER
INPUT TRANSDUCER
preamplifier
volume & tone controls
power amplifier
OUTPUT TRANSDUCER

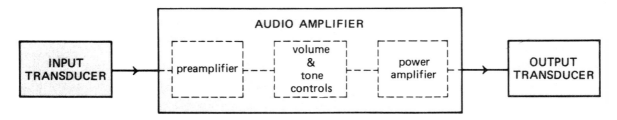

Figure 13.1

Input transducer

This may be a microphone, the pick-up of a record/compact disc player or the playback head of a cassette recorder. All change sound, produced in the first place by a source of speech or music, into electrical energy in the form of alternating a.f. voltages and currents.

Sound is received directly from the source by a microphone (see p. 40). In a record player it is stored on the wavy groove of the record and 'picked up' by a stylus and cartridge (see p. 41). In a compact disc player the sound is stored in reflecting 'pits' on the disc and picked up by a laser and photodiode. In a cassette recorder the sound is stored as variations in the magnetization of the tape and picked up by the electromagnetic head.

Audio amplifier

The electrical signals from the input transducer are too weak to operate the output transducer satisfactorily and have to be boosted by the audio amplifier. This consists of a **preamplifier**, incorporating a **volume control** to adjust the level of the sound from the whole system, and **tone controls** to enable high (treble) and low (bass) notes to be emphasized more or less. The output from the preamplifier feeds the **power amplifier** which ensures that enough power is supplied to the output transducer.

Output transducer

This is usually a loudspeaker but may also be headphones or an earpiece. These convert electrical energy into sound when a.f. currents and voltages are received from the audio amplifier.

Complete hi-fi system (music centre)

A complete hi-fi (high-fidelity) music centre and its block diagram are shown in Fig. 13.2(a) and (b). It comprises

(1) a record player (and/or compact disc player)
(2) a 3-band VHF/LW/MW radio tuner (p 57)
(3) a tape cassette deck
(4) an audio amplifier (pre- and power) into which the outputs from (1), (2) and (3) can be switched separately
(5) a loudspeaker system.

record player
radio tuner
tape cassette deck
amplifier
speakers

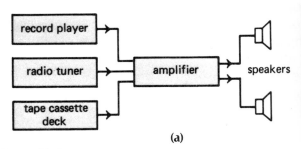

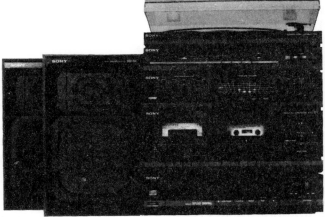

(a)

(b)

Figure 13.2

Questions

1 Why is a.c. in the frequency range 20 Hz to 20 000 Hz called audio frequency?

2 In the audio system of Fig. 13.3, what do X, Y and Z do?

X
Y
Z

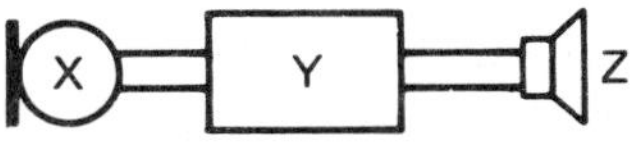

Figure 13.3

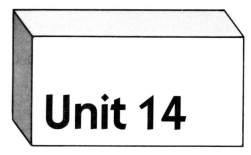

Unit 14 Radio Systems

Transmitter

The block diagram for a radio transmitter (sender) is shown in Fig. 14.1.

transmitting aerial
radio waves
microphone
a.f.
sound
modulator
modulated r.f.
oscillator
r.f.

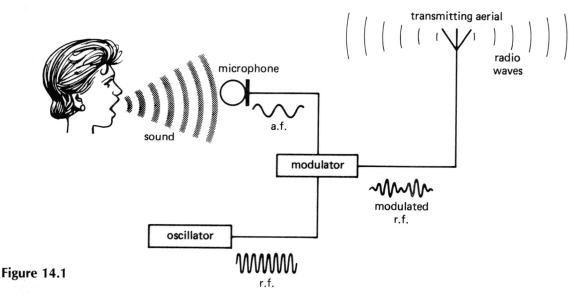

Figure 14.1

When sound (speech or music) falls on the microphone, audio frequency (a.f.) a.c. (20 to 20 000 Hz) is produced. To send out radio waves effectively, a **transmitting aerial** must be supplied with radio frequency (r.f.) a.c. (greater than 20 000 Hz). The a.f. signal has therefore to be combined in some way with the r.f. which acts as a 'carrier' for it.

A circuit called an **oscillator** generates r.f. of constant amplitude (wave size). This is fed into another circuit, the **modulator**, which changes the amplitude of the r.f. so that it has the same 'shape' as the a.f. When the modulated r.f. reaches the aerial it gives rise to radio waves that travel into the surrounding space. The wavelength of the wave depends on the frequency of the r.f.

Receiver

The various parts of a simple radio receiver are shown in Fig. 14.2.

radio
waves
receiving aerial
tuner
detector
audio
amplifier
speaker
radio
waves
modulated r.f.
from different stations
amplified
modulated r.f.
from one station
a.f.
amplified
a.f.
sound

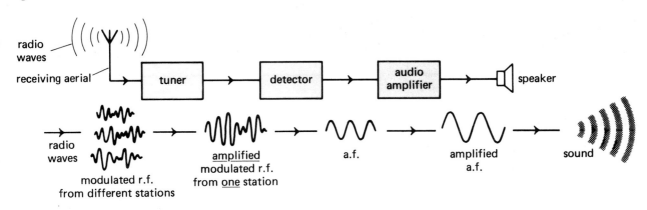

Figure 14.2

When radio waves strike a **receiving aerial** they create modulated r.f. currents in it that are small copies of those in the transmitting aerials from which they came. The **tuner** chooses *one* of the modulated r.f. currents from the aerial and amplifies it. The **detector** or **demodulator** separates the a.f. from the r.f. and passes the a.f. on to the **audio amplifier**, which boosts it so that the sound it produces in the **loudspeaker** is loud enough to be heard.

Questions

1 What does the modulator do in a radio transmitter? Why is it necessary?

2 What does the detector do in a radio receiver? Why is it necessary?

3 Using information published about radio programmes in national newspapers, draw up a table giving the wavelength *and* frequency of some stations you listen to.

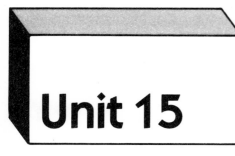

Unit 15 Feedback Control Systems

An electronic system may be required to keep a quantity such as the temperature of a room or the speed of an electric motor, more or less constant. This can be done by **feeding back** information from the output of the system to its input, in a way which enables the system to respond to any changes that occur. **Control** of the quantity to be kept steady is then achieved. Here are two examples.

Temperature control of a heater

A block diagram of a system to control the temperature of a room is shown in Fig. 15.1.

feedback
temperature selector
thermostat
electrical supply to heater
heater
room temperature

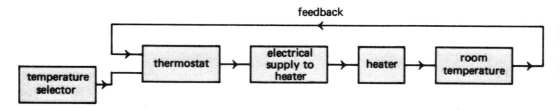

Figure 15.1

The required temperature is set by hand on the **thermostat**. If the setting is above the **room temperature**, the thermostat switches on the **electrical supply** to the **heater**. The room warms up and when its temperature reaches the one selected, the thermostat responds to this information, which is fed back to it from the air in the room, by switching off the electrical supply.

If the room cools and its temperature falls below the required value, the thermostat again responds and switches on the heater. In this way, temperature control by feedback is achieved.

The circuit in Figure 15.3 (page 59) shows how a thermistor can be used as a thermostat to control temperature.

Motor speed control

It is sometimes necessary for an electric motor to revolve at a steady speed, for example, when it has to drive a greater load. The block diagram for a speed controller system is shown in Fig. 15.2.

feedback
speed selector
error amplifier
electric motor
speed detector

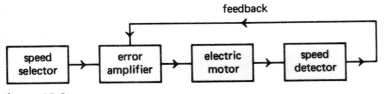

Figure 15.2

If the **speed detector** detects any change in the selected speed of the **motor**, it feeds back a signal to the **error amplifier** which makes the motor go faster or slower as required.

Question

1 In the circuit of Fig. 15.3 a fan is driven by an electric motor M which is controlled by a transistor. The transistor turns a relay on when the temperature rises and off when it falls.

(a) What is component X?

(b) When the temperature rises what change occurs in

(i) X

(ii) the current through the transistor and the relay coil?

(c) How does feedback occur in the circuit?

(d) What purpose does Y serve?

relay
+
X
Y
M

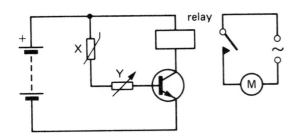

Figure 15.3

INSTRUMENTS

Unit 16 Meters

Ammeters and voltmeters

When a meter is connected to a circuit to make a measurement it should cause the minimum disturbance to the conditions which existed before.

An **ammeter** is inserted in **series** in a circuit. It must have a **low resistance** compared with the rest of the circuit, otherwise it changes the current to be measured.

A **voltmeter** is connected in **parallel** with the component, e.g. a resistor, across which the voltage is to be measured. It should have a **high resistance** compared with the resistor otherwise the total resistance of the whole circuit is reduced by the 'loading' effect of the voltmeter and the voltage to be measured changes.

Multimeters

A multimeter measures current, voltage and resistance, each on several ranges.

(A) Analogue multimeter In this type, Fig. 16.1, the deflection of a pointer over a scale represents the value of the quantity being measured.

Currents and voltages are measured by turning the selector switch so that the arrow on it points to the appropriate setting on the scale round it. (It is wise to set it on the highest range first to prevent damage to the meter.) The multimeter is then connected into the circuit as an ordinary ammeter or voltmeter would be (*observing the correct polarity*), see Units 2 and 3.

To make a resistance measurement, the multimeter leads are first held together, so making the external resistance between its terminals zero and the current through the meter (from its internal battery) a maximum. The leads

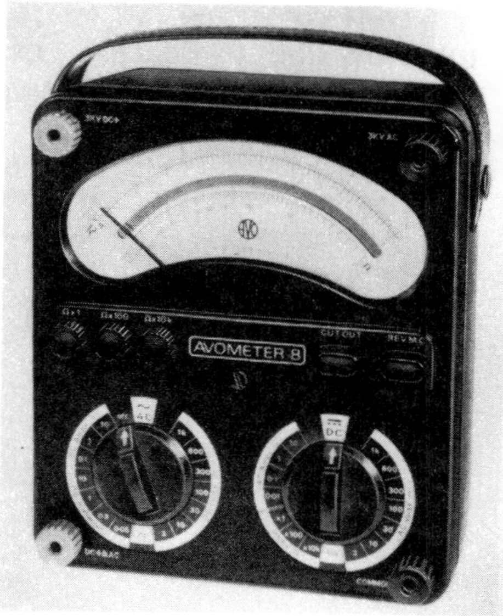
AVOMETER 8
DC
Figure 16.1

are then connected across the unknown resistance *R*. The current is now less and the pointer gives the value of *R* in ohms.

(B) Digital multimeter The measurement is shown on an LED or LCD (liquid crystal display) digital decimal display (Unit 7), often with four figures, Fig. 16.2.

Usually there are three sockets for making connections—(1) mA, (2) common and (3) V and Ω. For current measurements connections are made to (1) and (2). For voltage and resistance measurements (2) and (3) are used. Different ranges can be selected for each quantity.

You will find out in the next Unit how multimeters are used to locate faults in electronic circuits and components.

12.34
mA
V
Ω
S
COMMON

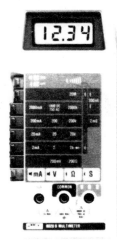

Figure 16.2

Questions

1 In Fig. 16.3 the circles are either ammeters or voltmeters. State what each is and the reading it would show.

2 Repeat Question 1 for Fig. 16.4.

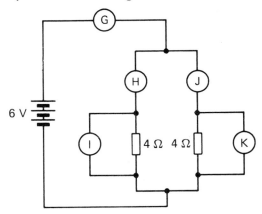

G
H
J
6 V
I
4 Ω
4 Ω
K

Figure 16.4

B
C
3 Ω
6 V
D
E
3 Ω
F

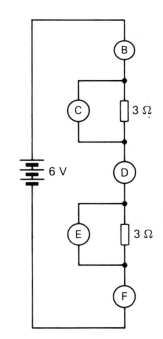

Figure 16.3

3 Do you think a measurement is more likely to be read wrongly on an analogue multimeter than a digital one?

Unit 17 Fault Finding

Some components are tested by using the fact that

(a) in **analogue** multimeters, the negative (black) terminal has positive (+) polarity (due to its internal battery), and

(b) in **digital** multimeters, the terminal marked 'mA' is usually positive (but this should be checked in the instruction booklet).

Diodes

A diode should give a *low* resistance reading when the cathode (the end with the band round it) is connected to the terminal with negative polarity and the anode to the terminal of positive polarity. The connections using an analogue multimeter are shown in Fig. 17.1. Reversing the connections gives a *high* resistance reading in a 'healthy' diode.

analogue multimeter
red (+) terminal but of negative polarity
low resistance reading
∞
1000
0
+
−
black (−) terminal but of positive polarity
cathode
anode
diode

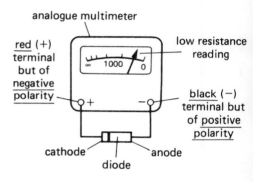

Figure 17.1

Transistors

In a transistor the resistance should be *high* between the collector (C) and emitter (E) for *both* methods of connection to the multimeter.

This enables the base (B) to be identified, since an npn transistor gives a *lower* resistance when the multimeter terminal of positive polarity (i.e. the black one marked −) is connected to B and the other terminal to E or C than it does with the leads reversed, Fig. 17.2.

∞
1000
0
+
−
E
B
C
n-p-n
low resistance
high resistance

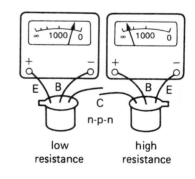

Figure 17.2

Capacitors

(A) Ordinary types If the resistance of the capacitor is less than about 1 MΩ, it is allowing d.c. to pass (from the battery in the multimeter), i.e. it is 'leaking' and is faulty. With large-value capacitors there may be a short initial burst of current as the capacitor charges.

(B) Electrolytics For the dielectric to form in these, a positive voltage must be applied to the positive lead of the capacitor (marked by a +) from the multimeter terminal of the positive polarity. When first connected, the resistance is low but rises as the dielectric forms.

Bulbs, fuses, connecting wire

Their resistance should be low if not they are faulty.

'Dry' joints

These are badly soldered joints which have a high resistance. In the circuit of Fig. 17.3, if there is a 'dry' joint at X the voltmeter reading to the right of X will be +6 V, and to the left 0 V, because there is a very high resistance at X.

R_2
X
R_1
+ 6 V
flying lead
V
0 V
+

Figure 17.3

Any other type of poor connection in a circuit shows up in the same way.

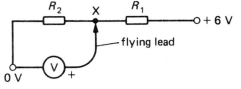

Questions

1 What is the sign of a 'healthy' diode?

2 Why would the LED in Fig. 17.4 not light up?

0 V
330 Ω
+ 6 V

Figure 17.4

3 Two of the connections X, Y, Z on a transistor, Fig. 17.5, were connected in turn to a multimeter on the resistance range. The resistances obtained ('high' or 'low') with the polarities shown are given in the table.

(a) Which connection is the base?

(b) Is the transistor 'healthy'?

red (+) terminal but of negative polarity
multimeter
black (−) terminal but of positive polarity
+
−
X Y Z
transistor

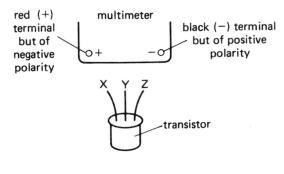

Figure 17.5

X	Y	Z	resistance
+		−	high
−		+	high
	+	−	low
	−	+	high
−	+		low
+	−		high

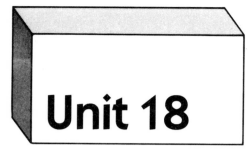

Unit 18 Cathode Ray Oscilloscope

Description

The cathode ray oscilloscope (CRO), Fig. 18.1, is one of the most important scientific instruments ever to be invented. It contains, like a television set, a **cathode ray tube** which has four main parts, Fig. 18.2.

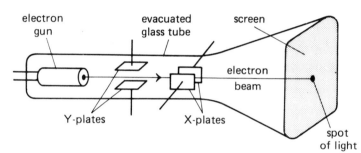

Figure 18.1

electron gun
evacuated glass tube
screen
electron beam
Y-plates
X-plates
spot of light

Figure 18.2

(A) Electron gun This shoots out a beam of electrons which travels at high speed along the middle of an evacuated glass tube. The number of electrons coming from the gun is controlled by the BRILLIANCE or BRIGHTNESS control on the front of the CRO. The FOCUS control alters the width of the beam.

(B) Screen A bright spot of light is produced on the screen where the beam hits it. A narrow beam produces a small spot.

(C) Y-plates These are two horizontal metal plates which deflect the beam vertically up or down when a voltage is applied to them via the Y-input terminals (often marked 'high' and 'low') on the front of the CRO. The Y-input voltage is usually amplified by an amount which depends on the setting on the Y-AMP GAIN control before it gets to the Y-plates.

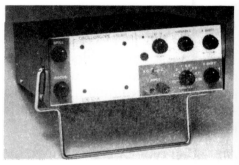

In Fig. 18.3(a) the voltage between the Y-plates is zero and the beam is not deflected.

In Fig. 18.3(b) the d.c. voltage makes the upper plate positive and the beam of negatively charged electrons is attracted upwards to it.

In Fig. 18.3(c) the 50 Hz a.c. input makes the beam move up and down so rapidly that it produces a continuous vertical line on the screen (which increases in length if the Y-AMP GAIN is turned up).

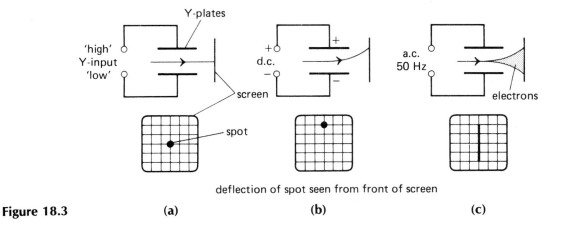

Y-plates
'high'
Y-input
'low'
screen
spot
+
d.c.
−
+
−
a.c.
50 Hz
electrons
deflection of spot seen from front of screen

Figure 18.3 (a) (b) (c)

(D) X-plates and time base The X-plates are vertical. The voltage applied to them comes from a circuit inside the CRO called the **time base**. It makes the spot sweep across the screen horizontally from left to right at a steady speed, determined by the setting of the TIME BASE control. At the end of the sweep the spot flies back very rapidly to its starting point on the left of the screen.

In Fig. 18.4(a), (b), (c), the time base is on. In (a) the Y-input voltage is zero, in (b) it is d.c. which makes the upper Y-plate positive, in (c) it is d.c. which makes the lower Y-plate positive. In all cases the spot traces out a horizontal line which appears to be continuous if the time base speed is high enough.

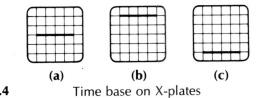

(a) (b) (c)

Figure 18.4 Time base on X-plates

Practical points

(1) The BRILLIANCE or BRIGHTNESS control, which is usually the ON/OFF switch as well, should be as low as possible when there is just a spot on the screen, otherwise screen 'burn' occurs which damages the fluorescent material on the screen. If possible it is best to defocus the spot or to draw it into a line by having the TIME BASE on.

(2) When preparing the CRO for use, set the BRILLIANCE (or BRIGHTNESS), FOCUS, X- and Y-SHIFT controls (the last two allow the spot to be moved 'manually' over the screen in the X- and Y-directions respectively) to their mid-positions. The TIME BASE and Y-AMP GAIN controls can then be adjusted to suit the Y-input.

(3) When the a.c./d.c. SELECTOR switch is in the 'd.c.' (or 'direct') position both d.c. and a.c. can pass to the Y-input. In the 'a.c.' (or 'via C') position, a capacitor blocks d.c. in the input but allows a.c. to pass.

Measuring voltages

A d.c. or a.c. voltage applied to the Y-input terminals (**time base off**) can be measured from the deflection of the spot if the Y-AMP GAIN control is calibrated (i.e. has a scale marked round it).

For example, if it is on 1 V/div (1 volt per division), Fig. 18.5(a), a deflection of 1 vertical division on the screen graticule (like graph paper) would be given by a 1 V d.c. input to the Y-terminals, Fig. 18.5(b). A vertical line 4 divisions long, Fig. 18.5(c), would be produced by an a.c. input of 4 V **peak-to-peak**, that is, of **peak** value 2 V (see Unit 2).

V/div
0.5
1
0.1
5
0.05
Y-AMP GAIN setting
(a)
1 div = 1 V
Y-input = 1 V d.c.
(b)
peak value = 2 V
peak-to-peak value = 4 divs = 4 V
Y-input = 4 V a.c. peak-to-peak
(c)

Figure 18.5

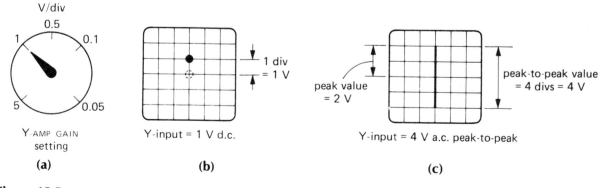

Displaying and measuring waveforms

In this widely used role the **time base is on** and the CRO acts as a 'graph-plotter' to show the waveform of the voltage applied to the Y-input, i.e. how it varies with time.

The display in Fig. 18.6(a) is for an a.c. supply voltage. If the Y-AMP GAIN control is on 5 V/div, the **peak-to-peak** value of the voltage is 4 divs = 4 × 5 = 20 V and its **peak value** or **amplitude** is 10 V.

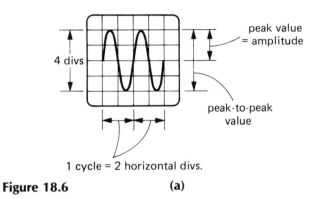

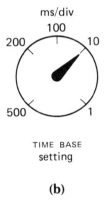

4 divs
peak value
= amplitude
peak-to-peak
value
1 cycle = 2 horizontal divs.

ms/div
100
200
10
500
1
TIME BASE
setting

Figure 18.6 **(a)** **(b)**

The **period** and **frequency** of the a.c. (see Unit 2) can be found if the TIME BASE control is calibrated. For example, if it is set on 10 ms/div, Fig. 18.6(b), the spot takes 10 milliseconds to move 1 division horizontally across the screen graticule. Then since 1 complete cycle occupies 2 horizontal divisions, we can say

$$\begin{aligned} \text{period} = \text{time for 1 cycle} &= 2\,\text{divs} \times 10\,\text{ms/div} \\ &= 20\,\text{ms} \\ &= 20/1000\,\text{s} = 1/50\,\text{s} \\ &\qquad (1000\,\text{ms} = 1\,\text{s}) \end{aligned}$$

Since 1 cycle occurs in 1/50 s, 50 cycles will occur in 1 s and so

$$\text{frequency} = 50 \text{ cycles per second} = 50\,\text{Hz}$$

Two other common waveform displays are shown in Figs. 18.7.

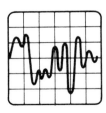

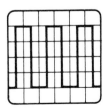

(a) Speech from microphone **(b)** Digital signal on microcomputer bus

Figure 18.7

Questions

1 When a d.c. voltage is applied across the Y-plates of a CRO via the Y-input terminals, the spot on the screen moves downwards, Fig. 18.8. Which plate, the upper or the lower, is connected to the positive of the d.c. voltage?

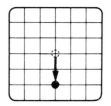

Figure 18.8

2 Which of the displays in Fig. 18.9 could appear on the screen of a CRO if an alternating voltage is applied to the Y-plates with the time base **(a)** off **(b)** on?

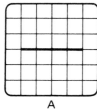 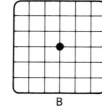 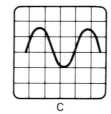 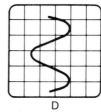 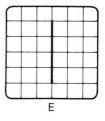

| A | B | C | D | E |

Figure 18.9

3 The waveform in Fig. 18.10(a) is displayed on a CRO. A student then alters *two* controls and obtains the waveform in Fig. 18.10(b). The two controls adjusted were
  A TIME BASE and Y-SHIFT
  B Y-AMP GAIN and X-SHIFT
  C Y-AMP GAIN and TIME BASE
  D FOCUS and Y-AMP GAIN
  E TIME BASE and FOCUS?

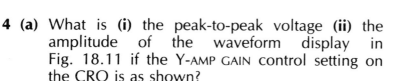

  (a)   (b)
Figure 18.10

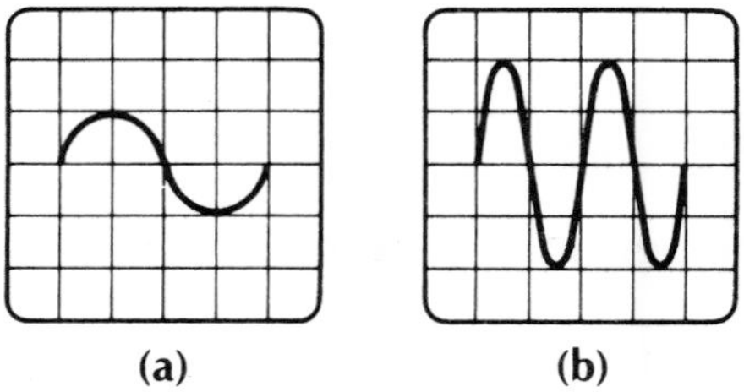

4 **(a)** What is **(i)** the peak-to-peak voltage **(ii)** the amplitude of the waveform display in Fig. 18.11 if the Y-AMP GAIN control setting on the CRO is as shown?

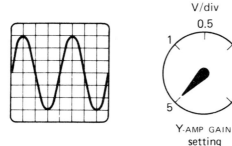

Figure 18.11

(b) Repeat (a) for the waveform in Fig. 18.12, which was obtained on another CRO with *different* Y-AMP GAIN control settings.
(**Note:** 1000 millivolts (mV) = 1 volt (V).)

mV/div
100
200
50
500
10
Y-AMP GAIN
setting

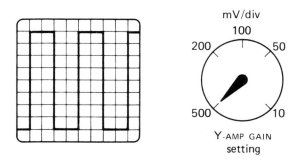

Figure 18.12

5 (a) What is **(i)** the period **(ii)** the frequency of the waveform display in Fig. 18.13 if the TIME BASE control setting on the CRO is as shown?

ms/div
100
200
10
500
1
TIME BASE
setting

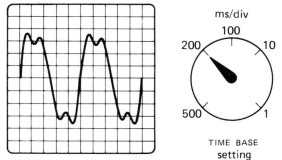

Figure 18.13

(b) Repeat (a) for the waveform in Fig. 18.14, which was obtained with a *different* TIME BASE control setting.
(**Note:** 1000 milliseconds (ms) = 1 second (s).)

ms/div
100
200
10
500
1
TIME BASE
setting

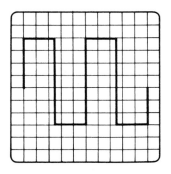

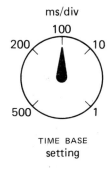

Figure 18.14

SAFETY

Unit 19 Dangers of Electricity

Mains supply

(A) Live and neutral wires The electricity supply from a power station is a.c. and is carried by two wires. The **neutral** wire (N), covered with **blue** insulation, is connected to earth and is at 0 V. The **live** wire (L), covered with **brown** insulation, is alternatively positive and negative and is the one that gives an electric shock if touched. **Remember**:

LIVE is BROWN **NEUTRAL is BLUE**

Every circuit is connected in parallel with the supply, that is, across the live and neutral, and so receives the full mains voltage, which is 240 V in many countries.

(B) Switches These should always be in the **live** wire, Fig. 19.1.

supply
N
L
lighting
circuits

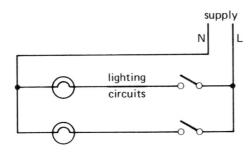

Figure 19.1

If they were in the neutral wire, lights and power sockets would have one side live when they were switched off. A shock could then be obtained by, for example, touching the element of an electric fire when it was switched off. This could be **fatal** if the person was 'earthed' by standing on a concrete floor or was in a damp environment (since water conducts).

(C) Power plugs The correct way to wire a three-pin plug is shown in Fig. 19.2. It has its own **fuse** (see Unit 20) in the **live** lead. The wires from the appliance are colour coded and must be connected to the corresponding pins on the plug, after the insulation has been removed from the end.

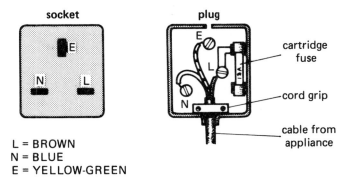

socket
plug
E
N
L
E
L
N
cartridge fuse
13A
cord grip
cable from appliance
L = BROWN
N = BLUE
E = YELLOW-GREEN

Figure 19.2

The third pin, the **earth** (E) pin, connects the metal case of the appliance by a wire with **yellow–green** striped insulation, to a wire behind the socket which is earthed, for example, by being connected to a metal water pipe. This earth connection is a safety measure to prevent electric shock should the appliance develop a fault. It causes a fuse to 'blow' (or, in newer installations, a circuit breaker to operate) which makes the circuit 'dead' and safe.

Sources of danger

It is important to be aware of possible sources of danger when working with electrical and electronic circuits.

(A) Live circuits Care is needed when testing live circuits and using devices that are connected to the mains supply. The **outer sheath** of the cable in a plug should be firmly secured by the **cord grip**, Fig. 19.2. Also, cables should be clamped inside cabinets to prevent any strain on the connections.

(B) Insulation This can wear, especially if it continually rubs where it enters the metal case of a cabinet. A rubber grommet offers protection, Fig. 19.3.

On circuit boards (see Unit 21), the conducting strips of copper foil should be separated enough to prevent unwanted connections and 'short circuits'.

cable
rubber grommet in hole in metal cabinet
metal cabinet

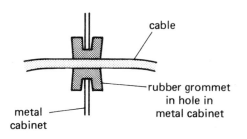

Figure 19.3

(C) Large capacitors These may hold a dangerous electric charge for a long time even though the equipment is disconnected from the supply. They can be discharged by holding a metal bar with a good insulating handle across the terminals.

(D) Hazardous vapours and dusts An electric spark or a device at a high temperature can ignite a mixture of air and flammable vapour (e.g. petrol) or fine dust (produced for example by grinding grain, sugar or coal). An explosion may even occur.

(E) Disposal of components These should never be burnt, especially old batteries.

Electric shock

An electric **current** passing through the body causes electric shock. It affects the heart (upsetting the rhythm and the flow of blood), the muscles and the nervous system. How severe the shock is depends on the **size** of the current (as shown in the table below) and the **time** for which it passes. Age, general health and moistness of the skin also affect it.

The size of the current depends on the voltage involved and the resistance of the body. The latter can be less than $1.5\,k\Omega$ if the skin is moist. In most accidents someone receives a 'shock to earth', and the better the contact that is made to earth (e.g. by standing on wet ground), the worse is the shock.

Current in mA	Effect
1	Maximum safe current
2–5	Begins to be felt by most people
10	Unable to let go and could become fatal
100	Probably fatal if through the heart

Questions

1 (a) Name the three terminals on a three-pin electric plug.
  (b) State the colour of the insulation on the wire connected to each terminal.
  (c) What is the purpose of the cord grip in the plug?

2 How can large capacitors in electronic equipment be dangerous?

3 (a) Name the electrical quantity which causes electric shock.
  (b) Why is the risk of a fatal shock greater for someone using electrical equipment outdoors (e.g. an electric lawnmower)?

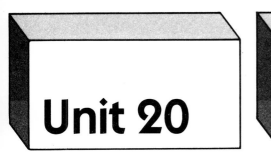

Unit 20 Safety Precautions

Fuses

A fuse is a short length of wire of material with a low melting point (often tinned copper), which melts and breaks the circuit when the current through it exceeds a certain value. A 3 A fuse may need 5 A to blow it at once; it will carry up to 3 A indefinitely. Two types of fuse are shown in Fig. 20.1.

fuse wire
symbol for a fuse
cartridge fuse
insulating holder

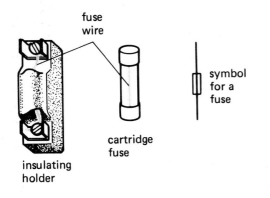

Figure 20.1

Two reasons for excessive currents are 'short circuits' due to worn insulation on connecting wires, and overloaded circuits. In such cases, without a fuse, the wiring would become hot (since for every cable there is a maximum safe current) and could cause a fire.

To calculate the fuse rating that is needed to protect a given appliance we use the expression

$$P = V \times I$$

where P is the power of the appliance in watts (W), V is the voltage across the appliance in volts (V) and I is the current through it in amperes (A) (see Unit 4).

This can be rearranged as $I = \dfrac{P}{V}$ and remembered from

as was done with $I = \dfrac{V}{R}$ (p. 18).

For example, if $P = 1\,\text{kW} = 1000\,\text{W}$ and $V = 240\,\text{V}$ then

$$I = \frac{P}{V} = \frac{1000}{240} = 4\,\text{A (approx.)}$$

A 5 A fuse would give adequate protection.

Residual current devices (RCD)

These are used as extra safety devices. They are especially suitable for plugging into sockets supplying power to outside portable appliances such as electric lawnmowers and hedgecutters where the risk of electric shock is greater (because the user is making a good earth connection via his feet). Their principle of operation is this. Normally the current in the live wire equals that in the neutral wire. However if a fault develops there is a *difference* between them and when it exceeds a safe level, the RCD breaks the circuit and switches off the supply. It is a fast-acting device which is sensitive to small current differences (e.g. 3 mA) and is reset for re-use simply by pressing a button.

Figure 20.2

Handling components

Electronic components can be damaged by incorrect or rough treatment. For example, if the lead-out wires from resistors, capacitors, diodes and transistors are bent too close to the component when they are connected into circuits, they may break.

When soldering, heat damage can occur, especially to semiconductors or devices, if a **heat sink** is not used (see **soldering**, page 80).

Some components, e.g. CMOS integrated circuits, are damaged by static electric charges (Unit 2) produced on their metal connecting pins if they touch insulators, e.g. plastics, clothes, in warm, dry conditions. For that reason, they are supplied in anti-static or conducting carriers and should not be handled unnecessarily when removed.

Questions

1 Why are fuses used in circuits?
2 Calculate the current rating of the fuse that is suitable with a 240 V supply for protecting
   (a) a 480 W appliance
   (b) a 3 kW appliance.
3 (a) What do the letters RCD stand for?
   (b) What is the purpose of an RCD?
   (c) When is an RCD especially useful?
   (d) What is the principle on which an RCD works?
   (e) State **three** advantages of RCDs over fuses.
4 State **two** ways in which damage can occur to electronic components when they are being connected into circuits.

PART 2 Building Circuits

Circuits can be assembled in different ways. Three ways are described below, using **S-DeC**, **matrix board** and **stripboard**. In the experiments and projects that follow, the S-DeC method is used because it allows circuits to be dismantled and new ones built with the same components. With matrix board the layout of the components and the wiring can be exactly as in the circuit diagram. For permanent circuits the stripboard method is suitable.

S-DeC

An S-DeC is a plastic box with a lid which has 70 numbered holes (Fig. B1). It has 14 metal contact strips under the lid, seven on each side of the box, as shown in Fig. B2. The strip under holes 1 to 5 automatically connects wires put into any one of these holes. The strip below holes 6 to 10 connects all the wires in these and so on.

control panel
slot for panel
slot for panel
lid
hole
S-DeC
metal contact strip

Figure B1

plastic insulation
resistor
bare wire
contact strip

Figure B2

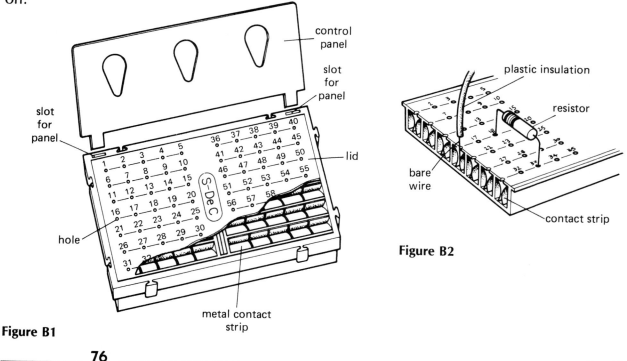

To make a connection push about 2 cm of *bare* wire *straight* into the hole (not at an angle) so that it is gripped by the contact strip. *Do not push it in too far* or use wires that are *dirty* or have *kinked ends*; this could damage the contacts. Bend leads on resistors and other parts as shown in Fig. B2 but *not too close* to the part or it may break off.

Use a wire link (Fig. B3) when two sets of holes have to be connected. Lengthen transistor leads by making 'joints' (Fig. B4) using plastic sleeving (tubing). You will have to do this to get all three leads into holes on the S-DeC.

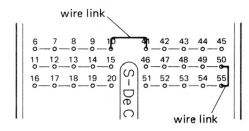

wire link
6 7 8 9 10 41 42 43 44 45
11 12 13 14 15 46 47 48 49 50
16 17 18 19 20 51 52 53 54 55
S-DeC
wire link

Figure B3

transistor
1
2
'joint'
push on
wire lead
1 mm bore plastic sleeving
tinned copper wire 22 gauge

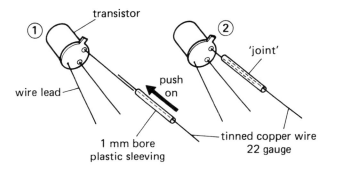

Figure B4

Wrap bare wire round and under lamp holder terminals before screwing them down (Fig. B5).

bare wire
1 mm bore plastic sleeving
lamp holder

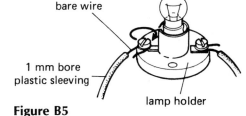

Figure B5

Wrap leads consisting of bare strands of wire round paper clips that have been partly opened (Fig. B6) to connect them to the S-DeC.

S-De C
earphone
insulation
bare strands of wire wrapped round clip
paper clip

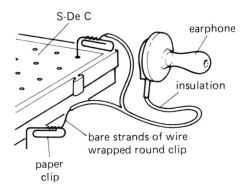

Figure B6

Connect wires to the 'lugs' on variable capacitors, variable resistors and loudspeakers (Fig. B7).

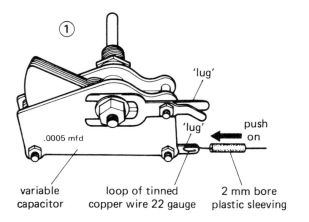

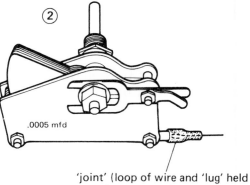

1. variable capacitor — 'lug' — loop of tinned copper wire 22 gauge — 2 mm bore plastic sleeving — push on — .0005 mfd

2. 'joint' (loop of wire and 'lug' held in contact by sleeving) — .0005 mfd

Figure B7

If these instructions are followed an S-DeC and components will give good service for a long time.

Matrix board

This is an insulating board containing a grid of regularly spaced holes, 0.1 inch apart (Fig. B8). Special terminal pins (Fig. B9(a)) are pushed through the holes, and leads of components and connecting wires wound round them so that they make good connections (Fig. B9(b)). Transistor leads are put through holes and each one bound to a terminal pin with a short length of wire (Fig. B10).

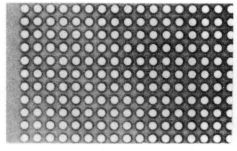

Figure B8

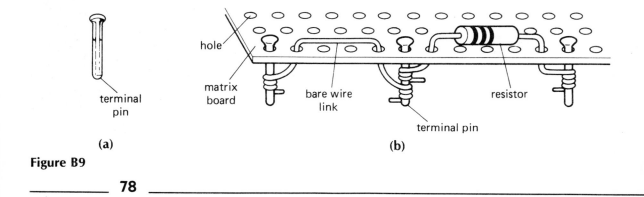

terminal pin

hole

matrix board

bare wire link

resistor

terminal pin

(a)

(b)

Figure B9

terminal pin
transistor
B
hole
matrix board
(cut away)
E
bare wire binding
transistor lead
to terminal pin
C
transistor
lead

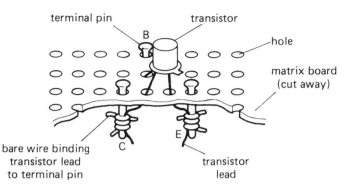

Figure B10

Stripboard

Stripboard (Fig. B11) has pierced copper strips, bonded to the insulating board on one side, to form the connections between the components. Leads from the latter are inserted from the other side of the board and soldered in place on the copper-strip side (see **Soldering** below).

Figure B11 **(a)**

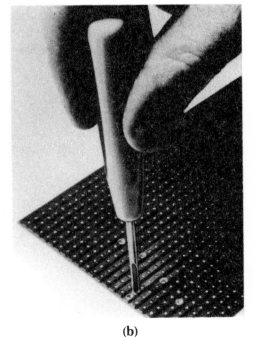

When the copper strip has to be broken (to prevent unwanted connections), a stripboard cutter like that shown in Fig. B11(b) is inserted into the hole where the break is required and rotated clockwise a few times. Alternatively, an ordinary twist drill held between the fingers and rotated will do.

This method of building circuits requires the layout of components to be planned, but the actual layout is similar to that used in the S-DeC method.

(b)

Soldering

A badly soldered joint can cause trouble which may be hard to trace. It has a dull surface and forms a 'blob'. A good joint is *shiny* with *only a little solder* in the joint. A 15 W soldering iron with a 1.5 mm or 2 mm tip is suitable for most purposes, but with ICs a 1 mm tip is better.

The steps in soldering a resistor to stripboard are shown in Fig. B12. The crocodile clip acts as a '**heat sink**' (to prevent heat damage to the resistor and is **essential when soldering diodes and transistors**). ICs are best mounted on holders soldered previously to the board.

1
solder
copper strip
soldering iron
crocodile clip
board
resistor
2
3
solder with arc-shaped shiny surface

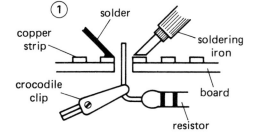

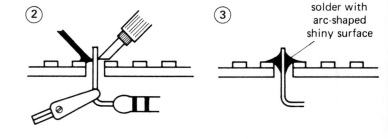

Tip of iron held on copper strip to heat it

Tip of iron moved to touch copper strip and resistor till molten solder fills joint

A good joint

Figure B12

Parts to be soldered should be clean (rubbing with emery cloth will ensure this) and grease-free, and the joint *should not be moved* before the solder solidifies.

Hints for success when building circuits

(1) Collect all the parts you need before starting.

(2) Be certain about which connections are which on transistors, integrated circuits and electrolytic capacitors. They can be damaged if connected wrongly. The markings on some transistors are easily rubbed off so do not finger them any more than you need to.

(3) After building a circuit do not connect the battery until you have
(a) checked the circuit carefully,
(b) made sure that bare wires, especially transistor leads, are not touching one another (or the can of the transistor if it is made of metal). If they do touch, short circuits and damage may occur.

(4) Take care to connect the battery the correct way round, as shown on the diagrams. In circuits with lamps or loudspeakers, disconnect the battery when you are not using the circuit, otherwise it will run down.

(5) If a circuit does not work after careful checking it may be that a transistor has become faulty, because at some time it was connected wrongly by accident. You can test it as described on page 62.

(6) The experiments and projects are best done in the order given; you will then follow things better. Do not be tempted to rush into building a radio before doing simpler jobs. S-DeC layouts are always given; however, after you have assembled a few successfully you may find it fun to work out your own arrangement from the circuit diagram.

EXPERIMENTS

Unit 21 Lamp Circuits

What you need

battery (4.5 V)
S-DeC (or other circuit board)
two lamps (6 V 0.06 A) and holders
connecting wire

What to do

Read Units 1–3 and *Building circuits* (pages 76–81) if you have not done so already.

(A) Simple circuit Connect the battery and one lamp as shown in Fig. 21.1. If all is well lamp L_1 should light up. Does it make any difference if the battery is connected the other way round?

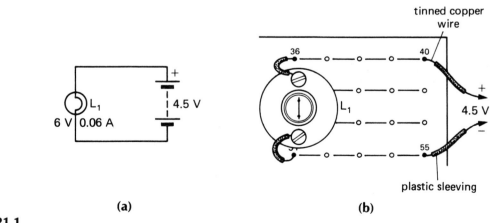

+
L1
4.5 V
6 V
0.06 A
(a)
tinned copper wire
36
40
+
L1
4.5 V
−
55
plastic sleeving
(b)

Figure 21.1

What is the voltage of the battery?

What is the voltage of the lamp?

Why is the lamp not fully bright?

(B) Series circuit Connect two lamps in series (i.e. one after the other) as shown in Fig. 21.2. How does the brightness of the lamps compare with that in (A)? What would you need to make them of about the same brightness as L₁ was in (A)?

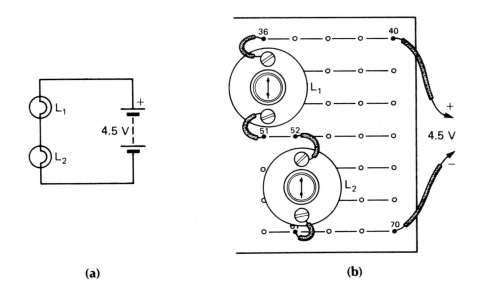

(a)   (b)

Figure 21.2

Unscrew L₁ from its holder till it goes out. What happens to L₂?

(C) Parallel circuit Connect two lamps in parallel (i.e. side by side) as shown in Fig. 21.3. How does their brightness compare with that in (B)?

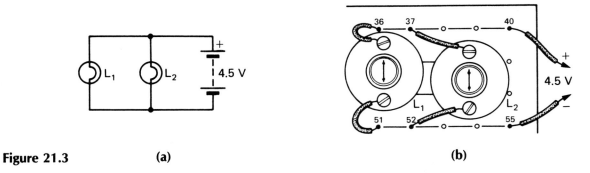

Figure 21.3   (a)   (b)

Unscrew L₁ from its holder. What happens to L₂ this time?

Unit 22 What Resistors Do

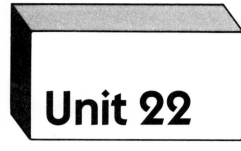

What you need

battery (4.5 V)
S-DeC (or other circuit board)
lamp (6 V 0.06 A) and holder;
resistors—100Ω (brown–black–brown),
1 kΩ (brown–black–red)
variable resistor—10 kΩ
connecting wire

What to do

Read Units 1–4 and *Building circuits* (pages 76–81) if you have not done so already.

(A) Fixed resistors Connect the circuit shown in Fig. 22.1 using a 100 Ω resistor for R_1. L_1 is just alight because R_1 has reduced the current through the lamp.

L1
R1
+
4.5 V

36
40
L1
51
52
R1
67
70
+
4.5 V
−

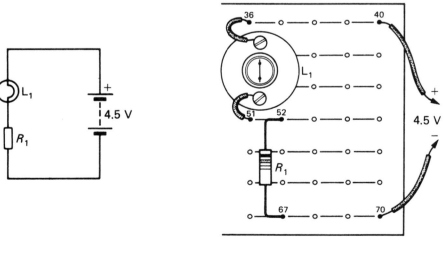

Figure 22.1 **(a)** **(b)**

Now use a 1 kΩ resistor for R_1; it makes the current too small to light L_1 even dimly.

(B) Variable resistor Make a 'dimmer' circuit by using a 10 kΩ variable resistor for R_1 as shown in Fig. 22.2.

Take leads from one *end* lug and the *centre* lug of the variable resistor to holes 52 and 67 on the S-DeC. The centre lug is usually made of thinner metal than the end lugs and more care is needed when making a joint with it. It helps if you press your thumbs against the bottom of the lug so that it cannot bend when you push the sleeving on it, as in Fig. 22.3.

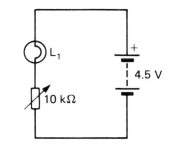

L1
4.5 V
10 kΩ
+

Figure 22.2

push sleeving
on to 'lug'
wire
press thumb
here against
centre 'lug'
2 mm bore
plastic sleeving
variable resistor

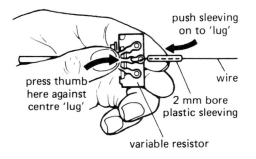

Figure 22.3

Rotate the spindle of the variable resistor slowly, first one way then right round to the other end. L_1 should get dimmer as the resistance increases (current decreases) and brighter as the resistance decreases (current increases).

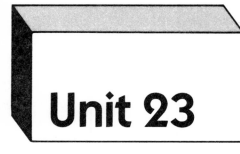

Unit 23 Diode, Thermistor, LDR

What you need

battery (4.5 V)
S-DeC (or other circuit board)
lamp (6 V -0.06 A) in holder
diode (e.g. OA91)
thermistor (e.g. TH3)
LDR (e.g. ORP12)
matches
torch
connecting wire

What to do

Read Units 1–8 and *Building circuits* (pages 76–81) if you have not done so already.

(A) Diode Connect a lamp L_1, a diode D_1 and a battery in series as shown in Fig. 23.1, with the anode of D_1 (the other end from the band) going to the + of the battery. L_1 lights, showing that current is passing through it due to D_1 conducting.

L1
D1
anode
cathode
D1
0A91
band
+
4.5 V
36
40
L1
51
52
D1
67
70
+
4.5 V
−

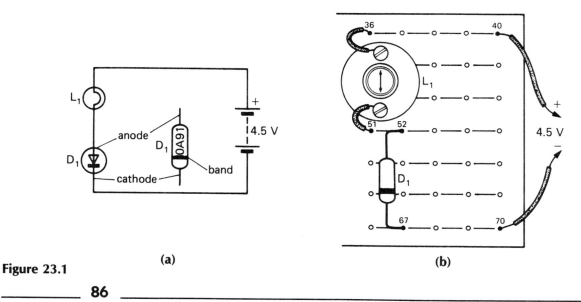

(a) **(b)**

Figure 23.1

Connect D_1 the other way round so that its cathode is joined to the + of the battery. Does L_1 light up? How does a diode behave differently from a 100 Ω resistor?

(B) Thermistor Replace D_1 in your circuit by a thermistor TH (Fig. 23.2). Does L_1 light up? Warm TH by holding a lighted match under it and watch L_1. Let TH cool.

When the resistance of TH is low, L_1 is lit. What lowers the resistance of TH?

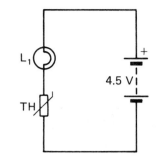

Figure 23.2

Does it make any difference if TH is connected the other way round?

(C) LDR Replace TH in your circuit by an LDR (Fig. 23.3). Does L_1 light up? Shine a torch on the LDR and watch L_1. Remove the torch.

When the resistance of the LDR is low, L_1 is lit. When does this happen?

Does it make any difference if the LDR is connected the other way round?

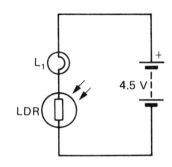

Figure 23.3

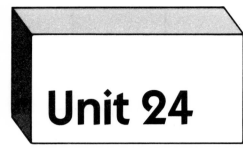

Unit 24 What a Transistor Does

What you need

battery (4.5 V)
S-DeC (or other circuit board)
two lamps (6 V 0.06 A) and holders
npn transistor (2N3053 or BFY51)
resistor 10 kΩ (brown – black – orange)
connecting wire (tinned copper 22 gauge)
1 mm bore plastic sleeving

What to do

Read Units 1–8 and *Building circuits* (pages 76–81) if you have not done so already.

Check that the case of the transistor is marked '2N3053' or 'BFY51'. Identify the emitter lead (E), the base lead (B) and the collector lead (C).

Lengthen the emitter lead (Fig. 24.1(a)) so that the transistor can be mounted on the S-DeC in the holes shown in Fig. 24.2(b). *Do not bend the leads too close to the bottom of the transistor* or they may break off in time.

Alternatively you could lengthen all three leads (Fig. 24.1(b)). None of them then needs to be bent but you must take care *not to push the lengthening wires too far into the sleeving* or they may touch one another or the metal case of the transistor and cause short circuits.

metal case
2N 3053
tag
1 mm bore plastic sleeving
these leads must not touch one another and E and B must not touch the case
C
B
E
tinned copper wire 22 gauge
(a)
2N 3053
C
B
E

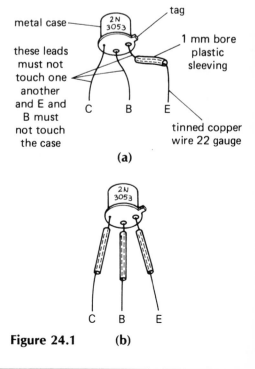

Figure 24.1 (b)

Now build the circuit as shown in Fig. 24.2. After mounting the transistor *make sure its leads are not touching where they come out of the can.*

collector
current
L_2
L_1
R_1
10 kΩ
B
C
E
Tr_1
2N3053
or
BFY51
4.5 V
+
base
current
collector current
+
base current
L_2
L_1
1
4
5
7
8
C
Tr_1
12
13
B
R_1
18
E
20
21
22
4.5 V
+
−

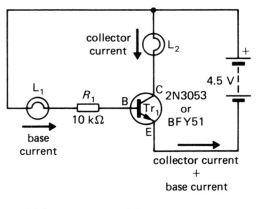

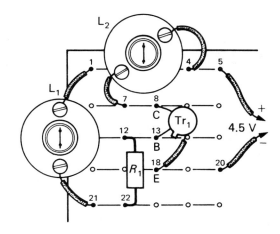

Figure 24.2 (a) (b)

L_2 lights up but not L_1. What does this show about the size of the collector current (which passes through L_2) compared with the size of the base current (which passes through L_1)?

Unscrew L_1 from its holder: the base current becomes zero and L_2 goes out. What do you conclude from this?

In a transistor the base current (the input) 'switches on' and controls the much greater collector current (the output). A transistor acts as a switch and as a current amplifier.

PROJECTS
Unit 25   Parking Light

[*] **Before attempting the projects** you should have read *Circuits and components* (Units 1–10), *Building circuits* (pages 76–81), and it is best to have done the experiments (Units 21–24).

A parking light for a car or a porch light can be switched on automatically as darkness falls by means of a light-dependent resistor (LDR).

What you need

battery (4.5 V)
S-DeC (or other circuit board)
LDR (e.g. ORP12)
two npn transistors (2N3053 or BFY51)
resistors—10 kΩ (brown–black–orange),
        22 kΩ (red–red–orange)
electrolytic capacitor (1000 µF)
lamp (6 V 0.06 A) and holder
connecting wire (tinned copper 22 gauge)
1 mm bore plastic sleeving

What to do

Check that the transistor is marked '2N3053' or 'BFY51'. Identify the emitter (E), base (B) and collector (C) leads (Fig. 25.1).

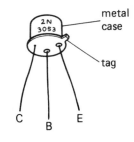

Figure 25.1

Lengthen either the emitter lead *or* all three leads (see Unit 24) so that the transistor can be mounted on the S-DeC in the holes shown in Fig. 25.2(b).

Build the circuit, Fig. 25.2, making sure after the transistor is mounted that its *leads are not touching one another* where they come out of the case.

R_1
10 kΩ
L_1
6 V
0.06 A
collector
current
base current
C
4.5 V
Tr
2N3053
or
BFY51
B
E
LDR
+
−
4.5 V
bare wire
1 mm bore plastic
sleeving
LDR
R_1
Tr
E
B
C
wire link
L_1

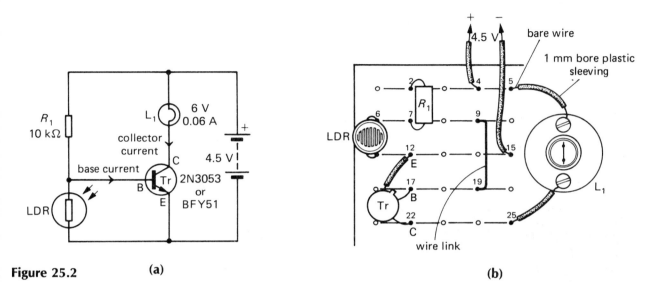

Figure 25.2 (a) (b)

L_1 should light up when the LDR is in the dark or is covered with a handkerchief.

How it works

When light shines on the LDR its resistance is low (about 1 kΩ). Most of the current flowing from the positive of the battery through R_1 finds it easier to return to the negative of the battery by way of the LDR rather than through the base of the transistor. As a result, the base current is too small to cause a collector current large enough to light L_1.

In the dark the LDR no longer acts as a by-pass for the base current because its resistance is much greater (about 10 MΩ). Most of the current through R_1 is then forced to flow into the base of the transistor. The base current, though still small, is more than before and is able to 'switch on' a collector current that is big enough to light L_1.

Two-transistor circuit

This is a more sensitive circuit; it switches on the lamp for a smaller change of light level. The emitter of Tr_1 is connected to the base of Tr_2 and the two transistors are called a **Darlington pair amplifier**. Before building the circuit lengthen *either* the emitter lead *or* all three leads on the second 2N3053 or BFY51, so that it can be mounted in the holes shown in Fig. 25.3(b).

R1
10 kΩ
C
B
Tr1
2N3053
or
BFY51
E
L1
6 V
0.06 A
C
Tr2
2N3053
or
BFY51
B
E
+
4.5 V
LDR

+
−
4.5 V
2
4
5
R1
6
7
9
LDR
1000 µF
12
13
E
17
18
Tr2
B
21
22
C
C
Tr1
26
29
B
31
33
E
wire links
L1

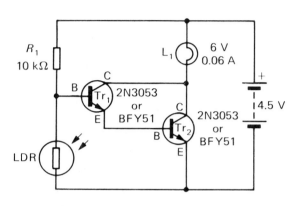

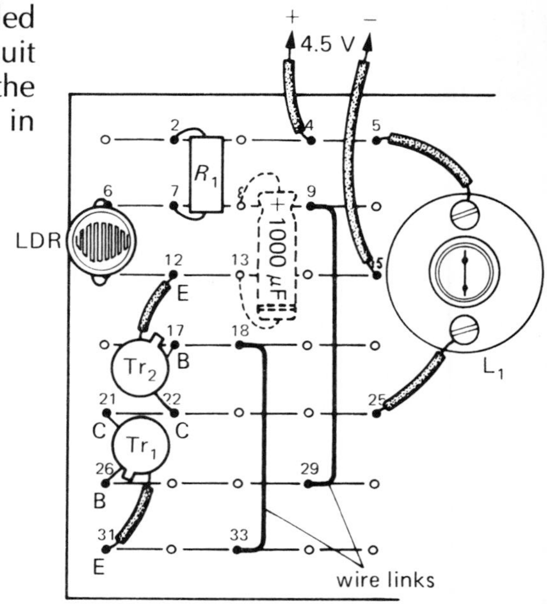

Figure 25.3 **(a)** **(b)**

Things to try

(A) Effect of R_1 Change R_1 from 10 kΩ to 22 KΩ. It now has to be darker before L_1 comes on.

(B) Delayed action light Connect a 1000 µF capacitor across the LDR, + lead to hole 8 and − lead to hole 13, as shown by the dotted lines in Fig. 25.3(b). L_1 comes on more slowly in the dark because current that would otherwise flow into the base of the transistor, charges the capacitor. The base current therefore increases less rapidly.

L_1 also goes off more slowly if light (from the headlamps of a passing car, for example) falls on the LDR because the capacitor gives up its charge (discharges) and keeps the base current flowing for longer. Test this by having the LDR in the dark (L_1 on) and shining a flashlamp on it for a jiffy. L_1 should dim a bit but not go out.

(C) Light-operated burglar alarm Remove the capacitor. Swap round the LDR and R_1, L_1 should now come on in the light and go off in the dark. The circuit could be used to detect an intruder shining a torch or switching on a light in a room 'guarded' by the LDR.

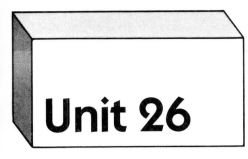

Unit 26 Flashing Lamp

A light is more likely to attract attention if it is flashing. Flashing lamps are used at road works and pedestrian crossings, on cars and as navigation lights.

POLICE

What you need

battery (4.5 V)
S-DeC (or other circuit board)
two npn transistors (2N3053 or BFY51)
resistors—100 Ω (brown–black–brown),
1 kΩ (brown–black–red),
two 10 kΩ (brown–black–orange)
electrolytic capacitors—two 100 μF, 10 μF
two lamps (6 V 0.06 A) and holders
connecting wire (tinned copper 22 gauge)
1 mm bore plastic sleeving

What to do

Check that the transistors are marked '2N3053' or 'BFY51'. Identify the emitter (E), base (B) and collector (C) leads (Fig. 26.1).

2N
3053
metal case
tag
C
B
E

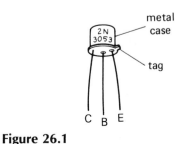

Figure 26.1

If you have not already done so, lengthen *either* the emitter lead *or* all three leads on both transistors (see Unit 24) so that they can be mounted on the S-DeC as shown in Fig. 26.2(b).

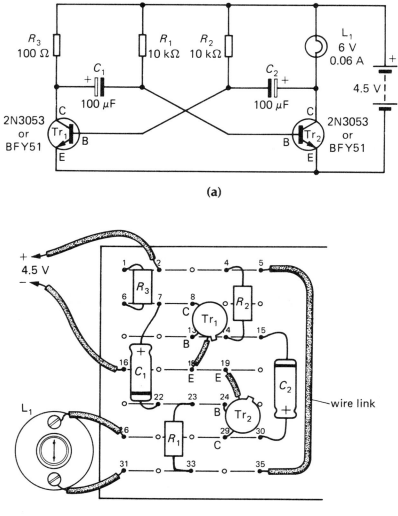

R_3
100 Ω
R_1
10 kΩ
R_2
10 kΩ
L_1
6 V
0.06 A
C_1
100 μF
C_2
100 μF
4.5 V
2N3053
or
BFY51
Tr_1
Tr_2
C
B
E

(a)

+
4.5 V
−
L_1
R_3
R_2
R_1
C_1
C_2
Tr_1
Tr_2
wire link

(b)

Figure 26.2

Build the circuit, Fig. 26.2, making sure that the electrolytic capacitors are the right way round and that the *transistor leads are not touching each other* where they come out of the bottom of the transistors.

If all is well, L_1 should flash 30 to 40 times a minute and be on and off for equal times.

How it works

The lamp flashes because each transistor is switched on and off in turn due to C_1 charging and discharging through R_1, and C_2 doing the same through R_2. The flashing rate depends on the values of $C_1 \times R_1$ and $C_2 \times R_2$.

The circuit is called an **astable multivibrator**.

Things to try

(A) Effect of C_1   Change C_1 from 100 µF to 10 µF. L_1 flashes faster (about 60 times a minute) and is on for longer than it is off.

(B) Effect of C_2   Make $C_1 = 100$ µF again, but change C_2 to 10 µF. The flashing rate will still be roughly 60 a minute but the 'on' times are shorter than the 'off' times.

(C) Effect of R_1   Make $C_2 = 100$ µF again, but change R_1 to 1 kΩ. The flashing rate stays at 60 per minute but the 'on' time is greater than the 'off' time (as in **A**).

(D) Effect of $C_1 \times R_1$ and $C_2 \times R_2$ Make $C_2 = 10$ µF leaving $C_1 = 100$ µF, $R_1 = 1$ kΩ and $R_2 = 10$ kΩ. The flashing rate is much faster and the on and off times are again equal. This is because $C_1 \times R_1 = 100 \times 1 = 100$, and $C_2 \times R_2 = 10 \times 10 = 100$.

(E) Two flashing lamps   Change C_2 to 100 µF and R_1 to 10 kΩ. Replace R_3 by another lamp in holes 1 and 6.

The lamps should flash one after the other as each transistor is switched on and off in turn.

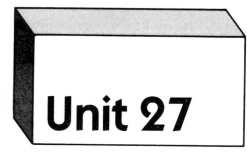

Unit 27

Electronic Organ

This is a chance to make your own electronic music.

What you need

battery (4.5 V)
S-DeC (or other circuit board)
two npn transistors (2N3053 or BFY51)
resistors—100 Ω   (brown–black–brown),   two   1 kΩ
        (brown–black–red),   2.2 kΩ   (red–red–red),
        two 3.9 kΩ (orange–white–red), two 4.7 kΩ
        (yellow–violet–red),   5.6 kΩ   (green–blue–
        red), 10 kΩ (brown–black–orange), 22 kΩ
        (red–red–orange)
disc ceramic capacitors—two 0.1 μF
crystal earphone
loudspeaker (2½ in, 4 to 80 Ω)
connecting wire tinned copper 22 gauge
1 mm and 2 mm bore plastic sleeving

What to do

Check that the transistors are marked '2N3053' or
'BFY51'. Identify the emitter (C), base (B) and collector
(C) leads (Fig. 27.1).

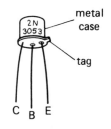

Figure 27.1

If you have not done so already, lengthen *either* the emitter lead *or* all three leads on both transistors (see Unit 24) so that they can be mounted on the S-DeC in the holes shown in Fig. 27.2(b).

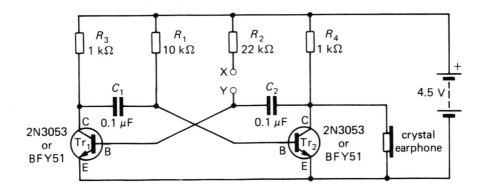

R3
1 kΩ
R1
10 kΩ
R2
22 kΩ
R4
1 kΩ
X
Y
C1
C2
0.1 μF
0.1 μF
+
4.5 V
C
B
E
2N3053
or
BFY51
Tr1
Tr2
crystal
earphone

(a)

insulated
wire link
bare wire link
+
4.5 V
−
R3
R2
R5
R6
R7
R8
R9
R1
R4
R10
C1
C2
Tr1
Tr2
X
Y
flying
lead
KEYBOARD
crystal
earphone

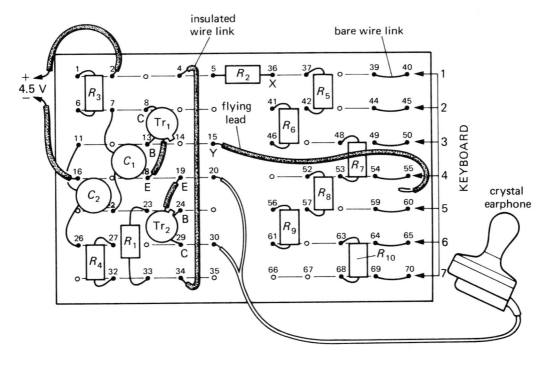

(b)

Figure 27.2

Put the circuit together, Fig. 27.2; making sure that when the transistors are in the S-DeC their *leads are not touching one another* near the case.

Touch the flying lead on each of the seven wire links (the 'keyboard') in turn (Fig. 27.3). They each give a different note. The lowest (Note 7) is given by the bottom link in holes 69 and 70 (most resistance); the highest (Note 1) by the link in holes 39 and 40 (least resistance). With a bit of luck you should be able to play a tune.

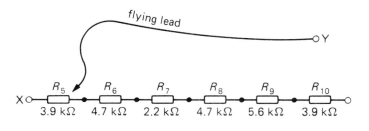

flying lead

R_5 3.9 kΩ R_6 4.7 kΩ R_7 2.2 kΩ R_8 4.7 kΩ R_9 5.6 kΩ R_{10} 3.9 kΩ

Figure 27.3

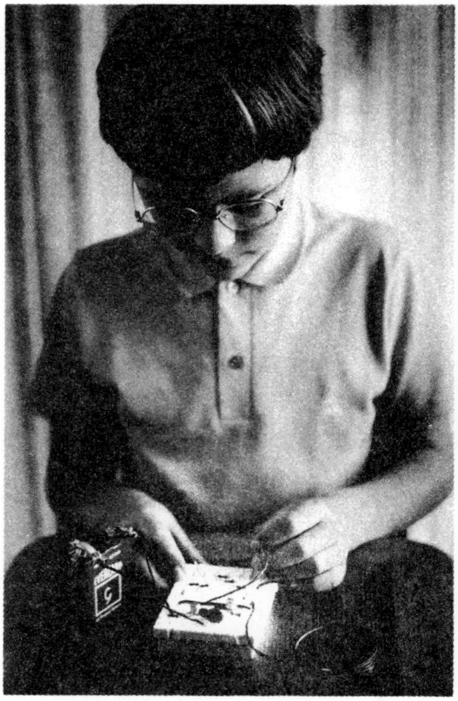

'Music' for *God save the Queen* The numbers tell you the notes to be played. *Note 1* is obtained by touching the wire link in holes 39 and 40, *Note 2* is given by the link in holes 44 and 45, and so on. When the numbers are close together you should play them quickly one after the other. When there is a star, make the note longer.

```
  6    6    5    7*        6 5
 God  save our  gra – cious queen

  4    4    3    4*       5 6
Long  live our  no – ble  queen

  5    6    7    6
 God  save the  queen

  2    2    2    2*       3 4
Send  her  vic – tor – ious

  3    3    3    3*       4 5
Hap – py  and  glor – ious

  4      3 4   5 6   4*      3 2
Long   to-o  reign ov – er  us

 1 3    4*    5*    6*
 God   save  the   queen
```

Figure 27.4

Connect another flying lead in hole 14. You now have a left 'hand' as well as a right to play on the keyboard. This should widen your repertoire!

How it works

The circuit is an **astable multivibrator** like that in the *Flashing lamp* project (Unit 26), except that the capacitors have much smaller values. This makes the transistors switch on and off too rapidly for a lamp to show the changes, but the rapid 'click-click-click-' caused in the earphone produces a note. The pitch of the note is decided by the position of the flying lead on the chain of six resistors (R_5 to R_{10}). For the highest note (the link in holes 39 and 40) the chain is not used at all.

Things to try

(A) Loudspeaker operation (with six notes) You will have to:

(1) remove the earphone from holes 20 and 30
(2) remove R_4 from holes 27 and 32
(3) remove R_{10} from holes 63 and 68
(4) remove the wire link from holes 69 and 70
(5) insert a 100Ω resistor in holes 30 and 66
(6) insert a loudspeaker in holes 35 and 67.

You can now entertain your friends as well!

(B) Mystery tune Here is the 'music' for a well-known tune, play it and see if you recognize it—there are no prizes for the correct answer but it is a favourite with certain football supporters! When there is a star, make the note longer.

6 4 3 2* 6 4 3 2*
6 4 3 2 4 6 4 5*
4 4 5 6* 4 2 2 3
3 4 3 2 4 6 5 6*

(C) Two-tone siren Touch in turn with a flying lead, two wire links that are next to each other. Doing it quickly several times will give the familiar two-tone sound of a British police car and ambulance siren.

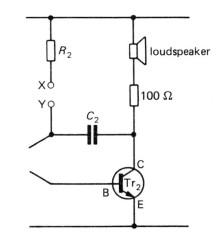

Figure 27.5

Unit 28 | 'Chip' Radio

In many parts of Britain this radio works from a ferrite rod aerial—no aerial wire or earth connection is needed. It has an integrated circuit (IC) which looks like a transistor but is a tiny 'chip' of silicon containing 10 transistors, 15 resistors and 4 capacitors. The 'chip' is nearly a radio on its own. With a few changes to the circuit it works a small loudspeaker.

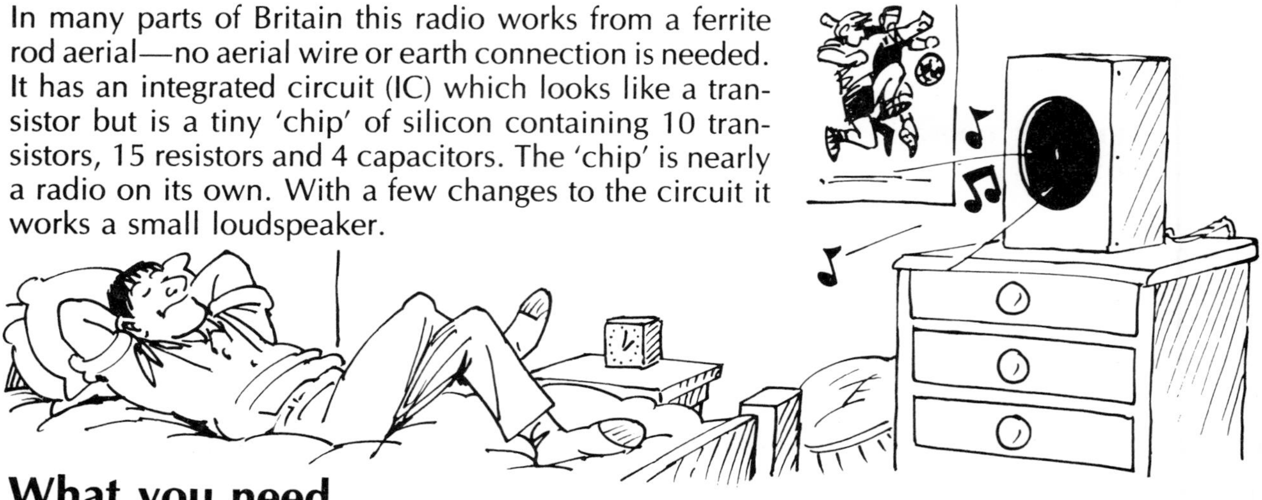

What you need

battery (4.5 V)
S-DeC (or other circuit board)
IC (ZN414 or ZN414Z)
two npn transistors (2N3053 or BFY51)
resistors—330 Ω (orange–orange–brown), 1 kΩ (brown–black–red), 4.7 kΩ (yellow–violet–red), 10 kΩ (brown–black–orange), two 100 kΩ (brown–black–yellow), 470 kΩ (yellow–violet–yellow)

variable capacitor (0.0005 μF)
electrolytic capacitor (10 μF)
disc ceramic capacitors (0.01 μF, 0.1 μF)
crystal earphone
loudspeaker ($2\frac{1}{2}$ in, 4 to 80 Ω)
ferrite rod (100 mm × 9 mm)
knob
tinned copper wire (22 gauge)
$7\frac{1}{2}$ metres enamelled copper wire (24 gauge)
1 mm and 2 mm bore plastic sleeving
two rubber bands
2 metres aerial wire

What to do

Check that the IC is marked 'ZN414' or 'ZN414Z' (Fig. 28.1(a)) and the two transistors '2N3053' or 'BFY51'. Identify leads 1, 2 and 3 on the IC (Fig. 28.1(a)) and the emitter (E), base (B) and collector (C) leads on the 2N3053s or BFY51s (Fig. 28.1(b)).

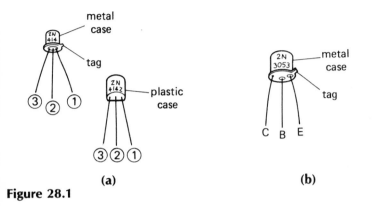

metal
case
tag
ZN
414
3
2
1
ZN
414Z
plastic
case
3 2 1
(a)
2N
3053
metal
case
tag
C B E
(b)

Figure 28.1

If you have not done so already, lengthen *either* the emitter lead *or* all three leads on one transistor (see Unit 24) so that it can be mounted in the holes shown in Fig. 28.2(b). Also lengthen the leads on the IC.

Using $1\frac{1}{2}$ metres of enamelled copper wire, wind a 50-turn coil on the ferrite rod. *You must scrape off* (with a penknife) *the dark reddish brown coating of enamel insulation from the ends of the wire* (so that the shiny copper can be seen) *where they are pushed into the S-DeC.*

'Join' 10 cm lengths of tinned copper wire to the lugs on the variable capacitor. (See page 77 for making 'joints'.) Slip 1 m bore sleeving on each length, leaving 2 cm of bare wire at the end which will be pushed into the hole on the S-DeC. Fix the variable capacitor to the control panel and put on the knob.

Build the circuit, Fig. 28.2, not forgetting the two wire links. Slot the control panel with the variable capacitor into the S-DeC. Connect the wire from the fixed plates to hole 25 and the wire from the moving plates to hole 35. **Check the circuit carefully**, making sure that the *transistor and IC leads are not touching one another or the metal cases*. When you connect the battery there should be a 'crackle' in the earphone.

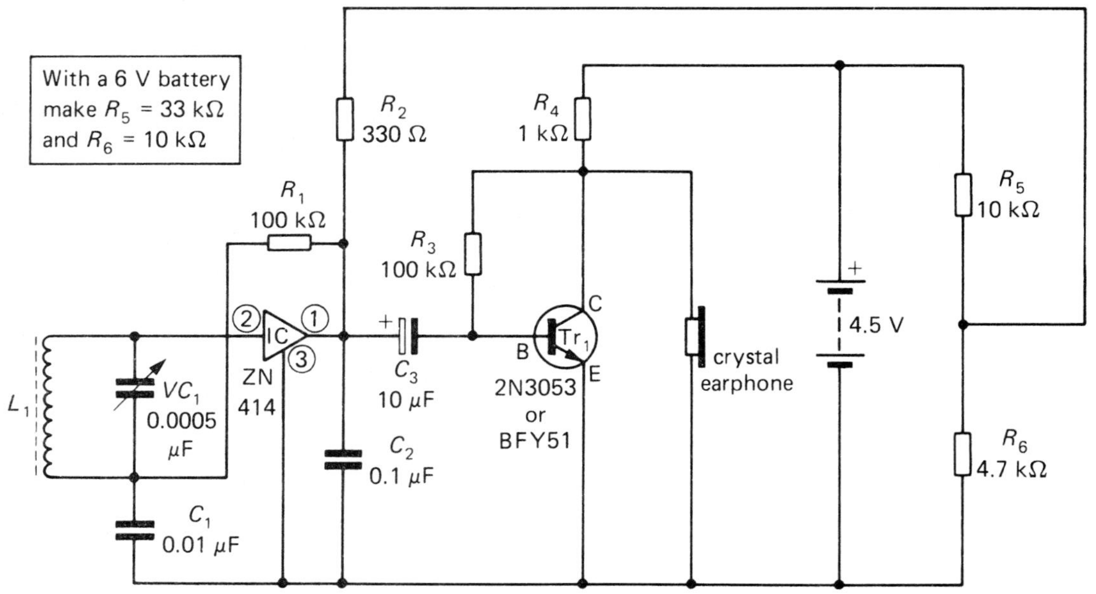
With a 6 V battery make R_5 = 33 kΩ and R_6 = 10 kΩ
R_2
330 Ω
R_4
1 kΩ
R_5
10 kΩ
R_1
100 kΩ
R_3
100 kΩ
+
4.5 V
C
B
E
Tr_1
crystal earphone
IC
ZN 414
L_1
VC_1
0.0005 μF
C_3
10 μF
2N3053 or BFY51
C_2
0.1 μF
R_6
4.7 kΩ
C_1
0.01 μF

(a)

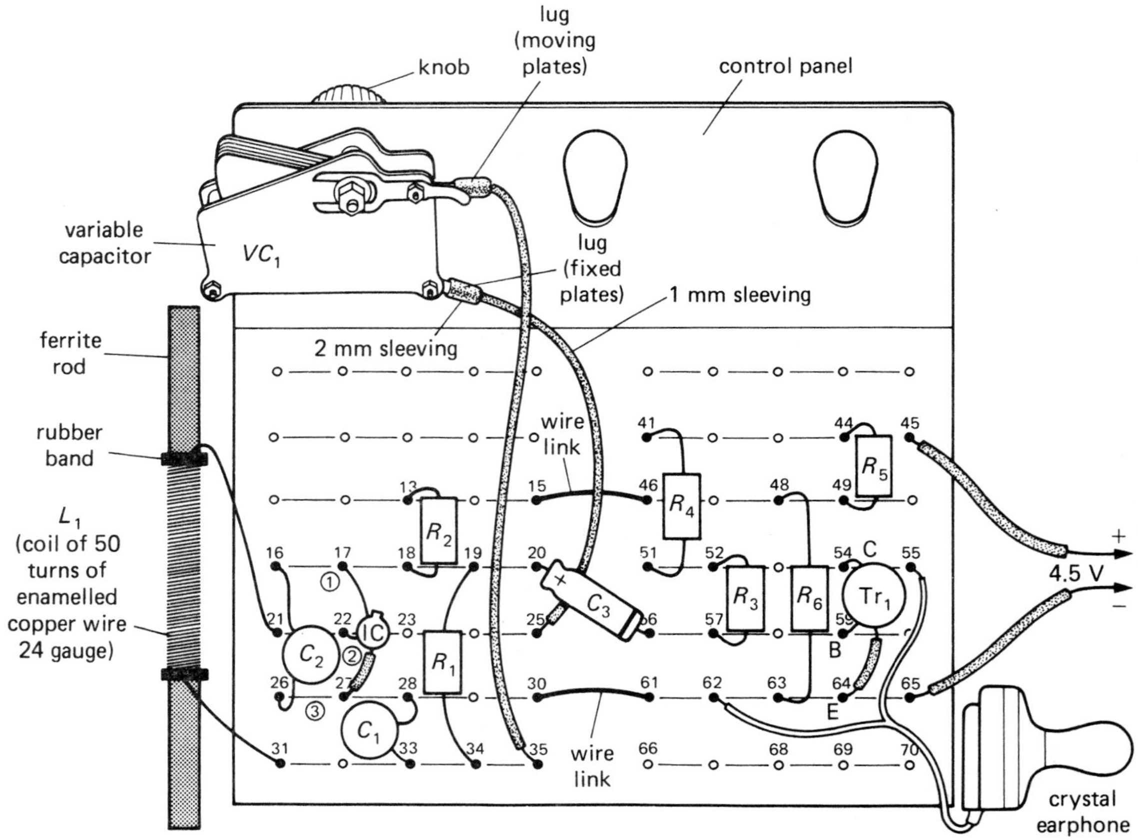
lug (moving plates)
knob
control panel
variable capacitor
VC_1
lug (fixed plates)
1 mm sleeving
ferrite rod
2 mm sleeving
rubber band
wire link
L_1 (coil of 50 turns of enamelled copper wire 24 gauge)
R_2
R_4
R_5
C_3
R_3
R_6
Tr_1
C_2
IC
R_1
C_1
wire link
4.5 V
+
−
crystal earphone

(b)

Figure 28.2

By carefully turning the knob on VC_1 you should be able to tune in medium-wave stations (in Britain, Radios, 1, 2 and 3, and local radio). *The ferrite rod aerial is directional, so slowly rotate the S-DeC for maximum volume.* If the signals are weak, try putting a 2-metre long aerial wire in hole 23 and fixing the other end as high as possible. If you live in a very poor reception area you may have to use the TV aerial to get good signals. After dark more distant medium-wave stations (e.g. Luxembourg) can be received.

32

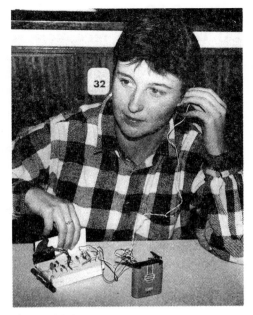

Figure 28.3

How it works

If you haven't read *Radio systems* (Unit 14), do so now. It will help you to understand the block diagram below.

aerial
tuner
detector
a.f. amplifier
earphone

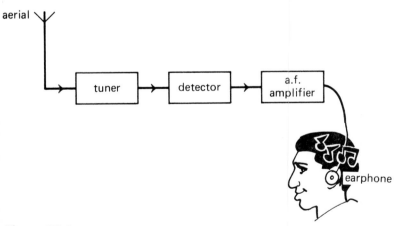

Figure 28.4

The ferrite rod acts as the aerial. L_1–VC_1 forms the tuner of the integrated circuit which is also the detector. The 2N3053 or BFY51 transistor is the a.f. amplifier.

The IC needs 1.5 V only. It is obtained by having R_5 and R_6 connected in series across the battery and tapping off the required voltage from R_6.

Things to try

(A) Long-wave reception Remove the 50-turn medium wave coil from the ferrite rod and replace it by a 200-turn coil wound from about 6 metres of enamelled copper wire. You should now receive long-wave stations (in Britain, Radio 4).

(B) Loudspeaker operation A second transistor Tr_2 is added and acts as a Darlington pair amplifier with TR_1. To build the new circuit you will have to change the old one by:

(a) removing the wire from the negative of the battery from hole 65,
(b) removing the earphone from holes 55 and 62,
(c) replacing R_3 in holes 52 and 57 by a 470 kΩ resistor,
(d) moving the wire link from holes 30 and 61 to holes 30 and 66,
(e) moving R_6 from holes 48 and 63 to holes 48 and 68,
(f) replacing R_4 in holes 41 and 51 by a small loudspeaker,
(g) lengthening the collector lead on another 2N3053 or BFY51 (for Tr_2) and mounting it so that the collector is in hole 55, the base in 65 and the emitter in 70,
(h) inserting the wire from the negative of the battery into hole 69,
(i) connecting an aerial in hole 23 if it is needed.

Figure 28.5 shows the circuit you should finish up with.

R2
330 Ω
loudspeaker
R1
100 kΩ
R3
470 kΩ
R5
10 kΩ
+
4.5 V
2
1
IC
3
ZN
414
C3
10 μF
C
B
Tr1
E
2N3053
or
BFY51
L1
VC1
C2
0.1 μF
C
B
Tr2
E
2N3053
or
BFY51
R6
4.7 kΩ
C1
0.01 μF

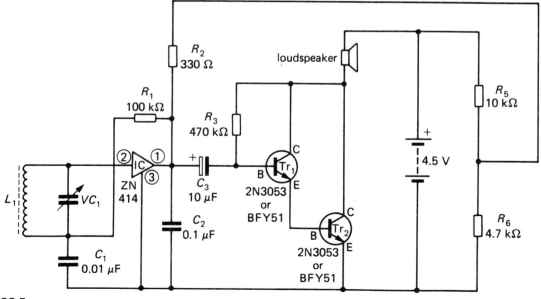

Figure 28.5

Components Needed

The following components are needed for the experiments and projects:

1	S-DeC
2	npn transistors (2N3053 or BFY51)
1	integrated circuit (ZN414 or ZN414Z)
1	photocell (e.g. ORP12)
1	thermistor (e.g. TH3)
1	germanium diode (OA91)
1	crystal earphone
1	loudspeaker ($2\frac{1}{2}$ in $4\,\Omega$ to $80\,\Omega$)
1	variable capacitor (0.0005 µF, e.g. Jackson Dilecon)
2	MES batten holders
2	MES lamps (6 V 0.06 A)
1	midget linear potentiometer ($10\,k\Omega$)
1	ferrite rod (100 mm × 9 mm)
1	knob
5 m	tinned copper wire, 22 gauge (20 grams)
2.5 m	plastic sleeving, 1 mm bore
0.2 m	plastic sleeving, 2 mm bore
7.5 m	enamelled copper wire, 24 gauge
1	crocodile clip
2	rubber bands, small
1	battery (4.5 V)
16	resistors, carbon, $\frac{1}{2}$ watt ($100\,\Omega$, $330\,\Omega$, two $1\,k\Omega$, $2.2\,k\Omega$, two $3.9\,k\Omega$, two $4.7\,k\Omega$, $5.6\,k\Omega$, two $10\,k\Omega$, $22\,k\Omega$, two $100\,k\Omega$, $470\,k\Omega$)
3	ceramic capacitors (two 0.01 µF, 0.1 µF)
4	electrolytic capacitors (10 µF, two 100 µF, 1000 µF)

Addresses

A **complete kit of components** for the experiments and projects can be bought (the '*Adventures with Electronics*' kit) from

Unilab Ltd, Clarendon Road, Blackburn, Lancs., BB1 9TA

or possibly obtained through local hobbies shops.

Firms supplying electronic parts are:

Electrovalue Ltd, 28 St Jude's Road, Egham, Surrey, TW20 0HB (catalogue available).

Maplin Electronic Supplies Ltd, P.O. Box 3, Rayleigh, Essex, SS6 8LR (catalogue available).

Many firms advertise in *Practical Wireless, Everyday Electronics* and other magazines. A firm which does this is:

Watford Electronics, 250 High Street, Watford.

If you have a local electronics shop you may find it worthwhile and more convenient to get parts there.

Beware of parts sold cheaply as 'untested' or 'manufacturer's surplus' or 'near equivalent to': they may be substandard.

Schools and colleges can obtain supplies from:

R.S. Components Ltd, P.O. Box 99, Corby, Northants, NN17 9RS (catalogue free).

S-DeCs are made by:

Roden Products, High March, Daventry, Northants, NN11 4RZ.

Answers

The world of electronics
1. Desk-top computer
2. Telecommunication satellite
3. Cardiograph
4. Personal stereo cassette player
5. Video recorder
6. Pocket calculator
7. Washing machine
8. Radar screen
9. Digital clock
10. Sewing machine
11. Petrol pumps

1 Circuit diagrams
1. A: cell, B: connecting wire, C: lamp, D: switch
2. L_1 goes out.
3. **(a)** L_1 stays on

   (b) See Figure A1.

4. **(a)** B **(b)** A **(c)** C

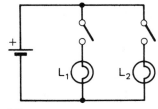

Figure A1

2 Electric current
1. **(a)** A_2 : 0.2 A, A_3 : 0.2 A

   (b) A_1 : 0.5 A
2. A_2 : 0.2 A, A_3 : 0.2 A
3. **(a)** A_1 : 0.3 A, A_3 : 0.3 A

   (b) See Figure A2.

4. **(a)** d.c. because the current, though changing in value, does not change in direction.

   (b) 1 cycle in 0.2 second, i.e. 1 cycle in $\frac{1}{5}$ second or 5 cycles per second = 5 Hz, therefore **(i)** period = 0.2 s and **(ii)** frequency = 5 Hz.

5. **(a) (i)** 1000 **(ii)** 500 **(iii)** 20

   (b) (i) 1.5 **(ii)** 0.3 **(iii)** 0.06

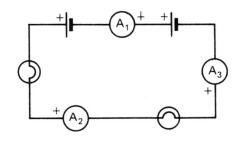

Figure A2

3 Voltage

1 **(a)** $4 \times 1.5 = 6\,V$
(b) $3 \times 1.5 - 1 \times 1.5 = 4.5 - 1.5 = 3\,V$
(c) $2 \times 1.5 - 2 \times 1.5 = 3 - 3 = 0\,V$

2 **(a)** V_2 : $3\,V$

(b) See Figure A3.

3 $x : 18,\ y : 2,\ z : 8$

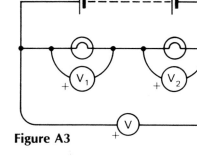

Figure A3

4 Resistors

1 **(a)** $10\,V/5\,\Omega = 2\,A$ **(b)** $10\,V$
(c) See Figure A4.
2 **(a)** $12\,V/4\,A = 3\,\Omega$
(b) $10\,\Omega \times 2\,A = 20\,V$
3 **(a)** $5\,mA \times 2\,k\Omega = 10\,V$
(b) $12\,V/3\,mA = 4\,k\Omega$
(c) $10\,V/5\,k\Omega = 2\,mA$
(d) $12\,V \times 3\,mA = 36\,mW$
4 **(a)** $1000\,\Omega = 1\,k\Omega$
(b) $47\,000\,\Omega = 47\,k\Omega$
5 **(a)** brown–black–black **(b)** brown–green–brown
(c) orange–white–red **(d)** brown–black–orange
(e) orange–orange–yellow **(f)** brown–black–green
6 **(a)** $1\,A$ **(b)** $1\,A$ **(c)** $3\,V$ **(d)** $6\,V$
(e) $3\,V + 6\,V = 9\,V$
7 **(a)** $4\,A$ **(b)** $2\,A$ **(c)** $12\,V$ **(d)** $12\,V$ **(e)** $12\,V$
8 See Figure A5.

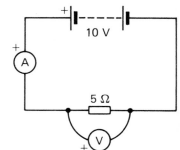

Figure A4

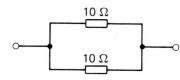

Figure A5

5 Capacitors

1 **(a)** Capacitance is $0.1\,\mu F$ and working voltage is
25 V.
(b) The *peak* value of a 240 V a.c. supply is 340 V
which exceeds the working voltage.
2 $2.2\,nF$, $100\,pF$, $4.7\,\mu F$
3 Connect a capacitor in series with the component.

6 Transformers

1 **(a)** $200/400 = 1/2$ (step up)
(b) $600/300 = 2/1$ (step down)
(c) $1/4$ (step up)
(d) $10/2 = 5/1$ (step down)
2 **(a)** $12\,V$ **(b)** $20\,V$ **(c)** 1000 **(d)** 4000
3 $100\,mA$

7 Diodes

1 L_2

2 (a) 5 V **(b)** 1 A **(c)** 5 Ω **(d)** 5 W **(e)** 1 W **(f)** 6 W

3 7 V/0.01 A = 700 Ω

4 (a) 3 V **(b)** 4 V **(c)** 40 mA = 0.04 A
(d) 4 V/0.04 A = 100 Ω
(e) 3 V × 5 mA = 15 mW

5 (a) (8 V − 3 V)/50 Ω = 5 V/50 Ω = 0.1 A = 100 mA
(b) 80 mA

8 Transistor

1 (a) ABE **(b)** ACE

2 B

3 200 mA/1 mA = 200

10 Transducers

1 (a) LDR **(b)** loudspeaker **(c)** filament lamp
(d) thermistor **(e)** electric motor **(f)** relay
(g) microphone **(h)** push-button switch

2 An input transducer has a non-electrical input and an
electrical output.
An output transducer has an electrical input and a
non-electrical output.

3 (a) brighter **(b)** dimmer

4 Hair dryer, food mixer, electric drill, extractor fan,
electric lawn mower, tumble dryer.

11 Logic systems

1 (a) OR **(b)** NOT **(c)** NAND **(d)** NOR **(e)** AND

2 (a)

A	B	C	Q
0	0	0	1
0	1	0	1
1	0	0	1
1	1	1	0

NAND gate

(b)

A	B	C	D	Q
0	0	1	1	0
0	1	1	0	1
1	0	0	1	1
1	1	0	0	1

OR gate

(c)

A	B	C	D	Q
0	0	0	1	1
0	1	0	1	1
1	0	0	1	1
1	1	1	0	1

3 A = AND B = OR C = NAND D = NOR
4 (a) AND **(b)** OR

12 Microcomputer systems

1 (a) Digital
  (b) To convert analogue to digital signals or vice versa.
2 (a) ROM, RAM
  (b) ROM: read only, permanent storage
    RAM: read and write, temporary storage
  (c) (i) ROM **(ii)** RAM

13 Audio systems

1 It produces an audible sound when fed to a loudspeaker, i.e. one which the human ear hears.
2 X: microphone, converts sound to electrical energy.
  Y: audio amplifier, boosts signal from microphone.
  Z: loudspeaker, changes electrical energy to sound.

14 Radio systems

1 Combines a.f. with r.f.
  Aerials only emit radio waves effectively when supplied with r.f.
2 Separates a.f. from r.f.
  Loudspeakers only produce sound when supplied with a.f.

15 Feedback control systems

1 (a) Thermistor
  (b) (i) Resistance decreases.
    (ii) Current increases.
  (c) The air temperature feeds back information to the thermistor and alters its resistance. This varies the base current to the transistor, switching it (and so also the relay and motor) on or off, as required.
  (d) Controls the temperature at which switching occurs.

16 Meters and measurements
1 B, D, F: ammeters reading $6\,V/6\,\Omega = 1\,A$
  C, E: voltmeters reading $1\,A \times 3\,\Omega = 3\,V$
2 G: ammeter reading $6\,V/2\,\Omega = 3\,A$
  H and J: ammeters reading $3/2 = 1.5\,A$
  I and K: voltmeters reading $1.5\,A \times 4\,\Omega = 6\,V$
3 Yes; it is easier to read the wrong scale, also the pointer may be between marks on the scale and an estimate has to be made.

17 Fault finding
1 It should have a 'high' resistance when connected in reverse bias and a 'low' resistance in forward bias.
2 It is connected in reverse bias.
3 **(a)** Y is the base because when + it has a low resistance with the other connection to X or Z.
  (b) Yes, because it has a high resistance for all other pairs of connections.

18 Cathode ray oscilloscope
1 Lower (since electrons have a negative charge and are attracted to the positively charged plate).
2 **(a)** E **(b)** C
3 C
4 **(a)** **(i)** 6 vertical divs $\times$ 5 V/div = 30 V
     (ii) 3 divs $\times$ 5 V/div = 15 V
  (b) **(i)** 8 divs $\times$ 500 mV/div = 4000 mV = 4 V
     (ii) 4 divs $\times$ 500 mV/div = 2000 mV = 2 V
5 **(a)** **(i)** 5 horizontal divs $\times$ 200 ms/div = 1000 ms = 1 s
     (ii) 1 Hz
  (b) **(i)** 5 divs $\times$ 100 ms/div = 500 ms = 0.5 s
     (ii) 1/0.5 s = 2 Hz

19 Dangers of electricity
1 **(a)** Live (L), Neutral (N), Earth (E)
  (b) L: brown, N: blue, E: yellow–green.
  (c) To stop connections being pulled loose in the plug.
2 They can store a large electric charge for a long time.
3 **(a)** Current
  (b) The person is making good contact with the ground through the feet.

20 Safety precautions

1 To prevent the wiring catching fire and to protect the appliance.

2 **(a)** $I = P/V = 480\,\text{W}/240\,\text{V} = 2\,\text{A}$: a 3 A fuse would be suitable.

(b) $I = P/V = 3000\,\text{W}/240\,\text{V} = 12.5\,\text{A}$: a 13 A fuse would do.

3 **(a)** Residual current device.

(b) To protect the user from electric shock.

(c) With outside portable appliances or wherever the user is making good contact with the earth.

(d) Faster-acting, more sensitive, more easily reset.

4 Leads from ends can break if bent too close to component; heat damage when soldering.

Index

Acknowledgements

Cover photograph by Anthony Price Advertising Photography.

Diagrams by RDL Artset.

Cartoons by John Erasmus.

Thanks are due to the following for permission to reproduce copyright photographs:
Pages 6–7: 1 IBM UK Limited; 2 British Telecom plc; 3 Science Photo Library Ltd; 4, 5 Sony (UK) Limited; 6, 9 Casio Electronics; 7 Hotpoint; 8 Racal Group; 10 The Singer Company UK Limited; 11 BP Oil Limited.
Figs 2.4(a), 3.2(a), 10.10(a), 18.1 Unilab Limited; 3.1(a), (b) Ever Ready Limited; 4.3(a), 4.5(a), 5.2(a), (b), (c), 5.3(a), 6.4(a), (b), 7.9(a), 8.1(a), 9.1(a), 10.2(a), (b), 10.4(a), (b), 10.5(a), 10.6(a), (b), (c), (d), 10.7(a), 10.9(a), 16.2, 20.2, B8, B11(a), (b) RS Components Ltd; 12.2 British Telecom plc; 12.3 Austin Rover; 13.2 Sony (UK) Limited; 16.1 Avo; 28.3 Tony Langham.